KT-392-489

DISPOSED OF
BY LIBRARY
HOUSE OF LORDS

Chinese Law and Legal Theory

The International Library of Essays in Law and Legal Theory

Second Series

Series Editor: Tom D. Campbell

Titles in the Series:

Freedom of Speech, Volumes I and II
Larry Alexander

Privacy
Eric M. Barendt

Comparative Legal Cultures
John Bell

Contract Law, Volumes I and II
Brian Bix

Corporate Law
William W. Bratton

Law and Democracy
Tom D. Campbell

Legal Positivism
Tom D. Campbell

Administrative Law
Peter Cane

International Trade Law
Ronald A. Cass and Michael S. Knoll

Sociological Perspectives on Law, Volumes I and II
Roger Cotterrell

Intellectual Property
Peter Drahos

Family, State and Law, Volumes I and II
Michael D. Freeman

Natural Law
Robert P. George

Commercial Law
Clayton P. Gillette

Competition Law
Rosa Greaves

Chinese Law and Legal Theory
Perry Keller

International Law, Volumes I and II
Martti Koskenniemi and David Kennedy

Constitutional Law
Ian D. Loveland

Interpretation of Law
D. Neil MacCormick and Fernando Atria

Human Rights
Robert McCorquodale

Anti-Discrimination Law
Christopher McCrudden

Medical Law and Ethics
Sheila McLean

Mediation
Carrie Menkel-Meadow

Environmental Law
Peter Menell

Criminal Law
Thomas Morawetz

Law and Language
Thomas Morawetz

Law and Anthropology
Martha Mundy

Gender and Justice
Ngaire Naffine

Law and Economics
Eric A. Posner

Japanese Law
J. Mark Ramseyer

Justice
Wojciech Sadurski

The Rule of Law
Frederick Schauer

Regulation
Colin Scott

Restitution
Lionel D. Smith

Company Law
David Sugarman

Freedom of Information
Robert G. Vaughn

Tort Law
Ernest J. Weinrib

Rights
Robin West

Welfare Law
Lucy A. Williams

Chinese Law and Legal Theory

Edited by

Perry Keller

King's College London

Ashgate

DARTMOUTH

Aldershot • Burlington USA • Singapore • Sydney

Published by
Dartmouth Publishing Company Limited
Ashgate Publishing Limited
Gower House
Croft Road
Aldershot
Hants GU11 3HR
England

Ashgate Publishing Company
131 Main Street
Burlington, VT 05401-5600 USA

Ashgate website: http://www.ashgate.com

British Library Cataloguing in Publication Data
Chinese law and legal theory. – (International library of
essays in law and legal theory. Second series)
1. Law – China 2. Law – China – Philosophy
I. Keller, Perry
349.5'1

Library of Congress Cataloging-in-Publication Data
Chinese law and legal theory / edited by Perry Keller.
p. cm. — (International library of essays in law and legal theory. Second series)
ISBN 1-84044-735-0
1. Law—China—Philosophy. 2. Law—China—History. I. Keller, Perry. II. Series.

KNN440 .C443 2000
349.51—dc21 00-029956

ISBN 1 84014 735 0

Printed in Great Britain by The Cromwell Press, Trowbridge, Wiltshire

Contents

Acknowledgements

The editor and publishers wish to thank the following for permission to use copyright material.

American Association for the Comparative Study of Law for the essays: Tingmei Fu (1993), 'Legal Person in China: Essence and Limits', *American Journal of Comparative Law*, **41**, pp. 261–97; Perry Keller (1994) 'Sources of Order in Chinese Law', *American Journal of Comparative Law*, **42**, pp. 711–59.

Journal of Asian Law, Columbia University School of Law for the essays: Donald C. Clarke (1996), 'Power and Politics in the Chinese Court System: The Enforcement of Civil Judgments', *Columbia Journal of Asian Law*, **10**, pp. 1–92; Carlos Wing-Hung Lo (1997), 'Socialist Legal Theory in Deng Xiaoping's China', *Columbia Journal of Asian Law*, **11**, pp. 469–86; Kam C. Wong (1996), 'Police Powers and Control in the People's Republic of China: The History of *Shoushen*', *Columbia Journal of Asian Law*, **10**, pp. 367–90.

McGill Law Journal for the essay: Daniel Rubenstein (1997), 'Legal and Institutional Uncertainties in the Domestic Contract Law of the People's Republic of China', *McGill Law Journal*, **42**, pp. 495–536. Copyright © 1997 McGill Law Journal.

Oxford University Press for the essays: Neil J. Diamant (1997), 'The Anatomy of Rural Family Revolution: State, Law, and the Family in Rural China, 1949–1966, Part One', *International Journal of Law, Policy and the Family*, **11**, pp. 149–91. Copyright © 1997 Oxford University Press; Minxin Pei (1997), 'Citizens v. Mandarins: Administrative Litigation in China', *The China Quarterly*, **152**, pp. 832–62. Copyright © 1997 The China Quarterly.

Sage Publications Ltd for the essays: William P. Alford (1999), 'A Second Great Wall? China's Post-Cultural Revolution Project of Legal Construction', *Cultural Dynamics*, **11**, pp. 193–213. Copyright © 1999 Sage Publications; Randall Peerenboom (1999), 'Ruling the Country in Accordance with Law: Reflections on the Rule and Role of Law in Contemporary China', *Cultural Dynamics,* **11**, pp. 315–51.

Texas Law Review Association for the essay: William P. Alford (1986), 'The Inscrutable Occidental? Implications of Roberto Unger's Uses and Abuses of the Chinese Past', *Texas Law Review*, **64** , pp. 915–72.

Washington University Publications for the essay: William C. Jones (1985), 'The Constitution of the People's Republic of China', *Washington University Law Quarterly*, **63**, pp. 707–35.

Yu Xingzhong (1989), 'Legal Pragmatism in the People's Republic of China', *Journal of Chinese Law*, **3**, pp. 29–51. Copyright © 1989 Yu Xingzhong.

Preface to the Second Series

The first series of the International Library of Essays in Law and Legal Theory has established itself as a major research resource with fifty-eight volumes of the most significant theoretical essays in contemporary legal studies. Each volume contains essays of central theoretical importance in its subject area and the series as a whole makes available an extensive range of valuable material of considerable interest to those involved in research, teaching and the study of law.

The rapid growth of theoretically interesting scholarly work in law has created a demand for a second series which includes more recent publications of note and earlier essays to which renewed attention is being given. It also affords the opportunity to extend the areas of law covered in the first series.

The new series follows the successful pattern of reproducing entire essays with the original page numbers as an aid to comprehensive research and accurate referencing. Editors have selected not only the most influential essays but also those which they consider to be of greatest continuing importance. The objective of the second series is to enlarge the scope of the library, include significant recent work and reflect a variety of editorial perspectives.

Each volume is edited by an expert in the specific area who makes the selection on the basis of the quality, influence and significance of the essays, taking care to include essays which are not readily available. Each volume contains a substantial introduction explaining the context and significance of the essays selected.

I am most grateful for the care which volume editors have taken in carrying out the complex task of selecting and presenting essays which meet the exacting criteria set for the series.

TOM CAMPBELL
Series Editor
The Faculty of Law
The Australian National University

Introduction

The essays collected in this volume represent an introduction to the law and legal theory of China[1] and provide a perceptive and well informed guide to a huge subject area of enormous depth and complexity. China's Confucian-based imperial legal system developed and flourished for more than 3000 years. Its final disintegration, following the collapse of the Qing dynasty in 1911, ushered in nearly a century of legal experimentation, development and intermittent disorder. As no single book could possibly offer a fully comprehensive discussion of this rich and diverse system of law, the essays in this volume were chosen to illustrate the best of English-language theoretical scholarship concerning law in China, whilst also introducing topics and issues from across the range of civil, criminal and administrative law.

The study of law in China is now a well established international field of research in which a number of exceptionally talented scholars write in English (see, for example, Turner *et al.*, 2000; Lubman, 1996, 1999; Alford, 1995; Potter, 1994). Nonetheless, outside of China, it is a comparatively small discipline which is centred in the United States – a society in which the strong influence of law and lawyers has happily coincided with a deep fascination with China. In general, English-language publications concerning Chinese law are dominated by the works of practitioners. Keen interest in the commercial potential of the China market has attracted the world's major law firms and fuelled the careers of many capable bilingual lawyers. Publications which feature articles on commercial law in China include *China Law & Practice*, *The China Business Review* and *East Asian Executive Reports*.

Most publications concerning law in China are, of course, written in Chinese and published in China. Not surprisingly, the writers of these essays and books enjoy many obvious advantages over researchers based outside China. They usually have better access to government officials and reports and, because they live and work within Chinese society, they are better placed to appreciate the strengths and weaknesses of the legal system. But, even in translation, their works are not readily understood by non-Chinese readers. Apart from a distinct formality of style, these works tend to be written in a coded fashion in which the writer avoids direct criticism or analysis of potentially sensitive issues. Legal scholars, much like other Chinese intellectuals, often signal their meaning in subtle ways that assume that the reader is an equally skilled participant who knows how to read between the lines.[2] The direct translation of these works into English is not often undertaken as so much of the meaning is lost in the effort.

China frequently provides an easy target for legal commentators who, on failing to discover a legal order aspiring sufficiently to European derived models, claim to find little of importance in what they do see. The Chinese legal system does undoubtedly throw up a host of theoretical and practical problems for Chinese lawyers and their foreign counterparts. Despite an abundance of governmental, workplace and social norms that touch all aspects of daily life, China is not a society in which the rule of law ideal has flourished. The autonomy of law – a strained concept in the best of circumstances – has had little opportunity to develop in a system in which the law, in its creation, interpretation and application, is so deeply permeated by considerations of power, convenience and intuitive justice.

The Chinese legal system therefore presents an interesting contrast to the experience of law in most Western countries. Under China's legal modernization programme of the 1980s and 1990s, a formal legal system of growing complexity has developed. But it is also one characterized both by eclectic borrowing from foreign legal systems and by the strong effects of contemporary, as well as traditional, cultural and political influences. English-language scholarship has responded in two distinct ways to this rapidly evolving, yet unusual, legal order.

First, the study of law in China has pushed academic lawyers to ask fundamental questions about the concept of law and to ask how current or historical Chinese legal regimes should be located within the various patterns of normative organization which might be called law. This effort has provoked much debate over the suitability of the various models or perspectives that have been used to analyse legal developments in China. In his essay, 'The Inscrutable Occidental? Implications of Roberto Unger's Uses and Abuses of the Chinese Past' (Chapter 1), William Alford criticizes the misapplication of analytical categories developed through the study of law in Europe and North America to the study of law in China. In this particular case, he argues that Unger misunderstood, and consequently misrepresented, the origins of imperial law. Furthermore, Unger employed a suspect evolutionary description of law in which China is used merely as an illustration of arrested development because of its apparent failure to mature into the type of 'legal system' which uniquely developed in Europe. Alford has frequently written about the need for Western observers to understand properly the historical, social and political context of Chinese law and to challenge their own preconceptions before deciding on its strengths and weaknesses. The theoretical challenge is to develop concepts of law which do justice to the richness of Chinese legal experience, but which also usefully relate that experience to the wider realm of legal theory.

Second, these efforts to theorize the nature of law in China have triggered an increasingly rigorous empirical approach to the study of Chinese law. It is now evident that the effort to gain a clearer understanding of the nature of Chinese law is often hindered by well established, yet over-rigid, views on the role of law in Chinese society. As Alford has pointed out, Confucian rhetoric denigrating the importance of law in the maintenance of social order has obscured the significant role that substantive and procedural law frequently played in imperial China (Alford, 1997, p. 389). The legacy of this Confucian rhetorical position continues to exert a strong influence on contemporary perceptions of the role of law in China. Moreover, Mao Zedong's own ambivalence towards the development of a system of socialist legality, shared by many other Communist Party leaders, has also encouraged other simplistic characterizations of contemporary Chinese law.

It is, however, only in recent years that legal scholars have attempted to look behind these misleading images. The upheavals of the Cultural Revolution era from 1966 to 1976 and the consequent novelty of much of the current legal order, as well as the secretive nature of communist policy-making and state administration, have limited the opportunities for serious research. But, as many of the essays in this collection demonstrate, there is a widely perceived need to test long-held assumptions and to produce a clearer picture of law in practice. The social scientific study of law is therefore at the forefront of contemporary research on Chinese law.

The 1990s witnessed a reawakening of Western interest in the history of Chinese law after a long period of relative inattention. Better access to documentary materials in China, as well as a growing awareness of the need to revisit old assumptions, has brought forth a number of important new publications (for example, Bernhardt and Huang, 1994; McKnight, 1992). But, given the extraordinary breadth and depth of this subject, there is still much ground-breaking work to be done. In his essay, Alford shows the continuing relevance of inquiry into the pre-imperial origins of Chinese legal thought and the later synthesis of Confucian principles of social order and statecraft with legalist-derived principles of law-based government. Alford and others have also done much to overturn the accepted wisdom that imperial law was merely a secondary mechanism used to impose order when clan organizations and other basic-level social groups failed to constrain their members. If further research confirms that law played a greater role in imperial, and even republican, China than hitherto presumed, this will alter critical underlying assumptions about the historical and cultural underpinnings of contemporary law. The indifference shown by Mao Zedong and others in the communist leadership towards the idea of government through law would, in particular, be seen more clearly as a characteristic of the current era.

The theoretical foundations of socialist law in China have not received broad attention in English-language legal scholarship. This is perhaps due in part to the difficulties faced by jurists in China in seeking to develop domestic legal theory beyond the blunt realities of Leninism. As Yu Xingzhong discusses in Chapter 2, the principles of socialist law in China are rooted in the instrumentalism espoused by A.Y. Vyshinsky, the Soviet prosecutor and legal theorist. In this view, the law is simply an instrument through which the Communist Party expresses the will of the people and suppresses their class enemies.

Vyshinsky's views are no longer a direct source of legal theory in China. The Communist Party has since declared that economic development, rather than class struggle, is the primary goal of the Chinese people. But to what extent is the Party willing to move beyond an instrumental conception of law? Writing a decade ago, Yu Xingzhong argues that, whilst Marxist theory had become little more than a rhetorical device, Chinese policy-makers have not relinquished their pragmatic instrumentalism. In a more recent comment (see Chapter 3), Carlos Lo concurs that the Party's legal doctrine is still fundamentally instrumentalist, but he also sees the Party's commitment to rule through law as a constraint on government discretion out of which further improvements may flow. Plainly, it is the Communist Party's monopoly on power that drives the instrumentalist circularity of published theoretical debate within China. Abandoning Vyshinsky's class-based conception of law, official doctrine now espouses a different materialist understanding of law. Positive law, properly conceived and created, should be rooted in, and reflect, the objective reality of social and economic experience in China. This new theoretical stance appears to mark a shift away from the instrumentalism of the past. However, the Communist Party remains the sole legitimate authority able to determine the correct nature of that objective reality and what policies and laws should result.

Although official legal doctrine is undoubtedly self-serving, we should not underrate the appeal of its underlying theoretical approach. In China there is still a strong intellectual belief in objective social and historical truth and in its revelation through 'scientific' inquiry. It is, moreover, important to distinguish legal practice from the doctrinal rationalizations offered by the Communist Party to justify its exclusive grip on all aspects of policy-making. Throughout most of its period in power, the Party has proclaimed and enforced norms of conduct as an important means of implementing its policies. The focus of scholarly research is consequently on the nature of these norms, their implementation and their effects on Chinese society. And whilst the dramatic growth of the legal system since 1979 attracts most attention, there is much still to be learned about the use of law in the Party's programme of social change in the pre-Cultural Revolution years.

In this respect, Neil Diamant's sociolegal study of the impact of the 1950 Marriage Law on family relations in rural China is especially interesting. In his essay, 'The Anatomy of Rural Family Revolution' (Chapter 4), Diamant challenges the idea that rural women could not avail themselves of their new legal rights under this legislation because of the restrictive nature of traditional countryside life. His research shows that, because of the importance which the Party attached to the radical reform of family relations, local cadres were mobilized to break down resistance to these emancipatory measures. In many localities young women were able to take advantage of the new law to escape or resist unwanted marriages. This shift in power within village society, and the consequent intensification of competition amongst men for sufficient income and status to gain a wife, had many unforeseen consequences for rural life. Diamant's work not only reveals the weaknesses of the accepted dichotomy between Chinese urban modernity and rural tradition, but also provides useful insights into the nature of women's emancipation in non-Western societies.

The Communist Party's effective use of the Marriage Law to spearhead its attempts to reform family relations should not, however, obscure the gradual stagnation of the legal system in the 1949–1966 Maoist period. The legal profession suffered heavily during the 1957 Anti-Rightist Campaign, and intermittent attempts to revive legal reform came to nothing with the abandonment of formal law during the Cultural Revolution. It is against this background that William Jones considered the adoption of China's present 1982 Constitution. In 1979 the Party, under Deng Xiaoping's leadership, had committed itself to a major programme of legal reform. But despite the appearance of new laws and regulations and the promise of many more, the prospects for meaningful constitutional law remained dim. The three preceding Constitutions certainly provided useful indications of the general political climate and direction of policy at the time of their adoption, but they never functioned as binding, effective charters delimiting the powers of state institutions or guaranteeing fundamental rights and responsibilities.

Jones' 'The Constitution of the People's Republic of China' (Chapter 5) offers an insight into the hopes and many uncertainties that marked the adoption of the 1982 Constitution. It is therefore a good indication of the achievements of the legal modernization programme that, in some important respects, the new Constitution has proven far more successful than expected. The key institutions of state have, to varying extents, grown into their constitutionally apportioned roles. To some surprise, the National People's Congress (NPC) is no longer an irrelevant rubber-stamp parliament and is now an important legislative institution. Moreover, some provincial-level people's congresses are beginning to develop along similar lines, providing a weak, but visible, presence operating within the axis of power that unites the provincial Communist Party structures and the provincial people's governments. It is, of course, true that these constitutional successes have been secured through the determined efforts of powerful figures in the Party hierarchy to build political and economic power bases out of these nascent state institutions. Nonetheless, the constitutional allocation of powers has been a significant point of reference in these personal and institutional rivalries.

The Constitution has been much less successful as a guarantor of individual rights and freedoms. Whilst it sets out a range of familiar civil liberties, no court or other body has been established to apply these principles to specific cases.[3] Consequently, the constitutional rights and freedoms of Chinese citizens can only be implemented once they are expressed in the form of national laws adopted by the NPC which can then be enforced by courts or other institutions. This indirect approach to the implementation of the Constitution has yielded some measurable progress. The 1989 Administrative Litigation Law and other laws and regulations on administrative law have created legal rights to judicial review and mechanisms to limit the abuse of administrative power (see Leung, 1998, p. 104). The revision of the Criminal Procedure Law in 1997 also contained noteworthy improvements in the protection of individual rights (see Wong, Chapter 10, this volume). But, in other cases, the necessary national implementing legislation is non-existent or drafted so as to merely confirm the enormous discretionary powers of the state.

The successes and failures of legal reform in China since 1979 have led many academic lawyers to question their basic assumptions about the paths of legal development. In Chapters 6 and 7 Randall Peerenboom and William Alford both perceptively argue that we must first shed our latent liberal democratic perspectives before we can properly understand the legal regime that China's leaders are attempting to foster. The post-Cultural Revolution leadership has supported legal reforms principally to promote economic development, maintain public order and to raise China's international credibility. These aims may support what Peerenboom calls a 'thin' theory of the rule of law, but they do not amount to a thicker liberal democratic vision of law. Yet the long-term direction of law reform and legal development in China remains unresolved. Eventually the country's educated, urban classes may demand a less instrumental and more autonomous form of law, but there are major political and cultural barriers to any fundamental shift in that direction.

China's legislative system is, for example, limited in its capacity to produce comprehensive, well designed legislation capable of effective enforcement. The interpretation and implementation of national legislation mainly occurs through the use of central and regional government administrative and regulatory powers. But these powerful administrative bodies are well equipped to turn the ambiguous language of national legislation to their advantage. As Perry Keller in 'Sources of Order in Chinese Law' (Chapter 8) explains, the State Council, the administrative arm of China's central government, and its provincial level counterparts, the people's governments, were experienced users of normative methods of government long before the resurrection of NPC law-making in the late 1970s. China's constitutional hierarchy of legislative and regulatory powers is therefore an awkward marriage of necessity between the theoretically supreme national legislature and the politically more powerful state bureaucracies. It is thus no surprise that one of the principal themes of legal reform since 1979 has been the effort to define and control the power of administrative bodies to make regulations.

These reforms have clearly advantaged the National People's Congress, which has gradually acquired a degree of genuine authority. Indeed, the question of whether national or regional regulations are consistent with the laws of the NPC is now a widely recognized issue of concern. Nonetheless, the resolution of that issue still lies principally in the hands of the State Council which enjoys powers – not shared by the courts or the NPC – to interpret and rescind secondary and tertiary regulations. There are also good reasons to believe that national legislation will continue to be drafted in ambiguous, adaptable language. First, China's political culture plainly supports the retention of broad discretionary powers by state officials. This flexibility is thought to be necessary for the government to react quickly to unforeseen events and to push new reforms forward. Chinese legal scholars have argued that, at this point in China's economic and political development, flexibility is more important than legislative stability (Zhu Suli, 1998, p. 429). Second, as an immense country that has paradoxically rejected a federal division of powers, China relies on a degree of ambiguity in legislative language to allow the adaptation of national laws to different regional and local circumstances.

In some legal systems the courts are able to determine the scope of legislative and regulatory powers through the device of constitutional and statutory interpretation, but in China the courts are not intended to operate as the final arbiters in matters of constitutional or legislative intent. Whilst they can provide a potential forum in which to determine the legal aspects of criminal, civil and administrative actions, the courts are, at the end of the day, merely one among several specialized administrative networks. They are therefore severely limited in their capacity to impose their decisions on other government bodies.

Donald Clarke discusses this issue in his thoroughly researched essay, 'Power and Politics in the Chinese Court System' (Chapter 9). He notes that the courts are something of an anomaly in China as their formal powers to award damages and other remedies cut across the skein of quasi-autonomous administrative networks into which China's system of government is divided. Normally, when administrative bodies in China are in dispute they will refer the matter to a common superior, sometimes even bringing the matter to the State Council for resolution. The courts, however, are attempting to enforce 'a set of rules that are essentially alien to the system: rules that purport to operate horizontally, across bureaucracies, and to bind all institutions and citizens equally' (p. 373). Judges in China are therefore understandably reluctant to grant a judgement which would place them in conflict with other government bodies. This is especially so when the body in question is connected to the local government which provides the court with its funding and other resources. Clarke suggests that the inability of China's courts to enforce property rights and contract rights reliably has important implications for theories of law and development. His research indicates that a consistently enforced system of property and contract law is not as important as previously thought for economic development. Chinese economic decision-makers must look elsewhere for sources of certainty and predictability that might otherwise have been provided by legally enforceable property and contract rights. These certainly include reliance on institutional and personal authority, as well as reliance on networks of mutually beneficial commercial relationships.

The Supreme People's Court (SPC) stands at the head of the national court system and its principal function is to supervise the decisions of the thousands of lower courts spread across the country (Finder, 1993). The SPC's main method for guiding these courts is through the interpretation of national laws. However, the Court hears very few actual cases and issues most legal interpretations through a variety of specialized administrative documents. It is in this role that Chinese jurists have argued that the SPC has usurped some of the functions of the National People's Congress (Finder, 1993, p. 183). In 1982 the Standing Committee of the NPC delegated the power to interpret national laws to the Court, but only so far as necessary for the resolution of cases before the courts. The Court has nonetheless issued several lengthy interpretative statements which are closer to supplementary legislation than narrowly framed judicial opinion. And whilst the Court has helpfully clarified many serious ambiguities in the law, the extent to which these interpretations are binding on other governmental bodies has yet to be fully resolved.

In the area of criminal law, however, the position of the Court is much clearer. The restoration of China's courts towards the end of the Cultural Revolution occurred as part of a general renewal of the formal criminal law process. Guided by the internal political–legal committees of the Communist Party, the courts function in close cooperation with the procuratorates and the public security organs. Consequently, the Supreme People's Court, as well as the lower courts, frequently enjoy less autonomy in criminal as compared to civil proceedings. In this tripartite system the avenues for lateral coordination between government bodies are clearer and more effective, but the demand for consensus is more intense. This is particularly true during periodic anti-crime drives, such as the 'Strike Hard' campaigns, when the three branches of the criminal justice system are mobilized to crack down on designated offences.

In the mid-1990s, the Chinese government initiated the reform and consolidation of the criminal law system, which had grown inexorably through the piecemeal issue of supplementary regulations and interpretations since its re-establishment in the late 1970s.[4] The revised Criminal Procedure Law, which took effect on 1 January 1997, introduced several important changes, including more transparent procedures, improved rights to counsel and limits on administrative determinations of guilt. The new law was also the culmination of a long-term effort to curtail the power of public security organs to detain suspects for 'shelter and investigation'. As Kam Wong's essay, 'Police Powers and Control in the People's Republic of China: The History of *Shoushen*', explains, these powers were originally developed in the early 1960s to control unauthorized population movement following the economically disastrous Great Leap Forward. 'Shelter and investigation' later became a convenient way to detain any person for weeks at a time without resort to the formal criminal process. Although these powers had no evident basis in national law, the convenience and flexibility of these powers ensured that many in the Party leadership remained convinced of their continuing necessity. The gradual clarification, curtailment and final abolition of 'shelter and investigation' is therefore a noteworthy success for legal reform in the criminal law sphere.

Other criminal law reforms have been less inspiring. Although the public security organs have lost the power to detain for 'shelter and investigation', they still retain substantial powers to sentence a person to 're-education through labour' for up to three years for anti-social offences that do not warrant a full criminal prosecution.[5] In addition, the recent revision of the substantive Criminal Law, welcome in some respects, has merely replaced the ill-defined crimes of 'counter revolution' with new ill-defined crimes that 'endanger state security'. In this respect, the criminal law system, which is the foundation stone of the Chinese legal order, remains the sphere best known for breathtaking discretion and naked instrumentalism.

In comparison, developments in administrative law – a relatively new element in the Chinese legal system – have introduced legal mechanisms which are potentially available to restrain the unlawful abuse of power (Potter, 1994; Finder, 1989). These mechanisms are principally located in the ground-breaking Administrative Litigation Law (ALL), adopted by the NPC in the spring of 1989 during the more relaxed political environment which preceded the Tiananmen student demonstrations. Since its enactment, the Chinese government has worked to flesh out the administrative law system through the adoption of four other major laws concerning the exercise of state administrative authority.[6] These laws have, in principle, imposed procedural requirements for administrative review or appeal procedures, clarified the scope of the state's obligation to compensate individuals for unlawful acts, curtailed the power of state bodies to impose fines or other administrative penalties and strengthened the legal basis for internal government investigations.

Despite a host of limitations and ambiguities, this set of administrative laws has opened up avenues to redress against the state – if not the Communist Party – which were once inconceivable in modern China. But the difficulties facing those who wish to make use of these opportunities are not to be underestimated. The primary purpose of these legal reforms is to improve the efficiency of government. To some extent they are merely a new twist in the central government's age-old quest to restrict the ability of local officials to act contrary to national policy without also fettering their abilities to implement those policies decisively and effectively. In substance, these laws constitute a fairly cautious empowerment of the individual against the state, by harnessing the power of public complaint in aid of government policy. China's administrative laws do not, however, empower anyone to contest the constitutionality or legality of any law or regulation.

Nonetheless, in Chapter 11 Minxin Pei argues that citizens have resorted to the Administrative Litigation Law more often and more successfully than some commentators have previously suggested. Pei's work is a superb example of the empirical research now being done at the cutting edge of Chinese legal studies. In researching his essay, 'Citizens v. Mandarins: Administrative Litigation in China', he has used court records to investigate the impact of the ALL on the behaviour of individuals seeking redress for grievances against state bodies. According to Pei, not only do Chinese citizens sue the government to protect their liberty or property only as a last resort, but the courts also remain reluctant to decide administrative law cases which endanger their relations with local government. However, the ALL has given political and economic entrepreneurs a potential lever which they are increasingly willing to use. In Pei's view, this trend in administrative litigation is part of a broader evolution in relations between state and society in China. Economic reforms have led to a much more diverse and sophisticated society in which citizens hold new expectations of government and are willing to voice their criticisms. In this changing environment the Administrative Litigation Law may well grow beyond the modest intentions of its drafters.

It is clearly in the economic field that the ALL has the most chance of realizing its latent potential. The remarkable growth of China's economy during the 1980s and 1990s has created many large, profit-driven corporate entities willing to defend their interests by any accepted means. But this growth has also seen a huge expansion in the range of activities regulated by the Chinese government which, in most cases, has followed its instincts to impose public law regulatory solutions on the market rather than encouraging parties to pursue their interests through civil law procedures. The possibilities for administrative litigation would therefore appear to be virtually endless.

For more than two decades, Chinese policy-makers have struggled to determine the direction and pace of economic reform and the appropriate role for the state in the new market economy. It is these concerns that have shaped the development of China's *sui generis* system of civil law, as legislative drafters have borrowed or invented legal concepts useful for the tasks at hand. The reception of foreign law therefore can be a rough and ready affair. Foreign legal concepts and principles, long familiar in other legal systems, have arrived in China shorn of many existing intellectual associations and fitted out for new purposes. This is certainly true of the civilian concept of the legal or juristic person (*fa ren*), introduced in 1987 in the General Principles of Civil Law. As Daniel Rubenstein points out in Chapter 13, this concept was borrowed to provide a legal structure on which to base the formal separation of state-owned productive and service enterprises from the state administrative structure; it was not intended to be a recognition in law of the formal equality in civil law of enterprises, individuals and government institutions.

Since its appearance, the legal person has gradually acquired greater substance in Chinese law, as Tingmei Fu explains in his essay, 'Legal Person in China: Essence and Limits' (Chapter 12). Having settled on a convenient legal form for state-owned enterprises, as well as approved collective enterprises, policy-makers then needed to determine the legal capacities of these new entities. Full autonomy on a free market model was, at that time, both impractical and ideologically unacceptable. These enterprises had charge of enormous state assets which, in theory, belonged to the Chinese people and they were also major social welfare providers for their employees. The legal person was therefore subject to close constraints, including a strict limited capacity rule. In the 1990s, the need for greater flexibility and autonomy was met through the adoption of the Company Law which builds on, but does not displace, the wider category of the legal person.

Contract law in China has evolved in an equally complex manner. Prior to Deng Xiaoping's initiation of economic reform and opening to foreign investment, contract was primarily an instrument of economic planning. Contract terms were normally imposed on the parties and implemented under the supervision of an administrative authority. Contractual obligations were also perceived differently in a Chinese cultural context. In a society in which responsibilities are traditionally defined by personal relationships, a sense of binding obligation to comparatively unknown parties could be weak or absent. It is thus not surprising that Chinese contract law has, until recently, developed under two distinct models. The 1981 Economic Contract Law governed contractual relations between non-governmental parties acting outside of the planned economy, whilst the 1985 Foreign Economic Contract Law governed relations between foreign and Chinese entities. The domestic law provided for considerably more government intervention in the contractual process, although neither law provided for complete autonomy of the parties. The final pillar of the contract law system, the Technology Contract Law, was adopted in 1987.

In his essay, 'Legal and Institutional Uncertainties in the Domestic Contract Law of the People's Republic of China' (Chapter 13), Daniel Rubenstein has written a clear and careful account of the development of domestic contract law since 1979, placing the law in its political and economic context and exploring the theoretical tensions within the law. Commercial lawyers have frequently neglected this side of the Chinese contract law system, concentrating their efforts on the law usually applied to foreign businesses. However, it is the evolution of domestic contract law that finally enabled the National People's Congress in 1999 to adopt a unified Contract Law which supports a much wider application of the principle of freedom of contract.[7] It will nonetheless take some time before the principles enshrined in the 1999 Contract Law begin to erode some pre-existing practices. There are certainly many Chinese companies which have enjoyed comparatively light regulatory control over their contractual relations for some time, and the new law reflects this reality. However, the old system, which encompassed not only the national contract laws but also a vast accumulation of special regulations and interpretations, also reflected the reality of bureaucratic power in China. The Contract Law contains notable compromises on questions of party autonomy and state intervention and no doubt these will be subject to varied interpretations. The adoption of a national law by the NPC is plainly an important event for any area of law as it signals political consensus within the leadership on a range of key principles and issues. But consensus at the top on matters of general principle has often failed to change practice at the local level.

Pitman Potter and Li Jianyong have also examined the problems of legal development in a transitional economy in their essay, 'Regulating Labour Relations in China: The Challenge of

Adapting to the Socialist Market Economy' (Chapter 14). The Chinese government has faced an enduring dilemma in the field of employment relations. As an avowedly socialist regime, it has always presented itself as a champion of the rights of workers and has introduced many employment structures and programmes which have provided real benefits for employees. Yet, as Potter and Li point out:

> . . . economic reform and the privatization (or at least corporatization) of production enterprises would appear to justify granting greater rights to workers in the areas of collective bargaining, work stoppages, and so on. Yet the regime also faces the need for continued economic growth, which mandates greater control over worker discipline even as it permits declining conditions of employment. (p. 527)

The 1995 Labour Law is, as a result, a strained and probably transitional compromise between the desire to maintain the levers of state control whilst also encouraging flexibility and adaptation.

The compromises underlying the Labour Law are expressed, as is usually the case in China's national legislation, in vague, formalistic language. The meaning of these provisions is worked out by national and regional officials through the issue of secondary and tertiary regulations as well as the constant issue of ad hoc notices and verbal instructions. But the day-to-day enforcement of this cascading hierarchy of law depends, as noted above, on local officials whose perspective is distinctly different from that of their superiors in Beijing or even the provincial capital. In particular, efforts to protect the rights of employees may well be clouded by close association with the managers of local enterprises.

The deterioration of working conditions is now a major concern in China and has given rise to an increasing number of strikes and other work-related disturbances. Nor has the 1995 Labour Law brought about any noticeable change in this worsening trend. Nonetheless, the enactment of the law has been a significant landmark. The existence of a national law has at least set out basic rights and responsibilities which have an enormous symbolic importance in setting the agenda for specific disputes and shaping public debate more generally. At the official level, the focus of debate has now moved from the discussion of labour rights in the abstract to the question of how the Labour Law is to be effectively implemented.

But whether the effective implementation of the Labour Law moves beyond the level of discussion and debate depends on the fate of the legal regime as a whole. The central leadership turned to law in the late 1970s to help make government administration work more efficiently and effectively. From this perspective, the promise of law has always been that it will curb the power of local officials and improve the central government's ability to implement its policies. Law is thus an instrument and a tactic in the struggle to centralize power. However, the government's economic reforms have unleashed a thrusting commercial society which is, in many ways, increasingly difficult to manage from Beijing. The central government's administrative structure does not reach into the lives of ordinary people and it must rely on local governments. Yet it is at the local level that legal reforms are most visibly in difficulty. The state, as a nationally organized entity, is no longer closely involved in day-to-day life. But far from giving space to an emergent and responsible civil society, what has arisen is a lucrative nexus between local officials and local commerce. In the new commercialized and consumer-driven China, it will require creative thinking and new methods if law is to achieve greater practical significance for ordinary citizens.

Notes

1 This book contains essays concerning the legal system of the People's Republic of China, but does not include the common law legal system of the Hong Kong Special Administrative Region, nor does it attempt to cover the civilian legal system of Taiwan.
2 On contemporary intellectual life in China, see Barmé (1999).
3 The NPC has the sole power to amend, interpret and supervise the implementation of the Constitution, but as yet has not established any special procedures for constitutional interpretation or supervision.
4 For an overview of recent criminal law reforms, see, *Wrongs and Rights*, and *Opening to Reform*, published by Lawyers Committee for Human Rights <http://www.lchr.org>.
5 Administration of Public Order Regulations 1982.
6 The 1990 Administrative Review Regulations, the 1994 State Compensation Law, the 1996 Administrative Penalty Law and the 1997 Administrative Supervision Law.
7 For commentary and translation, see Zaloom and Liu (1999, p. 15).

References

Alford, William P. (1995), *To Steal a Book is an Elegant Offense: Intellectual Property Law in Chinese Civilization*, Stanford, Conn.: Stanford University Press.

Alford, William P. (1997), 'Law, Law, What Law?', *Modern China*, **23**(4), pp. 398–419.

Barmé, Geremie (1999), *In the Red: On Contemporary Chinese Culture*, New York: Columbia University Press.

Bernhardt, Kathryn and Huang, Philip (1994), *Civil Law in Qing and Republican China*, Palo Alto: Stanford University Press.

Finder, Susan (1989), 'Like Throwing an Egg against a Stone? Administrative Litigation in the People's Republic of China', *Journal of Chinese Law*, **3**(1), pp. 145–224.

Finder, Susan (1993), 'The Supreme People's Court of the People's Republic of China', *Journal of Chinese Law*, **7**, pp. 124–224.

Leung, Conita (1998), 'Chinese Administrative Law Practice: Limitations and Prospects', *Hong Kong Law Journal*, **28**(1), pp. 104–117.

Lubman, Stanley (ed.) (1996), *China's Legal Reforms*, Oxford: Oxford University Press.

Lubman, Stanley (1999), *Bird in a Cage: Legal Reform in China after Mao*, Stanford, Conn.: Stanford University Press.

McKnight, Brian (1992), *Law and Order in Sung China*, Cambridge: Cambridge University Press.

Potter, Pitman B. (ed.) (1994), *Domestic Law Reforms in Post-Mao China*, Armonk, NY: M.E. Sharpe.

Turner, Karen, Feinerman, James and Kent, Guy (eds) (2000), *The Limits of the Rule of Law in China*, Seattle: University of Washington Press.

Zaloom, Anthony and Liu, Hongchuan (1999), 'China's Contract Law Marks a New Stage in Commercial Law Drafting', *China Law & Practice*, May, pp. 15–18.

Zhu Suli (1998), 'Paradoxes of Legal Development in China from the Perspective of Modernisation', *Hong Kong Law Journal*, **28**(3), pp. 428–39.

Part I
Theory and History

[1]

The Inscrutable Occidental? Implications of Roberto Unger's Uses and Abuses of the Chinese Past

William P. Alford*

> The problem faced by the observer remote in space or time is that he must approach the work from the standpoint of the conditions of his own existence and of his ideas about those conditions. He is not the maker of the work; his perspective on it differs from the maker's; and yet he must somehow incorporate the latter's perspective into his own to reach a complete comprehension of the artifact. He must solve the ambiguity of meaning. How can he do so unless he establishes a community of understandings and of values with the maker whose work he interprets or with the agent whose act he observes?[1]

There is a poignant irony to Roberto Mangabeira Unger's characterization of the dilemma that confronts those who would engage in serious

* Professor of Law, University of California, Los Angeles; B.A. 1970, Amherst College; LL.B. 1972, University of Cambridge; M.A. 1974, Yale University; M.A. 1975, Yale University; J.D. 1977, Harvard University.

I owe debts of gratitude to many people for the help that they provided me as I prepared this Article. In particular, I wish to thank two individuals, Professor Chang Wei-jen, Director of the Legal History Project of the Institute of History and Philology of the Academia Sinica on Taiwan and Professor of Law at National Taiwan University, and Roberto Mangabeira Unger of the Harvard Law School. Professor Chang for years has been a brilliant and unselfish source of inspiration and advice to me and countless other students of China's past. Although in this Article I am sharply critical of Professor Unger's work, I sincerely appreciate his willingness to share with me unpublished manuscripts in an effort to advance the scholarly enterprise. I also would like to express my appreciation for their support and guidance to many colleagues, students, and other individuals, including Richard L. Abel, Alison G. Anderson, Richard D. Baum, Chi-yun Chen, James V. Feinerman, William E. Forbath, Carole Goldberg-Ambrose, Wai-k'am Ho, Anna Marie Howell, Andrew C.K. Hsieh, Kenneth L. Karst, David N. Keightley, Christine A. Littleton, Steven R. Munzer, Frances E. Olsen, Peter Neumann, Susan Westerberg Prager, Arthur I. Rosett, Gary T. Schwartz, Steven H. Shiffrin, Phillip R. Trimble, Thomas W. Weidenbach, and Stephen C. Yeazell. Special thanks should also go to Frederick Smith and other friends at the Law Library of the UCLA School of Law for unstinting bibliographic assistance, the Career Development Program of the University of California, the Research Committee of the UCLA Academic Senate, the UCLA International Studies and Overseas Programs Committee, and the Dean's Fund of the UCLA School of Law for their financial support of my work; and Thelma Dekker, Genevieve Gilbert-Rolfe, and Margaret Kiever who patiently and skillfully transformed my illegibly word-processed drafts into a final product.

I have utilized major standard translations where I believe that they accurately convey the meaning of the original Chinese text. Chinese names are romanized according to the Wade-Giles system, with the exception of names of publications and authors in the People's Republic of China [hereinafter PRC] now regularly romanized according to the *pinyin* system.

I, of course, remain responsible for any opinions expressed and errors made in this Article.

1. R. Unger, Knowledge and Politics 110 (1975).

comparative study. Professor Unger describes it with perceptive grace,[2] and yet his own scholarship does not incorporate this insight.[3] Indeed, his failure to establish such "communit[ies] of understandings"[4] reveals the extent to which he is trapped within the very values of modern Western society that he, as a self-avowed "total"[5] critic, indicates he wishes to transcend.[6]

This Article focuses upon what may at first seem a subject best left for antiquarians or area specialists: Roberto Unger's treatment of the core of Chinese civilization—the period before the unification of China as an empire in 221 B.C.[7] The subject, however, is hardly arcane for Unger. Nor should it be for us, given his prominence[8] in and beyond the world of legal academe.[9] Ancient China occupies a position of considerable importance in Professor Unger's speculations about legal development in general.[10] It provides, he suggests, "a contrast case" that, when compared to the post-Renaissance West, "promises to deepen our insight into the complex relationship among modes of social organization, types of consciousness, and forms of normative order."[11] Although "the events that resulted in the Chinese imperial unification had much in common with those that produced the Western nation-states . . . their legal consequences," he asserts, "were very different."[12] As a result, the West was able to develop the rule of law that he characterizes as the cornerstone of the liberal state,[13] but the schools of thought that he treats as the foundation of Chinese civilization "shared assumptions that forbade them to defend the rule of law in the modern Western sense or

2. *See id.*; R. UNGER, LAW IN MODERN SOCIETY: TOWARD A CRITICISM OF SOCIAL THEORY 19 (1976) [hereinafter cited as R. UNGER, LAW IN MODERN SOCIETY].

3. *See infra* Part III.

4. R. UNGER, *supra* note 1, at 110.

5. *Id.* at 2.

6. *See infra* Part III.

7. In 221 B.C. the nation-states of the North China plain (which is considered the heartland of Chinese civilization) were for the first time unified into a single empire by the nation-state known as Ch'in. Although the dynasty established by Ch'in collapsed a mere sixteen years later, its empire lived on and expanded under the name of China. For more on the Ch'in unification, see D. BODDE, CHINA'S FIRST UNIFIER (1938).

8. *E.g.*, Shiffrin, *Liberalism, Radicalism and Legal Scholarship*, 30 UCLA L. REV. 201, 204 (1983); Leff, Book Review, 29 STAN. L. REV. 879, 880 (1977) (reviewing R. UNGER, KNOWLEDGE AND POLITICS (1975)). Shiffrin and Leff couple their recognition of Unger's contribution with highly insightful criticism of his work.

9. *See, e.g.*, Raskin, *The Law Wars*, L.A. Weekly, Dec. 13, 1985, at 37, col. 1.

10. *See infra* notes 58-63 and accompanying text. It should be noted that Unger suggests by way of caveat that there are limits to his use of the Chinese example to prove his points regarding "the historical bases of modern Western law," R. UNGER, LAW IN MODERN SOCIETY, *supra* note 2, at 48, but then proceeds to use that example without meaningful limits. *See id.* at 86-126. For more on Unger's use of caveats, see *infra* note 295.

11. R. UNGER, LAW IN MODERN SOCIETY, *supra* note 2, at 88.

12. *Id.* at 48.

13. *See id.* at 192.

indeed even to conceive of it."[14]

Unfortunately, it is Unger, rather than the ancient Chinese, whose assumptions have produced a failure of imagination. In his determination to use China to prove his points about the rise of the Western liberal state and in his failure to recognize the extent to which he presumes that his values are universal,[15] Unger is indifferent to the integrity of the Chinese past. Consequently, virtually every major dimension of his attempt to portray that past is exaggerated or misleading, if not simply wrong.[16] The inaccuracy of that picture obscures from Unger the broader character of Chinese civilization, casts doubt upon the soundness of his use of China as a "contrast case" to confirm assertions about the relation of law and society generally, and raises questions about the alternative to modern society that he endeavors to develop.

This study considers Unger's analysis of preimperial China with three central purposes in mind. Its principal objective is to examine Professor Unger's use of the Chinese past. This portrayal warrants attention both in itself and for what it tells us about Unger's attempts to theorize more broadly about legal development. Much controversy surrounds Roberto Unger and his work today.[17] But whether one admires[18] or is critical of[19] Professor Unger's scholarship—and there seems to be ample reason in his writing for both reactions—it ought not be disregarded.[20] Professor Unger is one of the most prominent figures in American legal academe today and his writing clearly has had an enormous impact upon

14. *Id.* at 106.

15. *See infra* Part III.

16. *See infra* Part II.

17. *See, e.g.*, *"Of Law and the River," and of Nihilism and Academic Freedom*, 35 J. LEGAL EDUC. 1 (1985).

18. *See, e.g.*, Monahan, Book Review, 61 SOC. & SOC. RES. 431, 432 (1977) (reviewing R. UNGER, LAW IN MODERN SOCIETY) ("One leaves this book with the feeling that a century from now scholars may still be poring over it, much as they do now with the works of Marx, Durkheim and Weber.").

19. *See, e.g.*, Richards, Book Review, 44 FORDHAM L. REV. 873, 874 (1976) (reviewing R. UNGER, LAW IN MODERN SOCIETY) ("[T]heoretical abstraction has the virtue of allowing Unger to indulge his preference for a style of portentous grandeur and prophetic apostrophe; its vice, however, is the deepest criticism of any theory, emptiness.").

20. Unger's stature and influence are such that the enterprise of speaking to the questionable picture he presents of preimperial China is worthwhile in itself. Many reviews of Professor Unger's work—especially of *Law in Modern Society*—assume that his depiction of distant cultures is correct. To the extent that they have considered this dimension of his work, reviewers, including some who have criticized other facets of his scholarship, have praised his breadth of knowledge. *E.g.*, Macdonald, Book Review, 57 SOC. SCI. Q. 700, 701 (1976); Monahan, *supra* note 18, at 432; Parsons, Book Review, 12 L. SOC. REV. 145, 146 (1977-1978); *see also* Parsons, *Law as an Intellectual Stepchild*, 47 SOC. INQUIRY 11, 36 (1977) (describing Unger's treatment of China as "a notable contribution").

For an illustration of the influence of Unger's views upon a general audience, see Miller, *Unger Lecture Concerns Comparative Tradition*, Harv. L. Rec., Jan. 30, 1976, at 14-15, col. 1; *id.* Feb. 6, 1976, at 11, col. 3 (letter of J.V. Feinerman); *id.* Feb. 13, 1976, at 11, col. 1 (letter of J.A. Cohen); *id.* Feb. 27, 1976, at 11, col. 1 (letter of S.B. Young).

contemporary legal scholarship.[21]

His prominence notwithstanding, an analysis of Professor Unger's work is not the sole object of this Article. Although his depiction of the Chinese past is deeply flawed, Professor Unger has at least raised for the consideration of an American legal audience the history and thought of the era that constitutes the foundation of Chinese culture. China is simply too important a civilization to be ignored by American academic lawyers engaging in comparative scholarship, in the formulation of general legal theory, or in speculation about the uniqueness and nature of our own legal heritage. This Article does not purport to present the last word as to the importance of preimperial China for an American legal audience. Indeed, our understanding of preimperial China has undergone such profound change during the past twenty-five years that any effort to generalize about that era should be received with great caution.[22] Rather, as a second objective, this Article hopes to consider preimperial China more thoroughly than has been done heretofore in an American law journal,[23] while recognizing that much more must be done if our thinking about law is to encompass China's rich legal tradition.

Professor Unger's problems in portraying the character of preimperial Chinese civilization emanate, at least in part, from his reliance upon frameworks of analysis that are far more restricted by the forms and values of modern liberal society than he imagines. The third and final goal of this Article is to examine those frameworks in order to stimulate further consideration of the difficulties that face those who engage in serious comparative legal scholarship.[24] We cannot escape the perspectives of

21. Typical of the attention paid Unger's work are two recent major articles in the *University of Pennsylvania Law Review*. Cornell, *Toward a Modern/Postmodern Reconstruction of Ethics*, 133 U. PA. L. REV. 291 (1985); Boyle, *The Politics of Reason: Critical Legal Theory and Local Social Thought*, 133 U. PA. L. REV. 685 (1985).

22. *See infra* notes 73-76 and accompanying text.

23. This is not a hard claim to sustain, given that during the past five decades only a single article principally concerned with any feature of preimperial China has appeared in any law journal published in the United States. That piece addressed only one aspect of international law in the preimperial era. Chen, *Equality of States in Ancient China*, 35 AM. J. INT'L L. 641 (1941). A very small number of articles published since then have considered in passing other aspects of early Chinese civilization. The most comprehensive such discussion does not purport to move beyond a brief treatment of the core of Confucian and Legalist thought regarding law. Lee & Lai, *The Chinese Conceptions of Law: Confucian, Legalist and Buddhist*, 29 HASTINGS L.J. 1307, 1307-12 (1978).

For more on contemporary scholarship on preimperial China, see *infra* notes 73-76 and accompanying text.

24. As Martin Shapiro has observed, American legal academe does not hold comparative scholarship in the highest regard. M. SHAPIRO, COURTS: A COMPARATIVE STUDY at vii (1982). In part, this may be attributable to the prevalence of the type of attitudes discussed with respect to Professor Unger *infra* Part III (including, for example, the assumption that Western legal development is far superior to that of other parts of the world). It also may be due in part, however, to the unwillingness of many comparativists to move beyond the descriptive in discussing foreign legal systems.

our own society.[25] Nor is it clear that we necessarily would wish to do so, even if we could. But, in any event, an awareness of the limitations that we face should commence and guide, rather than conclude, our inquiry.

This Article in Part I portrays Professor Unger's view of the relevance of an inquiry into law for social theorists and recapitulates the important role that he accords the Chinese example. Part II seeks both to provide a sinological critique of Unger's use of the Chinese past and to convey more closely the character of preimperial Chinese law, society, and thought. In so doing, it draws where possible upon materials that were available to Professor Unger at the time that he wrote about that era.[26] The reader may find that this discussion of Unger's treatment of preimperial China in Part II provides a great deal of detail about a new and strange topic, but that detail is both important in itself and as a basis for Part III.

The final Part of this Article considers the assumptions that undergird the frameworks through which Professor Unger endeavors to understand legal development and consciousness. In so doing, it considers not only the constraints that those assumptions impose upon his efforts to grasp the character of preimperial China, but also the limitations that they place upon his broader social theory and, in particular, his call for a new social order. Acknowledging the enormity of the task that confronts the serious comparativist, Part III also briefly suggests broad directions in which comparativists might proceed in seeking to minimize the type of problems evident in Professor Unger's work.

I

Law, for Professor Unger, is not merely one among many social artifacts from which the aspiring social theorist might choose at random.[27] To the contrary, in his view, law is a unique vehicle through which to understand society, for "[e]ach society reveals through its law the inner-

25. For a further discussion of these limitations, and efforts to deal constructively with them, see *infra* notes 413-18, 444-53 and accompanying text.

26. My discussion of Professor Unger's treatment of the "Chinese case" and its implications centers upon materials that were accessible to Professor Unger prior to the publication in 1976 of *Law in Modern Society* (which contains his principal discussion of preimperial China). R. Unger, Law in Modern Society, *supra* note 2. I have done so to portray fairly and fully the nature of Professor Unger's use of the Chinese past and because I do believe that valuable contributions to our understanding of China can—and should—be made by persons who are not area specialists. Given the richness of Chinese scholarship not available in translation at the time he wrote and the advances made in the study of preimperial China generally since then, I will at times draw upon material not available in Western languages before 1976. In each such instance, I will so inform the reader.

27. *See id.* at 47; *infra* note 350 and accompanying text.

most secrets of the manner in which it holds men together."[28] As such, "[l]aw seems a peculiarly fruitful subject of inquiry, for the effort to understand its significance takes us straight to the heart of each of the [three] major unsolved puzzles of social theory."[29] Law replicates the problem of method in social theory by at once being both descriptive and prescriptive;[30] law "bears closely upon the problems of social order" by mediating between public and private interests;[31] and law poses what he terms "the problem of modernity" by embodying the conflict between an ideology that values highly impersonal formal rules and a concern for substantive justice that at times may necessitate disregard of those very rules.[32]

If we are to begin to clarify the "relationship between law and society," Professor Unger informs us, we must eschew the timidity of the cultural relativists[33] and seek to organize legal experience into the "major sorts of law."[34] Only then will we be able to "describe the connections between species of law, on one side, and of society, on the other."[35] The typology that Professor Unger has generated for this task divides law into three distinct forms: "customary or interactional law,"[36] "bureau-

28. R. UNGER, LAW IN MODERN SOCIETY, *supra* note 2, at 47.

29. *Id.* at 44; *see also id.* at 3-46, 243-68 (discussing the predicament of social theory); *infra* Part III (briefly discussing Unger's social theory).

30. R. UNGER, LAW IN MODERN SOCIETY, *supra* note 2, at 44. For more on Unger's views on the problem of method in social theory, see *infra* Part III; *see also* R. UNGER, LAW IN MODERN SOCIETY, *supra* note 2, at 8-23, 245-62, 266-68; R. UNGER, *supra* note 1, at 106-19.

31. R. UNGER, LAW IN MODERN SOCIETY, *supra* note 2, at 44. Professor Unger's views on social order are considered *infra* Part III. *See also* R. UNGER, *supra* note 1, *passim*; R. UNGER, LAW IN MODERN SOCIETY, *supra* note 2, at 23-37, 127-33, 174-75, 262-65 *passim*.

32. R. UNGER, LAW IN MODERN SOCIETY, *supra* note 2, at 44. What Unger terms the "problem of modernity" is treated further at *infra* note 389. *See also* R. UNGER, LAW IN MODERN SOCIETY, *supra* note 2, at 37-40, 134-41; R. UNGER, PASSION: AN ESSAY ON PERSONALITY (1984) [hereinafter cited as R. UNGER, PASSION].

33. Professor Unger's disdain of cultural relativism is evident throughout his published work. *E.g.*, R. UNGER, *supra* note 1, at 193-95. He expressed these views even more sharply during a talk given at the Harvard Law School's East Asian Legal Studies Center in January 1976. Indicating that he was not afraid to pass judgment upon the moral vision of widely differing societies, Professor Unger stated that the core of what he would term Western civilization was, indeed, superior to its Chinese counterpart. Or, as his host at that talk, Professor Jerome A. Cohen of the Harvard Law School, summarized Unger's views in a sympathetic letter to the *Harvard Law Record*, "[H]e believes that the view that is implicit in the transcendent religions of Judaism, Christianity and Islam is superior to both the ethical worldliness and otherworldly spiritualism that have marked the culture of China and other societies." Harv. L. Rec., Feb. 13, 1976, at 11, col. 1; *see also id.*, Jan. 30, 1976, at 14-15, col. 1; *id.* Feb. 6, 1976, at 11-12, col. 3; *id.* Feb. 27, 1976, at 11, col. 1.

For a further discussion of the issue of cultural relativism, see *infra* notes 411-53 and accompanying text.

34. R. UNGER, LAW IN MODERN SOCIETY, *supra* note 2, at 47. Unger characterizes "the typological method" as "the most successful procedure yet devised to resolve this tension" between what he terms "systematic theory and historiography." *Id.* at 45. For more on his typology of forms of law, see *infra* notes 324-62, 390-453 and accompanying text.

35. R. UNGER, LAW IN MODERN SOCIETY, *supra* note 2, at 48.

36. *Id.* at 49.

cratic or regulatory law,"[37] and the "legal order or legal system."[38]

Customary or interactional law is law in "the broadest sense . . . simply any recurring mode of interaction among individuals and groups, together with the more or less explicit acknowledgement by these groups and individuals that such patterns . . . produce reciprocal expectations . . . that ought to be satisfied."[39] It lacks what he calls the attribute of being public, by which absence he means that it is "common to the entire society rather than associated with a centralized government that stands apart from other social groups."[40] And because it is not "positive," it is "inarticulate rather than expressed" and implicit rather than codified.[41] As a consequence, for him, customary law both describes what is and prescribes what ought to be without making a clear distinction between the two.[42]

Unlike customary law, bureaucratic law is both public and positive.[43] It "consists of explicit rules established and enforced by an identifiable government."[44] Although bureaucratic law does not wholly supplant customary law, Professor Unger believes it can arise only when a central state apparatus has separated from society and the concept of community has disintegrated to such an extent that unarticulated customary law is no longer sufficient.[45] Arising in this context, bureaucratic law "suffers" what Professor Unger terms an "internal conflict" between the "imperatives of instrumentalism and legitimacy."[46] By this he means the tension between written laws as, on the one hand, "mere devices of state policy [that] may be freely replaced whenever the views and interests of the rulers change"[47] and, on the other hand, rules embodying "some inherently right or necessary order . . . [that] government cannot or should not disturb."[48] He believes that all too many rulers, particularly outside of the modern West, have resolved this tension by using "a body of religious precepts" to cloak their instrumental use of law with an appearance of legitimacy, rather than imbuing law with what he sees as a

37. *Id.* at 50.

38. *Id.* at 52.

39. *Id.* at 49. For more on the breadth of Professor Unger's definition of customary law, see *infra* notes 345-50 and accompanying text.

40. R. Unger, Law in Modern Society, *supra* note 2, at 50.

41. *Id.*

42. *Id.* at 49.

43. *Id.* at 50.

44. *Id.*

45. *Id.* at 58.

46. *Id.* at 64-65.

47. *Id.* at 65.

48. *Id.*

truer legitimacy derived from genuine consensus.[49]

According to Professor Unger, the third of the major sorts of law—the legal order or legal system—"developed in modern Europe and, more precisely, in modern Europe alone, until taken from there to other parts of the world."[50] This "narrower concept of law"[51] differs from bureaucratic law not only in its public and positive nature, but also in its autonomy and generality.[52] The autonomy that Professor Unger has in mind has "a substantive, an institutional, a methodological, and an occupational aspect."[53] By that he means that the law does not embody "any [single] identifiable set of nonlegal beliefs or norms, be they economic, political, or religious"; is "applied by specialized institutions whose main task is adjudication";[54] "has a method . . . to differentiate it from [other forms of] discourse";[55] and requires for its ongoing vitality a specially trained core of professionals adept at legal argumentation.[56] This autonomy complements well what Unger terms "generality," which he defines as consisting of the ideals of "generality in legislation and of uniformity in adjudication."[57]

Professor Unger is led to the "Chinese case" by his effort to explain why the legal order, which he essentially sees as synonymous with the modern rule of law, is so assuredly a child of European culture.[58] The legal order, he suggests, can only arise in a society in which a "certain pluralism of groups" has emerged from the "breakdown of stable hierarchical relations among social ranks"[59] and in which there is "a transcendent view of the world, a view often accompanied by the elaboration of systematic bodies of sacred law."[60] This hypothesis, he indicates, could be both tested and refined "if we found a civilization that for some time remained alien to the rule of law ideal and contented itself with bureaucratic law."[61] In such a society, he posits, one would find the separation of state from society and the disintegration of community that he believes

49. *Id.*; *see also id.* at 131.
50. *Id.* at 86.
51. *Id.* at 52.
52. *Id.*
53. *Id.* at 52.
54. *Id.* at 53.
55. *Id.*
56. *Id.*
57. *Id.* Although Unger does suggest that the autonomy and generality that for him distinguish the legal order from bureaucratic law lie at the heart of the ideal of the rule of law, he never explains fully the exact relationship that he believes exists between what he terms the legal order and the rule of law.
58. *Id.* at 87; *see also id.* at 76-86.
59. *Id.* at 87.
60. *Id.*
61. *Id.*

are prerequisites to bureaucratic law, but one "would not anticipate the kinds of social order and of belief associated with the liberal state and transcendent religion."[62] It is, then, "to deepen our insight into the complex relationship among modes of social organization, types of consciousness, and forms of normative order" that Professor Unger leads us to "the comparison with China, as a contrast case."[63]

II

The stated focus of Professor Unger's inquiry into Chinese legal history is "particularly upon" the era from roughly 722 B.C. (the onset of the Spring and Autumn period[64]) to 221 B.C. (the foundation of the imperial state),[65] although his generalizations about the Chinese past are often cast so as to suggest a coverage of larger portions of Chinese history from the third millennium B.C.[66] to A.D. 1912 (the end of the imperial era).[67] To grasp the essence of the Chinese case, suggests Professor Unger, one should work through "three stages of analysis."[68] At the outset, it is necessary to examine the "period of Chinese history in which public, positive rules . . . seem to have had little importance," which he dates from 1122 B.C. to the mid-sixth century B.C.[69] The second phase of his analysis concerns the period from the mid-sixth century B.C. to 221 B.C. and is addressed chiefly to what he calls "the transformation period."[70] And finally, and most importantly, his inquiry considers how the "debates that took place among schools of thought" during this second era reveal the "social and cultural predispositions of different kinds of law."[71]

62. *Id.*

63. *Id.* at 88.

64. The Spring and Autumn [*Ch'un-ch'iu*] era which is most often dated from 722 to 481 B.C. takes its name from chronicles of the nation-state of Lu that document the history of those years both in Lu and the other nation-states of the North China plain. Tradition has it that the text known as the *Ch'un-ch'iu* was edited by Confucius (who was a native of Lu), although that view has less currency these days. C. HUCKER, CHINA'S IMPERIAL PAST 98-99 (1975).

65. R. UNGER, LAW IN MODERN SOCIETY, *supra* note 2, at 87.

66. Recent archaeological discoveries have tended to confirm Chinese assertions that a state may have existed in North China as early as the time of the so-called Hsia Dynasty (2205-1766 B.C.). *See* K.C. WU, THE CHINESE HERITAGE 106-43 (1982).

67. Unger is imprecise as to the period that he is covering when treating China in *Law in Modern Society*. One page after telling the reader that he will be focusing particularly upon China from 722-221 B.C., he commences a relatively extended discussion of the period running from 1122 to the mid-sixth century B.C.. *See* R. UNGER, LAW IN MODERN SOCIETY, *supra* note 2, at 88-96. At other points he seems to be generalizing about the full sweep of Chinese history from preimperial days through to the late imperial era. *See id.* at 87, 109.

Unger also sweeps across a broad expanse of time when briefly using the Chinese example in other works. *E.g.*, R. UNGER, PASSION, *supra* note 32, at 65-69.

68. R. UNGER, LAW IN MODERN SOCIETY, *supra* note 2, at 88.

69. *Id.* at 88-96.

70. *Id.* at 96-105.

71. *Id.* at 88, 105-09.

Texas Law Review Vol. 64:915, 1986

Any effort to assess Professor Unger's treatment of preimperial China should commence with an acknowledgement of the obstacles that limit efforts even to describe that era.[72] Notwithstanding the great advances made during the past two-and-a-half decades by Chinese and foreign historians, classicists, archaeologists, anthropologists, linguists, and others,[73] knowledge of preimperial China remains fragmentary in many respects and subject to substantial amendment, based upon often fortuitous findings.[74] Compounding the difficulty of deriving an accurate picture are the problems posed by the existence of a number of Chinese classics reputedly compiled during the preimperial era[75] whose accuracy

72. For a brief discussion of such obstacles and of sophisticated and often multidisciplinary efforts to overcome them, see KWANG-CHIH CHANG, EARLY CHINESE CIVILIZATION: ANTHROPOLOGICAL PERSPECTIVES at v-xi (1976); THE ORIGINS OF CHINESE CIVILIZATION at xix-xxix (D. Keightley ed. 1980); Keightley, *Akatasuka Kiyoshi and the Study of Early China*, 42 HARV. J. ASIATIC STUD. 267 (1982) .

73. Major work on preimperial Chinese civilization in general since 1960 includes GUO MORUO, ZHONGGUO GUDAI SHEHUI YANJIU [THE STUDY OF ANCIENT CHINESE SOCIETY] (1964); D. KEIGHTLEY, SOURCES OF SHANG HISTORY: THE ORACLE-BONE INSCRIPTIONS OF BRONZE AGE CHINA (1978); Cheng Te-k'un, *Some New Discoveries in Prehistoric and Shang China*, in ANCIENT CHINA: STUDIES IN EARLY CIVILIZATION (D. Roy and Tsuen-hsuin Tsien eds. 1978); Chou Hung-hsiang, *Chinese Oracle Bones*, SCIENTIFIC AMER. 135 (April 1979); KWANG-CHIH CHANG, SHANG CIVILIZATION 1-65, 369-70 *passim* (1980); THE ORIGINS OF CHINESE CIVILIZATION, *supra* note 72; HSÜ CHO-YÜN, HSI CHOU SHIH [WESTERN CHOU HISTORY] (1984); B. SCHWARTZ, THE WORLD OF THOUGHT IN ANCIENT CHINA (1985).

The work of a small number of PRC scholars—the most notable of whom are Liu Hainian and Qian Dagun—integrate the most recent such data on preimperial and early imperial law. *E.g.*, Liu Hainian, *Zhenyi Mingwen ji qi suo Fanying de Xi Zhou Xingzhi* [*The Zhenyi Inscriptions and the Criminal Justice System of the Western Zhou*], FAXUE YANJIU [STUDIES IN LAW] No. 30, at 81 (1984); Liu Hainian, *Yunmeng Qin Jian de Faxian yu Qin Lu Yanjiu* [*The Discovery of Qin Bamboo Strips and the Study of Qin Law*], FAXUE YANJIU [STUDIES IN LAW] No. 18, at 52 (1982); Qian Daqun, *Xi Zhou "San Shi" Kao* [*A Discussion of the "San Shi" of the Western Zhou*], FAXUE YANJIU [STUDIES IN LAW] No. 21, at 60 (1982); Liu Xuchuan, *Cong Yunmeng Qin Jian Kan Qin Dai de Jingji Fa* [*Observations on Qin Dynasty Economic Law Made on the Basis of the Yunmeng Qin Bamboo Strips*], FAXUE YANJIU [STUDIES IN LAW] No. 29, at 61 (1983).

What little work is now underway in the West on preimperial Chinese law is being done by sinologists, rather than academic lawyers. Two young specialists on early imperial China have completed an impressive translation of an important early legal document. McLeod & Yates, *Forms of Ch'in Law: An Annotated Translation of the Feng-chen Shih*, 41 HARV. J. ASIATIC STUD. 111 (1981). Professor A.F.W. Hulsewé also has recently published a worthy companion to his earlier book on Han law. A. HULSEWÉ, REMNANTS OF CH'IN LAW: AN ANNOTATED TRANSLATION OF THE CH'IN LEGAL AND ADMINISTRATIVE RULES OF THE 3RD CENTURY B.C. DISCOVERED IN YUN-MENG PREFECTURE, HU-PEI PROVINCE IN 1975 (1985). And Karen Turner Gottschang has written a doctoral dissertation that addresses with creativity and insight many questions that interest legal scholars. K. Gottschang, Chinese Despotism Reconsidered: Monarchy and Its Critics in the Ch'in and Early Han Empires (1983) (unpublished doctoral dissertation, University of Michigan Department of History) (available from University Microfilm International, Ann Arbor, Michigan).

74. The recent discovery in the PRC of a complete copy of the Han dynasty code, which is presumed to follow closely the code of the Ch'in dynasty, could well lead to further revisions of our thinking about late preimperial and early imperial Chinese law.

75. I have principally in mind those works referred to as the Five Classics—the *Shang-shu* or *Shu-ching* [*The Book of Documents* also known as *The Book of History*]; the *Shih-ching* [*The Book of Poetry*]; the *I-ching* [*The Book of Changes*]; the *Ch'un-ch'iu* [*The Spring and Autumn Chronicles*] (referred to in *supra* note 64); the *Li ching* [*The Book of Rites*] (which from the Han dynasty has been said to consist of the *Chou-li* [*The Rites of Chou*]; and the *Yi-li* [*Property and Rites*]). These

remains controversial in China and the West.[76] Nonetheless, even if we take account of the obstacles that face all scholars who would strive to understand preimperial Chinese society—and even if we limit ourselves to materials accessible to Professor Unger while he worked on *Law in Modern Society*—his portrayal of preimperial China must be seen as deeply flawed.

This Part offers a sinological critique of Professor Unger's treatment of preimperial China. It also uses a tripartite analysis, but not that of Professor Unger, for his methodology obscures more than it illuminates. Instead, this Part examines first his characterization of the nature of law in China prior to the sixth century B.C.; second, his assessment of both the breakdown of the political, social, and religious conditions that enabled custom to reign supreme and the concomitant rise of bureaucratic law; and third, his portrayal of the main currents of philosophical debate that marked late preimperial times. In each of these three stages, an effort is made to set forth fully Professor Unger's analysis prior to my own.

works are generally considered to be the "literary cornerstones of Chinese civilization." C. HUCKER, CHINA'S IMPERIAL PAST 98 (1975). Although all were translated into English long ago, Professor Unger makes no mention of any of these works, save for a single cryptic textual reference to the *Shih-ching*. R. UNGER, LAW IN MODERN SOCIETY, *supra* note 2, at 94. Nor do Unger's notes indicate use of a number of other major classics of the preimperial era, including the *Tso-chuan* [*The Commentary of Tso*] which discusses the *Ch'un-ch'iu* and is believed to have been written around 300 B.C.; the *Ta-hsüeh* [*The Great Learning*]; the *Chung-yung* [*The Doctrine of the Mean*]; the *Kuo-yü* [*Discourses on the States*]; and the *Chan-kuo Ts'e* [*Intrigues of the Warring States*].

A useful treatment of the validity of the Chinese Classics, particularly for a study of the Western Chou, available to Unger at the time he wrote *Law in Modern Society*, *supra* note 2, may be found in H. CREEL, THE WESTERN CHOU EMPIRE 444-86 (1970) (vol. 1 of THE ORIGINS OF STATECRAFT IN CHINA). Creel sees portions of *The Book of Documents*, *The Book of Changes*, and *The Book of Poetry* as especially credible contemporaneous sources for preimperial history. Two recent worthwhile treatments of these and other sources of early Chinese history are KWANG-CHIH CHANG, *supra* note 73, at 3-19, and B. SCHWARTZ, *supra* note 73, at 383-406. *See infra* notes 76, 93.

76. The traditional skepticism of many Western and some Chinese scholars prior to the archaeological and other advances of the past two decades is expressed in M. LOEWE, IMPERIAL CHINA 42-50 (1966).

For an absorbing discussion of modern political consequences of the debate over the authenticity of the Classics, see L. SCHNEIDER, KU CHIEH-KANG AND CHINA'S NEW HISTORY: NATIONALISM AND THE QUEST FOR ALTERNATIVE TRADITIONS (1971). *See also* KU CHIEH-KANG, THE AUTOBIOGRAPHY OF A CHINESE HISTORIAN 75-79, 83-87 (A. Hummel trans. 1931). For a view of the validity of the Classics quite different from Ku Chieh-kang's, see K.C. WU, *supra* note 66, at 322-395. *See also* W. DOBSON, EARLY ARCHAIC CHINESE (1962). Professor Dobson's meticulous comparison of major sections of *The Book of Documents* and early Western Chou (*c.* eleventh and tenth century B.C.) bronze inscriptions prove his strong evidence of the "integrity of these texts, and [is] a striking demonstration of the fidelity of their transmission." *Id.* at xv.

The validity of a famous early legal text is discussed in Pu Jian, *"Fa Jing" Bian Wei* [*An Analysis as to the Falsification of the Canon of Law*], FAXUE YANJIU [STUDIES IN LAW] No. 33, at 49 (1984). *See also* Pokora, *The Canon of Laws by Li K'uei: A Double Falsification?* 27 ARCHIV ORIENTALIA 96 (1959).

Texas Law Review Vol. 64:915, 1986

A. *Law in Early China*

1. Professor Unger's View.—Roberto Unger's stated central purpose in examining preimperial China is to distinguish why China was unable to move beyond bureaucratic law into a legal order. But in order to identify those factors, he contends that it is first necessary to understand the nature of earlier Chinese law and its relation to society. Prior to the rise of bureaucratic law between the mid-sixth and mid-fifth centuries B.C., Unger tells us, China provides "a wonderful example of a society almost wholly dependent on interactional law"[77] in which "written regulations or codes were still unknown."[78]

Unger seeks to explain how interactional law sufficed to guide early Chinese society by reference to the *li*.[79] The *li*, we are told, were not public, positive rules perceived to have been made by the state or, for that matter, by any person. "Indeed," suggests Unger, "they were not rules at all."[80] Instead, they "were more or less tacit models of exemplary conduct . . . transmitted as part of the experience of learning to participate in social relations . . . and they were formulated, when formulated at all, as moral anecdotes."[81]

The "more or less tacit models" that Unger suggests constituted the *li* had force, he continues, because they were the "living, spontaneous order of society."[82] Accordingly, they functioned with an "effortlessness" paralleling "in the realm of culture the predetermined course of instinct in the prehuman animal world."[83] "[P]erceived as customary forms of behavior intrinsic to particular social situations and positions . . . no clear lines were drawn [in *li*] between expectations about what persons of a certain rank would do in a given circumstance and views of what they ought to do."[84]

Embodying the "living . . . order"[85] of China prior to the sixth century B.C., the *li*, indicates Unger, "were hierarchical standards of conduct."[86] They took "for granted" the existence of a rigidly structured society and were "silent," as he suggests Chinese society was as a whole, "about responsibilities owed by the *chün-tzu* [the elite][87] to the *hsiao-jen*

77. R. UNGER, LAW IN MODERN SOCIETY, *supra* note 2, at 96.
78. *Id.* at 93.
79. *Id.* at 93-96.
80. *Id.* at 94.
81. *Id.*
82. *Id.*
83. *Id.* at 95; *see also id.* at 133.
84. *Id.* at 93.
85. *Id.* at 94.
86. *Id.* at 93.
87. The term *chün-tzu* literally translates as "son of the ruler" or "prince." Typically, it has

The Inscrutable Occidental

[the common people]."[88] As such, the Chinese world at this point lacked any notion that law could be used to distinguish state from society or otherwise significantly alter society.[89]

2. *Another View.*—At an initial "factual"[90] level, Unger's assertion that Chinese society before the sixth century B.C. was "almost wholly dependent" upon customary law and lacked anything approximating public, positive laws, needs substantial revision. There is abundant evidence—documented in Western languages at the time Unger wrote, including sources that he cites—that even prior to the establishment of the Western Chou state (in the 12th century B.C.[91]) Chinese society had public laws that may well have been written and that such laws continued to be a feature of that society throughout the remainder of preimperial history.[92] This is seen, for example, in a number of the great Confucian Classics and, in particular, throughout the *Shang-shu* or *Shu-ching* [*The Book of Documents*].[93] In the *The Book of Documents* one finds widespread and highly particular references to the law of the preceding dy-

been rendered as "gentlemen" or "worthies." For a discussion of Confucian efforts to redefine this label in moral terms, see *infra* notes 212-22 and accompanying text.

88. The term *hsiao-jen* literally translates as "little people." Typically it has been rendered as "commoner" or "common people." For a discussion of Confucian efforts to impart new meaning to this term, see *infra* notes 212-22 and accompanying text.

89. R. UNGER, LAW IN MODERN SOCIETY, *supra* note 2, at 95-96.

90. I use the word "factual" advisedly here, recognizing Professor Unger's critique of the fact/value distinction. *Id.* at 4.

91. The Western Chou period is generally dated from the fall of the Shang dynasty in 1122 B.C. to the transfer of the royal household to Loyang and formation of the Eastern Chou in 771 B.C.

92. *See, e.g.*, H. CREEL, *supra* note 75, at 161-93.

93. The most thorough effort at translating this difficult text is that of Bernhard Karlgren. Karlgren, *The Book of Documents*, 22 MUSEUM FAR EASTERN ANTIQUITIES BULL. 1-81 (1950) [hereinafter cited as Karlgren, *The Book of Documents*]; *see also* Karlgren, *Glosses on the Book of Documents (Part 1)*, 20 MUSEUM FAR EASTERN ANTIQUITIES BULL. 39-315 (1948); Karlgren, *Glosses on the Book of Documents (Part 2)*, 21 MUSEUM FAR EASTERN ANTIQUITIES BULL. 63-206 (1949). As indicated at *supra* notes 75-76, the validity of particular sections of *The Book of Documents* is far from settled. This, however, hardly seems to justify wholly ignoring the work, as Unger does.

In citing *The Book of Documents*, I have relied to the fullest extent possible upon sections of the work that are believed by major scholars of preimperial China to be authentic. I have, for example, drawn heavily from *The Announcement to K'ang*, *The Announcement to the Duke of Shao*, *The Announcement About Drunkenness*, *The Announcement Concerning Lo*, and other sections that Professor Dobson's research suggests are of high linguistic integrity. *See* W. DOBSON, *supra* note 76, at xv-xvi; *see also* H. CREEL, *supra* note 75, at 166 (stating that *Announcement to K'ang* is the oldest Chinese work dealing with law); K.C. Wu, *supra* note 66, at 67, 454 (discussing the authenticity of sections of *The Book of Documents*). Kwang-chih Chang suggests that oracle bones may confirm the extensive textual evidence provided by *The Book of Documents* to the effect that such law most likely existed by the late Shang and certainly by the early Chou. KWANG-CHIH CHANG, *supra* note 73, at 200-01. *Contra* A. HULSEWÉ, *supra* note 73, at 1 (in passing, placing the origin of extensive codified law in the early years of the Eastern Chou).

I have utilized translations drawn from Karlgren, save for those of the titles of sections of *The Book of Documents* which are drawn from James Legge's translation. J. LEGGE, THE SHOO KING 1-34 (vol. 3 of THE CHINESE CLASSICS) (2d ed.).

nasty, the Shang (also known as the Yin),[94] and even more comprehensive mention of the laws that the Chou applied soon after taking power from the Shang.[95] Thus, the *K'ang Kao* [*The Announcement to K'ang*] section of *The Book of Documents* reproduces a speech made by Wen, the first Western Chou king, that not only describes for his son K'ang specific punishments available for particular crimes, but also instructs him to observe carefully the limits of his legal authority and to see that these laws are administered in an appropriate yet fair fashion.[96] Whatever one might think of proceduralists, this hardly suggests reliance upon something akin to the instincts and drives of animals to communicate behavioral norms.[97] Other sections of *The Book of Documents* discuss the validity of Shang dynasty rules after the Chou conquest;[98] elaborate the range of punishments available under the Chou dynasty's public law;[99] speak in detail of how the laws are to be applied;[100] and consider the limitations of state-developed criminal law as a device to ensure social order.[101] These are among the many indicia that the Western Chou not only had public law but also recognized its importance in structuring society after coming to power in 1122 B.C.

Reliance upon public, positive rules did not die out during the Eastern Chou (which supplanted the Western Chou in 771 B.C.). Thus, for example, the *Tso-chuan* speaks of the Chin official Chao Tun's reform program of 621 B.C. during which Chin "rectified the laws concerning crime and regulated [the procedures for] trial and punishment."[102] This not only indicates that a body of public, positive law existed midway through Unger's first era, but also implies—as Professor Herrlee Creel has observed—that "there had been a code well before this time."[103] Nor was Chao Tun alone in his professional concern with law. In the *Shih-chi* [*Historical Records*], the famed Han dynasty historian Ssu-ma Ch'ien

94. *E.g.*, *The Canon of Yao, translated in* Karlgren, *The Book of Documents, supra* note 93, at 1-8; *see also* H. CREEL, *supra* note 75, at 165 (discussing references to Yin). The Shang, or Yin, is believed to have ruled from approximateiy 1766 to 1122 B.C. For background on the Shang, see generally KWANG-CHIH CHANG, *supra* note 73.

95. *E.g.*, *The Announcement to K'ang, translated in* Karlgren, *The Book of Documents, supra* note 93, at 39-43; *The Punishments of Lü, translated in id.*, at 74-78.

96. *See, e.g.*, *The Announcement to K'ang, translated in id.* at 39-43 *passim*, which instructs Chou officials as to the limits of their authority, and lines 19-23, which call upon officials to take steps to see that their "verdicts are correct and reliable."

97. *See supra* note 83 and accompanying text.

98. *E.g.*, *The Canon of Yao, translated in* Kalgren, *The Book of Documents, supra* note 93, at 5, line 22.

99. *E.g.*, *The Announcement to K'ang, translated in id.* at 40, line 10.

100. *E.g.*, *The Canon of Yao*, vol. 20, at 88-90, lines 1269-1270, *translated in id.* at 1-8.

101. *E.g.*, *The Announcement Concerning Lo, passim, translated in id.*, at 51-55; *The Announcement to the Duke of Shao, translated in id.* at 51, lines 20-21.

102. *Tso-chuan* 242:: 243-44 (Wen 6) *translated and quoted in* H. CREEL, *supra* note 75, at 166.

103. *Id.*

(*circa* 145-90 B.C.) recounts the biographies of many officials, reasonable and harsh, whose responsibilities led them to considerable involvement with and, in some instances, expertise in the law.[104]

Law during the years that constitute Unger's first phase was not wholly penal in nature. There is good reason to believe that the nation-states that later became China formed treaties from the eighth century B.C. onward.[105] Evidence exists indicating that the Chou developed rules regarding family responsibilities,[106] contractual obligations,[107] military conduct,[108] monetary affairs,[109] tax administration,[110] and other matters.[111] Thus, individuals who believed that persons with whom they had contracted had not lived up to their end of the bargain could seek recourse through the government.[112] Such data are too scanty to support the proposition that the Chou had a comprehensive civil law system but are certainly more than sufficient to cast doubt upon Unger's assertion that Chinese society during this era operated pursuant to unarticulated instinctual custom.[113]

There is more, too, to the *li* than Professor Unger's discussion sug-

104. 2 RECORDS OF THE GRAND HISTORIAN 413-51 (B. Watson trans. 1961) (Chapters 119 and 122 of the *Shih-chi*). Ssu-ma Ch'ien may have been presented these biographies in part to make points regarding the politics of his own age. Nonetheless, there is evidence from other sources regarding the existence of officials, and perhaps others, with special knowledge of the law, although they hardly appear to constitute the independent bar Professor Unger has in mind in speaking of the rise of the legal order. Professor Creel indicates that as early as the Western Chou certain officials may have concentrated upon legal matters, H. CREEL, *supra* note 75, at 169-73, 192-93, while Han Fei-tzu, among others, seems to acknowledge the existence of legal specialists when he urges the ruler to select as high officials person with "a feeling for the system of laws and regulations." Han Fei tzu, *On Having Standards*, in BASIC WRITINGS OF MO TZU, HSÜN TZU AND HAN FEI TZU, at 22 (B. Watson trans. & ed. 1967) (translations of each author numbered separately) [hereinafter cited as BASIC WRITINGS].

Finally, it is interesting to note that the Yün-meng excavation of Ch'in legal materials include 190 "Answers to Questions About the Ch'in Statutes." Those attempt to guide Ch'in officials in the explication of the law and suggest a higher level of training and legal acumen on the part of such officials than has typically been assumed. For an annotated translation of these, see A. HULSEWÉ, *supra* note 73, at 121-82.

105. *E.g.*, J. COHEN & CHIU HUNG-DAH, PEOPLE'S CHINA AND INTERNATIONAL LAW 4 (1974); HSÜ CHO-YÜN, ANCIENT CHINA IN TRANSITION: AN ANALYSIS OF SOCIAL MOBILITY, 722-222 B.C., at 58 (1965); C. HUCKER, *supra* note 75, at 36; Chen, *supra* note 23, at 641-43.

106. *See* Wang Yuanming, *Cong (Shi Jing, Zhao Nan, Xing Lu) Yi Shi Kan Zhou Dai de Susong [Observing a Chou Dynasty Case From One Poem (From the Shi Jing)]*, FAXUE YANJIU [STUDIES IN LAW] No. 32, at 82 (1984). *See generally* N. FEHL, LI: RITES AND PROPRIETY IN LITERATURE AND LIFE—A PERSPECTIVE FOR A CULTURAL HISTORY OF ANCIENT CHINA (1971).

107. H. CREEL, *supra* note 75, at 169-79, 183-88.

108. *Id.* at 179-80.

109. *Id.* at 133-60.

110. *Id.* at 153, 168.

111. *Id.* at 161-93. As Confucius indicated, "[The] Chou [founders] carefully attended to the weights and measures, [and] examined the [existing] body of laws . . . ." K. Gottschang, *supra* note 73, at 173.

112. H. CREEL, *supra* note 75, at 183-88.

113. R. UNGER, LAW IN MODERN SOCIETY, *supra* note 2, at 93-95.

gests. Most sinologists are of the view that the concept of *li* originated, during the Western Chou if not earlier, to encompass particular rituals that were meant to accompany set religious observances and sacrifices.[114] As these rituals were largely conducted by aristocrats, *li* gradually evolved into a code of conduct designed to regulate appropriate conduct, first among the nobility, and then more broadly.[115] Although it is hard to determine what participants in this code of behavior thought, there seems to be little support in the available historical record for Professor Unger's suggestion that the *li*, as customary law,[116] merged that which "happens" and that which "ought to be done."[117] To the contrary, there is considerable evidence from the Western Chou,[118] and even more from the Eastern Chou, suggesting a keen awareness of a gap between behavior and the standard of conduct called for by the *li.*[119] Nor is it correct, as Professor Unger states at another point that, "instead of a catalogue of explicit rules," the *li* were "more or less tacit models of exemplary conduct."[120] Particularly in their early incarnation governing religious ritual, but also later as they came to be codes of conduct, the *li* surely were specific, public rules.[121]

A more fundamental deficiency in Professor Unger's account of the *li* lies in his assertion that the *li*, which "touched upon all aspects of social life,"[122] paralleled Chinese feudal society in "its silence about responsibilities owed by the *chün-tzu* to the *hsiao-jen.*"[123] To the contrary,

114. *E.g.*, Bünger, *Genesis and Change of Law in China*, 24 LAW & STATE 66, 74 (1981) (discussing the original meaning of *li* as associated with sacrifice, its broadening to include other religious ceremonies, and its subsequent expansion into other spheres of life). This reading is in accord with the literal meaning of the term.

115. *Id.* at 213-16.

116. R. UNGER, LAW IN MODERN SOCIETY, *supra* note 2, at 93.

117. *Id.* at 49.

118. For information on the Western Chou, see generally H. CREEL, *supra* note 75.

119. *E.g.*, Confucius' statement to his disciple Tzu-chang regarding the modifications of the *li* by the Shang and Chou dynasties. THE ANALECTS OF CONFUCIUS bk. II, ch. 23 (A. Waley trans. 1938) [hereinafter cited as THE ANALECTS]. Note also his frequent expressions of disappointment in *The Analects* with the failure of those of noble birth to live up to the *li*.

120. R. UNGER, LAW IN MODERN SOCIETY, *supra* note 2, at 94. If "is" and "ought" are merged, presumably there is no need for "models of exemplary behavior." Benjamin Schwartz shows in his new book that the distinction was understood clearly in the period Unger analyzes. *See* B. SCHWARTZ, *supra* note 73, at 68; *see also infra* text accompanying note 417.

121. The complexity of the *li* is discussed by Bünger, who suggests that "their assignment to one of the traditional disciplines of European learning is not possible." Bünger, *supra* note 114, at 74; *see also* N. FEHL, *supra* note 106, at 216-18 *passim*; HYUNG KIM, FUNDAMENTAL LEGAL CONCEPTS OF CHINA AND THE WEST: A COMPARATIVE STUDY 51-52 (1981).

The breadth of the *li* is suggested by the *Chou-li* [*Rites of Chou*] and *I-li* [*Property and Rites*]. The former work lays out procedures of the early Chou government and the latter rules regarding official visits, marriage, mourning, and a range of other matters. Chinese tradition dates these works from the twelfth or eleventh century B.C., although recent scholarship suggests that they were probably written in the fourth or third century B.C. C. HUCKER, *supra* note 75, at 95-100.

122. R. UNGER, LAW IN MODERN SOCIETY, *supra* note 2, at 95.

123. *Id.* at 93.

the very core of *li* was their emphasis upon the obligations that flowed between both parties to any relationship. The *li* in their most rigid pre-Confucian form clearly envisioned a hierarchical world, not only along class lines (as Professor Unger suggests[124]) but also along those of gender and age.[125] They also, however, clearly provided that the person who enjoyed the loyalty or support of others by virtue of holding a superior position—be it socially, politically, or in the family—owed a commensurate obligation to those providing that loyalty or support.[126] As will be discussed below, this notion akin to a bond of obligation had vital implications in terms of law and social order that Professor Unger does not consider.[127]

B. The Political, Social, and Religious Context

1. Professor Unger's View.—The customary law that guided Chinese society for centuries largely gave way to a body of public, positive bureaucratic law, asserts Professor Unger, because of transformations in political, social, and religious life between the mid-sixth century and 221 B.C.[128]

In the centuries prior to the mid-sixth century that comprise Unger's first period, political power reposed nominally in the Chou king, but was in fact widely dispersed among local aristocrats who controlled fortress towns and the "fiefs" surrounding them.[129] These aristocrats together with members of the royal family and the *shih* (whom he com-

124. *Id.*

125. In *Passion*, Professor Unger tacitly acknowledges this, as well as the limitations thereby implied. R. UNGER, PASSION, *supra* note 32, at 67; *see also infra* note 402.

126. *E.g.*, THE ANALECTS, *supra* note 119, at bk. 11, ch. XII; *see also* W. EBERHARD, GUILT AND SIN IN TRADITIONAL CHINA 117 (1967).

To call Unger to task for failing to recognize the notion of reciprocal obligations found in early Chinese thought is not, of course, to endorse the conception of hierarchy underlying it.

127. *See infra* notes 304-23, 418 and accompanying text.

128. R. UNGER, LAW IN MODERN SOCIETY, *supra* note 2, at 88-89.

129. *Id.* at 88-91. Although Professor Unger states that the "implied analogy" between his first era and European feudalism is "in many respects inaccurate," *id.* at 88, he persists in using the language of feudalism to describe what he finds in early China. Not surprisingly, many other scholars, Marxist and non-Marxist alike, apply this language to Chinese history. Some sinologists, however, caution that use of the terminology of feudalism, fraught with overtones from European history, may hide as much of ancient Chinese society as it reveals. For example, David Keightley has observed that the use of the term "feudal enfeoffment" to characterize the granting by Western Chou rulers of land to loyal retainers suggests a more formal contractual relationship than available data indicates existed. He suggests "gift giving and receiving, rather than contractual agreements was the fundamental and traditional mechanism, both social and political, for linking the Chou King to his supporters." D. Keightley, The Western Chou as Social Polity: Vassalage Without Feudalism 7 (1982) (unpublished paper, available from the author) (quoting in part from D. Keightley, The Giver and the Gift: The Western Chou State as a Social Party (1981) (unpublished paper, available from the author)); *see also* Blakely, *On the "Feudal" Interpretation of Chou China*, in 2 EARLY CHINA 35-37 (1976); Kierman, *Feudalism*, in THE CAMBRIDGE ENCYCLOPEDIA OF CHINA 169 (B. Hook gen. ed. 1982).

pares to European knights), formed an elite organized "along hierarchical and hereditary lines."[130] Reflecting the "stability of the rank system,"[131] they stood in sharp distinction to the merchants and commoners. The former, Unger suggests, were insignificant politically or otherwise and so "occupied a distinctly subordinate position," and the latter were "mostly landless serfs" and slaves.[132] Religiously, this was an era marked by conceptions of the diety that had the potential to lead to either a faith of transcendence or one of immanence. But, contends Unger, the presence of these differing tendencies hardly disrupted a more basic normative homogeneity that served to reinforce the fixed nature of society and so made it possible for unarticulated custom to order Chinese civilization.

The stability that marked this first era, Professor Unger observes, began to erode in the mid-sixth century. Politically, the gradual "breakdown of the feudal system" during the transformation period led toward greater centralization and consequently set the stage for "the regimentation of society from above and for the development of doctrines of bureaucratic organization and social planning."[133] Socially, the neat, stable hierarchies of the preceding period began to crumble, with the result that "[p]ower began to flow away from the feudal aristocracies and toward the ruling princes and their counselors."[134] These advisors, who were "drawn largely from the *shih* stratum of the nobility," lacked the independent status of the feudal aristocracy and so owed their position largely to the princes with whom they were aligned.[135] The commoners, Unger tells us, also experienced change, as the " 'serfs' of the feudal society were transformed into tribute-paying tenants, and land was made more freely salable."[136] The net effect of these "changes" was to separate state from society and to dissolve the "highly integrated community of values and perceptions upon which the [foregoing] feudal order and its pervasive customary law depended," thereby creating the circumstances from which bureaucratic law would emerge.[137]

Although public and positive, the bureaucratic law of the transformation era, stressed Unger, differed greatly from that law which ap-

130. R.Unger, Law In Modern Society, *supra* note 2, at 90.
131. *Id.* at 95.
132. *Id.* at 90.
133. *Id.* at 97.
134. *Id.*
135. *Id.* at 97-98.
136. *Id.* at 98.
137. *Id.* at 99.

peared in European nation-states after the Renaissance.[138] Notwithstanding rhetoric that insisted upon "the importance of leveling all subjects before uniformly applied laws, . . . generality was always approached as an expedient with which to secure the sovereign's hold over the populace . . . ."[139] Autonomy also was missing, with the result that there were no clear lines between policy and law, no specialized courts to adjudicate disputes, no "constraints associated with the appeal to methods of legal reasoning,"[140] and "no profession of lawyers, as distinct from policy makers and experts in statecraft."[141]

The Chinese "failure to develop a European-type legal order"[142] from this new bureaucratic law is attributable, according to Professor Unger, to the absence in this era both of a " 'third estate' relatively independent from the governments of the centralizing monarchies"[143] and of a widespread belief in a transcendant God.[144] With respect to the former, he argues that the conditions and incentives that might have led to the establishment of a strong, autonomous merchant community or legal profession were lacking in preimperial China.[145] As for the latter, Unger suggests not only that the ambivalence within earlier Chinese religion was resolved in favor of a "commitment to immanence,"[146] but also that other potential external checks upon governmental power were absent because China both lacked a prophetic tradition[147] and "there was little contact with other societies to provide the experience of cultural diversity."[148]

2. *Another View.*—Professor Unger's characterization of the political, social, and religious circumstances of preimperial China presents a misleading picture of that society. In terms of the political life of that era, Professor Unger's most significant error lies in his assertion that the state did not begin to separate from society until the middle of the sixth century B.C.[149] Even if one chooses to accept his definition that the separation of state from society entails both "the evolution of social con-

138. *Id.* at 99, 104-05. For more on the significance of this comparison, see *infra* note 357 and accompanying text. *See also infra* Part III.
139. R. UNGER, LAW IN MODERN SOCIETY, *supra* note 2, at 104.
140. *Id.*
141. *Id.*
142. *Id.* at 99.
143. *Id.*
144. *Id.*
145. *Id.*
146. *Id.* at 99.
147. *Id.* at 100-101.
148. *Id.* at 100.
149. *Id.* at 96-99.

sciousness" and "the changing organization of society,"[150] textual and archaeological evidence clearly show that this process was well underway hundreds of years prior to the mid-sixth century.[151] Indeed, recent scholarship suggests that "Shang [fit] the definition of the state with regard to its legitimate force, its hierarchical ruling structure, and its social classes" almost a millennia earlier than Unger would have us believe.[152]

The picture of the nature of social organization in preimperial China painted by Unger is a limited one. His description of the breakdown of the traditional hereditary aristocracy and the rise to positions of political prominence by individuals of talent between the mid-sixth and mid-third centuries comports with the work of leading Chinese scholars.[153] But he is mistaken in his assertion that "[m]erchants had neither the incentive nor the chance to assert their own interests and to develop their own law."[154] The very scholars upon whose work he relies in describing the demise of the traditional aristocracy also make it abundantly clear that a rich, powerful, and independent merchant class (which had begun to develop centuries earlier) was much in evidence by the fifth century B.C.[155] Although merchants in preimperial China and post-Renaissance Europe did not occupy identical positions in society, considerable evidence exists suggesting that Chinese merchants were interested in promoting their own special class interests and had the political strength to do so.[156] For example, we know that an early Chou ruler had to form alliances with independent merchants to stay in power and that as a consequence, those

150. *Id.* at 58.

151. Sources available to Professor Unger indicating this include KWANG-CHIH CHANG, THE ARCHAEOLOGY OF ANCIENT CHINA 130-31 (1963); P'ING-TI HO, THE CRADLE OF THE EAST: AN INQUIRY INTO THE INDIGENOUS ORIGINS OF TECHNIQUES AND IDEAS OF NEOLITHIC AND EARLY HISTORIC CHINA, 5000-1000 B.C. 333-38 (1975); Keightley, *Religion and the Rise of Urbanism*, 93 AM. ORIENTAL SOC. J. 527, 527-38 (1973); *see also* Keightley, *The Late Shang State: When, Where and What?*, in THE ORIGINS OF CHINESE CIVILIZATIONS, *supra* note 72, at 523-64 (examining current data regarding the formation of the Chinese state, with an emphasis upon oracle bones).

152. KWANG-CHIH CHANG, *supra* note 73, at 364; *see* Keightley, *The Late Shang State: When, Where and What?*, in THE ORIGINS OF CHINESE CIVILIZATION, *supra* note 72, at 558; Baum, Ritual and Rationality: The Origins of Bureaucratic Culture in Ancient China (unpublished paper, available in the UCLA School of Law Library).

153. *See, e.g.*, HSÜ CHO-YÜN, *supra* note 105, at 99.

154. R. UNGER, LAW IN MODERN SOCIETY, *supra* note 2, at 99.

155. *See, e.g.*, HSÜ CHO-YÜN, *supra* note 105, at 11-13.

The world-renowned scholar of preimperial China, Kwang-chih Chang, is of the view that "undoubtedly traders played an important role in Shang society," KWANG-CHIH CHANG, *supra* note 73, at 241, which, in his view, was characterized by "highly sophisticated regional economic networks," *id.* at 366. Indeed, as he notes, the Chinese ideogram for the dynasty that ruled from 1766 to 1122 B.C., *Shang*, is also used in the term for commerce, *shang-yeh*. *Id.* at 241.

For further evidence of merchant activity during the Chou, see CHENG TE-K'UN, CHOU CHINA 298-99 (1963) (vol. 3 of ARCHAEOLOGY IN CHINA); H. CREEL, *supra* note 75, at 139-40; HSÜ CHO-YÜN, *supra* note 105, at 11-13.

156. *E.g.*, HSÜ CHO-YÜN, *supra* note 105, at 128.

merchants were able to exercise considerable power over him.[157] So, too, at the end of the preimperial era, the rich and powerful merchant Lü Pu-wei may have played the role of kingmaker of the state of Ch'in both figuratively (as "his support enabled one of the Ch'in princes to become king"[158]) and literally (as he is reputed to "have been the father of China's famous unifier, Ch'in Shih-huang-ti"[159]). That Lü and other merchants of the late preimperial era not only had an incentive to assert their own interests and to develop law to govern their activities, but actually did so, is suggested by the Ch'in unifier's efforts to bring commerce under the empire's yoke by replacing the varied local commercial practices and rules of preimperial China with a single state-controlled body of law.[160]

Professor Unger's discussion of the absence of natural law in preimperial Chinese society is also troublesome. He is essentially accurate in describing the multifaceted nature of religion during the early Chou.[161] The same cannot be said for his conclusion that the Chinese had abandoned all belief in a transcendent God by the transformation era[162] and so, lacked external higher standards against which the actions of secular authorities could be assessed and through which the restructuring of social arrangements might be imagined.[163] Major Western scholars as diverse as Joseph Needham,[164] Derk Bodde,[165] and J. J. L. Duyvendak,[166] whose works were available to Unger, share the view that the idea of the Mandate of Heaven [*t'ien-ming*]—a precursor of which

157. *Tso-chuan*, 662:664 (Chao 16), *translated and quoted in* H. CREEL, *supra* note 75, at 139 & n.23.

158. D. BODDE, *supra* note 7, at 10.

159. *Id.*

160. Those measures are described in *id.* at 170-75. *See also* A. HULSEWÉ, *supra* note 73, at 21-216.

It is important to note that the Ch'in effort to control commercial activity through unified state-imposed law was not successful. Ironically, from the early years of the Han dynasty (206 B.C. - A.D. 220) onward imperial Chinese merchants were far freer than post-Renaissance European merchants to develop their own law. *See generally* Bünger, *supra* note 114, at 81.

161. R. UNGER, LAW IN MODERN SOCIETY, *supra* note 2, at 91-92.

162. *Id.* at 99-101. Professors Huston Smith, Benjamin Schwartz, and Chi-yun Chen have written stimulating essays on this subject. *See* Schwartz, *Transcendence in Ancient China*, 104 DAEDALUS 57, 57-68 (1975); Smith, *Transcendence in Traditional China*, 2 RELIGIOUS STUD. 185-96 (1967); Chi-yun Chen, Once Again What is Taoism: Transcendency and *Axis Mundi* (March 16, 1985) (unpublished paper, presented at Southern California China Colloquium Symposium on Religion and Ideology in the Chinese Tradition, at UCLA) (available in UCLA School of Law library); *see also* B. SCHWARTZ, *supra* note 73, at 117-27, 138-45, 192-96.

163. R. UNGER, LAW IN MODERN SOCIETY, *supra* note 2, at 105.

164. J. NEEDHAM, *et al.* 2 SCIENCE AND CIVILIZATION IN CHINA 518-83 (1956). It should be noted that although it is far more admiring of China than Unger, Needham's epic history of Chinese science suffers from many of the difficulties of cross-cultural comparison described in Part III of this Article with reference to Unger's work.

165. Bodde, *Authority and Law in Ancient China*, 74 J. AM. ORIENTAL SOC. 46 (Supp. 17, 1954).

166. THE BOOK OF LORD SHANG 129-130 (J. Duyvendak trans. 1928).

may have been evident at least a millenium prior to Unger's second era[167]—and other forces accomplished in Chinese society many of the chief objectives that he sees as fulfilled by natural law in a Western context. In theory, the idea of the Mandate was that Heaven had endowed an earthly representative with the authority and responsibility to govern all civilized peoples.[168] That awesome authority and the duty of loyalty and obedience among the populace that went with it imposed upon the ruler—and, indeed, could only be justified by—an even more awesome responsibility to work for the welfare of the populace.[169] If the ruler failed to discharge that responsibility, as measured against universal and discernible standards that transcended the ruler, the people[170] could express their displeasure. Heaven then would remove its Mandate from the ruler[171] and provide it to one who would better heed the people and serve their welfare.[172] Thus, we are informed in *The Book of Documents* that the last Shang ruler "in his comments . . . had no clear understanding of the respect due to the people; he maintained and spread far and wide resentment and did not change. Therefore, Heaven sent down destruction on Yin . . . [and replaced it with the Chou] . . . . It was due to [such] excesses. Heaven is not tyrannical."[173]

The failure of Professor Unger to acknowledge the idea of the Man-

167. For more on the origins of the idea of the Mandate of Heaven, see Keightley, *The Religious Commitment: Shang Theology and the Genesis of Chinese Political Culture*, 17 HIST. RELIGIONS 211, 220 (1978); Keightley, Legitimation in Shang Chinese 43-45 (June 1975) (unpublished paper delivered at the Conference on Legitimation of Chinese Imperial Regimes) (available at the Wason Library, Cornell University). Useful Chinese works on this subject include FU SSU-NIEN, HSING MING KU HSÜN PIEN-CHENG [A CRITICAL ANALYSIS OF THE ARCHAIC MEANINGS OF THE CONCEPTS OF *Hsing* AND *Ming*] (1940); GUO MORUO, CHINGTONG SHIDAI [THE BRONZE AGE] (1945).

168. H. CREEL, *supra* note 75, at 44-45, 51-52, 82-87, 93-100; *see also* HYUNG KIM, *supra* note 121; P'ING-TI HO, *supra* note 151, at 333-38 (outlining the development of the Mandate of Heaven).

169. *See* Vuylsteke, *Tung Chung-shu: A Philosophical Case for Rights in Chinese Philosophy*, in LAW AND SOCIETY: CULTURE LEARNING THROUGH LAW 303-308 (1977). For more on the importance of the notion of reciprocal obligation in Chinese civilization, see *infra* notes 311-23 and accompanying text.

170. It is important to note that both in preimperial China and in post-Renaissance Europe one should use caution in speaking of the "people." In neither case did it include women, children, or slaves.

171. We ought not to forget that the notion of the Mandate of Heaven provided a convenient rationale for the Chou and others in Chinese history who subsequently wished to take power from established authority. The felt necessity of those throughout Chinese history who would aspire to power to couch their aspirations in these terms speaks to the force of this idea in Chinese civilization. H. CREEL, *supra* note 75, at 93-100.

172. In endeavoring to appreciate the significance of the removal of the Mandate of Heaven, we should remember that the emperor was known as the Son of Heaven and stood to lose his base of legitimacy if he lost the Mandate of Heaven. *Id. See generally* HOK-LAM CHAN, LEGITIMATION IN IMPERIAL CHINA (1984).

173. *The Announcement About Drunkenness, translated in* Karlgren, *The Book of Documents*, *supra* note 93, at 45. For a discussion of how the "evil characteristics" of the last Shang emperor, Chou Hsin, became a "traditional characterology" of "the 'bad last' ruler," see Wright, *Sui Yang-ti: Personality and Stereotype*, in THE CONFUCIAN PERSUASION 61-65 (A. Wright ed. 1960).

date of Heaven[174]—which is roughly akin to writing about the modern liberal state without mentioning the notion of the social contract—is accentuated by the inaccuracy of other remarks about the absence of a natural-law tradition in preimperial China.[175] To appreciate that China did not lack a prophetic or priestly tradition that might serve as a check upon secular authority, one need only consider either the prominence in China's moral tradition accorded Confucius and numerous other political figures who espoused doctrines of independence from corrupted authority rather than service to such rulers,[176] or the millennia-long tradition of Taoist and other prophets and priests.[177] Similarly, scant basis exists for the assertion that there was "little contact with other societies to provide the experience of cultural diversity."[178] To the contrary, even authors and sources cited by Unger show the existence both of a great deal of cultural diversity within the area that was unified into the Chinese empire in 221 B.C. and of extensive contact with people beyond that region.[179] And, although Unger portrays it as essentially a reaction-

174. For more on the Mandate of Heaven, see H. CREEL, *supra* note 75, at 44-45, 51-52, 81-100; PING-TI HO, *supra* note 151, at 333-38; B. SCHWARTZ, *supra* note 73, at 46-55, 110-11; Bodde, *supra* note 165, at 47-51.

175. Professor Unger also ignores the pertinence to a discussion of the existence of the idea of natural law in preimperial China of the ancient Chinese cosmological notions of the interaction of *yin* and *yang* and of the *wu-hsing* (five elements or agents). The early history of these ideas is not wholly clear, but even in the form they took long before the imperial unification, they suggest a strong linkage between events in the human and natural worlds. Crudely put, believers in this cosmology were of the view that if there were an imbalance of *yin* (the light or feminine force) and *yang* (the dark or male force) in either world, a reaction would ensue in the other. As later elaborated by Tsou Yen (*c.* 305-240 B.C.) and, more comprehensively, by Tung Chung-shu (*c.* 179-104 B.C.) these doctrines came to provide a basis for evaluating actions of the secular ruler. Indeed, the distinguished Western-educated Chinese scholar Hu Shih (A.D. 1891-1962) went so far as to suggest that Tung Chung-shu self-consciously wrote about the invocation of natural law long before anyone in the Western world. Hu Shih, *Natural Law in the Chinese Tradition*, 5 NATURAL L. INST. PROC. 148; *see also* Vuylsteke, *supra* note 169.

Yin-yang and *wu-hsing* cosmological doctrine also had an impact upon the administration of public, positive law in China, at least from the Han dynasty onward. Death sentences, for example, were not to be carried out in the spring and summer months—"these being seasons of rebirth and growth." D. BODDE & C. MORRIS, LAW IN IMPERIAL CHINA 44-45 (1967). For more on *yin-yang* cosmology in general, see B. SCHWARTZ, *supra* note 73, at 350-82.

176. *See* Needham, *The Past in China's Present*, *reprinted in* J. NEEDHAM, WITHIN THE FOUR SEAS 63-64 (1969).

177. *See* Mote, *Confucian Eremitism in the Yüan Period*, in THE CONFUCIAN PERSUASION, *supra* note 173, at 202, 206-09; Wai-k'am Ho, *Chinese Under the Mongols*, in CHINESE ART UNDER THE MONGOLS: THE YUAN DYNASTY (1968). For a discussion of Chinese traditions of dissent, see L. SCHNEIDER, A MADMAN OF CH'U: THE CHINESE MYTH OF LOYALTY AND DISSENT *passim* (1980).

178. R. UNGER, LAW IN MODERN SOCIETY, *supra* note 2, at 100.

179. *E.g.*, H. CREEL, *supra* note 75, at 194-241. Similarly, although Unger cites two works by Wolfram Eberhard, R. UNGER, LAW IN MODERN SOCIETY, *supra* note 2, at 276 n.33, 277 n.42, he fails to draw upon other material by Eberhard that goes to this very point. *See* W. EBERHARD, LOKALKULTUREN IM ALTEN CHINA [LOCAL CULTURES IN ANCIENT CHINA] 9-13 *passim* (1942). Recent highly sophisticated work in the history of linguistics confirms the range of peoples and cultures with which the early Chinese were familiar. Pulleyblank, *The Chinese and Their Neighbors*

ary force, the image prevalent in Chinese society of an earlier golden age appears to have had something of a "constitutional purpose . . . serv[ing] to hold . . . power within limits and . . . prohibit[ing] any decline into absolutism."[180]

C. The Philosophical Debate

1. Professor Unger's View.—Having exhausted the political, social, and normative arenas, Professor Unger turns for the third and final stage of his inquiry to "the debates that took place among schools of thought" during his transformation era.[181] These debates warrant attention, he suggests, both because these schools of thought provided the foundation upon which imperial Chinese law and political thought would be built and because the vision of the world they impart stands in sharp contrast to "the central tradition of modern Western social thought."[182]

Unger focuses upon "the struggle between the disciples of Confucius[183] and the *fa-chia*, the so-called Legalists,"[184] which he sees as the

in Prehistoric and Early Historic Times, in THE ORIGINS OF CHINESE CIVILIZATION, *supra* note 72, at 411-66. Even the peoples that were to become the imperial Chinese in 221 B.C. were hardly uniform culturally. *See* Keightley, *The Late Shang State: When, Where and What?*, in *id.* at 546, 550.

That non-sinologists, writing well before Unger, who had even fewer secondary works upon which to rely nonetheless took account of preimperial China's contact with other cultures is evidenced by Robert Adams in his celebrated study of the rise of urbanism. R. ADAMS, THE EVOLUTION OF URBAN SOCIETY 21-22 (1966). Indeed, Adams decided not to use early China as his "old world" example in that work in large part because preimperial China had had prolonged exposure to a range of influences, direct and indirect, from other societies. *Id.*

For a discussion of the sources upon which Unger did rely, see *infra* note 295.

180. Bünger, *supra* note 114, at 80. Bünger discusses briefly the power that this shared sense of the past exercised over definitions of what constituted an appropriate exercise of power. *Id*; *see* K. Gottschang, *supra* note 73, at 149.

For more on the content of that golden age, see *infra* note 217.

181. R. UNGER, LAW IN MODERN SOCIETY, *supra* note 2, at 106.

182. *Id.* at 109.

183. *Id.* at 106. In his discussion of Confucianism, Unger does not identify the thinkers to whom he is referring, other than to state that the "main doctrinal conflict" of the era in question involved "the disciples of Confucius." *Id.* His footnotes indicate that he consulted the works of Confucius (551-479 B.C.) and Mencius (*c.* 370-290 B.C.), as well as a number of secondary works that also touch upon other leading early Confucian thinkers. *See id.* at 276-79 nn.45-47.

Confucius is the latinized version of the honorific K'ung Fu-tzu (Master K'ung) that was used to refer to the philosopher K'ung Ch'iu. Born in the nation-state of Lu, Confucius endeavored to obtain political office first there and later elsewhere in North China. Some accounts suggest that he held high office (including the post of Minister of Justice in Lu), but more likely, at most he attained only a minor position in government. Confucius is celebrated for his teaching, the essence of which is said to have been compiled by his students into what are called *The Analects* [*Lün-yü*], and for his supposed role in editing a number of the great Chinese Classics.

For more on the thought of Confucius, Mencius, and Hsün-tzu, see *infra* notes 204-35, 366-70 and accompanying text. Additionally, the life of Mencius is described briefly *infra* note 216 and that of Hsün-tzu *infra* note 220. For a pioneering study of the history of Chinese legal thought, see YANG HUNG-LIEH, CHUNG-KUO FA-LÜ SSU-HSIANG SHIH [A HISTORY OF CHINESE LEGAL THOUGHT] (1937).

For an example of interesting recent scholarship in the PRC on the legal thought of the early

"main doctrinal conflict of the transformation era."[185] The Confucian disciples, he indicates, believed in the natural benevolence of individuals and of society. They were of the view that each person was imbued with "latent, preexisting notions of propriety" that had the potential of serving as "a tacit code of conduct."[186] This idea of a "natural pattern of moral sentiments waiting to be developed" was paralleled at the level of society, which was "perceived of as an association of groups, generated by a limited number of basic relationships."[187] For the Confucianists, suggests Unger, the state's function was both to provide "proper conditions of upbringing and government" in which individuals could develop their inner moral sense[188] and to "orchestrate and protect . . . rather than to destroy and supplant" societal order.[189]

Not surprisingly, Unger indicates, the Confucianists had a "distaste for positive and public rules."[190] The law of the state, they believed, "disregarded the true basis of social harmony . . . [and so] could lead only to greater dissension."[191] "Confucianism" instead "showed its devotion to customary law" as its adherents "accepted and reinterpreted the *li* of the feudal age" as their chief vehicle for regulating society.[192]

The Legalists, according to Unger, believed human nature to be bes-

Confucians, see ZHANG GUOHUA, 1 ZHONGGUO FALÜ SIXIANG SHI GANG [AN OUTLINE HISTORY OF CHINESE LEGAL THOUGHT] 77-125 (1983). Important recent Western scholarship on early Confucian thought includes B. SCHWARTZ, *supra* note 73, at 56-134; TU WEI-MING, CONFUCIAN THOUGHT: SELFHOOD AS CREATIVE TRANSFORMATION (1985).

184. R. UNGER, LAW IN MODERN SOCIETY, *supra* note 2, at 106. Unger is also not specific about the Legalist thinkers to whom he is referring. In his notes he does make mention of the works of two prominent Legalist thinkers, Shang Yang (*c.* 390-338 B.C.) and Han Fei-tzu (*c.* 280-233 B.C.), and also refers to a number of secondary works which do contain some discussion of other important preimperial Legalists. *Id.* at 278 n.45.

The use of the phrase *fa-chia* [Legalist] by Chinese and Western scholars alike to encompass Shang Yang, Han Fei-tzu, Kuan-tzu (*d.* 645 B.C.), Shen Pu-hai (*c.* 400-337 B.C.), Li Ssu (*c.* 280-206 B.C.), and a number of other less well-known figures derives from the emphasis of these individuals upon the utilization of law as a tool through which to regulate society. Some scholars believe that this term is misleading because it suggests more cohesion between these thinkers than was actually the case. *See* THE BOOK OF LORD SHANG, *supra* note 166, at 70; *cf.* H. CREEL, SHEN PU-HAI: A CHINESE POLITICAL PHILOSOPHER OF THE FOURTH CENTURY B.C. 135 (1974) (noting that "Shen Pu-hai was not a Legalist"). Others feel that the use of the term "Legalist" is confusing for Western readers in that it connotes something of a commitment to law in and of itself. Indeed, the ideogram for law [*fa*] had a broad range of uses in preimperial China, and is properly translated in different contexts to mean "model," "method," "technique," "rule," and "regulation," as well as law. For a discussion of the difficulties of translating *fa* precisely, see *id.* at 145-51.

For more on the Legalists, see B. SCHWARTZ, *supra* note 73, at 321-49; ZHANG GUOHUA, *supra* note 183, at 154-223; *infra* notes 236-56, 379-82 and accompanying text.

185. R. UNGER, LAW IN MODERN SOCIETY, *supra* note 2, at 106.

186. *Id.* at 107 (footnote omitted).

187. *Id.*

188. *Id.*

189. *Id.*

190. *Id.* at 108.

191. *Id.*

192. *Id.*

tial and "enslaved by the passions."[193] Concomitantly, they were of the view that the only order society had was that imposed by the state at any given time. As a consequence, they "wanted nothing more than to extend the powers of government . . . as an end in itself,"[194] whatever else their rhetoric may have suggested.

Believing order to be a wholly human-made imposition upon society, continues Unger, the Legalists saw no need to draw upon the past. Instead, to attain their goal of exercising temporal power, they turned to "coercively" imposed and enforced bureaucratic law,[195] which could be used in a ruthless fashion to control all aspects of society.[196]

Unger concludes his discussion of the core of Chinese civilization by observing that "[t]hough the theoretical assumptions about man and society made by the Confucianists and Legalists may have steered the two schools in opposite directions, both tendencies were incompatible with a rule of law doctrine."[197] Neither school believed, as did the "central tradition of modern Western social thought" that "men . . . deserve to be respected as individual persons."[198] And neither believed that "spontaneously generated social arrangements . . . ought to be protected as manifestations of individual and collective will."[199] In fact, the "tacitly shared assumptions" of Confucianism and Legalism were so powerful that they "forbade [the two schools] to defend the rule of law in the modern Western sense or indeed even to conceive of it."[200]

2. *Another View.*—Professor Unger's depiction of what he calls the "debates that took place among schools of thought" in late preimperial China warrants revision in two principal respects. First, in recounting what he terms "the main doctrinal conflict" of this era—that between the "disciples of Confucius and the *fa-chia*"[201]—he accurately reports certain broad features of each school of thought, but fails to consider vital dimensions of each school that significantly influenced its outlook on the very questions he believes are central. Second, he wholly ignores other schools of thought—such as the Mohists[202] and Taoists[203]—that were as

193. *Id.* at 107.
194. *Id.*
195. *Id.* at 106-109.
196. *Id.* at 109, 131.
197. *Id.* at 109.
198. *Id.*
199. *Id.* By "collective will" Unger means the will of private groups within the state. *See id.*
200. *Id.* at 106.
201. *Id.*
202. Mohism is a name given to the school of thought emanating from the writings of Mo-tzu (Mo-ti) who is reputed to have lived between the death of Confucius in 479 B.C. and the birth of Mencius approximately a century later. According to Han Fei-tzu, Confucianism and Mohism were

important at the time as those he discusses and that also shed further light on the issues that he generally deems most vital to understanding preimperial China.

Professor Unger correctly emphasizes the importance to early Confucian thought of the idea that each member of society possessed "latent, preexisting notions of propriety,"[204] that society contained an analogous moral order expressed through the five cardinal relationships[205] and that appropriate cultivation of these inherent norms and moral order was a prerequisite to the promotion of harmony both for the individual and for society.[206] A clear concomitant of this was a strong preference on the part of the Confucians[207] to utilize the *li* and morality in general, rather than formal written law, to regulate society.[208] But this does not mean that Confucian thought—and particularly that of those he calls the "disciples"[209]—was as limited to the "conservative notion of hierarchical community"[210] nor as opposed to "coercively imposed positive rules" as he suggests.[211]

It is true that Confucius and the leading expositors of his thought

two schools "well known for their learning." Han Fei-tzu, *Eminence in Learning*, in BASIC WRITINGS, *supra* note 104, at 118. The prominence of Mohism is confirmed by the eminent modern scholar Hu Shih who tells us that "Mohism seems to have had a very wide following for almost two centuries (430-230 B.C.)." HU SHIH, THE DEVELOPMENT OF THE LOGICAL METHOD IN ANCIENT CHINA 58 (2d ed. 1963).

For solid discussions of Mohist thought that were available to Unger, see YI-PAO MEI, MOTSE: THE NEGLECTED RIVAL OF CONFUCIUS (reprint 1973); Graham, *Later Mohist Treatises on Ethics and Logic Reconstructed from the "Ta-ch'u" Chapter of "Mo-tzu"*, 17 ASIA MAJOR 137 (1972). Recent discussions of the legal thought of Mo-tzu and his chief disciples may be found in ZHANG GUOHUA, *supra* note 183, at 126-40 and B. SCHWARTZ, *supra* note 73, at 135-72. *See also infra* notes 262-76, 371-75, and accompanying text.

203. Taoism in preimperial China was a philosophical tradition growing principally out of two works: the *Tao-te ching* [*The Way and Power*] and the *Chuang-tzu*. The former work is said to have been authored by Lao-tzu, who is reputed to have been an older contemporary of Confucius, but whose existence still has not been conclusively proven. The latter work is believed to have been the product of the late fourth century B.C. sage Chuang-tzu. For background on the Taoists, Unger might have considered a host of works, including H. CREEL, WHAT IS TAOISM? (1970); D. MUNRO, THE CONCEPT OF MAN IN EARLY CHINA 117-39 *passim* (1967); Lau, *The Treatment of Opposites in Lao Tzu*, 21 BULL. SCH. ORIENTAL & AFR. STUD. 349 (1958).

For a further discussion of some aspects of Taoism, see *infra* notes 277-93, 372-77 and accompanying text.

204. R. UNGER, LAW IN MODERN SOCIETY, *supra* note 2, at 107.

205. *Id.* at 107. The five cardinal relationships were those between ruler and subject, father and son, husband and wife, elder and younger brother, and older and younger friend. For background on the significance of Chinese family relationships, see generally FENG HAN-YI, THE CHINESE KINSHIP SYSTEM (1948).

206. R. UNGER, LAW IN MODERN SOCIETY, *supra* note 2, at 107-08.

207. *E.g.*, D. BODDE & C. MORRIS, *supra* note 175, at 19-23 (1967); LIANG CH'I-CH'AO, HISTORY OF CHINESE POLITICAL THOUGHT DURING THE EARLY TSIN PERIOD 48-49 (1930).

208. R. UNGER, LAW IN MODERN SOCIETY, *supra* note 2, at 105-109.

209. *Id.* at 106.

210. *Cf. id.* at 109.

211. *Id.* at 108.

were committed to hierarchical society, but it is also true that they strenuously advocated that, at least between the *chün-tzu* and *hsiao-jen*, the hierarchy be one in which merit and morality were more important than birth or wealth.[212] Whereas before the time of Confucius, the former term meant a prince or other man of noble birth and the latter signified commoners,[213] Confucius argued that a true *chün-tzu* was a man of noble moral character and that a *hsiao-jen* was a base individual.[214] This effort to maintain a hierarchy of relations based upon virtue, rather than material or other external standards,[215] was carried even further by the principal preimperial exponents of Confucian thought. Thus, we find Mencius[216]—one of the two most important such figures—affirming that "[even] Yao and Shun[217] were the same as anyone else"[218] and that "all men are capable of becoming a Yao or a Shun."[219] Similarly, we find

212. *See* D. MUNRO, *supra* note 203, at 112-16; V. RUBIN, INDIVIDUAL AND STATE IN ANCIENT CHINA: ESSAYS ON FOUR CHINESE PHILOSOPHERS 20-21 (1976) (S. Levine trans.); A SOURCE BOOK IN CHINESE PHILOSOPHY 15 (Wing-tsit Chan trans. & ed. 1963). There were, to be sure, limits to the Confucian ideal of a hierarchy based on merit. No matter how worthy they may have been morally, wives could not become husbands and so ascend to the pinnacle of the family hierarchy.

213. D. MUNRO, *supra* note 203, at 113.

214. *Id.* at 113-16; *see* THE ANALECTS, *supra* note 119, at bk. IV, ch. 11, in which Confucius declares that "gentlemen [*chün-tzu*] set their hearts upon moral force . . . commoners [*hsiao-jen*] set theirs upon the soil. Where gentlemen think only of punishments, the commoners think only of exemptions." Or consider Book IV, Chapter 16, in which it is said that "[a] gentleman takes as much trouble to discover what is right as lesser men take to discover what will pay." To be sure, as Hsiao Kung-chuan notes, Confucius at times used the term *chün-tzu* with reference to social rank. HSIAO KUNG-CHUAN, A HISTORY OF CHINESE POLITICAL THOUGHT: FROM THE BEGINNINGS TO THE SIXTH CENTURY A.D. 117-18 (F. Mote trans. 1979).

215. D. MUNRO, *supra* note 203, at 113-16.

216. Born a century after Confucius' death, Mencius (the latinized version of Meng-tzu, also known as Meng K'o) is said to have studied under pupils of Confucius' grandson. As was the case with Confucius, Mencius principally was a teacher and only briefly served in public office. Among the works discussing Mencius and his philosophy which were available to Unger are FUNG YU-LAN, A HISTORY OF CHINESE PHILOSOPHY 106-31 (1937); HSIAO KUNG-CHUAN, *supra* note 214, at 52-60; D. MUNRO, *supra* note 203, *passim*; Lau, *Theories of Human Nature in Mencius and Shyuntzyy* (sic) 15 BULL. SCH. ORIENTAL & AFR. STUD. (1953).

217. Yao and Shun were legendary early rulers of China subsequently regarded as models of benevolent and proper rule. Yao is described in a number of sources, commencing with *The Canon on Yao* section of *The Book of History* and including the *Confucian Analects* and Ssu-ma Ch'ien's *Historical Records*. Shun is discussed, *inter alia*, by Confucius, Mencius, and Ssu-ma Ch'ien. Nonetheless, a number of historians, particularly in the West, have been skeptical as to their existence. *E.g.*, K. LATOURETTE, THE CHINESE: THEIR HISTORY AND CULTURE 39 (2d ed. 1941) (speculating that Confucian scholars may have created these figures to lend their teachings "the sanction of antiquity"). In his recent study of preimperial China, K.C. Wu argues that recent archaeological data disproves the position taken by Latourette. Wu goes on to suggest that Chinese scholars eager to earn favor with their Western counterparts may have taken an unduly skeptical view of the possibility that Yao and Shun existed. *See* K.C. WU, *supra* note 66, at 35-44, 65-69.

Without suggesting an equivalence, it should be noted that the Chinese were not alone in appealing to a golden age to justify current activity. Harold Berman describes the "myth of a return to an earlier time" as "the hallmark of all the European revolutions." H. BERMAN, LAW AND REVOLUTION: THE FORMATION OF THE WESTERN LEGAL TRADITION 15 (1983).

218. MENCIUS bk. IX, pt. B, ch. 32 (D.C. Lau trans. 1970).

219. *Id.* at bk. VI, pt. B, ch. 2.

Hsün-tzu,[220] the other leading preimperial elaborator of Confucian thought, declaring that

> . . . any man who takes to heart the instructions of his teacher, applies himself to his studies and abides by ritual principles [*li*] may become a gentleman [*chün-tzu*] but anyone who gives free rein to his emotional nature, is content to indulge his passions and disregards ritual principles becomes a petty man [*hsiao-jen*].[221]

This emphasis upon character, rationality, and initiative would hardly seem to suggest that the Chinese felt that "men," if not women, "did not deserve to be respected as individual persons."[222]

The great preimperial Confucian thinkers also appear to have felt differently about public, positive law than Professor Unger suggests. Even Confucius did not dismiss the state's written law to the extent Professor Unger suggests.[223] Clearly, Confucius did not believe that such law was the best or most effective way through which to lead people to act properly.[224] Nonetheless, he recognized that formal law was an integral and necessary part of society as long as it included people who in practice proved not to be amenable to moral suasion.[225] Until society and human nature were brought into accord with the principles of the *li*—a process Confucius presumed would be lengthy[226]—it would be necessary to utilize this far less preferable tool to restrain those who could not be converted to propriety.[227]

220. Hsün-tzu (also known as Hsün K'uang) is said to have been born in the state of Chao sometime between 312 and 298 B.C. He briefly held public positions in the states of Ch'i and Ch'u, but, as did Confucius and Mencius, devoted his time principally to teaching. As is the fear of teachers past and present, his reputation is colored by the actions of his students, two of whom—Han Fei-tzu and Li Ssu—became leading Legalists. *See infra* notes 239-40. For more on Hsün-tzu, see FUNG YU-LAN, *supra* note 216, at 282-311; D. MUNRO, *supra* note 203, *passim*; Lau, *supra* note 216.

221. Hsün-tzu, *Man's Nature is Evil*, in BASIC WRITINGS, *supra* note 104, at 158. The conventional wisdom regarding Hsün-tzu, reflected in Watson's translation of the title of this essay, is that Hsün-tzu conceived of human nature as evil. Actually, a closer reading suggests that Hsün-tzu was somewhat less pessimistic about human nature. Hsün-tzu did see human nature as having a very real potential for evil. He also believed, however, that with serious efforts at self-cultivation—buttressed by a strong government setting a high moral example and utilizing formal written law—every person had the capacity to become highly moral.

222. *Cf.* R. UNGER, LAW IN MODERN SOCIETY, *supra* note 2, at 109.

223. *The Analects* contain a number of references to the need for laws. *E.g.*, THE ANALECTS, *supra* note 119, bk. XII, chs. 12, 13, bk. XIII, chs. 2, 3. For a thoughtful discussion of Confucian attitudes toward law, see Young, *The Concept of Justice in Pre-Imperial China*, in MORAL BEHAVIOR IN CHINESE SOCIETY 38, 40-46 (1981).

224. Recognizing the value of winning hearts and minds, Confucius is reputed to have said, "Govern the people by regulations, keep order among them by chastisements, and they will flee from you, and lose all self-respect. Govern them by moral force, keep order among them by . . . [*li*] and they will keep their self-respect and come to you of their own accord." THE ANALECTS, *supra* note 119, bk. II, ch. 3.

225. *See* HSIAO KUNG-CHUAN, *supra* note 214, at 113-14.

226. THE ANALECTS, *supra* note 119, bk. XIII, ch. 11.

227. *See id.*; R. AMES, THE ART OF RULERSHIP: A STUDY IN ANCIENT CHINESE POLITICAL THOUGHT 121 (1983).

Mencius and Hsün-tzu—upon whose work Professor Unger suggests he is focusing—viewed the written law of the state with less displeasure than their mentor. Although taking a rather more benign view of human nature than Confucius, Mencius recognized the important role that public, positive penal law had to play. Penal laws were necessary, he felt, even in the best of times. Thus, said Mencius, "men of superior character should fill the positions in the court . . . . If the ruler uses this . . . [opportunity] to make his policies and penal laws clear to the people, then other powerful states will be impressed."[228] Nor did Mencius restrict his interest in law to the criminal area, as he believed that administrative and economic arrangements could be facilitated through positive law.[229] To an even greater extent, Hsün-tzu saw formal state law not as an unpleasant expedient, but as an important and useful part of society that should be viewed affirmatively.[230] In his mind, law and *li* were not in opposition. Society, he believed, should regard the *li* as the embodiment of the moral principles toward which it should strive and should, accordingly, develop a formal criminal code that reflected the *li*.[231] Reliance upon such a code would not obviate the need for good rulers schooled in the *li* but could be highly salutary in helping them lead society toward realization of the ideals expressed in the *li*, given human nature.[232]

Professor Unger's treatment of the Legalists is no better. He is correct in indicating that the Legalists did not share the Confucian enthusiasm about the cultivation of internalized behavioral norms but instead advocated establishment of a strong central government that would brook no threat to its control over most areas of life.[233] Also accurate is his statement that the Legalists saw rigid adherence to formal written rules as the best way to attain that end.[234] Unger, however, is incorrect in dismissing the Legalists' underlying rationale by saying that they "wanted nothing more than to extend the powers of government . . . as an end in itself."[235]

228. MENCIUS, *supra* note 218, bk. II, pt. A, ch. 4 (Lau translation modified by the author). For a similar translation, see R. AMES, *supra* note 227, at 121.

229. MENCIUS, *supra* note 218, bk. III, pt. A, ch. 3.

230. *See* Hsün-tzu, *Human Nature is Evil*, in BASIC WRITINGS, supra note 104, at 157 *passim*; Hsün-tzu, *The Regulations of a King*, in *id.* at 33 *passim*.

231. R. AMES, *supra* note 227, at 230 n.36.

232. Hsün-tzu, *Human Nature is Evil*, in BASIC WRITINGS, *supra* note 104, at 162-63.

233. *See* Hsiao Kung-chuan, *Legalism and Autocracy in Traditional China*, 4 TSING-HUA J. CHINESE STUD. 108 (1964).

234. *See* Han Fei-tzu, *On Having Standards*, in BASIC WRITINGS, *supra note* 104, at 21 *passim*.

235. R. UNGER, LAW IN MODERN SOCIETY, *supra* note 2, at 107; *see also* R. UNGER, *supra* note 1, at 75 (where Unger equates Legalism and terrorism). *But see infra* notes 236-56 and accompanying text.

The Inscrutable Occidental

The most influential Legalist thinkers—Kuan-tzu,[236] Shang Yang,[237] Shen Pu-hai,[238] Han Fei-tzu,[239] and Li Ssu[240]—were deeply troubled by the chaos of their times, which they saw as destructive of political and social life for ruler and ruled alike. Having a decidedly less optimistic picture of the human potential for self-cultivation than the Confucians, the Legalists believed that the Confucian preference for reliance upon internalized behavioral norms had been corrosive of order at all levels of society and thus partially responsible for the turmoil of the

236. There is some doubt as to whether the text known as the *Kuan-tzu* actually was compiled by the individual known as Kuan-tzu (who also is said to have been known as Kuan Chung or Kuan Yi-wu). K. Gottschang, *supra* note 73, at 280-81. That text is widely considered, nonetheless, to be a strong statement of late preimperial Legalist views. LIANG CH'I-CH'AO, *supra* note 207, at 16. *See generally* W. RICKETT, GUANZI: POLITICAL, ECONOMIC AND PHILOSOPHICAL ESSAYS FROM EARLY CHINA 8-10 (1985); W. RICKETT, KUAN-TZU: A REPOSITORY OF EARLY CHINESE THOUGHT 8 (1965) (discussing why Kuan Chung is "identified with the [Legalist] school") [hereinafter cited as W. RICKETT, KUAN-TZU]. *But see* K. Gottschang, *supra* note 73, at 280 ("The *Kuan Tzu* has posed problems because it combines notions of law that fit in with neither Confucian nor Legalist thinking.").

237. Shang Yang, also known as Lord Shang and Kung-sun Yang, was born into a noble family in the state of Wei. One among many itinerant advisors of his times, he rose to a position of high political prominence in the state of Ch'in (which later was to found the first Chinese empire). *See* D. BODDE, *supra* note 7, at 1, 3-4. He is known for his advocacy of a series of measures designed to foster the centralization and rationalization of economic and political power, in part through the utilization of law. It is unclear whether he himself compiled *The Book of Lord Shang*, which expresses many of these ideas, or whether that work is the product of his followers. For more on Lord Shang, see THE BOOK OF LORD SHANG, *supra* note 166; SHANG YANG'S REFORMS AND STATE CONTROL IN CHINA (Li Yu-ning ed. 1977). There was a revival of interest in the Legalists during the Cultural Revolution (1966-1976) among the Legalists. *E.g.*, SHANG JUN SHU ZHU YI [AN ANNOTATED BAI HUA TRANSLATION OF THE BOOK OF LORD SHANG] (Gao Heng comp. 1975); *see also* Alford, *Of Arsenic and Old Laws: Looking Anew at Criminal Justice in Late Imperial China*, 72 CAL. L. REV. 1180, 1182 n.7 (1984).

238. A native of the state of Ching, Shen Pu-hai occupied low office in the state of Cheng prior to rising to the chancellorship of the state of Han. Professor H.G. Creel, who has written a book-length study of Shen, believes that he should be distinguished from the other so-called Legalists, because he was far more concerned with scientific principles of administration than with the use of law in itself, although Creel does recognize that Shen saw law as one major administrative vehicle. Shen envisioned a state that functioned according to clear, proven, and essentially immutable standards of administration (termed by him *shu* [techniques]). H. CREEL, *supra* note 184, at 135-162; *see* Bodde, Book Review, 36 HARV. J. ASIATIC STUD. 258 (1976) (reviewing H. CREEL, SHEN PU-HAI: A CHINESE POLITICAL PHILOSOPHER OF THE FOURTH CENTURY B.C. (1974)); Rosen, *Editor's Note*, 2 EARLY CHINA 29 (1976).

239. Han Fei-tzu was probably the most influential of Legalist thinkers. A student of Confucius' disciple, Hsün-tzu, Han Fei-tzu was a nobleman of the state of Han. He achieved a position of prominence in the state of Ch'in in the decades prior to the Ch'in conquest, but was purged by fellow Legalists. Among the many sources dealing with Han Fei-tzu that Unger might have consulted is FUNG YU-LAN, *supra* note 216, at 312-36. Interesting recent discussions of Han Fei-tzu's legal thinking include ZHANG GUOHUA, *supra* note 183, at 205-23, and LEO CHANG & WANG HSIAO-PO, HAN FEI SSU-HSIANG TE LI-SHIH YEN-CHIU [A HISTORICAL STUDY OF THE THOUGHT OF HAN FEI] (1983).

240. Li Ssu is not considered to have been a thinker of the magnitude of his Legalist forerunners. Nonetheless, this fellow student of Han Fei-tzu's authored Legalist tracts and, more importantly, became Prime Minister of the state of Ch'in. Li helped lead the Ch'in state through the imperial conquest, and later served as the first Prime Minister of China. For a full treatment of Li Ssu's life and thought, see D. BODDE, *supra* note 7.

age.[241] To their thinking, Confucianism led the ruler—who the Legalists saw as being no better morally than anyone else—to rule according to his private whims, rather than pursuant to clear and fixed principles.[242] It also encouraged state officials to vie with each other both for the ruler's ear and for personal privilege. Finally, it resulted in the unequal application of state law among the populace, thereby breeding resentment and cynicism, and undercutting loyalty to the state.[243]

The Legalists believed it imperative to instill a higher degree of order and coherence in political and social life, not simply as an end in itself, but as the only way in which the welfare of all members of society could be fostered. That end could best be attained, they felt, through clear and rigid public, positive laws that would regulate most areas of human endeavor.[244] Contrary to the impression imparted by Professor Unger,[245] many of the most prominent Legalist thinkers contended that these laws should apply equally to everyone, including the officials who administered them and even, some believed, the ruler himself.[246] Thus, we find Kuan-tzu saying,

> If [the ruler] does not conform to the law, governmental affairs will lack a constant standard. If he conforms to what is unlawful, his orders will not be carried out. If orders are issued yet are not carried out, it is because the orders do not conform to the law . . . . Therefore it is said: When prohibitions take precedence over [the ruler] himself, his orders will function among the people.[247]

Similarly, Han Fei-tzu argued that "if [the ruler] abandons fixed laws and depends upon personal judgments, even Yao is not capable of regulating a state . . . . On the other hand, let an average ruler observe the standards of law . . . [and he would not] go much amiss."[248] As a corollary to this idea of uniform application of the law, the Legalists urged that the law should be developed according to standardized procedures. The law should also be clear in order to be understood easily among the

241. *See* HSIAO KUNG-CHUAN, *supra* note 214, at 386-88.

242. *Id.* at 381-93.

243. *See* Han Fei-tzu, *On Having Standards*, in BASIC WRITINGS, *supra* note 104, at 21-29.

244. *Id.*

245. R. UNGER, LAW IN MODERN SOCIETY, *supra* note 2, at 107-08.

246. Kuan-tzu, Shang Yang, and Han Fei-tzu all speak of the need for rulers to adhere to the law if the state is to run properly. Han Fei-tzu at times even describes the ideal state for the ruler as being one of a veritable inactivity (reminiscent of the Taoist idea of *wu-wei* or purposive inactivity discussed *infra* note 290) in which clear and strictly applied laws would regulate the people. Han Fei-tzu, *On Having Standards*, in BASIC WRITINGS, *supra* note 104, at 21-29. Indeed, Shang Yang met his demise when, as Prime Minister of Ch'in, he endeavored to punish the son of his ruler for having broken the law. *See* SHANG YANG'S REFORMS AND STATE CONTROL IN CHINA, *supra* note 237, at 72-80.

247. Kuan-tzu, *On Conforming to the Law*, in W. RICKETT, KUAN-TZU, *supra* note 236, at 90.

248. Han Fei-tzu, *The Use of Men*, *quoted in* LIANG CH'I-CH'AO, *supra* note 207, at 121.

The Inscrutable Occidental

wide range of officials and local leaders to whom it was to be disseminated. And it should be administered by specialized officials trained in the law "who understand [its] . . . contents" and who are to be punished if they improperly apply it.[249] Moreover, believing that individuals were capable of responding rationally, Han Fei-tzu and other Legalists further insisted as a matter of policy that light offenses be severely punished so as to deter more serious crimes and to avoid the need to inflict even more severe punishments.[250]

To note that Kuan-tzu, Han Fei-tzu, and other major Legalist thinkers argued for the uniform application of publicly promulgated laws by specialized officials is not to suggest that Legalist philosophy presaged the rule of law as it has taken shape in modern Western society or even that Legalist thinkers in practice were able to implement the above-described principles. Although certain Legalist writings did deem it important that rulers neither disregard those laws handed down by their predecessors nor abuse their people,[251] ultimately even they acknowledged the authority of the ruler to alter the existing legal order.[252] Nor did Legalist philosophers propose regularized procedures through which the ordinary populace might seek effective redress against abuses of power or otherwise might participate personally in the governmental process.[253] Moreover, although not strictly pertinent to a discussion of Legalist theory, the harshly autocratic manner in which the Legalist oriented Ch'in state operated during its brief period of power[254] did little to enhance the image of Legalism, especially among the Confucian elite that subsequently dominated historical writing in imperial China.[255] None-

249. THE BOOK OF LORD SHANG, *supra* note 166, at 327-28; *see also supra* note 104.

An interesting latter-day parallel to (if not outgrowth of) this idea of official responsibility may be found in those provisions of imperial codes from the T'ang onward that virtually held officials to a standard of strict liability for unintentional errors. Relative at least to the contemporary West, imperial Chinese law reposed great power in the hands of adjudicators, rather than the parties to a case. By the same token, however, it called for the punishment of officials for inadvertent errors that would be unlikely to lead even to nominal punishment in the West. *See* Alford, *supra* note 237, at 1248 n.431 *passim.*

250. *See, e.g,* Han Fei-tzu, *The Five Vermin*, in BASIC WRITINGS, *supra* note 104, at 96, 104 (asserting that "[t]he best penalties are those which are severe and inescapable, so that people will fear them").

251. *Id. passim.* Or as Shang Yang wrote, "When the measures and figures have been instituted, law can be followed . . . . [A] ruler of men should pay attention to it himself." THE BOOK OF LORD SHANG, *supra* note 166, at 243.

252. *E.g.*, Han Fei-tzu, *The Way of the Ruler*, in BASIC WRITINGS, *supra* note 104, at 16-20.

253. D. BODDE, *supra* note 7, at 191, 195.

254. Although the Legalist-minded Ch'in applied the law with less status differentiation than Confucian scholars would have desired, recent scholarship suggests that Ch'in law still provided that officials receive lighter punishment than commoners. A. HULSEWÉ, *supra* note 73, at 7-8.

255. The order (reputedly given by the Legalist Prime Minister Li Ssu in 213 B.C.) to burn *The Book of Documents, The Book of Poetry*, and almost all other books espousing philosophies differing from that of the Ch'in state has, not surprisingly, hardly endeared the Ch'in or Legalism to subse-

theless, a fair reading of Legalist theory hardly suggests, as does Professor Unger, that the school was driven by nothing more than the desire to accumulate unbridled state power for its own sake.[256]

Professor Unger does not seek to survey preimperial Chinese philosophy. Nonetheless, because he refers to the then-current "debates" between schools of thought and, more importantly, because he generalizes broadly about preimperial Chinese society and consciousness, it is inappropriate that he omits any consideration of Mohism[257] and only briefly mentions Taoism.[258] These two schools were as prominent[259] as Confucianism and Legalism[260] during what he terms the transformation era and are relevant to his argument.[261]

Sharing the dismay of other major schools of thought over the disordered situation within which they lived, the Mohists believed that all human actions should be judged according to the degree to which they promoted the well-being of society's members,[262] regardless of social rank or position within the family. Concomitantly, the Mohists saw the Confucian view that social harmony required the observance of the obligations embodied in the five cardinal relationships as having curtailed

quent generations of Confucian scholars. The order to burn the books is described in D. BODDE, *supra* note 7, at 80-84, 162-66. The treatment of one major Legalist figure, Shang Yang, by Confucian and other historians from preimperial days to the present is traced in SHANG YANG'S REFORMS AND STATE CONTROL IN CHINA, *supra* note 237, at xiii-cxx.

Professor Unger notes that "Chinese imperial practice was built upon a mixture of the two, in which Legalist policies were often clothed in Confucianist language." R. UNGER, LAW IN MODERN SOCIETY, *supra* note 2, at 106. There is considerable truth to this, but it is also true both that Confucian thought significantly influenced the law, as indicated in the principal source that Professor Unger cites for the former proposition, CH'Ü T'UNG-TSÜ, LAW AND SOCIETY IN TRADITIONAL CHINA 267-297 (1965), and that Buddhism and Taoism also had considerable impact upon "imperial Chinese practice."

256. *See supra* note 235 and accompanying text.

257. *See supra* note 202 (regarding the prominence of the Mohists).

258. R. UNGER, LAW IN MODERN SOCIETY, *supra* note 2, at 99-100.

259. *See supra* note 203 (concerning the position of Taoism).

260. The presence of one additional school of late preimperial Chinese thought—the *ming-chia* [literally, the School of Names, but also known in English as the Logicians or the Dialectians]—should be noted. This school, which did not flourish after the imperial unification, had a deep faith, expressed through "dialogues, aphorisms and paradoxes," in the power of rational thought and logical method. A SOURCE BOOK IN CHINESE PHILOSOPHY, *supra* note 212, at 232. The existence of this school in preimperial China should lead us to think further about Professor Unger's statement in *Law in Modern Society* that "pre-Socratic philosophy inaugurated a rationalistic inquiry into nature that had no true analogue in China," R. UNGER, LAW IN MODERN SOCIETY, *supra* note 2, at 124, and his assertion in *Knowledge and Politics* that the antinomy of reason and desire is a product of the liberal state, R. UNGER, *supra* note 1, at 6.

261. *See infra* notes 371-75 and accompanying text (discussing the Taoist sense of an individual's capability of transcending existing societal arrangements).

262. Mo-tzu, *Universal Love*, in BASIC WRITINGS, *supra* note 104, at 39-49. The Mohist call for maximizing social welfare ought not to be confused with that of Jeremy Bentham and the Utilitarians. The "efficiency" that the Mohists had in mind was chiefly a repudiation of the waste that they saw entailed by elaborate Confucian rituals. For a brief discussion of Mo-tzu with attention to seeming similarities to the Utilitarians, see V. RUBIN, *supra* note 212, at 33-54.

rather than fostered overall welfare.[263] Instead, the Mohists advocated that each person adopt the principle of *chien ai*, which is typically translated as "universal love,"[264] but more accurately understood as a concern for all other persons commensurate to that one has for oneself. The Mohists felt that adherence to this principle of universal concern would both minimize the baleful effects of familial and other distinctions and better enable all members of society to recognize the true talent of other persons, whether strangers or family members.[265] This, in turn, would advance the interests of society both by strengthening an appreciation of common interest at a level far broader than that of the family and by engendering in the populace a support for their leaders based upon the recognition that those who led society owed their position to merit rather than to family ties.[266]

In this environment of universal concern, Mo-tzu saw government—and, with it, order—as emerging from the will of the populace,[267] although he was none too specific as to how that will was to be expressed in practice, particularly in the crucial initial phase of identifying those persons worthy to rule. Mo-tzu seems to have had a deep faith that within each level of community, from the simplest neighborhood through the state as a whole, adherence to the ideal of universal concern would enable "the most benevolent man" to become community head.[268] He also believed that before Mohist precepts became widely adopted, standards for each community should be set by the community head who, as the most benevolent man at that level, would be best able to give voice to those measures appropriate for that group.[269] Once Mohism had been adopted throughout the civilized world, leaders at each level of society would be able to refer to the level above for appropriate standards, with the emperor turning to Heaven for ultimate guidance.[270]

Given the character of community heads and the genesis of standards, Mo-tzu believed that the populace should therefore "identify oneself with one's superiors" and accept without question both the standards of judgment so developed and their particular application by the commu-

263. Mo-tzu, *Against Confucianism*, in BASIC WRITINGS, *supra* note 104, at 124-36.

264. *See* Mo-tzu, *Universal Love: Part III*, in *id.* at 39-49; Mo-tzu, *Moderation in Funerals*, in *id.* at 65-77.

265. Mo-tzu, *Universal Love: Part III*, in *id.* at 39-49. To be sure, not all distinctions were to be eliminated. Officials were entitled to privileges not available to the general populace, supposedly in order to aid them in governing.

266. *Id.*

267. The populace for Mo-tzu, as for all of the preimperial Confucian thinkers with the possible exception of the Taoists, should be read as the "male populace." *See supra* note 170.

268. Mo-tzu, *Identifying with One's Superiors*, in BASIC WRITINGS, *supra* note 104, at 34-38.

269. *Id.*

270. *Id.*

nity head.[271] Mo-tzu does not specify whether public laws would be necessary at the local level, but he is clear on the importance of such law at the level of the ruler of the state.[272] Thus, Mo-tzu tells us that

> [i]n ancient times, the sage kings devised the five punishments so as to bring order to the people. These [punishments] were like the main thread binding a skein of silk or the main cord controlling a net, by which the sage kings bound and hauled in those among the people of the world who failed to identify themselves with their superiors.[273]

The formation of standards by leaders did not mean for Mo-tzu that community heads were wholly free to exercise the authority that they derived from their communities without restraint. Mo-tzu urged rulers to select as advisors the most capable persons, regardless of station, and to take their counsel seriously.[274] Furthermore, justice was to be applied evenhandedly to the prominent, as evidenced by the example of a leading official in the state of Ch'in who insisted his son be executed for murder, notwithstanding the ruler's offer of a pardon.[275] Most importantly, Mo-tzu envisioned that Heaven might choose to topple a ruler who mistreated the people, much as it did away with the last Shang ruler, although he is vague as to how the populace might invoke this Will of Heaven [*t'ien-chih*].[276]

Professor Unger's omission of all but a single fleeting reference to Taoism in preimperial China[277] is equally unfortunate, for in many respects its principal works—the *Tao-te-ching*[278] and the *Chuang-tzu*[279]—speak to issues about which he is concerned. Both works sharply question the efficacy and the legitimacy of the structures, the standards, and even the consciousness of human society.[280] The *Tao-te-ching* criticizes reliance upon public, positive law, saying that "[t]he more laws are promulgated, [t]he more thieves and bandits there will be."[281] It is no less skeptical about the customary law embodied in Confucian morality,

271. *Id.*

272. *Id*; *see also* Mo-tzu, *Against Fatalism*, in *id.* at 120-21 ("[S]age kings issued statutes and published laws . . . to encourage good and prevent evil."); B. SCHWARTZ, *supra* note 73, at 149 (noting Mo-tzu's belief that criminal and civil laws, as enforced by the ruler, hold the state together).

273. Mo-tzu, *Identifying with One's Superiors*, in BASIC WRITINGS, *supra* note 104, at 38.

274. Mo-tzu, *Honoring the Worthy*, in *id.* at 18-33.

275. *Id.* at 31.

276. Mo-tzu, *The Will of Heaven*, in id. at 78-93.

277. R. UNGER, LAW IN MODERN SOCIETY, *supra* note 2, at 99-100.

278. A. WALEY, THE WAY AND ITS POWER: A STUDY OF THE TAO-TE-CHING AND ITS PLACE IN CHINESE THOUGHT (1934).

279. CHUANG-TZU: THE SEVEN INNER CHAPTERS AND OTHER WRITINGS FROM THE BOOK OF CHUANG-TZU (A. Graham trans. & ed. 1981) [hereinafter cited as CHUANG-TZU].

280. *See, e.g.*, id. at 43-61.

281. *Tao-tê-ching*, ch. LVII, *translated in* A. WALEY, *supra* note 278, at 211.

as it tells us "[i]t was when the Great Way [the *Tao*] declined [t]hat human kindness and morality arose."[282] The problem with both public, positive law and customary law, felt the Taoists, is that although each asserts a claim to legitimacy, both are but artificial constructs that human beings in their vanity would endeavor to impose upon the true order of heaven and earth, which "[regards] the Ten Thousand Things [everything] . . . as but straw dogs."[283] Indeed, human consciousness itself is but an artifice, as Chuang-tzu tells us in his celebrated story of how after awaking from a dream that he was a butterfly, he could not determine whether he was Chuang-tzu dreaming that he was a butterfly or butterfly dreaming that he was Chuang-tzu.[284] The task, then, is to purge one's mind of artificial constructs, which is what the *Tao-te-ching* means when it both calls for the attainment of "utter vacuity"[285] and declares that the best form of government is one in which the ruler keeps the people "vacuous" while "filling their bellies," in order that all might better try to comprehend the true order of nature.[286] Whether that order can be attained or even described is not altogether certain,[287] but for the Taoists the difficulty, if not the impossibility, of uncovering the *Tao* in no way vitiates the importance of striving to reach it.[288]

Given the language in which Taoist philosophy is expressed, its political import, not surprisingly, is far from clear. Some commentators have regarded Taoist philosophy as imbued with a commitment to individual autonomy and freedom, and with that, a belief in the capacity of individuals to restructure social arrangements creatively.[289] They have been particularly impressed with the Taoist disdain for the limitations that conventional legal and moral strictures would impose upon the spirit and its declaration that the best rulers were those who pursued a policy of purposeful inaction (*wu-wei*[290]) so that the people would scarcely

282. *Id.* ch. XVIII, at 165.

283. *Id.* ch. V, at 147.

284. CHUANG-TZU, *supra* note 279, at 61.

285. *Tao-tê-ching*, ch. XVI, *translated in* A. WALEY, *supra* note 278, at 162 (translation modified by the author).

286. *Id.* ch. III, at 145 (translation modified by the author).

287. *See id.* ch. I, at 141. It should be noted that the early Han emperor, Wen-ti (179-156 B.C.), did endeavor, albeit with limited success, to generate a program for the actual operation of government from Taoism. HSIAO KUNG-CHUAN, *supra* note 215, at 552-56.

288. *Cf. id.* ch. XXI, at 170.

289. *E.g.*, V. RUBIN, *supra* note 212, at 94-101.

290. The original Taoist notion of *wu-wei* appears to have meant that we should engage in purposive inactivity in order to allow the *tao* to take its course. This idea is echoed in the Legalist view that if the state were sufficiently well organized, it would run on its own, enabling the ruler to govern with a minimum of discretionary actions. *See* CHI-YUN CHEN, HSÜN YEH AND THE MIND OF LATE HAN CHINA 14-15 (1980); FUNG YU-LAN, *supra* note 216, at 331-35.

know that government existed.[291] Indeed, a few scholars have even gone so far as to suggest that preimperial Taoism implicitly called for rising up against improper authority.[292] Alternatively, however, one might take a far less sanguine view of the implications of Taoism for political life. The Taoist message that the best kind of government is one that rules unobtrusively after emptying the people's minds and filling their stomachs could be construed as an endorsement of totalitarianism. Whatever one's perspective, it is clear that Unger should have considered Taoism before presuming to opine on the assumptions about individuals and society that set the foundations of Chinese civilization apart from "the central tradition of modern Western social thought."[293]

III

Does it matter that Professor Unger appears to have taken a free hand in reconstructing the social organization, consciousness, and normative order of preimperial China? After all, he suggests at certain points that he is interested in using the Chinese example to test and clarify his broader speculations about the nature of legal development.[294] And, at other times he tells us that in invoking the Chinese case he hopes to "avoid most of the controversies that plague the literature" on preimperial China "and instead to focus on the main outlines of the standard interpretations" because "[t]he issue is what we can make of these interpretations if we take them for granted."[295] Moreover, he informs

291. *E.g.*, V. RUBIN, *supra* note 212, at 102, 106-08.

292. *E.g.*, *id.* at 112-14; *see also* Chi-yun Chen, *A Confucian Magnate's Idea of Political Violence: Hsün Shuang's (128-190* A.D.) *Interpretation of the Book of Changes*, 54 T'OUNG PAO 73, 112, 114 (1968).

293. R. UNGER, LAW IN MODERN SOCIETY, *supra* note 2, at 109. For a discussion of the role of Taoism in traditional Chinese politics, see YÜ YING-SHIH, LI-SHIH YÜ SSU-HSIANG [HISTORY AND THOUGHT] 10-20 (1976).

294. R. UNGER, LAW IN MODERN SOCIETY, *supra* note 2, at 48, 86-87.

295. *Id.* at 89. There is serious question as to whether Unger's sources constitute "the standard interpretations," and whether he provides the "main outlines" contained in them. He appears to have relied unduly upon the writings of certain continental sinologists writing before the Second World War (such as Alfred Forke and Marcel Granet) whose work was far from being standard by the mid-1970s. In so doing, he has either disregarded or made scant use of the scholarship of many more important and more interesting sinologists. The pertinent works of such prominent sinologists as Jean Escarra (*Le Droit Chinois*) and P'ing-ti Ho (*The Cradle of the East*), for example, are not mentioned. On the other hand, Professor Unger does cite the work of the eminent sinologist Herrlee Creel to support his portrayal of Chinese life between the foundation of the Western Chou in 1122 B.C. and the sixth century B.C., but makes no mention of the concept of the Mandate of Heaven, which Creel sees as central to understanding Chinese life during that time.

More revealing and, ultimately, of more concern than Professor Unger's use of secondary works by Western scholars, is his apparent lack of interest in what the Chinese have had to say about their own history. Although translations are available for the preimperial Chinese classics, he has little to do either with the major primary sources, *see supra* note 75, or with many of the leading interpretative works by Chinese available in Western languages.

It is also odd that Unger, who prides himself upon being such a fierce and independent critic of

the reader, the effort to form effective generalizations—especially across cultures—inevitably means that many historical events will be ignored[296] and that the consciousness of the actors being observed will not always be taken literally.[297]

The answer is that it does matter that Professor Unger has chosen to give us what he terms the "Chinese case" in the manner conveyed in *Law in Modern Society* and his other works, and not merely because he misconstrues data dear to the heart of area specialists in his effort to theorize broadly. Rather, it matters because in misconstruing so many and such important elements of those data he ultimately conveys a highly misleading picture of the foundations of Chinese civilization. And it also matters because the distorted nature of that picture raises serious questions as to the soundness both of his efforts to understand legal development generally and of his speculations regarding social order, social theory, and human nature.

To note that preimperial China had a greater ongoing belief in "a universalist standard by which to evaluate state law and to restrict government"[298] and a more diverse social order[299] than Professor Unger indicates is not to suggest that a closer consideration by him of the available data would have shown that the Chinese did in fact meet the historical conditions that his typology of law posits as necessary to move from bureaucratic law to a legal order. The problem revealed by Professor Unger's misportrayal of those two concerns and by the numerous other errors discussed in Part II of this Article is far more fundamental. It lies, instead, in that typology itself and in similar constructs that he employs in considering other aspects of Chinese society. For notwithstanding his self-described total criticism of liberal society,[300] his expressed interest in comparative scholarship,[301] and his stated desire to

established order, should so docilely and uncritically suggest that we take for granted "the main outlines of the standard interpretations" with respect to ancient Chinese history. If conventional Western liberal consciousness is problematic with respect to Western society, what warrants Unger's assumption that it is any less so when dealing with ancient Chinese society?

Unger's statements regarding the data he used in constructing his Chinese example are typical of the manner in which he issues caveats and then wholly disregards them.

296. *See* R. UNGER, LAW IN MODERN SOCIETY, *supra* note 2, at 8-23, 45-46.

297. *See id.* at 255.

298. *See supra* notes 161-80 and accompanying text.

299. *See supra* notes 153-60 and accompanying text.

300. R. UNGER, KNOWLEDGE AND POLITICS, *supra* note 1, at 1-3. Although Unger distinguishes sharply between liberal and postliberal society for some purposes, at other points he effectively treats them as one. This is not so much an inconsistency as a product of his belief that many dimensions of the former of which he is most critical are carried over into the latter, particularly in the West.

301. R. UNGER, LAW IN MODERN SOCIETY, *supra* note 2, at 41-43.

speak in universal terms,[302] Professor Unger's framework of inquiry so greatly favors the very forms and values of Western liberal society from which he typically sets himself apart[303] that it impinges upon his ability to discern the experience and consciousness of China and, in so doing, calls into question the utility of those constructs in general. It also suggests that his efforts to envision an alternative to modern society may be far more constrained by the forms and values of Western liberal society than he would like to think.

Part III of this Article illustrates how Professor Unger's treatment of preimperial Chinese law and consciousness is an outgrowth of the parochial nature of the constructs he employs. It then discusses how Professor Unger might respond to such charges, before examining briefly another possible approach to comparative legal study. The Part concludes by considering how Unger's use of the Chinese past points to problems in his efforts to envision a new social order that would move beyond the limits of modern society.

As depicted in Part II of this Article, Professor Unger has not merely mistaken a few idle facts as to the dating and content of early Chinese laws. To the contrary, he has failed to consider such crucial pillars of preimperial Chinese law as the notion of reciprocity found in the *li*,[304] the idea of the Mandate of Heaven,[305] the power of shared images of a just golden age,[306] and the Confucian effort to redefine the *chün-tzu* in moral terms.[307] Had Professor Unger examined these fundamental ideas he might have seen how in both Western Chou thought[308] and in preimperial Confucianism (particularly that of Mencius[309] and Hsün-tzu[310]) ethical considerations were intended to define the contours of state authority, and so, to inform and restrain the application of public, positive law.

The ancient Chinese state was not free to exercise unrestrained

302. *Id.*

303. Unger, of course, is not the first major Western commentator to suffer from such problems. Similar points might be made about Spinoza, Hegel, Marx, and Weber—upon all of whom Unger draws freely. *See* Alford, *supra* note 237, at 1190-91 nn.39-48.

304. *See supra* notes 122-27 and accompanying text.

305. *See supra* notes 164-75 and accompanying text.

306. *See supra* notes 217-19 and accompanying text. The recognition in history-conscious preimperial China of the power of the past may have tempered the exercise of power by those conscious of how their deeds would be portrayed in the future. For an illustration of this force, see K. Gottschang, *supra* note 73, at 46.

307. *See supra* notes 212-22 and accompanying text.

308. *See supra* notes 90-101, 114-19 and accompanying text. *See generally* H. CREEL, *supra* note 75.

309. *See supra* notes 216-19 and accompanying text; sources cited *supra* note 183.

310. *See supra* notes 220-21 and accompanying text; sources cited *supra* note 183.

power, as Unger suggests,[311] even in the presumed absence of specialized legal bodies[312] within which disputes could be adjudicated with the help of specialized legal personnel applying specialized legal rules. Positions of power, believed the Confucians, were to be occupied by individuals of high virtue,[313] whose particularly well-developed sense of morality and whose commitment to continue to improve their moral being[314] would regulate their discharge of official authority.[315] Moreover, the moral ethos embodied in the *li* and expressed in the concept of the Mandate of Heaven and the ideal of a golden age was meant to impose a fiduciary-like set of obligations upon those in positions of power and, concomitantly, to generate among persons occupying inferior positions clear and potentially enforceable expectations as to how that power would be exercised.[316] Thus, although the ruler was vested with considerable formal legal authority in order to discharge his duty to lead the people,[317] and although the populace typically deferred to his presumed greater wisdom and moral insight,[318] if the ruler exercised his power in violation of these ethical bounds, he could no longer be called a ruler. In that event, he neither warranted their loyalty[319] nor deserved to continue to exercise the Mandate of Heaven.[320] Paralleling this in family relationships was the sharp restraining impact that the *li* were meant to impose upon all those in positions of power.[321] To be sure, such constraints were not always adhered to in practice,[322] but we hardly find Professor Unger refusing to consider seriously either the theory of the rule of law or its prominence in Western consciousness merely because of the difficulties incumbent in its actualization.[323]

Professor Unger's failure to recognize that, at least in theory, moral ethos may have played a more prominent role in restraining state power

311. R. Unger, Law in Modern Society, *supra* note 2, at 52.

312. We still do not know enough to be certain that preimperial China did not have legal specialists of some sort. *See supra* note 104.

313. *See* Hsün-tzu, *The Regulations of a King*, in Basic Writings, *supra* note 104, at 37.

314. This ideal is expressed, for example, in the writings of the eminent late Han dynasty historian-philosopher Hsün Yüeh (A.D. 148-209). Hsün went so far as to suggest, in the words of Professor Chi-yun Chen, that an ideal ruler "must discipline his mind and regulate his conduct according to the highest standards of self-sacrifice set by the former Sage-kings." Chi-yun Chen, *supra* note 290, at 42.

315. *E.g.*, V. Rubin, *supra* note 212, at 18.

316. *See supra* notes 122-27, 162-80 and accompanying text.

317. *See, e.g.*, Liang Ch'i-ch'ao, *supra* note 207, at 161-167.

318. *See* V. Rubin, *supra* note 212, at 17-18.

319. *See supra* notes 164-77 and accompanying text.

320. *Id.*

321. *See supra* notes 125-26 and accompanying text; *see also* Vuylsteke, *supra* note 169, at 312.

322. *See, e.g.*, Baum, *supra* note 152.

323. *See* R. Unger, Law in Modern Society, *supra* note 2, at 56-57; *infra* text accompanying notes 423-26.

in preimperial China than in the modern West is not surprising, given the limitations of the typology through which he would have us consider law. Although advanced as universally valid,[324] his tripartite typology of legal forms is thoroughly imbued with the values of modern Western society[325] and unabashedly applied in order to clarify modern Western experience.[326] Thus, the typology presumes that legal development in all societies has followed a general evolutionary path toward greater progress[327] and equates that path with the historical conditions of Western society[328] and that progress with written rules.[329] Additionally, his typology reveals an implicit faith that, for all its glaring imperfections and contradictions, Western liberal society—through the specialized legal rules, institutions, professionals, and reasoning of its legal order—has done a better job of fostering expressions of "individual and collective will"[330] than any previous society, even if it is so inadequate that a new social order is now needed.[331]

The language in which Unger's typology is presented bears out its character. Customary law, we are told, is law in its most elemental form,[332] working with an effortlessness that parallels "in the realm of culture the predetermined course of instinct in the prehuman animal world."[333] All societies commence with it and in so-called "savage societies," "its dominion is almost exclusive."[334] When societies become more intricate through the separation and elaboration of the state, custom no

324. *See* R. UNGER, LAW IN MODERN SOCIETY, *supra* note 2, at 47-58.

325. *See infra* notes 327-62 and accompanying text.

326. *See* R. UNGER, LAW IN MODERN SOCIETY, *supra* note 2, at 48, 86-88.

327. Unger does not actually term his typological hierarchy evolutionary, but, as illustrated by the text accompanying *infra* notes 332-62, the language and manner in which it is presented strongly impart that impression. Initially, it may seem surprising that Unger should slip into this error in *Law in Modern Society*, given his rejection in *Knowledge and Politics* of the idea that the history of science is progressive. R. UNGER, *supra* note 1, at 128. And yet, as Arthur Leff has noted, Unger sees human nature as having a tremendous capacity for progressive moral development. *See* Leff, *supra* note 8, at 884. Still another sign of Unger's underlying attachment to the idea of progress lies in his view that the consciousness of modern society has advanced sufficiently beyond that of premodern society to enable contemporary humankind to discern heretofore unimagined alternative visions of social order. *See infra* notes 419-53 and accompanying text.

The idea of evolutionary progress does not seem to have had a significant premodern Chinese counterpart, notwithstanding the faith of Confucius and others that individuals and society could improve. For intriguing general discussions of the introduction of the idea of such progress, see J. PUSEY, CHINA AND CHARLES DARWIN (1983); B. SCHWARTZ, IN SEARCH OF WEALTH AND POWER: YEN FU AND THE WEST (1964).

328. *See* R. UNGER, LAW IN MODERN SOCIETY, *supra* note 2, at 66-86.

329. *See infra* text accompanying notes 332-62.

330. R. UNGER, LAW IN MODERN SOCIETY, *supra* note 2, at 109; *see supra* note 199.

331. For a discussion of that new alternative, see Unger, *The Critical Legal Studies Movement*, 96 HARV. L. REV. 561 (1983).

332. R. UNGER, LAW IN MODERN SOCIETY, *supra* note 2, at 49-50.

333. *Id.* at 95.

334. *Id.* at 50.

longer suffices, and it is necessary to move on to written law, even as elements of customary law are retained.[335] This initial level of public, positive law is a harsh one, composed as it is of coercively enforced state rules against which there is little check, with the result that persons under it are subject to the "arbitrary tutelage of the government."[336] Although many societies reach this level, only a select few have been able to "go on to develop . . . the legal order,"[337] which, has been the only one of his three forms[338] capable of fostering respect for "individual persons . . . [and] common understandings about right and wrong on the basis of . . . mutual respect."[339] To reach this third stage—with its unique regard for humanity—a society must, Unger suggests, exhibit the type of belief in a transcendent God and contain the plurality of interest groups that have been found only in Renaissance Europe.[340] In their absence, there was a "failure" in China,[341] which "contented itself with bureaucratic law,"[342] and in other societies,[343] to develop a legal order. Consequently, this pinnacle of Unger's hierarchical typology "developed in modern Europe and, more precisely, in modern Europe alone, until taken from there to other parts of the world."[344]

The undue modern Western orientation of Professor Unger's typology engenders other, more subtle problems. With its emphasis upon public, positive law, this typology leads us to focus only in the crudest fashion upon customary law, which Unger indicates is neither public nor positive.[345] All forms of custom, including the "largely tacit customs" of "savage" societies and what he suggests is the elaborate custom of modern liberal society that provides "the content of standards, like due care and reasonableness"[346] are grouped together without differentiation.[347]

335. *Id.* at 58-66.
336. *Id.* at 54.
337. *Id.* at 52.
338. *Id.* at 87.
339. *Id.* at 109.
340. *Id.* at 86-88.
341. *Id.* at 99, 105.
342. *Id.* at 87.
343. *Id.* at 110-26. Professor Unger endeavors in sixteen pages to survey "the sacred laws of ancient India, Islam, and Judaism . . . [and] Graeco-Roman legal history," as well as important dimensions of the social and religious milieu from which they arose. *Id.* at 110. Although he declares that a principal object in so doing is to "suggest how insights gained from the Chinese comparison could be qualified and developed," he makes only a few passing references to China that largely repeat, without additional elucidation, points of varying accuracy made earlier. *Id.* Nor do the brief comments offered on the five major civilizations mentioned above otherwise meaningfully qualify or develop further his use of the Chinese example. For more on the problems inherent in trying so readily to form judgments regarding cultures far removed in time and space, see *supra* notes 294-342, *infra* notes 344-453 and accompanying text.
344. R. UNGER, LAW IN MODERN SOCIETY, *supra* note 2, at 86.
345. *Id.* at 50.
346. *Id.* at 55.

Indeed, his definition of customary law—as "the accepted practices on the basis of which all communications and exchange is carried on"[348]—is so broad that it is not easily distinguishable from religion, language, or other habitual social activity. As a result, it is unclear how a study of this type of law tells us anything more about "the innermost secrets of the manner in which [a society] holds men together"[349] than would a serious study of ethics, religion, or other social practices.[350]

The typology is also problematic in its general presumption that legal development has always followed a basic evolutionary path and in its particular concern with transitions from "lower" to "higher" stages of legal development. These notions incline us to consider customary law, bureaucratic law, and the legal order in isolation from each other and from all but the most momentous of social forces. Unger tells the reader that he sees his different legal forms interacting with each other and with society,[351] and yet there is no niche in his typology for ongoing dynamic interaction between formal law and moral ethos short of the cataclysmic.[352] Nor are there places for either the type of public law described in detail in *The Book of Documents*[353] or the vision of Shen Pu-hai[354] and,

347. Contrary to Unger's implication, standards such as reasonableness and due care do not emanate wholly from custom. Legislative acts, administrative regulations, and judicial opinions presumably play a role in giving content to such standards.

348. R. UNGER, LAW IN MODERN SOCIETY, *supra* note 2, at 50. Indeed, Unger tells us at one point that customary law is "simply any recurring mode of interaction among individuals and groups, together with the more or less explicit acknowledgment by these groups and individuals that such patterns of interaction produce reciprocal expectations of conduct that ought to be satisfied." *Id.* at 49.

349. *Id.* at 47.

350. The assertion that law tells us more about the "inner-most secrets of the manner in which [a society] holds men together" is, of course, hardly value-free or necessarily universally valid. One could imagine making the argument that "society [best] reveals . . . [these] secrets" through its religion, ethics, approach to education, sexual practices, dietary habits, or a host of other social activities. It is ironic that Unger should here see law as having a unique message to impart, given his criticism of what he would term the liberal belief that law is distinguishable from morality and politics.

351. R. UNGER, LAW IN MODERN SOCIETY, *supra* note 2, at 47-86.

352. Both Unger's typology in general and its particular application to preimperial China presume a sudden leap from reliance upon unarticulated custom to the use by a state of full-blown codes. Although he suggests that custom continues to have force even after bureaucratic law or a legal order has been established, R. UNGER, LAW IN MODERN SOCIETY, *supra* note 2, at 54-55, there is no place in his typology for clearly articulated public rules that may be partially positive. Nor does the typology account for rules that are positive but not promulgated by the state, or for the situation where the state employs a modest number of isolated public, positive rules, rather than comprehensive codes, in conjunction with other tools of social control. Unger's failure to discern such intermediate possibilities may account for his taking statements that the Chinese did not have comprehensive codes until the seventh or sixth century B.C. to mean that no written rules were promulgated by the state prior to that time.

It should also be noted that Unger's typology does not account well for religious law.

353. *See supra* notes 93-101, 106-18.

354. *See supra* note 238.

to a lesser degree, Han Fei-tzu,[355] in which the affairs of state would operate according to clear and essentially immutable standards that are valued not for their direct enhancement of individual welfare, but for their fostering of the collective good. To the contrary, this typology essentially presents each legal form seriatim and with attention to social forces only as they evidence the preconditions needed to move from one evolutionary stage of law to the next.[356] The net effect, ironically, is to portray law far more statically and simplisticly than is warranted. In that respect Unger's typology mirrors his general depiction of China before the twentieth century as essentially unchanged from the formation of the Empire onward. His vision of a static China, which seems to underlie his presumption that preimperial China and post-Renaissance Europe are easily comparable, reflects an unfortunate misconception that still lingers in the very liberal society he so strenuously criticizes.[357]

The inadequacy of Unger's analysis also is evident in its failure to account for the transmission of legal forms across different societies. In his discussion both of early Chinese history and of the Confucian-Legalist debate, Unger suggests that, at least as early as the late preimperial period, the image of human beings and society dominant in Chinese civilization was incompatible with the values implicit in the rule of law.[358] Nor does he give any hint that this fundamental image was soon to change.[359] Similarly, he asserts that all other non-European societies lacked the social and cultural circumstances necessary to give rise to the legal order until that form was taken from Europe to other parts of the world.[360] Yet at no point does he indicate how societies, whose values differed so sharply from Europe's that they could not generate a legal order indigenously, were able suddenly to sustain that form of law after it was "taken" to them from Europe. Is Unger intimating that, through the colonial experience or otherwise, these societies rapidly developed both the belief in a transcendent God and the strong group pluralism that he sees as necessary to generate a rule of law?[361] Or is he telling us

355. *See supra* notes 239, 246; BASIC WRITINGS, *supra* note 104.

356. *See* R. UNGER, LAW IN MODERN SOCIETY, *supra* note 2, at 47-86.

A comparable point might be made about Unger's view of social order in general. He obviously is greatly concerned with moral questions and, indeed, sees profound social change emanating from an awareness of the gap between ideal and actuality. And yet, he devotes relatively little attention to showing the role that morality may play in society, short of these revolutionary transformations.

357. For an earlier example of the myth of a relatively static China, see K. LATOURETTE, *supra* note 217, at 340-41. Such views may tell us more about the observer than the observed.

358. *See* R. UNGER, LAW IN MODERN SOCIETY, *supra* note 2, at 86-109.

359. *See id.* at 86-88, 109.

360. *Id.* at 86.

361. Western missionaries, merchants, and military personnel all arrived in China in significant numbers during the first half of the nineteenth century. Christianity did not win large numbers of converts in China. *See* P. COHEN, CHINA AND CHRISTIANITY *passim* (1963).

that the power of the rule of law itself transformed the underlying values of these civilizations?[362] Or is this change explained by a link—which he has not drawn explicitly—to the modernization process? If this last possibility is the case, should not commitment to the rule of law be correlated to modernization rather than to intensity of belief in transcendence, unless he is equating modernization with a belief in transcendence?

Unger's efforts to portray what he would term the consciousness of preimperial China are no more satisfactory than his treatment of the interaction of law and moral ethos. His dismissal of Confucianism as espousing a backward-looking adherence to a rigid hierarchy of social positions,[363] of Legalism as but a pretext for the unbridled and terror-filled exercise of state power,[364] and of premodern Chinese civilization generally as culturally incapable of generating among its populace any serious sense that human beings could remake their social arrangements[365] shields from his view the depth and vitality of that which he seeks to describe. Had he approached preimperial China with a respect comparable to that he accorded to post-Renaissance European society, he might have appreciated that civilizations other than modern Western Europe have seriously considered the very tensions within social order that most concern him. He might have seen that Confucianism and, even more so, Taoist thought were each seized with the desire to reconcile their "sense of a latent or natural order in social life" with the human "capacity to let the will remake social arrangements."[366] The creative solution ultimately struck by the preimperial Confucians was to retain the essence of "natural order in social life," but to replace social position with moral worth as the principal requirement for filling certain of its slots, while generating legitimacy for such change through appeal to an ancient golden age.[367] In theory, the Confucians even recognized the dangers of both public and personal domination—an awareness of which Unger would ascribe chiefly to the modern age[368]—in their heavy emphasis upon the moral, almost fiducial obligations that accompanied all

362. One other possibility that Unger fails to discern is that non-Western societies may, in adopting legal forms of liberal society, have adapted those forms in light of underlying traditional values. This concern is addressed further *infra* note 389 and in Alford, On the Limits of "Grand Theory" in Comparative Law (address delivered at the Annual Meeting of the Association for the Study of Comparative Law, University of Washington, Seattle, Washington, Sept. 27, 1985) (forthcoming in 61 WASH. L. REV. (June 1986)).

363. R. UNGER, LAW IN MODERN SOCIETY, *supra* note 2, at 108, 131.

364. *Id.* at 107-08.

365. *Id.* at 86-109, 131-32.

366. *Id.* at 266.

367. *See supra* notes 204-22 and accompanying text.

368. R. UNGER, LAW IN MODERN SOCIETY, *supra* note 2, at 109.

positions of power.[369] Nor was their critique limited to the arena of the state, as they realized that a transformation of personal relations might serve to inspire significant institutional change.[370]

If Confucian solutions to the problems of social order left the basic shell of prior hierarchy intact and, more critically, did little to ease the burden of gender and age discrimination—problems that Unger does not recognize regarding China until *Passion*[371]—the Taoists were not quite so encumbered in their efforts to reconcile their "sense of a latent or natural order in social life . . . with the capacity and the will to remake social arrangements." The Taoists seem to have had an intense faith in the capacity of men, and perhaps of all human beings, to transcend the limitations of social arrangements within which they found themselves.[372] And yet, for all their skepticism about existing social arrangements, they did not deny the existence of a larger order.[373] Rather, they believed that each individual possessed the capacity to strive towards an understanding of that order.[374] That the Taoists seem also to have believed that such order probably could not be fully known should not be disconcerting to us, but rather should be seen as both a recognition on their part of the dynamism of social and natural life, and an appreciation by them of how structure shapes consciousness.[375]

Even those major schools of late preimperial Chinese thought least tolerant of the notion that people could reshape society in accord with a natural or latent order—the Mohists and the Legalists—did not reach such views lightly. It is true that the Mohists came to see society largely in fixed terms, as consisting of certain set social arrangements that people generally were not free to reconfigure.[376] But to the Mohists, this commitment to a particular form of society emerged from a collective agreement of the populace which was in accord with the Will of Heaven,[377] and was necessary to ensure the state of universal concern for all persons and, through that, the genuine community toward which they aspired.[378]

369. *See supra* notes 304-23 and accompanying text. As Karl Bünger has observed, "Advocates as well as opponents of a proposed enactment made every effort . . . to quote appropriate passages from the historical works and from the works of rites in support of their view." Bünger, *supra* note 114, at 79.

370. For an example of the Confucian belief that one could recast the nature of government through the personal, see THE ANALECTS, *supra* note 119, at bk. II, ch. 21; *see also* H. FINGARETTE, CONFUCIUS, THE SECULAR AS SACRED 37-56 (1972).

371. R. UNGER, PASSION, *supra* note 32, at 67-68.

372. *See supra* notes 277-93 and accompanying text.

373. *Id.*; sources cited *supra* note 203.

374. *See supra* notes 277-93 and accompanying text; sources cited *supra* note 203.

375. *See supra* notes 277-93 and accompanying text; sources cited *supra* note 203.

376. *See supra* notes 262-76 and accompanying text.

377. *Id.*

378. *Id.*

Furthermore, continued adherence to any set of societal arrangements was to be subject to an ongoing Mohist "utilitarian" test to ensure that it did in fact benefit all of society's interests.

The Legalists were scarcely more enthusiastic about the idea of people remaking social arrangements.[379] Yet they did not hesitate to remake what they saw as inappropriate social arrangements in a revolutionary fashion,[380] in addition to acknowledging that neither law nor society had remained constant through history.[381] Indeed, although building upon Taoism, their concern with equality represented a vision of society quite different from that embodied in the world around them.[382]

Unger does not discern the richness of preimperial Chinese consciousness because, with it as with the law, his analytical framework is far less universal than he presumes, and his focus is far more concerned with why China did not follow Europe's course than with the course it actually did follow. He readily both takes the great classical liberal social theorists to task for their failure to examine consciousness seriously enough[383] and declares that "to treat . . . understandings and values as mere shams is to assume that social relations can be described and explained without regard to the meanings the men who participate in those relations attribute to them."[384] Nonetheless, the standards that he implicitly sets forth for considering consciousness seem derived from Western experience, reflective of the values of Western liberal society, and applied (consciously or otherwise) so as to reaffirm the primacy of that model. Thus, preimperial Chinese consciousness is measured according to such criteria as the possession of a prophetic tradition in the Judeo-Christian sense,[385] the type of cultural diversity experienced in the Hellenic and Roman worlds,[386] and ultimately the belief in a single God whose will is partially withheld, but who promises to speak to humankind in a particular way.[387] This should not be surprising when we recall that a major goal of Unger's inquiry into consciousness is to ascertain what sets the modern Western world apart from its Western predecessors.[388] The very manner in which he poses the question assumes part of the answer.[389]

379. *See supra* notes 233-56 and accompanying text; sources cited *supra* note 184.
380. *Id.*
381. *Id.*
382. *Id.*
383. R. UNGER, LAW IN MODERN SOCIETY, *supra* note 2, at 41.
384. *Id.* at 56-57.
385. *Id.* at 99-101.
386. *Id.*
387. *Id.*; *see also* R. UNGER, *supra* note 1, at 290-95.
388. R. UNGER, LAW IN MODERN SOCIETY, *supra* note 2, at 134-37, 234-37, 265-66.
389. Indeed, much the same point might be made about Unger's discussion of what he charac-

The Inscrutable Occidental

In both *Knowlege and Politics* and *Law in Modern Society*, Professor Unger brings his considerable rhetorical powers to bear in arguing that any person engaged in worthwhile comparative inquiry must strive "to take the agent's purposes seriously, to grasp his conduct, as has often been said, from the actor's own point of view . . . and then to recode that message into the language of the observer's own culture."[390] The observer need not accept the agent's purpose as consonant with the agent's actions or endorse it as the observer's own. The comparativist must, however, appreciate the difficulty of the task, particularly across great expanses of time and space,[391] and work to establish a "community of understandings and of values . . . with the agent whose act he observes."[392] And yet lying at the heart both of Unger's typology of legal forms and the measures he uses to assess consciousness is the assumption that, although problematic, the rule of law and the consciousness of modern liberal society represent standards toward which all of humanity should have been aspiring until his formulation of a preferable alternative. That is not to say that Unger endorses the rule of law or liberal thought. Rather, it is to suggest that he presents them as more generative and protective of expressions of individual and collective[393] will than any other forms of law or consciousness,[394] even if he does so partially for rhetorical purposes to show that they are grossly deficient. So it is that in thinking about premodern China, Unger is concerned with the failure of the Chinese to develop the rule of law or "indeed even to conceive of it."[395] He does not ask either the more basic question of whether that is an appropriate inquiry, or the more interesting question of what alternatives Chinese society may have posed. And so it is that he does

terizes as the unique dilemma of modernity. Unger's presumption that there is a dilemma of modernity virtually requires him to localize certain behavior in time. Thus, Unger suggests that persons living in the modern world experience a tension "between belief and experience, between consciousness and organization" and between "the sense of a latent or natural order in social life . . . [and] the capacity to let the will remake social arrangements" for which there was no precedent in earlier times. *Id.* at 266. To note, as has been done in this Article, that there may have been something akin to the foregoing tension in preimperial China is not to intimate that early Chinese civilization and late twentieth century American society conceived of this tension in an identical fashion, but to suggest that it may not be as wholly a product of the modern era as Unger would have us believe. Indeed, it is arguable that the manner in which such tension is considered in certain of the societies that Unger calls modern (such as contemporary Japan and the PRC) may resemble the way in which it was thought of in preimperial China as much as it resembles the way in which such tension is experienced in the United States today.

390. R. Unger, Law in Modern Society, *supra* note 2, at 257.

391. R. Unger, *supra* note 1, at 110.

392. *Id.*

393. R. Unger, Law in Modern Society, *supra* note 2, at 109.

394. *Id.* at 86-109.

395. *Id.* at 106.

not consider how a more careful study of the Chinese past would have been enlightening not only about China, but about the West as well.

Professor Unger's likely defense to such charges would be that he views his comparative studies and, indeed, his entire social theory as being normative as well as descriptive.[396] As a consequence, he is not obligated to reflect in them the experience and consciousness of any particular culture or groups of cultures any more than he already has.[397] To heed this defense is not to suggest that Unger sees the comparative inquiry that informs his social theory as grounded upon anything but universals. He believes ardently that the acts of cultural comparison and the formulation of social theory presume the existence of "universal, though perhaps inarticulate, criteria of comparison"[398] and that one can "conceive of a unitary human nature that underlies all forms of social life."[399] Indeed, he contends that "to complete the resolution of the problems of method, social order, and modernity [which are his three components of social theory], one ultimately needs a view of human nature."[400] Rather, to heed this defense is to take seriously his statement that "the choice among possible views of humanity is likely to be itself influenced by moral and political perspectives that cannot be wholly justified by the view one chooses."[401] And it is to recognize that his moral and political perspectives lead him to embrace a vision of humanity that is heavily weighted toward the forms and values of part,[402] if not all, of Western liberal society.[403]

396. *Id.* at 42. Indeed, he rejects the fact-value distinction.
397. *Id.* at 42, 267.
398. *Id.* at 257.
399. *Id.* at 42.
400. *Id.* at 40.
401. *Id.* at 42.
402. At least in ***Knowledge and Politics*** and ***Law in Modern Society***, Unger pays little attention to the perspectives of women in Western liberal society (or anywhere else, for that matter). Indeed, many of the broad criticisms made in Part III of this Article with respect to his failure to take seriously the consciousness of foreign societies have parallels in his failure in the above-mentioned two works to incorporate the thinking and experience of women into his generalizations about social order and social theory. Scholars of comparative law and of feminist jurisprudence have a great deal to contribute to one another, especially until the perspectives of the subjects about which they are writing are more seriously incorporated into general theorizing about law.
403. Unger seems to recognize this without indicating any appreciation of its implications for comparative scholarship in *Knowledge and Politics* in which he describes his own doctrine of human nature as drawn from the "classic theory of human nature. All the great thinkers of Europe have contributed to its development, for it is the theoretical expression of that more basic insight into humanity no theory has managed to destroy." R. UNGER, *supra* note 1, at 198-99.

The perspectives in question permeate his vision of human nature and its imperatives. They are evident, for example, in his discussion of "individual freedom." Unger defines the "individual freedom" that he hopes will be attainable in the alternative he envisions to liberal society as, *inter alia*, "the basic liberties of membership [in voluntary groups], expression, and work," *id.* at 282, a definition no doubt appealing to many of us raised in the modern West. At no point, however, does he consider whether other cultures would choose either to define "individual freedom" in those terms

The Inscrutable Occidental

One is hard-pressed not to admire both Professor Unger's belief that there is a common bond uniting humanity and his candor in recognizing that his vision of that bond may not be wholly defensible even in terms of his own social theory.[404] Nonetheless, integral features of his critique of Western liberal society indicate that he ought to have accorded greater respect to conceptions of law, society, and human nature influenced by "moral and political perspectives" other than his own, even apart from the fact that it was he who invoked the Chinese example. A central focus of Unger's attack upon the rule of law—and liberal society—is his presumption that legal doctrine[405] (or indeed, any knowledge[406]) is incapable of being wholly neutral or objective. If all knowledge is ultimately so subjective, how can Unger so readily dismiss the experience and insight of preimperial China and other non-Western cultures in considering what distinguishes or fails to distinguish the development of law in the West? Similarly, in his attack upon both what he terms suprahistoricism (which he sees as wed to the notion that human nature has a single intelligible essence[407]) and what he describes as historicism (which he dismisses as so committed to localized detail as to preclude effective cross-cultural comparison[408]), Unger contends that human nature should be conceived of as "an entity embodied in particular forms of social life, though never exhausted by them."[409] And yet his inquiry is almost exhaustively focused upon those forms that comprise the "Christian-romantic tradition" that he describes in *Passion* as "our civilization."[410]

To take Unger to task for insisting upon a particular vision of social order and human nature at the same time that he argues for a world-view that recognizes subjectivity and multiplicity is not to urge upon him a cultural relativism that he would disdain. Unger and other comparativists close to the Critical Legal Studies movement[411] are correct in attacking those who presume that they somehow can stand apart from their own situation and view other societies in a value-free fashion. But

or to weigh what he encompasses within that term less heavily than other values. It is, after all, conceivable that others might believe that individual fulfillment—and, indeed, even freedom—is more likely to be reached through an emphasis upon genuine consensus than upon individual expression.

404. R. Unger, Law in Modern Society, *supra* note 2, at 42.

405. Unger, *supra* note 331, at 567-77.

406. R. Unger, *supra* note 1, at 3-5. It is ironic that Professor Unger at least implicitly believes that there is enough neutrality, objectivity, or shared understanding in language to enable him effectively to communicate his ideas to an international readership.

407. *Id.* at 245-47.

408. *Id.*

409. R. Unger, Law in Modern Society, *supra* note 2, at 260.

410. R. Unger, Passion, *supra* note 32, at 22-23.

411. *E.g.*, Frankenberg, *Critical Comparisons: Re-thinking Comparative Law*, 26 Harv. Int'l L.J. 411 (1985).

Texas Law Review Vol. 64:915, 1986

there are ways of approaching comparative legal inquiry other than through either Unger's tacit treatment of his values as universal or the naive, if well-meaning, relativistic notion that one can examine without judging.[412]

As I have sought to establish elsewhere,[413] another approach to comparative legal study emanates from a thoughtful appreciation of the difficulty of the task of comparative inquiry and a concomitant humility and diligence on the part of those engaged in that endeavor. The limitations that the subjectivity of knowledge and the confines of our particular perspectives impose should not be construed as a license authorizing us to make what we will of any situation. Nor should they be taken as a sign of surrender, suggesting that we abandon efforts at making judgments about other societies because we are unable fully to escape our own values in considering that which is foreign. Rather, those inescapable limitations should serve as a reminder of how vital it is that we commence any comparative inquiry by seeking rigorously to identify the values that shape our thinking, so that we might approach other societies with a better chance of recognizing how our orientation is likely to color what we see there.

With the foregoing as a departure point, we should strive to immerse ourselves thoroughly in all aspects of the history of any foreign society we would study. To do that, we must scrupulously seek out its "facts" while recognizing that there are no objective truths.[414] And we must imaginatively attempt to understand that society on its own terms, even as we acknowledge the impossibility of that endeavor and remind ourselves not to equate a society's consciousness and actuality. As we proceed through this inquiry, we must continually be open to the possibility of altering the conceptual frameworks through which we approached our subject in order to accommodate that which we find and so begin to construct a genuine "community of understandings." Such meticulous and empathetic, but not acritical, attention to the particulars of

412. For a strong defense of cultural relativism, see CULTURAL RELATIVISM: PERSPECTIVES IN CULTURAL PLURALISM (F. Herskovits ed. 1972). The debate between cultural relativists and their critics is discussed in Campbell, *Herskovits, Cultural Relativism, and Metascience*, in *id.* at v, and, with a great deal less sympathy for cultural relativism, in Bryan, *Cultural Relativism—Power in Service of Interests: The Particular Case of Native American Education*, 32 BUFF. L. REV. 643 (1983). The limits of cultural relativism are discussed *infra* text accompanying notes 413-18, and in Alford, *supra* note 362.

413. *See* Alford, *supra* note 362.

414. As Clifford Geertz has so masterfully shown, the same fact may hold a very different meaning in different societies. Consequently, he suggests, we must pursue a "thick description" of each society we would observe in order to understand the context that gives meaning to any particular fact. C. GEERTZ, THE INTERPRETATION OF CULTURES 6-7 (1973). *See generally* C. GEERTZ, LOCAL KNOWLEDGE: FURTHER ESSAYS IN INTERPRETIVE ANTHROPOLOGY 167-234 (1983).

other societies is necessary if we are to do more than see them in light of ourselves or judge them by standards derived exclusively from our experience. Even if we choose to assess others by our values, this effort will enable us to appreciate more fully what we are doing and, thus, help us to avoid unwittingly assuming that our thoughts and actions are universally valid. As with the *Tao*, the realization that the path we traverse may have no terminus hardly invalidates the significance of our journey.[415] To the contrary, it should serve as a beacon illuminating our course.

Had Unger approached ancient Chinese civilization with greater respect and rigor, he might have emerged with a clearer sense not only of the Chinese past. He might also have come away with an appreciation that a purportedly universal typology that fails to look beyond the forms of liberal society may conclude that those forms are more likely to be found in liberal society than elsewhere. Additionally, he might have understood that a framework for inquiry that incorporates more of the experiences of peoples living outside the West might prove more instructive about "the complex relationship among modes of social organization, types of consciousness, and forms of normative order."[416] Such a framework for inquiry might, for example, recognize that a serious societal commitment to the use of external standards to restrain secular authority need not be contingent upon the particular confluence of interest groups and images of the diety found in post-Renaissance Europe, and that such a commitment might be sustainable even if not supported by the institutions and skilled professionals of modern Europe.[417] And such a framework might move beyond noting the seeming absence in China and other distant civilizations of concerns stressed in the modern West to acknowledge those values upon which importance is placed in such societies. In so doing, it might consider how different societies define individual dignity, rather than assume *a priori* that the sense of it presented by Professor Unger is or should be shared by all.[418]

415. See *supra* notes 287-88 and accompanying text.

416. R. UNGER, LAW IN MODERN SOCIETY, *supra* note 2, at 88.

417. Unger suggests, for example, that because it relied almost exclusively upon customary law, Chinese society prior to his transformation era merged "is" and "ought." *See supra* text accompanying note 84. Had he not been so narrowly focused upon finding the forms of the modern West in ancient China, he might have realized that "[a]t its deepest level, the idea of the Mandate of Heaven presents us with a clear apprehension of the gap between the human order as it ought to be and as it actually is." B. SCHWARTZ, *supra* note 73, at 53.

418. *See supra* note 403.

In presuming that the values and practices of one part of humankind are the norm for all humanity and that other beliefs or behavior deviate from what is therefore normal, Unger commits the same type of error that Carol Gilligan has observed that psychologists such as Lawrence Kohlberg and Jean Piaget make in "equat[ing] male development with child development." C. GIL-

It is ironic that Professor Unger seems so little concerned with portraying China's history accurately, for history is crucial not only to Unger's scholarship but also to his belief that his writing serves attainable political objectives.[419] Unger turns to history not so much to demonstrate his erudition as to show that his vision of change cannot be dismissed as utopian. Parting company with those who would divide politics from philosophy, Unger views himself as offering in his scholarship a programmatic guide through which it might be possible to restructure society.[420] History, Unger indicates, evidences progression toward such a better[421] world while also providing a basis for the belief that human nature is capable of both imagining and realizing more humane possibilities for social structure and personality than have been witnessed to date.[422]

Unger is determined to work toward a new social order because he finds the rule of law—and the modern liberal state of which it "has been truly said to be the soul"[423]—ultimately unequal to the task of maximizing the realization of individual and collective will.[424] In his view, both the rule of law and the liberal state generally are beset with certain fundamental contradictions.[425] Through its call for the independent application of neutral principles by impartial adjudicators, the rule of law presumes an objective separation of legal doctrine from morality and politics that is neither attainable nor desirable.[426]

The epistemological problems that characterize the idea of the rule of law are mirrored within the liberal state in social organization, social theory, and individual personality, according to Professor Unger. At the level of social organization, a false confidence in the ability to divide rule from value cloaks and condones arbitrary public[427] and private domination[428] by the powerful in the name of legality and order. This is paralleled at the level of social theory by the conceit that it is possible and

LIGAN, IN A DIFFERENT VOICE: PSYCHOLOGICAL THEORY AND WOMEN'S DEVELOPMENT 10 (1982).

419. R. UNGER, *supra* note 1, at 230. For a discussion of similarities between Unger's concern with history and Hegel's, see Kronman, Book Review, 61 MINN. L. REV. 167, 181-82 (1976) (reviewing R. UNGER, KNOWLEDGE AND POLITICS (1976)); *see also* Cornell, *supra* note 21.

420. Unger, *supra* note 331, at 3-6.

421. As Unger has put it, "Our present historical condition makes possible a more complete resolution of the problem of self for the species as a whole and for each of its members." R. UNGER, *supra* note 1, at 230.

422. *Id. passim*; *see also* R. UNGER, LAW IN MODERN SOCIETY, *supra* note 2, at 243-68.

423. R. UNGER, LAW IN MODERN SOCIETY, *supra* note 2, at 192.

424. *Id.* at 109; R. UNGER, *supra* note 1, at 83-103.

425. R. UNGER, LAW IN MODERN SOCIETY, *supra* note 2, at 192-216.

426. R. UNGER, *supra* note 1, at 88-100.

427. R. UNGER, LAW IN MODERN SOCIETY, *supra* note 2, at 181.

428. R. UNGER, *supra* note 1, *passim*.

desirable to distinguish fact from value and the resultant formulation of theory that is unduly and artificially devoid of either political or metaphysical content in its striving toward objectivity.[429] And, at the personal level, it finds a counterpart, if not its genesis, in the illusion that it is both possible and healthy for reason and desire to traverse distinct paths.[430]

To escape the antinomies of liberalism, Unger believes it is necessary to develop new visions of social organization,[431] social theory,[432] and personality[433] that recognize the inseparability of reason and desire and are capable of melding individual autonomy with group solidarity to maximize each. Attainment of this end requires the reconciliation of "immanent order and transcendent criticism" so that humanity believes that "the practices of society represent some kind of natural order instead of a set of arbitrary choices" while at the same time realizing that they have the "capacity to let the will remake social arrangements."[434] Unger suggests that the key to such a reconciliation may lie in a "latent and living law . . . [which is] the elementary code of human interaction,"[435] for such a law expresses the moral vision of society. That law, he suggests, may best be effectuated through "the lawyer's insight," for "[t]hroughout history there has been a bond between the legal profession and the search for an order inherent in social life."[436] In his article on the Critical Legal Studies movement, he elaborates his vision of what this "latent and living law" will look like, at least for contemporary Western society.[437] That vision, a detailed consideration of which lies beyond the limits of this Article,[438] entails the development of an "enlarged" notion of legal doctrine that will openly acknowledge and embrace, rather than shirk from, politics.[439] It also calls for the establishment of a concomitant set of new rights the content of which is at once political, economic, social, and

429. R. UNGER, LAW IN MODERN SOCIETY, *supra* note 2, at 243-68.

430. R. UNGER, *supra* note 1, at 38-42.

431. *See* Unger, *supra* note 331, at 583-97.

432. R. UNGER, LAW IN MODERN SOCIETY, *supra* note 2, at 266-68.

433. R. UNGER, PASSION, *supra* note 32.

434. R. UNGER, LAW IN MODERN SOCIETY, *supra* note 2, at 266.

435. *Id.* at 242.

436. *Id.*

437. Unger, *supra* note 331, at 587. For the importance of his suggestion, akin to Marx's and many others, that the West will lead the way to a better world, see *infra* notes 443-53 and accompanying text.

438. For an interesting and not unsympathetic discussion of Unger's vision of a new society, see Hutchinson & Monahan, *The "Rights" Stuff: Roberto Unger and Beyond*, 62 TEXAS L. REV. 1477 (1984). Although they approach Unger from a very different perspective than I do, Hutchinson and Monahan also acknowledge limitations in his proposed new order.

439. Unger, *supra* note 331, at 576-83, 646-48.

psychological.[440] Through what Unger calls an ongoing "cultural revolution,"[441] these rights will empower individuals now subject to undue public or private domination without enabling them to exercise improper dominance over the lives of other persons.[442]

Unger's indifference to the experience of the Chinese threatens to undermine the legitimacy of the new order that he envisions. The alternative that he advances speaks of the need for developing a new universal notion of community that would reconcile a deeper and richer sense of solidarity than now exists in Western society with a respect for the integrity and autonomy of individual human beings.[443] Yet Unger makes no effort to consider how the traditions, present views, or broad imagination of the Chinese or, for that matter, any other people from outside the Western liberal world might shape or be accommodated by such a new world.

Supporters of Professor Unger might respond by contending that his vision of a reimagined order need not take account of Chinese or other non-Western experience because he is concerned with "work[ing] out the significance of this [new social] ideal for the contemporary and especially the advanced Western societies."[444] But is such a response justifiable? Even if one were to presume that Professor Unger's "work[ing] out" of his new society both was meant to be and could be isolated in the West, that hardly warrants his unwillingness to consider seriously non-Western experience in his efforts to restructure society so as to transcend what he perceives as the shortcomings of Western history. Unger himself recognizes in *Passion*, albeit belatedly and incompletely, that "[c]lassical Confucianism offers insights into the problem of solidarity that have never been surpassed by any other tradition of comparable influence."[445] Had he bothered to try to make use of such insights from China and other non-Western societies, he might well have structured his new society differently. For example, he might have appreciated just how heavily he relies for the attainment and maintenance of his new society upon complex formal legal mechanisms[446] and legal professionals possessing an expertise not shared by the citizenry as a whole.[447] And he might have

440. *Id.* at 576-675.

441. *Id.* at 586-602; *see infra* note 452.

442. Unger, *supra* note 331, *passim*.

443. R. UNGER, LAW IN MODERN SOCIETY, *supra* note 2, at 238-42, 262-66; *see* Unger, *supra* note 331, at 602-75 *passim*.

444. Unger, *supra* note 331, at 587.

445. R. UNGER, PASSION, *supra* note 32, at 66.

446. Unger, *supra* note 331, at 576-675.

447. R. UNGER, LAW IN MODERN SOCIETY, *supra* note 2, at 242; *see* Unger, *supra* note 331, *passim*.

understood more fully the role that ethics, education, and forces other than law can play in achieving certain objectives that he believes can only be reached through formal law.[448] Thus, he might have avoided replicating what he sees as the excessive legalism of liberal society[449] or, conversely, might have understood more fully the enormous implications of a call for "cultural revolution."[450]

Although the lessons that China might hold for improving Unger's vision of a new West alone dictate that he ought to have paid more attention to the non-Western world, there is another compelling reason that Unger should have been less parochial. Even if one were to accept Unger's statement that he is concerned with "work[ing] out" his institutional program for the West, clearly a revolution of such magnitude in the industrialized West would have enormous consequences for the rest of the world. If Unger means for his new society to reach beyond the West—and the expansive way in which he discusses it suggests that, at a minimum, he anticipates that it will spread[451]—does not his call for a new notion of community demand a far greater respect for "moral and political perspectives" of all peoples whom he would have be its members? And even if he does not envision that his new community would include the majority of the earth's populace, which, after all, lives outside

448. This is not to suggest, as Unger does in parts of his description of preimperial China, that a Chinese perspective on these concerns would dictate abandonment of all reliance upon public, positive rules. Even the most ardent of preimperial Confucians recognized the need for such law. *See supra* notes 223-32 and accompanying text. Rather, it is to recognize the important role that forces other than public, positive law can play in building society. *See supra* notes 114-27, 162-80, 204-32, 304-323 and accompanying text.

449. Dean Carrington might wish to rethink his suggestion that Professor Unger does not belong on a law faculty, given the inordinate role that Unger accords lawyers and legal education in the new society he envisions. *See* Carrington, in *"Of Law and the River," and of Nihilism and Academic Freedom*, *supra* note 17, at 10-11.

450. Unger does not appear to intend for his "cultural revolution" to replicate that of the PRC. Nonetheless, the Chinese experience does bear out the difficulty of controlling a movement undertaken not merely to bring about governmental and economic change, but also to transform a people's culture, including social practices and consciousness. For a credible and moving account of the PRC's experience by a participant, see LIANG HENG & J. SHAPIRO, SON OF THE REVOLUTION (1983).

451. *See* Unger, *supra* note 331, *passim*. Professor Unger states in this essay that he envisions his new society arising in advanced Western societies. *Id.* at 587. But the universal terms in which he speaks of human nature and of social organization suggest that he also assumes that this new society will eventually spread outward from the West to the rest of humankind, much as he believes that the legal order is capable of spreading. *See* R. UNGER, LAW IN MODERN SOCIETY, *supra* note 2, at 230.

It might be noted that, in its broad outlines, Unger's vision of a new order containing a complex of economic and social, as well as political and civil, rights may not be entirely as original as he intimates. For example, during the past two decades, suggestions often have been made in the context of the debate over international human rights that humankind's basic rights encompass economic and social, as well as political and civil, rights. Certain of these rights (such as the right to development) imply an ongoing transformation of the existing social and economic order. *See generally* Schachter, *The Evolving International Law of Development*, 15 COLUM. J. TRANSNAT'L L. 1 (1976).

of the West, does not the certain impact that massive change in the West would have upon such peoples require that he involve their ideas, if not their persons, in the creation of his new order?

Professor Unger correctly urges us to remember that scholarly activity has a greater impact upon the world of affairs than is typically assumed.[452] This insight is particularly apt with respect to highly influential faculty at leading law schools whose work seeks to shape the thinking of persons both within and beyond legal academe. Unger's treatment of China's past as unimportant, save as a manipulable foil for points about the West, is not without its political consequences. By presuming that the integrity of Chinese civilization is inconsequential and easily violable to serve our ends, he leaves the impression that this civilization is less deserving of scrutiny than those of the West and that we need not consider it with particular care as we seek either to understand or to transform the world. Sadly, modern history is all too replete with the consequences of this type of approach to China and other non-Western civilizations.[453]

Unger need not have emulated this undesirable trait of what he terms Western liberal society. Instead, he might have used his appreciation of scholarship's political force to impress upon us the need to incorporate the history and peoples of China and other distant civilizations into our thinking about building new and more humane communities. Ultimately, we may be no more able to attain such communities than we are now able to reach a genuine community of understandings with civilizations long separated temporally or otherwise. But, as with the attempt to build communities of understanding, the effort itself may be what matters most.

452. R. UNGER, *supra* note 1, at 29-30.

453. If the architects of United States involvement in Vietnam had had even a passing familiarity with the history of Sino-Vietnamese relations, they might have been more skeptical of the notion of a monolithic Communist menace sweeping domino-like throughout Asia. For more on the background of the molders of our Vietnam policy, see D. HALBERSTAM, THE BEST AND THE BRIGHTEST (1972).

For a portrayal of the role that Western scholarship denigrating the "Oriental" world has played in justifying and reinforcing European political subjugation of "Oriental" peoples, see E. SAID, ORIENTALISM (1978); Said, *Orientalism Reconsidered*, 1 RACE AND CLASS 1 (1985). Although Said focuses chiefly upon the Middle East and India, his general point holds true for China. Scholarly portrayals of foreign societies as "inferior" to our own—and particularly, as little concerned with individual or collective will—can have powerful political repercussions. To note the point is not to suggest that scholars abstain from forming strong judgments about other societies, but rather to implore that we do so only after careful and serious study provides a firm basis for any such judgments.

[2]

Legal Pragmatism in the People's Republic of China

BY YU XINGZHONG*

INTRODUCTION

Soon after its inception in 1949, the government of the People's Republic of China (PRC) abolished the old Nationalist laws and began building a socialist legal system. The new government rejected Nationalist legal theory, along with its laws, and sought to develop a new "socialist legality" to serve the needs of a socialist country. This process entailed a large-scale borrowing from the Soviet model. At the same time, it involved a campaign of criticism aimed at Western legal thought, especially American legal pragmatism,[1] which was associated by many PRC theorists with bankrupt Nationalist legal theory.[2] The subsequent development and reputed implementation of a socialist legal theory in China has been molded by a series of political upheavals, economic drives, and cultural movements.[3] The final

---

* Lecturer in Law, Northwest Institute of Politics and Law, Xi'an, People's Republic of China; visiting scholar, Columbia University School of Law, 1988-89. The author would like to express special gratitude to the Center for Chinese Legal Studies and the United Board for Christian Higher Education in China for their support and to Mimi Levy for her research assistance.

1. *See infra* text accompanying notes 5-7.
2. *See infra* text accompanying notes 14-27.
3. Chinese history since 1949 has been marked by successive political, economic and cultural movements. The most significant movements include: the "Three-Anti Campaign" against corruption, decay, and bureaucracy (1952); the "Five-Anti Campaign" against bribery, tax evasion, theft of state assets, and theft of state economic secrets (1952); the "Hundred Flowers Movement," an attempt to regain the support of intellectuals (1956); the ideological "Anti-Rightist Movement" (1957); the "Great Leap Forward," a combination of economic and technological reforms (1958); and the "Cultural Revolution" (1965-1976). *See generally* A. BARNETT, CADRES, BUREAUCRACY, AND POLITICAL POWER IN COMMUNIST CHINA (1967); J. TOWNSEND & F. SCHURMANN, IDEOLOGY AND ORGANIZATION IN COMMUNIST

product of this process is what is commonly called Chinese Marxist legal theory.[4]

The meaning and practical application of this theory, however, is far from evident. Recently, the PRC has again embarked on an economic and political renewal, re-introducing many of the capitalist legal structures and concepts that the early reformers sought to eradicate. Chinese legal theory is again in turmoil. Conservative Marxist legal theorists cling dogmatically to ideas that have proved sterile, even to the extent of justifying current reforms as consistent with Marxist doctrine. In reality, pragmatism dominates the approach of both conservatives and reformers alike.

An examination of the development of legal theory over the past 40 years reveals that part of the failure to develop a comprehensive and workable legal theory upon which a stable legal order can be built stems itself from the adoption by Chinese leaders of many of the tenets of the pragmatic approach to law that they had scorned in the early years. This commentary traces the development of legal theory in the PRC and attempts to give a new and critical evaluation of that theory. By way of conclusion, it points out the negative consequences of Chinese legal pragmatism and suggests a balance between pragmatism and the development of a stable legal order in China.

I. Foundations for Analysis of Legal Pragmatism in China

The Chinese approach to legal pragmatism bears little or no direct relation to Western or American legal pragmatism, as defined below. Instead, as used in this commentary, it describes a guiding concept peculiar to the Chinese legal system and Chinese legal philosophy. This concept is manifest in a number of aspects of the current legal system in the PRC, including: the resort to ad hoc legal measures, the separation of legal doctrine from practice, the overemphasis on instrumental facets of law, and the placement of policy before law.

An analysis of these and other aspects of contemporary legal pragmatism in China requires a brief background in two areas. First,

CHINA (2d ed. 1968); R. NORTH, CHINESE COMMUNISM (1966); Chen Shouyi, *Zhongguo Faxue Sanshinian*, in ZHONGGUO FAXUE WENJI (Collected Works on Chinese Law) 14 (1984).

4. Although there are different versions of Marxist legal theory, Chinese legal scholars accept only the classical or conventional theory. Classical theory is the basis of their efforts to combine the general principles of Marxism with the conditions specific to China. The thought of Andrei Y. Vyshinsky reflects the classical theory well. *See infra* text accompanying notes 28-35. For a discussion of the different versions of Soviet legal theory, see H. KELSEN, THE COMMUNIST THEORY OF LAW (1955).

although Western legal pragmatism as it developed in the United States differs from Chinese legal pragmatism, a comparison of the two enhances an understanding of the special characteristics of the Chinese approach. Second, because of its continuing influence, a look at traditional Chinese legal concepts is helpful.

A. *Pragmatism in the West*

Pragmatism, which began in the United States in the 1800s as an attack on traditional formalism, is a philosophy based on the belief that the truth, meaning, or value of ideas must be judged by their practical consequences rather than by a set of formalized, rigid, and timeless standards.[5] Legal pragmatism is an extension of philosophical pragmatism into the legal field. According to one legal historian, legal pragmatism began with Oliver Wendell Holmes, Jr., who explored "the process of thinking and inquiry which terminates in a rule or principle of law and upon the social facts, ideas, and beliefs which are 'the life of the law.' "[6] Roscoe Pound, the influential former dean of the Harvard Law School, also contributed greatly to the school of legal pragmatism. Pound associated pragmatism with "the adjustment of principles and doctrines to the human conditions they are to govern rather than to assumed first principles" and called for "putting the human factor in the central place and relegating logic to its true position as an instrument."[7]

B. *Traditional Concepts of Law*

Ancient China had a very powerful legal tradition, whose substance and uninterrupted history have been extensively discussed by both Chinese and Western scholars.[8] The ancient Chinese valued social harmony and believed that an ideal society did not require extensive legislation or litigation. Traditional Chinese moralism was embodied in the ruler who had responsibility for maintaining harmony. This moralism consisted of social norms that governed the

5. For a discussion of legal pragmatism, *see* E. PATTERSON, JURISPRUDENCE: MEN AND IDEAS OF THE LAW 465-500 (1953); R. SUMMERS, INSTRUMENTALISM AND AMERICAN LEGAL THEORY 22-6 (1982); Patterson, *Pragmatism as a Philosophy of Law*, in THE PHILOSOPHER OF THE COMMON MAN 172 (1940).

6. Patterson, *Pragmatism as a Philosophy of Law*, *supra* note 5, at 174-175, *quoting* O. W. HOLMES, THE COMMON LAW (1881). Holmes' only book, THE COMMON LAW, is regarded as a classic in the literature of pragmatic legal theory. Holmes' famous saying in this book, "The life of the law has not been logic: it has been experience," is regarded as at the core of legal pragmatism. *See* E. PATTERSON, *supra* note 5, at 504; R. SUMMERS, *supra* note 5, at 24.

7. Pound, *Mechanical Jurisprudence*, 8 COLUM. L. REV. 605, 609-10 (1908).

8. *See generally* D. BODDE & C. MORRIS, LAW IN IMPERIAL CHINA (1967); QU TONGZU, LAW AND SOCIETY IN TRADITIONAL CHINA (1961).

relationships between people, thus ensuring continuing harmony.[9] Law was an instrument of last resort. It was used by the emperors solely to maintain the hierarchal order by punishing criminals and deterring common people from crime.[10]

Ancient China had only criminal law. All legal transgressions were handled with criminal punishment.[11] Commoners feared law and legal institutions. They knew that when they violated the law they would be punished; but they did not think of law as something that could protect civil interests. Many assumed that a court summons, whatever its origin, was an indication of guilt. Law was not directed at the good, people believed; instead, its only purpose was to deter the potentially evil.[12] Thus the well-known proverb: "Law is meant for a base person but not for a gentleman *(fa bei xiaoren bu fang junzi)*." In short, law, in its limited form, was primarily a tool for dominance, not for protection of natural rights or individual interests.

The introduction of Western civilization into China during the 18th and 19th centuries resulted in significant changes within the political, economic and cultural structures of society. The preexisting social order was destroyed by several major political upheavals, and the legal tradition that was part of that social order was dismantled. Traditional notions at the heart of ancient Chinese law, however, remain influential today.

II. Early Development of Legal Theory in the PRC

The initial post-1949 development of Chinese legal theory consisted of two prominent movements: the first movement criticized Nationalist legal theory, and the second promoted a large-scale adoption of Soviet legal theory. This section will briefly review these two movements.

A. *Criticism of Nationalist Legal Theory*

After the overthrow of the Qing dynasty in 1911 and prior to the Communist takeover in 1949, the ruling Nationalists abrogated tradi-

---

9. *See generally id.*

10. *See* Liang Zhiping, *Zhongguo Fa de Guoqu, Xianzai yu Weilai: Yige Wenhua de Jiantao*, BIJIAOFA YANJIU, June 1987, at 17, 19-20.

11. For discussions on traditional Chinese legal procedure, *see* ZHOU MI, ZHONGGUO XINGFA SHI (A History of Chinese Criminal Law) 6 (1985); QIAO WEI, TANGLÜ YANJIU (A Study of Tang Codes) 504-514 (1985); ZHANG JINFAN, ZHONGGUO FAZHI SHIGANG (An Outline History of the Chinese Legal System) 201-303 (1985); LI JING, QINGLÜ TONGLUN (A Survey of Qing Codes) 405-514 (1985).

12. Mu Pingren, *Yu Youren Lun Fazhi Xiandaihua Shu*, BIJIAOFA YANJIU, June 1987, at 39, 42.

tional Chinese law remaining from imperial times, and enacted a new body of law based largely on European-style civil law. The primary models were the French, German, and Japanese civil codes.[13] Although the new legal structure was based on civil law, the Nationalists also invited American legal experts, including Roscoe Pound and others, to give advice on various aspects of legal theory. When the Communists took over in 1949 and embarked on various political and economic reforms, all bourgeois Western ideas, including Western law and legal theory, were severely criticized.

In February 1949, the Chinese Communist Party (CCP) issued "Instructions" ordering the abrogation and criticism of Nationalist laws.[14] These Instructions stated:

> The judicial organs should educate and transform the judicial cadres with a spirit that holds in contempt and criticizes the Six Laws of the Nationalists and all reactionary laws and regulations, and holds in contempt and criticizes all the anti-people laws and regulations of bourgeois countries in Europe, America and Japan. To accomplish this aim, they should study and master the concepts of state and law of Marxism-Leninism and Mao Zedong Thought, and new democratic policies, programmatic principles, laws, orders, regulations and decisions.[15]

This excerpt demonstrates that the objects of contempt and targets of criticism were not only the "anti-people" laws of the Nationalists, but also those of Japan, the United States, and European countries. Although the Instructions did not directly criticize preexisting legal theory, since laws and regulations are presumably formulated with the guidance of theory, criticism of Nationalist laws and regulations implies criticism of the underlying theory. "Anti-people" laws of bourgeois countries, moreover, stemmed from a bourgeois theoretical basis and would therefore also be subject to criticism in accordance with the Instructions.

---

13. FAXUE JICHU LILUN (Basic Theory of Jurisprudence) 164 (1984).

14. Zhongguo Zhongyang Guanyu Feichu Guomindang de Liufa Quanshu yu Queding Jiefangqu Sifa Yuanze de Zhishi (Instructions of the Chinese Communist Party Central Committee Relating to Abolishing the Complete Six Laws of the Guomindang and Establishing Judicial Principles for the Liberated Areas) (1949), *reprinted in* 2 FAXUE LILUN XUEXI CHANKAO ZILIAO (Reference Materials for the Study of Jurisprudential Legal Theory) 1 (1983) [hereinafter Instructions]. The Complete Six Codes of the KMT include the Constitution, the Civil Code and its related laws, the Code of Civil Procedure and its related laws, the code of Criminal Procedure and its related laws, the Administrative Laws, and the Military Laws.

15. *Id.*

After the CCP issued the Instructions, the political leadership initiated a campaign within Chinese legal circles in the 1950s to criticize the "old theory" of the Nationalists.[16] The objects of criticism included Western constitutionalism, the doctrine of separation of powers, judicial discretion, and presumption of innocence.[17] Many scholars focused their criticism on American pragmatic legal theory because they associated it with the legal philosophy of the Nationalists. Moreover, pragmatism was regarded by Marxist critics at that time as representative of the most reactionary of bourgeois legal theories. In the campaign against "old theory," scholars who were targets of criticism included Oliver Wendell Holmes, Roscoe Pound, and the Chinese intellectual Hu Shi, who was responsible for introducing pragmatism into the Chinese intellectual arena.[18]

In 1947, the Nationalist Ministry of Justice invited Pound to China to serve as a legal adviser.[19] He delivered three lectures on law in Nanjing and submitted to the Ministry of Justice a five-part program for improving the administration of justice.[20] Despite the fact that it is difficult to point to specific aspects of Nationalist law influenced directly by Pound and other legal pragmatists, in the minds of Marxist critics, their influence was considerable. For instance, one Marxist critic said, "The soul of Pound once occupied a significant position in the Chinese forum; his evil hands once made their way into the heart of China."[21]

It is interesting to note, however, that despite the Chinese view, Pound did not promote the direct adoption of Western legal principles in China. Instead, he argued that the Chinese should experiment with Chinese materials for solutions to Chinese problems.[22] Pound's view actually supports the policy, later frequently stressed by Chinese

---

16. *See infra* text accompanying notes 23-27.

17. *See* Yan Jingyao, *Zichan Jieji Xianfa de Xugouxing yu Weiji*, ZHENGFA YANJIU Feb. 1954, at 14; Kang Shuhua, *Zichan Jieji Sanquan Fenli Xueshuo de Xugouxing he Fandongxing*, ZHENGFA YANJIU, June 1959, at 47; Zhang Zipei, *Pipan Zichan Jieji Faguan Ziyou Yuanze*, ZHENGFA YANJIU, Feb. 1958, at 42; Wu Ningsu, *Pipan Zichan Jieji "Wuzui Tuiding" Yuanze*, ZHENGFA YANJIU, Jan. 1955, at 49.

18. *See* Li Da, *Hu Shi de Zhengzhi Sixiang Pipan*, ZHENGFA YANJIU, Jan. 1955, at 49; Yang Yuqing, *Pang De, Shiyong Zhuyi Faxue zai Zhongguo de Chuanbozhe*, ZHENGFA YANJIU Mar. 1955, at 13. *See generally* ZHONGGUO JINDAI ZHUMING ZHEXUEJIA PINGZHUAN (A Critical Biography of China's Famous Modern Philosophers) 693 (Ding Guanzhi & Xiao Wanyuan eds. 1983).

19. D. WIGDOR, ROSCOE POUND 277-78 (1974).

20. The three lectures were published under the title "Law and the Administration of Justice" by the Sino-American Cultural Service in 1947. For a description of his five-part program for improving the administration of justice, see Pound, *Law and Courts in China: Progress in the Administration of Justice*, 34 A.B.A.J. 275-76 (1948).

21. Yang Yuqing, *supra* note 18, at 13.

22. D. WIGDOR, *supra* note 19, at 277-78. *See generally* Pound, *supra* note 20.

Marxist legal theorists, that the Chinese legal system should be one with "Chinese characteristics." Nevertheless, Pound's Chinese critics found that since his theory of law was a part of the pragmatic school, it was to be condemned for its association with the Nationalists, and therefore he, too, was to be criticized.[23]

The criticism of Pound was cursory compared to the fire concentrated on Hu Shi and the Nationalist legal theory with which he was associated. Hu Shi (1891-1962), a Chinese philosopher, was educated at Cornell and Columbia universities. Upon his return from studying in the United States in 1917, Hu Shi sought to introduce pragmatism into China.[24] With this goal in mind, he invited John Dewey, his former teacher, to China in 1919.[25] Dewey's two-year sojourn throughout China resulted in a greatly enhanced enthusiasm for pragmatism in the Chinese academic community, and it became quite popular in the 1920s and 1930s.[26] Although Hu Shi was influential in many areas, he wrote little about law and his impact in the legal field was not readily apparent. Nevertheless, in the 1950s, Chinese Marxists, who condemned his role as a promoter of bourgeois pragmatism in the general philosophical arena, arbitrarily extended their criticism of him into the legal field as well.[27]

Ultimately, the campaign against legal pragmatism in the 1950s accomplished little, if anything. This campaign failed primarily because the dictates of Marxist ideology and the accompanying revolutionary fervor prevented scholars and others from carrying out their criticism in a dispassionate manner. As a result, scholars approached their critique with presuppositions about the faultiness of "bourgeois" Nationalist theory in general, and of pragmatism and Hu Shi's think-

23. *See* Yang Yuqing, *supra* note 18, at 14.

24. In the spring of 1919, Hu Shi delivered a series of lectures on pragmatism, and based on these lectures he published a long article entitled *Pragmatism*, which systematically deals with the development of pragmatism as a philosophy. Hu Shi, *Shiyan Zhuyi*, 2 HU SHI WENCUN 409 (1919). Convinced that scholarly thinking should be scientific, he believed that in philosophy, only pragmatism was scientific. Armed with the pragmatic method, Hu Shi devoted himself mainly to a series of academic studies and occasionally to politics. His major work in philosophy, *History of Chinese Philosophy*, appeared in 1919. HU SHI, ZHONGGUO ZHEXUE SHI DAGANG (1919). He also reexamined classical Chinese literature and encouraged the use of vernacular in literary works. In 1921, he published his collection of poetry, which was regarded as the beginning of new poetry in Chinese: HU SHI, CHANG SHI JI (Experiments) (1921).

25. GENG YONGZHI, HU SHI NIANPU (A Chronicle of Hu Shi) (1986). In a list of American pragmatic instrumentalists compiled by Professor Robert Summers, John Dewey was the only one who was a professional philosopher and who was not a lawyer. Yet Dewey's contributions to the philosophy of pragmatism were highly influential in the development of pragmatic legal theory. SUMMERS, *supra* note 5, at 22-23.

26. *See* ZHONGGUO JINDAI ZHUMING ZHEXUEJIA PINGZHUAN, *supra* note 18, at 25-27.

27. *See* ZHANG JINFAN, *supra* note 11, at 39; *see generally*, Li Da, *supra* note 18 at 51.

ing in particular. Chinese Marxist legal scholars of the 1950s did not fully appreciate the theory of legal pragmatism that they were criticizing. Their criticism was less an attempt to understand legal pragmatism than a general refutation of all things Western and "bourgeois," including all institutions and ideas associated with Nationalist thought.

B. *Borrowing from the Soviet Model*

Accompanying the campaign against legal pragmatism was a large-scale adoption by China of Soviet legal institutions and Soviet legal thought. Soviet advisors even helped the PRC government with the task of building a new "socialist legality."[28] The Soviet Union, as the first socialist state, was viewed by China as a world leader in theoretical, political, economic, and legal development. It was natural that the PRC, a newly proclaimed socialist state, should borrow from the Soviet model. The Chinese studied translations of the works of Soviet scholars in order to understand and develop a "socialist legality."[29]

Chinese legal scholars at the time were greatly interested in the work done by A.Y. Vyshinsky, a Soviet legal scholar of the 1930s, especially his definition of law, his typology of law, and his discussion on joint offenders.[30] The Soviet legal classification system, Soviet legal terminology, and even Soviet textbooks soon became familiar in law schools and legal departments across China.[31]

From the outset, however, the adoption of Soviet-style legal institutions was qualified. Chinese leaders took the pragmatic approach of selective adoption, aiming to adapt elements of the Soviet model to the unique Chinese experience. This approach required that they choose from and imitate those parts of the Soviet model that they felt met the needs of the ongoing political struggle in China. Of the leading Soviet legal theorists at the time, Vyshinsky appealed most to the pragmatic Chinese leaders.[32] Vyshinsky stressed the coercive aspect of law and regarded law as the instrument used by the ruling class to suppress antagonistic forces.[33] Chinese leaders in the 1950s, like those

---

28. Wu Jianfan, 22 COLUM. J. TRANSNAT'L L. 1; MacDonald, 6 DALHOUSIE L.J. 313.

29. Michael, *The Role of Law in Traditional, National and Communist China*, CHINA Q. 125, 136 (1962). For general discussions of Soviet legal systems, *see* J. HAZARD & I. SHAPIRO, THE SOVIET LEGAL SYSTEM (1962); E. JOHNSON, AN INTRODUCTION TO THE SOVIET LEGAL SYSTEM (1969); G. GUINS, SOVIET LAW AND SOVIET SOCIETY (1954).

30. Zhang Shanzu, *An Yang Weixingsiji dui Falü Kexue de Zhuoyue Gongxian*, ZHENGFA YANJIU, April 1955, at 51.

31. MacDonald, *Legal Education in China Today*, 6 DALHOUSIE L.J. 324 (1980).

32. *See* Zhang Shanzu, *supra* note 30, at 55.

33. For a discussion of Vyshinsky, *see* H. KELSEN, *supra* note 4, at 116-132. In the early

of the Soviet Union during the 1930s and 1940s, promoted a policy of class struggle. Convinced that law could be appropriately used as an instrument, Chinese legal scholars adopted Vyshinsky's model of legal theory. The choice of Vyshinsky's theory illustrates the beginnings of the Chinese-style pragmatic approach in law.

Although China has not looked to the Soviet model since 1960, its influence remains strong today, especially in its theoretical underpinnings. For example, the definition of the term "law" found in a 1984 Chinese legal dictionary is strikingly similar to one formulated by Vyshinsky in 1938. The Chinese dictionary defines law as "the aggregate of the rules of conduct enacted and approved by the state, expressing the will of the dominant class, the application of which is guaranteed by the coercive force of the state."[34] In comparison, Vyshinsky defined law as:

> the aggregate of the rules of conduct expressing the will of the dominant class and established in legal order, as well as of customs and rules of community life confirmed by state authority, the application whereof is guaranteed by the coercive force of the state to the end of safeguarding, making secure and developing social relationships and arrangements advantageous and agreeable to the dominant class.[35]

Another example of the lasting influence of the Soviet model is the retention of the Leninist notion that the Communist party, as vanguard of the proletariat, has the role of leading class struggle and guaranteeing the socialist transition. Despite the fact that the notion of class struggle rarely appears in political discussion today, the CCP still views itself as the vanguard of the PRC and is thus able to maintain its supreme authority in today's China.

III. Elements of Chinese Legal Pragmatism

In the decades following the initial legal developments discussed above, Chinese legal scholars have further developed what they call Marxist legal theory, despite the fact that Marx and Engels never formulated a systematic theory of law. This theory is summarized by the following excerpt:

> As is well known, the conventional legal theory in our coun-

30s, Pashukanis' ideas were predominant in Soviet legal circles, but in 1937 he was renounced and criticized. In the process of criticizing Pashukanis, Vyshinsky developed his own legal theory. *Id.*

34. Faxue Cidian (Jurisprudence Dictionary) (revised ed. 1984).

35. Soviet Legal Philosophy 336 (H. W. Babb trans. 1951).

> try is a theoretical system which is constructed by regarding antagonistic class relations as the basic elements, and which holds that "the existence of law rests on class and class struggle." According to this theory, (1) the origin of law — "law is an outcome of irreconcilable class struggle," (2) the essence of law—"law is an expression of the will of the ruling class," (3) the function of law — "law is an instrument with which the ruling class exercises its rule," (4) the development of law—"law will wither away with the disappearance of class." Furthermore, it holds that "law is a phenomenon unique to societies with classes." Because statements of the founders of Marxism about law were frequently quoted as "theoretical bases" for the theory, it has always been called Marxist legal theory and has been occupying predominant position in our legal field.[36]

The teaching of this Marxist legal theory comprises the primary prerequisite course of a legal education in China today.[37] The theory taught in schools, however, remains largely dogmatic, overly general, and distant from the needs of contemporary China. The aims of China's current legalization campaign — to build legal institutions, legislate a comprehensive body of law, and instill legal consciousness — stand in sharp contrast to the Marxist theory of the classroom. Moreover, these changes have been accompanied by the pragmatic approach taken by political leaders when dealing with today's realities. The divergence between the ideological abstractions of theory and the pragmatic approach to concrete day-to-day legal activities characterizes the Chinese legal scene today. This divergence has fueled recent jurisprudential debates in China. Since 1978, scholars have debated the class nature of law, the validity of current Marxist legal theory in China, and which direction the new "socialist legal theory with Chinese characteristics" should take.

The participants in these debates can be split into two different camps: one conservative, the other radical. The conservatives, largely composed of well-established political leaders, scholars, and other legal notables, maintain that the classical or conventional Marxist legal theory is scientific, correct, and unshakable.[38] They believe

36. Du Feijing & Wang Yongqing, *Makesi Zhuyi yu Faxue*, ZHONGGUO FAXUE, Feb. 1988, at 19 (quoted material is unattributed).

37. Although it is unclear exactly what contributions Mao has made to theory, the theory devised by Chinese legal scholars is said to contain elements of both "Marxism-Leninism" and "Mao Zedong thought." For Mao's ideas about law, *see* MAO ZEDONG SIXIANG FAXUE LILUN LUNWENXUAN (Selected Papers on Legal Theory of Mao Zedong Thought) (1985).

38. *See* Li Maoguan, *Guanyu Fa de Benzhi Shuxin de Tantao*, ZHONGGUO FAXUE, Jan.

that the class nature of law is the very characteristic by which Marxist legal theory gains its identity and that Marxist legal theory has revolutionized the philosophy of law.

On the other hand, the radicals, usually young scholars and occasionally well-known professors, do not agree that current Marxist legal theory in China has developed by combining basic principles of Marxism with the Chinese experience.[39] According to the radicals, Chinese Marxist legal theory only imitates Soviet legal theory formed and developed over four decades ago. In their view, legal studies today should concentrate on problems that need urgent attention — problems arising from the current reforms. Legal scholars, they add, should not confine themselves to the dogmatic methodology and rhetoric of the founders of Marxism. Instead, legal scholars should concentrate their efforts towards developing an innovative theory of Marxism truly suited to the Chinese situation.

The pragmatic approach towards developing a legal system in China has never been systematically explained by Chinese leaders or legal scholars. However, it plays a critical role in the legalization campaign in China today, as demonstrated in many statements made by political leaders. In addition, although the pragmatic approach largely responds to practical day-to-day needs, it also draws upon some of the basic tenets of Marxist legal dogma whenever theoretical justification is necessary.[40] Some theorists contend that Chinese Marxist legal theory is the outcome of practice that combines Marxist principles about law with Chinese actuality in light of the spirit of "seeking truth from fact."[41] However, as will be shown, the approach towards legalization is actually purely pragmatic, and despite much rhetoric, Marxist theory is largely ignored. It is ironic, therefore, that PRC legal scholars began in the early years by criticizing legal pragmatism and ended up adopting many of its basic tenets.

The Chinese pragmatic approach is manifest in the following characteristics: 1) it overemphasizes instrumental facets of law, 2) it regards law as an outcome of actuality, 3) it treats law as a servant of

---

1988, at 23; Guo Yuzhao, *Fa de Jiben Gainian de Zai Tantao*, ZHONGGUO FAXUE, Feb. 1988, at 29.

39. *See* Zhang Zonghou, *Faxue Lilun Bixu Biange he Gexin*, ZHONGGUO FAXUE, Jan. 1988, at 29; Du Paofu, *Lun Fa de Benzhi*, ZHONGGUO FAXUE, Mar. 1988, at 37; Du Feijing, *supra* note 36, at 18.

40. *See infra* text accompanying notes 53-57.

41. "Seeking truth from fact" is descriptive of a working style or attitude proposed by Mao Zedong and carried on by the successive CCP leaders. This style requires people to be practical and realistic but not subjective or idealistic in their work and life. More recently, Deng Xiaoping has adopted the term as a means of urging a move away from ideological argument.

policy, and 4) it does not treat individual legal rights seriously. As is shown below, these four characteristics are often camouflaged by and justified with Marxist dogma, while, in fact, they exist purely for pragmatic purposes.

Despite Marxist doctrine and past warnings against pragmatism, the Chinese legal system is developing pursuant to a purely pragmatic approach. For both Marxists and pragmatists, law is an instrument of the CCP. Theoretically, after establishing "actuality" (explained below), the CCP uses this instrument to legislate appropriate policy. Rights, as separate from and independent of duties, have no place in this process. Ultimately, since the purpose of law is to implement CCP policy, all enactment and revision of legislation follows the dictates of policy. The content of all law, therefore, is, in essence, an exact replication of CCP policy.

A. Law as an Instrument

Instrumentalism is a prominent component of both Marxist dogma and the pragmatic approach to legalization. Instrumentalists see law as an instrument for shaping society. Since 1949, this view has gone through two major stages. Immediately after the founding of the PRC, the CCP was primarily concerned with the extermination of antagonistic forces, seizure of national political power, and consolidation of victory.[42] Its goal at that time was to establish the proletarian dictatorship.[43] The CCP, as vanguard of the proletariat, was to lead society towards socialism. Extermination of antagonistic forces was considered critical to reaching this objective. Law was regarded as an instrument for class domination, an instrument that would allow the proletariat to dominate and thereby eventually extinguish the bourgeois class and all other reactionaries.[44]

Leaders thought law as an instrument should: 1) affirm and regulate the relationship between the ruling class and the ruled classes and between the oppressors and the oppressed, and suppress the resistance

42. *See* MAO TSETUNG (Mao Zedong), *On the Correct Handling of Contradictions Among the People*, in 5 SELECTED WORKS OF MAO TSETUNG 384 (1977); MAO TSETUNG, *On the People's Democratic Dictatorship*, in 4 SELECTED WORKS OF MAO TSETUNG 411 (1969).

43. MAO TSETUNG, *On New Democracy*, in 2 SELECTED WORKS OF MAO TSETUNG 339 (1967); MAO TSETUNG, *On the People's Democratic Dictatorship*, *supra* note 42, at 412; MAO TSETUNG, *New-Democratic Constitutional Government*, in 2 SELECTED WORKS OF MAO TSETUNG, *supra*, at 407.

44. FAXUE JICHU LILUN (A Basic Theory of Law) 181-189 (1984). The use of law as an instrument in today's China, although stemming from a different theoretical basis, is consistent with the traditional notion of law as an instrument of dominance. In fact, the Chinese leaders have unconsciously returned to such a traditional notion as they currently employ law in an instrumental fashion.

of the ruled classes; 2) affirm and regulate the relationship between the ruling class and its alliance; and 3) affirm and regulate the internal relations of the ruling class.[45] In the early years of political struggle, instrumentalism justified large scale suppression of "reactionaries" consistent with the stated purpose of suppressing the resistance of the ruled classes. Later, during the Great Leap Forward and the Great Proletarian Cultural Revolution, the absence of legal order highlighted the instrumental approach to law. Since law was only a tool, it was used only when necessary or desirable. These latter periods of class struggle emphasized extra-legal methods, and thus left the legal instrument aside.

As the political focus has moved from class struggle towards economic development, the primary role of law as an instrument has changed from serving class struggle to serving economic development. The CCP decided in December 1978 to shift the work priority from class struggle to economic development. Since then it has pursued a series of new economic policies designed to invigorate the internal economy and open China to the outside world.[46]

Thus, law is now an instrument serving the goal of economic development. Leaders have justified this change in CCP policy by concluding that "class struggle is no longer vital, since the exploiting class [in China] has been exterminated."[47] Law's instrumental role in the service of economic development is illustrated by the current CCP policy that all government leaders and economic units must use legal means, supplemented by other means, to maintain economic order.[48] The Marxist doctrinal justification for this new policy is sketchy. Theorists appear to reason that since the CCP retains its role as vanguard of the proletariat, its decisions are consistent with leading

45. *Id.* at 30-32.

46. *See* ZHONGGONG DANGSHI DASHI NIANBIAO 421 (1987). *See also* Communique of the Third Plenary Session of the Eleventh Central Committee of the Communist Party of China, *trans. in* Hsinhua News Agency, News Bulletin, Dec. 26, 1978, at 59, which states:

> While we have achieved political stability and unity and are restoring and adhering to the economic policies that proved effective over a long time, we are now, in the light of the new historical conditions and practical experience, adopting a number of major new economic measures, conscientiously transforming the system and methods of economic management, actively expanding economic cooperation on terms of equality and mutual benefit with other countries on the basis of self-reliance, striving to adopt the world's advanced technologies and equipment, and greatly strengthening scientific and educational work to meet the needs of modernization.

47. *See* Resolution on Certain Questions in the History of Our Party Since the Founding of the People's Republic of China (adopted by the Sixth Plenary Session of the 11th Central Committee of the Communist Party of China on June 27, 1981), *trans. in* BEIJING REV., July 6, 1981, at 37.

48. *See* FAXUE GAILUN (An Introduction to Law) 227 (1981).

China further down the path toward socialism. Moreover, theorists and political leaders use new slogans, like "socialism with Chinese characteristics," to legitimize the new policy.

B. Law as an Outcome of Actuality

For Chinese Marxist legal scholars, law is neither divinely endowed nor does it have anything to do with nature. These scholars rarely talk about such abstract values as "rationality" and "justice." Law is not understood in the context of relations between law and morality and rights and freedom as it is in many Western countries. The only source for law is "actuality" (*shiji*) as determined by the CCP. "Actuality" is relied on, almost ritualistically, as a justification for all legislation. In the early years, the CCP deemed that the "actuality" of class struggle was paramount. Now, the CCP perceives general economic construction as the guiding "actuality."[49] The relationship between "actuality" and law, while largely descriptive, seems to have become an essential component of Chinese Marxist legal theory. Actuality, moreover, is tied with the idea of "objective" (*keguan de*) determination of "actuality" and of the needs of development.

1. Doctrine

a. Actuality the Mother, Law the Child

Peng Zhen, the former Chairman of the Standing Committee of the National People's Congress of China, and a leader in the legal field, once offered this colloquy: "Is law subordinate to actuality or actuality to law? Who is the mother? Who are the children? Actuality is the mother. It produces law. Law and theories of law are the children."[50] Some legal scholars echoed this idea: "It is actuality and only actuality that is the source and foundation of law."[51] Peng Zhen's statement about law and "actuality" exemplifies today's pragmatic approach to legalization. The open-ended vagueness of the word "actuality" serves as an easy means to justify all actions.

Thus, because of this concept, those in the position to determine "actuality" possess a powerful means with which to make law and direct the course of social development. The outcome of such power can be desirable or catastrophic to society at large. For example, on

49. *See* ZHONGGONG DANGSHI DASHI NIANBIAO, *supra* note 46, at 422.

50. Speech by Peng Zhen, Fazhan Shehui Zhuyi Minzhu, Jianquan Shehuizhuyi Fazhi (Promoting Socialist Democracy and Perfecting Socialist Legality) (July 22, 1982), *reprinted in* FAXUE ZAZHI, May 1982, at 5, 6.

51. FAXUE JICHU LILUN, *supra* note 13, at 345.

the positive side, the "actuality" of the need for economic development has produced a series of laws that to date have been markedly successful in bringing foreign investment and foreign technology into China, as well as in stimulating internal growth. On the other hand, the "actuality" of the need to quicken the pace towards socialism led Mao to carry out the Cultural Revolution. More recently, sudden and arbitrary crackdowns on economic crime have been justified by pointing to the "actuality" of a rising threat to socialist society posed by bourgeois crimes.[52]

b. The role of "objectivity" in actuality

The view that "actuality" produces law derives in part from Marxist ideas about the need for continual legal reform. Chinese Marxist legal scholars believe that at each stage of social development laws appropriate to the adjustment of social relations in that stage of development must be enacted. Only then can there be harmony and consistency between the different laws and regulations and society.[53] When changes arise in society, the law should change to reharmonize the internal relations within society.[54] Thus, they believe that:

> Socialist law must develop and change in accordance with the development and change of economic, political, cultural and other conditions. This kind of change is embodied in the legislative process, where, in order to adapt to the *objective* needs of development, the process of enactment, revision, and abrogation of laws and regulations is continuously undertaken. (emphasis added)[55]

"Actuality" produces law that "adapt[s] to the objective needs of development."[56] It remains unclear, however, how one determines "actuality," or when a changed "actuality" warrants legal reform. "Actuality," apparently, is situational changes and needs. These situational changes and needs, moreover, are apparently "objective" and determined "objectively." Still, other than the vague concept of "actuality" in Peng Zhen's statement, or the idea of changing to meet

52. *See, e.g.*, Quanguo Renmin Daibiao Dahui Changwu Weiyuanhui Guanyu Yancheng Yanzhong Pohuai Jingji de Zuifan de Jueding (Resolution of the Standing Committee of the National People's Congress on Severely Punishing Those Who Commit Crimes that Seriously Sabotage the Economy) *in* ZHONGHUA RENMIN GONGHEGUO FALÜ HUIBIAN (A Collection of Laws of the People's Republic of China) 382 (1984).

53. FA DE JIBEN LILUN (A Basic Theory of Law) 294-95 (Ma Zhuyan, Shao Cheng, & Zhao Changsheng eds. 1987).

54. *Id.*

55. *See* FAXUE JICHU LILUN, *supra* note 13, at 350.

56. *Id.*

the objective needs of development articulated by Marxist doctrine, no key has been provided for knowing how "actuality" is determined. What is clear is that only the CCP is ultimately capable of assessing the "objective" needs for development and determining that "actuality" warrants legal reform.[57]

2. The Changing Constitution and Actuality

The frequent revision of the Chinese constitution reflects the changing "objective" determination by the CCP of "actuality." The PRC has promulgated four constitutions (in 1954, 1975, 1978, and 1982). Each of these four constitutions bears the mark of the political and economic environment in which it was produced. For example, the central political "actuality" of the early 1950s — the transition to a socialist state — was reflected in the provisions of the 1954 constitution.[58] Similarly, the 1975 "Gang of Four" constitution was strongly influenced by the "actuality" of the Cultural Revolution, and thus "the proletariat [was to] exercise all-round dictatorship over the bourgeoisie in the superstructure, including all spheres of culture."[59]

The new political "actuality" that led to the downfall of the Gang of Four necessarily also led to the need to revise the 1975 constitution. The new 1978 constitution brought back some of the principles of the 1954 constitution, laid out the new goal of "the four modernizations," and emphasized promotion of socialist democracy and elevation of science and education.[60] Even as early as late 1978, when, at the Third Plenary Session of the 11th Congress of the CCP, the present political and economic reforms were born,[61] leaders realized that yet another revision of the constitution was needed. Writing in 1982, when the new constitution was promulgated, Peng Zhen explained: "As the 1978 constitution cannot meet the needs of the current situation, fairly big revisions [were] made this time."[62] Even though the 1982 constitution was regarded by some as "the best of the

---

57. One leading Chinese legal scholar says: "Our people's democratic legal system should not be something prematurely and subjectively worked out. It must be gradually developed and perfected, from simplicity to complexity, in accordance with the 'actuality' and the objective requirements of political and economic development." FAXUE GAILUN ZILIAO XUANBIAN (Reference Material for an Introduction to the Science of Law) 107-108 (1984).

58. ZHONGHUA RENMIN GONGHEGUO XIANFA (The Constitution of the People's Republic of China) preamble (1954).

59. ZHONGHUA RENMIN GONGHEGUO XIANFA (The Constitution of the People's Republic of China) art. 12 (1975).

60. ZHONGHUA RENMIN GONGHEGUO XIANFA (The Constitution of the People's Republic of China) preamble (1978).

61. *See generally* ZHONGGONG DANGSHI DASHI NIANBIAO, *supra* note 46.

62. *See* Peng Zhen, *Explanations on the Draft of the Revised Constitution of the People's Republic of China*, BEIJING REVIEW, May 10, 1982, at 16.

four,"[63] changed "actuality," including the emergence of the private economy, required amendment in 1988.[64]

3. Legislation and Actuality

In the past forty years, the view that "actuality" produces law has played a significant role in Chinese legislative development. An overview of PRC legislation during this period helps to illustrate this idea. Beginning in 1949, upon the abrogation of the old Six Laws of the Nationalists, the legal work was to be conducted "in accordance with the new laws of the people."[65] These new laws did not as yet exist; they had to be created. The 1949 PRC government determined that the most urgent "actuality" at the time was the task of establishing the state machinery which was considered an essential component of the new proletarian dictatorship. Consequently, a series of laws and regulations pertinent to institutional arrangements was promulgated.[66] Later, in April 1952, when the leadership perceived that corruption was rife, this new "actuality" led to the enactment of anti-corruption legislation.[67] Law continued, in subsequent years, to be enacted according to the "actuality" as the PRC government determined it existed.

Late in 1978, the CCP decided that the preeminent "actuality" at that time was the need for domestic economic reform and development and a corresponding opening to foreign investment and trade.[68] This new "actuality" has necessitated more laws to encourage investment, protect investors, and introduce various market mechanisms

63. *See generally* Cao Haibo, *Disi Bu Xianfa Jiang Shi Woguo Zuihao de Yibu Xianfa*, in ZHANG YOUYU ET AL., 2 XIANFA LUNWEN JI (Essays on the Constitution) 16 (1982).

64. AMENDMENTS TO THE CONSTITUTION OF THE PEOPLE'S REPUBLIC OF CHINA (April 1988).

65. *See* Instructions, *supra* note 14.

66. *See, e.g.*, Zhongguo Renmin Zhengzhi Xieshang Huiyi Gongtong Gangling (Common Program of the Chinese People's Political Consultative Conference) (1949), in ZHONGYANG RENMIN ZHENGFU FALING HUIBIAN (1949-1950) (A Collection of Laws and Decrees of the Central People's Government 1949-1950) (1980); Zhonghua Renmin Gongheguo Quanguo Renmin Daibiao Dahui Zuzhi Fa (Organic Law of the National People's Congress of the PRC) (1954), in ZHONGYANG RENMIN ZHENGFU FALING HUIBIAN (1954-1955) 111-18 (1980); Zhonghua Renmin Gongheguo Guowuyuan Zuzhi Fa (Organic Law of the State Council of the PRC), in *id.*, at 123-32; Zhonghua Renmin Gongheguo Renmin Yanchayuan Zuzhi Fa (Organic Law of the People's Procuratorates of the PRC) (1954), in *id.*, at 133-38.

67. Zhonghua Renmin Gongheguo Chengzhi Tanwu Tiaoli (Regulations of the People's Republic of China for Punishing Corruption) (April 1952), in ZHONGYANG RENMIN ZHENGFU FALING HUIBIAN (1952) 29-32 (1980). For a brief discussion of the drafting of this regulation, *see* FAXUE JICHU LILUN, *supra* note 13, at 195-96.

68. *See generally* ZHONGGONG DANGSHI DASHI NIANBIAO, *supra* note 46.

into the economy.[69] Thus, economic law, in particular, has expanded rapidly in response to the demands of the current "actuality." China has gone through a complete cycle since 1949. For the first years after "liberation," except for the largest industries, much of the existing smaller private enterprise was allowed to remain. By the later 1950s, however, almost all of these sectors had been nationalized or collectivized. The response to the new "actuality" now requires a renewed privatization of certain sectors of the Chinese economy.

4. Administration and Actuality

"Actuality" also influences the administration of law in China. One pertinent example is in the area of law enforcement, where the punishment meted out for a particular crime varies with the political "actuality" at the time. If a criminal is so unfortunate as to be captured during an anti-crime campaign, he may receive the maximum punishment provided by the law, when the facts of his particular case might normally result in a lesser punishment but for the anti-crime campaign. When leaders are satisfied with the political and economic situation, lighter criminal penalties are likely to be imposed. Perceived instability leads to heavier penalties.[70] Thus, criminal penalties are determined by official perceptions of current "actuality," despite recent efforts to standardize the sentencing of criminals.

C. *Law as a Servant of Policy*

Assuming "actuality" is the mother of law, we must pursue further how "actuality" produces law. The medium which is needed to give effect to this "actuality" is none other than the fundamental principles and specific policies proclaimed by the CCP. Peng Zhen has supported this proposition: "What is law? Law is the finalization of

69. *See, e.g.*, Zhonghua Renmin Gongheguo Zhongwai Hezi Jingying Qiye Fa (Law of the People's Republic of China on Joint Ventures Using Chinese and Foreign Investment) (promulgated July 8, 1979), *trans. in* CHINA LAWS FOR FOREIGN BUSINESS (CCH) ¶ 6-500 [hereinafter CHINA L. FOR. BUS.]; Zhonghua Renmin Gongheguo Jingji Hetong Fa (Economic Contract Law of the People's Republic of China) (adopted Dec. 13, 1981), *trans. in id.* at ¶ 5-500; Zhonghua Renmin Gongheguo Waiguo Qiye Suodeshui Fa (Foreign Enterprise Income Tax Law of the People's Republic of China) (adopted Dec. 13, 1981), *trans. in id.* at ¶ 32-500; Gongshang Qiye Dengji Guanli Tiaoli (Regulations on Registration and Administration of Industrial and Commercial Enterprises) (adopted July 7, 1982), *reprinted in* JINGJI FAGUI XUANBIAN 67 (1984); Zhonghua Renmin Gongheguo Zhongwai Hezi Jingying Qiye Fa Shishi Tiaoli (Regulations for the Implementation of the Law of the People's Republic of China on Joint Ventures Using Chinese and Foreign Investment) (promulgated Sept. 20, 1983, amended Jan. 15, 1986), *trans. in* CHINA L. FOR. BUS., *supra*, at ¶ 6-550; Zhonghua Renmin Gongheguo Shewai Jingji Hetong Fa (Foreign Economic Contract Law of the People's Republic of China) (adopted Mar. 21, 1985), *trans. in id.* at ¶ 5-550.

70. FA DE JIBEN LILUN, *supra* note 53, at 324-25.

the Party's fundamental principles and specific policies. That is, it fixes the Party's fundamental principles and specific policies in legal form."[71]

Thus, through "actuality," all law is inextricably linked with CCP policy. The recent dramatic but smooth change from the view that law is an instrument of class struggle to the view that law is an instrument of economic development illustrates this link. The CCP first determines "actuality," then, through the medium of policy, promulgates appropriate laws and regulations. Scholars and political leaders have frequently debated the relationship between policy and law, but the dominant view still holds that CCP policy is the soul and foundation of law and contains the guiding principles for legislation.[72]

The purpose of law is only "to finalize, stipulate, and standardize that policy of the party which has proven correct and effective."[73] What is "correct and effective" is necessarily determined by the CCP. Anything inconsistent with the policy of the CCP is therefore neither correct nor effective. The process is simple: begin with CCP policy, articulate it into legal form, and the result is law. "Socialist law is an important and necessary tool for realization of the party's policy," observes one legal scholar. "It plays a particular and active role in the implementation of party policy."[74] Thus, law is always an expression of policy and has no independent status of its own.

In addition, the articulation of CCP policy into legal form bolsters the effectiveness of enforcement mechanisms. Standing alone, CCP policy is enforced by the disciplinary power of the party organization. Once clothed with the coercive power of the state and the universal applicability of law, it becomes even more powerful.

D. *Treatment of Individual Rights*

Overemphasis on the instrumental facets of law and on the notion that policy is the basis for law naturally and necessarily has led to the neglect of many fundamental jurisprudential categories. As mentioned earlier, discussions about "rationality" and "justice" are not found in contemporary Chinese legal theory, let alone studies of "rights." Discussion in the classroom setting centers only on general Marxist ideas; in the political setting it centers only on practical application. In neither case are rights treated seriously.

71. *See* Peng Zhen, *Guanyu Qige Falü Caoan de Shuoming*, in FAXUE GAILUN ZILIAO XUANBIAN, *supra* note 57, at 160.

72. *See* FAXUE JICHU LILUN, *supra* note 13, at 216-21.

73. Peng Zhen, *supra* note 71.

74. *See* FAXUE JICHU LILUN, *supra* note 13, at 219-220.

It cannot be said, however, that there is absolutely no mention of the word "rights" (*quanli*) in Chinese legal theory. Chinese Marxist legal scholars link "rights" of citizens with their "duties" (*yiwu*) to the state. There are at least three features of the Chinese Marxist concept of rights. First, it is believed that rights bear elements of a class nature, and that a distinction can be drawn between bourgeois and proletarian rights.[75] Bourgeois rights, by definition, protect the bourgeois and not the proletarian class. Similarly, proletarian rights serve the interest of their class. Second, Chinese Marxists argue that abstract or natural rights have never existed. A right is not inherent or inalienable, but rather something granted by the State and the dominant class. Legal rights are not a reflection of natural rights as they are in some Western legal systems, but rather, they are derived from citizenship. This concept of rights is inextricably linked to the notion that rights are granted by the state and are not inalienable. Since the state is capable of granting rights, then, undoubtedly, it is also capable of taking them back or changing them as it deems necessary.

Third, Chinese Marxist legal scholars believe rights are invariably qualified and incomplete. In their view, rights are not absolute, but relative, and must be accompanied by duties. They believe that there is no right that does not call for a duty, nor is there any duty that does not lead to a right. While you enjoy certain rights, you have a certain duty to perform and vice versa. A law textbook explains:

> Rights and duties, as two inseparable aspects forming the substance of a legal relation, exist in the whole (unity) of such legal relation. They are contradictory as well as unified. By "contradictory," it is meant that the two are quite different, have different meanings and different natures, and therefore shall not be confused. By "unified," it is meant that the two come into being simultaneously, are closely associated with and conditioned upon each other, and complement each other.[76]

Thus, the 1982 constitution stipulates that "[e]very citizen is entitled to the rights and at the same time must perform the duties prescribed by the Constitution and the law."[77] Law is understood, therefore, not as having the function of protecting rights. Instead, it is used both to grant and to restrict rights.

75. *See id.* at 386.

76. *See* FAXUE JICHU LILUN, *supra* note 13, at 390.

77. *See* ZHONGHUA RENMIN GONGHEGUO XIANFA (The Constitution of the People's Republic of China) art. 33 (1982).

Although there are many and varying interpretations of the concept of rights, these discussions are largely abstract. Chinese pragmatists see little practical or concrete use for such abstract rights in, for instance, creating social institutions or regulating the relationship between individuals and the government. In fact, rights that derived from something other than a grant from the state would considerably interfere with the freedom with which the CCP carries out its policies.

IV. Critique of Chinese Legal Pragmatism

As discussed, in today's China, the approach to the development of a legal system is purely pragmatic. This pragmatic approach is unacceptable. In all legal systems a certain amount of pragmatism is inevitable and necessary, for legislation is generally enacted in response to a situation that is thought to demand it. In an increasingly pragmatic world, the advantages and disadvantages of legal pragmatism are open to much debate. But in the particular instance of China, a purely pragmatic approach is most certainly harmful to the development of a comprehensive and stable legal order.

The adoption by Chinese Marxists of pragmatic approaches does not conflict, in their minds, with their own doctrine about the role of law. Marxists are both idealistic and pragmatic at the same time. They are idealists when they take an abstract and long term view of history and law; they are pragmatists when they are engaged in concrete and practical efforts. Marxists believe, for instance, that eventually the state, and with it the law, will wither away. In practice, a large network of laws and legal institutions is being built. In reality, this practice, which stands in sharp contrast to ideology, makes it increasingly less likely that the final outcome of this lawmaking will be a lawless society, which is a Marxist goal. Admittedly, many legal systems take a pragmatic approach and make use of the instrumental facets of law. However, the role of pragmatism in those legal systems differs in one crucial respect from its role in China. In the United States, for instance, pragmatism exists within the context of an established, sophisticated legal system, built on constant and inviolable principles. It is a society founded on the rule of law. In China, the emphasis on the instrumental facets of law lacks a similar foundation. Instead, tradition and Marxist dogma combine to promote an instrumentalist concept that affords virtually unlimited power to "proletarian" leaders to use law towards whatever ends they choose.

"Actuality" and "objectivity" are the major factors in the failure to bring about the rule of law in China. In Chinese jurisprudence all decisions are said to be objective. Thus, all legislation is justified as being the "objective" result of "actuality."[78] But Chinese legal pragmatism regards "actuality," as determined by the "objective" evaluation of the CCP, as the only standard for making and revising law. The broad majority of people who are not in a position to determine "actuality" do not have confidence in the law. For this reason, extra-legal settlement of disputes is preferred by many people. Even though China has already enacted many new laws, established new legal institutions, and implemented a publicity campaign promoting legal knowledge, indifference to law remains strong.

People's indifference to and mistrust of law can only be reversed with the creation of a true legal consciousness. Creating this legal consciousness necessarily involves bringing citizens into the process of making law and building legal institutions that can be relied upon, which are important components of the transformation from a society ruled by men to a society ruled by law.[79] Moreover, confidence in the new legal order can become complete only if people are convinced that the law equally binds and protects every individual. In this connection, a good understanding of the concept of rights will help foster a healthy legal consciousness. The importance and scope of this task has been neither fully understood nor adequately addressed in China.

The stated aim of creating a legal consciousness has been frustrated thus far by the CCP's persistence in relying on the instrumental function of law. Because only the CCP can make an "objective" determination of the "actuality" that is the source of policy, CCP policy and PRC law have become indistinguishable. Chinese legal pragmatists neglect the importance of the stability created out of lasting legal principles characteristic of societies which have instituted the rule of law. The continued pursuit of a purely pragmatic approach to legalization may have appeal in the short run — and the current economic and political reformers surely have benefited from its inherent flexibility — but, in the long run, it will undercut the goal of building a stable legal order.

Conclusion

If China expects to develop a lasting legal order, it must abandon pragmatism as it exists today. If the CCP continues to treat law merely as an instrument of policy, the establishment of the authority of law will remain illusive. To establish this authority, law must be

78. *See* Fa de Jiben Lilun, *supra* note 53, at 294-95.

79. *See* Liu Xin, *Renzhi yu Shehuizhuyi Fazhi Buneng Xiang Jiehe*, in Fazhi yu Renzhi Wenti Taolun Ji (Discussions of the Question of Rule by Law and Rule by Man) 88 (1981).

freed from the bondage of policy. At the same time, legal theorists must strive to develop a working theory of law that can serve as the true core of a comprehensive legal system.

Foremost among the tasks intrinsic to this goal is a thorough review of the basic jurisprudential categories common to many foreign legal systems that have been largely overlooked by many Chinese theorists until now. The role of individual rights and principles of legal justice will be one necessary focus of any such review. Any future pragmatic use of law must be strictly circumscribed by permanent principles that will remain relatively constant regardless of the direction of statutory reform. Failing this, the construction of a new legal order will remain an illusion that can be easily swept away by the change in direction of the current of any future policy.

[3]

SOCIALIST LEGAL THEORY IN DENG XIAOPING'S CHINA

CARLOS WING-HUNG LO*

I. INTRODUCTION

After assuming supreme power in the People's Republic of China in late 1978, Deng Xiaoping was most insistent that law was essential to socialist modernization and that Maoist legal nihilism had to be combated. He inaugurated a massive program to reform and restructure the legal system. Accordingly, the Party and State Constitutions were revised, law was codified, judicial organs were reorganized and the academic discipline of legal studies was revived. The aim was to replace what was referred to as the 'rule of persons' by the rule of law. By the time of his death in early 1997, much had been achieved. Though defects in the system remain and have been highlighted by many scholars, it is fair to say that China's socialist legal system has gone far beyond the old instrumental notion of safeguarding the rule of a Marxist Party. In the context of promoting economic modernization, law has increasingly been seen as the principal means for resolving conflict and maintaining social order. While many scholars have noted Deng's limited success in instituting the rule of law,[1] one must concede that China is no longer faced with the legal nihilism of the Maoist era.

---

* Carlos Wing-Hung Lo is Associate Professor in the Department of Management at the Hong Kong Polytechnic University, the author of *China's Legal Awakening: Legal Theory and Criminal Justice in Deng's Era*, and the Chief Editor of the *Asian Journal of Business & Information Systems*. The author would like to thank Mr. Robert Phay, the former Editor-in-Chief of this Journal, for reading and commenting upon earlier drafts and Prof. Bill Brugger for his generous help in revising this paper.

1. As most Sinologists and foreign jurists see it, Deng's contribution to China's legal system is still limited, since the Chinese legal system has still failed to satisfy the rule of law. *See generally* John Copeland Nagle, *The Rule of Law in Mainland China*, 2 AMERICAN ASIAN REV.157 (1996); Donald C. Clarke & James Feinerman, *Antagonistic Contradictions: Criminal Law and Human Rights*, 141 CHINA QUARTERLY 135 (1995); Robin Munro, *Rough Justice in Beijing, Punishing the "Black Hands" of Tiananmen Square*, 1 UCLA PACIFIC BASIN L. J. 77 (1991); Carlos W. H. Lo, *Criminal Justice Reform in Post-Crisis China: A Human Rights Perspective*, 27 HONG KONG L. J. 90 (1997).

But what sort of law are we talking about? This article argues that legal reform in China has to be seen within the context of a specific tradition of socialist law, developed originally in the Soviet Union. Of course, in many ways Deng moved away from a "Soviet model". He insisted that socialism (and almost everything else) had to be built with "Chinese characteristics". That did not mean that the Soviet-inspired socialist legal framework was to be abandoned. Its "socialist" content, however, had to be adapted to the thesis that China was in "the preliminary stage of socialism". That "preliminary stage" was to allow for a substantial commodity economy and an open-door economic policy. The market economy, justified by that formula, demanded forms of legal regulation unknown in the old planned and closed economy in which public ownership dominated. The Chinese approach has been very inventive.

Before we consider that inventive approach, let us consider the broad contours of the tradition of "socialist law". The "socialist theory of law" owes its origin to Vyshinsky, following Stalin's rejection of the notion that law and socialism were incompatible,[2] which had been articulated in the "commodity exchange school" represented by Pashukanis.[3] The socialist theory was strictly formulated to legitimate law in the socialist regime by bending elements of Marxist critical theory to serve an ideological purpose. It affirmed the positive value of law in "socialist transition" with the focus on differentiating socialist law from "bourgeois" law. Socialist law was seen not as a further development of bourgeois law, but as a new

---

2. *See* J.V. Stalin, *Report to the XVIII Party Congress*, *in* SOVIET LEGAL PHILOSOPHY 347 (Hugh W. Babb trans., Harvard Univ. Press 1951).

3. Before completely subjugating law to politics in the 1930s, Soviet theorists had attempted to develop what they considered to be "Marxist" law into a coherent *critical* theory. The views put forward were Marxist in the sense that they conformed to Marx's "base" and "superstructure" metaphor, his discussions on the relationship of law and ideology and his stress on the class character of law. At first theorists argued that law and socialism were incompatible. Such a thesis underpinned the critical theories of Stuchka, Reisner and Pashukanis, the most celebrated jurists of the time. Their point of view that "law was a bourgeois category that regulated relationships between isolated individuals in the process of commodity exchange" later became known as the "commodity exchange theory". Taking an economic reductionist position, such theorists argued that, since a commodity economy was the essential material condition for law, law would cease to exist as that commodity economy withered away. Since law was class-bound and conflict-ridden, Marxist theory precluded any idea of "socialist" (or proletarian) law. Meanwhile, law in the transition period, while a commodity economy still existed, was only a continuation of "bourgeois law". Above all, their obsession with "legal fetishism" prevented them from thinking about the necessity of law in a post-capitalist society. *See generally* P.I. Stuchka, *The Revolutionary Part Played by Law and State - A General Doctrine of Law*, *in* SOVIET LEGAL PHILOSOPHY, *supra* note 2, at 40; M.A. Reisner, *Law, Our Law, Foreign Law, General Law*, *in* SOVIET LEGAL PHILOSOPHY, *supra* note 2, at 71-109; E.B. Pashukanis, LAW AND MARXISM: A GENERAL THEORY (1981).

type of law which had grown out of the socialist revolution of the proletariat.[4]

The socialist theory was formulated on the basis of Stalin's instrumental approach. Law in socialist society was held to be the instrument of the state for the elimination of all capitalist residues, for the defense and the development of the socialist economy, and ultimately for the realization of communism.[5] Vyshinsky's theory held that socialist legal theory should specify the tasks and social functions of socialist law, its nature, its content and form as well as the condition for its withering away.[6] As for a general theory, it should cover the origins, development and the future of law in human societies. Within that model, Soviet jurists wrestled with the nature of law and its origins, the proper relationship between law and the economic base and the methodology of Marxist jurisprudence.[7]

The socialist theory was Marxist in the sense that it stressed the indissoluble link between the state and law, both historically and functionally. Law was conditioned by the state and had to be defined by reference to the state. It took on a political complexion; and legal theorists always had to refer to political theory, or more particularly to ideology. Socialist theory, therefore, was positivistic, seeing law as being laid down by the state and geared to serve the interests of the state until communism saw the state transcended. Its uniqueness, as summed up by Tay and Kamenka, lay in the "extra-legal presupposition about the nature and the function of law in the economic context, and in the rejection of law as independent of the state in practice".[8]

Has the wide adoption of market-oriented legislation based on Western models, particularly for the purpose of developing a "socialist market economy" under Jiang Zemin's leadership, made the socialist

---

4. S. A. Golunsky and M. S. Strogovich, *The Theory of the State and Law*, *in* SOVIET LEGAL PHILOSOPHY, *supra* note 2, at 386.

5. *See* A. Y. Vyshinsky, *The Fundamental Tasks of the Science of Soviet Socialist Law*, *in* SOVIET LEGAL PHILOSOPHY, *supra* note 2, at 308-9.

6. *See* A. Y. Vyshinsky, THE LAW OF THE SOVIET STATE 49-52 (1948).

7. *See generally* L.S. Jawitsch, THE GENERAL THEORY OF LAW 1-168 (1981). For discussion of the Soviet debate, *see* Sun Guohua, *Yijiao zhe xuyan [Foreword by the Translator and Proof-reader]*, *in* FA DE YIBAN LILUN [THE GENERAL THEORY OF LAW] 1-10 (Zhu Jingwen trans., Liaoning Renmin Chubanshe 1986).

8. A. Erh-Soon Tay & E. Kamenka, *Marxism, Socialism and the Theory of Law*, 28 COLUM. J. TRANSNAT'L L. 244 n. 23 (1985). Such a conclusion is drawn mainly from the studies of Hazard on Soviet law. *See generally* J. HAZARD, COMMUNISTS AND THEIR LAW: A SEARCH FOR A COMMON CORE OF THE LEGAL SYSTEM OF THE MARXIAN SOCIALIST STATES (1961) and MANAGING CHANGE IN THE USSR: THE POLITICO-LEGAL ROLE OF THE SOVIET JURIST (1983).

perspective obsolete? It seems both rash and simplistic to conclude that such a move has fundamentally changed the philosophical basis of the Chinese legal system. Western observers who have stopped paying attention to the continuing influence of the "socialist theory of law", simply because the Soviet Union has collapsed, may not be seeing the entire picture of legal reform in China. When considering China, one cannot overstate the ideological significance of the non-state sector. Nor should one overlook the fact that a definition of "socialist market economy" is still bent in the direction of the old statist teleology. As Gelatt notes, foreign legal concepts and traditions have been adapted within a broader framework of Marxian rule and have been accommodated to the basic principles of socialism. "The PRC leadership has never indicated an intention to use law in a way that would alter China's political or ideological foundations or 'basis'".[9] One should note, moreover, that while some law (criminal and administrative) enjoys a little autonomy from politics, economic law is much less autonomous and is not regarded as "mainstream". That will surely continue to be the case so long as the importance of public ownership retains its ideological dominance.

The tradition of "socialist law", therefore, remains important, and we must be careful not to negate Chinese socialist law in the name of Western legal theory, as warned by Lubman in reviewing the study of Chinese law in the United States: "[b]oth extreme cultural relativism and insistence on intellectual categories derived from Western legal systems have threatened to skew study (of Chinese legal system), with the latter trend more evident in recent years".[10]

This article discusses the evolution of socialist legal theory in China and in particular the changes resulting from Deng Xiaoping's reforms. While the old framework of socialist law remains, law has developed beyond crude Soviet instrumentalism. The subtlety of law's regulative function is now appreciated, and the way is open for seeing the relationship between the rule of law and democracy. This article will contrast Deng's approach to law with that of Mao Zedong. It will consider whether Deng laid down the basis for a uniquely Chinese legal theory in the context of Marxist jurisprudence. Finally, it will explore the future of Chinese socialist law under the leadership of Jiang Zemin.

---

9. *See* Timothy Gelatt, *Law Reform in the PRC after June 4*, 3 J. CHINESE L. 318 (1989).

10. Stanley Lubman, *Studying Contemporary Chinese Law: Limits, Possibilities and Strategy*, 39 AM. J. COMP. L. 294, 326(1991).

II. SOCIALIST LAW IN CHINA

A. *Mao's View*

We have noted that the Chinese legal system, though deeply influenced by the former Soviet Union,[11] was by no means a slave to Soviet formulae. The Chinese Communist Party was relatively free in formulating its own theory of law within the framework of Marxism-Leninism.[12] Mao, in fact, constantly challenged the positivistic notion of law inherited from the Soviet Union. By the mid-1950s, he had refused to conceal his dislike of the formal Soviet legal system; and that, amongst other things, informed the Sino-Soviet ideological split. Mao's hostility to formal law derived from his "philosophy of struggle", deeply affected by Marx's and Lenin's revolutionary theory:

> The state apparatus, including the army, the police, and the courts, is the instrument by which one class oppresses another. It is an instrument for the oppression of antagonistic classes; it is violence and not "benevolence".[13]

For Mao, law acted to restrict class struggle and a formal legal system could not adapt to rapidly changing revolutionary conditions. Thus, Mao persistently opposed the introduction of a purely legal order. From his class perspective, proletarian justice in socialist society demanded rejecting "bourgeois right", expressed in the principle of "all being equal before the law".[14] Mao's conception of law subsumed legal order and justice under a

---

11. *See* Richard Baum, *Modernization and Legal Reform in Post-Mao China: The Rebirth of Socialist Legality*, 2 STUDIES IN COMP. COMMUNISM 76, 76-77 (1986).

12. *See* JEROME COHEN, THE CRIMINAL PROCESS IN THE PEOPLE'S REPUBLIC OF CHINA, 1949-63: AN INTRODUCTION 71 (1968); *see also* Victor H. Li, *The Evolution and Development of the Chinese Legal System*, *in* CHINA: MANAGEMENT OF A REVOLUTIONARY SOCIETY 255 (John M. H. Lindbeck ed., George Allen and Unwin Ltd. 1972).

13. Mao Zedong, *On People's Democratic Dictatorship*, *in* 4 SELECTED WORKS OF MAO TSE-TUNG 418 (1977).

14. The rationale for class justice is enshrined in Article 43 of the "Statute of the Chinese Soviet Republic Governing the Punishment of Counter-revolutionaries" (1934) which provided lighter penalties for crimes committed by workers and peasants. The provision reads:"workers and peasants who commit an offence but are not leaders or major offenders may have their punishment reduced from that stipulated in the various articles of this statute regarding elements from the landlords and bourgeoisie who commit the same class of offence." *Quoted in* CARLOS W.H. LO, *The Legal System and Criminal Responsibility of Intellectuals in the People's Republic of China, 1949-82*, 2 OCCASIONAL PAPERS/REPRINTS SERIES IN CONTEMPORARY ASIAN STUDIES, No. 83 (1985). This tradition of "proletarian justice" continued in the principle of the "dictatorship of the proletariat" and later more explicitly in Mao's distinction between two categories of contradiction after the communist regime was established in 1949. See Mao Zedong, *On the Correct Handling of Contradictions Among the People*, 5 SELECTED WORKS OF MAO TSE-TUNG 384-421 (1977). For a discussion on justice under Mao, see Lo, *The Legal System and Criminal Responsibility of*

broader framework of politics and ideology: law was simply an instrument to be wielded by the Party in fostering class struggle and socialist transition.

Law, defined as an instrument of class struggle, was to be implemented not so much by formal judicial organs as by mass participation in political campaigns and mass movements.[15] Mao put strong emphasis on its educational function in inculcating the masses with communist ethics.[16] Of course, Soviet law did that too,[17] but Mao's emphases were different. Mao's ideal (communist) society was based on his particular vision of communist ethics which had to be achieved here and now and could not be postponed until a communist society rendered law unnecessary.[18] As communist ethics developed, law lost its authority. And that was nowhere more the case than when Mao's frustration with the slowness of the Soviet model led to his ideas on "uninterrupted revolution" in 1957. The result was the Anti-rightist Movement and the Great Leap Forward where "politics took command" and the value of law was negated. Eventually Mao declared that law was useless.[19]

B. Conceptions of Law under Deng Xiaoping

Unlike that of Mao, Deng Xiaoping's approach towards law was pragmatic. Drawn largely from his bitter political experiences, Deng's conception of law was geared to practical goals. After resuming leadership in late 1978, Deng developed policies geared to rebuilding and strengthening the Chinese legal system. As we have noted, he saw law as necessary to maintain social order for socialist modernization. Putting forward the slogan "develop Marxist ideology under the new historical

---

Intellectuals, op. cit, at 83-84.

15. *See generally* JAMES P. BRADY, JUSTICE AND POLITICS IN PEOPLE'S CHINA: LEGAL ORDER OR CONTINUING REVOLUTION? (1982).

16. For discussion of the educational function of law in Mao"s conception of the legal system, see LO, *supra* note 14, at 6-10.

17. The educational function of Soviet law was stressed by Vyshinsky, Golunsky, Strogovich and Chkhikvadze. *See generally* Vyshinsky, *supra* note 5; Golunsky and Strogovich, supra note 4; Article 3 of the "Law Concerning the Judicial System of the U.S.S.R. and the Union and Autonomous Republics" (1938) prescribes that "the court in all its activities is educating Soviet citizens in a spirit of devotion to their fatherland and to the cause of socialism; it is unswervingly precise in carrying out Soviet laws- care for socialist property, labor discipline, an honorable attitude towards the state and social duty, and respect for the rules of all socialist life.") from D. A. Funk, *Lesson of Soviet Jurisprudence: Law for Social Change Versus Individual Rights*, 7 IND. L. REV. 466 (1974) (quote amended for stylistic reasons). For detailed discussion, see *id.* at 466-72.

18. For a clearer picture of Mao's vision of the ideal society, *see* LO, *supra* note 14, at 24. See also BRADY, *supra* note 15.

19. SHAO-CHUAN LENG AND HUNGDAH CHIU, CRIMINAL JUSTICE IN POST-MAO CHINA: ANALYSIS AND DOCUMENTS 16-17 (State University of New York Press 1985)

conditions of China",[20] Deng did not return to all features of the Soviet model but insisted on searching for a "Chinese" path to the development of a socialist legal theory. His aim was to free China from the constraints of both Soviet ideas and Mao's theory of the state and law but he retained some basic features of the old socialist ideology. His insistence in 1979 on the "four cardinal principles" - the socialist road, the dictatorship of the proletariat, the leadership of the Party, and Marxism-Leninism and Mao Zedong Thought - makes that clear.

Deng's approach was incremental. While proclaiming unswerving adherence to his "four cardinal principles", he nevertheless affirmed the fundamental role of legal institutions in socialist society. But Deng did not see that approach as contradictory. Here he distinguished between ideology and political practice. Ideology was the source of the Communist Party's legitimacy to rule. The "four cardinal principles" were the foundation of that ideology. In practice, however, they should not be seen as extra-legal and should appear in legal form if they were to be accorded supreme authority. Deng had no doubt "law was the highest authority".[21]

As Deng saw it, if one was single-mindedly to pursue the goal of socialist modernization, what had become known as the "rule of persons" had to be replaced by the "rule of law". Here Deng's position was clear-cut. He bluntly opposed the "rule of persons": "Very often, what leaders say is taken to be the law and anyone who disagrees is called a law-breaker. Such law changes whenever a leader's views change".[22] That approach should be eradicated!

Deng's pragmatic leadership style resulted in action-driven legal principles, not just ideological maxims. Insisting on the slogan "there must be laws for people to follow", Deng demanded the completion of legal codes. His second slogan was that "those laws must be observed". Third, he demanded that "law breakers must be dealt with accordingly", and fourth that "law enforcement must be strict". Finally, he maintained that all were "equal before the law".[23] Those practical principles provided workable, simple and straightforward guidelines for legal reform. Of the five principles, Deng was particularly concerned with those dealing with the observance and implementation of law. The criteria for evaluating law and the legal system were its ability to improve people's material life, to

---

20. *See e.g.*, Deng Xiaoping, *Opening Speech*, *in* THE TWELFTH NATIONAL CONGRESS OF THE C.C.P. 3 (Foreign Languages Press 1982).

21. Deng Xiaoping, *Implement the Policy of Readjustment, Ensure Stability and Unity, 25 December 1980*, *in* SELECTED WORKS OF DENG XIAOPING (1975-1982) 339 (Foreign Languages Press, 1984).

22. Deng Xiaoping, *Emancipate the Mind; Seek Truth from Facts and Unite as One in Looking to the Future, 13 December 1978*, *in* SELECTED WORKS OF DENG XIAOPING (1975-1982), *supra* note 21, at 157-58.

23. See Carlos W. H. Lo, *Deng Xiaoping's Ideas on Law: China on the Threshold of a Legal Order*, ASIAN SURV., July 1992, at 649-65.

foster "spiritual civilization" in the socio-cultural area and to promote democracy in the political realm.[24] Yet, in the absence of a coherent theoretical formulation, Deng's random views could be bent in the direction of expediency, especially when one came to consider the relationship of the Party to the law and the relation of law to democracy.

For Deng, it was best that the development of the legal system and democracy proceed gradually in a manner corresponding to economic progress. Although believing that Party interventions in that process should be minimized, Deng regarded some degree of Party direction and supervision as essential if chaos was to be prevented. The denunciation of the "rule of persons" was intended to remind Party cadres to exercise their leadership role within the boundaries permitted by law. Even class struggle (so much as it still existed) had to be geared to legal order and to be handled by the legal system. Above all, the core of Deng's legal ideas rested on his practical principles which were taken as legal maxims by the regime. His vision of Chinese society was legally-regulated, with socialist democracy as the political foundation. Yet Deng acknowledged that it would take a long time to achieve that goal. To make the legal order work, Deng saw it as vital to raise the level of the nation's legal consciousness. Education was the appropriate means to produce a large pool of qualified legal professionals to operate the legal order. In short, "political stability and social unity" should be the over-riding concern within the overall policy of "promoting democracy and strengthening the legal system".

III. Toward a Chinese Socialist Theory of Law

The above approach was eclectic. It was clear enough that Deng did not have, and never had, a coherent theory of law; he merely had some preliminary ideas on the orientation of law when he put forward the legal reform proposals after the Third Plenum in 1978. And yet his ideas on law had unparalleled significance in Chinese history due to the fact that he provided a leadership which understood the positive value of law and which brought to an end the legal nihilism enshrined in Mao's legal thought. His conception of law had gone beyond the narrow Soviet instrumentalist justification of Party rule and had advanced towards a basis for criticizing arbitrariness. He had come to realize that the repressive function of law should be seen in terms of a notion of public order much deeper than simply eliminating enemies of the revolution. Deng believed that legal regulation was important to socialist modernization and opening up China to the rest of the world. However imperfectly, Deng's view of law

24. Deng Xiaoping, *On the Reform of the System of Party and State, 18 August 1980*, *in* SELECTED WORKS OF DENG XIAOPING (1975-1982), *supra* note 21, at 304-9.

had begun to comprehend the importance of a democratic setting to safeguard people's political rights against arbitrary rule and bureaucratism. It understood law's highest authority and its universality both in formulation and in application. Such was to be the basis of a new theory of socialist law.

But the implementation of law was constrained. Ideologically Deng's "four cardinal principles" set the boundaries. The term "socialist road" referred to maintaining a dominant planned economy, supplemented by a limited market economy. The "dictatorship of the proletariat", now defined more loosely than hitherto as much the same as "people's democratic dictatorship", could allow for a degree of democracy based on a comprehensive legal system. Party leadership, moreover, was tempered by the expressed need for public supervision. Finally, "Mao Zedong thought", in its new formulation, demanded that one concentrate on the practicality of Marxism in tackling the realties of China.[25] On the one hand, the "four cardinal principles" were designed to provide an ideological safeguard against the possibility that emancipating the mind from dogmatism could lead to the negation of Marxism. On the other hand, the fact that they were interpreted as *living* anti-dogmatic principles offered much hope for emancipation. As one might expect, there was much debate on how to uphold them, particularly in light of the injunction to "build socialism with Chinese characteristics" and its application to law.

First priority was given to preserving social order. Second came the development of the socialist economy, and third was the promotion of democracy within a framework of political stability. Since the Party under Deng saw law as a function of socialism, the more liberal the vision of socialism (such as in Zhao Ziyang's "preliminary stage", and most recently in Jiang Zemin's "socialist market economy"), the more the scope of law was broadened. Conversely, the more conservative the notion of socialism (such as that held by Li Peng and some veterans), the more narrow the jurisdiction of law would be.

Chinese jurists assumed the task of constructing a new theory of law, upon which the Chinese legal system could be based. Inspired by Deng's desire to create a socialist legal order, progressive Chinese jurists began to review critically the Vyshinsky-style Soviet legal theory with a view to going beyond narrow instrumentalism. In an unprecedentedly relaxed

---

25. See RESOLUTION ON C.C.P. HISTORY 76-83 (Foreign Languages Press 1981). For the main features of the policy-line adopted by the Eighth Party Congress, see ZHONGGUO GONGCHANDANG LIUCI QUANGUO DAIBIAO DAHUI ZHONGYAO HUIYIJI (II) [COLLECTION OF IMPORTANT DOCUMENTS OF ALL FORMER NATIONAL CONGRESSES OF THE COMMUNIST PARTY OF CHINA, PART II] 74-81 (Renmin Chubanshe, 1983). For details, see generally EIGHTH NATIONAL PARTY CONGRESS OF THE COMMUNIST PARTY OF CHINA (DOCUMENTS) (Foreign Languages Press, 1981). *See also* Deng Xiaoping, *Uphold the Four Cardinal Principles, 30 March 1979*, *in* SELECTED WORKS OF DENG XIAOPING (1975-1982), *supra* note 21, at 171-86.

atmosphere they held protracted debates. But those debates were far from adventurous and remained within official parameters specified by Deng's "four cardinal principles". In a pragmatic atmosphere jurists felt that their best strategy was not to provoke leaders by pushing too far ideas about democracy but instead to show that the de-politicization of law yielded concrete benefits. All understood that the dictatorial nature of the regime and socialist legality could best be achieved without challenging the official ideology. Nevertheless there were some telling gains, as described below.

Jurists did much to discredit pure instrumentalism and, reversing the mode of thinking dominant in the 1960s, overturned ideas about the primacy of the "rule of persons" in favor of the "rule of law".[26] They refuted the former concept, which dated from long before Vyshinsky, and stressed the incompatibility of formal law and socialism by referencing to later attempts to place law in a "socialist" context. Jurists made much of the out-dated nature of traditional Marxist legal studies[27] and their inability to offer an adequate explanation of socialist law in a situation where class confrontation had "basically come to an end".[28] They went on to launch an unprecedented challenge to ideas about the "class nature of law" and to advocate radical ideas about the "social nature of law".[29] Increasingly one saw jurists attempting to persuade orthodox Marxists that law could be de-politicized by reference to current Chinese social and economic realities under the rubric of a "socialist legal system" and a "socialist system of legal studies with Chinese characteristics".[30] The aim was to create a new legal "ideal-type".

No new comprehensive theory resulted, yet in the rejection of ideas about the class nature of law one saw rationales for future theoretical developments. Some progressive scholars such as Wu Shihuan, Wan Bin and Zhang Zhonghou, in groping for a Chinese "socialist theory of law" and fighting legal nihilism, took the first step in what may become a new comprehensive structure. Wu Shihuan, a jurist from Zhongshan University, was emphatic that one should break away from the idea of "taking class

26. For the most comprehensive discussion in this respect, see Yu Haozheng, *Renshi Yu Fazhi Wenti De Taolun Yao Shenmo Xianshi Yiyi?* [*What are the Practical Implications of the Discussion on the Question of "Rule of Persons" and "Rule of Law"*], 7 MINZHU YU FAZHI [DEMOCRACY AND THE LEGAL SYSTEM] 8 (1980).

27. Xia Zhi, *Dui Makesizhuyi Faxue Tifa De Shangque* [*Questioning the Formulation of Marxist Jurisprudence*], 1 FAXUE [LEGAL STUDIES] 8 (1987).

28. Zhang Zhonghou, *Dui Fa De Sange Jiben Gainian De Zhiyi* [*Queries on Three Fundamental Concepts of Law*], 1 FAXUE [LEGAL STUDIES] 4 (1986).

29. Zhou Fengju, *Fa Shi Danchun De Douzheng Gongju Ma* [*Is Law Purely an Instrument for Class Struggle?*], 1 FAXUE YANJIU [LEGAL RESEARCH] 37 (1980).

30. *Guanyu Jiaqiang Faxue Jiben Lilun Yanjiu De Changyi* [*Proposals for Strengthening Research on the Basic Theory of Law*], 11 FAXUE [LEGAL STUDIES] 2 (1982).

struggle as the key link".[31] Wan Bin, a liberal jurist from Shanghai, argued strongly that Marx and Engels had never built up a coherent theory of law and that the traditional Marxist theoretical system of law as propounded in China was strictly an invention of Soviet jurists.[32] The leading figure of this new wave of thought was perhaps Zhang Zhonghou, visiting professor at the Jilin University Law School, who, by denouncing the idea that "class nature is the unique property of law", argued that the traditional theory of legal studies ought to be thoroughly "rejuvenated".[33] Indeed, all progressive scholars insisted that law was determined by "objective regularities" of social development and not by class struggle.[34] Zhang was the most thorough. In rejecting class as the sole determinant of law, he argued that class nature was a product of social nature. The essential properties of law were social, coercive and normative - none of which could be reduced simply to class.[35] This resulted in the view that while class struggle was transient, social regulation would last forever. Those reforming endeavors ended with the abandonment of a Vyshinsky-type socialist theory of law and simple economic reductionism in favor of law and legal studies "with Chinese characteristics".

With the triumph of progressive scholars over the conservative jurists concerning the manner in which China should be governed after 1982, the orientation of a new approach to law was set. The dominance of progressive thinking on law in Chinese jurisprudential circles since then has provided a theoretical basis for jurists to develop China's own "socialist theory of law". Many advocates of that theory argued that the philosophical basis for the socialist theory should rest on Marx's own ideas on law rather than on the Soviet tradition. These boiled down to a methodological injunction to start from the economic and social realities of present day China. To many, it appeared obvious that (given the transition to socialism) law was socially determined and no longer class determined, and that the essential properties of law were social, coercive and normative - none of which could be reduced simply to class. Since law had a social

31. Wu Shihuan, *Faxue Yeyao Tupo Yi Jieji Douzheng Wei Gang De Moshi [Jurisprudence Should Also Break Away from the Model of Taking Class Struggle as the Key Link]*, 8 SHEHUI KEXUE PINGLUN [DISCUSSIONS ON THE SOCIAL SCIENCES] 73 (1985).

32. Wan Bin, *Chuantong Faxue De Gaige Yu Makesihuizhuyi Faxue De Fazhan [The Reform of Traditional Jurisprudence and the Development of Marxist Jurisprudence]*, 4 SHEHUI KEXUE [SOCIAL SCIENCES] 6 (1986).

33. *Faxue Lilun Yao Gengxin - Ji Zhang Youyu He Zhang Zhonghou De Yixi Tan [Theories of Jurisprudence Need to Be Renewed - The Record of the Discussion Between Zhang Youyu and Zhang Zhonghou]*, RENMIN RIBAO [PEOPLE'S DAILY], Mar. 31, 1986, at 5.

34. *Zhongguo Faxue Hui Faxue Jichu Lilun Yanjiu Hui Chengli Dahui Congshu [Summary of the General Meeting on the Establishment of the Research Institute of the Basic Theories of Jurisprudence of the Society for Chinese Jurisprudence]*, 3 ZHONGGUO FAXUE [LEGAL STUDIES OF CHINA] 57 (1985).

35. *Guanyu Fa De Benzhi He Zuoyong [On the Nature and Function of Law]*, ZHONGGUO FAZHI BAO [NEWSPAPER OF THE CHINESE LEGAL SYSTEM], Oct. 31, 1986, at 3.

rather than a class character, it should be a social regulator instead of an instrument of class struggle.[36] In socialist society, all people should be (and, in contrast to the situation in "bourgeois society", in reality could be) equal before the law. Consider Zhang Zhonghou's definition of the changed nature of law in socialist society:

> Law is the aggregate of rules of conduct, made and confirmed by the state or other organs of social management, the application of which is safeguarded by the coercive force of the state or these social organs to regulate social and people's relationships. In a society characterized by class conflict, law possesses a distinct class nature, expressing the will of the ruling class. In societies characterized by class harmony, law performs mostly the functions of co-ordinating economic relationships and regulating human relationships. In classless society, law's instrumental function in class struggle will vanish and law will turn completely to perform the task of social management.[37]

The liberal discussions of law in Chinese jurisprudential circles revealed gaps between the expectations of officials and intellectuals. After 1982, the Party leadership, adopting a very favorable attitude towards law, regarded it as an effective means by which to implement its reform program. An instrumentalist view still prevailed but there had been a change in the end which the instrument was to serve. Gradually to install a comprehensive legal order in China was seen as serving the Party's views on economic reform and preserving Party rule. But that kind of instrumentalist end implied an increasingly salient non-instrumentalist way of thinking. Once Party rule was constrained to rule through law, de-politicization grew apace. Understanding the implications, scholars welcomed the Party's position. Yet there remained major differences in officials' and scholars' interpretation of the application of the "rule of law".

Put bluntly, the real relationship of the Party to law was central. When one considers that "leadership by the Party" was the first of Deng's "four cardinal principles", one has to explore the Party's real relationship to law. What had changed? Clearly there had been a move from the situation in Mao's era where the Party had enjoyed absolute leadership over the judiciary. Party policy at that time had been described as the "soul" of

---

36. *See* Carlos W. H. Lo, *Rejecting the Socialist Theory of Law: Reforming Chinese Legal Studies in the 1980s'*, 7 CHINA INFORMATION 1 (1992).

37. *Guanyu Fa De Benzhi He Zuoyong*, *supra* note 35, at 3.

the people's democratic legal system and had a status higher than law.[38] After the Third Plenum in 1978, that attitude began to change. Since Deng Xiaoping held that "law was the highest authority", his "four cardinal principles" had to appear in legal form (as noted above); but it was not always clear just what that implied. Party leaders were unequivocal in claiming the Party and its cadres were no longer above the law in routine operations – a rejection of the old view that "Party policy was the soul of law". Leaders such as Peng Zhen spoke of a harmonious relationship between law and Party policy, since both represented the "will of the ruling class"; and that view was strongly promoted after 1984. Law and Party policy were held not to be substitutable, since they performed different roles in achieving Party objectives. Law, moreover, could only be amended in accordance with Party policy by prescribed legal procedures. There were enough contradictions in that formulation to cause much confusion.

The Party's approach here was ambivalent and often muddled. One was not always clear about the exact meaning of law being "supreme" (or the highest authority) in a "socialist" context, since the Party had consistently rejected what it considered to be the Western "bourgeois" notion of "the supremacy of law".[39] If law were genuinely supreme, the Party was subordinate to law and under the supervision of the judiciary instead of *vice versa*. That was a question of subordination of the Party, not one of a harmonious relationship. In any case, talk of a harmonious relationship was idealistic; law and policy would inevitably clash, as they did in all countries. The point was not to extol harmony but to specify supra-political mechanisms for conflict-resolution. Note also that while the Party talked of the primacy of law, the phrase "leadership of the Party" was inserted into the "Preamble" of the 1982 Constitution. The highest law in the land was formally subordinated to a political party; the Constitution which allowed for political manipulation. Clarity was sorely needed; but clarity was too dangerous and might impair legitimacy.

While Party spokespersons were muddled, many of the legal scholars could be more consistent. Any policy which conflicted with law, they felt, should be void. Nevertheless, it was usually much too dangerous to challenge the principle of Party leadership in the name of legality. Often lip-service was paid to Party leadership or the issue explicitly avoided, while scholars concentrated on the issue of judicial independence and independent administration of law. Some, however, were quite explicit in

---

38. Li Shiwen, *Ba Youpai Sufan Weifa De Fanlun [The Rebuttal of the Rightist Fallacy on the Liquidation of Counter-revolutionaries]*, ZHENGFA YANJIU [STUDIES IN POLITICS AND LAW], 1957, at 33. *See also On the People's Democratic Dictatorship and the People's Democratic Legal System,* CHINESE L. & GOV'T, Summer 1968, at 4.

39. The Party's ambiguous attitude toward the proper relationship between Party policy and law manifests a rejection of the notion of "the supremacy of law."

examining the practical implications of the "supremacy of law" after 1983. Law as the expression of the will of the people, they felt, should command the Party.

IV. THE FUTURE OF CHINESE SOCIALIST LAW

Many observers have concluded that the intellectual debate on legal questions has been overly abstract. Such a viewpoint, which demands practical guidelines for the judicial system, coincides with the Party stance that "legal studies in China lag far behind legal practice", misreads the implications of the debate on law in post-Mao China. It has been instructive to study how jurists may work on technical aspects of criminal justice without a clear vision of socialist legal order. But they grope for one. Unlike the West or even the former Soviet Union, law is still in a confused state and is full of conceptual uncertainties; legal studies are in complete turmoil. But the scope of legal reform has gradually been appreciated and crucial questions have emerged.

What sort of legal order does the Party intend to create? What purposes are served by establishing a legal system? What is the status of that legal system in socialist society ideologically and practically? What is the proper relationship between law and politics? What is the relationship of law to Party policy? To what extent should law protect people's democratic rights? Finally, what is to be pursued in criminal justice - formal justice or class justice? All of these questions determine the nature of the legal system to be installed in China and, in turn, dictate the direction of legal reform, the legal system and the legal values with which the people are to be inculcated. Searching for answers to those questions, scholars aim to provide a solid foundation for the structural framework of legal studies in China. In short, without clear ideas about a socialist legal system, Chinese jurisprudence can have no long-term goals.

But there is reason for optimism. Belief in law is now seen as positive rather than negative in socialist society. This development is similar to occurrences in the post-Stalinist Soviet Union. Breakthroughs in Soviet legal development came mainly from intellectual efforts. Despite the poverty of legal practice in the Stalinist era, Soviet jurists explored the nature of socialist law deeply enough to formulate a legal vision clear enough to guide the development of law. Thus the former Soviet Union could embark on sweeping legal reforms after Khrushchev. Much can be learned from Soviet experience. After all, Leninist hostility to law was replaced by a positive assessment. That was the spirit in which Chinese scholars tried to forge a "socialist legal system" in the early years of legal reform. Although discussions were contained within an old framework of "socialist law", discarding taboos led to considerations of the "heritability of law" and the extent to which Chinese scholars might learn from Western experience.

More significantly a comprehensive review of "Marxist jurisprudence" led to re-organization of the entire discipline of legal studies. Revival of legal studies determined the professional values and morality of legal professionals. Legal education, so important for socialization, was essential to transform the legal values of an entire population in the long-run. But the Party still rules. Scholars propose, but the Party disposes. Yet the Party is poorly-equipped in knowledge of law. Once it had decided whole-heartedly to establish a comprehensive socialist legal order, it required the services of jurisprudential circles. Its control is limited. Suffice it to say that the extent to which Chinese jurisprudential circles can exercise tutelage depends on the Party's commitment to transforming China from a police state to a legal society. China's quest for a socialist market economy under Jiang's leadership has raised our hopes.

But one should remember the circumstances under which Jiang came to power - the crackdown of 1989. After that crackdown one heard a reaffirmation of the need for more traditional Marxist legal studies,[40] and a reaffirmation of a class-centered approach[41] held sway for a time. But one still heard the voices of progressives,[42] and conservatives were cautious.[43] Scholars still refused to take Marxist theory as dogma[44] and

40. A handful of articles and speeches re-asserting the theme of taking Marxism as the proper perspective in conducting legal studies appeared between August 1989 and 1991. The most significant ones are: *Zai Falu Xue Lingyu Jianchi Makesizhuyi [Upholding Marxism in the Realm of Legal Studies]*, ZHONGGUO FAXUE [CHINESE LEGAL STUDIES], Sept. 1989, at 121-23; Zhang Youyu, *Woguo Faxue Bixu Yi Makesizhuyi Faxue Wei Zhidao [Chinese Legal Studies Must Be Guided By Marxism]*, QIUSHI [SEEKING THE TRUTH], Apr. 1990, at 14-20. As for speeches, see Zhang Youyu, *Tantan Faxue Yanjiu Lilun [Talks on the Studies of Jurisprudence]*, FAXUE TIANDI [FORUM FOR LEGAL STUDIES], Feb. 1991, at 1-3; Chen Pixian, *Faxue Yanjiu Bixu Jianchi Makesizhuyi Zhidao [Legal Studies Must Uphold the Guidance of Marxism]*, FAZHI RIBAO [LEGAL SYSTEM DAILY], May 29, 1991, at 1.

41. On the restoration of a class perspective of law in the wake of the "June Fourth" incident, see Ji Xuedong, *Guanyu Fa De Benzhi Shuxing De Jige Wenti [Certain Questions on the Essence of Law]*, JIANGXI SHEHUI KEXUE [SOCIAL SCIENCES OF JIANGXI], Feb. 1990, at 113-117; Zhou Huiguo, *Lun Falu De Jieji Xing He Shehui Xing Zhi Zheng [On the Contention Between the Class Nature and Social Nature of Law]*, NANJING DAXUE XUEBAO [JOURNAL OF NANJING UNIVERSITY], Apr. 1990, at 6-12; Wei Zailong, *Lun Faxue De Yanjiu Fangfa [On the Research Method of Legal Studies]*, 4 FAXUE PINGLUN [COMMENTARIES ON LEGAL STUDIES] 1 (1991).

42.. For the latest discussions in this respect, see Yang Haikun, *Zhongguo Shehuizhuyi Fazhi De Lilun Yu Shijian [Theory and Practice of the Chinese Socialist Rule of Law]*, FAXUE YANJIU [LEGAL RESEARCH], Jan. 1991, at 9-14.

43. Such a sentiment was fully expressed by Sun Guohua, one of the most celebrated conservatives from the Department of Law, People's University of China. *See* Sun Guohua, Guo Huacheng, and Chen Guoqing, *Falu Xue Yanjiu Shinian [A Decade of Studies on Law]*, FALU XUEXI YU YANJIU [STUDYING AND RESEARCHING LAW], Feb. 1990, at 1-7. *See also* Guo Daohui, *Yong Makesizhuyi Zhexue Yanjiu Faxue [Employing Marxist Philosophy to Study Jurisprudence]*, ZHONGWAI FAXUE [LEGAL STUDIES IN CHINA AND OTHER COUNTRIES], Feb. 1992, at 45-61.

44. *See* You Junyi, *Shi "Gengxin" Shi Fujiu? Xuexi Makesizhuyi Falu Guan De Yidian Tihui ["Reforming" or Restoring the Past? Some Insights Gained from the Study of the Marxist Perspective of Law]*, SHEHUI KEXUE [SOCIAL SCIENCES], Apr. 1990, at 9-12; Liu Delin, Wu Yiping,

persisted with the quest for a distinctively Chinese approach to law and legal studies.[45] Eventually the importance of creativity in legal studies was stressed.[46] There was a new flourishing of creative debate, carrying on where the debates of the 1980s had been truncated.[47] All this was designed to accommodate the idea of a "socialist market economy",[48] which now seems irreversible.

Jiang Zemin, in adopting the mantle of rule, seems to have emulated Deng Xiaoping.[49] He appears to have continued Deng's insistence on market reform within a context of stability. He has reaffirmed commitment

---

Zhengque Lijie Makesizhuyi Faxue Sixiang [Correctly Understanding Marxist Legal Thought], YANCHENG SHIZHUAN XUEBAO, Apr. 1990, at 23-26; Zhang Wenxian, Ma Xinfu, Zheng Chengliang, *Xin Shiqi Zhongguo Falu Xue De Fazhan Yu Fansi [Development and Reflections on Chinese Legal Studies in the New Era]*, ZHONGGUO SHEHUI KEXUE [SOCIAL SCIENCES IN CHINA], June 1991, at 167-80.

45. For the latest review on this subject, see generally WANG YONGFEI & ZHANG GUICHENG, ZHONGGUO FALU XUE YANJIU ZONGSHU YU PINGJIA [SUMMARY AND ASSESSMENT OF CHINESE LEGAL STUDIES] (1992).

46. *See* Zheng Yongjiu, *Chuangxin, Zhongguo Falu Xue De Genben Siwei [Creativity, the Thought Underpinning Chinese Legal Studies]*, FAXUE [LEGAL STUDIES], July 1992, at 2. See also his earlier article, Zheng Yongjiu, *Falu Yu Fazhan - Jiushi Niandai Zhongguo Fa Zhexue De Xin Guandian [Law and Development - New Ideas of Chinese Philosophy of Law in the Nineties]*, ZHONGWAI FAXUE [LEGAL STUDIES IN CHINA AND OTHER COUNTRIES], Apr. 1992, at 5-10; and more recently Chen Zhen, Shi *"Zhengque Yindu" Haishi Wudu [Is it a "Correct Guide" or An Incorrect One?]*, ZHONGGUO FAXUE [LEGAL STUDIES OF CHINA], May 1995, at 48-56; and Liu Chang, *Duoyuan Shidai Yu Duoyuan Faxue [An Era of Pluralism and Pluralism in Jurisprudence]*, XUE YU TANTAO [STUDY AND EXPLORATION], Mar. 1995, at 96-100.

47. For the details of debates on law in the 1980's, see Lo, *Rejecting the Traditional Socialist Theory of Law*, supra note 36. For a summary of latest developments, see Zhang Shaoyu, *Falu Sue Yaniu Zongshu [A Summary of Research in Legal Studies]*, FAXUE YANJIU [LEGAL RESEARCH AND STUDIES], Jan. 1995, at 3-8, and Li Lin, *Zouxiang Ershiyi Shiji De Falu Xue [Toward the Legal Studies of the Twenty First Century]*, ZHONGGUO FAXUE [LEGAL STUDIES OF CHINA], May 1995, at 122-24, and *Falu Xue De Gaige Yu Fazhan [The Reform and Development of Legal Studies]*, FALU KEXUE [LEGAL SCIENCE], Mar. 1995, at 3-18.

48. *See, e.g.* Sun Guohua, Zhu Jingwen, *Dui "Falu Ying Yi Shehui Wei Jichu" Zhi Wojian [My Personal Views on "Law Should Take Society as its Basis]*, FAXUE [LEGAL STUDIES], Nov. 1992, at 8-11; Liu Han, Xia Yong, *Falu Xue Mianlin De Xin Keti [New Topics to Be Faced by Legal Studies]*, FAXUE YANJIU [LEGAL RESEARCH AND STUDIES], Jan. 1993, at 3-11. For those dealing specifically with the market economy, see in particular Shi Tong, *Shichang Jingji Yu Falu Xiandaihua [Market Economy and the Modernization of Law]*, FAXUE [LEGAL STUDIES], Jan. 1993, at 1-6; Fang Shirong, *Fazhi Yu Shichang Jingji Xiang Shiying De Ruogan Wenti Tantao [Inquiries on Cetain Issues Concerning the Mutual Adjustment of the Legal System and the Market Economy]*, ZHONGNAN ZHENGFA XUEYUAN XUEBAO [JOURNAL OF MIDDLE-SOUTH CHINA LAW AND POLITICAL SCIENCE INSTITUTE], Feb. 1993, at 1-5; Wang Shuwen, Lun Jianli *You Zhongguo Tesi De Shehuizhuyi Shichang Jingji Falu Tixi [On the Establishment of a System of Law with Chinese Characteristics for the Socialist Market Economy]*, ZHENGFA LUNTAN [POLITICS AND LAW FORUM], Apr. 1995, at 7-11. For latest developments, see Qiu Chunlan, *Shichang Jingji Yu Fazhi Jianshe Yanjiu Zongshu [A Summary of the Studies on the Market Economy and the Construction of the Legal System]*, SHOUDU SHIFAN DAXUE XUEBAO [JOURNAL OF BEIJING NORMAL UNIVERSITY], Apr. 1995, at 76-79.

49. *See generally Jiang Leaves His Mark on the Media*, SOUTH CHINA MORNING POST, Oct. 3, 1997; *Backing for Jiang Ideology*, SOUTH CHINA MORNING POST, Jan. 26, 1996.

to the regulative functions of law in a market economy[50] and has promoted new economic legislation.[51] He has renewed emphasis on establishing legal infrastructure, re-enforcing judicial independence, improving the quality of legal personnel, training lawyers and promoting popular legal awareness.[52] As noted before, his approach is instrumental but with far-reaching consequences. But, one must remember, there remain other objects of an instrumentalist approach beyond economic development. Jiang has made it quite clear that cultural and ideological purity may not be sacrificed for temporary economic growth.[53] The authority and validity of Marxism still appears to stand beyond challenge.[54] Thus Jiang still appears to adhere to a repressive view of law rather than to emphasis on human rights; evidence of such a view may be seen in the treatment of dissidents such as Wei Jingsheng and Wang Dan and instructions given to the media to toe the Party line.[55] To retain legitimacy Jiang has resorted to old ideas of ideological conformity.[56] The regime has adopted a "strike-hard" policy in cracking down on violent and hard-core crimes.[57] The punishments are harsh and the legal proceedings are rushed.

V. CONCLUSION

Despite the events of 1989, it is fair to say that Deng's conception of law has generally advanced beyond a simple instrumental concern with Marxist political rule. Although instrumental concerns remain and are painfully re-emphasized time and again, law has increasingly been seen as a social regulator and as a mechanism for effective administration. Law has increasingly been seen both as a channel for economic modernization (instrumental perhaps, but in a much broader sense than before) and,

---

50. Jiang Zemin, *Accelerating Reform and Opening-Up*, BEIJING REVIEW, Oct. 26 - Nov. 1,1992, at 23. Since then, the regime has been busy with economic legislation and improving legal facilities for a new economic order. *See Legal Service for Economic Order*, BEIJING REVIEW, Aug. 9-15, 1993, at 4; *Reform Brings Out Corporate Law*, BEIJING REVIEW, Sept. 6-12, 1993, at 24-25; and *Lawyer System Reform to Match Market Economy*, BEIJING REVIEW, Nov. 6-12, 1993, at 4.

51. For a summary of economic legislation between 1993-95, see *Continued Improvement in Chinese Legislation*, BEIJING REVIEW, Jan. 8-14, 1996, at 22-24.

52. Id.; *see also Political Reform, Next Target*, BEIJING REVIEW, Dec. 21-27, 1992, at 4.

53. *See Political Reform, Next Target*, *supra* note 52 at 9-14.

54. *See generally Party Stresses Value of Marxist Foundations*, SOUTH CHINA MORNING POST, June 11, 1996

55. *Media to Remain in Hands of Party*, BEIJING REVIEW, Feb. 12-18, 1996, at 6; *see generally also Press Reminded to Toe Party Line*, SOUTH CHINA MORNING POST, Apr. 22, 1996; *Hardline Jiang Propagandists for Promotion*, SOUTH CHINA MORNING POST, July 3, 1996.

56. *See supra* note 49.

57. For example, it was reported that in the three-month period between April and June 1996 over a thousand executions had taken place; *Crime Purge Sees 98 More Executed*, SOUTH CHINA MORNING POST, July 25, 1996, at 7; *see generally also Courts to Step Up Executions*, SOUTH CHINA MORNING POST, May 2, 1996.

despite rather severe crises, is coming to be seen as the principal means to resolve conflict and to regulate social order. Yet one is always conscious of the fact that Deng always saw "rule by law" occurring under Party tutelage, and Jiang seems to continue to hold that position.

In the revived legal studies, which Deng sponsored, one detects a strong demand for a new socialist theory of law upon which to base the legal system, independent of that of the former Soviet Union. "Chinese characteristics" have been stressed and content may be given to that term when one considers that the Chinese political economy differs from that of the former Soviet Union in that it is a mixed economy operating in a more open way. This is what "the preliminary stage of socialism" and later, "the socialist market economy" boils down to; and as such has major implications for Chinese law, demanding a new socialist conception to accommodate a regulatory legal regime. Yet it has been difficult to break away from Soviet-style thinking, so long as the supreme status of Party leadership remains unshakable. The "socialist rule of law" remains limited.

Yet one must not be too pessimistic. The fact that jurists could eradicate legal nihilism is impressive. It enabled jurists to entrench the "rule of law" in Chinese legal thinking. Discrediting the thesis of "class will", moreover, after years of heated debate, is considerable progress. Law has been considerably de-politicized and such de-politicization has intensified demands for formulating China's own socialist theory, capable both of expounding legal issues and guiding legal reform. A specifically Chinese form of legal theory and jurisprudence is vital if institutional changes are to continue and is vital to developing a popular legal culture.

The demise of the Soviet Union should not deter scholars from considering the continuing importance of China's inherited "socialist theory of law". Yet, clearly, the demise of the Soviet Union will impel Chinese jurists to move further away from Soviet frames of reference. In the long-term, more and more Western approaches to law will be adopted. In the meantime, however, legal scholars will be most remiss if they ignore China's attempts in recent years to employ Marx's ideas as the philosophical basis of law, China's realities as the empirical source of law, social nature as the essential properties of law, the economic base as the chief determinant of law, and regulation and protection of people's democratic rights as the major functions of law.

[4]

International Journal of Law, Policy and the Family **11**, *(1997)*, 149–191

THE ANATOMY OF RURAL FAMILY REVOLUTION: STATE, LAW, AND THE FAMILY IN RURAL CHINA, 1949–1966 PART ONE

NEIL J. DIAMANT*

ABSTRACT

This article, which is in two parts, takes a new look at how the 1950 Marriage Law of the People's Republic of China shaped family dynamics in rural areas between 1949 and 1966. In contrast to previous studies which have depicted the law (which banned arranged marriages, bigamy, concubinage and made it easier to divorce, among other things) as ineffectual in changing family relations, and rural society as basically stable and patriarchal throughout this period, this article demonstrates that Chinese peasants, women in particular, clamoured to take advantage of many of the law's articles, particularly those expanding the right to divorce. This happened even as many women and men still held what we would consider 'traditional' views towards the sexual division of labour. The result of the law, in combination with other state policies (such as collectivization and the famine after the Great Leap Forward), was a notable shift in power away from family elders and village men towards young women, who sometimes used their rights to a 'free love' marriage and divorce to pursue goals the state considered quite unorthodox. Rather than emphasize stability and patriarchy, this article argues for a reconceptualization of law-induced social change in China that emphasizes fluidity and power shifts. This case of family change in rural China also suggests that there is little incompatibility between an understanding of sexual *in*equality as the natural order of things and the willingness to take an active role in changing one's family situation. Achieving gender 'equality', a principle concern of western feminists and often the criteria by which they judge women's progress in the Third World, was not a precondition for social change in the rural Chinese family. Part One deals primarily with the revolutionary period and Part Two with the period of consolidation of the revolution and the impact of collectivization.

In times of change, it is not uncommon to find that popular anxieties over its direction, pace, and nature are expressed in conflicts over 'proper' family behaviour, structure, and the role of the state in regulating family relations. Whether this is because growing up in a family is the one experience most people share despite other social differences, or

* Department of Political Science, Tel. Aviv University, Ramat Aviv, Israel, diamant@spirit.tau.il.

because in many societies the family is seen as the most elementary and fundamental form of social institution, what happens to the family is frequently seen as emblematic of societies' problems, as well as its aspirations. Now, amid the breathtaking changes of the end of the twentieth century, the family is the centre of political, and by implication moral, debate. Old consensuses are questioned: in the US, policies and laws concerning the family and celebrated as 'emancipatory' during the heyday of the civil rights movement are now criticized as too 'liberal' because of increasingly high divorce rates. At the same time, new definitions of 'proper' family structure are being struggled over, seen most recently in the debate over same-sex marriages. Not surprisingly, politicians, sometimes to their peril, have became involved in these debates. In the last several years, several state legislatures have attacked as harmful to women and children 'no fault' divorce laws enacted in the 1960s and 1970s (Johnson, 1996; Whitehead, 1993), even though many legislators themselves have been divorced several times. In countries with weaker liberal traditions, the debate has been equally intense, although played out in a different ways. In Ireland, the legislature and church are at loggerheads about whether to even allow divorce (Clarity, 1995), but in the Ivory Coast, conflicts over divorce have been overshadowed by those concerning the legality of polygamy (French, 1996).

Current debates over the 'proper' family structure and the state's role in regulating family relations have largely overlooked these issues' heavy historical baggage. From Plato to Hegel, the family, and its relationship to the state, has been used as a model and metaphor for the 'good', 'ethical' society. In Plato's *The Laws*, for instance, the state was conceptualized as a union of households and families, and his proposed legislation concerning marriage, property, and inheritance were shaped by the crucial role he attached to the family in affairs of state (Okin, 1982). Aristotle, by contrast, defined the family in *opposition* to the state; men could become moral and rational persons only by leaving the 'feminine' sphere of the family (*oikos*) and participating fully in the public, cum male, sphere of the *polis* (Elshtain, 1982). In the *Persian Letters*, Montesquieu condemned the arbitrary rule of the reign of Louis XIV by comparing his management of state affairs to the way an 'Oriental' master of a harem controls his women and slaves (Shanley and Stillman, 1982). Perhaps as a result of this, some scholars have argued that the French Revolution itself was a form of freeing oneself of authoritarian national parents and replacing them with a another family, whose children were able to act as autonomous individuals (Hunt, 1992). Hegel, who wrote at a time when many families were sundered by industrialization and urbanization, envisioned the family as an institution whose strength might foster the individualism and sense of ethics necessary to fully participate in the public sphere. The ethical state, according to

Hegel, was grounded both in the family and civil society (Landes, 1982).

Debates about the role of the family in the social order have not been limited to philosophers. What was a side interest of theirs has been taken up with more zeal by theorists and practitioners of revolution. Robespierre, Marx, Engels, and Lenin have all heeded, albeit in different ways, socialist theorist Ferdinand Lasalle's call to 'reconstruct' their societies 'from the ground up', by staging 'a revolution with regard to love, sexual life and morality' (Müller-Freienfels, 1978). This desire was frequently manifested in the enactment of radical changes in the previous regime's family law. In France, in 1792 revolutionaries also promulgated a new family law to weaken the power of the Church and clergy over family and moral matters. Central to this new legislation was the reconceptualization and redefinition of marriage as a contract rather than a pact between man, woman and God (Traer, 1980). As one pamphlet from the time stated, divorce 'follows from individual liberty, which would be lost in any indissoluble commitment (Hunt, 1992). In Russia, similar changes in family law were legislated. Seeking to fulfil Marx and Engels' promise of a more egalitarian society, the Supreme Soviet declared a new family law (which also made divorce much easier to obtain than under the previous regime) only eleven months after the Bolshevik Revolution. In these cases of social and political revolution, family reform was only partially successful: in cities, and particularly among educated and literate women, many took advantage of liberalized family laws, but the farther one went out into the countryside, the fewer divorces there were. Peasants remained largely untouched by the new state policies (Phillips, 1980; Juviler, 1977; Geiger, 1968).

As one of the most revolutionary states of the twentieth century, China was not an exception to this pattern. Family reform was on the agenda of the Nationalist Party, or KMT (which was in power in mainland China between 1928–49), since the early 1920s, and in 1931 the state passed its first Family Code. Due to political distractions such as the Japanese invasion of Manchuria and growing Communist strength, however, this Code was not put into practice outside of large cities such as Shanghai (Berhardt, 1994). The Communists, for their part, promoted their own version of a family law in the 1930s, but higher priority was given to mobilizing peasants for revolution and fighting the KMT on the famous 'Long March'.

After successfully encircling cities from the countryside and capturing state power, in 1950 the Communists were finally in a position to implement its new family law, which was simply called a 'Marriage Law'. In fact, the scope of the law encompassed far more than marriage. The goal of the law was to replace the 'feudal' marriage system with one that emphasized Western notions of the good marriage legislated since the French revolution. Free choice marriages based on love and contractual mutual consent (Article I of the law) were to take the place of the now banned practices of arranged marriages, polygamy, concubinage, and use of matchmakers, all said to be the vestiges of the 'feudal' system. As in the French and Soviet cases, divorce procedures were simplified; in cases of arranged marriages, Article 17 held that should one party seek to divorce, a divorce should be allowed after mediation. With this expanded notion of choice in marriage and divorce, the party anticipated a dramatic reduction in young people's suffering at the hand of their elders, and a concomitant rise in 'harmonious' relationships.

To date, the literature on the impact of the 1950 Marriage Law has largely confirmed findings of other scholars of revolutionary family law; change, seen through the prism of divorce, has been depicted as a predominately *urban* phenomenon. Laws aimed at the emancipation of young women and men through giving them a widened latitude to choose their own mates were said to have threatened the ability of poor rural men to continue the patrilinial line. Given the choice of who to marry, few women would choose to marry poor men. After political campaigns to enforce the 'Marriage Law' ended in 1953, the state, according to this view, did little to promote family change through law. As a result marriages continued to be arranged by parents, and divorce, due to the structure of rural communities and marriage practices in which women married out of their home village into their husbands', was almost non-existent. As anthropologists Sulamith and Jack Potter wrote, 'In the new society as in the old society, women fell between two stools. . .They literally had nowhere to go after a divorce. . .In spite of the fact that the right [to divorce] existed in theory, the social structure made it a practical impossibility' (Potter and Potter, 1990). During the 1950s and 1960s, rural family structure thus remained patriarchal and stable. Given the value western writers place on 'change', such stability has been given as evidence to indict the Communists for hypocrisy and false promises of women's liberation (Johnson, 1983; Stacey, 1983; Wolf, 1985).

This article takes a new look at what happened to the rural family during the heyday of Chinese Communist radicalism, a period usually referred to the Maoist period (1949–66). In it, I show that the rural Chinese family was hardly as stable or even patriarchal as portrayed in the secondary literature; women (and some, but fewer, men) took advantage of the Marriage Law well after 1953. My article chronicles the dramatic changes that took place in the rural Chinese family. Some of these were the direct result of the new law; others were a byproduct of other policies, such as rural collectivization and mass mobilization in the mid-1950s, the devastating famine after the Great Leap Forward (1958–61), and the introduction of market oriented economic reforms in the early 1960s. By emphasizing the extent of change rather than stability in the Chinese countryside, my findings reverse the conventional wisdom on state-family relations in rural China during the 1950s and 1960s.

Evidence for my arguments come largely from hitherto closed archives in the Peoples' Republic. During 1993–4 I was allowed access to archival documents of several agencies involved in dealing with the family–the Chinese Women's Federation, Bureau of Civil Affairs (which was responsible for registering marriage and uncontested divorce) and courts. Usually hand-written and stamped 'secret', these reports are far more candid, and probably more truthful, about problems the state encountered trying to implement the new family law than reports published in newspapers and other journals. Because they did not serve any propaganda purpose, few of these documents underwent official censorship. In terms of location, the archives I chose represented the gamut of the urban-rural divide (See Map on following page). I examined archives in the rural suburbs of Shanghai and Beijing, areas some fifty miles away from the city centre where residents did not spend all of their time in cultivation but worked at least part-time in some form of industry. The second type of area was far more rural, located in the Southwestern Province of Yunnan. There, there was little industrialization to speak of, and peasants lived in villages remote from urban centres. If changes described below in the suburbs might be at least partially explainable by their proximity to urban centres, in Yunnan the city influence was virtually non-existent. Evidence of significant rural change in Yunnan therefore is of utmost importance because evidence of significant change there would falsify previous arguments that there was little change in rural China, and its remoter areas in particular.

1. THE IMPACT OF LAW, 1950–66

As noted earlier, scholars of Chinese family law have generally agreed that it was in urban, rather than rural, areas where people proved most willing to take advantage of the new law. Reasons for why urbanites and not peasants were both willing and able to take advantage of the law were usually derived from certain assumptions about the nature and location of 'modernity' and 'tradition'. Only cities, according to this view, allow their residents the opportunity for the sophistication, education, and individualism necessary to learn about and use progressive new laws. 'Urban life and work', according to Kay Anne Johnson, 'could provide greater *freedom from* traditional structures and patrilineal authority' (Johnson, 1983). Peasants, by contrast, are said to face overwhelming obstacles when trying to exercise newly-endowed rights. Not only are they generally less exposed to new ideas about the family (as family reform discourse is invariably located in city-based universities),

Political Map of China. Research was based in areas marked with (x).

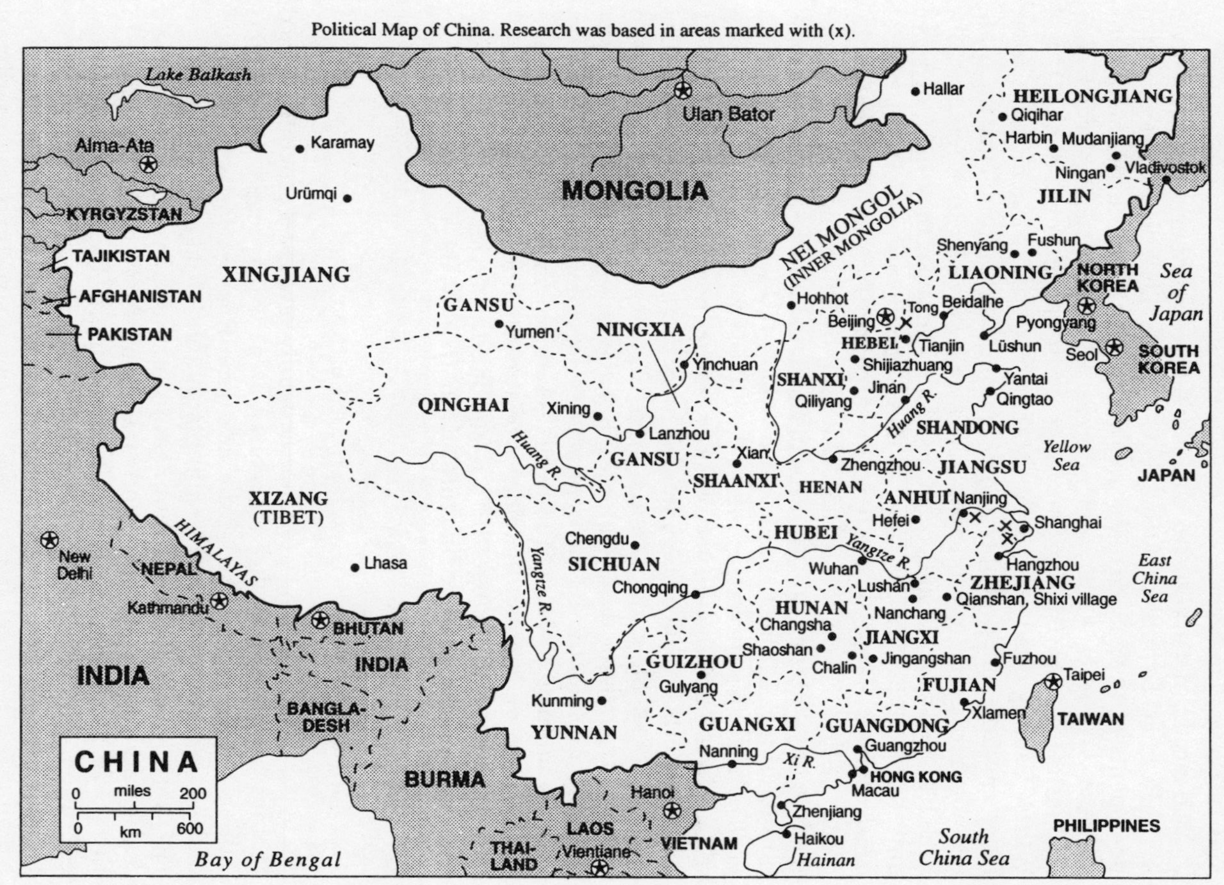

but their identity, interests, and social networks are tightly tied to communities, which are generally said to favour stability over change and maintaining male authority over the family (Worobec, 1991). Because of this, quests said to be the epitome of individualism, such as leaving one's family and filing for divorce, are easily stifled. Divorce in 'traditional society', Edward Shorter has argued, was 'virtually non-existent' (Shorter, 1975).

Marxist ideas about the emancipatory effect of factory labour made it even more reasonable to have expected little rural change after the promulgation of the new Marriage Law. Unlike workers who had already left supposedly tight-knit rural communities for more anonymous, free-wheeling cities and were now earning a wage, peasants were still tied to their land, community, and by 1950–2 – when the Marriage Law campaigns were enforced – 'preoccupied' with land reform (Johnson, 1983). Geography also made divorce even easier for urbanites. Because communication in cities was more developed, and the legal apparatus 'more accessible to women and young people', Johnson suggests, groups favouring change were 'more likely to learn about and be able to use the Marriage Law than women in more remote rural areas (Ibid). Johnson succinctly summarizes these arguments:

> one of the main points at which the complex of modernizing-urbanizing-industrializing factors is thought to induce family change is where such factors begin to disrupt traditional kin patterns and to deprive the family's patriarchal elder of the ability to provide and control the economic and social role opportunities of its members. At the same time, [in cities] new economically viable alternatives for individual family members become available outside the family. . .Urban areas, far more than rural areas, contained the seeds of the cultural family change which marriage reformers sought to encourage. . . [among] the relatively small numbers of women workers. . .and among students and intellectuals (Johnson, 1983).

Socio-legal theories of court use, as well as historical evidence, confidently associated willingness to take advantage of new laws with the modern features of urban living (Buxbaum, 1978). Where relations between parties to a case are close (as in a village), legal scholars such as Donald Black, William Felstiner and Pyong-choon Hahm have argued, chances are *less likely* that they will seek out state law. As Black (1989) puts it, 'the relational distance between the parties. . .is one of the most powerful predictors of legal behaviour yet discovered. *The closer people's relations are, the less law enters into their affairs*. A grievance between people such as relatives or old friends is likely to result in less law than the same grievance between casual acquaintances or strangers'. In such communities, Felstiner (1974) and Hahm (1969) have suggested, mediation rather than adjudication is the preferred method of dispute settlement, because mediators can be sensitive to the disputants' demands only if they are familiar with local norms and 'share the social and cultural experience of the disputants they serve'. The history of past family reform events in revolutionary states have confirmed Black's Theorem. As noted earlier, in France and the Soviet Union, those who took advantage of the liberalized divorce clauses were urbanites, intellectuals in particular, not peasants in remoter areas of the country.

2. PRELUDE TO THE MARRIAGE LAW: THE IMPACT OF LAND REFORM

New evidence suggests that land reform, rather than being an obstacle to social change, was a major factor leading to peasants' willingness to go to court to sue for divorce. Even on the Southwest frontier, where land was scarce and the state weak (in a way similar to the 'Wild West' in US historical lore), reports indicated an increase from 520 divorce cases in 1950 to 6,600 cases in 1953, a twelve-fold rise during the years land reform was implemented.[1] Others noted that the divorce request rate doubled and sometimes tripled before and after land reform.[2] What explains this unanticipated, dramatic rise?

Land reform was crucial to family change for several reasons. First, it resulted in the mass execution of landlords and village leaders under the previous regime, thereby 'loosening' social structure and inspiring feelings of fear of the state. At the same time, land reform generated legitimacy. This positive 'experience of the state' was transposed to how peasants felt presenting their problems to state authorities. Second, reforming land gave peasants a tangible resource, ie, land confiscated from pre-1949 élites, which they used to negotiate their way out of marriages and families. Finally, land reform, in combination with the Marriage Law, provided peasants with a less tangible resource *in language*. Even though most peasants were neither literate nor well-versed in Enlightenment thought, words such as 'emancipation', 'liberation', 'freedom' provided them with a powerful weapon to leave marriages, as well as engage in sexual practices roundly condemned by the regime.

A. *Land Reform as 'Experience of the State'*

Conducted between 1949 and 1952, land reform was almost invariably violent. Land reform 'work teams' and cadres from county and district governments were sent to villages to mobilize peasants in struggle sessions and 'people's courts in which landlords and 'local bullies' were often summarily executed. William Hinton's account of land reform in Long Bow Village in North China remains the classic account of peasants' 'experience of the state'. In one struggle session, told to Hinton by the Chairman of the Peasant Association,

> when the final struggle began Ching-ho [a landlord] was faced not only with those hundred accusations but with many more. Old women who had never

spoken in public before stood up to accuse him. Even Li Mao's wife – a woman so pitiable she hardly dared to look anyone in the face – shook her fist before his nose and cried out, 'Once I went to glean wheat on your land. But you cursed me and drove me away. Why did you curse and beat me? And why did you seize the wheat I had gleaned?' Altogether over 180 opinions were raised. Ching-ho had no answer to any of them. He stood there with his head bowed (Hinton, 1966).

Friedman, Selden, and Pickowicz, writing about the experience of Wugong village in central Hebei Province, (also in North China) also comment on the violent, and often unpredictable, nature of the land reform campaigns. Because Wugong lacked many individuals who could be clearly labelled as 'class enemies' – a requisite for political struggle – CCP leaders chose a man whose 'crime' was being the son of someone who was said to have bullied villagers, gambled, abducted widows, raped and slept with prostitutes. Held accountable for the crimes of his father, this man, named Li Dalin

was dragged before the crowd. Li Rui. . .was carried up on stage to denounce Li Dalin. People were silent as she poured out her grief. When she finished, the crowd engulfed the hapless Dalin and beat him for the sins of his father. . .Bound and dragged through the lanes, Dalin was smashed, twisted, and bullied, crippling his back. He was forced to confess to these alleged crimes, then jailed in the headquarters of the Poor People's Association (Friedman *et al*, 1991).

In these cases, land reform was manipulated to serve personal, and sometimes lineage oriented goals. Yet, even with these miscarriages of justice, Hinton's account also shows that the idea of 'emancipation' (*fanshen* in Chinese) became part of the peasant vocabulary, as those who owned no land or rented out land received land confiscated from the pre-1949 village élite.

Recently published gazetteers from rural China reveal not only the violence of land reform, but its equalizing nature as well. In Qingpu county in the Shanghai suburbs, prior to land reform, those later classified as 'poor' and 'middle' peasants represented 87.8 per cent of the local population, but owned only 27.5 per cent of the land; landlords who were 4.6 per cent of the population owned 51 per cent.[3] After land reform, the land-ratio balance was changed dramatically in favour of peasants who owned little to no land. The land confiscated from landlords was distributed to approximately 50,000 poor and hired peasants; every household received a parcel of land, and each individual in the peasant household received their own plot.[4]

In the Southwestern province of Yunnan, which was home to a panoply of ethnic minority groups, land reform served to exacerbate ethnic tensions and make the state and courts arbiters of community conflicts. According to official land reform policy, local officials were required to study differences in land holding patterns in different areas of the province (such as mountains and valley basins), as well as consider the ethnic composition of each area. Land reform should commence only after investigation, and if there were a sufficient number of poor peasant 'backbone' cadres. Implementing land reform, moreover, should not increase the hostility between ethnic groups or strike a crippling blow against élites; cadres should 'emphasize each group's common interests'.[5] Unfamiliar with the history of ethnic tensions in the area, policy-makers seemed to have been unaware that many communities had few common interests to begin with. Land reform intensified these disputes by throwing very tangible rewards and punishments up for peasants to grab.

The account of the rent reduction, return deposit, land reform movement in a county gazetteer gives few hints as to how land reform was implemented in practice, stating only the barebone facts: 1,046,907 *mu* (one mu is 1/6 of an acre) of 'feudal land' was confiscated and distributed to 957, 367 landless peasants. Farm animals, equipment, homes, and grain belonging to landlords were also confiscated. Local ruffians (*eba*), bandit leaders, and landlords were attacked and struggled. In the end, the gazetteer claims, land reform achieved a 'basic change' in rural land relations.[6]

Fortunately, recently published intra-party documents from the early 1950s and archival sources allow us to fill in some of these omissions. Land reform in Yunnan was greatly complicated by the area's political history, class structure, ethnic composition, and gender relations. To mobilize peasants to participate in struggle sessions against landlords, cadres first had to assure peasants that the area – one of the last bastions of KMT resistance – was militarily secure, and that later on landlords would not be able to take revenge. In Yunnan, this was a difficult task. Even by 1953, Nationalist soldiers and other predatory groups were still hiding in mountain lairs. For many, standing up and making a bold accusation against one's former landlord was simply too risky. Landlords and other pre-1949 power-holders took advantage of peasants' wariness during the rent-reduction campaign by spreading rumours that the Nationalists would soon return to Yunnan, and when they did, peasants who made accusations would be executed. As a result, many peasants were reluctant to air their grievances publicly.[7]

Previous patterns of ethnic conflict also affected land reform. In one village, for instance, Han and a minority group called the Yi lived together in the same community, but had a very brittle relationship. Between 1920s and 1950s, Yi controlled most of the village sand, renting it out to Han at very high interest rates. Tensions continued well into the early 1950s. When the Communists established health clinics in the village, Han and Yi would sit separately, and when two Yi assumed posts at the county seat, a dispossessed Han landlord organized 3,000 to struggle against the Yi. To retaliate, the Yi organized an attack against several Han. Conflicts prevalent earlier in the century over land use and water rights continued to divide the two communities.[8]

These complications in village land and ethnic relations were difficult to fit into the simplistic formulas and classifications of land reform. In the above village, the Yi had the most land, but were not well-represented in county and district government. Were they the exploitative landlord class or victims of Han ethnic chauvinism? If the latter was the case, they should be struggled, but if local cadres were to implement Beijing's conciliatory policies towards minority customs and traditions, Yi, as an oppressed minority, should not be subject to struggle. Official policy tried to steer a middle course: poor peasants of all ethnicities could unite to struggle against Han landlords, but minority peasants should take the lead in struggling against landlords of their own ethnicity.[9] Cadres, however, persisted in advocating struggle.[10] When peasants did not mobilize on their own accord, they used force.

Redistributing land did not remove the sources of ethnic tensions as originally hoped. Instead, in many cases the violent struggle over land widened pre-existent cleavages in rural society by terrorizing local élites, older people, and the village rich, much as it did in the suburbs of Shanghai and Beijing. When a minority group (the Miao) installed a rich peasant as chairman of their Peasant Associations, cadres threatened a violent purge. The chair, terrified, committed suicide. Other Miao then panicked, fleeing the village.[11] In an Yi community, a 40 year old Yi woman was murdered by hanging.[12] Elsewhere, there were complaints of cadres beating minority village headmen, secretly organizing unauthorized 'Poor Peasant Associations' to encourage peasants to withhold rent payments, and itching to struggle local leaders calling them 'village bullies'. Some headmen, fearing struggle, abrogated their traditional responsibilities in the village completely. At minimum, many showed passive resistance. Some headmen told peasants, 'if you have a problem, go to your government, not me!'[13]

Land reform did not resolve long-standing conflicts over land either. Cadre radicalism raised villagers' expectations of the possible, particularly among the poorest peasants. All over the province there were reports of poor landless peasants making 'new demands' and 'taking initiative', with a concomitant rise in the number of land disputes handled in district governments and courts.[14] But these demands were difficult to fulfil–particularly in the minority-dominated mountains where there was little arable land. One Yi complained to senior Han officials, 'In Luquan county the minorities are mostly in the high mountains. There are only a few landlords and not a lot of land. During land reform, the fruits of struggle were also few'. A Miao said, 'In our county the Miao are in the high mountains, and have suffered bitterness for several thousand years. Now, with land reform, we want to switch places with the landlords in the valley basin'.[15] Officials who rejected these proposals as too radical could still not escape peasants' new demands. With land reform, the more intractable intra-ethnic disputes over land became, the greater became the Government's role resolving them.

Patterns of gender relations were also shaped by land reform, albeit not in ways the state anticipated. When peasants heard that land would be distributed on the basis of the number of persons per household, many took in 'adopted daughters-in-law' (young girls who would grow up in the household and then marry their son), thinking that in this way they could increase their land allotment.[16] Mobilization of women was not easy. Initially, women were very reluctant to participate in land reform, fearing retribution from both landlords and their families. Some women, fearing their husbands were going to political meetings to have illicit sex, hindered their participation by accusing them of wandering eyes, or forcing infants into their arms to take along to meetings.[17] Women with children were reluctant to participate because they were afraid of exposure to the light of shooting stars: many believed that a child who was exposed to such light would be cursed and soon die.[18] Others did not understand land reform policy, fearing that land rights would be turned over to the head of the household, not to them individually.[19] In other cases, women who left their homes and their children to attend meetings, or to participate in mutual aid teams, found upon their return that their children had accidentally burned in fires, bitten by dogs, drowned in ponds, or were poisoned by eating plants.[20]

As cadres persisted and 'speak bitterness' sessions began, officials soon found women to be quite radical, speaking openly and bitterly about their past experiences, exposing past offences and raiding landlords' homes for their hidden stashes of cash (women, given their knowledge of the 'private sphere' were said to be especially good at this).[21] Yet, contrary to the Party's expectation that young women would criticize landlords for their 'class oppression', startled cadres found women spontaneously criticizing their husbands and in-laws as the main two sources of their oppression. Old women in Yunnan who spoke bitterness about how they were treated by landlords soon found themselves facing their daughter-in-laws, who, encouraged by the 'speak bitterness' example, began to 'speak bitterness' about their oppression. One report commented, 'as soon as middle-aged women accuse the landlord of crimes, young women, as well as some young men, begin accusing their parents and grandparents. We encounter this problem very frequently'. These women, the report complained, 'do not see class oppression, only their in-laws and husbands'.[22] Such accusations, coming as they did in the immediate wake of land reform, led some men to panic. In one county, rumours spread that the International Women's Day Holiday (8 March) would be used to 'kill, arrest, and monitor men'. Fearing persecution, men wandered around villages crying, and refused to participate in meetings.[23]

Accusations against in-laws and husbands often went hand in hand with demands for divorce. Reports show that the divorce request rate doubled and sometimes tripled before and after land reform.[24] Nevertheless, women seeking divorce (women were the overwhelming majority of plaintiffs) rarely received help from local Women's Federation representatives. These officials were extremely harried with work they considered more important, such as production, and saw 'women's work' as a burden. When women came to them with land and family-related problems, they would say, 'Leave me alone. Go to court'.[25]

B. *Blurred Boundaries I: State Reactions to the Marriage Law*

In many areas of China, the implementation of the Marriage Law occurred either immediately after or during land reform. In Yunnan and the rest of the Southwest, Provincial court directives instructed their subordinate administrative units that the Marriage Law campaign 'must be combined' with land reform, land reform investigation, agricultural production, legal reform, and clearing the court docket.[26] The merging of these campaigns meant that rural political officials often framed the Marriage Law in the political methods and discourses of land reform. This framing was evident in the very wording of the law. Fresh from their land reform experience, cadres mistakenly called the 'Marriage Law' (*hunyin fa*) campaign a 'Marriage *Reform*' (*hunyin gaige*) campaign, even in official reports.[27] Associated with this wording was a certain conception of time: if land relations could be speedily reformed through land reform, cadres reasoned, why not marriage relations and family structure as well? One instructor was thus forced to tell cadres, 'Implementing the Marriage Law can't be done in one or two days. It's not like land reform that has a deadline. Marriage reform is slow'.[28]

The linguistic overlap between land reform and the Marriage Law suggested that older men and women would serve as convenient targets for the campaign: the Marriage Law, after all, targeted the 'feudal' marriage system in the 'old society', and the older generation were the most obvious representatives of 'feudalism'. During cadre study sessions in one township near the Shanghai suburbs, for instance, village and township cadres, using a militaristic metaphor originating in their recent civil war experiences, suggested that, 'the only way to solve any problems is to line everyone up to see who are our friends and who is the enemy', otherwise, 'it's [the law] only propaganda and won't accomplish anything'. During the movement these officials looked forward to convening 'people's courts' to prosecute old women in the village.[29] As one state official argued, 'during land reform we reformed land; in the Marriage Law we should reform grandparents'.[30] In a village in the

Beijing suburbs, village officials proclaimed, 'in this movement grandfathers have turned into landlords!'[31] Sometimes the criterion for struggle was even broader. In Shanghai's suburban Yangsi district, officials hoped to struggle and then execute 'anyone who has marriage problems'.[32]

In the early phases of the Marriage Law campaign, cadres often acted upon their interpretation of the Marriage Law as a struggle against older people and those against whom cadres had other sorts of grievances. In one township, work team members, together with local cadres, convened an ad hoc people's court to handle marriage disputes. During one of the court hearings, a man named Yu Mingxian was accused by someone of abusing his daughter-in-law. Hearing this accusation, Yu, most likely fearful for his life after witnessing the execution of landlords and others deemed Communist enemies, fell to the ground and began knocking his head against it, screaming that he was falsely accused.[33] In a township in Qingpu county, a Women's Federation official 'regretfully' said, 'In our village there's an old woman who abused her daughter-in-law. We didn't investigate the situation but instead organized a struggle session against her, ordered her to confess, and submitted her to a beating. But after several days the conflict with her and her daughter-in-law has become worse. Now the situation is really serious'.[34]

When reports of struggle sessions and unauthorized convening of people's courts were received by district and county party committees, orders were sent down to remind village cadres that the Marriage Law campaign was not the same as previous campaigns conducted against various 'enemies of the people', such as landlords, bandits, and former government officials. They instructed local officials to use 'persuasion' and 'education' rather than violence to resolve marriage disputes, all while adhering to the basic spirit of the Marriage Law – 'protecting the rights of women'. Policy now emphasized 'tight control' over the movement in order to prevent peasants from panicking.[35] In meetings, higher level officials would tell gathered cadres, 'When you go back don't make irresponsible remarks and be disciplined'.[36] With the issuing of these orders, cadres breathed a sigh a relief. Their personal behaviour inside the family was often far from exemplary (many were guilty of spousal abuse, for instance), and many were just as afraid of being investigated during the campaign as others; they, too, witnessed the power of the party during land reform. As one remarked, 'If I hadn't learned this report I would have committed a big mistake when handling marriage problems'.[37] Fearing punishment if they were to handle a case incorrectly, cadres often adopted a 'hands off' approach towards problems they encountered for fear of 'deviating' from policy and being accused of being responsible for someone's death. At this point, higher authorities complained that control over the movement was 'too tight: cadres do not dare explain the policy and also do not dare handle any questions'.[38]

For plaintiffs, the road to court and district governments – institutions which were authorized to handle divorces – often began with these fears in local government institutions. Fearing being held responsible if they handled a dispute incorrectly, village officials sometimes perfunctorily dispatched women to districts and courts.[39] In other cases, however, plaintiffs had to make more than one effort to obtain the proper documentation. As one township cadre confessed: 'In the past women would come to the township government to divorce or break off their engagement but I would always put them off. Sometimes they would come five times before I introduced the case to the district'.[40] This led to cases of serious abuse,[41] as well as to a crackdown on local officials. In January 1952 in Tong County, the county party secretary instructed courts in no uncertain terms to accept divorce cases even without a letter of introduction from district, township, or village officials. Moreover, he instructed them to accept oral testimony as sufficient evidence 'because the people's cultural level has not yet been sufficiently raised' and they thus could not write. 'Written testimony', he wrote, 'is an unnecessary limitation, and should be immediately cancelled'.[42]

C. *Blurred Boundaries II: Social Transposition between Land Reform and the Marriage Law*

How did family elders react to these political and legal developments? Such a question is crucial to answer, since if ever there were barriers between an individual peasant and divorce, these barriers were likely to be erected within the family and local state institutions (Johnson, 1983). Below I flesh out how land and marriage reform together interacted both to weaken the authority of family elders and community while at the same time inspiring popular legitimacy.

When the Marriage Law campaigns reached their high tides in Winter 1951 and Spring 1953, elderly peasants had much to fear. As noted above, cadres who had only a vague impression about the articles of the law organized 'speak bitterness' sessions (in which peasants would speak about how difficult life was before the Communists arrival), land reform-style struggle sessions, mass meetings and 'people's courts, where violators of the Marriage Law were summarily sentenced. In Tong county near Beijing, for instance, the state executed an old woman for having driven her daughter-in-law to suicide. After witnessing this, some young women exclaimed, 'we've been liberated! In the past we were abused by in-laws and grandparents; now, we should get back at them a bit!'[43] Not surprisingly, events such as these sometimes resulted in panic among older men and women. In one community, for instance, seven older women witnessed CCP organizers mobilizing young women and heard them air their family grievances. Together, the seven secretly formed a pact according to which, 'if one has to confess they will all go on stage together; if one is sent to detention, they'll all go to prison together'.[44] In another village, in an 'old people's meeting' work team members found participants 'very worried' and 'stunned'. One man warned, 'These days are the eye of the hurricane!'; Old Lady Zhang went to the work team and asked, 'Does everyone with an arranged marriage have to divorce?'; and the father of another peasant lamented, 'Marriage Law, Marriage Law! Get rid of the old society! When you get rid of the old society, we old folks will also be gotten rid of too!'[45] In another county, older men said 'grandfathers have all turned into landlords!'[46]

Suicide statistics from Shanghai's rural suburbs from 1951–3 lend some support to these anecdotal data. Broken down by sex, women accounted for 69 per cent of suicide attempt cases (n = 128). Here, Chinese suicide is at variance with international patterns. In different time periods in the US (1970s), England (Victorian and Edwardian periods) and Singapore (1968–1971) men generally committed suicide more often than women, sometimes by a 4:1 ratio (Anderson, 1987; Kusher, 1989; Hassan, 1983). More consistent with international patterns, however, is the correlation of age and sex with suicide. Among female suicide attempts in China, the average age was twenty-five, but among men, the average age was almost ten years older – thirty-four years old. While there were only four women over forty years old (4.7 per cent of all women), among men, those over forty accounted for 22 per cent of cases.[47] Given the tensions generated by successive political campaigns, most of which targeted pre-1949 power holders who were almost invariably older men, it would not be unreasonable to suggest that some of these suicide cases resulted from cadre excesses and sudden, unsettling, power shifts within the rural family.

Fearing political trouble, struggle sessions, and imprisonment, elderly Chinese peasants frequently, but reluctantly, adopted a passive approach to their children's marital affairs at the very same time that young men and women asserted their new rights to 'freedom'. Similar to complaints lodged against village officials, scores of reports indicated that parents felt that they 'dare not intervene' with their children's affairs. In Tong county, an old woman complained, 'Now it's "marriage freedom" [so] if my son marries a "broken shoe" (a promiscuous woman), there's nothing I can do about it. What's the point of caring whether she gives him face and is pretty? Now the government is promoting this idea [of marriage freedom], so I have no choice [but to accept it]'.[48] The Tong county Marriage Law committee confirmed this account by noting that 'some old people now no longer dare try to control their children's marital affairs. As a result, some youths get married while still under age, and mistakenly emphasize that this is their right of "marriage freedom" '.[49]

In the Shanghai suburbs as in the North, the elderly showed similar reluctance to intervene in the family. In Yangjing district near Shanghai, one woman, Li Xiaomei, was widowed at twenty-eight and wanted to remarry someone else. Her in-laws refused, afraid she would take away their one grandson. 'Now', she said, 'I'm thirty-six and have suffered for eight years. But Chairman Mao is now the leader and widows can remarry. My in-laws do not dare intervene any longer. One time I went to a relative to stay for two days. When I came back, they made an ugly face. They objected to my leaving, but wouldn't say anything'.[50]

D. *Community, Legitimacy and Language*

As Li Xiaomei's testimony hints, there was more to the image of the Chinese Communist party than a prosecuting and executing organization. Although some peasants were reluctant to 'bring up old scores' in highly political forums for fear of getting family and friends into political trouble,[51] many young and old women took advantage of 'speak bitterness' meetings to speak openly of their difficulties prior to the arrival of the Communists. Despite differences in age and status, many women nonetheless shared common experiences: poverty, early death of parents, becoming an adopted daughter in a hostile home, widowhood, and abuse. One old woman, for instance, looked at a picture of a man beating a young woman and cried out 'That's me! That's me!' Another woman was forced to abort several children and almost died of internal bleeding. At the speak bitterness session she said, 'I was reincarnated too early, [ie before the Communists] that's why I suffered too much'.[52]

Linguistic residues of land reform, as well as a general confusion concerning the conceptual and social boundaries of 'revolution' and 'distribution', also help explain why peasants sometimes welcomed the new family law. In rural areas, peasants framed Marriage Law in terms similar to those of land reform. During the later campaign, the party distributed land and rice to the poor peasants; now, with marriage reform, the party would 'distribute', or 'assign' women to poor peasants. One older woman remarked, 'You young people have nothing to worry about now. The government will give you wives'.[53] In districts near Shanghai, old people said, 'after the Marriage Law we won't have to worry about our children's marriage any longer'.[54] But how would such 'distribution' take place, and who should be allocated to who? Here, land reform discourse of 'equalization' also shaped criteria for marriage. During a Marriage Law question and answer session in Fujian Province in Eastern China, a peasant asked, 'How should we get married?' The cadre replied, 'The good will marry the good and the bad will marry the bad'.[55] In Zhennan township near Shanghai, cadres said, 'the Marriage Law will even things up: the good will marry the good, the bad the bad, cripples will marry cripples and the blind will marry the blind'.[56]

Linguistic confusion over the name of the law itself sometimes combined with the transposition of land reform discourse. The official name of the law was the 'Marriage Law' (*hunyin fa*), the word 'marriage' – in both Chinese and English – serving as a noun. During the course of the campaign, however, muddle-headed village cadres often misinterpreted the noun *hunyin* (marriage) as the verb for 'to get married' (*jiehun*), and subsequently called the law 'a get married law' (*jiehun fa*)![57] Convinced that the CCP was legislating marriage, some acted accordingly. In Tong county, for example, cadres called the law a 'get married law' and convened a mass meeting to force villagers to marry. As a result, seventy-year-old widows panicked, afraid local officials would soon 'assign' them a man.[58] Further away in Fujian Province, a party secretary confessed to having written down all the names of a village's bachelors and widows, and upon meeting one in the street would take out his list and tell them to pick someone out.[59] In another area, when villagers saw Marriage Law work team members entering their village they would yell out, 'the wife allocation work team has arrived!' and village women asked, 'When we are assigned, is it OK if I not be assigned to a hunchback?'[60]

By casting the party and state as 'matchmaker', peasants transposed the state's role concerning land to its role governing the family. In the above example, the woman who asked not to be assigned to a hunchback did *not* question the legitimacy of 'allocation', but only *to whom* she would be assigned. It is also possible that this transposition reflected traditional notions of public and private. In Chinese political thought, the state was conceived of as a family. The state leader, like the father, was responsible for maintaining peace and harmony for everything under his realm. After decades of social and political turmoil, many peasants welcomed renewed state intervention in the reordering of society. Mao's call for 'harmony' within family relationships in the Marriage Law may have resonated with these traditional conception of the role of the state in society. When speaking bitterness, some older peasant women thus praised Chairman Mao for land reform, as well as being concerned about ordinary people's family matters. As one woman said, 'Chairman Mao is great. He cares about everything, even our family relationships'.[61]

In addition to language that was derivative of political campaigns such as land reform, peasants were also influenced by language that had at its very heart the notion of 'choice'. Article I of the Marriage Law called for 'free choice' marriages based on 'love', rather than marriages arranged by parents and relatives. Peasants – despite their low level of literacy – took the language of the law very seriously, much to the dismay of more literate comrades in the Women's Federation and other government agencies. The new political language of 'freedom', 'choice', and the associative term 'liberation', gave women a powerful way to justify their love, desire, and pursuit of upward mobility through marriage. A Women's Federation report from a county in the frontier province of Yunnan found that:

many [peasants] misunderstand the Marriage Law. They blindly emphasize that the Marriage Law 'liberated' them. This is the case for some women in particular, who have become very unconventional and dissolute in their sexual relations. They have several partners at once, and often switch among them, choosing whichever man appeals to them on that particular day. They also flirt with many men.[62]

Similar interpretations of the Marriage Law were common even among ethnic minorities, who often had an antagonistic relationship to the central state, and in areas where the state refrained from enforcing the new law.[63] Owing to the lack of communication infrastructure on the frontier, word of mouth and rumour frequently substituted for formal political communication. Even though many minority areas did not hear a formal announcement of the law, minority women, like their Han Chinese counterparts, were still influenced by its language. Young women, one report found,

understand 'freedom' as allowing them to behave rashly in sexual relations. If they are criticized by the court or by other peasants, they feel that their 'freedom' is being infringed upon. Others who genuinely seek freedom might encounter the resistance of their family or the Peasant Association. If they do, they are incensed that their freedom is being limited and resist. Some even commit suicide or abuse and kill their own children to get revenge.[64]

In one case, a women from the Yi minority argued that the Marriage Law's clause of marriage freedom, 'allowed her to get together with five men at a time and have sex without a formal marriage'.[65] In another county, a court investigation noted that some peasants, 'have a one-sided view of the meaning of marriage freedom: they think marriage freedom' means that there are no limitations at all, and that parents should have no say whatsoever as to who we should marry'.[66]

Women's perception that they now have 'absolute' marriage freedom frequently resulted in sort of a rural 'marriage-divorce roundabout': women would marry, argue with their husbands, and then either run off to a government office or back to their parent's home, and from there, demand divorce on the basis of their new freedoms. The court took a critical stance towards this behaviour by attributing such marriages to the fact that many women 'misunderstand marriage freedom' and then 'carelessly marry'.[67]

The court, for its part, frequently granted these divorces, sometimes in 100 per cent of cases.[68] Court officials, like many others in state bureaucracies, feared that *not* supporting women in marriage claims was a 'violation' of state policy. Moreover, being far away from villages and lacking telephones and other modern technological amenities, few had the resources to verify plaintiffs' claims. As a result, reports on judicial behaviour complained that courts granted divorces if plaintiffs were 'determined', even if their reasons for divorce were considered unjustified (such as divorcing a husband because of baldness, a bad leg, eyes, and so forth). One report lamented, 'If the couple are determined, the court grants a divorce. . .they don't do any investigation before deciding if a case should be dismissed'. The lack of a strong rural investigatory apparatus gave peasants wide berth to fabricate testimony to secure divorce. As one report found,

In courts, plaintiffs often exaggerate or lie about certain reasons for divorce. They say that their free marriages were actually arranged by a matchmaker; that their spouse is sleeping around when they're not; that because they're in different production teams they are never together when they are always together; that they're abused when they are treated well, or that they have no feelings towards one another only because they had one or two arguments or fights.[69]

But there were other reasons, in addition to determination, why courts and other government agencies found it relatively easy to grant divorces. Peasants all over China received land during land reform, which they were able to use as a bargaining chip in their divorce cases. For courts trying to figure out how to resolve knotty marriage disputes, land could easily be used to reach an amicable settlement. In court cases, courts would simply divide a parcel of land in half, assign one half to the husband and the other to his wife and in this way settle the case. For instance, in a village in the Shanghai suburbs, there were four divorce cases (4 per cent of total households), and all were said to have been 'straightforwardly and quickly resolved'. In another village, a woman surnamed Zhou wanted to divorce her husband because he suffered from schistosomiasis. During mediation she offered him some of her land in return for his agreement to a divorce. He was satisfied with this settlement, and did not ask for anything else. Within ten minutes, the case was resolved and the two returned home.[70] County court mediation cases confirm the important role land played in facilitating equitable divorce settlements.[71]

The above descriptions of how the Marriage Law was implemented are from the years 1950–3, a period when the Communists mounted two nation-wide campaigns to implement the law. Struggle sessions, terror, panic, and other such reactions were largely responsible for local officials and courts' willingness to grant divorces, even when they held in contempt the women who petitioned for divorce.[72] After 1953, however, there were no more campaigns to implement the law. For some scholars, this signalled the state's retreat from its previous commitments to improve the lives of women, especially in rural areas; the state, according to this view, returned to the patriarchal roots of peasant China. As Friedman, Selden and Pickowicz write, 'Though women were brought into the work force and the schools, and women's rights to property ownership and divorce were written into law, no practical challenge was mounted to the values, practices, and institutions and male supremacy' (Friedman *et al*, 1991). As a result, 'divorce was almost non-existent in rural areas' after the end of the second Marriage Law campaign in 1953 (Honig and Hershatter, 1988). Was this in fact the case? Once having awarded peasants new rights, was the state able to retract them just by not launching another campaign?

New evidence shows that rights, and particularly the language of those rights, once granted, are difficult to take away. Peasants continued to divorce after the end of Marriage Law campaigns in 1953, continued to invoke the language of freedom, and continued to use the Marriage Law to gain leverage against husbands and families. In 1962, for instance, there were as many divorces (for reasons that will be explained in Section 3, dealing with the impact of famine), as in 1953, even though the state did not make a special effort to enforce the law.[73]

An investigation of the marriage situation in Wuxiang county in Shanxi Province in North China reveals the extent to which divorce strengthened the hand of women in rural families, even after the earlier campaigns. Unlike areas of South China which were conquered by the Communists only in late 1949 and early 1950, Wuxiang county was classified by the Communists as an 'old liberated area', meaning that it was 'liberated' in 1946. The Marriage Law was implemented in the region in 1947, and mutual aid teams organized in 1948. As a result of these changes, the report found, almost as many women as men participated in agricultural labour, brides rode on trucks instead of traditional 'bridal sedans' to marriage ceremonies, domestic violence was reportedly less frequent, and 'free marriages' more common. Still, old attitudes persisted: women wanted to rely on men to provide the bulk of the household income, and men continued to believe that women worked best at home.[74]

The most dramatic changes were not in views towards the sexual division of labour or notions of gender 'equality' (a major concern of Western feminist theory) but rather, in how legal changes such as the right to divorce continued to change power relations in the family. Peasant women were tenacious in using the Marriage Law to raise their status in the family, as well as to acquire material possessions. Sometimes, even the threat to divorce was enough to cower men into submission. According to an investigation report, 'men are afraid their wives will divorce them, so they give into their every whim. They buy them whatever they want. If their wives do not feel like working, they don't dare say anything'. In one mutual aid team, investigators found, five out of nine households experienced instances in which 'the wife refused to work, but the husband did not dare say anything to her'.[75]

In some cases, the right to divorce led peasant women to demand radical changes in the domestic division of labour. Usually, men worked in the fields while their wives remained at home caring for the children and cooking for the family. After the work day was over, men came home and expected that a meal would be ready to eat. Some women found this arrangement unsatisfactory. Village women, the report complained, 'loaf around at home and don't cook' but instead demanded that their husbands 'cook and serve them', even after they returned home tired from work. Complaints were ineffective. When husbands 'tried to reason with them', the women reportedly 'threatened to divorce'. Such threats were carried out: marital relations in the township were called 'fluid', and so-called 'rash divorces' – usually initiated by women – were said to be 'relatively common'. In one village, 25 per cent of all married couples under the age of twenty-five were either divorced, or in the process of divorce within a sixteen-month period.[76]

Even better testimony to the lasting impact of the Marriage Law after 1953 were conflicts over adultery and divorce among wives of active soldiers. In China, most soldiers hail from rural areas, and often spend months away from their families or fiancées. For women who remained in villages when their husbands were in the army, life alone among men (single and married) was extremely difficult. Not only did they have to resist the temptation for sex for long periods, but they also had to maintain the family income without their husbands' labour. The state, for its part, tried to convince them to remain faithful to their husbands, but was slow to provide the means that made their families less dependent on the mobilized soldier.[77] In addition, the state tried to protect soldiers' marriages through Article 19 in the Marriage Law, which required that women seeking to divorce their soldier-husbands first obtain his written consent; without such consent, divorce would be extremely difficult. Women thus found themselves caught between a rock and hard place: the state was slow to provide them with subsidies but made it difficult for them to change partners. One result of this was that soldiers' wives became highly dependent on local officials, who did have access to scarce resources, such as good job assignments, welfare allowances, grain and meat supplies, and the like.

Reports from the 1950s and 1960s attest to the tensions and temptations of military families of soldiers in their villages. During 1955, a county court in Yunnan Province handled twelve cases of violations of the Marriage Law's Article 19. Of these cases, eight were reported to have been perpetrated by pre-1949 village élites and 'local hoodlums', but the other four by 'basic-level cadres, especially village cadres and militia heads who used their position as an excuse to conduct night-time investigations to have sex with soldier's wives'.[78] A report on military marriages in another southern province found that, in one administrative district, there were over 1,100 cases of 'destroying military marriages', including 330 that resulted in pregnancy. Among the perpetrators were twenty-three county and district cadres and 149 township and village cadres; others were ordinary peasants and militiamen.[79]

Despite the violation of Article 19, soldier's wives and their cadre lovers were frequently remorseless when confronted by central state investigators and other peasants. Emboldened by their relationship with officialdom, many peasants pressed for divorce. Some were quite bold when explaining their behaviour. One such woman argued, 'My husband's out making revolution. Because of this I'm at home and am so busy I have no spare time. How come this isn't considered working for the revolution? How come the party only looks after him? In a couple of years the spring of my youth will pass'.[80] To justify their violation of Article 19, some women invoked the Marriage Law's Article 1, which granted them 'marriage freedom' in cases of arranged marriages. In Yunnan Province, a soldier's wife named Wang Gongmei wrote a petition to the county court demanding 'marriage freedom' because 'her parents arranged the marriage'. This marriage was not formally registered; the couple married the traditional way, by having a feast. The court sent the case to the district government, which 'rashly' granted her a divorce without bothering to contact Wang's mobilized husband, as was required by law. The district reasoned: 'Having a feast doesn't mean you're married; to marry you have to go through formal procedures. The marriage was thus invalid in the first place'.[81]

The law's language of marriage 'freedom' contributed to a fluid family structure in other ways. Even after 1953, peasant women used the law to marry against their parents wishes, marry to gain material possessions and divorce several times should their first or second husband not satisfy them. For state officials who expected peasants to have good 'socialist' marriages (ie monogamous, based on mutual understanding, affection and common political stance towards the regime) peasants' willingness to marry and divorce in rapid succession was a major irritant. In the Beijing suburbs of North China, a 1954 party report on the marriage situation complained that a woman named Wang Xiuyun 'has slept with 4–5 men, and the village party secretary has already slept with her twice'. In other rural areas, the report continued, 'some women publicly live together with 3–4 men'. The result was said to be 'chaos' in marital relations and many out-of-wedlock marriages.[82] Farther south in Yunnan, an investigation found that, 'in rural areas, illicit sex, adultery, and seducing minors is very common. Sexual relations are particularly chaotic among youth'.[83] In Northern Jiangsu, the Provincial Women's Federation reported, 'many couples get married because they have already had sex and she is pregnant' only to divorce several days later. Children who were the product of such relationships were sometimes killed or abandoned by their parents.[84]

The rapid expansion of mutual aid teams into larger scale agricultural co-operatives and the concomitant politicization of the countryside during 1956–7 apparently had little effect on peasant marriage and sexual practices, or the language they used to justify their affairs. In 1956, the Women's Federation in Jiangsu Province complained that women 'flirt with three men at a time', 'trick men into giving them engagements gifts and then refuse to talk to them again', marry only for money without any regard for the age or political class of their spouse, and 'divorce after using up all their husbands' money', sometimes only a few days after marriage.[85] A 1958 article by a law student on the causes of divorce in the countryside pointed out that, in 'some backward rural areas', peasants 'misunderstand the meaning of free marriage', and marry on the basis of fleeting moments of passion. Two months later, they petition for divorce, telling the judge: "I didn't know that he was 10 years older than me", or "I didn't know that s/he was married and already had children" '. The student also found that some peasants were frequent visitors to court compounds. A woman named Huang Dezhen, he complained, was only nineteen, but had divorced and married four times between 1950–8. Huang divorced her last husband on account of an illness that caused baldness. The casual way Huang dealt with her relationships irritated the student: 'A 19-year-old could not even see if her husband had hair on his head or not!' he griped (Fei, 1958). Rural parents – their authority weakened by campaigns and changes in the economy, appear to have played little role in these affairs. As one mother commented, 'no one now dares to intervene in other people's freedom to divorce; it's just that it will be embarrassing if our children divorce *many times*'.[86]

3. THE IMPACT OF COLLECTIVIZATION

How did collectivization, the process through which individual and family plots were appropriated by the state and amalgamated into larger units, contribute to divorce during the mid-1950s? In the above pages I focused primarily on the impact of law on the family. In the section below I turn to the impact of other state policies, with particular reference to the economy and agriculture. Although treated in different sections, there was considerable overlap between the implementation of the law and other policies. As noted earlier, the Marriage Law, and its divorce clause in particular, continued to affect social structure even after the formal campaigns ended. How the right to divorce intersected with other state policies during the 1950s will be discussed below.

Two hypotheses come to mind when considering how collectivization might shape family relations. The first is suggested by the analysis of the previous section. If having land improved the chances of obtaining a divorce, then policies that took away that very land would likely make divorce that much more difficult. Another hypotheses, suggested by Marx and Engels, would be that divorce might actually become *easier*, because parental authority over property would be further weakened. New evidence gives partial support to both: divorce continued largely for reasons suggested by Marx and Engels, but at a lower rate than during the early 1950s. (See Appendix I for the divorce trend between 1951–61).

How did collectivization begin? In July 1955, Mao Zedong, impatient with the pace of rural socialist transformation after the end of land reform and worried about a 'rightist' resurgence in the countryside, insisted that more villages form what were then called 'agricultural producers co-operatives', or 'APC's', even though there was widespread reluctance to form larger units (Schurmann, 1968; Friedman *et al.*, 1991). Hard-working peasants were reluctant to join co-ops with lazy and/or weaker peasants, fearing the latter would not contribute their fair share. Adding to these worries was the regime's insistence that collective units be as 'politically pure' as possible. Both cadres and ordinary peasants preferred to work with rich peasants and landlords rather than poor peasants, believing that poor peasants were poor because they were either weak, lazy, or scoundrels, even if they were the politically privileged class.[87] Gender issues complicated matters further: the government encouraged women to participate in agricultural labour, but was slow to organize child care facilities. In some instances, couples divorced because one spouse wanted to join the co-op but their spouse refused, or because one spouse did not work hard once in.[88] Men did not make the conflict between household chores and agricultural labour any easier for women. If women wanted 'equality' with men, they reasoned, why shouldn't they haul the same loads and work the same number of hours?[89]

Family relations during these years were further strained by other polices associated with rural collectivization. The mid-1950s witnessed massive public work projects to repair roads, dikes, and canals. Young men were mobilized on a massive scale to complete these projects, leaving behind families to tend to their land. For women unaccustomed to hard physical labour, such work was not easy. According to a 1956 report by the Jiangsu Province Women's Federation,

> when male peasants leave to repair dikes, women are left by themselves to look after 6–7 *mu* of land. As a result, work is very intense. They have no time to look after the household, no time to wash clothes, prepare food etc. . .[90]

Because men were either unavailable or unwilling to assist with household chores, the extra burden of caring for children during this mass mobilization fell upon women and older peasants who could not work outside of the home. Forced to take care of the household and agricultural work without their husbands' assistance, peasant women during these years had little time for anything except work.

For some family elders, caring for many children in their old age was a burden deemed 'too heavy to carry'. According to one report, the elderly had 'three fears': of 'being bothered', children getting sick, or else fighting with each other.[91] Living either separately from their children, or saddled with extra responsibilities at home, many were left dependent on the goodwill of their children to provide for them.

State efforts to provide the elderly with minimal welfare provisions sometimes made their situation even worse. Some sons, daughters, and daughter-in-laws believed that, with collectivization, the state, rather than the family, would provide for all of their parents' needs. This allowed them to feel less guilty about neglecting them. In other cases, however, neglect was more calculated. A report on civil disputes in Hebei province, for instance, found that collectivization reduced the number of land disputes, but increased the number of cases involving children neglecting their parents. Children either believed that the state welfare programme obviated the need for their care, or calculated that there would be few costs in neglecting parents because 'they can't inherit the land anyway' (Li and Tian, 1957).

By the late 1950s, there were signs that neglect of elders had become increasingly common. Usually, elderly peasants suffered at the hand of their own families. Reports found that daughters-in-law used divorce, control over the private sphere of the household, mobility, and revolutionary political language to abandon their in-laws, abuse them, or drive them to suicide. In 1958, for example, a police investigation in Yunnan reported an alarming rise in the number criminal cases involving the abuse, poisoning, murder, and abandonment of parents 'since the high tide of collectivization'. Involving both cadres and ordinary peasants, the report concluded that

> most abuse cases are the result of children hating that their parents are old and cannot work. Usually the son and daughter-in-law collaborate. In other cases, the daughter-in-law initiates the beating and the son joins in, fearing that if he goes against her, she will petition for divorce. For instance, the wife of one Xiao Yuxian hates that her mother-in-law is poor and dependent on her work. Because of this, Yuxian's wife refuses to feed her. She threatens her husband and mother-in-law by saying that she will return to her parents home and divorce in order to get what she wants. . .[In another example], the wife of Xiao Zuxian doesn't allow her husband to talk with his mother. If he does, she refuses to give him anything to eat.[92]

State intervention did little to alleviate the plight of ageing parents. Daughters-in-law could wield political language like a cudgel, intimidating officials, husbands, and in-laws alike. For instance, a woman named Hu Longren despised her mother-in-law and refused to feed her. At the dinner table, Hu's mother-in-law pleaded for some food. Hu refused, and told her that, 'Even if this food was shit, I still wouldn't give it to you!' Close to starvation, Hu's mother-in-law brought the matter to the attention of the township government. Officials tried to mediate the cases several times, but without success. During the meeting, Hu confounded the officials by yelling and accusing them of 'supporting the old and oppressing the young'. Nor were in-laws spared the wrath of political language. A woman named Yang Yuzhen berated her mother-in-law, 'You're just like a landlord! All you do is eat and exploit people! Why don't you work!?' Other women called the collective's welfare programme 'exploitation', because it contradicted the socialist principles of 'to each according to his work', and 'you eat what you can work'.[93]

In addition to political language, mobility was another resource that gave young women leverage over elderly parents and in-laws. Hobbled by old age, or perhaps bound feet, there was little parents could physically do to prevent daughters, daughters-in-law, and sometimes sons, from running away from the village. In the Beijing suburbs, for instance, a 1954 report noted several cases of family conflicts caused by 'young men and women ignoring parents who threaten to cut them off and then leaving the village to go get married'[94] Running away was instigated not only by desire to elope. In Luquan county, Yunnan, a woman named Li Jiaying (nineteen years old) married one Bai Zhongshan (twenty-three). They met in March 1956 and married fifteen days later. Two weeks after the marriage, Li argued with her mother-in-law and then 'ran back to her parents' home and petitioned for divorce. Other women ran off because they were unaccustomed to the difficult physical effort demanded in agricultural work. Having been raised to sew, cook and the like, some found more physical labour intolerable. To escape a life of such work, some opted to leave their spouse and his family. In Yunnan, a report criticized a woman named Li Xiuying for divorcing despite a happy marriage. Li, the report complained 'frequently ran away' because she 'hated to work'.[95]

Elderly Chinese peasants were terribly upset over this turn in their fate. Some tried to bring their children to township government legal departments, hoping that the state would intervene on their behalf. Township officials, busy with organizing communes and production schedules, rarely assisted. Others took solace in the company of other women. In one village, several abused old women got together and 'told each other that they shouldn't be happy if they have a son, or unhappy if they don't. If they don't have children and are old, they can still go to the commune and get welfare'. Other elderly found relief in death. Shocked at how 'their world had changed', some committed suicide, believing that the next world would surely be better than the present one.[96]

The state's explanation of children's unfilial behaviour toward their parents was remarkable in its admission of past and present political error. During the Marriage Law campaigns, party officials confessed, 'we attacked the feudalism of old people, abuse, etc, without any mention of the need to respect and support the elderly. As a result, bourgeois selfishness took root'. Also responsible were post-collectivization property arrangements and fear of losing a wife and daughter in a divorce. This led sons to collaborate with their wives against their parents. Neighbours and relatives, even as they witnessed elderly starving to death and committing suicide, did not intervene because they 'have gotten used to the young no longer caring for the old'.[97]

Further contributing to rural family instability were changing land relations, which often made severing family and marital relationship a simple matter. After having their land seized, peasants now viewed the state as the 'guardian' of unwanted family members as well. This perception gave women and men free reign to act on their own worst instincts. The Jiangsu Province Women's Federation reported that, since collectivization, there had been many instances of parents abandoning their children, and Communist party officials abandoning their wives. When a child is born, the report noted, 'they place it on the steps of government offices in the hope that the government will raise it. After giving up the child, the woman leaves and tries to get a job as a nursemaid'.[98] Viewing the co-operative as guarantor of the needy also extended to children born out of wedlock, even when fathers were classified by the regime as 'counter-revolutionaries'. In the countryside around the city of Nanjing, the Jiangsu Women's Federation reported that

> Not a few 15–16 year-olds become pregnant out of wedlock. There are also family members of counter-revolutionaries whose husbands are in labour reform who are now pregnant. There are even cases of incest. In all these cases, the women give birth and insist that the government help them take care of the children. If the government doesn't agree, they curse, yell, and scream at the cadres.[99]

Separating from undesirable wives was also less complicated now that land was collectivized. In Chuansha county near Shanghai and in Yunnan, male cadres who 'looked down upon their peasant wives' because they were 'crude' or illiterate frequently petitioned for divorce, or else deliberately provoked conflicts to force their spouses to initiate proceedings. After divorce, they ignored their responsibility towards their families, believing that the collective would now take care of them.[100]

Conflicts over property settlements in divorce cases were also eased by collectivization. A 1957 court report from Yunnan found that among divorcing peasants 'there are very few disputes over post-marital property'. Such disputes arose in only two out of the fifty-five divorce cases the court handled. The court attributed this to the fact that, between 1953–7, women had been participating in production, paid according to their work, and were therefore no longer dependent on their husbands or families. Property settlements remained problematic only in relationships involving a sick spouse, or in households in which many family members were unable to work.[101]

What complicated divorce settlements was not male opposition to divorce, as has been suggested by some scholars (Johnson, 1983; Stacey, 1983). Collectivization, after all, eased the burden on some men by providing their wives with alimony payments and the like. Moreover, men might be just as frustrated with their wives (for gambling and adultery in particular) as wives were with their husbands.[102]More problematic from the state's perspective was women's mobility between their parents and husbands' homes.[103]In Yunnan Province, for instance, the county court handled a case involving a woman named Shao Hongying, who 'returned to her parent's home' after one month of marriage. During the courtship and month of marriage, Shao on several occasions 'ran back and forth' between her husband's home and her own. The court persuaded her not to divorce, but Shao demanded that the court solve her 'grain allocation problem'. The court found that in cases such as Shao's, a common problem arose when work points and grain were distributed in two different locations (work points were distributed at husbands' homes). Should women divorce and their families not receive an extra grain ration, families might have difficulty feeding them. To resolve this problem, the court ordered that when women returned to their parent's homes after divorce, their families should receive an extra grain allotment.[104]

Collectivization was important also at the level of the language court officials used to decide cases. Many judges applied socialist principles of 'equality' to settle post-divorce disputes over land and property, sometimes at the expense of fairness. Two investigation reports by an intermediate court in Yunnan complained that lower courts were 'excessively egalitarian' in settling property disputes because they ignored differences in parties' individual circumstances. Instead, they divided property and land perfectly equally between husband and wife, with no regard for how much each party brought to the marriage. In other cases, courts sided with women by granting them the lion's share of property and land, prompting complaints that such decisions were unenforceable at the village level (Li and Tian, 1957).

In comparative perspective, the relative ease with which divorce cases were settled after collectivization is not all that surprising. In other collectivized economies, divorce is also quite common, and facilitated by the lack of concern over alimony payments, property, and land settlements. In the Israeli kibbutz, for instance, divorce does not affect one's status, occupation, income, or future prospects because the kibbutz assumes responsibility for both partners' livelihood. There are, of course, disincentives to divorce. In such a small community, encounters with estranged spouses are unavoidable. Nonetheless, the divorce rate on the kibbutz (as of 1982–3) is only slightly lower than major metropolitan areas, but still higher than the national average (Kaffman, Shoham, Palgi, and Rosner, 1986).

A. *Famine and the Family: The Impact of the Great Leap Forward*

Although sharing features of common property and land, the Israeli kibbutz differed from the collective in China in important ways, most significantly in organization and the amount of resources available to individual members and families. On the kibbutz, members join voluntarily, and can now enjoy a level of prosperity equivalent to some western European countries. In China, by contrast, during the high tide of collectivization peasants were often coerced into communes, and remained destitute after they entered (Friedman *et al*, 1991). As China hurtled towards the Great Leap Forward in 1958, peasants were mobilized to join massive public work projects, often working around the clock to the point of complete exhaustion. Peasants were ordered to build backyard furnaces and smelt their cooking utensils in sufficient quantity to enable China to catch up to England's steel production within sixteen years. When men were away, women, who were generally less experienced than men in fieldwork, were forced to take up the slack in the fields. As a result, many villages failed to bring in the fall harvest(MacFarquhar and Fairbank, 1987).

By 1959 and 1960, the results of the Great Leap's utopianism were slowly becoming apparent. Many areas of China, but particularly in the arid North, suffered famine on a massive scale. In poor Anhui Province in central China, peasants excavated corpses for food and scraped bark from trees. Others abandoned communes in search for food in more hospitable locales; in Hebei Province, there were reports that migrants fled to the Northeast, and there established new communities. Rural political administration in the province, already in chaos after the massive amalgamation of co-operatives into full-scale communes, could do little to prevent massive migration, food riots, and raids of granaries (Friedman *et al*, 1991). The food supplies that were available were shipped to urban areas, where inhabitants rarely suffered from starvation throughout the Leap years, although they did live at subsistence levels.

The post-Leap famine, like famines elsewhere (Hane, 1981; Fitzpatrick, 1994), strained family relations to a breaking point. Competition for scare resources pitted the young against the old, and spouses against each other. Liu Shaoqi, the Chinese Head of State during those years, privately admitted that, during the Great Leap, 'people starved and families were torn apart' (Friedman *et al*, 1991). It was these family tensions, and the migratory survival strategies they produced, that contributed heavily to the rash of divorces in 1961–2. Evidence suggests that women usually initiated divorce. In Kunshan county near Shanghai, there were 104 registered divorces in 1958, 178 in 1959, and 465 during the peak of the famine in 1961. Compilers of the county gazetteer attributed divorce to the fact that some women, as in earlier periods, 'blindly ran away' because of economic hardship.[105] In Lufeng county in Yunnan, too, women were also the majority of plaintiffs, but men also initiated many proceedings.[106] Family elders, who had already lost a great deal of influence during the Marriage Law and collectivization, were often abandoned and left to die of starvation. Few were in a position to prevent women and men from 'blindly running away'.

Contributing heavily to these divorces was the organizational and social chaos resulting from the Great Leap, which removed some obstacles on the road to divorce. Commune officials who implemented the radical policies and were then left scrambling to pick up the pieces could do little to prevent divorce. It is also possible that officials might actually *encourage* villagers to leave in order to have fewer mouths to feed.[107] Commune mediation committees were also in disarray, as hungry officials tended to their families' needs. As state layers built up between peasants and courts during 1954–8 peeled away, there remained few administrative structures between villages and the courts.

Even as the extent of the disaster of the Great Leap Forward became clear, the top CCP leadership was slow to respond with emergency measures. Mao Zedong was reluctant to admit that his economic policies were misguided, and there were few brave enough to risk his wrath by explicitly criticizing him. In 1959–60, factional struggles and purges in the leadership made it difficult to devise, let alone implement a coherent new economic policy. Only in 1961, after a series of investigations into the economic situation of the countryside and Mao's grudging withdrawal from the 'front line' of politics, were a series of economic measures approved to ameliorate the famine and raise peasant production and living standards. Known as the '60 Articles', the new economic policy reduced the amount of cereals peasants were required to deliver to granaries and increased welfare expenditures to rural areas. In mid-1961, peasant households were allowed to restore cultivation of private plots; other small-scale peasant enterprises, such as weaving, raising pigs, chickens, ducks and the like, were also sanctioned. Products from these household enterprises could then be sold in reopened rural markets. Throughout the early 1960s, however, these policies only partially improved peasant income; many areas of China remained dirt poor, even if they were better off than during the Great Leap (MacFarquhar and Fairbank, 1987; Union Research Institute, 1971).

How did the aftermath of the Leap and the economic policies of the '60 Articles' shape family relations? Evidence shows that economic policies that rewarded work and opened markets also gave material incentives to families to commit rather severe violations of the Marriage

Law's ban on arranged marriages, bigamy and 'commercial marriages'. According to party and government reports after the Great Leap, the years 1961–6 witnessed a widespread revival of 'feudalistic' marriage practices, such as arranged and coerced marriages, bride prices, exchanging gifts, wedding feasts, and underage marriages.[108] At the same time as these 'feudal' marriage practices spread, however, the number of divorce cases was as high in 1963 as 1953 in areas as ecologically and economically different as the Shanghai suburbs and Yunnan. How can we explain these seemingly paradoxical outcomes?

The post-Leap economic policy allowing the expansion and revival of household plots, rural markets, and the work point system gave peasants incentives to circumvent the Marriage Law and avoid political class-based relationships. Post-Leap marriages, many of which were formed exclusively on the basis of material considerations, often proved highly fragile and contributed to the higher divorce rate. According to many reports, state officials often 'took the lead' violating the law. Since the '60 Articles' policy gave incentives to households to increase sideline production, cadres augmented their household labour force by buying wives and adopting or purchasing young girls for their boys to marry when their came of age, or a *tongyangxi* relationship. In one Yunnan commune, for instance, a production team leader and CCP member cited purely economic reasons to justify his adoption of a thirteen-year-old girl for his young son:

> Since the promulgation of the 60 Articles, everything is calculated on the basis of work points. If I bring in a young girl, even though she won't add to the labour force in the short term, I can still increase my income by having her raise pigs and ducks and do household work. When she's at home, more adults can work in the fields. This way we can collect more work points.[109]

In addition to the desire to increase work points, cadres also adopted daughters-in-law because many perceived that, after the Great Leap, the Communist Party was abandoning communes in favour of a land tenure system based entirely on household plots. In another commune, another production team leader gambled that the party would liberalize land policy even further and adopted a young girl:

> In 1961, the party abandoned the policy of collective dining halls. In 1962, the party restored some land and farm animals to households. In 1963, it's possible that all land will be returned to households. I have a son, so the earlier I bring in a young daughter-in-law, the better. That way there will be more people in the household. When land is distributed back to the household [on the basis on the number of people per household] we can then get an extra piece of land.[110]

Witnessing party officials bringing in *tongyangxi*, peasants who were able to afford the expense followed suit. In one district in Yunnan, sixty households were reported to have brought *tongyangxi* into their families.

Of these, five were families of commune cadres, ten were production team leaders, and thirteen were party members; the rest were 'ordinary' peasants. With political leaders violating the law, few peasants feared retribution. When outside work teams criticized peasants for this practice during the Socialist Education campaign, some peasants responded, 'The cadres lead and the masses follow'.[111]

Behind the cadres' confidence that they would not be prosecuted for violating the Marriage Law was a acute awareness of their own importance in the community. With their connections to higher level of government, local officials were perfectly placed to secure scarce resources (such as food) for themselves, family and friends. This enhanced power was not lost upon parents and relatives of young village women. Success in selling a daughter into a cadre family would virtually guarantee the family's survival in the post-famine years; the more money one could get for a daughter, the better off parents would be, even if the daughter eventually divorced. Many parents were thus anxious to arrange marriages for their young daughters, and demanded a high price for their 'hand'.[112] Because women were willing to divorce, sometimes after only a few days, a high bride price might give them added incentive to stay in place.[113]

Parents were not the only ones demanding a high price for daughters. Young women were not mere pawns or putty in their parents' hand; they had both agency and ambition, and demanded a lot for themselves. In the post-Leap period as in previous years, prior to consenting to a proposed marriage young peasant women presented suitors with a shopping list of demands. Reports from the 1960s criticized women for making excessive demands for such lists, which included large apartments, cash, watches, alarm clocks, wool blankets, clothes, leather shoes and purses, a formal photograph, a meal with candy and pork, in addition to a night on the town to see opera performances. In relatively well-off Songjiang county, men had to sew three to four woollen pants and build an extra room for their new bride as a condition for marriage. Without the extra room, women refused even to consider the match. Similar demands were made in poorer areas farther away from cities. In Wujiang county in Jiangsu Province, women reportedly demanded eight '*zi*'s': a gold earring (huan *zi*), a gold ring (jin *zi*); a silk quilt cover (chou bei mian *zi*), a multi-coloured quilt (hun tan *zi*), to ride in a bridal sedan (zuo qiao *zi*), have a pig killed (sha zhu *zi*) and have a two-room apartment (liang jian fang *zi*), in addition to some cash (qian *zi*). According to the report, 'women will agree to marry only after receiving all of this'. As during the early 1950s, young women refused to marry peasants unless there was absolutely no other alternative.[114] In demanding a high price for their agreement to marry, some women seemed to have been very aware of their clout in the marriage market. Using their right to divorce, women gravitated towards those men with more means, such as cadres and other wealthier peasants. Women often pressed their advantage to the hilt. As reports from the Shanghai suburbs remarked, 'It's easy for young women to find a partner. Because of this, they have very high demands: a big apartment, furniture, gifts, strong workers, and good looks'. A marriage's failure was not cause for concern. With many available men, women could easily remarry, even if they had already lost their virginity. As one woman explained, 'Even if I divorce I'll always be able to find a husband. All I have to do is not make so many demands'.[115]

The multiple marriages of a peasant woman named Chen Qiaolin is a case in point. Prior to her marriage, Qiaolin 'flirted and talked about marriage with three different men', until finally agreeing to marry a worker at the railroad bureau. Married in August 1961, Qiaolin soon spent the 600 *yuan* the railroad worker gave her as a gift for marriage. After her marriage, she flirted with three other men: Chen Zhongyuan, a state purchasing agent, and two truck drivers, Liu Zhong, and Wang Shaochang. Qiaolin decided that purchasing agent Chen could offer her the best of two worlds – access to food supplies and extensive travel opportunities within the county. Qiaolin then had sex with Chen, and sued to divorce her railroad worker husband. After the railman heard of these developments, he chased after Qiaolin, but when he grabbed her, Qiaolin turned and socked him on the nose, breaking it. Furious, the railman complained to the court that, 'If you have money you can stay married; if you don't, you can forget about your wife'.[116]

Qiaolin's case was not an isolated incident.[117] Investigations of female party officials often complained that cadres, who were supposed to serve as examples to the rest of the population, also used divorce as a method to advance themselves materially. In Yunnan, the county party committee complained that, 'some female cadres, because they want money, material possessions, and to have a good time, have cheated men by accepting gifts from three men at a time and promising to marry each of them'. In Jinshan and Qingpu counties near Shanghai, women reportedly 'returned to their parents' homes after they spent all their husband's money, and the husband and his family were no longer able to afford them'.[118] In one county, the director of the Women's Federation was criticized for using 250 *yuan* of pilfered money to divorce her husband, supposedly because he had tuberculosis, and remarrying soon afterwards.[119]

Male officials, who were also in a position to offer access to scarce resources, were quick to take advantage of the post-Leap economic difficulties to improve their family situation and enhance their personal status. Whereas female cadres tended to use marriage and divorce to increase their material resources, men preferred instead to have affairs and multiple marriages, probably to increase their 'face' among other cadres; in China, having more than one wife had traditionally been a way to demonstrate wealth and status. In 1963 in a commune in Yunnan, four out of six party members at the commune level had more than one wife, and adultery and 'chaotic sexual relations' were said to be 'common'. In one district in the commune, the deputy party secretary 'used his position and ability to allocate jobs' in order to commit adultery with eight women. Another cadre at a key gastronomic post–Ji Guofu of the food storage facility–pilfered 2000 *yuan* of goods, a good deal of pork to 'have illicit sex with over 20 women, including several wives of soldiers'.[120] In other cases, cadres abducted other peasants' wives, had menage-à-trois, and exchanged wives amongst themselves. Few of these relationships were kept secret. In one commune, for instance, the production team leader 'openly committed bigamy' with a beautiful nineteen- year-old, inviting enough guests to their illegal wedding to fill fifteen tables. Peasants who witnessed these officials complained, 'These days it's impossible to control the cadres'.[121]

Cadres were not the only peasants able to use the new economic policies to attract *tongyangxi*, lovers, and wives. In Yunnan, some peasants picked up their meagre belongings and moved to wherever they could collect more work points in return for their labour. With their notebook of workpoints, all they needed to do was record the number of points they had earned (with an official seal) and then proceed to a public granary to collect their rations. Along the way, some collected wives, many of whom were eager to find a hard-working and enterprising man. One peasant was reported to have three wives, all living in different villages. Other peasants from the village complained that this man 'was hardly ever at home working. . .He lives a couple of days in one place, fools around, and goes somewhere else for several days'. Other peasants committed 'bigamy' by taking advantage of the chaos in marriage registration bureaux. Anxious to increase their welfare allotment, peasants registered to marry several times, each time at a different locale. Having secured these 'marriages', they would then file for benefits at different agencies. Lacking telephones and other communications equipment, neither grain nor marriage bureaux were able to verify their true marriage situation. From 1958 to 1963, reports indicated a three-fold increase in the number of rural bigamy cases. Many of these cases were attributed to the registration bureaux' 'casually giving out documentation' and not investigating peasants' family situation.[122]

Unlike cadres who could use their access to scarce resources to attract lover and wives, poorer families unable to muster such resources had no choice but to rely on their own efforts. In a county near Shanghai, there were reports that poor fathers did not allow their sons to be drafted into the military in order to help build an extra room for a new daughter-in-law. If the son were to leave home to join the PLA, the productive capacity of the household would be drastically reduced. Lacking the income earned from his work, the family would not be able to add the room, and the son would forever remain a bachelor.[123]

Desperate peasants might also resort to illegal means to raise funds. In Yunnan, a Women's Federation report noted that 'very many' poor peasants robbed, gambled, sold drugs, and engaged in black market trade in order to raise funds to marry or purchase *tongyangxi*. On occasion, these efforts paid off. In one commune, a peasant named He Shicai won 340 *yuan* during three successive nights of gambling. He used 280 *yuan* of his profits to purchase a ten-year-old girl for his nine year-old son.[124] Peasants who lacked He Shicai's luck at the gambling table remained in difficult straits, however, and were said to express strong support for the CCP's Marriage Law.[125] Even though the law made it easier to divorce, the law also banned the 'commercial marriages' that placed them at a clear disadvantage. Only with state intervention, some argued, could poor men afford wives.

Peasants who despaired because they were unable to purchase wives might have taken heart at the fact that cadres and peasants who managed to purchase *tongyangxi* often found themselves without their new wife soon after the completion of the transaction. Short of locking *tongyangxi* or brides in rooms or killing them, there was little husbands' families could do to prevent new daughter-in-laws from running away, usually back to their natal homes. In a county in Yunnan, for example, nine out of twenty-five women who were married in 1962 (most were between sixteen and seventeen years old and had arranged marriages) 'had already returned to their parents' homes and broken off relations', and five were reportedly about to follow suit.[126] Although most of these cases seem to have ended with the woman running back to her parent's home, it is also likely that some ended up in court, where a more formal resolution to a marriage could be had.

4. CONCLUSION

Evidence presented in this essay challenges several important characterizations of Chinese rural life in the secondary literature. During the mid-1950s and 1960s, peasants did not, as other scholars have suggested, remain 'tied to the land' or stuck within a rural social structure that allowed no mobility or possibility to extract oneself from unsatisfactory relationships. Throughout the period under discussion, the Marriage Law, in combination with other state economic policies, had profound influence both on social family structure and power relations within the family; there was a clear power shift away from family elders to members of the younger generation, women in particular. Taking advantage of their new rights in the Marriage Law, many women sought out relationships outside of what the state considered permissible boundaries. These included relationships based solely on material considerations, or those initiated and consummated for pleasure for pleasure's sake. What is perhaps most ironic about China's family law during the 1950s and 1960s was that the law condemned the 'feudal' marriage system without considering any *benefits* of the system of arranged marriages. Arranged marriages, even though they resulted in many unhappy relationships, had the benefit of making sure that poor men had a reasonable chance of securing a spouse. The system compromised individual happiness for a modicum of stability. But when the Marriage Law opened up the marriage market, women took advantage of their new opportunities to pursue a greater degree of upward mobility than was possible under the old system. This placed poorer men in an extremely precarious position in the new marriage market. The result was a deterioration in social stability and security, as poor men engaged in high risk, illegal ventures to get their hands on the necessary funds to marry. This does not suggest that arranged marriages are 'better', but only that they served a purpose. 'Loosening' social structure via the Marriage Law benefited many, but also came at a price.

Even though the Marriage Law, collectivization, and the Great Leap Forward reverberated strongly within the family, it would be difficult to argue that all the changes described above were the *intended* result of these policies. In the case of the Marriage Law, the law's lingering linguistic residue lasted far longer than the campaigns to enforce the law. In the case of collectivization and the '60 Articles' policy, there was no way the state could have predicated the rise in abuse against family elders, illegitimacy, abandonment of spouses, marriage-related corruption and bigamy. State policy, whether legal or economic, clearly was important, although in many cases the impact on the family was only incidental, the unintended by-product the laws and policies.

Let us now return to the comparative question that opened this essay. Earlier I noted that in the two other major modern revolutions, the impact of the laws was primarily in urban than rural areas; the farther away one moved away from cities, the fewer divorces there were. Clearly this was not the case in China, where there were many divorces even in the most remote areas of the country. Why was this case? The explanation, I believe, lies in the nature of the Chinese revolution itself. In France and in Russia, the revolutions were urban based, and brought to power men with a strong urban orientation. Only after cities were taken did the revolution spread to rural areas. At least until the victory of the North Vietnamese and the Vietcong in Vietnam and the Khmer Rouge take-over in Cambodia in the 1970s, only in China was the revolution based in *rural* areas and from there spread to cities. Only Chinese peasants underwent the emancipatory process of land reform, and later the devastating famine on the scale of the Great Leap Forward. Most importantly, only in China did the revolution bring to power poor and often uneducated peasants, whose muddle-headedness in implementing the Marriage Law resulted in many divorces. Classifying China as just another revolutionary state without noting and emphasizing its *rural* component is to gloss over what was most important about it.

APPENDIX I:

Registered Divorces
(i.e. not including court divorces)
in Songjiang county (outside of Shanghai), 1951–1961

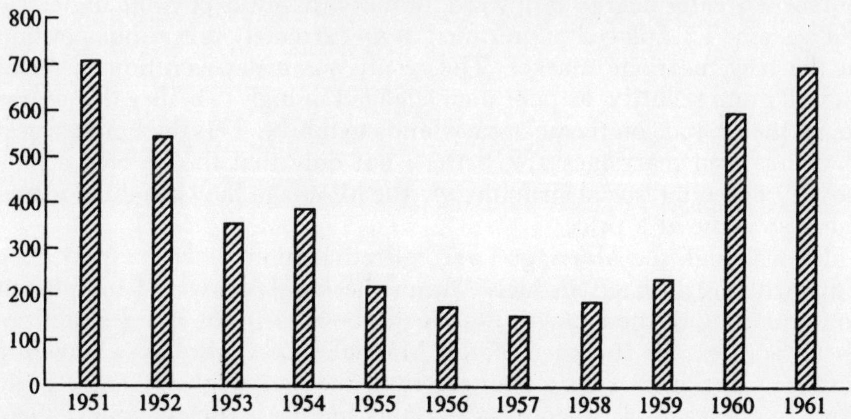

Source: 'Shanghai shi Songjiang xian hunyin dengji qingkuang', (Situation of Marriage Registration in Songjiang County), Songjiang County Archives, 8–1–32, at.32.

NOTES (ARCHIVAL AND PRIMARY CHINESE)

In the article, archival sources are abbreviated as follows:
BMA = Beijing Municipal Archives (Beijing)
CXA = Chuxiong Prefectural Archives (Yunnan Province)
JPA = Jiangsu Provincial Archives (Jiangsu Province)
QPA = Qingpu County Archives (Qingpu County, near Shanghai).
SMA = Shanghai Municipal Archives (Shanghai)
SJA = Songjiang County Archives (Songjiang County, near Shanghai)
TCA = Tong County Archives (Tong County, near Beijing)
YNA = Yunnan Provincial Archives (Yunnan Province)

[1] Rates are calculated on a household basis. On the 100 per cent divorce rate see CXA 4–4–A, at 138. For the divorce rate in Chuxiong see CXA 16–3–A1, at 185. In Guangtong county, Dianwei township, the divorce rate was 6 per cent (twenty couples in 304 households). See CXA 16–5–B1, at 21. On Mianyang district, An county, Sichuan, see CXA 16–5–B1, at 8. The report indicated ninety-seven couples divorcing in one township (Huaxi). According to the 1992 An county gazetteer (at 125), there was an average of 2,167 households per township in 1944. In addition, fifty-two adopted daughter-in-laws returned home. For the statistic on 14 per cent of the Lisu minority in Gezhi township returning home and demanding divorce see YNA 103–1–45, at 149. On the increase of cases at the district see CXA 16–3–A1, at 184. In Shanghai, by contrast, using the same measure of divorces per household, slightly over 1 per cent divorced in the years 1951, 1952, 1953. See SMA C31–2–369, at 38.

[2] CXA 16–8–B1, at 69; CXA 16–3–A1, at 180.

[3] *Qingpu xian zhi*, at 200.

[4] *Baoshan xian zhi*, at 153–4.

[5] *Chuxiong xian zhi*, vol II, at 117. Wang Lianfang writes of three 'contradictions' in land reform in border areas: between the party and minorities and GMD remnants, special agents, between different minority groups, and between upper and lower class people within minorities groups. See Wang Lianfang, *Minzu wenti lunwenji* (A Treatise on Minority Problems) (Kunming: Yunnan Renmin Chubanshe, 1993) at 273– 4.

[6] *Chuxiong zhou zhi*, vol II, at 115–19.

[7] Wang Lianfang, at 31; CXA 16– 8–B1, at 3.

[8] Wang Lianfang, at 10–11.

[9] Wang Lianfang, at 59.

[10] Wang Lianfang, at 54.

[11] Wang Lianfang, at 89.

[12] CXA 11–1–14B–1, at 134.

[13] Ibid, at 164, 121–2.

[14] Wang Lianfang, at 73, 141.

[15] CXA 11–1–14B–1, at 140.

[16] YNA 89–1–15, at 42.

[17] CXA 16–8–B1, at 2.

[18] Ibid, at 3.

[19] CXA 4–1–A1, at 27.

[20] CXA 16–8–B1, at 68.

[21] CXA 16–6–B1, at 32–3.

[22] CXA 4–1–A1, at 27.

[23] CXA 4–2– 1 (1952), at 80.

[24] CXA 16–8–B1, at 69; CXA 16–3–1, at 180.

[25] CXA 16–6–1, at 33, 35.

[26] YNA 103–1–45, at 150.

[27] CXA 16–3–A1, at 18–20; CXA 16–15–B1, at 137.

[28] CXA 16–15–B1, at 138.

[29] SMA A71–2–1859, at 55.

[30] SMA A71–2–1859, at 84.

[31] BMA 84–1–32, at 41.

[32] SMA A71–2–1864, at 75.

[33] SMA C32–1–4, at 81.

[34] QPA 11–2–1, at 13.

[35] SMA A71–2–1859, at 96.

[36] SMA A71–2–1859, at 109.

[37] SMA A71–2–1864, at 82.

[38] SMA A71–2–1859, at 99, 96.

[39] QPA 48–2–31, at 120; SMA A71–2–1958, at 30.

[40] QPA 48–2–31, at 85.

[41] In one case a woman named Zhou Shuling, whose parents both died, filed for divorce at the township government. Her husband, a local physician, agreed to the divorce but not to the property distribution. Township officials could not solve the problem and passed it on to the district, who also did not help. In the meantime, her mother-in-law threatened to commit suicide several times. The local police arrested her for a night as a warning, but she was opposed to the divorce. One night the entire family ganged up on Zhou and beat. The local police found out and arrested the entire family. Zhou was then sent to a local town to recuperate. The District Woman's Federation investigated the case and recommended an immediate divorce with a judicial unit (*shenpan zu*). See 'Case of Mao Bokang and Zhou Shuling of Baonan township, Maojiatang selected area', SMA A71–2–958, at 49.

[42] TCA 3–1–31, unpaginated report.

[43] TCA 7– 1–4, at 108–9. The same report also noted a disturbing rise in the frequency of violence directed at older people. In some areas in Tong county, young women refused to give enfeebled in-laws any food or clothes.

[44] BMA 84–1–32, at 41.

[45] SMA A71–2–1855, at 38–9.

[46] BMA 84–1–32, at 41.

[47] SMA A71–2–1861.

[48] TCA 1–2–31, at 14.

[49] TCA 1–2–31, at 10.
[50] SMA A71–2–1858, at 28.
[51] Ibid, 4.
[52] Ibid , at 5.
[53] Ibid, 6.
[54] SMA A71–2–864, at 70; SMA A71–2–1858, at 27.
[55] SMA E81–2–117, at 90.
[56] SMA A71–2–1856, at 69.
[57] SMA A71–2–1859, at 90; SMA A71–2–1863, at 11.
[58] TCA 1–2–31, at 14.
[59] SMA E81–2–117, at 61.
[60] SMA E81–2–117, at 96.
[61] SMA A71–2–1855, at 31; SMA A71–2–1856, at 6
[62] YNA 87–1–82, at 47.
[63] The following is based on reports specifically indicating ethnicity, unlike the accounts above which are vague in this regard.
[64] CXA 11–4–14B1, at 126.
[65] CXA 16–12–B1, at 62.
[66] CXA 11–96–14B–1, at 55; YNA 89–1–55, at 37.
[67] YNA 89–1–82, at 40.
[68] CXA 4–4–A1, at 38.
[69] CXA 11–96–14B–1 (1957) at 56.
[70] QPA 48–1–13, at 101–2.
[71] QPA 58–2–51.
[72] CXA 11–4–14B–1, at 86
[73] SJA 8–1–32 (1964) at 32.
[74] QPA 48–2–59 (1955) at 78.
[75] QPA 48–2–59 (1955) at 79.
[76] QPA 48–2–59, at 78–9.
[77] In 1954 the Bureau of Civil Affairs in Chuxiong found that welfare work among military dependants was erratic, and in some cases military dependants were ignored altogether. See CXA 16–13–B1, at 64.
[78] CXA 16–12–B1 (1955) at 58–0.
[79] CXA 11–77–14B–1, at 22.
[80] BMA 84–3–28 (1954) at 46.
[81] CXA 16–13–B1, at 64
[82] BMA 84–3–28 (October 1954) at 45–6.
[83] CXA 16–12–B1, at 55.
[84] JPA 35 (1956) at 29–30.
[85] JPA 35 (1956) at 29–30.
[86] YNA 89–1–55 (1955) at 37. Emphasis mine.
[87] CXA 16–14–A1 (Oct 1955) at 263.
[88] CXA 11–96–14B–1, at 54.
[89] CXA 16–14–A1 (August 1955) at 256; CXA 16–18–B1 (August 1954) at 168.
[90] JPA 35 (1956) at 28.
[91] CXA 16–18–B1 (1954) at 168.
[92] CXA 16–65–B1 (September 1958) at 171.
[93] CXA 16–65–B1, at 172.
[94] BMA 84–3–28, at 40.
[95] CXA 11–96–14B–1 (1957), at 54, 56. According to the report, twelve out of eighty divorce cases in 1956 were caused by fights between the husband's mother and her daughter-in-law: 'the mother-in-law yells at her daughter-in-law over trivial matters, and the latter disobeys'. In other cases, daughters-in-law refuse to care for their mothers-in-law, and insist that the 'mutual aid team take care of her instead'. For other mid-1950s cases of women returning to their natal home over arguments with their mother-in-laws see CXA 16–27–A1, at 29. These cases note that women were 'incessantly returning to their natal homes' after arguments, returning to their husbands after several days, arguing again, and once again 'returning to their natal home'.
[96] CXA 16–65–B1, at 172.
[97] CXA 16–65–B1, at 172.

[98] JPA 35 (1956) at 28, 31. The report stated that ignoring responsibility was particularly common, 'especially after collectivization'.

[99] JPA 35 (1956) at 30.

[100] CXA 16–27–A1 (1957) at 30.

[101] CXA 16–27–A1 (1957) at 33–4.

[102] In a random sample of twenty court cases from Qingpu, adultery was the main cause of divorce among male petitioners in both 1955 and 1965.

[103] Prior to collectivization and the household registration system, peasant women worried that their 'freedom' to move between her husband's and natal homes would be curtailed. They also worried that 'women's rights' would no longer be protected. See CXA 16–48–A1 (December 1956) at 142.

[104] CXA 16–27–A1 (1957) at 34.

[105] *Kunshan xian zhi* (Kunshan county gazetteer) (Shanghai: Shanghai Renmin Chubanshe, 1990) at 546, 566. The difficult economic situation was also cited in the dramatic increase in cases in Jinshan county, near Shanghai. According to the gazetteer, there was an average of 200 cases every year between 1954–62, but in 1962 and 1963 there were over 400 cases per year. See *Jinshan xian zhi* (Jinshan county gazetteer) (Shanghai: Renmin Chubanshe, 1990) at 696.

[106] CXA 16–B1–75 (March 1963) at 89. Women were petitioners in 57 per cent of cases.

[107] I am grateful to Joseph Esherick to pointing this out.

[108] Most all reports in my collection from this period document, or at least make it a point to criticize, the revival of these practices. The series in Chuxiong labelled '16–75–B1' are particularly useful in this regard.

[109] CXA 16–75–B1 (March 1963) at 52.

[110] CXA 16–75–B1, at 52.

[111] CXA 16–75–B1, at 52–3.

[112] In Chuxiong, in the twenty to twenty-nine-year-old category, women outnumbered men by roughly 2000 people. See *Chuxiong zhou zhi* (Chuxiong Prefecture gazetteer), (Beijing: Renmin Chubanshe, 1993) vol I, at 319.

[113] CXA 16–85–B1, at 34–5; CXA 16–75–B1, (March 1963) at 73.

[114] CXA 16–85–B1, at 36; CXA 16–77–B1 (1963), at 57; On Songjiang see SMA C31–2– 79, at 88; For Jiangsu see JPA 1898 (April 1965) at 14.

[115] SMA C31–2–1106 (March 1966) at 58; SMA C31–2–979, at 88.

[116] CXA 16–75– B1 (March 1963) at 92.

[117] For other cases in both the pre and post Leap periods see reports in CXA 11–96–14B–1, at 53; JPA 35, at 29–30; BMA 84–3–28, at 45; TCA 7–1–8, at 42; SMA C31–2–469, at 69, 72; CXA 11–97–14B–1, at 64.

[118] SMA C31–2–979, at 88; CXA 16–75–B1 (March 1963) at 74.

[119] CXA 16–55–B1 (March 1963) at 65.

[120] CXA 16–82–B1 (1963) at 16.

[121] CXA 16–75–B1, at 52–3; CXA 16–75–B1 (March 1963) at 57.

[122] CXA 16–75–B1 (March 1963) at 73; CXA 16–77–B1, (October 1963) at 43.

[123] SMA C31–2–1106 (March 1966) at 58.

[124] CXA 16–85–B1, at 37. CXA 16–92–B1 (January 1966) at 27.

[125] CXA 16–77–B1 (March 1963) at 58; SJA 8–1–37, at 139.

[126] CXA 16–75–B1 (April 1963) at 53.

REFERENCES (SECONDARY SOURCES)

Anderson, Olive (1987) *Suicide in Victorian and Edwardian England* (Oxford: Clarendon Press) 45.

Bernhardt, Kathryn (1994) 'Women and the Law: Divorce in Republican China', in Kathryn Bernhardt and Philip C.C. Huang (eds) *Civil Law in Qing and Republican China*, (Stanford: Stanford University Press) 187–213.

Black, Donald (1989) *Sociological Justice* (Oxford: Oxford University Press) 11.

Buxbaum, David (1978) 'Family Law and Social Change: A Theoretical Introduction', in his edited volume *Chinese Family Law and Social Change in Comparative Perspective* (Seattle: University of Washington Press).

Clarity, James (1995) 'Irish Cabinet Backs Lifting Ban on Divorce', *The New York Times* 9.

Elshtain, Jean, (1982) 'Aristotle, the Public-Private Split and the Case of the Suffragists', in her edited volume *The Family in Political Thought* (Amherst, Mass: University of Massachusetts Press).

Fei, Yuke (1958) 'Luetan chuli nongcun diqu hunyin wenti de tihui', (Handling peasants' marriage problems) *Zhengfa Xuexi*, vol 5–6, 53–9.

Felstiner, William (1974) 'Influences of Social Organization on Dispute Processing', *Law and Society Review*, vol 9, No1, 74, 79, 83.

Fitzpatrick, Sheila (1994) *Stalin's Peasants: Resistance and Survival in the Russian Village after Collectivization* (New York and Oxford: Oxford University Press).

French, Howard (1996) 'For Ivory Coast Women, New Battle for Equality', *The New York Times*, 4 June.

Friedman, Edward and Mark Selden and Paul Pickowitz (1991) *Chinese Village, Socialist State* (New Haven: Yale University Press).

Geiger, Kent (1968)*The Family in Soviet Russia* (Cambridge: Harvard University Press) 253.

Hahm, Pyong-choon (1969) 'The Decision Process in Korea', in Glendon Schubert and David J. Danelski (eds) *Comparative Judicial Behaviour: Cross-Cultural Studies of Political Decision-Making in the East and West* (New York and Oxford: Oxford University Press) 24–5.

Hane, Mikiso (1982) *Peasants, Rebels, and Outcasts: The Underside of Modern Japan* (NY: Pantheon).

Hassan, Riaz (1983) *A Way of Dying: Suicide in Singapore* (Singapore: Oxford University Press) 174.

Hinton, William (1966) *Fanshen: Documentary of a Revolution in a Chinese Village* (NY: Vintage) 137.

Honig, Emily and Gail Hershatter (1988) *Chinese Women in the 1980's* (Stanford: Stanford University Press) 206.

Hunt, Lynn (1992) *The Family Romance of the French Revolution* (Berkeley: University of California Press).

Johnson, Dirk (1996) 'No-Fault Divorce is under Attack', *The New York Times*, 2 December.

Johnson, Kay (1983) Anne *Women, the Family and Peasant Revolution in China* (Chicago: University of Chicago Press.

Juviler, Peter H (1977) 'Women and Sex in Soviet Law', in Dorothy Atkinson, Alexander Dallin and Gail Lapidus (eds) *Women in Russia* (Stanford: Stanford University Press) 311.

Kaffman, Mordecai, Sheryl Shoham, Michal Palgi, and Menachem Rosner (1986) 'Divorce in the Kibbutz: Past and Present', *Contemporary Family Therapy*, vol 8, No 4 (Winter) 301–16.

Kushner, Howard (1989) *Self-Destruction in the Promised Land: A Psychocultural Biology of American Suicide* (New Brunswick: Rutgers University Press) 95.

Landes, Joan B. (1982) 'Hegel's Conception of the Family', in Elstein, *The Family in Political Thought* (Amherst, Mass: University of Massachusetts Press).

Li, Yangxi and Tian Ye (1957) 'Hubei sheng nongcun minshi jiufen de diaocha' (An investigation of rural civil disputes in Hebei Province), *Zhengfa Yanjiu*, vol 4 (March) 31–4.

MacFarquhar, Roderick and John K. Fairbank (eds) (1987) *The Cambridge History of China*, Vol 14 (Cambridge: Cambridge University Press) ch 7–8.

Muller-Freienfels, William (1978) 'Soviet Family Law and Comparative Chinese Developments', in David Buxbaum (ed) *Chinese Family Law and Social Change in Comparative Perspective* (Seattle: University of Washington Press) 331.

Okin, Susan Moller (1982) 'Philosopher Queens and Private Wives: Plato on Women and the Family', in Jean Elshtain (ed) *The Family in Political Thought* (Amherst, Mass: University of Massachusetts Press) 44–9.

Phillips, Roderick (1980) *Family Breakdown in Late 18th Century France: Divorces in Rouen, 1792–1803* (Oxford: Clarendon Press) 92–4.

Potter, Sulamith and Jack Potter (1990) *China's Peasants: The Anthropology of a Revolution* (Cambridge: Cambridge University Press) 263.

Schurmann, Franz (1968) *Ideology and Organization in Communist China* (Berkeley: University of California Press) 442–4.

Shanley, Mary Lyndon and Peter Stillman (1982) 'Political and Marital Despotism: Montesquieu's *Persian Letters*', in Elstein, *The Family in Political Thought* (Amherst, Mass: University of Massachusetts Press).

Shorter, Edward (1975) *The Making of the Modern Family* (NY: Basic Books) 7.

Stacey, Judith (1983) *Patriarchy and Socialist Revolution in China* (Berkeley: University of California Press).

Traer, James F. (1980) *Marriage and the Family in 18th Century France* (Ithaca: Cornell University Press) 131.

Union Research Institute (1971) *Documents of the Chinese Communist Party Central Committee, September 1956–April 1969* (Hong Kong: Union Research Institute) vol 1, 719–22.

Whitehead, Barbra (1993) 'Dan Quayle Was Right', *The Atlantic Monthly*, vol 271, No 4 (April).
Wolf, Margery (1985) *Revolution Postponed: Women in Contemporary China* (Stanford: Stanford University Press).
Worobec, Christine D. (1991) *Peasant Russia: Family and Community in the Post-Emancipation Period* (Princeton: Princeton University Press).

[5]

THE CONSTITUTION OF THE PEOPLE'S REPUBLIC OF CHINA

WILLIAM C. JONES*

The 1982 Constitution of the People's Republic of China,[1] like its many predecessors, purports to establish a government that appears quite recognizable to Westerners. It bears an obvious relation to both the United States[2] and Soviet constitutions,[3] though it has some unusual

---

* Professor of Law, Washington University, St. Louis.

1. I have used the following sources for the Chinese texts of the constitutions: 1949 Common Program, 1 XIAN FA ZELIAO XUANBIAN, SELECTED MATERIALS ON CONSTITUTIONAL LAW [hereinafter referred to as CONSTITUTIONAL MATERIALS]; the 1954 constitution is found in *id.* at 150; the 1975 constitution is found in *id.* at 293; the 1978 constitution is found in *id.* at 303; and the 1982 constitution is found in the official pamphlet edition, which contains the report of the drafting committee. I have used the following English translations from which all translations in the text are taken: Common Program, FUNDAMENTAL LEGAL DOCUMENTS OF COMMUNIST CHINA 34 (A.P. Blaustein ed. 1962); 1954 constitution, SELECTED LEGAL DOCUMENTS OF THE PEOPLE'S REPUBLIC OF CHINA 1 (J. En-pao Wang ed. 1976); 1975 constitution, *id.* at 65; 1978 constitution, official translation in separate booklet published by Foreign Languages Press (1978); 1982 constitution, official translation in separate booklet published by Foreign Languages Press (1982).

2. Most constitutions are modeled to some extent on the United States Constitution because it is one of the oldest and easily the best known. The similarities with the Chinese constitution lie primarily in the structure of the constitution. In both, the powers of the most important organs of government are set out in general terms, and the organs are similar: Congress, the Administration and the Judiciary. Yet there are differences, particularly in the Administration where, in China, the existence of the bureaucracy is recognized (arts. 30-32). And there are some additional institutions in China such as the Central Military Commission (art. 93) and the Procuracy (arts. 129-133). China is a unitary rather than a federal state, so the treatment of local matters is quite different. Still, the document as a whole is close to the form of the United States Constitution and it includes a bill of rights. *See infra* note 7.

3. The principal similarity of the Chinese constitution to that of the Soviet Union seems to me to lie in the presence of ideological statements and the prominence of economics, in other words, the clear recognition of Marxism as the official doctrine of the state. Thus, the preambles in both constitutions refer to the struggle to overturn capitalism and to establish socialism. Both define themselves as socialist states. China: "The People's Republic of China is a socialist state under the people's democratic dictatorship led by the working class and based on the alliance of workers and peasants." Art. 1. The U.S.S.R.: "The Union of Soviet Socialist Republics is a socialist all-people's state expressing the will and the interests of the workers, the peasants, and the intelligentsia, and of the working people of all the nations and nationalities of the country." Art. 1. The Soviet constitution devotes chapter II to the "Economic System." The Chinese constitution devotes thirteen articles in its first chapter, "General Principles," to economics. Arts. 6-18.

There are also institutional similarities. The Chinese procuracy is obviously of Soviet origin. *See* Ginsburgs & Stahnke, *The Genesis of the People's Procuracy Procuratorate in the People's Republic of China,* THE CHINA Q. 1 (1964); *The People's Procuratorate in Communist China: The Period of Maturation, 1951-1955, id.* at 53 (1965); *The People's Procuratorate in Communist China: The Insti-*

characteristics. Power is said to belong to the people, but it is exercised by what looks like an indirectly elected parliament, the National People's Congress.[4] Congress enacts—or formally approves—legislation. But in addition, it elects the President, who is the head of state; the Premier, who is head of the government, that is, the bureaucracy; and the top officials in the courts, the procuracy, and a number of other organizations.[5] Congresses at lower levels, such as the provinces and counties, exercise similar powers at their levels. That is, they choose the local administrative chiefs such as governors in the case of provinces, mayors, countyheads, etc. They also choose the presidents of the courts and the chief procurators at their levels.[6] Citizens are guaranteed the usual political rights such as freedom of speech, assembly and religion,[7] as well as the new social and economic rights such as the right to remunerative employment, retirement benefits and the like.[8]

The most unusual feature is Congress. It is not really a parliament in the usual sense, both because it is too large (around 3,000 members)[9] and because it meets too seldom (once a year) actually to initiate legislation

---

tution Ascendent, 1954-1957, id. at 82 (1968). The use of standing committees of larger bodies, such as a congress, to do the real work of those bodies, is also a common feature of the two constitutions. See the provisions on the Presidium of the Supreme Soviet, arts. 119-124. The Standing Committee of the National People's Congress is dealt with primarily in articles 65-69.

4. Art. 59. The actual process of election is controlled by the Election Law for the National People's Congress and Local Congress of 1979. CONSTITUTIONAL MATERIALS, *supra* note 1, at 336, amended by Fifth National People's Congress, Dec. 10, 1982, translated in SUMMARY OF WORLD BROADCASTS, PART III: THE FAR EAST, (Dec. 18, 1982 FE/7212/C/1) [hereinafter cited as SWB].

5. Arts. 62 & 79. The term that the Chinese now translate as "President" [*Zhuxi*] is normally translated as "Chairman," as in "Chairman Mao." I do not know the reason for the change.

6. Art. 101.

7. Art. 33 provides that all citizens are equal before the law; art. 34 gives the right to vote, and to be elected, to all citizens over 18 years old, except to those "deprived of political rights according to law;" art. 35 gives rights of "freedom of speech, of the press, of assembly, of association, of procession and of demonstration;" art. 36 gives freedom of religious belief; art. 37 declares that the freedom of persons is inviolable, that no one can be arrested except by order of the court of procuracy, and that unlawful searches of the person are prohibited; art. 38 guarantees personal dignity; art. 39 protects against unlawful searches of houses; art. 40 guarantees the confidentiality of correspondence; art. 41 gives the right to criticize and make complaints to officials.

8. Art. 42 declares that citizens have the right and duty to work; art. 43 declares working people have the right to rest; art. 44 says the state will prescribe a system of retirement for workers and staff in enterprises and organs of the state; art. 45 declares that citizens have the right to material assistance from the state and provides for the blind and other disabled persons; art. 46 declares that citizens have a right to an education.

9. The number varies from session to session. *See* C.E. WENG, CONTEMPORARY CHINESE POLITICS 109 (2d ed. 1958) [hereinafter cited as WENG].

on its own.[10] In fact, it is not intended to initiate legislation. Its primary function is to elect and remove the important officials of government, including a standing committee that can act as Congress when the latter is not in session.[11] The actual control of the government is in the hands of the Premier and the top officials of the ministries. Legislation is supposedly the task of the Standing Committee of the National People's Congress.[12] The Premier, government officials and Standing Committee are responsible to Congress, but only in an ultimate sense: Congress selects them and can remove them from office.[13] There is no parliamentary responsibility in the sense of a system whereby a government that fails to get a majority in parliament on a vote of confidence falls. The process of election of Congress is unusual. The Constitution provides that citizens elect representatives to local people's congresses directly.[14] These congresses elect delegates to the congress of the next superior level and so on up the line to the National People's Congress. At present there are only three levels in the process: the local congresses, provincial congresses (or the equivalent), and the National People's Congress.[15] Thus, citizens vote directly for members of local congresses. These congresses elect the members of the provincial congresses, and the latter choose the members of the National People's Congress.

In other words, the constitution purports to establish a rather interesting system of government. One might wonder how a large number of problems that seem to be presented will be resolved. For instance, how will the Chinese solve the problem of divided control between the local congresses and top level officials in Peking? The problem is most obvious in the case of the courts. While, as indicated, local courts are appointed by local congresses and are responsible to them,[16] appeals from their decisions lie to the higher courts and in some cases to the Supreme People's

10. The point is made by the Chinese themselves. *See, e.g.*, Wang, *The New Constitution Strengthens the Standing Committee of the National People's Congress*, in A GUIDE TO THE CONSTITUTION OF THE PEOPLE'S REPUBLIC OF CHINA [*Zhonghua Renmin Gongheguo Xian Fa Jianghua*] 110 (1983) [hereinafter cited as CHINESE CONSTITUTION.]

11. Arts. 61 & 67.

12. Art. 67. There are some statutes that only Congress can enact—notably amendments to the constitution, arts. 62(1) & 64.

13. Art. 62(5)-(8) (power to appoint); art. 63 (power to dismiss).

14. Art. 59.

15. Art. 5 lists the level below the national level; art. 97 sets out the election process. *See also* FOREIGN BROADCAST INFORMATION SERVICE (FBIS), Electoral Law of the PRC for the NPIC and Local People's Congresses of All Levels, in DAILY REPORT 12 (Jul. 27, 1979).

16. Arts. 101 & 128.

Court in Peking. These higher courts are charged with supervising the lower courts.[17] Who controls? The courts or the Congresses? The same problem exists in all ministries because all ministries exercise ultimate control over local levels, and yet local officials are said to be responsible to the local congresses that appoint them.

Such questions, and many others, are interesting for students of government, but unless there are some radical changes in China, we shall never know the answers. The constitution seems to bear no relation to the actual government of China. Citizens enjoy neither civil[18] nor economic rights.[19] Congresses are in fact rubber stamps that do as they are told by whoever is in power at their level.[20] The meetings of a congress are ceremonial occasions. No doubt they afford a welcome opportunity for their members to travel, see friends, and make contacts. Perhaps they are significant as meeting places for important people because congress members are normally persons of some significance. In that way they may serve as significant parts of the actual government of China.

But it is fairly clear which governmental structures exercise power in China, at least in a formal sense, and the National People's Congress and

---

17. Art. 127.

18. It is perhaps enough to cite the case of Wei Jingsheng, one of the leaders of the short-lived "Peking Spring" movement, when some young people expressed themselves very freely in making criticisms of the government. Wei was sentenced to 15 years on what seem to me to have been trumped-up charges. *See* Jones, *Due Process in China: The Trial of Wei Jingsheng*, 9 REV. OF SOC. L. 55 (1983). To be sure, this was before the 1982 constitution, but freedom of speech was also guaranteed in the 1978 constitution, art. 45, and the people who put Wei in prison are the people who still govern China and who promulgated the 1982 constitution. Wei is still imprisoned. For reports on a number of political prisoners, see AMNESTY INTERNATIONAL, CHINA: VIOLATIONS OF HUMAN RIGHTS 5-51 (1984). One might also note the "Cultural Pollution" campaign of 1983-84. *See* Schram, *Economics in Command? Ideology and Policy Since the Third Plenum*, THE CHINA Q. 418, 437-48 (1984). This was used to dampen discussion in at least one university. But citation is otiose. Some of the "freedoms" are so qualified in the text that they are meaningless. Thus, art. 36 guarantees freedom of religion but states that "Religious bodies and religious affairs are not subject to any foreign domination. . . ." In practice, this means that many persons cannot practice their religion, notably Roman Catholics and Tibetan Buddhists.

19. China is a poor country and does well to keep its citizens from starving to death. It does not always succeed in that. "Retirement" as such is not guaranteed to farmers and perhaps some kinds of workers. All are supposed to get material assistance when they are old. Art. 45. But one hears that one of the reasons peasants are not cooperating with the birth-control program is that they believe sons are the only dependable social security. It might be added that China has a significant unemployment problem, although it is disguised by such terms as youth waiting for assignment. *See, e.g.*, WENG, *supra* note 9, at 255.

20. The Chinese would of course deny this. I can only say that I have never seen any evidence of independence. Even Professor Weng who has tried to find examples of independent action regards Congress as pretty subservient. *See* WENG, *supra* note 9, at 111.

the local congresses are not among them. China is a country that is governed by a highly centralized bureaucracy that is more or less under the control of the Communist Party.[21] The Army remains a great power that is not usually directly involved either in the government or Party, but that may become so at any time. Of course it is not clear at all just how control is exercised either within the Party or by the Party on external organizations such as ministries, to say nothing of the Army. The situation at the lower levels is especially murky, but it is difficult to understand how things work even at the more visible top levels. Deng Xiaoping is nominally an official who is chairman of a committee that supervises the Army; he is subordinate, on paper, to Congress. He has never held the very top posts in either the government or Party. Yet it is quite clear that if Deng were to go to E Mei Shan to contemplate nature and observe the sacred monkeys for an extended time, E Mei Shan is where the government of China would be. Congress could continue to hold performances in Peking or not. It would not affect the way things ran. For that matter, the Politburo could continue to hold its meetings and make pronouncements, but unless it was clear that Deng agreed, it would not be wise to rely on these actions.[22]

What is true of the 1982 constitution was also true of its predecessors. The written constitution was not the place to start if one wanted to know what the government of China was really like. One might say that the written constitution had little to do with the actual constitution, that is, the real structure of government. Though it should be said that the 1975 and 1978 constitutions were a little closer to reality than the rest, because they both emphasized the importance of the Communist Party.[23] In other respects, however, they shared the remoteness from reality of their fellows. In view of this, it is tempting simply to dismiss Chinese constitutions as trumpery designed to provide an occasion for flights of oratory at the time of their adoption.[24] There is much to be said for this point of

21. This does not mean that every order from the center is automatically obeyed nor that local organizations have no independence. As a matter of fact, they are often quite resistant and hard to control. But the organizational chart is quite clear. And by and large the center gets what it wants.

22. He is Chairman of the Central Military Commission, which was created by the 1982 constitution, art. 93. This position is subject to the National People's Congress. Art. 63(3).

23. 1975 CONST. art. 2; 1978 CONST. art. 2(24).

24. There is quite a lot of that. *See, e.g., PLA Delegates Discuss New Constitution*, SWB (Dec. 3, 1982, FE/7199/C/99):

> . . . said that inclusions of provisions for building socialist spiritual civilization is of great significance. He said communist ideology is the core of socialist spiritual civilization of which Lei Feng was an exemplar . . . every PLA fighter should emulate Lei Feng, foster a

view. Indeed, it may be the only rational position to take on the question of the content of Chinese constitutions.

This is not to say that written constitutions play no role in the Chinese polity. They clearly have one function: The adoption of a constitution is a signal that a significant change has taken place in the government or in society, and that it is conceived to be long-lasting. The first constitution, the so-called "Common Program" in 1949, signified that the Communists had won the civil war against the Nationalists and had formed a completely new government for China. The 1954 constitution showed that the new government regarded itself as firmly established. Military and political control were complete. There was no significant problem with foreign or domestic enemies, and the foundations of a socialist state had been laid. The 1975 constitution indicated that what might be called the leftist faction believed that it had won decisively the bitter intra-party struggle of the Cultural Revolution and was in a position where the adoption of a new constitution would solidify its control. The 1978 constitution indicated how mistaken the leftist faction was, and affirmed what was apparently believed to be the permanence of the coalition that overturned the "Gang of Four." This belief was in turn pretty firmly exploded by the end of the same year in the Third Plenum of the Eleventh Session of the Central Committee. This signaled the establishment of Deng's primacy. The change was confirmed by the 1982 constitution whose promulgation purports to indicate a complete rejection of the Cultural Revolution and all "leftist" ideas and a return to the good old days of the 1950s. If the former pattern continues, then the failure to promulgate a new constitution when Deng passes from the scene might indicate a belief—or perhaps just a hope—of the ruling powers that they would continue to govern. Or it might mean that a fight was going on and it was not yet clear who had won. Of course something might have happened to the Chinese polity and it might mean that a more impersonal and permanent system of government had been established. Whatever

---

> deep love for the motherland and the people, and for labour, science and socialism, display the communist spirit and be a vanguard in building socialist spiritual civilization. . . .

See also the reactions of Chinese People's Political Consultative Conference observers at the National People's Congress: "all an historic event . . .," "an achievement gained through a struggle and a summary of experience," "It is paid for with blood." FBIS, Report CPPCC meeting in Renmin R:Bao, in DAILY REPORT K8 (Dec. 9, 1982). Peng Zhen in presenting the constitution to Congress said, "When our one billion people all cultivate the consciousness and habit of observing and upholding the constitution and fight against all acts violating and undermining the Constitution this will become a mighty force." SWB (Dec. 7, 1982, FE/7202/C/16).

happens, the promulgation of a new constitution, or the failure to promulgate one, will be an event of great political significance.

There is not much question that constitutions play this role in China. The question is, do they have any other significance, since they do not establish or describe the apparatus of government nor determine the rights of citizens. It seems pretty clear that they perform at least one additional, though related, function. Apart from merely signaling a change in power or in the political and economic conditions of the country, constitutions also tend to show the direction that their promulgators plan to take in governing China. This will take the form both of indications of actions that the new government plans to take and of a basic ideological statement. The result is that constitutions can indeed be regarded as the source of law in the People's Republic of China just as they are declared to be.[25] But the term "constitution" has a different meaning from the one normally given to it in the West. The constitution is not written for the ages. It is a statement of current policy. When the policy changes, the law ipso facto changes. Indeed the change in the operative rule may antedate the change in the wording of the constitution. For instance, when, in the 1950s, the ownership of agricultural land was converted from cooperative and individual property to commune or collective property, and then in the late 1970s and 1980s was changed back again, it was because the rulers of China believed that collective or individual operation of the land, as the case might be, was the best way to solve the problem of increasing agricultural production at that time. Once this decision was made, an appropriate system of land ownership was adopted. Eventually the constitutions were changed to reflect the new policy. But the law in an operative sense had changed long before. Policy in China *is* law. It does not merely influence law.[26]

---

25. The preamble, in its last paragraph, states that the constitution "is the fundamental law of the state." It must be taken by all as "the basic norm of conduct." One of the articles by Wang Zhengzhao and Lin Yuhui in a book on the constitution prepared by the People's Daily Press, CHINESE CONSTITUTION, *supra* note 10, at 12, which is entitled *The New Constitution is our Country's Basic Law*. It says that the constitution is the basic law because (1) its content sets out the basic principles of law such as the necessity for constructing socialist modernization, the nature of the state, and the economy, but it does not go into detail; (2) any law that is in conflict with it is without effect; and (3) it is enacted and amended in a different way.

26. The 1954 constitution recognized the existence of state, cooperative, individual, and capitalist ownership, art. 5. The formation of cooperatives was encouraged, arts. 7 & 8. But individual ownership of land by peasants is protected, art. 8. It was anticipated that no more than one-third of the peasant households would form "lower-level producer cooperatives," in which the individuals retained ownership but farmed cooperatively and split the profits, by the end of 1957. However, in

Presumably this is a perfectly correct way of looking at law and the constitution in a Marxist society. Law is an instrument that the ruling class uses to exert social control. It is an aspect of the superstructure.[27] The only real law is dialectical materialism. The governing structure in a country like China is the Communist Party, which establishes—and disestablishes—institutions as seems desirable in order to achieve the ultimate goal of communism. A constitution is a general summary of present policy. Laws are more particularized statements of policy. For this reason, an ideological statement is even more important than a concrete statement of economic or social policy because it serves as the basis of such policies. Particular policies must be appropriate to the current stage of society's development. This stage will be made clear in the ideological statement. For example, the most important change in the 1975 constitution from the 1954 constitution was the change in the phrase "China is a people's democratic state"[28] to "China is a state of the dictatorship of the proletariat."[29] This indicated that there had been a change

---

1955 Mao decided that the pace should be accelerated and the country was almost completely collectivized by 1957, having passed through cooperatives into socialist collectives in which there was no individual ownership and peasants were rewarded for their work. Communes that unified political and economic control appeared in 1958. *See* M. MEISSNER, MAO'S CHINA 140-60, 230-41 (1977) [hereinafter cited as MEISSNER]. But the constitutional provisions on land ownership were not changed until 1975. The 1978 constitution stated that there were two types of ownership of the means of production: state ownership and collective ownership (communes), art. 5. Within the commune there was ownership by: the commune, the production brigade and the production team. Farming of private plots for personal needs subject to predominance of the collective economy was permitted, art. 7. In 1977, prior to the time the constitution was promulgated, "household contracting" had begun in some areas. Under this system the procurement contract was made with an individual household rather than a team or brigade. Once its quota was met, it could dispose of the surplus for its own benefit. The system has many variations. By 1982 it dominated in China. The changes were effected by a series of Central Committee Documents. The constitutional change recognizing (more or less) individual responsibility was promulgated in December 1982. 1982 CONST. art. 14. For a summary of these developments, see Walker, *Chinese Agriculture During the Period of Readjustment 1978-83*. THE CHINA Q. 783, 786-89 (1984).

27. *See* Wang Shuwen, *The Basic Characteristics of the New Constitution*, CHINESE CONSTITUTION, *supra* note 10, at 21. He states that constitutions are important component parts of the superstructure. According to Lenin, there are two types: the "real constitution" and the "written constitution." The real constitution determines the nature, content and character of the written constitution. Wang then indicates how the four written constitutions (the Chinese never call the Common Program a constitution) reflect their real constitutions. The only good ones are those of 1954 and 1982. The latter reflects the conclusions of the Third Plenum such as the four basic policies and the Four Modernizations.

28. 1954 CONST. art. 1.

29. 1975 CONST. art. 1. This change in phrasing was the principal subject of the publicity in favor of the 1975 constitution when it was promulgated. *See* Cohen, *China's Changing Constitution*, 76 THE CHINA Q. 794 (1978) [hereinafter cited as Cohen].

in the nature of the state and society. Even more important, it was regarded as emphasizing the fact that there would be a continuation of the class struggle against, among others, enemies at home. And in turn this meant a continuation of the Cultural Revolution. On the other hand, the switch to the phrase "People's democratic dictatorship" in the 1982 constitution[30] signals the elimination of the class struggle, and that indicates that the Cultural Revolution will not be revived. At least in the current stage of development, the policy of advancing the Four Modernizations rests on this foundation. The various measures in furtherance of foreign trade, including the Joint Venture Law[31] and the individual responsibility system, are aspects of the Four Modernizations campaign. Thus the ideological statement is the basis of a general statement, which serves as the basis of concrete statutes.

Of course, one cannot regard any of these ideological or policy statements as permanently binding, but if a statement is fairly recent and seems to be in accord with current conditions and attitudes, it is a good indication of where the leadership expects to go. A clear statement of policy may, in consequence, be of considerably more value than a more detailed set of rules. As a result, the preamble is generally the most important part of the constitution. Thus the statements in the preamble to the 1982 constitution that emphasize the importance of modernization and the necessity to make use of foreign capital and almost to eliminate class struggle[32] may be rather more significant to a person who is contemplating a joint venture than a whole portfolio of legal materials of the usual type.

A description of Chinese constitutions is, therefore, a description of the way the documents called constitutions relate to the social, economic and political conditions that existed when they were promulgated and to the actions taken and contemplated by those who promulgated them. It has a continuing relationship with those conditions, and changes accordingly. A Chinese constitution must, in consequence, be seen as part of a

30. Art. 1.

31. Enacted July 1, 1979, translated in SWB (July 16, 1979, FE6/63/C/22).

32. The preamble to the 1982 constitution keeps the concept of the class struggle, but only just. After making it clear that the exploiting classes no longer exist as a class, it states that the class struggle will have to go on for a long time against foreign and domestic enemies. However, in the official commentary, it is pointed out that according to the 1981 census, 99.97% of those over 18 years old had the right to vote and be elected. In other words, they were not "exploiters" who had been deprived of their political rights. The exploiting classes have diminished greatly in size. Still the country has to fight the enemy within and without. So, dictatorship is preserved. *Id.* at 56.

process and can only be understood if one has some sense of this development. This has been true since the very beginning of the People's Republic of China.

The People's Republic of China came into existence formally in 1949 immediately after the enactment of the Common Program.[33] The Common Program was, as indicated above, a response to the victory of the Communists in their long war with the Nationalists. Its purpose was to solemnize this victory and to indicate where the country was to go. The main task of the new government was to assure its control and to eliminate the effects of decades of war and neglect. At the same time the government was committed to Marxism-Leninism-Mao Zedong Thought. It wished to establish the basis for socialism in China, but without scaring people. The program began by declaring that China was a people's democratic state that carried out the people's democratic dictatorship on the basis of an alliance of workers and peasants.[34] The tasks of the new nation were to complete the war of liberation,[35] to destroy the special rights of imperialist countries in China, and to confiscate bureaucratic capital and return it to the ownership of the democratic society. The nation should gradually change feudal and semifeudal ownership into a system whereby the farmers owned the land. It should protect rights and advance China from an agricultural into an industrial country.[36] It must establish equality of the sexes[37] and eliminate counter-revolutionary and imperialist Guomindang antirevolutionary activity. In necessary cases, it must, according to law, take away the political rights of persons involved in such activities.[38] In foreign affairs, China is united with those countries which love peace and freedom and particularly the Soviet Union and the People's Democracies.[39] There were a number of more particular provisions connected with the establishment of new social conditions such as the necessity for workers to participate in

33. The Common Program was enacted by the Chinese People's Political Consultative Conference on September 29, 1949. 1 COLLECTED LAWS AND REGULATIONS OF THE CHINESE CENTRAL PEOPLE'S GOVERNMENT [Zhongyang Renmin Zhengfu Faling Huipian] 17 (1945-50). The People's Republic of China came into being on October 1, 1949. Central People's Government Announcement of the People's Republic of China, *id.* at 28.

34. Art. 1.

35. Art. 2.

36. Art. 3.

37. Art. 6.

38. Art. 7.

39. Art. 11.

management.[40]

The policy was carried out pretty much as written. By 1954, all significant opposition was quelled except in Taiwan; a successful war had been fought against the United States; the economy was rehabilitated and progressing; nationalization had begun.[41] As the preamble to the 1954 constitution announced, "the necessary conditions have been created for planned economic construction and gradual transition to socialism." Thus the time was ripe for a new constitution—the first to be given the name of "constitution." The preamble stated that during this time of transition to socialism, there was to be a "broad people's democratic united front." State ownership, cooperative ownership, individual ownership, and capitalism could all exist, though it was implied that capitalism was only temporary. In foreign affairs, "China has already built an indestructible friendship with the great Union of Soviet Socialist Republics and the People's Democracies."

In the body of the constitution, China was again defined as a "people's democratic state led by the working class and based on the alliance of workers and peasants."[42] Article 4 is perhaps the most significant. It provides: "The People's Republic of China, by relying on the organs of state and the social forces, and by means of socialist industrialization and socialist transformation, ensures the gradual abolition of systems of exploitation and the building of a socialist society." Several sections follow in which it is stated that different groups, such as individual workers and capitalists, will be "helped and guided" to enter into cooperatives or state-controlled activity.[43] Capitalists are forbidden to engage in "unlawful activities which injure the public interest, disrupt the social-economic order or undermine the economic plan of the state."[44] "Feudal landlords" and "bureaucratic landlords" continue to be deprived of political

40. Part IV, Economic Policy, arts. 26-40, sets out the government's policy, which is, essentially, to permit and encourage capitalism under state control, while making the state economy the principal factor. Art. 32 deals with workers' participation in management.

41. MEISSNER, *supra* note 26, at 59, 60, 73-80, 92-97.

42. Art. 1.

43. Art. 7 states that the state encourages, "guides and helps" the development of cooperatives, which are "the chief means for the transformation of individual farming and individual handicrafts." Art. 8 provides that the state "guides and helps" individual peasants to form cooperatives. The policy of the state in regard to rich peasant economy is to eliminate it. Under art. 9, handicraft workers are to be "guide[d] and help[ed]" into cooperatives. Under art. 10, the good aspects of capitalist industry and commerce are permitted but the state "encourages and guides their transformation into various forms of state-capitalist economy."

44. Art. 10.

rights. Treasonable and counter-revolutionary activities are suppressed.[45]

Socialist transformation, in the sense of a change in ownership relations, came very quickly thereafter. By 1958 almost all agricultural land had been collectivised and all industry had come under state control. The individual sector of the economy had ceased to be of much importance.[46] In some ways it was time for a new constitution. Indeed, the issue was raised by Mao Zedong.[47] But the completion of the transition to socialism (if that is an accurate description of what happened) was almost immediately succeeded by a number of disturbances that delayed the adoption of a new constitution.

The two most important occurrences were the Great Leap Forward in 1958[48] and the Cultural Revolution in 1966.[49] These two events were very complex. Opinions vary enormously as to what caused them and what they mean. There is no space to discuss these matters here. There is, however, one element that is common to both of these events that has been very important for Chinese constitutional development. This is the issue of the persistence of and the necessity for the class struggle in China after the goals of nationalization of the economy and the establishment of political and military control had been achieved.

There is no question that the exploiting classes in the usual sense of the term had been eliminated. Many members of those classes—landlords, capitalists, officials in the former government, etc.—had been killed or imprisoned. Their ownership rights in the means of production had been confiscated and their organizations were destroyed. But China's revolution was not complete. Both agricultural and industrial production were far too low. What should be done to improve them? If one believed that the class struggle was essentially over, then the emphasis would be on physical conditions. One might feel that the chief obstacles to China's march towards socialism were essentially the objective material condi-

45. Art. 19.

46. D. PERKINS, MARKET CONTROL AND PLANNING IN COMMUNIST CHINA 13-17 (1966).

47. JOINT PUBLICATIONS RESEARCH SERVICE, MISCELLANY OF MAO TSE-TUNG THOUGHT [Maoze dong sixiang wan sui] (1949-1968) PART I, 138 (Feb. 20, 1974). It is reported that Mao said on December 12, 1958, "The issue of integrating politics and the commune, for example, was not passed by the People's Congress, nor is it in the constitution. Many parts of the constitution are obsolete, but it cannot be revised now. As for surpassing the U.S., we will formulate a written constitution."

48. The Greap Leap is discussed in MEISSNER, *supra* note 26, at 204-52.

49. The Cultural Revolution is discussed in MEISSNER, *supra* note 26, at 309-58.

tions of poor transportation, a low educational level, poor technology, and lack of skilled personnel and of capital to make improvements and the like. In short, one might concentrate on what could be called "productive forces."

On the other hand, if one believed that the basic problem was always political and that development comes from changing ownership relationships, or, one might say, the class struggle, then the problem was to locate the class that must be struggled against. One could, of course, continue to badger the survivors of the old exploiting groups and their descendants. And, as a matter of fact, the constant harassment of persons with a bad class background was a feature of Chinese life until quite recently. But it is obvious that this is not enough because these people had little power. Who did? High officials and members of the Communist Party. If these people were harboring feudal or bourgeois thoughts, they must be struggled against. They had become an exploiting class.[50] But ultimately—according to one very influential view—the battle was subjective. We must all struggle to rid ourselves of restrictive feudal or bourgeois thinking, to rid ourselves of the ego.[51] If these political problems were attacked first, the solution to economic and social problems would appear.

Of course, it does not do to regard the upholders of these views as completely separate. All Marxists believe in the importance of the class struggle and that political questions, as they understand the term, are very important. No one in China questions the necessity for improved irrigation and the use of computers. But there are great differences in emphasis and these differences are reflected in the constitutions that have been promulgated since 1975.

It is not clear just who was in control of China in 1975, but it is pretty clear that the group favoring emphasis on the class struggle was in control of the media. Apparently this group also controlled the government sufficiently to cause a new constitution reflecting their views to be

50. See the discussion of "old classes" in Whyte, *Inequality and Stratification in China*, 64 THE CHINA Q. 698-705 (1976).

51. See report on Jiang Qing by Roxanne Witke in COMRADE CHIANG CH'ING 339 (1977):

> Chiang Ch'ing concluded her remarks on a cherished subject, the problem of the Ego. That subjective aspect of revolutionary transformation was always (and most emphatically in our interview) at the forefront of her consciousness, and seemingly was her sense of the heart of the Cultural Revolution. Making revolution, she said in effect, was simultaneously an introverted and extroverted experience, a personal and public affair. Conflicts were not only external—between the enemy and ourselves—or internal—among ourselves, as Chairman Mao had argued. They must be waged *within* oneself—*against* the so-called Ego.

promulgated, because the preamble made it very clear that this constitution was the product of those who emphasized the class struggle. It provided:

> Socialist society covers a considerably long historical period. Throughout this historical period, there are classes, class contradictions and class struggle, there is the struggle between the socialist road and the capitalist road, there is the danger of capitalist restoration and there is the threat of subversion and aggression by imperialism and social-imperialism. These contradictions can be resolved only by depending on the theory of continued revolution under the dictatorship of the proletariat and on practice under its guidance.[52]

These ideas are pervasive in the 1975 constitution. It is what might be called a very Maoist document.[53] Almost all traces of the former social system had disappeared.[54] The Communist Party is the core of leadership of the whole Chinese people. "The working class exercises leadership over the state through its vanguard, the Communist Party of China."[55] References to capitalists and other parties had disappeared. Essentially the only property relationships that are recognized are collective or state property,[56] though very grudging permission is given for private plots and handicrafts.[57] The emphasis is on struggle. Administrators must "put proletarian politics in command, combat bureaucracy, maintain close ties with the masses and wholeheartedly serve the people. Cadres at all levels must participate in collective productive labour."[58] "The proletariat must exercise all-round dictatorship over the bourgeoisie in the superstructure, including all spheres of culture."[59] Article 13 more or less describes and endorses the Cultural Revolution. It provides:

> Speaking out freely, airing views fully, holding great debates and writing

52. 1975 CONST. preamble.

53. Though there is some question whether or not Mao approved of it since he did not attend either the meeting of the Party Central Committee prior to the meeting of the National People's Congress at which the constitution was promulgated, or the Congress itself. *See* M-h Yao, *The Fourth National People's Congress and Peiping's Future Direction* in THE NEW CONSTITUTION OF COMMUNIST CHINA 324, 327-8 (M. Lindsay ed. 1976).

54. There is no reference to capitalism or, for that matter, to landlords except as persons deprived of political rights. Art. 14.

55. Art. 2.

56. Art. 5.

57. Art. 7. Private plots are permitted so long as the "development and absolute predominance of the collective economy of the people's commune are ensured." Art. 9 permits ownership of income from work, savings, houses, and "other means of livelihood."

58. Art. 11.

59. Art. 12.

> big-character posters are new forms of carrying on socialist revolution created by the masses of the people. The state shall ensure to the masses the right to use these forms to create a political situation in which there are both centralism and democracy, both discipline and freedom, both unity of will and personal ease of mind and liveliness, and so help consolidate the leadership of the Communist Party of China over the state and consolidate the dictatorship of the proletariat.[60]

The standing committees of local congresses are replaced by "revolutionary committees."[61] In regard to legal procedure, the constitution provided that: "The mass line must be applied in procuratorial work and in trying cases. In major counterrevolutionary criminal cases the masses should be mobilized for discussion and criticism."[62]

It is difficult to determine the extent to which China was actually governed by these precepts, but there is no question that between the time when the constitution was adopted in 1975 and the death of Mao in September 1976, the "leftists" who, as indicated above, seem to have controlled the media, made strenuous efforts to promote these views. During the summer before Mao's death, there was a vigorous campaign against Deng Xiaoping and his doctrine of emphasizing "productive forces."[63] There was a lot of favorable publicity given to the Cultural Revolution with perhaps a hint at its revival.[64] This period is included in what the present government calls ten years of turmoil. It could also be classified as a period in which the doctrine of viewing the class struggle as the key link was the keystone of official government policy.[65]

Almost immediately upon Mao's death, things began to change. The group—later characterized as the Gang of Four—who had presumably been behind this constitution were imprisoned and new people began to take over.[66] One of the first notable changes in policy involved educa-

60. Art. 13.

61. Art. 22.

62. Art. 25.

63. The discussion of the campaign against Deng Xiaoping is based upon *Two Systems, Lessons of Teng's Crimes,* CHINA NEWS ANALYSIS (1976). *See also* B. BRUGGER, CHINA: RADICALISM TO REVISION 1962-1979, 170-96 (1981).

64. *See, e.g., The Great Cultural Revolution Will Shine Forever,* PEKING REV., at 14 (July 2, 1976), *The Making of a Young Actress, id.*; *Advance Along the Road of the Great Proletarian Cultural Revolution, id.* at 16.

65. *See, e.g.,* the translation of the official commentary to the 1975 constitution in SELECTED LEGAL DOCUMENTS OF THE PEOPLE'S REPUBLIC OF CHINA 93-95 (J. En-Pao Wang ed. 1976), where it is said that "our main task is to . . . persist in continued revolution. . ." and a statement of Mao Zedong is quoted: ". . . there are still classes, class contradictions and class struggles. . . ."

66. See B. BRUGGER, *supra* note 63, at 194-96, 201, 202.

tion.[67] The entire system of university admissions was changed. In the early 1970s admission was, in theory, based primarily on work experience and political reliability and not on academic qualifications as we understand the term. The course of study emphasized practice more than theory and the length of time spent in the university was shortened. In 1977, soon after the fall of the Gang of Four, this was changed to a system that based admission on an extremely competitive examination more or less of the western type. The courses of study became much more academic and longer. There were changes in other fields as well. Foreign contacts were encouraged and imports increased.[68] There were purges of those who had sided with the Gang of Four, and there was a "reversal of verdicts" of those who were said to have been unjustly accused of various things—usually counter-revolutionary activity—during the Cultural Revolution.[69] The government was a rather strange alliance. It included both Deng Xiaoping and Hua Guofong, the man who had replaced him after his downfall in April 1976.[70] In the midst of all this, the 1978 constitution was promulgated.[71] It reflected the unresolved conflicts in the government.

The new constitution retained the general ideological line of the 1975 constitution, but there were some modifications. Thus, in the preamble, China is still said to be a country under the dictatorship of the proletariat and the Cultural Revolution is still a great victory. But there is a slight relaxation in the cry for the class struggle. Intellectuals are now included in the worker-peasant alliance by means of the "mass line," which was to be expanded and strengthened as a sort of united front. The big task is to preserve the revolution and to make China a modern country by the end of the century by achieving the Four Modernizations.

In the text there is the same compromise. Most of the language is the same as in the 1975 constitution, but some changes have been made. For instance, the rural people's commune is no longer defined as "an organi-

---

67. *See* Pepper, *Chinese Education After Mao: Two Steps Forward, Two Steps Back and Begin Again?*, THE CHINA Q. 1 (1980).

68. See, for instance, the statement about a 26.8% increase in exports in the first half of 1979 and the establishment of new institutions to encourage trade and the import of technology, in *Quarterly Chronicle and Documentation*, THE CHINA Q. 881, 886 (1979).

69. *See Quarterly Chronicle and Documentation: (b) The Campaign Against Lin Piao and the 'Gang of Four'*, and *id.* (c) *The Leadership*, THE CHINA Q. 157, 158, 173 (1979).

70. Deng was rehabilitated and reappeared as Vice-Chairman of the Party by mid-1977. B. BRUGGER, *supra* note 63, at 202-03.

71. The 1978 Constitution is discussed in detail in Cohen, *supra* note 29.

zation which integrates government, administration and economic management."[72] Instead, it is a "socialist sector" of the economy.[73] In the article on improving production, instead of saying that the state by "grasping revolution . . . improves the people's material and cultural life step by step . . .,"[74] the 1978 constitution says that the state "adheres to the general line of going all out, aiming high and achieving greater, faster, better and more economical results in building socialism . . . and it continuously develops the *productive forces* so as to consolidate the country's independence and security and improve the people's material and cultural life step by step."[75] The term "productive forces" was anathema to the Gang of Four because it indicated that one was not emphasizing the importance of the class struggle as the key to development.

The 1978 document also eliminated the statement that the proletariat must "exercise all-round dictatorship over the bourgeoisie in the superstructure."[76] Education and science again became primary aims of the state.[77]

There were some structural changes as well. The procuracy was restored[78] as well as the use of "people's assessors" in the trial of cases.[79] The accused had a right to a defense, and while the masses were to be drawn in for discussion and suggestions in major counter-revolutionary or criminal cases,[80] there was no statement that the mass line must be generally used.[81] In the part dealing with the legislature, the powers given to the National People's Congress and to its standing committee are set out in much more detail[82] than in the 1975 constitution.[83] It was believed by some that these provisions strengthened Congress.[84]

It is hard to say whether any of these changes in the language of the constitution would have had any effect whatever on the actual government of China even if the constitution had remained in effect. But as it

72. 1975 CONST. art. 7.
73. 1978 CONST. art. 7.
74. 1975 CONST. art. 10.
75. 1975 CONST. art. 11.
76. 1975 CONST. art. 12.
77. 1978 CONST. art. 13.
78. 1978 CONST. art. 43.
79. 1978 CONST. art. 41.
80. *Id.*
81. 1978 CONST. art. 22.
82. 1978 CONST. art. 25.
83. 1975 CONST. arts. 17 & 18.
84. Cohen, *supra* note 29, at 809-12.

happens, before the year 1978 was out, the political situation changed radically. The Third Plenum of the Eleventh Central Committee Meeting of the Party was held in December.[85] Its report announced the end of the class struggle and made the Four Modernizations the country's main task. This meeting signaled the basic victory of Deng Xiaoping and his group in the struggle for control of the Party—though mopping up operations still go on. In August 1980, the Central Committee of the Communist Party recommended the establishment of a committee to revise the constitution.[86] Soon thereafter the National People's Congress established a constitutional revision committee.[87] The 1982 constitution is what they came up with. In June 1981, at the Sixth Plenum of the Central Committee, Hua Guofeng resigned as Party Chairman and Hu Yaobang, a follower of Deng, was selected to replace him.[88] These events indicated that the Deng group was in firm control of both the Party and the government, at least at the top levels.

In the period since Deng took power, the most visible aspect of political life in China has been the emphasis on the Four Modernizations. Or, one might say, industrialization at almost any cost. This campaign, if one can call it that, pervades every aspect of Chinese life. In fact, though not in name, collective ownership of agricultural land is being scrapped in favor of a sort of limited individual ownership under the label of the "individual responsibility system."[89] Foreign investment is sought ea-

---

85. The Third Plenum is discussed in B. BRUGGER, *supra* note 63, at 218-19.

86. Proposal of the Central Committee of the Chinese Communist Party Regarding the Revision of the Constitution and the Establishment of a Constitutional Revision Committee [*Zhongguo Gongzhan Dang Zhongyang Weiyuanhui Guanyu Xingai Xianfa He Chengli Xianfa Xingai Weiyuanhui*] of August 30, 1980, in CONSTITUTIONAL MATERIALS, *supra* note 1, at 375.

87. Resolution of the Third Session of the Fifth National People's Congress of the People's Republic of China Regarding the Revision of the Constitution and the Establishment of a Constitution Revision Committee [*Zhonghua Renmin Gongheguo Ti Wu Jie Quanguo Renmin Daibiao Da Hui Ti San Ze Huiyi Guanyu Xingai Xianfa He Chengle Xianfa Xiugai Weihuanhui*] of September 10, 1980, CONSTITUTIONAL MATERIALS, *supra* note 1, at 379.

88. *See Quarterly Chronicle and Documentation*, THE CHINA Q. 547, 548 (1981).

89. *See* Schell, *A Reporter at Large: The Wind of Wanting to Go It Alone*, THE NEW YORKER 65-73 (Jan. 23, 1984) [hereinafter cited as Schell]. *See also supra* note 26. The Chinese would, of course, deny that land farmed under the individual responsibility system is "owned" by the cultivator because it cannot be sold or even rented. Even if the peasants were not busy finding ways around these prohibitions—as one assumes they are—the rights they do have constitute ownership as this term is defined in the RESTATEMENT OF PROPERTY § 10 comment b (1936). The recent *Circular of the Central Committee of the Chinese Communist Party on Rural Work During 1984*, THE CHINA Q. 132 (1985), allows households to enter into contracts to use land for 15 years or more. This is "ownership" by almost any definition. While land "may not be bought or sold, may not be leased to a thid party and may not be transferred as building plots for housing or for any other non-agricul-

gerly and foreigners are even permitted to develop and, in effect, to own China's natural resources such as oil.[90] Internally, private capitalism at a low level, such as handicraft industry, hauling, restaurants, etc., is permitted.[91] It is reported that shares will soon be sold in Chinese enterprises and that both Chinese and foreigners will be permitted to buy them.[92] In other words, private and even foreign ownership of the means of production is now permitted (although considerable intellectual energy is expended to deny this). Education is also being emphasized and changed. Its chief goal now is to produce high-quality experts in large numbers. Education is now an elite system that relies on competitive examinations, foreign experts and foreign training for its staff, a complete reversal of the radical egalitarian theories of Chairman Mao. The new officials in the Party and government, at least at the top levels, tend to be people with university educations.[93]

In valuating these changes, it is instructive to look back at the campaign that was conducted against Deng Xiaoping during late 1975 and 1976.[94] That is roughly the period between the promulgation of the 1975 constitution and the death of Mao. This campaign began with the attack on Deng's theories of education. It was alleged that he advocated that there be more attention to theory, less to practice. He advocated downplaying the worker-peasant teams. He was accused of having said, "The greatest tragedy of these years is that study has been abandoned and everything is work and trade."[95] He is supposed to have said that universities should train scientists and cadres and "universities" which train people to become peasants and workers should be abolished.

The general attack on Deng's ideas that followed in the next few months quoted speeches in which Deng is alleged to have criticized campaigns as a waste of time that harmed old Party members who were

---

tural use," *id.*, the contract can be transferred with the consent of the collective. *Id.* It is said that the peasants expect the leasehold to become "property" after 15 years and in the meantime there is a brisk trade in them. Kueh, *The Economics of the 'Second Land Reform' in China*, THE CHINA Q. 122, 128 nn.10-12 (1985).

90. The Joint Venture Law is available in both English and Chinese in 1 CHINA'S FOREIGN ECONOMIC LEGISLATION 1 (1982).

91. *See* Schell, *supra* note 89, at 43-58.

92. As to possible foreign ownership of shares in Chinese concerns, see *Peking firms may seek Hong Kong listing*, South China Morning Post, July 6, 1984, at 1.

93. *See* WENG, *supra* note 9, at 251-54.

94. This is based on CHINA NEWS ANALYSIS No. 1044 (June 18, 1976). *See also* B. BRUGGER, *supra* note 63, at 177-95.

95. CHINA NEWS ANALYSIS, No. 1044 (June 18, 1976).

falsely accused of being revisionists. He objected to the criticism of intellectuals. He emphasized science and technology. In general he advocated the development of productive forces as opposed to the class struggle. He said, quoting Mao, "The criterion of good or bad is whether production force is released or tied down."[96] He advocated purchasing foreign technology on credit, using Chinese resources to pay for it. He advocated the use of material incentives both in industry and agriculture to raise production.

Thus the positions for which Deng was criticized have become the official program of the Chinese government and the basis of the 1982 constitution. This could have been predicted: So long as Deng and his group are in power, this will continue to be the program (unless they change their minds). If what have been his opposition are in power, one can expect a shift in emphasis from productive forces to the class struggle. At any rate, these are the principles that govern China now and they form the basis of the new constitution just as the ideology of previous groups has governed the constitutions they promulgated and the policies they followed.

The ideological message of the 1982 constitution is very clear. The preamble begins with the usual history of the struggle of the Chinese people against feudalism and imperialism. However, it emphasizes China's long and glorious history and the role of Sun Yat-sen in overthrowing the Manchus. These are both new features of the standard history. Then there is a summary of the history of the People's Republic of China. The Cultural Revolution—emphasized in the 1975 and 1978 constitutions—is ignored. In sum, the "people's democratic dictatorship led by the working class and based on the alliance of workers and peasants, which is, in essence, the dictatorship of the proletariat, has been consolidated and developed."[97] The basic task at this stage is to achieve the Four Modernizations.[98] The class struggle is basically over. It is essential to rely on workers, peasants and intellectuals in achieving modernization; there must be a "broad patriotic united front."

In the constitution's text, this message is continued. Article 1 states that China is a people's democratic dictatorship. This phrase is apparently a code term that means that the class struggle is down-played. It is especially valuable for intellectuals and former capitalists—two groups

96. *Id.*

97. 1982 CONST. preamble.

98. The Four Modernizations are: industry, agriculture, defense, and science and technology.

very important for the Four Modernizations—who can be classified as "people" or even "workers," but who are a little difficult to characterize as "the proletariat." If these groups participate in the dictatorship, then they are less likely to be targets of it. In the case of the dictatorship of the proletariat, anyone who is not a member of the proletariat is a likely target for dictatorship. The consequences can range from inability to get work or an education to execution as an enemy.

The Four Modernizations are not mentioned by name in the text, but their spirit governs. In the 1975 and 1978 constitutions, the state administers the individual economy in an effort to eliminate it. Now the individual economy is a complement to the "socialist public economy," and "the state protects the lawful rights and interests of the individual economy."[99] Article 14 summarizes the present economic program:

> The state continuously raises labour productivity, improves economic results and develops the *productive forces* by enhancing the enthusiasm of the working people, raising the level of their technical skill, disseminating advanced science and technology, improving the system of economic administration and enterprise operation and management, instituting the socialist system of responsibility in various forms and improving organization of work.[100]

State and collective enterprises are given some independence.[101] Foreign investment is allowed.[102] The state awards achievements in scientific discoveries. Article 25 provides: "The state trains specialized personnel in all fields who serve socialism, increases the number of intellectuals and creates conditions to give full scope to their role in socialist modernization."[103]

All of this is in line with the preamble and with what Deng preached before he got to power and practiced thereafter. In other words, China is a state that is dedicated to the principles of Marxism-Leninism-Mao Zedong Thought, but which at the present time must concentrate on building up its productive forces. When the aims of the Four Modernizations are achieved, China will presumably be able to advance to a stage closer to socialism. Because the intellectuals by that time will be in control of both Party and state, their positions would seem to be assured, so

---

99. 1982 CONST. art. 11.
100. 1982 CONST. art. 14.
101. 1982 CONST. art. 16.
102. 1982 CONST. art. 18.
103. 1982 CONST. art. 25.

that this would be socialism with a very different face from that contemplated in 1975 and 1978.

The activities of the government since the 1982 constitution was promulgated are in accordance with these aims. And that is perhaps one of the points to notice about Chinese constitutions. To say that policy is law is not to say that China's political system is lawless, or unpredictable, or subject to the whim and caprice of its leaders. The official policy of a country like China is normally hammered out after lengthy discussions. Once established, it is likely to continue for a long while. If a group that is in power wishes to change policy, there will probably be many signals. And if an opposing group comes to power, it is likely that one will know beforehand much of what it plans to do. Still, there is more uncertainty and more change than there is in a system such as that of the United States, in which policy tends to be crystallized into "law." The policy against over-concentration in industry is held in varying degrees of esteem by different administrations, but none has felt it possible formally to repeal the antitrust laws. But in China, every policy, every law, can be completely changed within a very short time.

Such changes are now going on. What will happen next? If past practice continues, then this constitution will remain in force as long as the present group remains in power, unless its policies should change considerably. In the event of a significant political or policy change, there would be a formal constitutional change. This would presumably be of no surprise to the Chinese, who are at least as aware as we are of the transitory nature of their constitutions. Indeed, they sometimes say as much. A member of the Chinese People's Political Consultative Conference is supposed to have said in regard to the 1982 constitution: "Will the new constitution become a mere scrap of paper as the 1954 constitution became. . . ?"[104] The Chinese must also be aware of the fact that institutions of government such as the courts and congresses have no real power and that a constitutional guarantee such as a guarantee of freedom of the person or the right to have a trial uninfluenced by "Administrative organs, public organization or individuals"[105] and the like, is pretty empty. Officials must, in other words, be aware of the facts that not only can all their policies and laws change if they lose out in a power struggle, but also they themselves run a serious risk of personal harm if this should

104. FBIS, DAILY REPORT K8 (Dec. 9, 1982).

105. Art. 126.

happen. It has already happened to these officials during the Cultural Revolution—and before, for that matter. It seems reasonable to assume that they do not wish for it to happen again. Consequently, they seem to have a great desire for stability, and they have attempted to make this constitution different from its predecessors in order to get that stability. They have attempted to substitute law, as we understand the term, for policy. They have done this by means of certain provisions in the constitution itself,[106] and by means of a vigorous campaign for the "rule of law" in China.[107]

It is difficult to know what significance to give to these or any other institutional changes in Chinese constitutions, because all we have to go on are the constitutions themselves and the Chinese commentaries. The Chinese commentators make no effort to ask how things will actually work. Instead they write about Chinese constitutions in the way an American might write about a new state constitution. They discuss every institution as if it functioned exactly as one would expect from reading the text. This is almost never true. It often seems that none of the institutions that are dealt with at length in the constitutions have any importance at all. Consequently, what does it matter if there are changes in the functions that are supposedly given to the institutions? It would matter, of course, if there were a strong desire on the part of very powerful people to have the changes mean something. There are hints in the new constitution and its official commentary that this may be the case now. What seems to be intended is to create institutions that will have some actual power and thus to create a government that is at least distanced from the Party, if not completely removed from its control.[108]

106. Consider for example the treatment of art. 5, which provides that "no law . . . shall contravene the Constitution," and all "state organs, the armed forces," etc., "must abide by the Constitution and the law." Both the Congress, art. 62(2), and its Standing Committee, art. 67(1), are to enforce this apparently. The problem of constitutionality is discussed in one standard commentary under the chapter heading "The new constitution strengthens the stipulations for defending the constitution" [*Xin Xianfa Zhajiangle Xianfa Bao Zhangde Guiding*]. The authors list four ways in which the new constitution provides this protection: (1) it strengthens the supervisory power of the Congress and its Standing Committee; (2) it gives the standing committee power to declare acts and regulations unconstitutional; (3) it provides that all agencies and citizens must respect the constitution; and (4) it requires a super-majority of Congress to amend the consitution. There is no discussion of how all this will work. There seems to be a feeling that if there are words in a statute that say someone has a "right," then he does. *See* W. ZHAOZHE & C. YUNSHENG, GUIDE TO THE NEW CONSTITUTION [*Xin Xianfa Jianghua*] 224-27 (1983).

107. *See supra* note 19. *See also The Use of the Legal Weapon*, CHINA NEWS ANALYSIS (June 18, 1984).

108. The 1982 Party Constitution, adopted three months before the State Constitution, is in

The outlines of such a government are anything but clear. They may not always be clear to the authors. One clue to what is intended may be found in the seven changes in governmental institutions in the new constitution that are said by the draftsmen in their official commentary to be particularly significant.[109] These changes were:

1. The power of the National People's Congress is increased because more power is given to its standing committee. Because the standing committee can meet frequently and is much smaller than the Congress as a whole, it can exercise power effectively. This is something that the Congress cannot do.
2. The position of President of the Republic is restored.
3. A military affairs control committee is established. It is appointed by the Congress and responsible to it. Formerly the armed forces were under the Party's control (at least that is what the constitutions said).
4. The Premier is made responsible to Congress for the actions of the government. Each ministry operates under a system whereby the minister is responsible for the action of his ministry to the Premier. A system of auditing is instituted both at the national and local levels in order to strengthen the supervision of fiscal matters.
5. The local government authorities have been strengthened under central leadership. The congresses of provinces and cities under direct rule exercise supervisory authority over local governments, which operate under a system whereby the chief administrator is responsible.
6. The communes have been deprived of all political functions, which now go to the "township." This clarifies political responsibility.
7. Certain high officials, such as the President and members of the Standing Committee of the National People's Congress, may not serve more than two terms.

These provisions seem to be designed to create an hierarchical system of government with the apex in the Premier. Each unit has a head who is responsible to the next higher level and so on up to the top. The Premier is in turn nominally responsible to the National People's Congress, but in fact this means that he is responsible to the Standing Committee. The Committee will, in all probability, be more or less self-perpetuating be-

---

harmony with this view. It provides in the preamble that "The Party must conduct its activities within the limits permitted by the Constitution and the laws of the state." 25 BEIJING REV. at 8 (1982). In 1980 when this constitution was being drafted, Deng Xiaoping, in a speech delivered to the Political Bureau of the Party, stated that the Party should be separated from the government. The Party would establish general principles but would strengthen the state structure. Policy would not be a substitute for government. HSIA & JOHNSON, THE CHINESE COMMUNIST PARTY CONSTITUTION OF 1982: DENG ZIAOPING'S PROGRAM FOR MODERNIZATION (1984).

109. Speech by Peng Zhen printed in Chinese edition of 1982 constitution, *supra* note 1, at 66-69.

cause, in view of the indirect nature of the electoral process, radical changes in the composition of the Congress are unlikely, and the Standing Committee is clearly intended to control Congress. Hence what one has is very similar to the system of the government in an American corporation. The organization is run by its permanent bureaucracy, the President and his subordinates, but there is a very real power of ultimate supervision by a self-perpetuating board of directors. In China, however, there is the troublesome memory of a long-term power holder—Mao Zedong—that is no doubt fresh in people's minds. So no one is permitted to stay in a top job for more than two terms. One curious aspect to this system is that it is, in some ways, more in harmony with the theories of Sun Yat-sen than the government that now exists in Taiwan.[110]

Dr. Sun believed that political power should be distinguished from governmental power. A strong government was not to be feared so long as the government is ultimately controlled by the people in the exercise of their political power. Government consists of making, enforcing and interpreting rules as well as recruiting personnel for government and investigating its work. The mass of the people cannot do these things. But the people can control the government by exercising four political powers: suffrage, initiative, referendum and recall. In a country as large as China, they cannot exercise powers directly as they might, perhaps, in a Swiss canton. Hence they act through the people's Congress. The Congress is not a legislature. It does not make laws in the usual way. Rather, it elects the leaders of the government, one branch of which makes laws (the legislative yüan). The people, acting through their representatives, the Congress, can elect or remove all top officials. The people can initiate legislation or have it referred to them for approval (referendum). But the initiative and referendum are as extraordinary in China as they are in the United States. Normally people simply elect top officials of the government and supervise their work by getting periodic reports. This is, of course, the way the National People's Congress is supposed to work.

110. The Constitution of the Republic of China (Taiwan) provides for direct election to the Legislative Yüan—the body that actually legislates, art. 64, as well as to the Congress, art. 26. As indicated in the text, Dr. Sun wanted elections only to the Congress, which was to elect the Legislative Yüan. *See* P.M.A. LINEBARGER, THE POLITICAL DOCTRINES OF SUN YATSEN 89-121, 209-23 (1937) and W.Y. TSAO, THE CONSTITUTIONAL STRUCTURE OF MODERN CHINA 96-113, 130-45 (1947). The Tsao book reprints the translations of the texts of the Chinese Constitution of 1946 (in force in Taiwan), *id.* at 275, and the draft constitution of 1937, much closer to Dr. Sun's ideas, *id.* at 238.

There are also, to be sure, many differences between the 1982 constitution and the ideas of Dr. Sun and his followers.[111] Still, if one looks only at what the constitution says about the political as opposed to economic institutions of China and at what it says about international relations, one cannot help wondering about the possible influences of Dr. Sun—who has never been repudiated by the Communists. At the present time, even those economic provisions of the constitution that encourage individual farmers to control the land they farm and benefit from it seem to be a sort of echo of Dr. Sun's famous program of giving land to the tiller. Dr. Sun attempted to assimilate western democratic ideas and institutions into traditional Chinese ideas and institutions in order to create a system that would work in China. If the present constitution is in fact influenced by Dr. Sun, its draftsmen are emphasizing the Chinese tradition as the foundation of their government. There seems to be some hint of this in the preamble in the midst of many protestations of loyalty to Marxism-Leninism.[112] Connecting the present government to Chinese tradition is an obvious way of giving the government a basis for existing independent of the Party.

Regardless, however, of whether the leaders of China are the ardent followers of Marxism-Leninism-Mao Zedong Thought that they purport

111. The most obvious difference is that Dr. Sun proposed to have the government administration divided into five divisions, or Yüan: Legislative, Judicial, Administrative, Examination and Control. Y-S SUN, SAN MIN CHU-I 144-49 [Lecture Six]. The first three divisions are taken from the U.S. Constitution and the last two from traditional Chinese institutions. The table of organization for the government established by the 1982 constitution of the People's Republic of China envisages a Congress which formally enacts legislation that is actually drafted by its standing committee and special committees subordinate to it, not a Legislative Yüan that is quite separate. The government supervised by the congress has three or four parts: the State Council (equivalent to Dr. Sun's Administrative Yüan); Central Military Commission; People's Courts; and People's Procuracy. (The last two are treated together). On the other hand, one of the principal features of Dr. Sun's program for China was the idea of "tutelage." China was not yet ready for direct elections nationwide because it had no experience with democracy. Hence the Guomindang controlled the country and conducted elections first at the local or county level. When all the counties in a province were electing their local government, the province was then ready to have province-wide elections. When half the provinces were democratic, there could be elections to Congress. LINEBARGER, *supra* note 104, at 210-214. The system of indirect elections established in the 1982 constitution is certainly compatible with this, although it is not exactly the same. It is curious that the idea of a standing committee of the People's Congress, which was rejected by the drafters of the Guomindang constitution, was strongly advocated—for much the same reasons given by Peng Zhen—by Professor Tsao, who seems clearly to be a disciple of Dr. Sun. TSAO, *supra* note 110, at 112-13.

112. See preamble provisions on China's long history and Sun's role in overthrowing the Manchus.

to be, or closet devotees of the Three People's Principles, it is still not clear that the governmental institutions described in the constitution will ever operate independently of the Party. The Party at the present time is not, after all, a small band of enthusiastic revolutionaries. It is an enormous bureaucracy with tens of millions of members. For thirty-five years, membership in the Party has been the principal road to power and the perquisites of power such as housing, food, education, health care, travel, and the like.[113] The vast majority of persons now living in China have never known anything else. All of the persons who are in the top positions in the government are also important Party members. The two things go together. It is hard to see those Party members who are, for example, Standing Committee members, getting rid of Party control of the electoral process. Though it was suggested recently by one of the most authoritative observers of China that the current Chairman of the National People's Congress, Peng Zhen, who was vice-chairman of the committee that was said to have drafted the constitution, is attempting to make the Standing Committee of the National People's Congress a rival power-center to the Politburo of the Communist Party because Zhen is not a member of the Politburo. He is said to have significant support.[114] If this is an accurate assessment, it is interesting. Even if it does not mean that power has shifted from the Party to governmental institutions, Zhen's attempt would mean that they, particularly the Standing Committee, have become fora in which battles for Party control might be fought. Hence they would acquire some real life as opposed to the merely formal existence they have had heretofore. Of course such importance, even if it exists, may be short-lived. Mao Zedong created extra-Party organizations, notably the Cultural Revolution Small Group and the Red Guards, when he had apparently lost control of the Party apparatus. He used these new organizations to destroy the leaders of the Party (sometimes in a very literal sense).[115] But once this was accomplished, he simply put his men into control of the Party. The new organizations disappeared or ceased to have much power. Moreover, if there is some sort of struggle for power going on now between Deng and Peng, it is a struggle between two octogenarians. It is not clear that its outcome will have any long-term significance. Although of course it may.

There is another development that might make the institutions created

113. *See* WENG, *supra* note 9, at 135.

114. L. LaDanay, *China's New Power Centre?*, FAR EASTERN ECON. REV. 38 (1984).

115. *See* H-Y LEE, THE POLITICS OF THE CHINESE CULTURAL REVOLUTION 1-10 (1978).

by this constitution different from those created by its predecessors. That is the development of a legal profession. China has never had a significant legal profession in the western sense outside of the Treaty Ports such as Shanghai where there were extraterritorial courts. Even the vestiges of a western (or even Soviet) system pretty much disappeared after 1958. There were courts, but it is not clear what function they fulfilled. There was clearly no general system of criminal courts in a western sense. Nor were there lawyers.[116] Beginning in the late 1970s, however, there has been a determined movement to change this situation. Laws and law books proliferate. Law departments are being established or re-established in universities. University-level institutions and special courses are being formed to give training in law to judges, most of whom were military men and had no legal training.[117] If this activity continues, it will mean that there will be a very large number of people in a well-entrenched bureaucracy—the courts and procuracy (though will the security administration continue to dominate?)—who have been trained to think in terms of law as something independent of policy. There will be other trained lawyers throughout the bureaucracy. This is already true of the foreign trade organs.

It would be foolish to suppose that all of these individuals will have acquired a passionate fondness for civil rights and due process, although it is clear that at least those who have studied law in law departments have had access to western legal materials, including constitutional law materials.[118] It does seem possible, however, that they will serve to form a core of resistance to rapid change outside the normal channels, such as to something like the Cultural Revolution. If one wished to rid oneself of an opponent, a "trial" for counter-revolutionary acts would be used rather than a mass meeting. The "trial" of the Gang of Four is of interest in this context because previously trials were not used in purges of

116. For my views on the system as of 1975, see Jones, *A Possible Model for the Criminal Trial in the People's Republic of China*, 24 AM. J. COMP. L. 229 (1976). See Peng, *Importance of Improving China's Legislation*, BEIJING REV. no. 35, 16 (1984), for an official view of the legal situation in China since liberation.

117. *See, e.g.*, Li, *Legal Education Surges Ahead*, 26 BEIJING REV. 22 (1985); *Spare-time college helps train judges*, China Daily, Feb. 18, 1983; *Socialist legal system making good progress*, *id.*, Dec. 12, 1983; *Major plan adopted to train jurists*, *id.*, Jan. 7, 1984.

118. For example, CONSTITUTIONAL MATERIALS consists of five volumes and includes most of the major constitutional documents of the western world, including the Magna Carta, The Petition of Right, the U.S. Declaration of Independence and Constitution, and the Declaration of the Rights of Man. It had an initial press run of 15,000 copies and was freely available throughout the country.

Party leaders.[119]

Despite this apparent desire for change and the measures that seem to have been taken to bring it about, it is far too early to say whether the new constitution will in fact effect some changes or simply go the way of its predecessors. Much depends on how long Deng stays in power and on who succeeds him. To make any predictions on how the Chinese constitution will fare in the midst of these events, one must be able to predict the immediate future of Chinese politics, and few would wish to attempt that.[120] All that one can say is that from 1949 to the present, Chinese constitutions have not played a western role of describing and prescribing the forms and powers of governmental institutions and the rights of citizens, although they purport to do so. Rather, they have signaled political and ideological change. The more recent changes have involved a bitter and violent dispute over the issue of the continuation of the class struggle thirty years or so after liberation. Those who oppose continuation of the struggle are now in power. They have attempted in every possible way to prevent a reversal of their programs. Doubtless the most important method that they have used is the traditional one of purging the party and replacing supporters of the old group with their own people.[121] They have devoted much attention to building up mass support. But they have also attempted to make some institutional changes in the Chinese government that may make it more resistant to change. And they constantly emphasize the importance of law as opposed to policy, and have sponsored the development of a legal system and a legal profession. Only time will tell what they have accomplished.

119. As a "trial" it was a farce, but it was interesting that the Chinese used a public show trial to get rid of defeated opponents. Previously, people just disappeared. Sometimes they were publicly attacked, but there was no trial-like proceeding. For the early purge of Gao Gang and Rao Shushi, see F. TEIWES, POLITICS AND PURGES IN CHINA 166-210 (1979). Two prominent leaders were accused primarily of "factionalism" and trying to seize power. They were accused anonymously at the Fourth Plenum of the Seventh Central Committee Meeting in 1954, and were publicly attacked at the National Conference of the Party in 1955. Sometime in between Gao committed suicide. There was a "verdict," but no trial. The Teiwes book discusses all of the important purges up to the Cultural Revolution.

120. Of course if one had to guess, it would be that what is likely to emerge is something like the system in the Soviet Union: stable, but very authoritarian and controlled, and rather corrupt. The Soviets are said to believe that China will have to adopt their system, though of course they do not characterize it as I have. *See* T. Oka, *China charts its own course*, The Christian Science Monitor, June 30-July 6, 1984, at 14 (int'l ed.).

121. This present campaign to "consolidate" the Party has in fact been characterized as a purge by one well-informed observer. *See* HSIA & JOHNSON, *supra* note 108, at 30-31.

[6]

RULING THE COUNTRY IN ACCORDANCE WITH LAW

Reflections on the Rule and Role of Law in Contemporary China

RANDALL PEERENBOOM
UCLA Law School

◇

ABSTRACT

This article examines rule of law in China. Part 1 distinguishes between (i) substantive or thick theories of rule of law that incorporate elements of political morality, such as particular economic arrangements, forms of government, or conceptions of human rights; and (ii) formal or thin theories of rule of law that focus on features that any legal system must possess to function effectively as a system of laws. Although China does not endorse liberal democracy or a liberal conception of human rights, nevertheless the legal system is intended to serve many of the same general purposes as legal systems elsewhere. Accordingly, thin versions of rule of law are applicable to China. Part 2 then measures the performance of China's legal system against the benchmark of certain features generally accepted by advocates of a thin theory of rule of law.

Key Words ◇ China ◇ foreign investment ◇ legal development ◇ legal theory ◇ rule of law

While much of the debate about legal reform in China takes rule of law as the benchmark, there seems to be little agreement as to what rule of law is or how to measure it. Many legal scholars in particular share Judith Shklar's fear that rule of law 'may well have become just another one of those self-congratulatory rhetorical devices that grace the public utterances of Anglo-American politicians' (Shklar, 1987: 1). Not only is there no accepted definition of rule of law, there is not even agreement on how to go about defining it. On the one hand, there are those that favor a substantive understanding of rule of law that incorporates elements of political morality such as particular economic arrangements (usually capitalist), forms of government (usually democratic), or conceptions of human rights

Cultural Dynamics 11(3): 315–351. [0921–3740 (199911) 11:3; 315–351; 010176]

(usually liberal). For example, the 1959 International Congress of Jurists in New Delhi declared:

> The function of the legislature in a free society under the Rule of Law is to create and maintain the conditions which will uphold the dignity of man as an individual. This dignity requires not only the recognition of his civil and political rights but also the establishment of the social, economic, educational and cultural conditions which are essential to the full development of his personality.[1]

On the other hand, there are those who prefer a more limited understanding of rule of law that emphasizes its formal or instrumental aspects – those features that any legal system allegedly must possess to function effectively as a system of laws, regardless of whether the legal system is part of a democratic or non-democratic society, capitalist or socialist, liberal or theocratic, and indeed regardless of whether the legal system is a good one or an evil one (Raz, 1979; Summers, 1993).[2] As Joseph Raz notes,

> If rule of law is the rule of the good law then to explain its nature is to propound a complete social philosophy. But if so the term lacks any useful function. We have no need to be converted to the rule of law just in order to believe that good should triumph...
>
> A non-democratic legal system, based on the denial of human rights, on extensive poverty, on racial segregation, sexual inequalities, and religious persecution may, in principle, conform to the requirements of the rule of law better than any of the legal systems of the more enlightened Western democracies. (Raz, 1979: 211)

Typical candidates for the more limited normative purposes served by thin theories of rule of law include: preventing anarchy and Hobbesian war of all against all (Fallon, 1997; Walker, 1988); securing government in accordance with law—rule of law as opposed to rule of man—by limiting at least some forms of arbitrariness on the part of the government (Dicey, 1885); enhancing predictability, which allows people to plan their affairs and hence promotes both individual freedom and economic development (Hayek, 1944); and providing a fair mechanism for the resolution of disputes (Gaus, 1994). Perhaps the most formal and substantively minimal basis for rule of law is that suggested by Raz, who takes as his departure point the 'basic intuition' that law must be capable of guiding behavior (Raz, 1979).

Although proponents of a robust substantive theory of rule of law may take issue with all that is left out of thin theories, it is important to appreciate just how much can be derived from a minimal starting point such as the ability of law to guide behavior. To serve that purpose, laws must exhibit certain formal characteristics. They must be publicly promulgated (open and transparent), prospective, consistent, and relatively clear and stable.[3] In addition, they must be implemented: if laws are not enforced in practice, people will quickly realize that there is no need to follow the law and adjust their behavior accordingly.

A variety of institutions and processes are also required. The promulgation of law assumes a legislature and the government machinery necessary to make the laws publicly available. It also assumes rules for making laws. Congruence of laws on the books and actual practice assumes institutions for implementing and enforcing laws. While informal means of enforcing laws may be possible in some contexts, modern societies must also rely on formal means such as courts and administrative bodies. Furthermore, if the law is to guide behavior, laws must be applied and enforced in a reasonable way that does not completely defeat people's expectations. This implies normative and practical limits on the decision-makers who interpret and apply the laws and principles of due process or natural justice such as access to impartial tribunals, a chance to present evidence, and rules of evidence.

Proponents of a formal or instrumental conception of the rule of law point to several advantages of a thin theory over a thick substantive one. First, even a limited conception of rule of law has many important virtues. Although just what these virtues are and the normative weight they are to be assigned will depend on how thin the theory is and a number of practical and normative issues, thin theories of rule of law at minimum promise some degree of predictability and at least some limitation on arbitrariness. By narrowing the focus, a thin theory highlights the importance of these and other rule-of-law virtues.

Second, a thin theory allows for focused and productive discussion of rule of law among persons of different political persuasions. As Robert Summers notes,

> A substantive theory necessarily ranges over highly diverse subject matter, and thus sprawls in its application. On a full fledged substantive theory, arguments and criticisms purportedly in the name of the 'rule of law' tend to be arguments and criticisms in the name of too many different things at once. (Summers, 1993: 137)

Being able to narrow the focus of discussion and avoid getting bogged down in larger issues of political morality is particularly important in cross-cultural dialogue between, for example, American liberals and Chinese socialists or Muslim fundamentalists.

Third, as a practical matter, much of the moral force behind the rule of law and its enduring importance as a political ideal today is predicated on the ability to use rule of law as a benchmark to condemn or praise particular rules, decisions, practices, and legal systems (Fallon, 1997: 43). To the extent that there is common ground and agreement on at least some features of a thin theory of rule of law, many of the theoretical and practical problems associated with normative valuations in a pluralist society and world are avoided. Criticisms are more likely to be taken seriously and result in actual change given a shared understanding of rule of law.

Of course a thin theory of rule of law is no panacea. A fully developed thin theory would need to include among other things an account of the values, purposes, or ends of rule of law; the requisite characteristics of laws; the institutional arrangements needed to give effect to rule of law; and a theory of interpretation. Clearly, there is plenty of room for disagreement.[4]

For starters, why these purposes? Even the limited purposes of rule of law suggested by thin theories need justification. For instance, many argue that the reason for valuing predictability is that it enhances freedom and allows people to make plans, and thus respects human dignity (Finnis, 1980: 272; Raz, 1979: 221). Underlying this view is a liberal view of the self as moral agent that emphasizes autonomy and the importance of making moral choices. But not all ethical traditions share this view of the self or place such importance on making choices. The dominant Chinese view of the self as social and the Confucian emphasis on doing what is right rather than the right to choose (Peerenboom, 1998) call into question justifications of rule of law that appeal to this interpretation of human dignity.[5]

As for the characteristics of laws, several are vague—what precisely is meant by consistent? Some laws may be inconsistent at the level of purpose but not in specific provisions. Moreover, all of the required traits admit of degrees and exceptions. Some laws are clearer than others. Sometimes laws are changed and even made effective retroactively. Further, at times the various elements conflict. Replacing a number of vague rules with clearer ones would enhance predictability in one way—yet at the same time it could increase instability and hence detract from predictability in another.

A thin theory must also address a number of other controversial (and in some cases unsolvable) issues. Is separation of powers necessary (and what exactly does it entail)? Is judicial review necessary? A free press? An independent legal profession? While it is generally agreed that an independent judiciary is required, how independent should the judiciary be? Should judges be allowed to make law by supplementing or modifying the law in light of the particular circumstances and general considerations of equity even if that diminishes predictability? Should administrators have the same powers? When interpreting laws, should judges and administrators stick to the plain meaning of the statute or should they take into consideration other factors such as its purpose?

A full-blown thin theory of rule of law would attempt to resolve these and other issues based on limited formal or substantive content and the values that flow from rule of law so conceived. But the rule of law is but one component of the larger legal and political order. As noted, it is compatible with great injustice. Thus the question arises as to the relation of rule of law to the legal and political system as a whole. When are the values gained by adherence to rule of law to give way to other values? This is not a question that can be answered internally from within the walls of a thin theory of rule of law. At the end of the day, the question turns on larger issues of political morality and a vision of a just society, whether liberal, libertarian, socialist, or communitarian.

Proponents of a more robust substantive approach to rule of law claim that these are the important issues anyway: the relation of the rule of law and indeed law more generally to economic development, democracy, and human rights. Their objection to thin theories is not (or at least not primarily) that there is room for disagreement over particular elements, that the rule of law is achievable only to a degree or even that there is as yet no fully developed thin theory that justifies the particular choice of purposes, characteristics, institutions, and values. Rather than disagreement, the reaction is to say, 'ok, so what?'[6] But two points bear emphasis: first, there is general agreement about many of the basic features of a thin or instrumental rule of law; second, as a strategy for cross-cultural comparisons, it makes sense to begin from common ground, and thus start with a thin account of the rule of law.

In Part 1, I examine various purposes that law and the legal system are meant to serve in contemporary China, some associated with thin theories of rule of law and some with more substantive conceptions. My purpose is not to present a full-blown substantive theory or even a full-blown thin theory. Rather, my objective is to demonstrate that the ends law and the legal system are supposed to serve in socialist China, while similar in a broad sense to the ends law and the legal system are intended to serve in western liberal democracies, differ in important ways that raise many of the large political issues that proponents of thin theories wish to avoid; nevertheless, despite such differences, there is enough common ground to support a thin theory of rule of law along the lines sketched earlier. Given such common ground, assessing China's legal system against the benchmark of rule of law principles is meaningful both as an external and internal critique.

In Part 2, I focus on certain generally accepted elements of a thin theory of rule of law. The elements selected are not meant to be exhaustive. Limitations of space prevent a comprehensive appraisal of China's legal system in light of rule-of-law standards, although enough is said to provide a fair sense of the current state of China's legal system. Judged by the selected rule-of-law standards, China's legal system, while it has made tremendous progress over the last 20 years, stands in need of considerable improvement, as is widely acknowledged in China. But more important than the particular diagnosis of the health of China's current legal system is an understanding of the complexity of the situation and the diversity of factors that cut in different directions and affect different elements in different ways. The elements were selected in part for what they reveal about China's legal system and the challenges it faces in complying with rule-of-law standards and relying on law as a source of order. They also call attention to some of the issues that would need to be addressed to develop a full-blown thin theory of rule of law and even more so a full-blown substantive theory. A thin theory to some degree and a substantive theory to an even greater degree would need to take into consideration the influence of China's ethical, political, and philosophical traditions, culture, socialist ideology, current level of economic development, government structure, legal institutions, and a host of other such contingent factors. Indeed, one of the most challenging issues is to determine the extent to which even thin rule-of-law theories will vary during periods of great economic and political transition—an issue confronting many of the former Soviet Union countries and also China, as the latter undergoes the transformation from a centrally planned economy to a more market oriented economy.[7]

1. The Purposes of Law and the Rule of Law

At the most abstract level, law and the rule of law are means to achieve a just, good, or normatively appealing society. But positing justice or a good society as the end is vacuous: justice and a good society simply function as place-holders for more particular values or ends. Liberals will define justice and a good society in terms of liberal values; libertarians in terms of libertarian values; communitarians in terms of communal values; socialists in terms of socialist values.

On a less abstract level, law and the rule of law have often been considered necessary (i) to constrain the arbitrary acts of the government (Wang, 1998; Jiang Mingan, 1997; Ying, 1997; Liu Hainian, 1998); (ii) to facilitate and ensure economic development (Wang, 1998; Jiang Zemin, 1996; Shen, 1998); (iii) to protect the individual against the state (Wang, 1998; Li, 1998; Li and Zhang, 1997); and (iv) to provide a fair mechanism for resolving disputes (Liu Hainian, 1998). As indicated, each of these candidates has also been offered in support of rule of law in China. Of course, these intermediate purposes or ends may themselves be interpreted in a variety of ways. For instance, liberals interpret protection of the individual against the state in terms of a liberal conception of human rights that emphasizes the freedom and autonomy of the individual. Others may assign less importance to individual freedom and autonomy and more to communal values or social stability, and hence draw a different balance between the rights of individuals and the needs of the state. Moreover, there are a number of possible institutional arrangements consistent with these goals. Thus, while many consider constitutional review by a court constitutionally independent of the legislature essential if law is to be used to curtail arbitrary acts of government, China—like some other countries that adopt a parliamentary system—does not. Finally, it bears recalling that rule of law is relative: no country's legal system will have a perfect score on every possible rule-of-law indicator.

Limitations on Arbitrary Acts of Government

Perhaps the most commonly accepted purpose of the rule of law is to limit the arbitrary acts of government. The historical roots for the modern western understanding of rule of law can be traced back to the struggles between the parliament and the English monarchy in 17th-century England, where the banner of rule of law was raised to resist the arbitrary economic and political acts of the King (Dicey, 1885; Walker, 1988).[8] Many of the ideas most closely associated with rule of law today grow out of this fundamental goal, including the notion of a government of laws not men, the supremacy of the law, equality of all before the law, separation of law and politics, separation of powers, and in particular an independent judiciary.

So central is the notion of a government limited by law to most people's understanding of rule of law that many would deny the mantle of rule of law to any legal system that does not impose meaningful constraints on the ruling elite, preferring to characterize such systems as rule *by* law. Rule by law is associated with instrumentalism, where law is a mere tool of the state (Baum, 1986). There is no separation of law and politics, law is not supreme, and the dictates and policies of the rulers trump laws.

Whether contemporary China is best described as a rule by law or rule of law (in this limited sense) has been the subject of much discussion (Alford, 1999; Dowdle, 1999; Epstein, 1994; Hintzen, 1999; Yu, 1989). It is important to distinguish the issue of whether law is meant in theory to impose meaningful constraints on the Chinese Communist Party (CCP) and government officials from whether it does so in practice. If as a theoretical matter law is not meant to impose meaningful constraints on the ruling elite, then China would not be considered a rule-of-law state at all (on this definition). On the other hand, failure to provide meaningful constraints in practice is often a matter of degree. Accordingly, China might be considered a rule-of-law state, albeit a flawed one.

Support for the view that law is meant to impose meaningful constraints on the government in theory and does so at least to a considerable extent in practice is readily available. The excesses and injustices of the Cultural Revolution led many of China's leaders to advocate a rule of law as a way of reining in the CCP and the state. As a result, the 1982 Constitution incorporated the basic principles of a government of laws not men, the supremacy of the law, and the equality of all before the law. Article 5 confirms that the state shall uphold the dignity of the socialist legal system; that all state organs, armed forces, political parties, enterprises, and institutions must abide by the law; and that no organization or individual is privileged to be beyond the Constitution or the law. Article 33 declares that all citizens are equal before the law.

Moreover, since 1978, China has embarked on an ambitious program of legal reform and institution building. Much effort has gone into developing and improving the professionalism of the legislature, judiciary, legal profession, procuracy, and public security. China has passed numerous laws and regulations aimed at strengthening these institutions, including the

Organic Law of the People's Courts, Judges Law, Lawyers Law, Procuracy Law, Police Law, and the recently amended Criminal Law and Criminal Procedure Law. In addition, the government has devoted considerable resources to professional training and upgrading the quality of personnel in all of the key institutions.

The establishment of an administrative law system that gives individuals the right to challenge the decisions of administrative officials has been one of the most remarkable features of the post-1978 legal reforms. While much of the impetus for rule of law in the immediate aftermath of the Cultural Revolution arose from within the CCP by leaders who had personally suffered from the arbitrary and lawless acts of the state, those outside the CCP have also called for rule of law and equality before the law as a means to discipline corrupt officials and protect themselves from abuse by administrative personnel. The Administrative Litigation Law, Administrative Supervision Law, State Compensation Law, and other administrative laws and regulations go a long way toward creating a system that holds government officials accountable for their acts, although problems remain both in the laws themselves and even more so in their execution.

As an empirical matter, there can be little doubt that law increasingly matters in contemporary society. Li Peng's stepping down as premier after completing the two terms permitted under the Constitution and accepting a lower position as head of the National People's Congress (NPC) exemplified a respect for law and the Constitution that would have been unheard of during the Mao period. The CCP showed similar deference to law in 1993 when it withdrew an amendment to the Constitution that it had submitted directly to the NPC in violation of proper procedures. Moreover, notwithstanding a wide gap between laws on the books and actual practice and a tendency among many to circumvent or ignore the law, most laws are followed most of the time by most people.[9]

Yet despite such positive signs, there continues to be considerable debate as to whether law in theory is meant to constrain the government and CCP, as well as concerns about the actual effectiveness of law as a constraint in practice. At the center of the theoretical debate is the tension between the leading role of the CCP and the notion of supremacy of law. PRC legal scholars have struggled to reconcile the CCP's role with a rule of law in which the law is supreme (Hintzen, 1999; Keith, 1994; Jiang Lishan, 1997; Liu Hainian, 1998; Wang, 1998; Zhang Qi, 1998). It is important to stress, however, that few today advocate a return to a rule by man (*ren zhi*) system in which the dictates of CCP leaders supersede laws (Jiang Lishan, 1997). Nor do most deny the need to rule the country in accordance with law or challenge the core idea that law is necessary to limit the arbitrary acts of the state. Further, those who argue for a leading role of the CCP generally do so on the basis that there is no contradiction between the CCP exercising leadership and the supremacy of the law. Others simply accept that the two cannot be reconciled and advocate that law should be supreme.

But to pose the issue in terms of whether the CCP or the law is supreme is not particularly helpful. The question is too abstract to lend itself to a meaningful answer. The debate is better posed in terms of two issues: the relation of law to morality; and who has the right to decide such matters as the proper ends for society, whether rule of law is the best means to achieve such ends and when following the law should give way to more important substantive normative values.

Every legal system must address the question: why should law be supreme? If law and the rule of law are means to some substantive end such as a just society, there could conceivably be situations where the law and the rule of law must give way to more important values. In the West the general debate about law is often framed in terms of natural law versus positive law, with natural law imposing additional moral constraints on positivist rule of law and allowing for the possibility that positivist laws must give way in certain instances to other normative values. In the context of thin theories of rule of law, the debate is over the compatibility of civil disobedience and equity (roughly, the authority of judges and administrators to deviate from the letter of the law in the name of general moral principles and justice) with the rule of law.

The discussion may be further focused by distinguishing two situations. The first is where the normal operation of law is suspended, for example during periods of martial law. The second is where in specific instances certain laws are set aside to secure other values.

All states allow for the possibility of suspending the normal system of law in emergency situations. What distinguishes a rule-of-law state from a non-rule-of-law state is the manner in which the decision to suspend the normal operation of law is reached and the frequency. In a rule-of-law state, the decision to impose martial law is itself rule-governed. The executive cannot simply impose martial law willy nilly but must follow proper procedures. Even if the executive has the military power to declare martial law, rule of law requires that the executive abide by the law. Ultimately, what prevents the executive from abusing its power in such a situation is respect for law and a rule-of-law culture.[10] China has passed laws stipulating the proper procedures for imposing martial law and thus appears to endorse, as a matter of official policy anyway, the view that even the suspension of rule of law in cases of emergency should be governed by law.

When particular laws may be set aside to secure other values is a more difficult theoretical issue. One of the criticisms of rule of law is that it tends to degenerate into rule fetishism. Rule of law promotes obedience to laws, whether such laws are good or bad, appropriate in the particular context or not.[11] While most people would allow that in some cases laws should give way to higher values,[12] they may disagree about the particular instances when laws should give way, who has the right to decide, the standards for making the decision, whether the discretion ceded the decision-maker to follow the rules is subject to review and if so by whom, and so forth.

Just as individuals may differ over such issues, so may societies given their different ethical traditions. Western ethical traditions have tended to focus on establishing the proper rules to guide interpersonal interactions, whether the Ten Commandments, the Kantian Categorical Imperative, the utilitarian principle of maximization of the good, or Rawls's two principles of justice.[13] Moreover, such rules tend to be abstract and universally applicable to all contexts. Accordingly, westerners may be more willing than others to accept a narrowly circumscribed rule of law that sacrifices equity and particularized justice for the virtues of generality, equality, impartiality, and certainty that result from limiting the discretion of the decision-maker. In contrast, Chinese ethical traditions, whether Confucian, Daoist or Maoist, have rejected rule ethics and universal principles in favor of a context-specific, pragmatic, situational ethics (Peerenboom, 1993). In the past, Confucian and Daoist sages were responsible for determining what was best in a given situation based on their own judgment rather than by appeal to fixed laws or universal ethical principles. More recently, socialist leaders and government officials have claimed the same right. Indeed, one of the most striking features of the legal system in China today is the wide discretion ceded government officials to interpret and implement the law.[14]

China may well differ from other countries with respect to the ease with which law may be shoved aside to accommodate other values. Nevertheless, theoretical disagreement over this issue does not call into question the basic premise that law is to be supreme or that law is meant to constrain the arbitrary acts of the government. To be sure, the effectiveness of law as a restraint on the government will depend in practice on how easily law may be shunted aside. Further, at some point, routine disregard of the law will raise questions as to a society's commitment to the rule of law, though it is important to bear in mind that there may be other explanations why laws are not followed, including that the laws are poorly drafted, unworkable in practice, or the product of a bygone era and out of step with present-day realities.

The debate over the supremacy of law and the leading role of the CCP also raises questions about who has the right to make certain decisions. If rule of law is a means to an end, then the issue arises as to what the end should be, whether law is the most appropriate means to the end, when the value to be gained by adhering to law should give way to more important values, and so on. In a general sense, democratic societies afford the right to make such decisions to the people. Citizens choose the substantive ends for society by electing candidates who then pass laws that reflect the substantive values of their constituencies. In theory, the people also have the right to choose their form of government, including the institutional arrangements that will give effect to the rule of law, when they ratify the constitution or refrain from amending it once ratified.

In China, such decisions have not been left to the people but made by the ruling elite. One of the differences between China's socialist rule of law and a liberal democratic one is that such fundamental decisions in China are reserved for the CCP in its role as vanguard of the people.[15] However, as we have seen, a thin version of rule of law is compatible with non-democratic forms of government.

Setting aside such theoretical issues, many would argue that despite its avowed commitment to the supremacy of law and a government of laws rather than men, in practice China continues to endorse an instrumental rule by law that fails to measure up to even a thin account of rule of law. In support, they point to an ambivalent attitude toward law among the 'principal state architects' of the Chinese legal system and in particular the desire to retain ultimate authority over the system (Alford, 1999; Corne, 1997a); continued CCP influence on or interference with the legislature and courts; a number of shortcomings in PRC institutions and law that make it difficult for law to serve as a meaningful constraint on government officials and the CCP, including vagueness of many laws and the wide discretionary authority ceded administrative officials to make, interpret, and implement laws; examples of flagrant use of the law as an instrument of state power; and the continued failure of the legal system to protect the civil and political rights so central to liberal democracy.[16]

While it is no doubt true that many both within and outside of the Party leadership have ambivalent views about the role of law in China today,[17] it is also likely that different leaders hold different views, that many of them have not thought through their positions in a systematic way, and that their views are therefore likely to be inconsistent in some respects and, at least for some of them, 'soft' and subject to change. There also appear to be generational differences, with younger people, particularly those trained in law or exposed to the West, tending to view law as more autonomous and less instrumental. Moreover, while the views of Party leaders are clearly important to the future development of the legal system, whether they will be determinative is debatable. First, differences among Party elites both in the substance of their views and the firmness with which they hold such views make it difficult to predict how their views will be translated into action. Second, the development of the legal system hinges on more than the ideas of the top leadership. Rule of law is a function of institution building and legal consciousness raising. Progress has been made and continues to be made in both of these areas. Moreover, the development of China's legal system has been and will continue to be in part a response to objective forces, including the needs of a market as opposed to a centrally planned economy; the demands of foreign investors; international pressure, as evidenced in the amendment of the Criminal Law and Criminal

Procedure Law and China's accession to various human rights treaties; GATT requirements, should China become a member of the World Trade Organization (WTO); and the ruling regime's desire for legitimacy, both at home and abroad.

That said, that the CCP leadership continues to set the parameters for what is permissible in Chinese society is undeniable. For instance, the CCP continues to exert influence over the courts in a variety of ways. While people's congresses are formally empowered to appoint judges, in practice judges are often selected by the CCP Political-Legal Committee on the same level and the choices rubber-stamped by the people's congresses (Clarke, 1996).[18] Most senior judges, including the members of the adjudicative committee of the court, which has the ultimate authority to decide any case before the court, are CCP members. Further, judges still discuss important political cases or cases with difficult legal issues with the Political-Legal Committee (Finder, 1997). More generally, the CCP exercises control over the court by setting general policies, implicitly accepted by judges, within which the courts must operate.

Similarly, the CCP continues to dominate the NPC and major government posts through the nomenklatura system of appointments (Lieberthal, 1995; Tanner, 1994). As a result, most key positions are staffed by CCP members. Direct elections of government officials are limited to the township and county levels. While the NPC has begun to shed its rubber-stamp image, it has voted down just one law (Dowdle, 1997: 6) and has yet to refuse to ratify any of the government-sponsored candidates for a top post.

On the other hand, although China still lacks a truly independent and autonomous legislature or judiciary, direct intervention in the particular cases by the CCP has lessened in recent years (Finder, 1997), as has the direct influence of the CCP on the legislative process (Tanner, 1994). Moreover, one must avoid the assumption that rule of law requires particular institutional arrangements, such as US-style separation of powers or a particular type of judicial independence or constitutional review. A thin theory of rule of law is compatible with a variety of institutional arrangements. China rejects separation of powers in favor of a system in which the legislature is supreme. Thus, each of China's four levels of courts is responsible to the people's congress at the equivalent level, which supervises its work, appoints and removes judges, and provides financial funding. As in many civil law systems, courts in China do not have the power formally to make law. The highest legislative authority, the National People's Congress, is responsible for promulgating basic laws. Moreover, the power of courts to interpret laws and regulations is limited in China. The NPC, through its Standing Committee, is responsible for interpreting laws and the Constitution. While the NPC delegated the right to interpret laws to the Supreme Court, the Court was only given the right to interpret laws where necessary for judicial work.[19] Further, and perhaps most importantly, neither the Supreme People's Court nor any other court has the right to interpret or declare invalid administrative regulations or regulations passed by the people's governments or people's congresses, although courts may refuse to enforce a regulation contrary to superior law.

Although these limitations on the authority of the courts may make it more difficult for the courts to play a leading role in ensuring that government actors are bound by law, they do not in themselves add up to a repudiation of the rule of law, or at least thin versions of that ideal. Apart from the ways in which courts are funded (and the degree of direct influence by the Party), China's court system is similar to that in some European civil law countries.

Similarly, worries that the wide discretion afforded administrative officials to make, interpret, and implement regulations is inconsistent with the rule of law are not unique to China (Corne, 1997a). Many westerners raise the same objections (Fallon, 1997). Clearly many of China's practices in the administrative area are at odds with the rule-of-law ideal (Liu and Wang, 1998). The inherent and delegated authority of administrative agencies to make law is vast; the limits on such authority unclear. Moreover, there is no gainsaying the fact that administrative agents are afforded considerable discretion and flexibility in interpreting and implementing laws. Yet whether the system is designed to promote rule by law rather than rule of law is debatable. There are a variety of legitimate practical and theoretical reasons for wide discretion and flexibility afforded administrative officials.[20] Moreover, although the power of courts to rein in administrative officials is limited, there are a number of internal and external channels to challenge administrative decisions.[21] To be sure, the effectiveness of the various channels in practice appears limited. Thus one of the issues that even a thin theory of rule of law would have to address is just how much discretion and flexibility is compatible with the rule of law. Even if we accept, as we must, that realization of the rule-of-law ideal is always a matter of degree, a fully developed thin theory of rule of law would need to provide an account of deviations from the ideal that are so serious as to be incompatible with the rule of law. China's deviations from the rule-of-law ideal in administrative law area are more than sufficient to conclude that it is a flawed rule of law. But then many countries also score poorly in this area. Whether at the end of the day China's deviations are so different in kind or magnitude to characterize the legal system as a rule by law rather than a (deeply) flawed rule of law depends on where one draws the line.

Arguably the best evidence for the view that law in China, in practice if not in theory, is best described as rule by law is the 'instrumental' use of law to carry out government and CCP policy. One does not have to look far to find examples of the continued use of law as a tool of the state, including the use of economic laws as an instrument of state-planning; the acceleration of state-owned enterprise reform after the 15th Party Congress; the policy-driven anti-crime Strike Hard campaign; and the use of the criminal law and the administrative punishment reform-through-labor to harass and detain political dissidents on trumped-up charges.

Of course, law is used as an instrument to realize government and social policy everywhere. Thus a distinction must be drawn between an acceptable instrumentalism and a pernicious one. Opponents of instrumentalism contrast instrumentalism with an autonomous legal system. In such a system, law serves as an independent source of normative order and legitimacy. Laws must be made in accordance with proper procedures. They must be applied in certain ways—impartially by administrators acting within their legal authority or by unbiased judges who base their decisions on the laws rather than personal relations or CCP dictates. Moreover, an autonomous legal system implies that law and the legal system will be sufficiently independent from the political process to serve as a check on government. At minimum, the government must express its will through proper legal channels.

In most instances, the CCP restricts itself to proper channels, relying on laws rather than policies to rule. However, even when it does so, the fact that the legislature and courts are less than fully autonomous detracts from the legitimacy of the processes and contributes to the perception of instrumentalism. This perception is fortified by cases of instrumentalism in its most pernicious form, such as the 1989 declaration of martial law where the CCP ignored the proper procedures; the ongoing reliance on the policy-driven Strike Hard campaign rather than the criminal law to crack down on crime; the arrest, detention, and imprisonment of dissidents and other political activists; and the continued insistence that wayward CCP members be subject to internal Party discipline rather than criminal sanctions meted out by the courts.

Yet care should be taken not to diminish the extent to which most laws are made and applied without undue influence from the CCP nor to overstate the importance of select examples of CCP policies trumping the law. Arguably, such violations of the rule of law should be seen as the exception rather than the rule and as a reflection of the reality of power politics rather than as an endorsement of an instrumental rule by law over a rule of law that imposes meaningful constraints on the ruling elite. China is currently undergoing a transition. Old habits die hard (Li, 1998: 149; Liu Hainian, 1996: 26). While serious deviations in practice exist, on the whole China would seem to be moving toward a system in which laws do impose meaningful constraints on both the CCP and the government.

Economic Development and the Market Economy

Rule of law is often linked to the rise of modern capitalism, free markets, and clearly defined, legally enforceable property rights. Max Weber's sociological analysis of law emphasized that rational rules not only promote predictability and thus enhance economic efficiency and contribute to economic development; they also enhance the legitimacy and authority of law in that they are more likely to be normatively acceptable to the people (Rheinstein, 1954). Apart from clearly defined property rights, rule of law on this view entails generally applicable, transparent, fairly and consistently applied laws sufficiently normatively acceptable to the populace that most people will follow them voluntarily.

Since 1978, China has viewed legal reform and the creation of a socialist legal system as integral to economic development. After the Cultural Revolution, Deng Xiaoping and other leaders decided that the major problem confronting China was not class struggle but economic growth. China was declared to be in the primary stages of socialism. Before China could reach the hallowed ideal of a communist society, it would first have to pass through a capitalist phase. One of Mao's mistakes was to try to leapfrog over the capitalist stage. Accordingly, Deng announced that to get rich was glorious and threw open the doors to foreign investment.

In the last two decades, China has embarked on radical economic reforms intended to transform a centrally planned economy into a 'socialist market economy'. While China has endeavored to create a rational and predictable legal framework for investors both foreign and domestic, numerous problems remain in practice. Many of the problems with respect to compliance with the formal or thin aspect of rule of law in China, such as the rapid change in laws, the poor quality of the drafting, and the inconsistencies between laws and policies and lower and higher level laws, are due in part to the fact that China is currently in a transitional state (Cai, 1999).

Protection of the Individual: Liberal Democracy and Human Rights

The notion that rule of law is necessary to protect the individual against the state is closely associated with the idea that rule of law imposes limits on the arbitrary acts of the state. Yet limiting the arbitrary acts of government is not an end in itself. One imposes limits on the government for a particular purpose. For many, the purpose is primarily to ensure economic predictability and enhance efficiency. Many liberals would add that the purpose is (also) to protect the rights and freedoms of individuals.

In his *Second Treatise on Civil Government*, John Locke combined the notion of rule of law as imposing limitations on executive discretion with a liberal democratic conception of human rights. Rule of law was necessary to ensure that the state and majority did not trample on the rights of individuals. Moreover, Locke argued that for laws to effectively constrain executive discretion and protect the individual against the arbitrary acts of the state *and the majority*, there must be a separation of powers between the executive, legislature, and judiciary.

Many in China have argued for rule of law on the grounds that it would protect individuals against the type of arbitrary abuses of power that characterized the Cultural Revolution. Yet even if one accepts that the purpose of rule of law is to protect the individual against the state, there are different possible understandings of what that entails. One's particular conception of this purpose of the rule of law will depend on one's general political beliefs. Democrats will understand protection of the individual to entail democracy and the civil and political rights necessary to ensure meaningful democracy. Welfare liberals will understand protection of the individual to entail the recognition of not only civil and political rights but social, economic, and cultural rights such as the right to education and work, the free choice of employment, and so on. Libertarians will interpret rule of law to require not only limited government and minimal intervention in the economic area but also a minimal role for the government in the social realm so as to ensure the maximum amount of individual freedom and autonomy.

Although a few people in China hold the view that rule of law and the protection of the individual are to be understood in terms of liberal democratic values and institutions (see e.g. Li and Zhang, 1997), most do not. The socialist leadership remains opposed to democracy except in a most limited sense, restricting direct elections to the village and county level. Moreover, the view that democracy will not work in China and that strong (neo-authoritarian) leaders are needed because the masses are incapable of governing themselves—a view with deep historical roots in China—remains widespread, even among reform-minded intellectuals.

While the number of people who support democracy in China remains limited, the number who endorse a liberal understanding of human rights and relation of individual to society is even more limited. Most reject the basic premises of liberalism, many of which are at odds with China's philosophical and ethical traditions, including: (i) the fact of pluralism—i.e. the empirical view that people disagree as to what is good for them and for society and the normative view that they reasonably disagree; (ii) the importance of autonomous moral choice; and (iii) the belief that people know best what is in their own best interest and that the state shows respect and treats people equally by remaining neutral and allowing the people to choose the ends for society through elections (Peerenboom, 1998). Similarly, the anti-majoritarian function of rights that lies at the core of liberal democracies remains all but ignored in China, presumably because most Chinese would find abhorrent the idea that the rights of an individual trump the will of the majority, the interests of the community, and the good of the society (Peerenboom, 1995). Many also question whether, as a practical matter, liberal democracy has produced a more morally attractive society. For many if not most Chinese, western liberal democracies tilt the scales too much in favor of the individual to the detriment of the community.

But the refusal to accept liberal democracy and liberal values does not rule out the possibility of a morally attractive society governed in accordance with law. Accordingly, the temptation to read a particular political agenda into rule of law should be resisted by maintaining a distinction between thin and substantive theories of rule of law.

Dispute Resolution

One of the main purposes of rule of law is to provide a fair mechanism for resolution of disputes. The importance of rule of law to dispute settlement in the West is due in part to the acceptance of pluralism and the belief that individuals not only disagree about what constitutes the good for themselves and society but that they reasonably disagree. In this view, society consists of diverse individuals each pursuing his or her own interests and ends, which inevitably leads to conflict. However, because people have different values, there is no common normative standard to judge which interests and ends are correct. Since people cannot agree on a substantive basis for resolving conflict, they first agree on fair procedures for choosing social ends. Democracy is one procedural response: value disputes are settled and social ends chosen by voting. Rule of law is another response. Parties take their disputes to court, where in theory impartial judges, constrained by rules of evidence, determine the facts and then on the basis of precedents and/or publicly promulgated statutes, reach a decision. Again, the emphasis is on proper procedures. Disputants are guaranteed a fair trial, though not necessarily one that will result in the victory of good over evil, truth over falsehood, justice over injustice.

Historically, most Chinese political theorists have rejected the inevitability of pluralism and the belief that there is no substantive normative basis on which to reconcile disparate views, in favor of an optimistic faith in the possibility of a harmonious resolution to disputes. All interests, including the interests of the individual and the state, are reconcilable, and harmony is attainable, as long as the leadership is able to provide correct moral and ideological guidance (Nathan, 1985). Similarly, individual disputes are assumed to be resolvable as long as the parties are sincere and willing to compromise. Traditionally, Confucians rejected law as a primary means of resolving disputes in favor of informal mechanisms for dispute resolution allegedly more conducive to harmony. Today, the emphasis on informal means of dispute resolution continues to be one of the distinctive features of law in China.

On the other hand, recently discovered legal materials and court documents have shown that historically Chinese were much less hesitant about litigating than previously assumed (Huang, 1994). Moreover, the sharp rise in law suits in recent years suggests that contemporary Chinese are increasingly willing to rely on the courts to sort out conflict. While litigation was virtually non-existent in 1979, the total number of law suits reached 5.26 million in 1996, a jump of almost 16 percent over 1995. Further, while litigation has been increasing, mediation has been decreasing in popularity.

Reliance on the courts to settle disputes indicates that law and the legal system are increasingly important sources of order in China. But a legal system must meet certain minimal rule-of-law requirements—such as impartial adjudicators and fair procedures—if it is to serve effectively as a means of resolving disputes. [22]

2. *Basic Features of a Thin Theory of the Rule of Law*

China's socialist legal system is meant to serve many of the purposes normally associated with rule of law: limits on arbitrary government action, predictability and economic development, protection of the individual, and resolution of disputes. While each of the general purposes raises important issues of political morality that separate socialists from liberals, a thin theory of rule of law need not address such issues to the same degree as a substantive theory.

Although rule-of-law proponents of different political persuasions may disagree sharply over the fundamental values that rule of law is intended to secure, they generally disagree less when it comes to the basic functional requirements of rule of law. Libertarians, liberals, communitarians, and socialists stand on common ground in accepting that rule of law requires procedural rules for law-making; laws must be made in accordance with such rules to be legally binding; laws must be public and readily accessible, prospective, generally applicable, consistent, relatively stable; they must be enforced and fairly applied in practice; and on the whole laws must be sufficiently acceptable to most people such that most people respect the laws and are willing to follow them most of the time.[23]

To be sure, there is still considerable room for disagreement about the relative importance of the various elements, the degree to which a particular element such as consistency must be satisfied, the particular institutional means to realizing the various elements, whether other elements are also required, and so forth. But this is to be expected, in part because of the difference in ends that rule of law is intended to serve, and in part because of historically contingent factors such as a country's political traditions, ethical systems, level of economic development, and so on. While a fully developed thin theory of rule of law would address such issues, that is not the goal here.

China has committed itself to a government of laws not men, to ruling the country in accordance with law. Focusing on some of the more functional criteria of rule of law sheds light on the extent to which law actually serves as a source of order in contemporary China and the obstacles to greater reliance on the law as a means to bring about a normatively attractive Chinese society, however that may be conceived.

Law-Making: Proper Procedures

If order is to be predicated on laws, there must be a way of verifying whether laws are valid and legally binding, i.e. (i) they are made by an entity with authority to make laws; (ii) the entity was acting within its scope of authority; (iii) the entity followed proper procedures; and (iv) the regulations are not inconsistent with superior legislation. China has passed a number of laws setting out the procedures for law-making. Yet numerous problems remain (Li, 1997). Indeed, so many regulations fail to meet these minimal criteria that one scholar has concluded:

> The disparate mass of laws and regulations which makes up the formal written sources of Chinese law does not possess sufficient unity to be regarded as a coherent body of law. In their disarray, the sources of Chinese law seem barely capable of providing the basic of point of reference which all complex systems of law require. (Keller, 1994: 711)

One of the problems is the sheer complexity of the system. As Peter Corne notes, 'At first glance the PRC legal system appears almost unintelligible. It consists of multiple levels of laws, regulations, sub-legal documents and explanations, each with, up until now, ill-defined legal status and effect' (Corne, 1997b: 1). A number of entities have or have been given the right to legislate, resulting in a bewildering and inconsistent array of laws, regulations, provisions, measures, directives, notices, decisions, explanations, and so forth, all claiming to be normatively binding and treated so by the creating entity.

The opaqueness of the legislative process further exacerbates the problem. China has gone some way toward making the legislative process more transparent, particularly with respect to national level laws passed by the National People's Congress. Such laws usually take longer to pass, and input is sought from a variety of sources at different stages, often including foreign experts (Tanner, 1995). Yet lack of access to the law-making process, particularly with respect to the passage of regulations and other normative documents by local congresses, governments and administrative entities, often results in poor quality and inconsistent legislation that frustrates the rational expectations of those subject to law and undermines China's own professed policy objectives.

Significantly, a Legislation Law is currently under consideration, which in the present version calls for publication of all or part of draft laws and hearings and conferences open to the public and may also clarify the lines of authority for law-making (Li, 1997).

Transparency: Laws must be Public and Readily Accessible

Throughout the 1980s, foreign companies repeatedly decried the unfairness of being subject to inaccessible internal (*neibu*) regulations that thwarted their efforts at rational decision-making. Although internal regulations are much less of a problem today, they continue to exist in all areas.

In many cases, regulations are hard to track down once issued, even when they are not internal. There is currently no central publishing place for all legislation, and indeed no requirement that all legislation be made public. Many rules (*guizhang*) and other normative documents (*qita de guifanxing wenjian*) are never published and may not be relied on by the courts as law, although in practice the issuing administrative entities often treat them as having the binding force of law (Corne, 1997a: 73, 170). In addition, many rules and other normative documents passed by local congresses and governments are only published in obscure local newspapers, making it virtually impossible for anyone to know exactly what rules apply at any given time in any given place.

While there are currently a number of electronic databases available in China, all are far from comprehensive, particularly with respect to local regulations. Only one promises to be an on-line service like Westlaw or Lexis. Although the technology would now seem to be available to address the problem, a law or regulation requiring all entities to report immediately all rule-making is also required.

Awareness of Laws

Widespread ignorance of the law undermines the rule of law and the ability of law to function as a source of order. Overall, the level of legal consciousness remains fairly low in China (Zhang Qi, 1998: 129), which is perhaps understandable given that the legal system has been rebuilt virtually from scratch since 1979. Despite efforts to publicize major laws (Li, 1998: 154), lay people are often unaware of even the most basic laws. The sheer numbers of new rules, problems with access to laws and regulations once issued, and complexities in law-making that often result in conflicting rules only exacerbate the problem.

In the business world, few of those running companies, particularly state-owned enterprises, have been trained in law (or for that matter economics or business management). Moreover, although PRC companies are starting to hire in-house counsel or outside lawyers on a retainer basis, many continue to conduct business without the benefit of legal advice. Government officials, for their part, often reveal an almost shocking ignorance of basic rules and fundamental legal concepts.

Even many lawyers have at best a tenuous grasp of the law. It is still possible to qualify as lawyer without a college education in law, or even a college education at all, and without passing the bar exam. As of 1996, only 25 percent of China's lawyers had college degrees, while another 46 percent had completed *dazhuan* degrees obtained through two or three years of study, either in full-time universities, part-time colleges, or night schools, or through correspondence courses and self-study (Zhang and Hu, 1996: 42). Thus almost 30 percent of China's lawyers have no formal education beyond high school.

Moreover, even if one has attained a college degree, it need not be in law. And even if one has a law degree, that hardly means one is qualified to practice. Legal education in China tends to emphasize memorization of black letter law rather than critical reasoning and ability to analyze and solve problems. Graduates even from the very top schools are generally much less prepared to assume responsibilities as practicing lawyers than their counterparts from foreign legal systems. Given that many lawyers find it easier and more effective to rely on personal relations and connections rather than legal analysis and arguments to obtain approvals and win cases, there is little incentive to master the law.

China is striving to professionalize the various arms of the legal system. The last few years have seen national legislation on judges, the police, the procuratorate, and prisons. Judges, prosecutors, and police are all subject to higher education requirements and better training. Prior to the Judges Law, for example, there were no objective qualifications for judges other than that one be a cadre, and in practice, many judges were demobilized army officers with no legal education and often no formal education beyond high school. The new law requires at minimum a college education for new judges, while judges already in office prior to the new law who do not meet the educational requirements must undergo training.

China's efforts to increase the level of professionalism deserve to be acknowledged and applauded. Nevertheless, the task is daunting, and much work remains to be done. As of year end 1995, 80 percent of judges had at least *dazhuan* qualifications, but among their counterparts in the procuracy only 58.3 percent had similar qualifications (China Law Yearbook, 1997).

Quality of Legislation

While the quality of legislation has improved remarkably over the last 20 years, much legislation remains poorly drafted and characterized by excessive generality and vagueness, omissions, undefined terms, inconsistencies, and a lack of practical experience and appreciation for law-making hierarchies on the part of the drafters (Corne, 1997a; Howson, 1997).

Poor drafting continues to undermine the attempts of China's legislators to use law as a means of achieving order and of the regulated to rely on law to protect their interests. Of course one can point to examples of poor drafting in any country. Moreover, what appears to be poor drafting is often a reflection of hard negotiations, political compromise and the need on the part of the drafters to mediate the conflicting interests of different constituencies. That said, all too often the only possible explanation for the many omissions, inconsistencies, contradictions, and related maladies that plague much PRC legislation is simply poor drafting, in many instances due to lack of practical experience on the part of the drafters (Li, 1997).

The generality and vagueness of many PRC laws are attributable to a variety of reasons (Jiang Lishan, 1997: 41). Many of China's laws are modelled on the laws of civil law countries, which typically are more general and broadly drafted than statutes in common law countries. Moreover, China is a large country currently undergoing profound social and economic changes. Conditions in the poor inland and western regions differ dramatically from those in the fertile valleys and coastal cities in the east. As a result, laws and regulations are broadly drafted to allow sufficient flexibility in implementation to meet local conditions. Numerous laws expressly delegate wide discretion to lower level governments or administrative organs to fill in the gaps by issuing implementing rules and to interpret the laws in such a way as to ensure that the laws fit the particular circumstances. A traditional emphasis on particularized justice characteristic of the Confucian tradition, socialism's emphasis on uniting theory and practice, and the pragmatic orientation of current leaders also favor laws that are often statements of general principles that must then be interpreted and applied to the particular situation by local officials and administrators. As the de facto ultimate authority, the core leadership of the CCP presumably favors general laws since it can effect change whenever policy changes by simply ensuring that laws are implemented in accordance with the new policy.

Regardless of the reasons, the excessive generality and vagueness of PRC laws, coupled with the wide discretionary powers conferred on local authorities to implement the laws, undermine the predictability and certainty of law. At minimum, they increase transaction costs by making it more difficult, time-consuming, and expensive to figure out just what the rules are at any time in a given place.[24] At worst, they breed corruption and a reliance on connections that erode the normative force of law.

No Rapid Changes

Rapid change in laws or the ways laws are interpreted or implemented defeats the expectations of those governed by the rules and contributes to a sense of unfairness that undermines the legitimacy and normative force of the law. Yet PRC laws and regulations are often subject to rapid change: sometimes the law itself changes; sometimes the law does not change but the application or interpretation does; and sometimes the law changes but the application does not.

Of course regulations change everywhere, particularly in the economic area. Moreover, sometimes interpretation and implementation of existing laws will change or new laws will be issued that meet with resistance in practice or do not produce the degree or type of change expected by the drafters of the laws. Nevertheless, China is extreme both with respect to the rapidity with which large number of laws change and changes in implementation or the lack of any such change even though the laws have changed.

In fact, many of China's laws are passed on a provisional or experimental basis. If the experiment proves successful, the regulations are made permanent. There are a number of reasons for this approach, including the pragmatic orientation of China's leaders, the socialist emphasis on informing theory with practice, and the current realities of China, in particular the wide diversity between regions and the need to carry out massive reforms in uncharted territories. Again, however, experimental laws detract from the stability of law.[25] The fear that the experiment will come to an end or the rules will be modified make it difficult to rely on existing laws.

Consistency

One of the most striking features of the legal system in China is the frequent inconsistency between laws and policies, the number of inconsistent laws and regulations, and especially the number of lower level regulations that conflict with superior legislation. According to a study in the mid-1980s in Hebei, Beijing, and Tianjin, about two-thirds of local regulations were inconsistent with the Constitution (Corne, 1997a: 152).

Given such a large number of inconsistent regulations, some scholars have appealed to a more relaxed understanding of consistency. In Corne's view, consistency in the PRC refers to consistency with the spirit rather than the letter of superior legislation (Corne, 1997a: 147). Moreover, as long as the enacting body is acting within the scope of its delegated or inherent authority, regulations that on their face conflict with superior regulations need not be considered inconsistent. Given the need to make laws applicable to particular contexts, such inconsistencies are apparently not only tolerable but desirable. Thus, Donald Clarke has argued that the de facto view of constitutional order in the PRC is that the higher the level at which a legal norm is promulgated, the less legally relevant it is. While Clarke notes the government may not expressly endorse such a view, it would appear, as he points out, that in practice the Constitution is largely a political manifesto, NPC laws represent broad statements of policy, and State Council rules are what people are really supposed to follow (Clarke, 1997).

While flexibility in applying general rules to specific situations may be desirable, in many cases the reasons for conflicting rules have less to do with a concern for particularized justice than with power grabs among

China's various bureaucracies. As one commentator notes, 'the expansion of legislative powers to so many central and regional state bodies has in effect brought the rivalries and disorder of Chinese bureaucracy directly into the legislative structure' (Keller, 1994: 733). The transition to a market economy has exacerbated inter-agency conflicts. Recent downsizing reduced the number of ministries from 40 to 29, with the number of government officials to be slashed by 50 percent, intensifying the desire among the survivors to make themselves seem needed. The struggle for turf among administrative departments often leads to a variety of departments claiming jurisdictional authority over the same area and issuing conflicting rules to protect their institutional interests.

Similarly, one of the biggest reasons for conflicting regulations is the desire on the part of local governments to promote local interests. Economic reform has resulted in greater autonomy for local governments. It has also resulted in fewer subsidies from the state. As a consequence, local governments often pass regulations that conflict with national legislation in an effort to promote investment.

Ideological struggles are also a factor. Two of the areas most rife with inconsistencies and conflicts between lower and higher level legislation are land and labor, in part because they are undergoing rapid reform as part of the transition from a centrally planned economy, but also due to their ideological importance. Mao rose to power on the promise of land reform. Allowing private ownership of land, even in the form of leaseholds, was a major step toward redefining socialism with Chinese characteristics. Similarly, laborers are supposedly the backbone of socialism. Breaking the iron rice bowl by giving employers the right to freely hire and fire employees and pay them according to their performance suddenly made China appear less like the workers' paradise and more like the much maligned capitalist enemy. Some inconsistencies therefore may be attributed to differing views among China's political factions.

Whatever the reasons, inconsistencies and conflicts in rules create obstacles to a law-based order. Conflicting rules create uncertainty for the regulated, who are not sure which laws to follow. For instance, if investors prefer to take advantage of more flexible lower level laws, they then live in fear that the central authorities will one day crack down on rogue local legislators and officials who exceeded their authority.

As damaging to rule of law as the existence of conflicting rules is the lack of a practical way to sort out the conflicts. While on paper there are ways to reconcile inconsistencies in China, in practice there often are no effective means to do so (Chen, 1992: 90–2; Li, 1997). The power of constitutional supervision resides in the NPC and its Standing Committee. Because the CCP rejects separation of powers, there is no independent constitutional review body. Thus the NPC polices itself. Not only has the NPC yet to strike down any of the laws of its Standing Committee as unconstitutional, the Standing Committee has yet to annul any lower level enactments on grounds of unconstitutionality. Similarly, while there are various means to resolve inconsistencies between national and lower level legislation and among lower level legislation, in practice it is difficult if not impossible to resolve the conflicts. The NPC Standing Committee, State Council, and lower level people's congresses have all been reluctant to intervene.

Fair Application of Laws: Due Process

At the heart of rule of law understood as an instrument for dispute resolution is due process and the fair application of laws. Due process requires at minimum a transparent decision-making process; limits to the discretion of the decision-makers and ways to challenge their decisions; procedural rights such as the right to a hearing, prior notice, the opportunity to present and refute evidence; and impartial adjudicators.

China has problems in all of these areas. One of the peculiarities of litigation in the PRC is that cases are often decided outside the courtroom. In the past, many decisions were made prior to trial in accordance with the dictates of CCP personnel, despite official prohibitions against this practice of *xianding houshen* (decision first, trial later). While today CCP intervention in particular cases is lessening, judges still discuss important cases with the CCP Political-Legal Committee, which oversees the courts and is the de facto power responsible for appointing and removing judges, and with the adjudicative committee, which consists of the president of the court and other senior judges and is responsible for handling difficult cases (Finder, 1997). More typically, judges are subject to outside interference by administrative officials seeking to avoid liability under the Administration Litigation Law or pressured by local government officials to find in favor of local companies for fear that a negative judgment could result in fewer profits and therefore less tax revenue for the local government (Gong et al., 1993). Judges are also courted by the parties to a suit and their lawyers, wined and dined, and in many cases bribed, despite prohibitions against such behavior (Gong et al., 1993; Cai, 1999).

Often even more impenetrable than the judicial decision-making process is the administrative approval process. Although China is currently transforming from a centrally planned economy to a more open market economy, the government maintains control over the economic sphere by subjecting a wide variety of transactions to approval, and in many cases, multiple approvals. While in most instances approval authorities must issue a decision within a specific amount of time and state their reasons if approval is denied, in some cases there are no time limits, while in other cases the authorities are not even obligated to give their reasons for rejecting an applicant.

Some administrative departments even refuse to answer queries about regulations that they passed or are responsible for interpreting. The result is that the regulated are forced to curry favor with the regulators by taking them to dinner or offering gifts just to obtain information from public servants whose job it is to provide such information. In some instances, cash-strapped departments refer callers to consulting companies, set up by current or former employees of the department, which will handle inquiries or direct them to the proper party for a fee.

Further, as noted earlier, administrative entities in China are given wide latitude in implementing regulations, many of which they themselves have passed. Moreover, despite the passage of the Administrative Litigation Law and the Administrative Reconsideration Regulations, many of the discretionary acts of administrative officials in interpreting regulations are not subject to further review either by the courts or by superior organs in the administrative hierarchy. The right to interpret regulations without fear of challenge confers on administrative officials considerable power, which can be easily abused and lead to inconsistency or arbitrariness that defeats reliance on law as a source of normative order, undermines the predictability that allows rule of law to promote economic development, and detracts from the legitimacy and normative authority of laws.

Conformity of Law and Practice: Laws must be Enforced

One of the striking revelations for western lawyers practicing in China is the wide gap between the laws and actual practice. Despite repeated calls by the government for stricter implementation, laws continue to be ignored or flouted on a regular basis by local government officials, administrative ministries, domestic and foreign companies, law firms, individuals, the CCP, and even the courts.

Local governments are particularly egregious offenders. For instance, China has sought to limit foreign investment in the retail industry, issuing national regulations that allow the establishment of just 22 joint ventures in 11 cities on a trial basis, all to be approved centrally. Yet local governments, thumbing their noses at Beijing, have approved some 300 retail joint ventures. Shanghai alone has approved more than 40 (Stevenson-Yang, 1998). The central authorities are clearly aware of the illegal approvals and from time to time have issued notices threatening to crack down. Each time, after waiting out the storm, local authorities have continued to approve more retail ventures.

Financially pressed and in some cases corrupt, local government and administrative officials have been particularly prone to abuse their authority by imposing illegal and random fines, fees, and other charges on companies, both domestic and foreign. In 1995, unauthorized charges on foreign and domestic companies amounted to almost $4 billion. In 1996, the amount jumped to over $7 billion for state-owned enterprises alone

(Freshfields, 1998). According to one report, the Guangxi government recently eliminated 60 types of illegal charges levied against foreign invested enterprises by some 24 departments (*East Asia CIEC Economic Brief*, 1997). McDonalds alone was subject to 31 different fees.

Local companies regularly ignore the law in countless ways, most noticeably in the failure to comply with environmental regulations and pay taxes. Due diligence with regard to local companies invariably turns up problems such as the failure to comply with establishment procedures and obtain the requisite approvals, failure to register mortgage agreements, irregularities in holding board meetings or passing resolutions, and so forth.

PRC companies are not the only ones who ignore the rules. Foreign investors do so as well. Many have established representative offices that routinely exceed their business scope by engaging in direct business activities. So commonplace is the practice that the tax authorities require the representative offices to pay taxes, although in theory representative offices should not be engaging in direct business and therefore should have no revenues.

Individuals also regularly disregard the law: tax evasion is rampant; smoking in public continues despite regulations and signs expressly prohibiting it; bicyclists, motorists, and pedestrians routinely ignore traffic rules, even in the presence of traffic police. At the other end of the spectrum, the CCP shows its disdain for laws when it declares martial law without following proper procedures; relies on the Strike Hard campaign rather than criminal laws to attack crime; interferes with the courts in politically sensitive cases; and delays the trial of former Beijing Mayor Chen Xitong on corruption charges for over two years.

Indeed, even the courts fail to follow the rules. By some estimates, anywhere from 25–40 percent of domestic court judgments go unenforced (Clarke, 1996). The main reason is local protectionism, where judges bow to pressure from local government to find in favor of local companies for fear that a negative judgment could result in fewer profits and therefore less tax revenue for the local government. Court officials also regularly violate court regulations and their professional responsibility obligations when they meet with parties and their lawyers outside the courtroom. Some financially pressed courts have knowingly accepted cases for which they lack jurisdiction or in some cases conspired with the parties to make up facts or causes of actions that would provide such jurisdiction in order to meet quotas on the number of cases accepted and obtain the fees from hearing such cases. In his 1997 report to the national legislature, the President of the Supreme People's Court admitted that some courts abuse their authority in execution proceedings and stated that further measures on execution proceedings were planned.

This is not to suggest that China is lawless chaos. Laws are observed in most instances. Moreover, the reasons for such a wide gap between law and reality are many. Sometimes parties simply are not aware of or do not understand the law. Central–local tensions are also a problem: local governments violate central regulations out of the perceived need to promote local investment. Oftentimes, practice is ahead of the law. Despite their best efforts, Chinese law-makers frequently cannot keep up with the pace of economic reform. Laws and regulations cannot be produced fast enough to meet the demands in a very fluid environment, and as a result practice forges ahead out of necessity. In some cases, officials, companies, and individuals ignore or circumvent laws because they feel the laws are poorly drafted, unfair, or simply unworkable. At other times, parties simply make the commercial decision that breaking the law is worth the risk given the potential profits, the risk of probability of being caught, and the likelihood that they will be subject to serious punishment even if caught.

The gap between law and practice is also a function of China's legal culture, if by that one means 'those parts of the general culture—customs, opinions, ways of doing and thinking—that bend social forces toward or away from law and in particular ways'.[26] Two related features of China's legal culture merit attention: the lack of respect for and the low status of law; and a willingness to set aside the law whenever it is in one's interests to do so, often in the name of finding flexible ways around rules (*biantong*).

Normative Acceptability of Law: Respect For and Willingness to Follow Laws

The relatively widespread disregard for law whenever it is convenient calls into question the status and normative authority of law in China. For law to serve as a source and means of order in society, people must have sufficient respect for the law to follow it even when doing so is not in their immediate interest. Arguably, compliance could be obtained by coercion. However, coercion-based compliance does not ensure respect for law or contribute to the legitimacy of law (Epstein, 1994). Such respect and legitimacy requires that law be normatively acceptable to the majority of citizens.

There are a variety of factors that undermine the normative authority of law and make it difficult for the populace to accept and respect law as a source of order in China today, including traditional attitudes toward law as an inferior albeit necessary means of achieving social order; the persistence of a pernicious instrumentalism; the fact that other sources of normative order, whether the CCP, local officials, or personal connections (*guanxi*), are still often more important than law and the view that power and position trump law; corruption in the legal system (Cai, 1999); the weakness of legal institutions and in particular the courts, both institutionally in terms of their place in the administrative and constitutional structure and in terms of the powers granted them under specific laws such as the Administrative Litigation Law; and the lack of participation by the general populace in the process of making the laws.

3. Conclusion

Rule of law means different things to different people. Many liberal democrats have assumed that it incorporates or promotes certain liberal values or requires particular forms of government such as democracy or particular institutional arrangements such as separation of powers and an independent judiciary with constitutional review powers. Of course one may define rule of law as one chooses. But then one should not be surprised if China does not fit the bill, given the differences in the ends that rule of law is meant to serve in China. To criticize China's legal system for not realizing goals that it was never intended to realize is not very constructive. Liberal democrats and human rights advocates who believe Chinese citizens would be better off if China endorsed democracy and/or liberal values and a liberal conception of human rights would be better served by addressing such moral and political issues directly rather than by insisting on a particular understanding of rule of law.

On the other hand, law is more important today as a means to achieve social order than perhaps at any time in China's long history. Perhaps this is an inevitable response to modernity. The traditional emphasis on harmony and informal means of dispute resolution is increasingly at odds with the reality of a contemporary pluralistic society. With trade and foreign investment growing daily, China has now become an integral part of the world economy. China is now also a member of the world community, having signed a number of international treaties and rights conventions. As a result, it is expected to meet certain minimal standards. And if China enters the WTO, it will be subject to a number of additional rule-of-law constraints. Moreover, China has turned toward law as a means of achieving order for purely domestic reasons. Many of these reasons are broadly similar to those cited by others in support of rule of law, though interpreted differently in light of the commitment of China's leaders to socialism, China's traditions, and contemporary values.

Although the ends served by rule of law in China may differ from the ends rule of law serves elsewhere, China's legal system must still meet certain minimal functional criteria if the legal system is to play the role it is intended to play. There is room for disagreement over particular criteria, the means by which they are to be satisfied, and the degree to which they must be satisfied for law to serve the purposes it is intended to serve in China. Nevertheless, the failure of China's legal system to satisfy to some reasonable extent any or most of the basic functional criteria commonly associated with rule of law would make it impossible for China to achieve its own professed goals and to rely on law as a source of order.[27]

Measured against a variety of functional criteria, China's legal system has made remarkable progress in the last 20 years. At the same time, it has a long way to go. But this is widely acknowledged in China, and efforts are being made to improve the system. To be sure, the process will take time. There are numerous obstacles to greater reliance on law to govern the country and a variety of causes for such obstacles.

Some obstacles are practical and lend themselves to a technological solution, such as the lack of an on-line database that would make all normatively binding regulations readily available. Some are caused at least in part by the transition from a centrally planned economy to a more market oriented economy, such as the rapid change in laws, the experimental nature of laws, the numerous inconsistencies, the wide discretion afforded officials, and the wide gap between practice.

Many of the obstacles may be attributed to institutional causes. As typical of civil law systems, laws in China tend to be general; administrators are given wide-ranging discretion; courts are relatively weak; and judges and lawyers tend to function more like civil servants than their common law counterparts. China has adopted a system in which the NPC is supreme, thus reducing the stature and authority of the courts. The way courts are funded and judges appointed also contributes to rampant local protectionism and undermines the authority of the courts and the rule of law. The lack of effective means to reconcile conflicts is largely an institutional problem. Even if the Constitution is to play a different role in China than in other countries and not be directly justiciable, thus reducing the need for effective constitutional review bodies, there must still be effective methods for resolving conflicts between local and national regulations.

Ideology is also a contributing factor. For instance, the socialist emphasis on uniting theory and practice favors vague, experimental regulations and wide discretion to local authorities with respect to implementation. More negatively, the tendency toward pernicious instrumentalism and to shove law aside when convenient may be traced to traditional socialist views of law as a coercive tool of the state.

Some of the shortcomings in China's legal system have historical roots. The fact that the legal system had to be rebuilt virtually from scratch is one of the main explanations for the frequent lack of pertinent laws, the low level of professionalism of judges, lawyers, administrators, and much of the poor drafting and problems in implementation.

Cultural factors also play a role. Traditionally, China has lacked a rule-of-law culture in which law was held in high esteem. The willingness to rely on connections to circumvent the law, the emphasis on substantive justice and the view that morality trumps law, the tendency to afford wide discretion to decision-makers, all have deep cultural roots. At the same time, the temptation to essentialize Chinese culture must be avoided. Chinese society is changing and Chinese culture is changing along with it. While traditional beliefs and practices may present obstacles to the adoption of certain institutions and shape the way the legal system operates and laws are applied, cultural restrictions are not insurmountable.

Although many of the problems faced by the legal system in China are not unique to China, the particular set of issues confronting China obviously is unique to China. Thus it should come as no surprise that China's legal system and version of rule of law differ from those of other countries. Nevertheless, over time China's legal system most likely will become more like the legal systems of other countries, even as it maintains its differences.

NOTES

I would like to thank William Alford, Carine Defoort, Randle Edwards, and Geor Hintzen for their helpful comments and criticisms. I owe a special debt of gratitude to Mike Dowdle, with whom I have had countless conversations about rule of law in China, and whose probing questions have shaped many of the ideas presented in this article.

1. Cited in Raz, 1979: 210–11. See also Rule of Law Foundation, Rule of Law Principles, URL (consulted in May 1999) http://www.rol.org/htmfiles/ what.htm. On the Chinese side, Li (1998), Liu Hainian (1998) and Sun Xiaoxia (1998) favor a substantive definition that incorporates rights. Sun even cites the 1959 International Congress of Jurists. In summarizing the views of legal scholars at a national conference on good governance and the rule of law, Zhang Qi (1998) notes that most legal scholars maintain that the rule of law must include substantive elements of political justice.
2. While many legal scholars agree that rule of law is compatible at least theoretically with evil empires, several also note that in practice the two tend to be incompatible because even thin accounts of rule of law impose restraints on rulers that tyrants and dictators are not likely to tolerate. Tyrants and dictators would have no need to comply with the rule of law. If they did so, it would only be for strategic reasons (Finnis, 1980: 272; Summers, 1993: 139).
3. One typical feature of thin theories of rule of law that does not follow from the requirement that law be capable of guiding behavior is that laws be 'general'. The basic idea is that laws must not be aimed at a particular person and that similarly situated people should be treated equally. However, as Raz notes, laws may be both general and discriminatory (by treating all members of a particular race in the same way, for example). Raz does not object to particular rules but requires that they be made in accordance with open, clear, and stable rules. But the generality of law is also based on the rule-of-law ideal of limited government. Laws should apply to both officials and citizens alike. The requirement that law guide behavior is unclear as to scope: *whose* behavior?
4. A quick comparison of the lists of rule-of-law elements of Fallon (1997), Fuller (1976), Raz (1979), Summers (1993), Walker (1988) reveals both common ground and a number of differences.
5. This is not to deny that predictability is valuable for other reasons (economic development) or even that the ability to plan one's affairs is valuable to some degree in China (see e.g. Liu Hainian, 1998). However, the weight attached to

the ability to plan affairs and the reasons given in support are likely to be different in China.

6. Consider Shklar's comments on Fuller's eight requirements of a rule of law: 'as a legal ideal for us there is little to either accept or reject in this conventional list of lawerly aspirations. It is its moral status that ... seems unsure' (1987: 13).
7. For instance, during such periods, laws will tend to be less stable and change more frequently. Moreover, the gap between law and reality may also be somewhat greater as old laws that are no longer applicable are ignored; at the same time, people may not yet be aware of or have assimilated the new rules.
8. Others trace the notion of rule of law back as far as Aristotle (Shklar, 1987).
9. One would expect of course that most rules are followed most of the time if for no other reason than that in most cases the rules presumably accord with one's interests or at least do not impose significant compliance costs.
10. Similarly, respect for law and the principle that no one is above the law help explain why Nelson Mandela or Bill Clinton respond to a summons to appear before a grand jury.
11. A law may be overinclusive or underinclusive with respect to the goal which the law is supposed to achieve, leading to unanticipated and unjust results. Accordingly, Lawrence Solum (1994) argues for an Aristotelian virtue-centered reading of rule of law that emphasizes the virtuous character of judges who decide cases on the basis of the particular circumstances in the name of equity. Solum notes that tailoring law to a particular case is not the same as aligning law and morality, which might require a general change in the law (e.g. if the law allowed slavery or some other form of racial discrimination, a judge might refuse generally to enforce all such laws). Macedo (1994) and Burton (1994) question whether Solum's emphasis on particularized justice in the name of equity is consistent with rule of law. Valcke (1994) considers the related issue of the compatibility of civil disobedience with rule of law broadly construed.
12. See Rene David (1984) for a discussion of the way different legal systems attempt to incorporate or appeal to higher values.
13. There are of course exceptions, including Aristotelian ethics, pragmatism, and situational ethics.
14. The largely unfettered discretion of government officials is due to a number of factors in addition to a cultural preference for situational ethics. For instance, China's legal system is modelled on civil law systems, which generally afford wider discretionary authority to administrators than common law systems. Similarly, the readiness of local officials to shunt laws aside in particular instances or to deviate from the letter of the law is a function of the generality and vagueness of PRC laws (also a common civil law trait), loopholes in the Administrative Litigation Law, lax enforcement, corruption, and an increasing willingness of local governments to pursue their own interests.
15. At a 1996 seminar on law in China, many of the participants struggled in their attempts to reconcile the supremacy of law with the need for law to conform with morality. However, few explicitly endorsed rule of man. Even the most conservative scholars accepted the need to rule the country by law and to limit the arbitrary acts of the state. At the same time, they sought to protect the traditional perogatives of the elite to determine the ends which rule of law would serve and to decide when rule of law should give way to other ends and values.

What they rejected was the liberal democratic view of rule of law that would turn such decisions over to the people. Such elitism is common among Chinese intellectuals, and not surprising in that it serves their own self-interests (Hintzen, 1999).

16. Strictly speaking, the last objection raises issues of political morality that exceed the scope of a thin theory of law, as noted in the discussion of protection of the individual below.
17. PRC scholars often point out that the emergence and development of rule of law in China has been largely a top–down, government orchestrated movement in response to urgent economic needs, as opposed to a more evolutionary process arising out of civil society as in the case of Europe (Jiang Lishan, 1998a, 1998b; Su, 1998). Accordingly, they question whether the CCP and government will continue to support the development of rule of law when it begins to restrict seriously their authority and power.
18. Some scholars have recommended that Political-Legal Committees be eliminated, starting at the grassroots level. See the comments of Cui Min (Editorial Office, 1998: 8).
19. Nevertheless, despite this restriction, the Court has increasingly assumed responsibility for interpretation of key laws in light of the Standing Committee's abdication in this area.
20. Of course, there are also many illegitimate reasons as discussed below.
21. The Administrative Reconsideration Law and Administrative Supervision Law provide the basis for internal challenges to administrative regulations and acts. External channels include legislative supervision by the NPC, people's congresses and the Ministry of Supervision as well as supervision by the CCP (Corne, 1997a: 243–81).
22. This is not to claim that all legal systems will resolve disputes in the same way. For instance, China traditionally emphasized substantive justice over procedural justice, as evidenced by an emphasis on confessions, opportunities to appeal a decision all the way up to the emperor, imposition of harsh punishments on those who falsely accused others, the use of torture to obtain the truth and a relatively low level of concern for procedural issues. Today, the legal system continues to emphasize right results over procedural niceties. Thus, despite rules against illegal searches, evidence obtained in violation of proper procedures is not excluded. Similarly, while China adopts a system of one appeal, supposedly final judgments may be challenged by the parties, courts, and procuracy pursuant to a procedure known as adjudicative supervision. A fully developed thin theory of rule of law would need to address the compatibility and desirability of these evidentiary rules, legal procedures, and normative orientation with the rule of law.
23. While the last requirement is somewhat unusual, it is not unknown. Walker (1988: 28) includes general congruence of law with social values as one of the requirements of a thin theory of rule of law, although he notes: 'In a sense we may be cheating a little by making this fourth point an element or part of the definition. Strictly speaking, it is a limit on the model, not an ingredient of it. The rule of law could theoretically exist without this requirement being satisfied. But … it would not last long.' Similarly, Raz's notion that people should be ruled by law *and obey it* suggests that the normative acceptability of the law

and respect for law would be advantageous if not absolutely necessary (since presumably people could be coerced to obey the law).

24. On the other hand, vague and general rules may be desirable, particularly during a period of transition, in that clear and specific rules designed for a centrally planned economy may quickly become inappropriate for a market economy. The governed will not know whether the rules will continue to be applied and will need to spend time contacting the authorities to confirm the point. To the extent that laws are not applied, the gap between law and actual practice increases, with possible negative consequences for predictability and certainty. For an argument against clearly defined rules in a transitional context, see Dowdle, 1999.
25. For a view that rapid changes do not necessarily defeat the expectations of people, see Jiang Lishan (1998b).
26. Friedman (1975), cited in Lubman (1997).
27. For critical views of whether even the minimal requirements of rule of law are applicable and desirable in China's context or more generally in the context of transitional states see Dowdle, 1999; Su, 1998. See also Jiang Lishan, 1997, 1998a, 1998b, for discussion of the costs of rule of law and the applicability of particular rule-of-law criteria such as stability of laws to China (though Jiang ultimately concludes that China has little choice but to develop its economy and for that rule of law is necessary).

REFERENCES

Alford, W. (1999) 'A Second Great Wall? China's Post-Cultural Revolution Project of Legal Construction', *Cultural Dynamics* 11(2): 193–213.

Baum, R. (1986) 'Modernization and Legal Reform in Post-Mao China: The Rebirth of Socialist Legality', *Studies in Comparative Communism* 14(2): 69–104.

Burton, S. (1994) 'Particularism, Discretion and the Rule of Law', in *Nomos*, xxxvi, *The Rule of Law*, (ed.) Ian Shapiro, pp. 178–204. New York: New York University Press.

Cai Dingjian (1999) 'Development of the Chinese Legal System since 1979 and its Current Crisis and Transformation', *Cultural Dynamics* 11(2): 135–66.

Chen, A. (1992) *An Introduction to the Legal System of the People's Republic of China.* Hong Kong: Butterworths.

China Law Yearbook Editorial Department, ed. (1997) *Zhongguo falu D nianjian* (China Law Yearbook), p. 1056. Beijing: China Law Yearbook Publishing House.

Clarke, D. (1996) 'Power and Politics in the Chinese Court System: The Enforcement of Civil Judgments', *Columbia Journal of Asian Law* 10: 1–125.

Clarke, D. (1997) 'State Council Notice Nullifies Statutory Rights of Creditors', *East Asian Executive Reports* 19: 9–15.

Corne, P. (1997a) *Foreign Investment in China*. Hong Kong: Hong Kong University Press.

Corne, P. (1997b) 'China's Legal Structure', in *A Guide to the Legal System of the PRC*, pp. 1–10. Hong Kong: Asia Law and Practice.

David, Rene (1984) 'Source of Law', in *International Encyclopedia of Comparative Law.* The Hague: Martinus Nijhoff.

Dicey, A.V. (1885) *The Law of the Constitution* (10th edn, 1959). New York: St Martin's Press.

Dowdle, M. (1997) 'The Constitutional Development and Operations of the National People's Congress', *Columbia Journal of Asian Law* 11: 1–125.

Dowdle, M. (1999) 'Heretical Laments: China and the Fallacies of "Rule of Law" ', *Cultural Dynamics* 11(3): 287–314.

East Asia CIEC Economic Brief (1997) 'China: Elimination of Extra Fees Aids Foreign Investment' (30 Sept.).

Editorial Office (1998) 'Yifa zhiguo yu lianzheng jianshe yanjiuhui jiyao' (Summary of Key Points of Conference on Ruling the Country according to Law and Good Governance), *Faxue Yanjiu* 4: 3–17.

Epstein, E. (1994) 'Law and Legitimation in Post-Mao China', in Pitman Potter (ed.) *Domestic Law Reforms in Post-Mao China*, pp. 19–55. Armonk, NY: M.E. Sharpe.

Fallon, R. (1997) ' "The Rule of Law" as a Concept in Constitutional Discourse', *Columbia Law Review* 97: 1–56.

Finder, S. (1997) 'The Structure and Operation of Chinese Courts', in *A Guide to the Legal System of the PRC*, pp. 17–30. Hong Kong: Asia Law and Practice.

Finnis, J. (1980) *Natural Law and Natural Rights.* Oxford: Clarendon Press.

Freshfields (1998) 'Foreign Investment: Combating Irregular Fees', *China Notes* (Jan.): 1–3.

Friedman, Lawrence M. (1975) *The Legal System: A Social Science Perspective.* New York: Russell Sage.

Fuller, L. (1976) *The Morality of Law* (13th printing). New Haven, CT: Yale University Press.

Gaus, G. (1994) 'Public Reason and the Rule of Law', in *Nomos*, xxxvi, *The Rule of Law*, ed. Ian Shapiro, pp. 328–53. New York: New York University Press.

Gong Xiangrui, Fu Zhubian, Zhang Shuyi and Jian Mingan (1993) *Fazhi de lixiang yu xianshi* (The Ideal and Reality of the Rule of Law). Beijing: China University of Politics and Law Press.

Hayek, F. (1944) *The Road to Serfdom.* Chicago, IL: University of Chicago Press.

Hintzen, G. (1999) 'The Place of Law in the PRC's Culture', *Cultural Dynamics* 11(2): 167–92.

Howson, N. (1997) 'Flood of Legislation Clears the Way for New Corporate Forms—But are they Worth it?', *China Joint Venturer* (July/Aug.): 7–11.

Huang, P. (1994) 'Codified Law and Magisterial Discretion', in Huang and K. Bernhardt (eds) *Civil Law in Qing and Republican China,* pp. 142–86. Stanford, CA: Stanford University Press.

Jiang Lishan (1997) 'Zhongguo fazhi gaige he fazhihua guocheng yanjiu' (Study of the Process of China's Legal System Reform and Rule of Law Development), *Zhongwai faxue* 6: 35–46.

Jiang Lishan (1998a) 'Zhongguo fazhi daolu chutan (shang)' (Preliminary Examination of China's Road to Rule of Law—Part I), *Zhongwai faxue* 3: 16–28.

Jiang Lishan (1998b) 'Zhongguo fazhi daolu chutan (xia)' (Preliminary Examination of China's Road to Rule of Law—Part II), *Zhongwai faxue* 4: 21–33.

Jiang Mingan (1997) 'Yifa xingzheng shi jianli fazhi guojia de ti zhong ying you zhi yi' (Administrating According to Law should be Included in the Meaning of Establishing a Rule of Law Country), *Xingzheng faxue yanjiu* 1: 1–15.

Jiang Zemin (1996) Addresses Legal System Forum. Beijing.

Keith, R. (1994) *China's Struggle for the Rule of Law*. New York: St Martin's Press.

Keller, P. (1994) 'Sources of Order in Chinese Law', *American Journal of Comparative Law* 42: 711–59.

Li Buyun (1997) 'Guanyu qicao "Zhonghua renmin gongheguo Lifafa (zhuanjia jianyigao) de ruogan wenti"' (Several Issues in the Experts Draft of the PRC Legislation Law), *Zhonguo Faxue* 1: 11–19.

Li Buyun (1998) 'Shixing yifa zhiguo jianshe shehui zhuyi fazhi guojia' (Establish a Socialist Rule of Law State by Implementing Ruling the Country in Accordance with Law), in Ministry of Justice (ed.) *Zhonggong zhongyang fazhi jiangzuo huibian* (CCP Politburo Legal System Symposia Collection), pp. 133–55. Law Publishing Company (Falu Chubanshe). Beijing.

Li Buyun and Zhang Zhiming (1997) 'Kuashiji de biaojun: yifa zhiguo, jianshe shehuizhuyi fazhi guojia' (The Cross-Century Target: Ruling the Country According to Law, Establishing a Socialist Rule of Law State), *Zhongguo faxue* 6: 18–25.

Lieberthal, K. (1995) *Governing China.* New York: W.W. Norton.

Liu Cuixiao and Wang Jianrong (1998) 'Xingzheng faxue yanjiu shuping' (Critical Commentary on Administrative Law Research), *Faxue yanjiu* 20 (Jan.): 102–13.

Liu Hainian (1996) 'Yifa zhiguo: zhongguo shehuizhuyi fazhi jianshe de lichengbei' (Ruling the Country According to Law: A New Milestone in the Construction of China's Socialist Legal System), *Faxue Yanjiu* 3: 24–36.

Liu Hainian (1998) 'Beilun shehuizhuyi fazhi yuanze' (General Discussion of Socialist Rule of Law Principles), *Zhongguo faxue* 18: 5–15.

Lubman, Stanley (1997) 'Sino-American Relations and China's Struggle for the Rule of Law', *Columbia University East Asian Institute Reports* (Oct.): 19.

Macedo, S. (1994) 'The Rule of Law, Justice and the Politics of Moderation', in *Nomos*, xxxvi, *The Rule of Law*, ed. Ian Shapiro, pp. 148–77. New York: New York University Press.

Nathan, A. (1985) *Chinese Democracy*. Berkeley: University of California Press.

Peerenboom, R. (1993) *Law and Morality in Ancient China: The Silk Manuscripts of Huang-Lao*. Albany, NY: SUNY Press.

Peerenboom, R. (1995) 'Rights, Interests and the Interest in Rights in China', *Stanford Journal of International Law* 31: 359–86.

Peerenboom, R. (1998) 'Confucian Harmony and Freedom of Thought: The Right to Think Versus Right Thinking', in Wm. Theodore de Bary and Tu Weiming (eds) *Confucianism and Human Rights,* pp. 234–60. New York: Columbia University Press.

Raz, J. (1979) 'The Rule of law and its Virtue', in *The Authority of Law*, pp. 210–29. Oxford: Clarendon Press.

Rheinstein, M. (1954) *Max Weber on Law in Economy and Society.* Cambridge, MA: Harvard University Press.

Shen Zongling (1998) 'Yifa zhiguo yu jingji' (Ruling the Country According to Law and the Economy), *Zhongwai faxue* 3: 1–15.

Shklar, J. (1987) 'Political Theory and the Rule of Law', in A. Hutchinson and P. Monahan (eds) *The Rule of Law: Ideal or Ideology?* pp. 1–16. Toronto: Carswell.

Solum, L. (1994) 'Equity and the Rule of Law', in *Nomos,* xxxvi, *The Rule of Law,* ed. Ian Shapiro, pp. 120–47. New York: New York University Press.

Stevenson-Yang, A. (1998) 'Retail Roundabout', *China Business Review* 25(1): 43–9.

Su Li (1998) 'Ershi shiji zhongguo de xiandaihua he falu' (Twentieth Century China's Modernization and Rule of Law), *Faxue yanjiu* 20 (Jan.): 2–15.

Summers, R. (1993) 'A Formal Theory of Rule of Law', *Ratio Juris* 6(2): 127–42.

Sun Xiaoxia (1998) 'Fazhi guojia ji qi zhengzhi jiegou' (Rule of Law State and its Political Structure), *Faxue yanjiu* 20 (Jan.): 16–26.

Tanner, M.S. (1994) 'The Erosion of Communist Party Control over Lawmaking in China', *China Quarterly* 138: 382–403.

Tanner, M.S. (1995) 'How a Bill Becomes a Law in China: Stages and Processes in Lawmaking', *China Quarterly* 141: 39–64.

Valcke, C. (1994) 'Civil Disobedience and the Rule of Law: A Lockean Insight', in *Nomos*, xxxvi, *The Rule of Law*, ed. Ian Shapiro, pp. 45–62. New York: New York University Press.

Walker, G. (1988) *The Rule of Law*. Melbourne: Melbourne University Press.

Wang Jiafu (1998) 'Guanyu yifa zhiguo jianshe shehui zhuyi fazhi guojia de lilun he shijian wenti' (On Governing the Country in Accordance with Law: Theoretical and Practical Issues in Establishing a Socialist Rule of Law State), in Ministry of Justice (ed.) *Zhonggong zhongyang fazhi jiangzuo huibian* (CCP Politburo Legal System Symposia Collection), pp. 116–32. Law Publishing Company (Falu Chubanshe): Beijing.

Ying Songnian (1997) 'Yifa xingzheng lunwang' (Overview of Administrating in Accordance with Law), *Zhongguo faxue* 1.

Yu Xingzhong (1989) 'Legal Pragmatism in the People's Republic of China', *Journal of Chinese Law* 3(1): 29–52.

Zhang Geng and Hu Kangsheng, eds (1996) *Zhonghua renmin gongheguo lushifa quanshu* (Compendium of the PRC Lawyers Law). Beijing: Lantian Publishing.

Zhang Qi (1998) 'Fazhi de lixiang and xianshi' (The Ideal and Reality of Rule of Law), *Zhongwai faxue* 2: 128–9.

BIOGRAPHICAL NOTE

RANDALL PEERENBOOM is Acting Professor of Law at UCLA Law School, where he teaches courses on Chinese law. He has a BA in Philosophy (University of Wisconsin-Madison), MA in Chinese Religions and PhD in Chinese Philosophy (University of Hawaii), and JD (Columbia University). He is the author of numerous works on Chinese philosophy and law, including *Law and Morality in Ancient China* and *Lawyers in China* (Lawyers Committee on Human Rights, 1998). He practiced law in China with a major international firm, 1994–8, and is currently co-editor of the revised *Doing Business in China*. His current research interests include the rule of law in China, human rights, administrative law reform, legal theory and commercial law. *Address*: UCLA Law School, Box 951476, Los Angeles, California, 90095–1476, USA.
[email: peerenbo@law. ucla.edu]

[7]

A SECOND GREAT WALL?

China's Post-Cultural Revolution Project of Legal Construction

WILLIAM P. ALFORD
Harvard Law School

◇

ABSTRACT

This article examines the PRC's post-Cultural Revolution project of legal development, the largest such undertaking in world history. It commences with a review of the achievements and shortcomings of legal construction in the PRC over the past two decades. The article then probes the rationale for and nature of this project, in so doing endeavoring to situate it historically. In its final section, the article suggests ways in which we might think of assessing China's efforts at constructing a legal system within a single generation.

Key Words ◇ autonomy ◇ convergence ◇ human agency ◇ instrumentalism ◇ legal development

The People's Republic of China's (PRC) post-Cultural Revolution project of legal development is an event of epic historic proportions. No other major modern society has endeavored in so short a time to reconstruct its legal system in so extensive and novel a fashion. Indeed, one might say that in its magnitude, this undertaking offers something of a contemporary societal analogue to another unparalleled Chinese construction project—the building, during the 3rd century BCE, of the Great Wall. As with the Wall, the project of post-Cultural Revolution law reform has the potential to recast China's internal dynamic, even as it seeks to shape China's interaction with the world beyond its borders. Will it, as some suggest has been the case with the Wall, prove an enduring structure, playing a key role in bringing definition and order to China over time, or will it, as others contend about the Wall, be no more than a porous edifice that not only fails to provide the protection it purports to offer but fosters a false security masking internal decay?[1]

This question is one that, of course, defies a ready or definitive answer—

Cultural Dynamics 11(2): 193–213. [0921–3740 (199907) 11:2; 193–213; 008644]

most especially as the mortar binding the bricks of this project has barely begun to set. The present article ventures preliminary thoughts about China's project of post-Cultural Revolution legal development both for its inherent importance and for the further questions it raises about Chinese reform beyond law, the nature of legality more generally, and the challenges that confront those of us from outside involved in this process as observers or participants or both—recognizing throughout that the vastness of this topic surpasses even that of Qin Shihuang's Great Wall.

The PRC's Project of Legal Construction

At first glance, the edifice of legality constructed over the 20 years since the post-Cultural Revolution effort at legal construction was launched is, at least in formal terms, a very considerable structure to behold. Starting in the late 1970s with little more than a skeletal constitution that was basically an attack on established institutions of governance, and a small number of generally worded statutes that typically derived much of their meaning from Chinese Communist Party (CCP) policy pronouncements in what, after all, was said to be a civil (or code-based) legal system,[2] the PRC has since developed an extensive body of laws, regulations, and other legal enactments. Chinese officials proudly report the promulgation during this period of more than 300 laws by the National People's Congress (NPC) (the supreme organ of state) and its Standing Committee, more than 700 regulations by the State Council (the central government's executive and administrative arm), more than 4000 regulations by subnational people's congresses and their standing committees, and more than 24,000 other legal enactments by the ministries arrayed under the State Council and their subnational counterparts (with more, undoubtedly, being added as this article is being written).

The fruits of the two decades of formal legal development are many. The PRC has an elaborate constitutional document that sets out a range of political, economic, and social rights, as well as 'organic' laws designed to define the legal status, structure, and responsibilities of the congress, the courts, the procuracy, and other key state institutions. It also possesses a General Principles of the Civil Law containing inter alia, examples of the type of overarching, defining principles regarding civil legal acts, ownership, and obligations that one would anticipate finding in the book on general principles of a civil code drafted in the German tradition; basic laws (*jiben fa*) laying out key rules regarding criminal law, criminal procedure, marriage, and the like—many now in their second generation; and a range of other statutory and regulatory enactments, including many in areas of the law new to the PRC concerning issues such as inheritance, corporations, intellectual property, the environment, and legal profession. Indeed, official and quasi-official sources point to the size of China's body of legal enactments as an indication of how far Chinese legal construction has proceeded (Li Bian, 1997: 23).

This vibrancy in law-making has been accompanied with unprecedented efforts to put in place the personnel needed to operate such a legal system. Whereas China had some 32,000 persons working in its court system (including judges and associated administrative personnel) in 1960, that number is 10 times larger today (Alford and Fang, 1994). Law schools and programs providing legal training short of a degree have proliferated in comparable ways—now reaching well into the hundreds. But these numbers pale, in turn, relative to a legal profession that has grown from 3000 in 1980 to over 120,000 today, with plans to add roughly 30,000 over the next two years and to bring the total to 300,000 by the year 2010—which, in absolute terms, is likely to leave China by that date with more lawyers than any nation, save for the United States (Alford, 1995a: 22–3; Peerenboom, 1998).

The foregoing is not simply a question of the state creating structures on paper. China's citizens are increasingly availing themselves of these legal processes. During 1996, China's courts heard 5,264,619 cases—more than 15 times the number of those heard in 1960 and almost 16 percent more than were heard in 1995 (again to make use of the penchant of PRC authorities for statistics). The media, the arts, and social survey research, whether conducted by Chinese scholars, foreigners, or both, all suggest a growing awareness on the part of the populace of formal legality. This is poignantly illustrated, for example, by Zhang Yimou's 1992 film *Qiu Ju da guansi* (The story of Qiu Ju) which, albeit with something of a tongue in cheek quality, concerns the efforts of a rural woman to invoke formal legal processes to attain the justice that she believes has been denied her by more traditional dispute resolution. And it is confirmed by the impressive rural field work of Xia Yong and his colleagues (Xia Yong, 1995).

One could go on, but even discounting the lingering effects of the traditional fascination with numerology and of the residue of a state planning mentality that seeks to reduce all to the quantifiable, it is clear that China has laid in place many of the formal building blocks of a new post-Cultural Revolution legal system. The crafting of these major building blocks having been noted, however, one need not peer terribly hard to discern shortcomings in these foundations.

Turning first to the Constitution, it is true that the PRC's current document provides a panoply of rights, including some—such as the right to employment and to social security—not found in the constitutions of certain of the industrialized advanced liberal democracies. But having documents termed constitutions is, of course, not the same as constitutionalism—if we construe the latter term as the sustained effort to rise above immediate political dictates and restrain the exercise of power in order to preserve higher freedoms or minority rights. The PRC constitution may well state a set of desired ends, but as the late Zhang Youyu, one of China's most eminent legal scholars wrote in 1989, it is not intended to have direct legal effect (quoted in Chen, 1992: 46). To date, the Constitution has yet to be successfully invoked to constrain the exercise of governmental or party power, the Supreme People's Court has instructed lower-level courts not to rely on it in deciding cases, and the body that enacted it—the National People's Congress—is, through its Standing Committee, the body ultimately charged with interpreting it (Liu Nanping, 1997: 95; Cai Dingjian, 1995: 227–9).

Moving beyond the Constitution, for all the advances in the drafting of laws and regulations in recent years, many very substantial problems remain. China does have a burgeoning body of legal enactments, but, in all too many instances, as Perry Keller has skillfully depicted, there is an important lack of clarity as to which units of government are authorized to enact and interpret this welter of rules and on what basis (Keller, 1994: 738–42).

On the law-making side, Chinese as well as foreign experts are hard put to identify a consistent principled basis to distinguish, for example, between basic and other laws passed by the NPC; between regulations enacted by state agencies pursuant to delegated, as opposed to inherent, authority; and between detailed rules that the Supreme People's Court periodically issues under the broad rubric of interpretations and those promulgated by non-judicial administrative actors (Keller, 1994: 743–9; Liu Nanping, 1997).

My concern here is not a formalistic one about the neatness of categories, but rather the very fundamental question of how one is to understand and ultimately delimit one's legal obligations. This difficulty is, in turn, exacerbated by the vagueness and internal inconsistency of many laws. The former problem is evidenced, for example, by one set of consumer protection regulations that declare violators shall be dealt with 'sternly', whatever that might mean (Guojia jingwei, 1986: 104–7), while the latter is illustrated by the recently revised air quality law which first empowers local environmental protection departments to exercise unified supervision and control over air pollution, but then reduces their enforcement powers vis-a-vis enterprises owned or run by the state to mere recommendations *(Zhonghua renmin*, 1995: arts. 3 and 13).

Vagueness and inconsistency are, to some degree, a part and parcel of every legal system, but in the Chinese case they are compounded by an additional set of concerns. One is the apparent authority various state agencies have not only to make, but also to interpret, their own legal enactments, free of any requirement that their own deliberations or any external review be transparent, particularly at a time when many such actors are busy churning out rules designed in part to justify their continued existence as China changes. A second is the relative absence of meaningful standards for sorting out potential or actual conflicts (whether at the national level or the subnational level or between national and subnational units of government)—as official assertions that conflicts do not exist because China is a unitary state in which higher level norms always prevail over lower simply are untenable (Keller, 1994: 749–51). And a third is the sense of the state, at least in the criminal area, that its own laws are inadequate to discharge the purposes for which they were enacted, in the absence of a concerted political campaign, as evidenced in the recent *yanda* (Strike Hard) campaign in which Amnesty International estimates that thousands were executed (Agence France Presse, 1997; Amnesty International, 1996).

Somewhat analogous points might be made regarding the institutions and personnel undergirding these laws. As Anthony Dicks has shown in the *China Quarterly*, although Chinese courts are more active than ever before, their capacity to bind administrative actors, not to mention the Communist Party, remains limited which, in his words, 'necessarily throws doubt on the authority of the courts as exponents of a generalized and universally applicable view of the law' (Dicks, 1995: 109). The courts are, as Donald Clarke has argued, in many respects, possessed of no greater authority than any other *xitong* (or administrative system). So it is, for example, that the enforcement of judgments, even against state agencies, remains a critical problem in the PRC (Clarke, 1995, 1996).

One reason why the courts have been experiencing such difficulties may have to do with their personnel. As recently as five years ago, approximately one-fifth of China's judges had completed their tertiary education (and many in fields other than law) (Alford and Fang, 1994). Although serious efforts have been expended in recent years to close the gap, it remains true that a considerable portion of China's middle-aged judges are superannuated People's Liberation Army officers, transferred over out of the belief that the army had too many people and the judiciary too few and that the skills involved in officering were much the same as those needed in judging.[3] Younger judges tend to have had more formal training, but they continue to be drawn from the ranks of the Communist Party, to be subject to its ongoing oversight, and, in the view of some observers, lack the dedication to public service and integrity of their elders drawn from the army.[4] And, in general, many judges seem to be experiencing considerable difficulty in accepting the type of novel, if still modest, adversarial role provided to defense counsel in the 1996 revisions to the criminal procedure law, according to early reports regarding its implementation (Fu Hualing, 1998: 47).

Notwithstanding the posture of superiority that some PRC lawyers adopt these days towards the judiciary, the legal profession is neither appreciably better educated, more independent, nor a consistent force for the improvement of the legal system. The Ministry of Justice continues to set quotas for new lawyers, much as line production ministries in the planned economy determined how much steel or cooking oil the state needed. One result is that China over the past 17 years has licensed more than three times more people to practice law than the number of people who have earned degrees in law. Although the Ministry has indicated that it now sees its role as one of macro, as opposed to micro, management of lawyers, the leadership of the All China Lawyers Federation—which is supposed to be the voice of the legal profession itself—has included well-placed former Ministry officials, some, at least, with limited legal training or experience. And misconduct by lawyers, including bribery of judges and other officials, is a serious problem, at least according to anecdotal data gleaned by this author in the course of interviews with Beijing legal professionals.[5]

So, too, there is a need to look beyond raw data in assessing the significance of citizen engagement with the law. Cases filed are, indeed, way up but the vast majority of these concern small-scale economic disputes, divorce, and other interactions between citizens, rather than efforts by citizens to avail themselves of legal processes to cabin state power or halt abuses by errant cadres. Citizens may have invoked China's administrative litigation law on an annual average of 50,000 times during the decade of the 1990s (Pei Minxin, 1997: 836) but that pales before reports in *Cheng Ming* that in 1995 alone the Communist Party's internal disciplinary mechanism expelled more than 1,000,000 cadres and other Party members, chiefly for reasons of corruption and other inappropriate conduct (Luo Bing, 1996: 6–8).

There is, in view of such problems, a temptation to dismiss China's post-Cultural Revolution project of legal construction, including the ways in which it has drawn on the experience of the United Kingdom, United States, Germany, Japan, and other advanced industrialized states, as insincerely undertaken, ill-conceived, or incompetently executed. To do so, however, would be a mistake that would not only limit our comprehension of that project, but would deny us the opportunity to ponder the broader questions that it raises about both the full spectrum of Chinese reforms and the nature of law, whether in China or more generally.

Simply stated, it seems to me that the principal state architects of China's post-Cultural Revolution law reform project have a genuine ambivalence toward their undertaking. On the one hand, they wish to reap the advantages of liberal legality in terms of its perceived capacity to support economic growth, engage the international community, and legitimate the existing regime. On the other, however, they aspire to do so without being unduly subject to its constraints, either in the more obvious sense of explicit limits of the type that liberal legality places on the exercise of political authority, or in the more subtle ways that adherence to a system of consistently and visibly enforced rules tends to limit even the well-intentioned exercise of discretion by those in power. In effect, this design is the counterpart in law of the larger effort to carry out a substantial transformation of the economy without a commensurate relinquishing of political control. It should lead those of us interested in law to ask such fundamental questions about our field as what are the most vital features of legality that distinguish it from politics, what is the relationship between a society's law and larger values and institutions, and, most cogently, to what degree is it possible to divide legality in the manner to which those crafting law reform in China aspire.

The Rationale for Law Reform in the PRC

We might commence our effort at understanding this process better by looking further into the rationale behind it—so long as we keep in mind as we describe these broad motivating factors that there have been differences of opinion among officials and scholars, within the parameters of permitted discourse (and even at times as to those bounds) as evidenced, for example, by the debates that accompanied, and delayed, the promulgation of laws in such diverse areas as copyright, corporations, and criminal procedure (Alford, 1995b: 66–94).

Among the most important reasons that the Chinese leadership launched and continues to support the project of legal construction are:

1. the reconstruction and further development of core institutions of governance that were decimated during the turmoil of the 1950s, 1960s, and 1970s—such as the Ministry of Justice, which was eliminated in 1959, and the procuracy, the prosecutorial functions of which were absorbed by the police and courts from 1969 through 1978;
2. displaying a Weberian faith in the relation of economic and legal development, the facilitation of the transition from a largely planned economy to one more driven by market forces (and, with it, the development of rules and structures to accommodate the devolution of a growing measure of economic authority from a limited number of administrative agencies to a much broader array of actors wishing to undertake a far more varied range of transactions);
3. the maintenance of order, particularly in the face of the social forces unleashed by the foregoing events, that, for example, have spawned an unauthorized internal migration that official sources have put at as many as 100 million people (which, if true, would be double the size of the population of South Korea) (Canye wengao, 1995: 1), eroded the moral authority of the ruling party, and led a range of actors, including even subnational units of government, to behave in ways the center deems inconsistent with its interests;
4. legitimation at home and abroad—by distinguishing the post-Cultural

Revolution regime from its predecessors, enlisting the law to disseminate norms nationally, and acquiring the perceived attributes of modernity (as, for example, during the debate over patent law of the early 1980s when one proponent argued that if over 100 countries already have such law, clearly so should the great Chinese people) (Alford, 1995b: 68);

5. engagement—both affirmatively and defensively—with an international community which, for good or ill, employs the language of legality and increasingly penetrates into areas once seen as international affairs, ranging from the treatment of dissidents, to the fuels factories use, to the benefits workers in state-owned enterprises receive, and
6. the provision of an outlet for Chinese citizens seeking redress for their grievances against fellow citizens and, in a much more circumscribed fashion, against selected local officials acting contrary to central authority—as, for example in the more than 1.25 million reviews of Cultural Revolution criminal convictions carried out in 1978–82 and in more recent drives commenced by Beijing to prevent wayward local cadres extracting extralegal fees from the peasantry (*Renmin ribao,* 1998: 1).

In pursuit of these and other ends, China has not been shy about drawing on the legal systems of foreign jurisdictions and, in particular, such major industrialized democracies as the United Kingdom, Germany, Japan, and especially the United States. It has devoted tens of millions of dollars of its own resources and of those provided by multilateral organizations and foreign governments, foundations, universities, businesses, law firms, and private citizens, as well as a great deal of effort, to the following sorts of endeavors:

- sending abroad thousands of China's most promising personnel in legally related fields, particularly to common law countries, to study and practice law—some of whom have returned to occupy key positions within legislative drafting, legal academic and other relevant circles;
- receiving thousands of foreign judges, professors, lawyers, and others for purposes from wide-ranging lectures on law to consultancy on specific legal issues (Seidman and Seidman, 1997: 9–12);
- studying foreign laws as the PRC prepared its own new legislation, as, for example, in the case of the patent law—with respect to which the laws of more than 100 jurisdictions (including Taiwan and Hong Kong) were reviewed (Alford, 1995b: 69); and
- making foreign law a staple in undergraduate legal education and a growing component of training programs for judges, prosecutors, and lawyers, while also calling upon officialdom broadly better to familiarize itself with the law in general (a fair proportion of which bears the imprint of foreign models). Even the senior leadership—including

President Jiang Zemin, Premier Zhu Rongji, and the head of the National People's Congress, Li Peng, among others—not long ago sat through a series of lectures on domestic and international law designed to convey its support for the dissemination of legal knowledge (Xinhua, 1998a).

Nonetheless, even as they have devoted scarce monies and extensive energies to the introduction of foreign law, China's leaders have sought to keep within sharply circumscribed bounds what many of us who work in the law in those countries from which China is drawing most heavily consider the single most important feature of such legality—namely, the aspiration that law enjoy autonomy and not be subordinated to politics. In this skeptical, postmodern age of ours, I doubt that many of us would want to make the claim that our legal systems—or, for that matter, any other human institutions—are ultimately capable of standing wholly beyond politics. Indeed, the very goal of distinguishing law from politics is itself the product of a particular set of political values, especially regarding limits on the exercise of political power which that goal of legal autonomy is, in turn, meant to reenforce. But that, it seems to me, does not diminish—and it may even enhance—the importance of our seeking, however imperfectly, to craft and maintain legal institutions that aspire to stand beyond politics and that ultimately may—through their transparency and predictability, universality and fairness of application—serve as a reference against which even the well-intentioned actions of the powerful may be assessed and, perhaps, checked.

To put it bluntly, this is not something that the principal state architects of Chinese legal construction desire. To the contrary, even as they have sought to develop China's post-Cultural Revolution legal system, they have endeavored to retain ultimate authority over it. Consider, for example, the irony of the most recent 15th Congress of the Communist Party in which China's leaders called on the nation to embrace the rule of law, even as the Party remains unambiguously above it—as evidenced in a host of ways, including its immunity from suit under the Administrative Litigation Law (which has been much publicized as the principal vehicle through which Chinese citizens are to seek redress for abuses of power) on the grounds that the law only applies to state organs of which the Party is not one, and the continuing use of Party discipline, rather than law, as the primary instrument to deal with wayward officials and other cadres (Pei Minxin, 1997: 835). Or think about how strenuously and quickly the President of the Supreme People's Court in 1989 defended the use of force against citizens who occupied Tiananmen Square and in 1997 called for the state to squelch all targets of the Strike Hard campaign (Alford, 1990: 177; *Zuigao renmin fayuan,* 1996: 25–7). Or look further into the ways in which the generality and opacity of so much Chinese law, its underdevelopment in terms of procedures and remedies available to the populace (at least relative to many other states), and the ongoing lack of a clear differentiation between courts and other state organs all have the effect, whether fully intended or not, of placing considerable unchecked discretion in the hands of officialdom and party.

To note all this—and the many other examples one might add—is not to attribute all difficulties with Chinese law to the role of the Communist Party. Center–regional tensions, local protectionism, bureaucratism, the speed with which the economy and society are changing, inexperience with the law, poverty, and the desire for personal aggrandizement, are among the many factors that are to some measure distinguishable from, even if exacerbated by, law's relative absence of autonomy from the Party. Nor is it to suggest that Chinese law has failed to take on any life of its own or even that the leadership is wholly unaware of the value of predictability in the law—an appreciation of which it would seem to have at least in the economic arena. Rather, it is to throw into relief the particular design of China's post-Cultural Revolution project of legal construction and the ways in which foreign legality is being adapted as a part thereof.

Undergirding this design is a very mechanistic view of officially promulgated law—as fundamentally a tool or technology that can be readily detached from one setting to apply in a second very different context in order to accomplish particular state objectives—as if one were simply borrowing the working drawings pursuant to which the Great Wall in Badaling was built to reconstruct a section in Mutianyu. Stated differently, this vision seems to presume that, as China seeks to utilize the language and forms of law initially crafted in a liberal democratic context, the economic can be separated from the political, rules from culture, and substance from procedure and institutions in ways that I suspect Marx, Weber, the authors of the *Da Qing Lü Li* (The Statutes and Substatutes of the Great Qing Dynasty), or their predecessors who crafted earlier Chinese codes, and many others might well have found surprising.

Some observers may suggest that we, at least, ought not to be surprised that the present Chinese leadership might hold such a mechanistic view of legality, given that its top tier—including virtually all members of the Communist Party's Politburo's Standing Committee—is today filled with engineers such as Jiang Zemin, Li Peng, and Zhu Rongji (all of whom, it also should be noted, were trained in the USSR) and has never included an individual educated in the law, save for a few hours of lecture late in life. Indeed, well into the 1990s, no regular member of the 200-odd person Central Committee of the Chinese Communist Party was a lawyer or law graduate and, in what surely must be a record among major nations, far fewer than 1 percent of the 3000 delegates to the national legislature have been lawyers—which, in the Chinese setting, may be a telling fact, given the central role that the Constitution accords the NPC not only in promulgating

China's laws, but also in serving as the supreme organ of state and the final arbiter of the Constitution and laws it enacts.[6] Of course, in noting this paucity of the legally trained in important positions in China we need to remember that the PRC's law schools were effectively closed from the late 1950s onward for almost two decades as well and also be mindful of the general 'generational' trajectory from soldiers to engineers to lawyers evident in Taiwan, Korea, and certain other jurisdictions.[7]

Tempting though it might be, it would be misleading to attribute this sense of law as an instrument that can be readily detached from one context and applied to another setting simply to the background of China's leaders in engineering or even in Leninism—given that this approach has both noteworthy historical antecedents and strong, if somewhat unexpected, exponents in today's international community. Historical continuities are all too easy to overstate and all too difficult to prove, but the attitude of today's leaders toward foreign law resonates with that of many of their predecessors and perhaps most notably, that of the Self-Strengthening movement of a century ago. At its core, this movement was a response to the grave circumstances in which the Chinese state found itself by virtue of a combination of severe internal turmoil and foreign depredations (Kuo and Liu, 1978: 491–5; Duara, 1995: 206–8). China could best strengthen itself and so deal effectively with such challenges both at home and abroad, its leaders felt, by employing practical techniques developed by the outside world while holding dear to Chinese values for all essential matters. Encapsulated in the classic *ti-yong* formulation (pursuant to which China was to be the 'essence' and foreign learning an 'instrument'), this effort found concrete manifestation in the establishment during the latter half of the 19th century of the Zongli yamen (a forerunner of a modern foreign office) and the Tungwen guan (a school for foreign languages), the development of state arsenals, shipyards, and factories, and early efforts to translate and begin to deploy principles of foreign and international law.

Notwithstanding the talents of leaders such as Feng Guifen, Zeng Guofan, Li Hongzhang, Liang Qichao, and others, however, the self-strengtheners and their immediate progeny not only failed in this effort to enlist western techniques to serve Chinese essence, but in the process came to question just what comprised the Chinese essence they were endeavoring so earnestly to preserve. And perhaps in no area did this attempted patchwork produce a less satisfactory result than in law, given two sets of tensions: one between the values underlying the western legality the self-strengtheners sought to borrow and the ends toward which they sought to deploy it, and the other between the rhetoric and reality of legality in the hands of a West all too ready in its relations with China to invoke law to serve power (Cohen and Chiu, 1974; vol. 1: 8–12).

It is important to appreciate that there is nothing uniquely Chinese about instrumental approaches to legality. Again, somewhat ironically, the international community today is reinforcing such an attitude toward law in China in at least two distinct regards. The first lies in the ways in which the governments of the major industrialized democracies are at times willing to slight even their own law and its underlying values and ideals in the service of economic interests—in a manner reminiscent of their 19th-century forerunners—thereby confirming the more cynical of Chinese leaders in their belief that law is nothing but a malleable tool of such interests and compounding the difficulties confronting those in China who might take a more nuanced view of law. Witness, for example, the dexterity with which the United States has over the past few years shamelessly attempted to dance around the requirements of its non-proliferation and export control laws so as to be able to sell nuclear and other lucrative equipment to China, or consider the ways in which most major European nations have arguably skirted their international human rights obligations by refusing to support even the mildest of resolutions to examine China's record before the United Nations Human Rights Commission, for fear of losing Airbus and other sales (Roth, 1997). Or ponder the willingness of the US in 1996 to condone Beijing's efforts to tighten control over all media—including the mandatory re-registration of all printing presses in the nation, the prohibition of the importation of new equipment without state permission, and the stationing of police in every industry making compact discs—in return for a promise of greater intellectual property protection (Alford, 1996, 1997a: 143–4).

A second, and perhaps more subtle way in which the international community has, somewhat unwittingly, reinforced the current Chinese leadership's vision of legality lies in the approach that a number of significant multilateral, foreign governmental, and nongovernmental organizations have taken in their technical legal assistance work in China. Each has touted the role that law can play in nation building while studiously avoiding associated political questions or implications, as if to suggest that the 'technical' side of law that might foster economic development can somehow be neatly extricated from its more political dimension. To paraphrase one high-level representative of a major multilateral institution, the major multilateral financial institutions deal in economics, not politics.

At one level, this is certainly understandable. A central message many working with the law hope to impart to China is that law and politics should be distinct. In addition, as a practical matter, many of the non-Chinese entities in question have an official mandate to avoid the explicitly political (even if various of their agents hope that technical legal development will over time spur political change), while few of us engaged with China on legal affairs wish unnecessarily to jeopardize our working relationships there. But at another level, whether intended or not, this approach perpetuates the notion that the developmental benefits to be derived from a greater use of legality can be attained principally through the promulgation of what one PRC student of mine has termed 'lovely laws', without confronting difficult, inherently political questions regarding the limiting of official discretion, the devolution of significant authority to independent adjudicators, greater citizen access to legal redress, and ultimately, the subjugation of the Communist Party to law.

Evaluating China's Post-Cultural Revolution Project of Legal Construction

For all the accomplishments of Chinese law reform, there are reasons to wonder about the extent to which China's new wall of legality serves the purposes envisioned by its principal architects in the leadership. From some perspectives, such uncertainty as to the success of Chinese law reform may seem very odd. After all, given China's present and projected prosperity, it would seem that law must be working reasonably well, at least in terms of the goals envisioned by its chief state architects. Since the end of the Cultural Revolution, the PRC has lifted tens of millions of its citizens out of grinding poverty (World Bank, 1997: 1–2). Its economy grew at a rate of close to 10 percent annually for many years, it attracts more foreign direct investment than any other developing nation, and the World Bank, among others offering essentially sanguine predictions, suggests that China is well positioned to increase its gross domestic product some sevenfold over the next generation alone (World Bank, 1997).

The inquiry, I would suggest, needs, however, to be a good deal more probing in at least three important respects, even as we remember that societies, including the advanced industrialized democracies, that accord legality considerably more autonomy also have very serious problems of their own.

First, even in relatively straightforward economic terms, it seems clear that the unwillingness of China's leaders to cede the law greater autonomy—and the consequences thereof in terms of transparency, predictability, and fairness—have and will cost China dearly. Foreigners contemplating transferring technology or capital to China typically demand and sometimes receive a healthy premium to compensate for the legal system's shortcomings, if they are even willing to part with their upper-end technology. Figures on foreign direct investment need seriously to be reassessed in the light of the large amount of PRC money routed, at times illegally, through Hong Kong back into China to take advantage of tax holidays and the large amount of PRC money headed offshore, some of it illegally. And we need to be mindful that predictions of dramatic growth of the type that the World Bank and others enjoy making presume the effective operation of a legal system capable of facilitating the thorough transformation and future fair operation of China's banking, fiscal, accounting, and statistical systems—each of which, at present, is at a minimum, facing very serious problems that pose potentially significant obstacles to China's extraordinary rate of growth (Pei Minxin, 1998: 321–2; Lardy, 1998).

But there is more to assessing the effectiveness of Chinese law reform than economic statistics, even appreciating the difficulty of attributing causality as we cast our glance upon society more broadly. In considering the quality of life, for example, we need to recognize that more people are enjoying a higher degree of personal freedom, so long as they avoid the political, than at any point in the history of the PRC—and that the growth, relative to earlier years, of predictability and fairness in the law surely is one among a number of reasons for this (Ching, 1998: 57). At the same time, however, we must acknowledge that the weakness and relative lack of autonomy of the legal system contribute importantly to—and are, in turn, exacerbated by—a range of other problems. These include:

- the ways that pervasive corruption and conflicts of interest not only waste vast public resources, but also eat at the foundations of trust so central to any society and especially one undergoing wrenching transformations and experiencing rapidly widening inequality;
- the drag of bureaucratism—in terms of a proliferation of quasi-, pseudo-, and extralegal licensing, regulatory, and other requirements by state agencies and officials taking advantage of the confusion rife within the Chinese legal system to use law to justify their continued post-reform existence, fend off their bureaucratic rivals, and fill their coffers—at the very time that China's leadership indicates that it hopes to put the economy on more of a market footing and release domestic entrepreneurial energies (Manion, 1996: 167);
- the limiting of ready legal and administrative outlets through which growing pent-up grievances by workers and others might find constructive resolution, especially given the ineffectuality of China's state-run unions (Karmel, 1996: 128–31);
- the deleterious impact on the public health and natural environment of unenforced environmental and associated laws (Smil, 1993: 194–5); and
- the failure to develop—or even begin with real candor to discuss openly how best to develop—an effective and visible mechanism for addressing through law center/subnational tensions, such as the local protectionism that not only impedes the flow of goods nationally but also inclines judges and local officials (whose salary and working and living conditions are controlled locally) to favor local litigants over those from afar, be they firms or itinerant workers from elsewhere in China or foreign enterprises (Lubman, 1997).

Third, any assessment of the effectiveness of the approach toward legality pursued by China's leaders also needs to take account of the ways in which it is received by the citizenry. Our capacity to ascertain this is, to be sure, somewhat constrained by the paucity of survey research and by lingering questions as to the candor of responses on issues of potential political sensitivity, but, without being flip, possibility of either acceptance or rejection by the populace of the program of post-Cultural Revolution legal reform poses challenges to its architects.

Certainly, at first glance, popular acceptance would seem to be just what the regime desires, but as the cases of celebrated dissidents such as Guo Luoji and Dai Qing illustrate in an admittedly exaggerated form, those who would take the law literally (redolent as parts of it are with the language of liberal legality) potentially confront the state with a Hobson's choice—at least in some instances (Alford, 1993: 49–55). In effect, they are forcing the state either, on the one hand, to follow through on rights it apparently has promised, but which, at least in some instances, it may not have fully intended to deliver or the consequences of which it may not have fully appreciated, or, on the other hand, to risk seeing its legitimacy tarnished for failing to adhere to its own law. Indeed, a somewhat similar point might be made about some of the expanding body of persons working in the law who—whether for reasons of professionalism or personal pecuniary interest or both—have growing reason to take the law seriously. Rejection, of course, is, if anything, more troublesome. China may not yet be democratic, but without popular support, it is difficult to imagine the law coming alive and, without legitimacy of the type that the law is intended to help engender, it is difficult to envision Beijing being able to carry through with the plans it has announced further to transform the economy and society.

Presuming that a wall of legality constructed without a foundation of autonomy may not long endure, are we warranted in assuming that, following its demise, China will instead embrace liberal legality?

There is a surprisingly broad array of people who, with varying degrees of self-consciousness, in effect subscribe to a notion akin to what some Chinese leaders like to call *heping yanbian* (peaceful evolution) of which the idea of legal evolution might be termed a prime component. The most obvious are those—in the spirit of Francis Fukuyama—who say that we are at the end of history and it is only a matter of time before our norms and practices, including the basic tenets of our conception of legality, secure universal acceptance (Fukuyama, 1992). Scarcely less direct are certain economists—such as Thomas Rawski and Gary Jefferson—who although not phrasing their arguments in terms of the end of history see classical laissez-faire economics and associated legal institutions as being so clearly preferable to any set of alternatives that only the foolhardy could reject them (Jefferson, 1997: 581; Alford, 1997b: 597). Of somewhat similar mind are many in the foreign and international development community whose legal technical assistance work is premised on the assumption that the repeated use by China of law even in a fairly instrumental fashion will foster a climate that will ultimately lead to a more liberal legality. And there are even some in Chinese leadership circles who voice very strong doubts about the appropriateness of the values of liberal legality but seem, by virtue of the very vigor with which they urge resistance to these values, to be acknowledging their capacity to spread (Xinhua, 1998b).

I think it misleading, if not potentially pernicious, though, to presume the progressive development of liberal legality for at least three reasons. First, such a view understates the degree to which the problems confronting efforts to foster legal development in China are entrenched and enduring. For example, such troubling dimensions of the contemporary Chinese legal scene as the indistinctness of administrative and adjudicatory functions, the relative lack of transparency in governmental processes, the systematic difficulty in bringing the law to bear on officialdom, and the unwillingness of the center adequately to fund the administration of justice at the local level all have deep and abiding roots in Chinese soil (Alford, 1984: 1192–6). Other problems—such as the Communist Party's extralegal interference in the state's legal processes in ways big and small, ranging from Strike Hard-type campaigns to the routine involvement of party cadres in mundane cases affecting their interests—arguably may be of more recent vintage, but are not necessarily any less tenacious.

Second, although it may seem at odds with the foregoing point, the assumption that China will perforce converge with liberal democracies, in effect, suggests a single path of development with ourselves as its natural endpoint. That carries with it the danger of overstating both the posited and realized virtues of our own approach, while also obscuring other possibilities that the Chinese experience might yield. After all, it would seem that one could extol the need for a legal system to provide fundamental transparency, predictability, universality, and fairness without necessarily suggesting that it replicate all dimensions of the American, German or Japanese experience or that of any other legal system committed to the rule of law.

Third, and perhaps most importantly, assumptions of inevitability by their very nature devalue the role of human agency—by which I mean the capacity with which we are endowed to make choices, for good or ill, and the responsibility attendant upon the choices we make. As such, however unwittingly or modestly, these assumptions diminish our humanity and that of those we study.

In rejecting a relatively linear notion of convergence, I want to emphasize that I am neither subscribing to a vision of Chinese civilization as fundamentally lacking in the cultural resources upon which a less instrumental, more autonomous legal order might be built nor, more generally speaking, contending that culture is as confining as Samuel Huntington and others who argue in terms of eternally distinct civilizations would have us think (Huntington, 1996: 40–55).

Turning to the first point, it seems to me, for example, that the central Confucian premise that the exercise of power ought to be accompanied by a profound sense of responsibility to those over whom said power is held—an important component of which surely encompasses justice and fairness—should be heartening to those aspiring to construct a richer legality than now obtains in official circles in Beijing (Schwartz, 1985: 102–9). Similarly, there is much worthy of further consideration in Taoist ideas of a higher standard against which the actions of state authority might be assessed; in Buddhist beliefs in the centrality of compassion and decency to all life, and even in the pre-imperial *fajia* (or Legalist) determination that all human endeavor be subordinated to a single set of rules—not to mention the more popular conceptions of justice evident in the type of mediation processes that Michael Palmer (1987: 252–8) has so insightfully studied or that permeate Chinese fiction from the Bao Gongan tales of the medieval era to at least some parts of the *fazhi wenxue* (legal system literature) of today (Kinkley, forthcoming).

As concerns my second point, it would seem that essentialist understandings of Chinese culture as somehow fixed and lacking the capacity to change are simply untenable in light of the insights generated by historians and social scientists over the past two decades. Moreover, the growing professionalism of numerous Chinese whose careers lie in the law, the burgeoning of an unprecedentedly large middle class, and both the desire and pressure China feels to be a part of an international order that is reaching into the lives of its citizens in ways scarcely imaginable even a decade ago are phenomena that carry with them a potential impetus for further change.

Stepping back, then—with respect to culture no less than with regard to convergence—we need to eschew inevitability and its unwarranted assumption that, as concerns law, China will follow one or the other of two paths prescribed by either world or Chinese history. The challenge of building a legal system that aspires to treat law as sufficiently distinct from politics to yield the benefits of transparency, universality, predictability, and fairness on a regular basis (even if in practice it may not always realize that distinction and accomplish that end) and the particular form that such a system might take in any given society are not preordained matters, but themselves require intensely political decisions as to how properly to bound that which is political. This, in turn, brings us back to the centrality of human agency, which we ignore at our peril if we wish to discern and assess the patterns that mark this and any future Chinese efforts at legal construction.

NOTES

This is a revised version of the Annual Lecture of the Centre of Chinese Studies of The School of Oriental and African Studies (SOAS) of the University of London and a Golden Jubilee Lecture of the SOAS Faculty of Law originally given in November 1997. I wish to thank Anthony Dicks, John Ohnesorge, Dane Peacock, Randall Peerenboom, Yuanyuan Shen, and especially Michael Palmer for their various roles in making this piece possible, and gratefully acknowledge the support of my dean, Robert Clark, and the Harvard Law School. None bear any responsibility for the views stated herein.

1. The complex history of the Wall and its significance in Chinese civilization is the subject of Waldron, 1990.
2. To be sure, the 1975 Constitution of the PRC superseded the more elaborate Constitution of 1954. For more on the state of PRC law at the end of the Cultural Revolution, see Chen, 1992.
3. The army, incidentally, had need for fewer officers not because of an overall reduction in armed forces, but because hundreds of thousands of its troops have in recent years been transferred into the People's Armed Police—that part of the armed force whose job is the maintenance of internal order.
4. Author's interviews, Beijing, October 1997.
5. Author's interviews, Beijing, September–December 1997.
6. As recently as the mid-1990s, fewer than 0.1 percent of the 3000 delegates to the National People's Congress were lawyers (Zhang Zhimin, 1995). It should be noted, in fairness, that an increasing number of NPC staffers have legal training and that legal academics have been involved in law drafting in recent years.
7. Consider, for example, the course of development in both Korea and Taiwan which over the past three decades have moved from dominance by military figures (Park Chung-hee and Chiang Kai-shek, respectively) to more technically oriented leaders (Kim Young-sam and Lee Tung-hui) and which now include a number of lawyers among aspirants for national political office (a majority of candidates for the presidency in Korea in 1997 were lawyers, while the two chief candidates for president in the ROC, Ma Ying-jeou and Chen Shui-bian, are both lawyers). In evaluating these statistics, it is worth noting that there are fewer than 7000 admitted lawyers in Korea (including both prosecutors and judges).

REFERENCES

Agence France Presse (1997) '3,500 Executed in China's Strike Hard Campaign' (14 April).

Alford, William (1984) 'Of Arsenic and Old Laws: Looking Anew at Criminal Justice in Late Imperial China', *California Law Review* 72: 1180–256.

Alford, William (1990) 'Seek Truth from Facts'—Especially When They are Unpleasant: America's Understanding of China's Efforts at Law Reform', *UCLA Pacific Basin Law Journal* 8: 177–96.

Alford, William (1993) 'Double-Edged Swords Cut Both Ways: Law and Legitimacy in the People's Republic of China', *Daedalus* 122(2): 45–69.

Alford, William (1995a) 'Tasselled Loafers for Barefoot Lawyers: Transformation and Tension in the World of Chinese Legal Workers', *China Quarterly* 141: 22–38.

Alford, William (1995b) *To Steal a Book is an Elegant Offense: Intellectual Property Law in Chinese Civilization.* Stanford, CA: Stanford University Press.

Alford, William (1996) 'A Piracy Deal Doesn't Make a China Policy', *The Wall Street Journal,* 17 July: A14.

Alford, William (1997a) 'Making the World Safe for What? Intellectual Property Rights, Human Rights and Foreign Economic Policy in the Post-European Cold War World', *New York University Journal of International Law and Politics* 29(1–2): 135–52.

Alford, William (1997b) 'Of Jeffersonian Visions: A Critique of Gary Jefferson's "China's Economic Future" ', *Journal of Asian Economics* 8(4): 597–603.

Alford, William and Fang Liufang (1994) 'Legal Training and Education in the 1990s: An Overview and Assessment of China's Needs', report for the World Bank (unpublished).

Amnesty International (1996) *No One is Safe*. London: Amnesty International.

Cai Dingjian (1995) 'Constitutional Supervision and Interpretation in the People's Republic of China', *Columbia Journal of Asian Law* 9: 219–45.

Canye wengao (1995) (Reference Documents) 'Jingying yimin yu xinxing dachengshi: zhanlue' (Bold immigrants and newly developing large cities: a strategy), unpublished.

Chen, Albert (1992) *An Introduction to the Legal System of the People's Republic of China.* Singapore: Butterworth.

Ching, Frank (1998) 'US Press Shifting on China', *Far Eastern Economic Review* (16 July): 57.

Clarke, Donald (1995) 'The Enforcement of Civil Suit Judgments: China', *China Quarterly* 141: 65–82.

Clarke, Donald (1996) 'Power and Politics in the Chinese Court System: The Enforcement of Civil Judgments', *Columbia Journal of Asian Law* 10: 65–82.

Cohen, Jerome and Hungdah Chiu (1974) *People's China and International Law*, vols 1 and 2. Princeton, NJ: Princeton University Press.

Dicks, Anthony (1995) 'Compartmentalized Law and Judicial Restraint: An Inductive View of Some Jurisdictional Barriers to Reform', *China Quarterly* 141: 82–110.

Duara, Prasenjit (1995) *Rescuing History from the Nation: Questioning Narratives of Modern China*. Chicago, IL: The University of Chicago Press.

Fu Hualing (1998) 'Criminal Defence in China: The Possible Impact of the 1996 Criminal Procedural Law Reform', *China Quarterly* 153: 31–46.

Fukuyama, Francis (1992) *The End of History and the Last Man.* London: Hamish Hamilton.

Guojia jingwei (1986) (The State Economic Commission) 'Bufen guochan jiayong dianqi "sanbao" guiding' (Provisions on the 'three responsibilities' [system] for certain domestic made electronic appliances) 30 July 1986, in Guowuyuan fazhiju (ed.) *Xiaofeizhe chuanyi baohu falu zhinan* (A handbook on the protection of consumer rights and interest), pp. 104–7. Beijing: Falu chuban she (reprinted in 1993).

Huntington, Samuel (1996) *The Clash of Civilizations and the Remaking of World Order*. New York: Simon & Schuster.

Jefferson, Gary (1997) 'China's Economic Future', *Journal of Asian Economics* 8(4): 581–95.

Karmel, Solomon (1996) 'The Neo-Authoritarian Dilemma in the Labor Force:

Control and Bankruptcy vs. Freedom and Instability', *Journal of Contemporary China* 5: 111–33.

Keller, Perry (1994) 'Sources of Order in Chinese Law', *American Journal of Comparative Law* 42: 711–59.

Kinkley, Jeffrey (forthcoming) *Chinese Justice, the Fiction, Law and Literature in Modern China*. Stanford, CA: Stanford University Press.

Kuo, Ting-yee and K.C. Liu (1978) 'Self-Strengthening: The Pursuit of Western Technology', in John King Fairbank (ed.) *The Cambridge History of China: Late Ching 1800–1911*, Pt 1. Cambridge: Cambridge University Press.

Lardy, Nicholas (1988) *China's Unfinished Economic Revolution*. Washington, DC: Brookings Institution Press.

Li Bian (1997) 'Legal System Develops Apace', *Beijing Review* 40 (12–18 May): 23.

Liu Nanping (1997) *Opinions of the Supreme People's Court: Judicial Interpretation in China*. Hong Kong: Sweet and Maxwell.

Lubman, Stanley (1997) 'There's No Rushing China's Slow March to a Rule of Law', *Los Angeles Times* (19 Oct.): M2.

Luo Bing (1996) 'Mijian xielu zhonggong zuzhi fulan' (Secret document exposes decay in Communist Party organization), *Cheng Ming* 225: 6–8.

Manion, Melanie (1996) 'Corruption by Design: Bribery in China's Enterprise Licensing', *Journal of Law, Economics and Organization* 12(1): 167–95.

Palmer, Michael (1987) 'The Revival of Mediation in the People's Republic of China (1) Extra-Judicial Mediation', *Yearbook of Socialist Legal Systems*, 219–77.

Peerenboom, Randall (1998) *Lawyers in China: Obstacles to Independence and the Defense of Rights*. New York: Lawyers Committee for Human Rights.

Pei Minxin (1997) 'Citizens or Mandarins: Administrative Litigation in China', *China Quarterly* 152: 832–63.

Pei Minxin (1998) 'The Political Economy of Banking Reforms in China, 1993–1997', *Journal of Contemporary China* 7: 321–50.

Ren Jianxin (1997) *Zuiguo renmin fayuan gongzuo baogao* (The work report of the Supreme People's Court).

*Renmin ribao (*1998) 'Qieshi zuo hao dangqian jianqing nongmin fudan gongzuo' (Conscientiously do a good job of current work on the alleviation of illegal exactions on the peasantry), overseas edn (July 28): 1.

Roth, Kenneth (1997) 'Human Rights Watch Holds News Conference for Release of its 8th Annual Survey of Human Rights Practices Worldwide', *FDCH Political Transcripts* (4 Dec.).

Schwartz, Benjamin (1985) *The World of Thought in Ancient China*. Cambridge, MA: Harvard University Press.

Seidman, Ann and Robert Seidman (1997) 'Not a Treasure Chest, a Tool Box: Lessons from a Chinese Legislative Drafting Project', in Ann Seidman, Robert Seidman and Janice Payne (eds) *Legislative Drafting for Market Reform: Some Lessons from China*, pp. 1–32. London: Macmillan.

Smil, Vaclav (1993*) China's Environmental Crisis: An Inquiry into the Limits of National Development*. Armonk, NY: M.E. Sharpe.

Waldron, Arthur (1990) *The Great Wall of China: From History to Myth*. New York: Cambridge University Press.

World Bank (1997) *China 2020: Development Challenges in the New Century*. Washington, DC: World Bank.

Xia Yong (1995) *Zhongguo gongmin chuanli fazhan yanjiu* (Toward an age of rights: a study of the development of the rights of Chinese citizens). Beijing: Zhongguo zhengfa daxue chubanshe.

Xinhua (New China News Agency) (1998a) 'Law Lecture for Senior Chinese Officials Held', in Lexis-Nexis Xinhua file (12 May).

Xinhua (New China News Agency) (1998b) 'Party Leader Emphasizes Social Stability', in Lexis-Nexis Xinhua file (29 December).

Zhang Zhimin (1995) 'Dandai Zhongguo de lushi ye: yi minquan wei jiben chidu' (Lawyers in contemporary China: a civil rights perspective), *Bijiaofa Yanjiu* (Journal of Comparative Law) 9: 1.

Zhonghua renmin gongheguo daqi wuran fangzhi fa (1995) (The Air Pollution Prevention and Control Law of the People's Republic of China).

Zuigao renmin fayuan gongzuo baogao (1996) (The work report of the Supreme People's Court) in Zhongghuo falu nianjian bianji bu (Law Yearbook of China Editorial Department) *Zhongguo falu nianjian* (Law Yearbook of China), pp. 25–30. Beijing: Falu nianjian chubanshe.

BIOGRAPHICAL NOTE

WILLIAM P. ALFORD is Henry L. Stimson Professor of Law and Director of East Asian Legal Studies at the Harvard Law School. Professor Alford is the author of *To Steal a Book is an Elegant Offense: Intellectual Property Law in Chinese Civilization* (Stanford University Press, 1995) and numerous articles about Chinese legal affairs and international law. He has taught at UCLA and Georgetown and lectured at various universities in the PRC. He is a graduate of Amherst College, the University of Cambridge, Yale University and the Harvard Law School. *Address*: Harvard Law School, Cambridge, MA 02138, USA. [email: alford@law.harvard.edu]

Part II
Specific Issues

[8]

PERRY KELLER

Sources of Order in Chinese Law

A person cannot live in China long without becoming aware of the complex, interwoven web of social rules which governs every aspect of Chinese life. The normative richness of life in China is inescapable. And yet paradoxically China has also become notorious for the unreliability of its laws which are so often said to be irrelevant to the resolution of disputes or the expectation of commercial conduct. This reputation is of course an oversimplification. In countless circumstances Chinese officials and private citizens do turn to lawyers or to the courts for assistance.[1] But nonetheless it is a reputation that is more often than not well deserved.[2]

How then can this dissonance between the normative strength of Chinese society and the weakness of its formal legal order be explained? At one level we need look no further than the formal legal system itself. The chronic disorder of Chinese legislation undoubtedly lies behind many of the problems of the country's legal system. Lawyers and officials in China engage in a daily struggle to make sense of vague, inconsistent laws of often questionable legislative authority. The disparate mass of laws and regulations which makes up the formal written sources of Chinese law does not possess sufficient unity to be regarded as a coherent body of law. In their disarray, the sources of Chinese law seem barely capable of providing the basic point of referance which all complex systems of law require.[3]

PERRY KELLER is lecturer in law at King's College London. Research for this article was supported in part by grants from the British Academy, ESRC and the Chinese Academy of Social Sciences. I wish to thank Bill Alford, Neil Duxbury, Tom Gibbons, Jane Henderson and Martin Loughlin for their comments on earlier drafts.

1. Since 1979 Chinese lawmakers have issued several thousand laws and regulations. Although there are at present no published collections or data services containing all Chinese central and regional laws and regulations, the publication of Chinese legislation has improved dramatically in recent years and several useful compilations are now available. These include, *Zhonghua Renmin Gongheguo Falü Quanshu* (The Complete Laws of the People's Republic of China), (Jilin Renmin, Jilin, 1989), (supp. 1990); *Difangxing Fagui Xuanbian* (selected Regional Regulations), (Zhongguo Jingji, Beijing, 1991); *Zhonghua Renmin Gongheguo Falü Jieshi Jicheng* (Compilation of Normative Interpretations of Law), (Jilin Renmin, Jilin, 1990), (supp. 1991).

2. See, for example, Kaye, "Disorder Under Heaven," (9 June 1994) Vol 157 *Far Eastern Economic Review* no. 23, 22-23 for a recent account of China's law and order problems.

3. The expression "sources of law" has of course many possible meanings. In this article I have adopted the definition articulated by Alan Watson in his book *Sources of Law, Legal Change and Ambiguity* in which he describes sources of law as expressed,

This is not to suggest that the disarray of Chinese legislation is the root cause of all China's problems of legal development. Indeed, any evaluation of the legislative and regulatory documents which compose China's positive law must inevitably include reference to the equally difficult issues of legal interpretation and doctrinal development. In addition, there are well known aspects of Chinese state administration and legal culture which work against the uniform application of legal rules. Selective and often arbitrary law enforcement as well as widespread public indifference to legal rights, procedures and remedies are important features of the Chinese legal landscape.

Nonetheless, the development of positive law in China is a discrete story which is of overwhelming significance to any understanding of Chinese law. In China's contemporary legal order, which so tightly restricts judicial law making, legislative sources of law provide the primary vehicle for the conscious construction of law's formal boundaries and internal relationships. Yet it is particularly difficult to identify the boundaries and relationships of positive law in China. Since the post-Mao reforms began in the late 1970's, the country's leaders have authorized the gradual construction of a complex hierarchy of legislative categories and powers based on pre-existing institutions and means of administrative control. However, as this article describes, the interpretation and application of the sub-statutory categories of Chinese law remains under the tight control of the administrative bureaucracies of the state. The consequences of this are twofold. These categories of law are often inseparable from the administrative process itself and, as a result, they are easily distorted or abused in the course of factional and institutional power struggles.

Nor is it particularly easy to determine the provenance of this legislative structure or its conceptual basis. Chinese law making officials work within a constellation of influences, and whilst many of these can be readily identified, their specific effects are not so easily perceived. China possesses, for example, a highly sophisticated Confucian based legal history which once formed the philosophical backbone of imperial law and continues to resonate in contemporary legal culture. The country has also undergone a series of experiments in the reception of foreign law. German and Soviet law have in particular served at different times as models for the re-invention of China's legal order. Yet the impact of indigenous and foreign ideas regarding the nature of law and its positive forms has varied tremendously through the turbulent decades of recent Chinese history. Even now,

---

linguistic formulations which are accepted as authoritative by the courts and other institutionalized decision makers. Alan Watson, *Sources of Law, Legal Change and Ambiguity* Introduction, xi (1985).

as China is experiencing rapid economic and social change, approaches to law and law making continue to evolve.

The purpose of this article is to examine the development of formal sources of law in the People's Republic of China. Whilst the article focuses on the current programme of legal modernization which was initiated in 1979, it also examines the important historical influences which affect contemporary law making. The article is especially concerned with the ways in which ideas concerning the proper organization of positive law have been adapted to the political and administrative realities of China. It also explores how different approaches to order and rationality in law have influenced the development of the formal sources of Chinese law.

Imperial Edicts and Republican Codes

In December 1978 the Central Committee of the Chinese Communist Party endorsed a programme of economic modernization.[4] This programme was the centrepiece of China's new, far reaching strategy of economic revival and political stabilization. Having turned the corner on the upheavals of the Cultural Revolution era (1966-1976), China's leaders decided that economic development should be the cornerstone of national policy for the 1980's. In a further break with the policies of Mao Tse-tung, the leadership included legal modernization within their programme of reform.[5] Many senior Party officials and their families had endured terrible personal suffering during the Cultural Revolution. For some, the reconstruction of legal order offered protection against further political instability.[6] Many within the leadership also perceived that law could improve the effectiveness of central control over the Party and state bureaucracies as well as over the general public. They were persuaded that the creation of positive legal rules would restrict the authority of individual officials and thereby introduce greater certainty and predictability into state administration.[7] Beyond these purely domestic considerations, the enactment of trade and investment legislation was also seen as a prerequisite for the attraction of needed foreign investment.[8]

The Party's endorsement of legal modernization in 1978 marked the first phase of a lengthy and as yet still incomplete law reform programme. It was not, for example, until 1986 that legislative officials completed a series of major changes to the framework of positive

4. Jonathan D. Spence, *The Search for Modern China* 656 (1990).
5. Id., at 658.
6. Wu Daying & Liu Han, *Zhongguo Shehuizhuyi Lifa Wenti* (Issues in Chinese Socialist Legislation) 63 (1984).
7. Tanner, "The Erosion of Party Control over Law Making in China," (1994) *China Quarterly* No. 138, 57-79, at 61.
8. Kevin J. O'Brien, *Reform without Liberalization* 158-59 (1990).

law with a final extension of legislative powers to regional People's Governments and selected local authorities.[9] During this eight year period, China's legislative authorities created a complex, tiered hierarchy of law making powers and legislative categories.[10] The result of these labours did not however reflect any particular theoretical approach to the development of formal sources of law. China's legislative structure is, as described below, a highly pragmatic response to political and institutional pressures. But whatever its pragmatic virtues, it is also a legislative system riddled with ambiguities and inconsistencies which have had a significant impact on the character of contemporary Chinese law.

In turning away from the legal nihilism of the Cultural Revolution, China's law makers did not of course embark on the legal modernization programme with an entirely blank slate. They were inevitably aware of the country's own highly sophisticated legal tradition and were certainly not ignorant of various attempts made in this century to introduce western derived legal institutions and substantive law to China. There is however little to be gained in attempting to fix the exact importance of these influences on contemporary events or even the extent to which they have merged over time. The issues involved are beyond precise analysis and any specific conclusion must surely depend on the particular individuals, events and places concerned. Nonetheless, the predominant historical influences on contemporary law making are easily discerned and are essential to any informed appreciation of contemporary Chinese law.[11]

There is little overt evidence of a direct link between China's imperial legal order and the one more recently established under the People's Republic of China. Apart from a few conceptual and organizational terms preserved in contemporary legislation, the past seems to have largely disappeared.[12] However, the influence of China's once dominant Confucian ethos is readily apparent in the variant strains of modern Chinese legal culture. In the Confucian conception of state and society, law was far more than a mere instrument of imperial will. Law represented a body of coercive rules deeply embedded within broader philosophical and moral norms concerning proper per-

9. Difang Geji Renmin Daibiao Dahui he Difang Geji Renmin Zhengfu Zuzhi Fa, (The Regional People's Congresses and Regional People's Government Law) 1979, as amended 1986, *Zhonghua Renmin Gongheguo Changyong Falü Daquan* (Compilation of the Commonly Used Laws of the P.R.C.) 1992 edition, (Felu, Beijing, 1992) (herein after "*Changyong*"), 121.

10. See chart at page 728.

11. William Jenner's recent work, *Tyranny of History: The Roots of China's Crisis* (1992), is an interesting essay on the importance of Chinese history to the country's current political and social difficulties.

12. Many terms used to designate legislation, such as "tiaoli" which is now used to designate minor primary laws or major secondary regulations, were standard terms used in imperial statutes.

sonal and social conduct.[13] Consequently the doctrinal coherence of the law and its consistency in application was derived more from this philosophical and moral context than from a formalist interpretation of legislative texts. Chinese society has in many respects held to this contextualist approach to law. There continues to be a widely held belief that the application of positive law should be subject to extra legal considerations, such as the relationship and circumstances of the parties and the demands of commonly held standards of justice.[14]

Despite the abandonment of the imperial legal system earlier in this century, there is an unmistakeable connection between China's traditional legislative practices and contemporary law making.[15] The founders of the Communist Party, even as they set out to change China, were themselves the product of late imperial society, "educated in its schools and culture and soaked in its values."[16] It is not surprising therefore that they and their followers were not only influenced by the substance of pre-revolutionary law and legal culture, but also by the ideas imbued in the organization and expression of positive law. Perhaps the most interesting parallel which exists between late imperial and contemporary sources of law in China lies in the dichotomy which exists between the formalistic and symbolic use of primary legislation and the flexible and pragmatic use of sub-statutory rules.

This dual approach to legislative order reached its most advanced form under China's last dynasty, the Qing (1644-1911). The Manchu founders of the Qing chose to retain many aspects of the governmental order of the preceeding Ming dynasty, including its system of law.[17] The Ming legal order was also in many ways based on the institutions and laws of earlier dynasties, however it also had many of its own characteristics, including an especially rigid view of the role of primary legislation.[18] The founder of the Ming, Zhu Yuanzhang, expressed the central principle of Ming legislation in his

13. For a general introduction to law and Confucianism in late imperial China, see Derk Bodde & Clarence Morris, *Law in Imperial China* (1967). See also, Alford, "Arsenic and Old Laws: Looking Anew at Criminal Justice in Late Imperial China," 72 *Calif. L. Rev.* 1180 (1984).

14. For an historical analysis of these influences, see Fan Zhongxin & Zheng Ding, *Qing Li Fa yu Zhongguoren* (Human Relations, Reason, Law and Chinese People) (1992).

15. This influence is directly visible in the work of contemporary legislative commentators, see for example Guo Daohui, *Zhongguo Lifa Shidu* (China's Legislative System) 148 (1988).

16. Jenner, supra at n. 11, 35.

17. William Jones provides a useful overview of the Qing legal system in the introduction to his book, *The Great Qing Code* 1-28 (1994).

18. Ma Xiaohong, "Zhongguo Fengjian Shehui Liang Lei Falü Hingshi de Xiaozhang Ji Yingxiang," (The Growth, Decline and Influence of the Two Forms of Law in Chinese Feudal Society) 5 *Faxue Yanjiu*, 73-78 (1993). See also Ma Xiaohong, "Shilun Zhongguo Fengjian Shehui de Falü Xingshi," (A Discussion of the Forms of Law in Chinese Feudal Society) 2 *Zhongguo Faxue*, 110-17 (1991).

maxim, "the decreed laws (*lü*) shall not change."[19] By this he meant that the primary code of laws reflected eternal and universal principles and must therefore be adhered to and passed on unchanged.[20] The Ming code was an archaic, tersely worded text rooted directly in the seventh century code of the Tang dynasty. And whilst it contained a sophisticated body of norms based on general principles and possessed an observable harmony, it was often difficult to interpret or apply directly to specific facts.[21] In adopting the Ming code with few changes as their own principal legal code, the Qing founders placed severe restrictions on the further development of imperial law. By preserving this text as a sacred document, alterable only in rare circumstances, Qing officials were forced to rely increasingly on alternative legislative techniques to circumvent the rigidity of the code. These principally involved the use of subordinate forms of law to provide legislative solutions for problems which could not be resolved by reference to the code. In practice, Qing magistrates gave more weight to officially approved supplementary rules, official interlinear commentaries and even case precedents, than they did to the code itself.[22] Private commentaries also became important as official aids to the elucidation of the code's obscure language.[23]

In accepting this state of affairs, Qing law makers, like those in many other societies,[24] were, it seems, not especially concerned by the general lack of coherence in the organization of positive law. They were however not unaware of the problems which ambiguous statutory language could cause for legal administration. Qing authorities in fact carried out several revisions to the ever increasing corpus of sub-statutory rules and case examples in efforts to eliminate outdated or ambiguous provisions from these supplementary sources of law.[25] But despite these efforts to improve the clarity of the law, the Qing code, the primary source of textual ambiguity, was left largely untouched. The need to work around the impediment of the code was therefore a major factor in the development of positive law forms during the Qing. As a result subordinate forms of positive

19. Ma Xiaohong, id., 5 *Faxue Yanjiu* 75 (1993).

20. Zhu Yuanzhang's insistence on the maintenance of a body of fundamental, positive legal norms can be traced in part to the "legalist" strain in imperial Confucian legal doctrine which emphasized the importance of well publicized, coercive, positive rules of law to good governance.

21. Jones, supra at n. 17, 3.

22. Geoffrey MacCormack, *Traditional Chinese Penal Law* 53 (1990).

23. Fu-mei Chang Chen, "The Influence of Shen Chihch'i's CHI-CHU Commentary Upon Ching Judicial Decisions," in Cohen, Edwards & Chang, *Essays on China's Legal Tradition* 170-221 (1980).

24. Watson, supra at n. 3, xii.

25. MacCormack, supra at n. 22, 53. See also J. Cheng, *Chinese Law in Transition, The Late Ch'ing Law Reform* 90 (Ph.D. Thesis, Brown University, 1976), (avail. SOAS Library, London).

law displaced these rules as the principle sources of law.[26] Legislative development was therefore a disorderly business fashioned around the formal, symbolic importance of the primary norms of the code and based on a range of flexible, sub-statutory forms of law.

Disorder in the organization and expression of positive law does not necessarily lead to incoherence in the content of the law. In the view of most Qing officials and scholars, positive law derived its coherence from its Confucian and imperial context.[27] The organizational deficiencies of the law were remedied by a scholarly knowledge of Confucian philosophical and moral doctrines and the classical texts on which they were based, as well as a practical understanding of imperial legal administration and the norms and expectations of local society. It was only in the last decades of the dynasty, as China experienced an increasing influx of foreign ideas, that Qing officials were directly confronted with concepts of radical legal autonomy and the rationalization of legal structures which those concepts implied.

The upheavals of the nineteenth century brought an end to the dominance of Confucian orthodoxy within China. In the face of widespread economic and social turmoil as well as European territorial encroachment, many Chinese intellectuals looked elsewhere for the means to revitalize the state.[28] A growing number believed that China should adopt the apparent hallmark of the powerful European states; constitutional government based on a strong, well defined legal order.[29] In 1902 the Qing court acceded to reformist demands and initiated a programme of administrative modernization. As part of this programme, officials were specially appointed to oversee the reform the Qing legal system which was to include the drafting of a series of criminal and civil law codifications based on western legal models.[30] And whilst conservatives within the court were able to frustrate the application of much of this legislation, the project itself laid the foundations for legislative reforms during the Republican era (1911-1949) which followed.

The late Qing law reformers enjoyed reasonably good access to European civil and common law materials, principally through diplomatic collections gathered abroad and contacts with European legal scholars. But it was Japan, a country which also possessed a related Confucian heritage, that furnished a convenient model for the reception of western legal concepts.[31] At the turn of the century, Japan's

26. Ma Xiaohong, supra at n. 18, 74.

27. Fu-mei Chang Chen, supra at n. 23, 209.

28. Spence, supra at n. 4, p. 245. See also, Wu Shuchen, "Fa Yuan," (The Source of Law) 2 *Zhong Wai Faxue* 47-52, 49 (1989).

29. O'Brien, supra at n. 8, 13.

30. Cheng, supra at n. 25.

31. Henderson, "Japanese influences on Communist Chinese Legal Language," in Jerome Cohen (ed.) *Contemporary Chinese Law* 158 (1973).

Meiji government had already acquired decades of experience in the translation and adaptation of European law. In 1898 the Japanese had felt sufficiently confident in their mastery of European law to adopt the German civil code, the *Burgerliches Gesetzbuch* (BGB), only two years after its German promulgation. The apparent success of Japan's programme of political and economic modernization provoked strong Chinese interest. Many Chinese officials and scholars gained their first thorough appreciation of European civil law concepts of legislative organization through these Sino-Japanese exchanges.[32]

The exposure of the Chinese to the German civil code is particularly significant. The BGB represents a remarkably sustained attempt to realise a formalist idealization of law's coherence and rationality within the form and structure of positive law.[33] In this attempt to elaborate a consistent statement of the principles of civil law through careful organization and precise phrasing, Chinese jurists discovered a novel conception of formal law which profoundly affected legislative development during the republican period and continues to echo dimly in contemporary legal reform. It was not however until Chiang Kai-shek's Nationalist Party consolidated its control over the central regions of China in the late 1920's that another comprehensive reform of Chinese law was attempted. The Nationalist programme of legal reform centred on the adoption of codifications of constitutional law, criminal law, criminal procedure and administrative law. These codifications, known as the Six Codes, were heavily indebted in both organization and substance to German legislative precedents. They remain the basis of the Nationalist legal order in Taiwan and more recently have become a source of inspiration for law makers and academics within the People's Republic of China (PRC).[34]

The promulgation of the Six Codes in the 1930's appeared to herald China's complete reception of the Romano-German civil law tradition. However, the implementation of Nationalist law was largely restricted to major urban areas under the central government's control.[35] Undermined by corrupt and authoritarian central administration, semi-autonomous regional warlords, civil war with the

32. Id. at 169.

33. See Konrad Zweigert & Hein Kotz, *An Introduction to Comparative Law* 149-62 (2nd ed. 1992).

34. Writer's interview with members of the Institute of Law, Chinese Academy of Social Sciences, April 1992. E. Epstein refers to the contemporary educational uses of Nationalist law in, "Law and Legitimation in Post-Mao China," in Pitman B. Potter (ed.) *Domestic Law Reforms in Post-Mao China* 19-55, 34 (1994).

35. John King Fairbank, *China: A New History* 301 (1992). For a specific example, see Zelin, "Merchant Dispute Mediation in Twentieth-Century Zigong, Sichuan," in Kathryn Bernhardt & Philip Huang (eds.) *Civil Law in Qing and Republican China* 249-86 (1994).

Communists and finally war with Japan, the Nationalist legal regime had little impact on Chinese society.

Soviet Theory and Chinese Bureaucracy

When the Communist Party came to power in 1949 it possessed an experience of law and administration which was rather different from that of the Nationalists. In their remote rural base areas, the Communists had created a style of administration adapted to the Party's proclaimed tasks of political and social revolution. The simple legal system developed by the Party in these wartime conditions consisted of major principles and rules of conduct concerning the suppression of political opposition and common crimes as well as reforms concerning land holding and the structure of the family.[36] The structure of these laws tended to be simple and transitory. Processes of enactment and distinctions of form were largely unnecessary in a system where the commands of Party leaders carried overriding authority.[37]

As the Communist Party secured its victory over the Nationalists, it began to build on its administrative experience in the base areas to create a new legal order. Well before the official founding of the PRC, the Central Committee decreed the complete abolition of the Six Codes and all other Nationalist legislation.[38] But in view of the rudimentary state of the Communist legal system, the Central Committee also ordered that where the "new laws of the people" did not exist, judicial work should be carried out in accordance with the policies of the Party.[39] In effect, this decree formalized the legal authority of Party policy directives, which in the early years of the PRC served as the mainstay of Communist administration. The awkward balance created between law and Party policy set out in this decree exemplifies what was to become the enduring conundrum of the Communist legal order; how is it possible to assert the authority of law within a state founded on Leninist principles of Communist party supremacy?

Whilst content to avoid the use of formal laws or legal procedures in most areas, the Communist leadership moved quickly to create a constitutional foundation for the new state. The Common Programme, a temporary constitutional instrument issued in 1949, set out a general structure for national, regional and local administra-

36. Wu Daying and Liu Han, supra at n. 6, 20. O'Brien, supra at n. 8, 20-25.
37. Wu Daying and Liu Han, id. at 18.
38. Guanyu Feichu Guomindang Liufa Quanshu Yu Queding Jiefangqu de Sifa Yuanze de Shishi, (Directive Concerning the Abolition of the Nationalist Six Codes and the Establishment of Principles of Law in the Liberated Areas), issued by the Central Committee of the CCP, February 1949, *Zhonghua Renmin Gongheguo Falu Quanshu*, supra at n. 1, 1426.
39. Id.

tion.[40] And although the Common Programme had little practical significance in the militarized administration of the early People's Republic, it did create an important precedent for subsequent Chinese legislative practice. Its drafters sought to balance ideological and practical demands for a strong, unitary state with the equally important need to allow for regional diversity. Their solution was to include a grant of subordinate law making power to regional and local governments.[41] This in effect created a multi-tiered hierarchy of legislation in which law making authority at each level was, in principle, circumscribed by the content of all higher level laws and regulations.

During the early 1950's, Soviet legal theory, in particular the work of the Stalinist jurist and chief prosecutor A.Y. Vyshinsky, had a decisive impact on the construction of Chinese socialist law. Chinese theorists embraced Vyshinsky's rigid positivist view that law is a formal, normative expression of the will of the ruling class, as formulated and enforced by the state in the interests of that class.[42] In a socialist state, according to Vyshinsky, the Communist Party, as the representative of the ruling proletariat, should enjoy absolute control over the creation of positive law by the organs of the state. The Party should also determine the form and content of these laws according to the requirements of its evolving programme of economic and social development.

The consolidation of Chinese Communist legal doctrine brought about an increasingly decisive break with the legislative concerns of the republican era. Vyshinsky's Leninist rejection of any autonomy of law from politics carried with it an abandonment of rationality as an essential characteristic of law. There was no longer a theoretical imperative to achieve internally constructed order and consistency of meaning in the law, either through the positive language of legislation or through its doctrinal elaboration. This is not to say that consistency in legal doctrine or practice was no longer of any importance. However its appeal to Chinese administrators was clearly only functional. Having rejected capitalist rule of law theories, coherence in

40. Zhongguo Renmin Zhengzhi Xieshanghuiyi Gongtong Gangling, (The Common Programme of the Chinese People's Political Consultative Conference), *Zhonghua Renmin Gongheguo Zuzhi Fagui Xuanbian* 3 (Selected Organizational Laws of the P.R.C.) (1985) (hereinafter *Zuzhi Fagui*).

41. Liu Han, "Zhongguo Xianxing Zhengzhi Tizhi he Fazhi de Lishi yu Xianzhuang," (The History and Circumstances of China's Current Political Structure and Legal System), in Wu Daying & Liu Han (eds.), *Zhengzhi Tizhi Gaige Yu Fazhi Jianshe* (Political Structural Reform and Legal Construction) 1-77, 54 (1991).

42. Yu Xingzhong, "Legal Pragmatism in the People's Republic of China," 3 *Journal of Chinese Law* 28-51, 36 (1980). See also, Xu Yongkang, "Qianping Weixinsiji Falu Lilun," (A Short Review of Vyshinsky's Theory of law) 6 *Faxue* 1-3 (1988). For an account of Vyshinsky's life and work, see Sharlet & Beirne, "In Search of Vyshinsky: The Paradox of Law and Terror," in Piers Beirne (ed.) *Revolution in Law* 136-56 (1991).

law only appealed to the extent that it improved the effectiveness or convenience of state administration.[43]

The Communist Party's instrumental conception of law marked an official return to a much more contextualist approach to the issue of legislative meaning. According to Chinese adaptations of Vyshinsky's work, the function of law is to express, in a positive, normative form, current Party policy.[44] The Party therefore holds incontrovertible authority over the determination of the content of the law. But by giving absolute primacy to Party policy and denying the validity of any dissenting interpretation of the needs of socialist development, Party leaders ensured that statutory language could not provide a basis from which to challenge Party authority. Official doctrine has therefore ensured that the authority of any law is in practice contingent on its accurate reflection of the current state of Party policy. Laws which are in this sense inaccurate require re-interpretation, amendment or, as is frequently the case in China, may simply be ignored.[45]

In fashioning its new legislative order, Party leaders adopted the Soviet principle that all state power should rest exclusively in the hands of a supreme legislature.[46] This principle was expressed in the PRC's first fully fledged constitution which was promulgated in 1954 by China's new national legislature, the National People's Congress (NPC).[47] In this Soviet inspired Constitution the NPC rescinded the legislative structure established by the Common Programme in 1949 and radically centralized the exercise of law making powers. Only the NPC and its executive body, the Standing Committee, retained authority to enact national laws (*falü*) or decrees (*faling*).[48] Regional and local governments, with the exception of autonomous minority

43. Liberal theories of the rule of law make greater demands on legal coherence. The essential liberal requirement that there should be a distinct separation of law and politics necessarily implies that law should possess a high degree of internal rationality and coherence capable of supporting the consistent application of legal principles and rules without direct resort to external political considerations. A useful account and defense of liberal legal theory can be found in Andrew Altman, *Critical Legal Studies: A Liberal Critique* (1990).

44. Chen Hanfeng, "Zhengdang, Zhengce, Quanli, Falü Zhi Guanxi," (The Relationship of Political Parties, Policy, Power and Law) *Fazhi Ribao* 3 (30 October 1987).

45. One of the more significant examples of this practice occurred in 1987, when the Party approved experimental land leases in selected areas despite constitutional and legal prohibitions on land leasing. Keller, "Legislation in the People's Republic of China," 23 *U. Bri. Colum. L. Rev.* 653-88, 658 (1989).

46. For a discussion of Soviet legislative principles, see Rene David & John Brierly, *Major Legal Systems in the World Today* 226-30 (3rd ed. 1985). Also see, Huskey, "A Framework for the Analysis of Soviet Law," 50 *The Russian Review* 53-70 (1991).

47. O'Brien, supra at n. 8, 29. In this article all references to the NPC include, where relevant, reference to the Standing Committee of the NPC.

48. Articles 27 and 31, Zhonghua Renmin Gongheguo Xianfa 1954 (Constitution of the PRC), *Zuzhi Fagui*, supra at n. 40, 7 and 9.

areas, were stripped of all formal legislative power.[49] The 1954 legislative structure accommodated Soviet doctrinal requirements and also responded to the leadership's desire to curb the growth of regional powerbases.[50] It did not however produce a framework which could sustain a workable system of law. The country clearly could not be governed on the scanty output of a national legislature which met in two week annual sessions, or even its somewhat more productive Standing Committee, which met in poorly attended, monthly sessions.[51] But it is also obvious that the Party never intended that it should be, because the development of normative administration was already occurring elsewhere.

The use of positive norms in Communist administration emerged out of early Party and state systems of bureaucratic communication. In the first years of the People's Republic, the Communist Party found that its documentary communication systems, developed in the base areas, could not meet the demands of national government. After initially relying on inherited Nationalist government documents and procedures, the Party developed its own complex methods of written and verbal bureaucratic communication.[52] As these methods evolved, officials and academics began to use the Soviet derived term normative documents (*guifanxing wenjian*) to refer to all administrative directives purporting to establish or modify norms of public or official behaviour.[53] Documents of this type were issued at all levels of the administrative hierarchy, from the State Council down to village and neighbourhood authorities. They appeared in innumerable forms and were used to set general principles as well as precise rules of conduct. Throughout most of the Communist era, normative documents have constituted the basis of normative administration. Indeed, as this article describes, China's current legal order was in many respects developed out of the pre-existing normative document system.

For some Chinese officials, the 1954 constitutional changes created an obvious conflict between the express restriction of most formal law making powers to the NPC and the widespread use of normative documents by other state bodies. As the courts had no

49. Liu Han, supra at n. 41, 56.

50. Maurice J. Meisner, *Mao's China* 130-33 (1977).

51. O'Brien, supra at n. 8, 75.

52. Oksenberg, "Methods of Communication within the Chinese Bureaucracy," 57 *China Quarterly* 1-39, 36 (1974).

53. Writer's interview, supra at n. 34. The term 'normative document' (*guifanxing wenjian*) is most frequently used to refer to any document issued by state or quasi state bodies which has a normative content. In this broad sense, 'normative documents' include both formal laws and administrative directives. In this article 'normative document' is used in a narrower sense to mean, for the sake of clarity, a document having normative content but which is not included in the recognized categories of formal law.

power to challenge the authority of normative documents or legislation, there appeared to be little more than a procedural distinction between these two categories. In some instances, normative documents were even issued using common legislative designations, such as the much favoured term "*tiaoli*" (regulations).[54] In 1956 Mao Tse-Tung addressed this issue when he stated that, "under the *Constitution*, legislative power is concentrated at the centre. But where central policies are not violated and it is in accordance with the needs of the situation and the work at hand, localities may issue regulations ("*zhangcheng, tiaoli, banfa*"). The *Constitution* certainly does not prevent this."[55] In this statement Mao accomplished two important things. First he decisively affirmed the authority of normative documents. Second, by endorsing the role of normative documents he forestalled any argument that formal law should move beyond the general principles expressed in the NPC legislation and become more specific and technical in character. The Chinese legal order therefore effectively remained split between the formal legal powers of the NPC, which symbolized the unitary nature of the state, and the administrative powers of the central and regional bureaucracies to issue and enforce normative documents.

The enactment of the 1954 Constitution marked the beginning of a period of legal reform which some officials expected would produce a comprehensive body of substantive law patterned after the Soviet model.[56] In a short period of time legislative drafters made considerable progress in creating important draft legislation, including a criminal and a civil code. However the onset of the Anti-Rightist Campaign in 1957 brought an abrupt end to any hopes of replacing institutional reliance on Party and state administrative directives with even a basic core of substantive legislation. During this devastating political campaign to identify and silence the Party's critics, advocates of greater legal control over the Party's activities were purged from legal and academic institutions.[57] The 1950's legislative programme did not recover from this onslaught. Draft legislation was shelved and the NPC did not enact any further legislation for another two decades.[58] Despite the apparent return to political stability during the early 1960's, many of China's leaders, in particular Mao Tse-tung, had come to believe that law in any form represented an unnecessary fetter on the Party's ability to govern and develop a

54. See, *Zhonghua Renmin Gongheguo Fagui Huibian* (1955) (Collected laws and Regulations of the PRC) (1956) which contains several State Council normative documents that are styled as 'regulations' *tiaoli*.

55. Liu Han, supra at n. 41, 55.

56. Guo Daohui, supra at n. 15, 3.

57. Wu Daying & Liu Han, supra at n. 6, 57. See also Liu Han, supra at n. 41, 41 and O'Brien, supra at n. 8, 45.

58. Guo Daohui, supra at n. 15, 4, and O'Brien, id. 49.

socialist society.[59] Legal bureaucracies, such as the Ministry of Justice, were gradually abolished as the role of law in state administration continued to be downgraded.[60] What remained of the formal legal order and its institutions finally disappeared in the chaos of the Cultural Revolution era (1966-1976).[61]

The Return to Legal Modernization

Chinese legal literature usually portrays the Cultural Revolution as a time in which there was literally no law at all; an era of legal nihilism "bereft of the laws of man or heaven" (*wufa wutian*).[62] But whilst anarchy and civil war threatened in its initial phase, military forces soon restored a semblance of central authority. And even though government administration during these years was characterized by mass mobilization campaigns, there is abundant evidence that administrative authorities continued to rely on normative documents to implement policy through much of this period. Even Chinese public records show only a three year hiatus in the issue of national level directives in important areas such as the regulation of industry and commerce.[63] The re-establishment of Party and State bureaucratic systems in the early 1970's coincided with a recorded increase in the use of normative documents, some of which have been retrospectively accorded the status of law.[64] However, as Guo Daohui points out, these instruments were not produced by designated law making bodies or through fixed procedures and were otherwise indistinguishable from the administrative process itself.[65] Not only were they produced in a non-systematic, piecemeal fashion, they were not governed by what H.L.A. Hart would describe as authoritative *secondary rules* capable of determining their validity. The use of normative documents during the Cultural Revolution therefore only amounted to an informal system of law in the broadest possible sense. But the experience of normative governance acquired through the issue and implementation of these regulatory instruments subsequently provided the wellspring for China's current programme of legal modernization.

59. O'Brien, supra at n. 8, 47.

60. O'Brien, id. at 45-49.

61. Id. at 59. Wu Daying and Liu Han, supra at n. 6, 59.

62. Guo Daohui, supra at n. 15, 4.

63. Zhou Zhenxiang & Zhao Jingchun (eds.), *Xin Zhongguo Fazhi Jianshe Sishi Nian Yaolan* (A Survey of Forty Years of New China's Legal Construction) 361 (1990).

64. See, for example, Guanyu Tushu Banben Jilu de Guiding, (Regulations Concerning Records of Book Editions), issued by the Publications Office of the State Council, 7 December 1972, contained in *Zhonghua Renmin Gongheguo Xianxing Xinwen Chuban Fagui Huibian* (*1949-1990*) (Collected Press and Publication Regulations of the PRC Currently in Effect) (1990).

65. Guo Daohui, supra at n. 15, 4.

The Communist Party officially renewed its interest in law reform in 1978 with the Central Committee's ratification of Deng Xiaoping's ambitious plans for economic revival. Legislative officials were instructed to dust off the draft legislation of the 1950's and prepare these and other new laws for promulgation. However, as legal reform gathered pace, it became apparent that the constitutional allocation of law making powers was at odds with the needs of the new legislative programme as well as the realities of bureaucratic power. Under the cautiously reformist *Constitution* of 1978, the NPC and its Standing Committee retained exclusive authority over the enactment of law.[66] Legislative planners were consequently faced with the same problem that Mao Tse-tung had papered over in his declaration of 1956. China's cumbersome supreme legislature was simply not equipped to deliver the torrent of legislation required if China was to move to a legally based system of administration.

In theory the Communist Party could have reconstituted the NPC and its Standing Committee to work throughout most of the year considering and enacting legislation. The NPC could also have delegated the authority to issue subordinate regulations for specific national laws to central or regional administrative bodies. But this model, in which all law issues directly or indirectly from a single legislative authority, would have flown in the face of the practical divisions of state power within China. The State Council, along with the commissions, ministries and other departments under its authority, was and still is the central administrative organ of the national government. At provincial and local levels, People's Governments and their departments have served a similar function. At the outset of the legal modernization programme, these bureaucracies were not only the experienced centres of government administration in China, they also formed important institutional power bases within the structure of the Communist Party. During this transitional period, I suggest, powerful interests within these bureaucracies demanded formal recognition of their quasi-legislative functions.

The extension of law making authority to these bodies was not long in coming. By 1979 the Central Committee had already acknowledged the need to decentralise administrative power and had caused the NPC to enact legislation extending subordinate law making powers to the provincial level People's Congresses.[67] Three years later, the NPC completely overhauled the country's formal legislative

66. Article 20, Zhonghua Renmin Gongheguo Xianfa 1978, (Constitution of the PRC), *Zuzhi Fagui*, supra at n. 40, 21. For a general description of this Constitution, see Cohen, "China's Changing Constitution," (1978) *China Quarterly*, No. 76, 794-841.

67. Article 7, para one, Zhonghua Renmin Gongheguo Difang Geji Renmin Daibiao Dahui he Difang Geji Renmin Zhengfu Fa, supra at n. 9, 122.

structure with the adoption of China's current constitution.[68] The last extension of legislative power came in 1986 when the NPC granted law making powers to regional People's Governments and to selected local People's Congresses and People's Governments.[69] (This structure is set out on the chart at page 728 below). However, as this article describes, the acquisition of law making powers has been a mixed blessing. It has brought expectations of order, coherence of meaning and even openess which pose a threat to the secrecy and flexibility of administrative practice. The failure to meet these expectations has no doubt fueled theoretical arguments within China that these administrative rule making powers cannot properly be described as 'legislative powers'.

China's legislative structure combines two different forms of legislative hierarchy. The first is a unified hierarchy of institutional bodies possessing law making authority. This hierarchy is crowned by the full NPC and descends directly through its Standing Committee to the State Council. Below these central government institutions, law making powers are divided between the territorial bureaucracies of regional and local government and the functional bureaucracies of central government administration. The special powers granted to the autonomous minority area legislatures provide the third leg to this division of law making authority.

The second is a hierarchy of legislative categories, which can be simplified into three levels. Primary legislation stands at the top of this pyramid, just below the *Constitution* in legal authority. This type of legislation is often narrowly categorized as "*falü*," a term which is usually translated as "law" and hence gives rise to considerable confusion in foreign accounts of Chinese law. At the second legislative level, there are "*fagui*" which are issued in different forms by the State Council and the regional People's Congresses. Although the term "*fagui*" is usually translated as "regulations," there are in fact many other Chinese legislative terms which, out of a lack of English language alternatives, must also be translated as 'regulations'. This provides yet another source of confusion in the use of English language translations of Chinese law. Finally, at the tertiary level, there are "*guizhang*" which are issued in different forms by central government ministries and regional and local governments. This term is also commonly translated as "regulation." This article adopts the terms "secondary regulations" and "tertiary regulations" to maintain a clear distinction between these two categories. The special legislative category of "*autonomous and special regulations*" (*zizhi &*

68. Zhonghua Renmin Gongheguo Xianfa 1982 (Constitution of the PRC), *Changyong* 1.

69. Article 7, para. two Article 51, Zhonghua Renmin Gongheguo Difang Geji Renmin Daibiao Dahui he Difang Geji Renmin Zhengfu Fa, supra at n. 9, 122 and 130.

danxing tiaoli) created for autonomous minority areas rests uneasily in a poorly defined space between the primary and secondary legislative levels.[70]

Although the development of formal sources of law in China has been driven by the practical interests of state administrative bureaucracies, theoretical arguments have also had their influence. In resurrecting the theme of legal modernization, Party officials returned to the theoretical doctrines as well as the draft legislation of the 1950's.[71] Vyshinsky's instrumentalism reappeared in force. Even official pronouncements on the need to institute the "rule of law" in place of the "rule of men," made plain that law should still be subordinated to Party policy.[72] Yet since the early 1980's the intellectual climate in China has changed beyond recognition. In the legal sphere, the growth of a community of academics, officials and professionals involved in legal affairs has engendered a more sophisticated understanding of China's own legal history as well as the function of law in contemporary Chinese society. In periods of relative tolerance, legal writers have even been able to express new views on the relationship between the Communist Party and the laws of the state.[73] Without challenging the ultimate authority of the Party, writers have also argued for the creation of a rationally ordered and internally consistent legislative order.[74] For some officials and academics, the reorganization of positive law on a more coherent basis is essential if law is to become the pre-eminent framework for public and private life.[75]

70. *Autonomous and special regulations* are a problematic category of subordinate law. In principle they are the legal instruments which designated minority area administrations use to pursue special policies related to ethnic needs. However legislative commentators have yet to show convincingly how they are to be distinguished from other subordinate legislation. (See, for example, Liu Jinghai, Minzu Quyu Zizhifa Shishi Zhong de Jige Wenti' (Several Issues concerning the Implementation of the Minorities Autonomy Law) (1991) 5 *Zhongguo Faxue* 41-45.) Therefore, for the purposes of this article, any observations made regarding *regional regulations (difangxing fagui)* should be regarded as applying, *mutatis mutandis*, to *autonomous* and *special regulations*.

71. Yu Zingzhong, supra at n. 42, 37.

72. A useful summary of the officially approved theory of socialist legal construction in China is contained in the *Shehuizhuyi Fazhi* (Socialist Legal System) entry of the *Faxue* (Legal Science) volume of the *Zhongguo Dabaike Quanshu* (The Chinese Encyclopedia) (1984).

73. See, for example, Ding Bangkai, "Dang Zheng Fenkai de Faxue Sikao," (Thoughts on the Legal Aspect of the Separation of the Party and the State) 3 *Faxue Yanjiu* 15 (1988).

74. Zhao Qingpei, "Lifa Tixi Helihua," (The Rationalization of the Legislative System) in Sun Wanzhong (ed.) *Lifaxue Jiaocheng* (Legislative Studies Text) 215 (1990).

75. Writer's interviews with legal academics and legislative officials, Comparative Law Conference, Beijing University, April 1992.

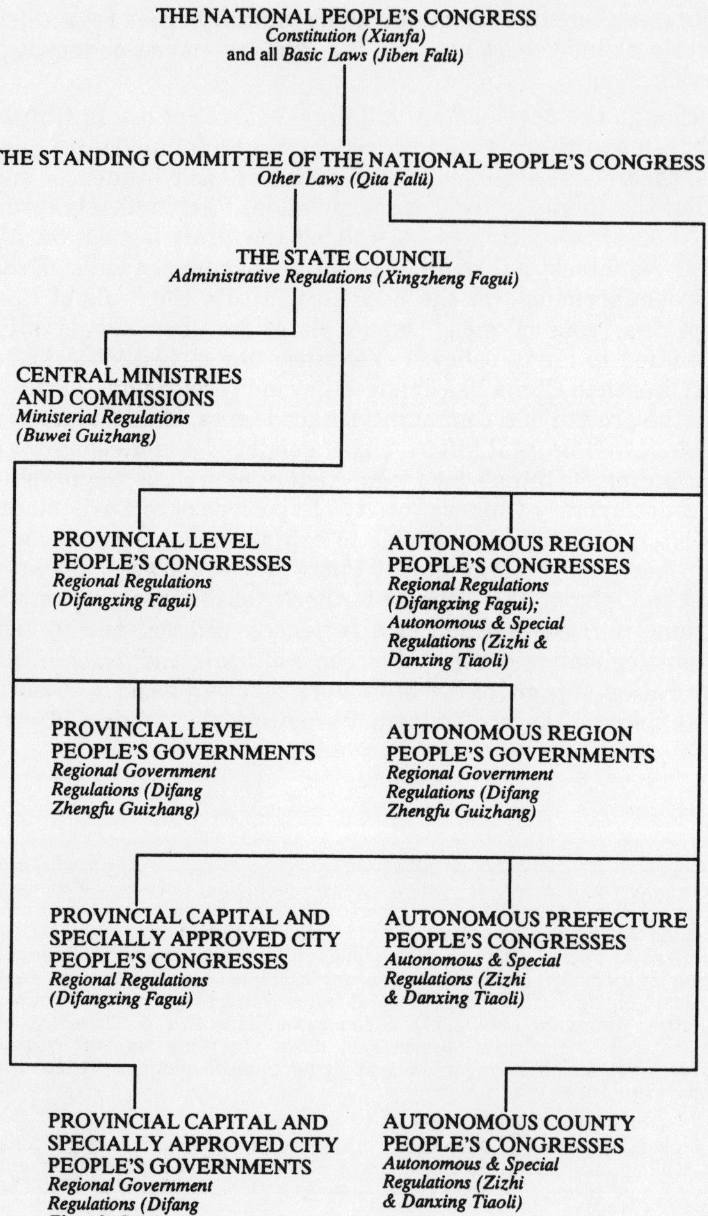

THE LEGISLATIVE STRUCTURE OF THE PEOPLE'S REPUBLIC OF CHINA[76]

76. Adapted from Liu Han, supra at 41, chart No. 15, 57.

Nonetheless, the importance of these ideas should not be overstated. As described below, China's legislative structure has yet to approach the formal rationality and coherence promoted by these officials and academics. Chinese legislative practice is more often characterized by narrow instrumentalism than by the bending of administrative practice to the demands of legal consistency. Moreover, many officials involved in the development of Chinese law appear content that the legal system should derive consistency and coherence primarily from the dictates of Party and state policy and perhaps even the commonly held values of Chinese society.

Sources of Law and Party Supremacy

The strength of China's formal legislative structure lies in its recognition of the normative activities of the administrative bureaucracies. While this structure does not give legal status to all normative documents issued by these bodies, it does provide them with legislative categories with which they can clothe the issue of major norms and commands with the status of law. But in devising a structure of positive law so firmly based on pre-existing administrative practice, China's legal planners laid the foundations for much of the disharmony of contemporary law. As the content of Chinese law has ballooned since 1979 through the issue of thousands of laws and regulations, the resulting confusion has thrown the structural shortcomings of the legislative system into stark relief.

The foremost of these shortcomings is surely the ambiguous relationship between the constitutional supremacy of the Communist Party and the authority of the law. Despite tentative efforts made during the late 1980's to separate the functions of the Party and the state, the Party continues to carry out the core functions of state administration.[77] The drafters of the 1982 *Constitution* attempted, rather unsatisfactorily, to resolve the Party/state relationship through a provision which requires that all organizations, including political parties, abide by the law.[78] However, the *Constitution* also confirms the supreme authority of the Communist Party over all institutions of the state and of society.[79] This equivocal formulation has provided a flexible framework on which to rest Party doctrines which assert that law is an instrument for the execution of Party policies and is therefore in essence a mature form of those policies.[80]

---

77. Saich, "Much Ado About Nothing: Party Reform in the 1980's," in Gordon White (ed.), *The Chinese State in the Era of Economic Reform* 149-74, 169 (1991).

78. Article 5, 1982 Constitution, supra at n. 68, 4.

79. Preamble, id.

80. Peng Zhen, "Guanyu Qige Falü Caoan de Shuoming," (Explanations Concerning Seven Draft Laws) in *Faxue Gailun Ziliao Xuanbian* (Selection of Legal Outline Material) 160 (1984).

The Communist Party is responsible for the initiation of political, economic and social change through the issue of policy directives. According to orthodox legislative theory, primary legislation should only be used to consolidate these changes after the objectives of Party policy have been achieved.[81] In recent years academics and legislative officials in China have engaged in a protracted debate concerning the use of "pre-emptive legislation" (*chaoqian lifa*). Proponents of doctrinal reform have urged that legislation be used to initiate social change, arguing that a reliance on Party policy directives undermines the authority of the law.[82] Traditionalists have countered that such a change would be contrary to the established Chinese Marxist doctrine that law is a superstructural response to changes in the economic and social base.[83] Needless to say, such a change would also limit the flexibility of Party and state administration. The orthodox view therefore remains that legislation ought to be a response to and not an instigator of change.[84] Legislative principle also dictates that once laws are enacted they should remain "stable" (*wending*) and should therefore only be amended where absolutely necessary.[85] In this respect primary legislation has come to represent the stable core of Chinese law in a way which is curiously reminiscent of the symbolic role performed by the principal rules of the Qing code.

The requirement that positive law should only be used to consolidate changes initiated through administrative measures is reflected in the legislative principle that national laws should not be enacted until the relevant circumstances are "ripe" (*chengshu*).[86] That is to say, not until the institutions and personalities involved have reached a consensus on the principles and rules which should govern the area of concern.[87] Should any immediate problems arise in the course of experimental reforms before the circumstances are judged to be ripe for legislation, interim regulatory measures are normally used. Administrative practice in this area appears to be ad hoc and therefore it is difficult to generalise regarding the types of interim measures used. In some cases authorities have introduced reforms almost exclusively through the issue of normative documents setting

---

81. Guo Daohui, supra at n. 15, 155. For political and other reasons, some important Party policies, such as the national "one child" birth control policy, have not been enshrined in legislation, although the proportion of major policies receiving a legislative basis has risen significantly in the past decade. Tanner, "Organization and Politics in China's Post-Mao Law Making System," in Potter, supra at n. 34, 53-96, 87.

82. He Jinhua, et al., "Lifa Chaoqian Yu Sifa Chaoqian Bitan," (A Discussion of Pre-emptive Legislation and Pre-emptive Legal Administration) 4 *Faxue* 9-15 (1991).

83. Id.

84. Writer's interview with members of the Institute of Law, Chinese Academy of Social Sciences, August 1993.

85. Guo Dahui, supra at n. 15, 136.

86. Guo Daohui, supra at n. 15, 161.

87. Id. at 163-64.

out changes in Party and state policy.[88] Whilst in others, secondary or tertiary regulations have been issued to provide a more formal basis for experimental changes.[89] Reforms are usually confined to specific regions or localities on the basis that some areas are more economically or socially advanced and therefore better suited to the reform in question.[90] If successful, many reforms are later implemented nationally, often accompanied by formal legislation. However, detailed examination of the experimental reform process is rare because of the Communist Party's deliberate concealment of its role in state administration.[91]

The attractions of this incremental approach to change are fairly obvious. Bureaucrats are able to tinker and experiment endlessly before committing themselves to legislation. But reliance on Party authority to pre-empt legislation has blurred the boundaries of positive law. Chinese legislation is perpetually in half focus as it fades into its background context of Party decisions and policy documents. It consequently fails to achieve a separate identity as the formal source of Chinese law. The continued reliance of Chinese decision makers on policy directives and makeshift regulations to introduce reforms clearly compromises any movement towards a legislative model in which the formal sources of law provide a coherent foundation for interpretation and doctrinal elaboration. It also underscores the ambivalence of many Chinese legislative officials towards such a model.

Nominal Legislatures and Nominal Law

One of the few enduring features of the Chinese legislative system has been the position of the People's Congresses as the sole organs of state power. These soviet style bodies were ushered in under the 1954 *Constitution*.[92] In addition to the supreme National People's Congress, these bodies were also mandated for all provincial,

88. Chang, "Deciding Disputes: Factors That Guide Chinese Courts in the Adjudication of Rural Responsibility Contract Disputes," *Law & Contemp. Probs*, 101-46, 107 (1989).

89. For example, China's recently enacted Company Law was preceded by a wide range of provincial legislative measures. Kaye & Cheng, "Babes in the Bourse," (16 July 1992) 155, *Far Eastern Economic Review* 48-50, 49.

90. Huang Xianping, "Difang Lifa ji qi Shijian Yiyi," (Regional Legislation and its Practical Significance), in Tang Xiaokui, Ouyang Zhen and Huang Xiangping (eds.) *Difang Lifa Bijiao Yanjiu* (Comparative Research into Regional Legislation) 1-11, 3 (1992).

91. Lieberthal, "Introduction: The Fragmented Authoritarianism Model and Its Limitations," in Kenneth G. Lieberthal & David M. Lampton, *Bureaucracy, Politics, and Decision Making in Post-Mao China* 1-30, 28 (1992).

92. O'Brien, supra at n. 8, 29. Their current constitutional basis rests on Articles 57 and 96 of the 1982 Constitution, supra at n. 55, 9 and 16.

prefectural, county and lower levels of territorial administration.[93] Like the NPC, they have had a chequered history. After a period of rapid development in the mid-1950's, regional and local People's Congresses withered away in the leftward shift of Chinese politics and only reappeared in the 1980's. Moreover, the Communist Party has at all times kept a firm grip on these institutions, controlling the environment in which they function as well as their internal organization and working procedures.[94]

Between 1954 and 1979 China's legislative structure seemed to be one dimensional; the NPC held exclusive constitutional authority to make laws.[95] This state of affairs easily accommodated a rigid, soviet inspired division of the legal activities of the state into legislative (*lifa*), administrative (*xingzheng*) and judicial (*sifa*) categories. In theory the NPC was the sole institution in China possessing the legislative authority necessary for the creation of law. Regulations issued by minority area People's Congresses, to say nothing of the innumerable normative documents issued by Party and state bodies, did not have the status of formal law. They were merely instruments of administration and hence could in principle only be used to interpret and apply legislation adopted by the NPC.

Since the extension of law making powers in the early 1980's, Chinese legislative officials have attempted to redefine the concept of legislation (*lifa*) to take account of these changes. There now appears to be a general consensus that the present system can be described as a "unitary, two level, multi-layered" (*yiyuan, erji, duoceng*) legislative structure.[96] This formulation is intended to reflect two key aspects of the Chinese legislative system. Firstly, it is a unified system, in as much as NPC legislation may in principle extend to any subject matter. Secondly, legislative authority is divided between central and regional levels of authority, within which there are further distinctions concerning the exercise of legislative powers.

But this convoluted phrase is in reality more a device to conceal differences than a useful definition. Whilst some officials lay stress on the overall unity of the legislative structure and the consequent

93. O'Brien, "Chinese People's Congresses and Legislative Embeddedness," *Comparative Political Studies*, 80-107, 85 (April 1994).

94. Information regarding Party control of the People's Congresses is not widely available. However, O'Brien's article, id., 90-91, provides useful observations as do M.S. Tanner's article, "Organization and Politics," supra at n. 81, 63-63, and Liang Yanmin and Wang Xiangming's article, "Dui Difang Renmin Daibaio Dahui Zhidu de Tantao," (Investigation of the Regional People's Congress System) 3 *Faxue Zazhi* 30 (1988).

95. 1954 and 1978 Constitutions, supra at n. 48 and 66.

96. Huang Xiangping, "Difang Lifa de Diwei he Tezheng," (The Position and Characteristics of Regional Legislation), in Tang Xiaokui, supra at n. 90, 10-20, 12-17. See also, Yuan Jianguo, "Lifa Tizhi," (Legislative Structure), in Sun Wanzhong supra at n. 75, 70-103, 73-74.

importance of national law,[97] others have emphasized the breadth and flexibility of the concept of legislation and the importance of regional law.[98] And even amongst the latter, there are critical differences of opinion over which powers should legitimately be included within the legislative framework.[99] Whilst one can take a cynical view of these arguments, given that the views of many of these writers are evidently coloured by their institutional connections,[100] the issues involved are anything but academic. They concern the relative authority of different categories of positive law and the balance of power between the institutions who control these categories. In this respect they are a direct reflection of the bureaucratic conflicts endemic to Chinese state administration.[101]

The complexity of the legislative hierarchy clearly presents an obstacle for those Chinese officials who wish to develop a more rational and coherent system of sources of law. The extension of legislative powers to so many central and regional state bodies has in effect brought the rivalries and disorder of Chinese bureaucracy directly into the legislative structure.[102] Administrative bodies which hold law making powers are now able to enhance the status of their policy positions and claims to administrative jurisdiction through the issue of regulations.[103] The legislative system has seemingly failed to develop a sufficient armoury of procedural and definitional rules which can be used by central authorities to control these aggressive uses of legislative power. If formal sources of law are to be used to promote coherence within the law generally, they at least require organizational rules which dictate the scope of legislative competence and the precedence of differentiated legislative authority. Chinese legislative officials have however struggled unsuccessfully to define the scope of institutional power or to define the nature of the laws and regulations these bodies issue.

These problems begin with the status of primary legislation. In some respects the position of NPC law seems unassailable. The NPC is constitutionally the supreme organ of state power and its laws can-

97. Cai Dingjian, "Lifa Quan yu Lifaquan Xian," (Legislative Power and the Legislative Competence) 5 *Faxue Yanjiu* 3-9, 2 (1993).

98. Huang Xiangping in Tang Xiaokui, supra at n. 90. Yuan Jianguo, supra at n. 96, 70-74.

99. Id.

100. Tang Xiaokui and the other contributors to *Difang Lifa Bijiao Yanjiu*, supra at n. 90, are, for example, all officials working under the Standing Committee of the Human Province People's Congress; whereas the contributors to *Lifaxue Jiaocheng*, supra at n. 75, are all officials within the State Council Legislative Bureau.

101. D. Lampton, discusses the nature of Chinese bureaucratic conflict in his article, "A Plum for a Peach: Bargaining, Interest and Bureaucratic Politics in China," in Lieberthal, supra at n. 91, 33-57.

102. See Lampton, id., regarding bureaucratic conflicts.

103. See infra at n. 168 and accompanying text.

not be validly contravened by any subordinate law.[104] There is however a significant weakness in the NPC's apparent legislative supremacy. Although subordinate regulations can be used directly to implement specific primary legislation, they can also be issued to carry out the issuing body's administrative responsibilities and need not be linked to any particular NPC law. As some Chinese commentators assert, the powers to issue secondary and tertiary regulations have their own basis in the constitutional allocation of administrative responsibilities and can therefore be used without a specific delegation of legislative authority from the NPC.[105] However, this line of argument has rather damaging implications for the coherence of the legislative structure. It implies that the only restrictions placed on subordinate regulations are firstly, that they do not contravene NPC law and secondly, that they are within the administrative competence of the issuing body. But many Chinese academics and officials resist this conclusion as it robs primary legislation of any reserved substantive content and renders it a purely functional legislative category.[106]

Yet defining the reserved content of NPC legislation has proven to be a difficult task.[107] At present, there are few constitutional or statutory provisions relevant to this issue and the solutions derived from legislative practice tend to raise more questions than they answer. Semi-official commentaries suggest that certain basic matters should only be dealt with through NPC legislation, including the creation of significant rights and obligations affecting Chinese citizens as well as the enactment into law of major political, economic or social policies.[108] Subordinate regulations should therefore only be used to give these rights and obligations or policies greater specificity.[109] The problem of course lies in determining what is a new right or obligation or a new policy, and what is merely a clarification of an existing one; a difficulty not made any easier by the characteristically vague language of NPC legislation.[110] Nonetheless there is a certain

---

104. NPC legislation is in principle limited to the *Basic Laws* of the full NPC and the *other laws* of the NPC Standing Committee, but in practice most "Resolutions" (*Jueyi*) and "Decisions" (*Jueding*) of the NPC are to some extent normative and are therefore commonly included in compendia of NPC laws. See for example, *Zhonghua Renmin Gongheguo Falu Quanshu*, supra at n. 1.

105. Zhang Shaoyu (ed.), "Jiaqiang Dui Difang Lifa Gongzuo de Yanjiu," (Improving Research on Regional Legislative Work) 1 *Faxue Yanjiu* 64-69, 65 (1991).

106. Cai Dingjian, supra at n. 97, 7-8.

107. Legislative officials within the central government are currently considering proposals for a *Legislative Standards Law* (*Lifa Biaozhun Fa*) to resolve many of the uncertainties of the legislative structure. Writers interview, supra at n. 34.

108. Zhou Xiaohong, "Guanyu Lifa Quanxian Deng Wenti de Yanjiu Zhongshu," (Survey of Research Concerning Legislative Competence and Other Issues) 1 *Zhongguo Faxue* 115-19, 115 (1992).

109. Id. See also, Yuan Jianguo, supra at n. 96, 91.

110. See infra at n. 192 and accompanying text.

logic to these efforts. Distinctions between different categories of positive law only make sense if different consequences flow from those distinctions. Here at least there is an effort to develop potentially useful distinctions out of the formal categories of law.

Developing a principle of exclusive NPC authority over certain substantive matters is not entirely impractical, but would require greater discipline than has so far been evident in Chinese legislative or judicial practice.[111] After a decade of vigorously pragmatic law making, major reforms would be necessary to bring about a meaningful assertion of the NPC's legislative authority. Legislative officials would need to begin by sorting out the muddled distinction between *basic laws* enacted by the full NPC and *other laws* enacted by the NPC Standing Committee.[112] In principle NPC *basic laws* are reserved for fundamental national legislation. Yet in many cases the full NPC and the Standing Committee have enacted substantially similar legislation.[113] Although the failure to articulate the distinction between these two types of NPC laws has few practical consequences, as the Party leadership is unlikely to permit any overt conflict breaking out between the full NPC and its leadership body, the Standing Committee, it does set a prominent precedent for inconsistent legislative practice.

Legislative officials would also need to reconsider the effects of the decision made during the mid 1980's to delegate major elements of the NPC's legislative competence. During that period the NPC approved three delegations of power to the State Council, including a broadly worded authority to make laws concerning the national programme of economic reform and opening to foreign countries.[114] Given the uncertain nature and scope of NPC legislative powers, or indeed the constitutional origins of its authority to delegate its powers, it is hard to identify the exact content of these delegated powers, beyond perhaps a vague power to legislate major state policies or to enact fundamental rights and obligations in these areas.[115] These delegations were moreover made virtually carte blanche; without time limits, supervisory procedures or methods for identifying which

111. See infra at n. 205 and accompanying text.

112. Tanner, supra at n. 81, 59.

113. For example, the Xingshi Susong Fa (Criminal Procedure Law) 1979 *Changyong* 467, was enacted by the full NPC, whereas the Minshi Susong Fa (Civil Procedure Law) 1992 *Xin Fagui* was enacted by the NPC Standing Committee.

114. Guanyu Shouquan Guowuyuan Zai Jingji Tixhi Gaige he Duiwai Kaifang Fangmian Keyi Zhiding Zanxing de Guilding he Tiaoli de Jueding, (Decision concerning the Delegation of Authority to the State Council to the State Council to Enact Temporary Regulations in Matters Concerning the Economic Reform and the Opening to Foreign Countries), *Zhonghua Renmin Gongheguo Falü Quanshu*, supra at n. 1, 86.

115. M.S. Tanner suggests that the decision whether a law is to be enacted through the NPC or under the State Council's delegated power is a matter to be negotiated in each case by officials from the Party centre, State Council and NPC. Tanner, supra at n. 81, 59.

State Council regulations are based on these powers.[116] As a result, the State Council's ordinary *administrative regulations*, which are in principle subordinate to NPC law, are outwardly indistinguishable from those issued under the authority of the delegated NPC powers.[117]

The proposition that certain subject matters are reserved to the NPC is further undermined by the use of subordinate regulations to implement experimental reforms. Whilst central or regional Party directives are the usual source for new political, economic or social policies, trial implementation is often effected through subordinate regulations and normative documents.[118] For example, in recent years various experimental company law regulations appeared in several of the economically advanced provinces and cities.[119] Before the enactment of the national Company Law in 1993, these measures permitted the local resolution of problems related to the emergence of joint stock companies and also paved the way for national legislation. Whilst this approach to law reform has many practical advantages, it clearly weakens the NPC's claim to legislative supremacy.

The attempt to provide a definitive characterization of the relationship between NPC law and State Council regulations has been mirrored on a smaller scale at the regional level. The Chinese state structure is based on a symmetrical replication of the institutions and structure of central government at regional and local levels. Thus the division of legislative authority between the NPC and the State Council is mirrored in a similar division between lower level People's Congresses and People's Governments. Accordingly, the People's Congresses are entitled to issue secondary regulations called *regional regulations*, (*difangxing fagui*), and the equivalent People's Governments are entitled to issue tertiary regulations called *regional government regulations*, (*difang zhengfu guizhang*).

During the 1980's, regional Party authorities resuscitated the largely non-existant regional People's Congresses and started to use them to issue regional legislation, thereby giving formal legal status to regional Party policy.[120] As these *regional regulations* began to appear in quantity, legislative officials and academics were confronted with two problems of principle. The first was the need to create a workable theoretical distinction between NPC laws and regional People's Congress legislation. Few, if any, challenged the basic principle that regional law exists to implement national legisla-

116. Id.
117. Zhou Xiaohong, supra at n. 108, 116.
118. Guo Daohui, supra at n. 15, 177.
119. Kaye & Cheng, supra at n. 89.
120. O'Brien, supra at n. 93, 91.

tion in the context of local circumstances.[121] A similar consensus has not emerged regarding the practical application of this principle. Many questions have yet to be satisfactorily answered: for example, how far can the provisions of national laws be strained to accommodate local circumstances? Indeed, is it acceptable for regional authorities to act within the spirit if not the letter of national legislation and go so far as to 'modify' (*biantong*) national law to suit local conditions?[122] Chinese commentators are divided on these issues and many would admit that an adequate functional division between national and regional law has yet to be found.[123] The institution with the best claim to authority over this issue, the Standing Committee of the NPC, has so far provided little guidance. The Standing Committee holds exclusive power to rescind *regional regulations* on grounds of illegality and could therefore use this authority to refine the legislative structure. But the Standing Committee has acted cautiously and has in fact never formally used these powers of rescission.[124] But it is perhaps unrealistic to ask that any single institution take on the intractable task of defining the division of power between China's central and regional authorities.

The second major problem in this area is the identification of a plausible distinction between *regional regulations* and *regional government regulations*. Some Chinese commentators have proposed a functional differentiation.[125] Zhang Shangong argues that the People's Congresses should be used to enact regulations implementing NPC legislation and People's Governments should be used to issue regulations implementing State Council legislation. This solution obviously harmonizes with the Chinese theoretical distinction between legislative and administrative organs of the state. But it has little practical value, as it ignores the confusion of powers caused by the delegation of NPC legislative competence to the State Council. Moreover, it does not address the question of which body should issue regulations in situations where directly relevant national law is non existent. However Zhang rightly comments that recent attempts to

121. See Wu Daying & Liu Han, supra at n. 6, 9-10, see also Yang Zongke, "Lun Woguo de Zanxingfa Tizhi," (A Discussion of the Structure of China's Provisional Laws) 6 *ZhongWai Faxue*, 8-14, 12 (1991).

122. Ouyang Zhen, "Difang Lifa de Zhidao Sixiang he Jiben Yuanze," (The Guiding Thought and Principles of Regional Legislation), in Tang Xiaokui, supra at n. 90, 48-66, 62.

123. See, for example, Zhang Shangong, "Lifa Quanxian Tizhi," (The Structure of Legislative Competence), in Zhang Shangong & Xu Xianghua (ed.), *Lifaxue Yuanli* (Principles of Legislation) 89-112, 109 (1990).

124. Xu Xianghua, "Lifa Zhikong," (The Control of Legislation), in Zhang Shangong & Xu Sianghua, id., 186-202, 195. Between 1979 and 1991 regional and specially approved local People's Congresses enacted more than 2000 *regional regulations*. Sun Changjun, "Difang Lifa de Zhiguan Fanwei," (The Authority and Scope of Regional Legislation) in Tang Xiaokui, supra at n. 90, 21-36, 24.

125. Zhang Shangong, supra at n. 123, 110.

identify substantive divisions of legislative authority between regional People's Congresses and People's Governments have been overly abstract and impractical.[126] Propositions that People's Congresses are exclusively responsible for "major issues related to the locality"[127] or "major issues relating to substantive rights and obligations"[128] surely do no more than gloss over an unresolved problem.

There is of course a certain artificiality to these debates. They are founded on the principle that the People's Congresses enjoy a special role as the representative organs of the people and that *regional regulations* should consequently be qualitatively distinct from *regional government regulations*. Indeed, many insist that the latter instruments are not law at all.[129] But what is not accounted for in these public debates is the role of the Communist Party in guiding the legislative process. The provincial level Party Committees are the real centres of regional power. These bodies decide major issues and transmit those decisions to the Party or state institutions concerned. The Party leadership is consequently the ultimate source of all legislation, regardless of its content, form or the institution through which it is issued. Nor do these debates acknowledge the dominance of the state bureaucracies over these nominal legislatures. The departments of the regional and local People's Governments carry out the day to day work of government administration and are therefore the effective instruments of policy implementation. By contrast, the People's Congresses are well known to be the weakest institutions in the triangle of Party Committee, People's Government and People's Congress[130] and in many instances lack sufficient financial resources or technical expertise to carry out their apparent responsibilities.[131]

Bureaucratic Power and Legislative Deference

China's contemporary legislative structure arose out of the tangled administrative structures and practices of the often turbulent decades of Communist rule. It is therefore not surprising that Chinese legislative processes are dominated by the administrative bureaucracies which pre-existed this latest programme of legal modernization. But the ability of these bureaucracies to dominate the production and enforcement of law rests on more than their formal authority to issue some forms of secondary and tertiary regula-

126. Id., 109.
127. Huang Xiangping, supra at n. 90, 10.
128. Yuan Jianguo, supra at n. 96, 95.
129. Huang Xiangping, supra at n. 90, 6.
130. O'Brien, supra at n. 93, 86.
131. Shi Taifeng, "Shehui Xuqiu yu Lifa Fazhan," (Social Needs and Legislative Development) 1 *Zhongguo Faxue* 15-22, 18 (1991).

tion. These bodies have a more complex and pervasive hold on the Chinese legal system.

There are three principle sources of this dominance. The first lies in the superior position of the administrative bureaucracies as institutional power bases within the Communist Party. For example, the individuals who hold leadership positions within the State Council not only outnumber their equivalent colleagues within the NPC Standing Committee organization, but also invariably outrank them within the Party leadership.[132] At the regional level, a provincial governor is usually the first Deputy Party Secretary of the province. Whereas the head of the provincial People's Congress Standing Committee invariably holds a lower rank within the Party and often lacks direct access to key Party sub-committees.[133]

A second source of administrative dominance arises out of the law making process itself. Most Chinese laws, regardless of their place in the legislative hierarchy, are initially drafted within the state bureaucracies. At the central government level, the ministries and other departments of the State Council not only issue their own tertiary level *ministerial regulations*, but they also draft the State Council's secondary level *administrative regulations* and most of the NPC's primary level *basic laws* and *other laws*.[134] And whilst it is true that these drafts are frequently amended by the NPC, the ministries are still able to set the primary agenda and often control implementation.[135] In the regions, the administrative departments of the People's Governments play a similar role in producing both tertiary level *regional government regulations* and secondary level *regional regulations*.[136]

The control of law drafting by state administrative bodies is of course not unique to China. The regulatory nature of contemporary law demands a wealth of technical knowledge and administrative experience which legislative bodies typically do not possess. Consequently, in many western states the preparation of legislation has gradually shifted into the hands of administrators, leaving national legislatures with less effective control over the structural and substantive development of positive law. The responses to this change are equally well known. Many legislative bodies have created new structures and procedures to counter the decentralizing effects of administrative law making. In Britain, for example, this has included

132. O'Brien, supra at n. 94, 92.
133. Id.
134. Writer's interview with officials of the State Council Legislative Bureau, April 1992. The NPC Standing Committee's principal staff support body, the Legislative Affairs Commission (*Fagongwei*) has been responsible for drafting a number of important laws of general application, such as the General Principles of Civil Law.
135. Tanner, supra at n. 81.
136. Zhang Shaoyu, supra at n. 105, 67.

the creation of select committees designed to improve Parliament's policy making functions as well as planning and implementation of legislation.[137]

In China, despite the growing importance of legislative bodies, legislative control over the law making process is especially fragmented and ineffective. In recent years the NPC has acquired greater importance in the national law making process, shedding some of its reputation as a "rubber stamp parliament". If its delegates are not able to vote down legislation approved by the Party centre, they are able to make significant changes to legislative bills, at least outside the sensitive state and public security areas.[138] Yet the NPC clearly does not possess sufficient institutional autonomy to impose its authority over the legal system. The NPC's relative importance is perhaps best explained as an aspect of the fragmentation of power in China's central government. The inability of the Party's leadership to find a concensus on many issues has effectively allowed the Party's decision making arena to broaden and extend into the principle institutions of the state.[139] The NPC therefore provides an additional forum in which powerful interests can seek to influence the transformation of policy into legislation. Some local or regional People's Congresses play a similar role.[140] However the situation varies from province to province depending on the division of Party authority in each area.

There does not appear to be any single institution within the Chinese system of government which has either the authority or desire to impose order on the legal system. It certainly is not the Chinese courts, which are restricted in their powers of interpretation and are not permitted to declare any law or regulation invalid.[141] The administrative bureaucracies are equally unlikely candidates. Whilst they clearly dominate the legislative process, they are far too divided amongst themselves to provide a basis for the effective control of the legal system. Rivalry between these bodies is in fact one of the principal reasons why Chinese law making is such a cumbersome and disorderly affair, proceeding at times with little regard for the cost or likelihood of effective implementation.[142] Nor should one look

137. Philip Norton, *The British Polity* 302 (2nd ed. 1991).
138. Tanner, supra at n. 7, 68.
139. Tanner, supra at n. 81, 86.
140. O'Brien, supra at n. 93, 88-89.
141. See infra at n. 206 and accompanying text.
142. Li Shishi, "Fazhan yu Wanshan Woguo Lifa Sikao," (Thoughts on the Development and Perfection of China's Legislation) 2 *Zhong Wai Faxue* (1991). Writer's interviews with members of the Institute of law, Chinese Academy of Social Sciences April, 1992 & August, 1993.

The field of contract law provides a prominent example of the way in which the powerful position of the State Council and its ministries causes fragmentation in China's legislative order. Chinese contract law is not only subject to the Economic Contract Law 1993 (Jingji Hetong Fa, *Xin Fagui*), and the Foreign Economic Contract

to the Communist Party to rationalize the legislative process. The Party is too closely enmeshed in state administration to stand above the struggles of the state bureaucracies.[143]

A third source of bureaucratic dominance within the Chinese legal order lies in China's unusual division of authority over the interpretation of law. In 1981 the NPC Standing Committee issued a Resolution (*jueyi*) which partially delegated its own exclusive power to interpret NPC legislation to other state bodies.[144] The Standing Committee retained authority over fundamental interpretational issues, but delegated powers to the Supreme People's Court and Supreme People's Procuratorate to interpret NPC law where necessary for judicial and procuratorial work.[145] This formal confirmation of the Supreme People's Court's powers has in fact proven to be one of the most important developments of the legal modernization programme. In the face of the Standing Committees' virtual abdication of responsibility for legal interpretation during the 1980's,[146] the Supreme People's Court has emerged as the principal source of authoritative interpretation of NPC legislation.[147] Indeed, some observers are hopeful that the court will ultimately strengthen the role of law in Chinese society and, in doing so, counter balance the influence of the administrative institutions of the State.[148]

Law 1985 (Shewai Jingji Hetong, *Changyong* 278), but is also governed by a host of regulations governing specific forms of contract, such as the *Contracts for the Sale and Purchase of Industrial Mineral Products Regulations* (Gongkuang Chanpin Gouxiao Hetong Tiaoli, *Changyong* 230) or the *Contracts for the Waterborne Transport of Goods Implementing Regulations* (Shuilu Huowu Yunshu Hetong Tiaoli, *Changyong*, 261). This confusing situation has arisen not so much by design, but as a consequence of the division of administrative authority over contract issues. Ministries responsible for various aspects of the economy, such as mining or water transport, have merely asserted their right to control contract issues related to their spheres of administrative authority. (Cheng & Rosett, "Contract with a Chinese Face: Socially Embedded Factors in the Transformation from Hierarchy to Market," 5 *Journal of Chinese Law* 143-244, 206 (1991).)

143. In these circumstances, it is not surprising that whilst Chinese civil law clearly shows the substantive influence of German law, its haphazard organization is at odds with the German interest in the careful, rational ordering of positive law. Bernstein, "The PRC's General Principle from a German Perspective," 52 *Law & Contemp. Probs.* 117-28, 123.

144. Guanyu Jiaqiang Falu Jieshi Gongzuo de Jueyi (Resolution Concerning the Strengthening of Legal Interpretive Work), *Zhonghua Renmin Gongheguo Falu Quanshu* supra at n. 1, 86.

145. Id.

146. The NPC Standing Committee focussed its attention during the 1980's on the enactment of new legislation. It did not begin to issue interpretations of law in its own name until 1990, although its legislative staff unit, the Legal Affairs Commission (*Fagongwei*) has issued a number of legal interpretations over the past decade. Some of these are contained in *Zhonghua Renmin Gongheguo Falü Jieshi Jicheng*, supra at n. 1.

147. See infra at fn. 211 and accompanying text.

148. Finder, "The Supreme People's Court of the People's Republic of China," 7 *Journal of Chinese Law* 111-90 (1994).

The Standing Committee Resolution also gave formal recognition to the role of state administrative bodies in legal interpretation. It provides that specific questions concerning the application of NPC law arising outside of the procuratorial and judicial processes should be decided by the State Council and its subordinate bodies. The Resolution is moreover equally significant for the matters that it does not address. When it was issued in 1981, the Resolution represented a reasonably complete treatment of the interpretation of formal law, even though it only dealt with NPC and regional People's Congress legislation.[149] But despite the subsequent creation of new categories of positive law, the Resolution was not amended. Nor was any other authoritative instrument issued to deal with the changed situation. The Resolution simply does not address the question of who should interpret State Council *administrative regulations* or People's Government *regional government regulations*.

The doctrinal reasons for this omission are fairly obvious. As a legislative body, the NPC Standing Committee is only empowered to make rules for the interpretation of legislative law (*lifa*). It has no jurisdiction over the interpretation of administrative law (*xingzheng fa*).[150] As a result, administrative law makers have been left to enjoy exclusive authority over the interpretation of their own secondary and tertiary regulations.[151] Even the Supreme People's Court has no authority to make formal pronouncement on the meaning of these regulations, although the courts may refuse to enforce a regulation which is contrary to national law.[152] The state administrative bureaucracies have thus successfully retained control over both the issue and interpretation of their own regulations. The full measure of their success can only be appreciated if one considers the progress they have also made in establishing the principle that all secondary and tertiary regulations should be recognized as formal sources of law.[153] It is no small feat for an administrative body to enjoy formal rights of interpretation over the regulations it has issued and also to require that the courts enforce those regulations as rules of law.

---

149. The Resolution did not include reference to the interpretation of *autonomous and special regulations* issued in recognised minority areas, however by analogy to *regional regulations* these would presumably be interpreted by the Standing Committee of the regional or local People's Congresses which issued them.

150. Writer's interview with officials of the State Council Legislative Bureau, October, 1988.

151. The State Council has recently attempted to assert closer control over the interpretation of *administrative regulations* through newly issued guidelines. Guanyu Xingzheng Fagui Jieshi Quanxian he Chengxu Wenti de Tongzhi (Notice concerning Issues of Competence and Procedure in the Interpretation of Administrative Regulations), *Zhonghua Renmin Gongheguo Xin Fagui Huibian* (hereinafter *Xin Fagui*) (Zhongguo Fazhi, Beijing, 1988-present) (1993) No. 2, 144.

152. Writer's interview with officials of the Supreme People's Court, April, 1992.

153. See infra at n. 185 and accompanying text.

The Imperceptible Boundaries of Law

Legislative reform has not been a high priority for China's state bureaucracies. Having achieved formal recognition of their law making activities in the constitutional reforms of the early 1980's, they have proceeded cautiously in further defining the nature of their legislative authority. Nonetheless, academic and official concern over the fragmented and even chaotic state of sub-statutory law has lead to a number of individual reforms. These have largely involved the establishment of procedures governing the issuing of different types of regulations. The most important of these reforms occurred in 1987 when the State Council approved rules governing the issue of *administrative regulations (xingzheng fagui).*[154] These regulations have legal effect throughout China and rank only second to NPC legislation in importance. Since 1987 all *administrative regulations* must be approved by the State Council Standing Committee or by the Prime Minister personally before promulgation. They must also bear one of three specific legislative titles and should also be published on issue.[155] The 1987 rules did not however provide any new guidance on the relationship between *administrative regulations* and NPC legislation. They merely confirm the principle that *administrative regulations* may be issued by the State Council for the purposes of national administration. They do not address the difficult problem of defining a substantive distinction between NPC and State Council law. Nor do they address the absence of any formal distinction between *administrative regulations* issued under the State Council's own powers and those issued under powers delegated by the NPC.

The 1987 rules do however sharpen the formal and procedural distinctions between *administrative regulations* and the State Council's own normative documents.[156] Since 1987 any document issued in accordance with the these rules is by definition an *administrative regulation*. Any other document issued by the State Council must therefore be a normative or other administrative document. Another State Council directive, also issued in 1987, sets out form and content requirements for routine administrative documents issued within the central government.[157] Certain types of document defined in this di-

---

154. Xingzheng Fagui Zhiding Chengxu Zanxing Tiaoli, (Provisional Regulations Concerning the Formulation Procedures for Administrative Regulations) *Zhonghua Renmin Gongheguo Falu Quanshu*, supra at n. 2, 1375.

155. Article 3, id. These titles are *tiaoli, guiding* and *banfa* which can be translated as "regulation," "rules" and "methods".

156. The State Council's authority to issue normative documents rests on Article 89(1) of the 1982 Constitution (supra at n. 68, 14.) which authorizes the issue of 'administrative measures' (*xingzheng cuoshi*) and 'decisions and orders' (*jueding & mingling*).

157. Guojia Xingzheng Jiguan Gongwen Chuli Banfa, (Method for the Treatment of Documents Issued by State Administrative Organs) (issued 1981, amended 1987, 1993) *Xing Fagui.*

rectory, such as 'directive' (*zhishi*) and 'notice' (*tongzhi*), are frequently used for normative purposes, such as the issue of administrative interpretations of law.

Nonetheless the creation of formal procedures governing the issue of *administrative regulations* has only created a weak barrier between these regulations and State Council normative documents. The only substantive distinction between the two categories would appear to be one described by Zhan Zhongle.[158] He suggests that the State Council cannot rely on its NPC delegated powers to issue normative documents which create rights or obligations affecting Chinese citizens or which implement major policies. It may only use *administrative regulations* to accomplish these ends. However, these familiar vague phrases leave administrative bodies with considerable freedom to determine when a matter must be dealt with by regulation or by normative document. The ambiguities present in this area are such that State Council officials have even argued that both *administrative regulations* and State Council normative documents should be regarded as having force in law.[159] Certainly any examination of published central government normative documents reveals that many are clearly intended to have binding legal effect.[160]

Since 1987 efforts to strengthen the legislative system through procedural reform has extended to the lower level bodies which issue tertiary regulations (*guizhang*). These regulations appear in two forms: *ministerial regulations* (*buwei guizhang*) which are issued by central government ministries and other departments; and *regional government regulations* (*difang zhengfu guizhang*) which are issued by provincial level and specially authorized local governments. They are also the most controversial aspect of China's formal sources of law. Indeed, some Chinese commentators argue that these regulations are merely instruments of administration and cannot therefore be included within the structure of positive law.[161]

Recent procedural reforms do not seem to have brought significant change to the organization of tertiary regulations. In many cases these changes have only created modest procedural boundaries between tertiary regulations and normative documents issued by the same bodies.[162] Often the only clear distinction lies in the requirement that a regulation must receive the personal approval of the highest ranking official in the administrative body concerned. The

158. Zhang Zhongle, "Lun Xingzheng Fagui, Xingzheng Guizhang Yiwai de Qita Guifanxing Wenjian," (A Discussion of Normative Documents Outside the Field of Secondary and Tertiary Regulations) 2 *Zhongguo Faxue*, 108-13, 110 (1992).

159. Yuan Jianguo, supra at n. 96, 92.

160. Many of these are contained in *Zhonghua Renmin Gongheguo Falu Guifanxing Jieshi Jicheng* (Collected Normative Interpretations of Law of the People's Republic of China), (Jilin Renmin, 1989) (Suppl. 1990).

161. Huang Xiangping, supra at 90, at 6.

162. Writer's interview, supra at n. 34.

Minister of Public Security is, for example, expected to give formal approval to any tertiary regulations issued by the Ministry of Public Security (*Gongan Bu*). Consequently the formal distinction between tertiary regulations and normative documents is often difficult to perceive. According to one legislative official, there are between 10,000 and 40,000 tertiary regulations presently in force in China. The exact number depends on which types of document are defined to be within this category of law.[163]

Commentators opposed to the recognition of tertiary regulations as sources of law have voiced two general criticisms. Firstly, these regulations are frequently inconsistent with the relevant provisions of superior laws and regulations.[164] This is in part a consequence of inadequate methods of administrative control. Having virtually excluded the judiciary from any role in determining the validity of subordinate regulations, the State Council has relied on a variety of methods to identify and resolve inconsistencies between tertiary regulations and superior law. But these methods are only sufficient to deal with the worst abuses of law making power at subordinate levels.[165] There are simply too many tertiary regulations for the State Council's legislative staff to deal with them adequately and, in any event, claims of legislative inconsistency are not easy to prove. Primary and secondary legislation is usually drafted with deliberate generality and flexibility of language.[166] Consequently, it is often a matter of subjective opinion as to whether a particular tertiary regulation is inconsistent with the letter or spirit of superior legislation.[167]

The second general criticism made regarding tertiary regulations is that they are frequently used improperly to extend the issuer's field of administrative competence.[168] This problem is rooted in the principle that the legislative competence of a body authorized to issue tertiary regulations is defined by the scope of its assigned administrative responsibilities. However, these responsibilities are often set out in loose terms which allow for the inclusion of new technological or social developments within the existing divisions of administrative authority.[169] As a result, issuing regulations which purport to gov-

163. Id.

164. Zhou Xiaohong (rapporteur), "Dui Difang Lifa "Bu Xiang Dichu Yuanze" de Tantao," (Inquiry into the "Principle of Non-contravention of Superior Law" in Regional Legislation) 1 *Zhongguo Faxue* 122-24, 123 (1993).

165. Writer's interview, supra at n. 34.

166. See infra at n. 191 and accompanying text.

167. Shi Taifeng, supra at n. 131, 18.

168. Guo Daohui, supra at n. 15, 169. See also, Tanner, "Organizations and Politics," supra at n. 81, 65.

169. In 1988 the State Council issued an internal document clarifying the administrative responsibilities of central government ministries and other departments in order to reduce jurisdictional conflict. However, these responsibilities are still

ern a new area of concern has become a useful way of claiming administrative authority over that area.[170]

In the view of some officials and academics, tertiary regulations should simply be excluded from any description of the legislative sources of Chinese law.[171] There is certainly some force to this argument. Tertiary regulations seem wholly lacking in the self binding characteristic of law. There are only minimal substantive and procedural restrictions governing their use and they are also subject to the exclusive interpretational authority of the bodies that issue them. The legislative work of ministries and regional governments in China can however be seen from another perspective. Edward Epstein argues that many of these bureaucracies work towards the promotion of technical, formally rational rules in their own areas of authority.[172] It is possible therefore that, whilst these authorities often undermine the general coherence of Chinese law through their own law making activities, they do in fact create smaller pools of coherence within the overall disorder of the legal system.

In their present form tertiary regulations clearly represent a disruptive element in the organization of Chinese law. However, asserting control over the use and content of tertiary regulations would require the assertion of control over the bodies which issue these substatutory instruments. But a radical change of this nature is unlikely to occur in China's consensus driven system of government which suffers from intense personal and institutional rivalries.[173] Indeed, institutional cooperation and decision making in China has been likened by one American scholar to "protracted guerilla warfare".[174] Bureaucratic rivalry is of course an inevitable aspect of any system of administration. But in China's case, the problem is exacerbated by the sheer size and complexity of government and the bifurcated authority of Communist Party and state institutions. Moreover, in recent years the central government's authority over state administration has weakened considerably through the growth of regional and, perhaps more strikingly, local power.[175]

broadly framed. Writer's interview with officials of the Legislative Bureau of the State Council, April 1992.

170. One example of this sort of jurisdictional conflict arose out of official concern over the spread of AIDS into China from abroad. In 1990 the Ministry of Communications and the Ministry of Health both issued *ministerial regulations* requiring the crews of Chinese ocean going ships returning from abroad to undergo health checks. Unfortunately each ministry required that these take place at hospitals under its own authority, possibly in hopes of monopolizing the resulting fee revenue. (Related to the writer by a member of the Institute of Law, Chinese Academy of Social Science.)

171. See, Huang Xiangping, supra at n. 90, 6.

172. Epstein, supra at n. 34, 27.

173. Lampton, supra at n. 101, 38-39.

174. Id. at 37.

175. G. Segal, *China Changes Shape*, Adelphi Paper #287 (International Institute for Strategic Studies 1993).

It should not therefore be surprising to find that arguments over the status of tertiary regulations are often rooted in other more overtly political disputes concerning the allocation of institutional power. This can be seen quite clearly in the legislative problems which have arisen out of the deep tensions which exist between central and regional authority in China. This tension was brought into the legislative structure in the early 1980's when regional and selected local People's Governments were granted the power to issue tertiary regulations.[176] The commissions and ministries of the State Council had of course already received this power under the 1982 *Constitution*.[177] There are consequently two forms of tertiary regulations and the power to issue them straddles the great administrative division between the functionally defined central government ministries and the territorially defined People's Governments.[178]

A major problem now exists in determining the relative authority of these two forms of law. Central ministries and provincial level People's Governments are at the same level in the Chinese administrative hierarchy. As a result, every administrative issue which affects a ministry as well as a provincial government requires its own unique accommodation of their interests. In principle, neither has the administrative authority to impose its will on the other. The legislative consequence is that law making officials cannot agree on a procedural principle to resolve conflicts between central and regional tertiary regulations.[179] The parties to any clash of regulatory interests must negotiate a solution or ultimately refer the issue to the State Council.[180]

In 1988 the hitherto academic controversy over the status of tertiary regulations emerged as one of the principle obstacles to the enactment of the much awaited Administrative Litigation Law (*Xingzheng Susong Fa*).[181] This national law, which introduced judicial review of administrative action into the Chinese legal system, includes a provision which defines the categories of positive law on which the courts may rely in determining the legality of any administrative action.[182] During the drafting process, officials within the State Council argued that, despite valid criticisms, tertiary regulations should nonetheless be included within the scope of this provision. In their view, which they and many commentators continue to

176. See supra at n. 69 and accompanying text.
177. Article 90, 1982 Constitution, supra at n. 68.
178. Lampton, supra at n. 101, 38.
179. Zhou Xiaohong, supra at n. 108, 118.
180. Writer's interview, supra at n. 134.
181. Zhang Shuyi, "Examination of Several Controversial Issues in the Administrative Litigation Law (Draft)," 24 *Chinese Law and Government* No. 3, 47-53, 50 (1991).
182. Article 52, Xingzheng Susong Fa (Administrative Litigation Law), *Changyong* 149-57, 155.

hold, these lower level regulations constitute the effective legal basis of Chinese government administration.[183] They argue that primary legislation (*falü*) and secondary regulations (*fagui*), are drafted in general language which cannot be used to determine whether specific acts committed by government officials are unlawful. Only tertiary regulations provide sufficient detail to resolve their issues.

In the final version of the Administrative Litigation Law, the drafters struck a compromise which compels the courts to 'consult' (*canzhao*) relevant tertiary regulations when deciding administrative cases.[184] However, according to State Council officials, this term simply means that the courts must implement tertiary regulations unless they can be shown to be contrary to superior law.[185] This interpretation of the law is in effect no more than a restatement of the State Council's original argument that tertiary regulations should be recognized as the third tier of the legislative structure. Given the institutional weaknesses of the Chinese courts, it is probably an interpretation that they are willing to accept.[186]

Yet the problems which tertiary regulations pose for the orderliness of Chinese law pale into insignificance when the full dimensions of China's normative document system are considered. Almost every institution in China, whether governmental, industrial or otherwise, issues and enforces rules of some kind. The term normative documents encompasses all these institutional rules.[187] In theory, lower level normative documents are easily distinguished from formal positive law by the fact that they are issued by institutions which lack the necessary authority to issue secondary or tertiary regulations. According to legislative authorities, they cannot therefore be directly enforced in the courts or be used as the basis for the imposition of fines or penalties.[188]

Nevertheless, these rules have many law like characteristics for those who are required to obey their provisions. They are after all enforced by the administrative bodies that issue them and, anecdotal evidence suggests, many judges give considerable weight to them in deciding how to apply formal laws and regulations.[189] The uncertain status of normative documents exposes the essential problem of China's legislative structure. The formal boundaries of positive law are only significant if there is also a practical distinction between norms that are within or without those boundaries. In China, it

183. Zhang Chunfa, "Zhengfu Guizhang de Ruogan Wenti," (Certain Issues Concerning Government Regulations) 1 *Faxue Yanjiu* 15-19, 16 (1991).
184. Article 53, *Xingzheng Susong Fa*, supra at n. 182.
185. Writer's interview at n. 134. See, Zhang Chunfa, supra at n. 183, 17.
186. See infra at n. 215 and accompanying text.
187. Zhang Zhongle, supra at n. 158, 112.
188. Writer's interview with officials of the Legislative Office of the Beijing People's Government, April 1992. Zhang Chunfa also addresses this issue, supra at n. 183.
189. Writer's interviews with Chinese lawyers and judges, 1988, 1989 & 1992.

seems that there is often no difference in practice whether a norm is, for example, contained in a tertiary regulation or merely in a county government normative document.

Some Chinese commentators have argued that the solution is to create an additional tier of regulations which would give formal legal status to major normative documents issued by county level People's Governments.[190] But such an extension of law making authority would firstly further complicate and decentralize the country's legislative structure. For this reason the proposal is unlikely to win the support of officials in Beijing who favour a more coherent and centrally dominated legal order. Secondly, this proposal would merely enlarge the sphere of formal law and leave the law/normative document distinction intact and unresolved.

Language, Meaning and Legislation

China's approach to legal interpretation, in which the issuers of laws and regulations retain important powers of interpretation, has had a distinctive effect on the development of legislative language. Unlike those countries in which the courts dominate the work of legal interpretation and therefore create the rules of interpretation, doctrines of legal language have largely emerged in China in the form of guidelines for legislative drafters.

The fundamental principle of Chinese legislative drafting is that primary legislation should be both "general" (*yuanzexing*) and "flexible" (*linghuoxing*).[191] This principle received Mao Tse-tung's imprimatur in the 1950's when he expressly praised the new 1954 *Constitution* for its generality and flexibility.[192] These qualities have since remained central to accepted Chinese doctrines of law making and are colloquially referred to by legislative officials as the policy of "preferring the coarse to the fine" (*yicu bu yixi*).[193] The justification offered for this principle is that national legislation must be general and flexible so that it can be both implemented throughout the country and also adapted to local conditions.[194] The principle of general-

190. Wang Lianchang, "Shilun Xiafang Difang Guizhangquan," (A Preliminary Discussion of the Extension of the Power to Issue Regional Tertiary Regulations) 4 *Faxue Zazhi* 12-16, 14 (1988).

191. Guo Daohui, supra at n. 16, 136. These principles reveal a close parallel with the Chinese imperial legislative tradition. In his work, Ma Xiaohong has highlighted the generality of language which characterized late imperial (Ming and Qing) legislation (Ma Xiaohong, supra at n. 18, 113). Moreover, it is this generality which contemporary Chinese legislative theorists praise when invoking the views of imperial law makers in support of contemporary policies. Guo Daohui, supra at n. 15, 147.

192. Guo Daohui, "Lun Lifazhong Yuanzexing he Linghuoxing Jiehe," (A Discussion of the Synthesis of Generality and Flexibility in Legislation) 1 *Faxue Pinglun* 15-19, 15 (1987).

193. Writer's interview, supra at n. 34.

194. Guo Daohui, supra at n. 191.

ity and flexibility therefore captures the essential concept of Chinese law making that legislation must reflect the unitary nature of the state while satisfying the needs of regional diversity. It also accords with the principle of legislative stability (*wendingxing*),[195] as it permits the effective amendment of the law through changes in interpretation rather than through alterations to the actual text.

Chinese law is also intended to be educative. This can be seen in the requirement that legislation should be drafted in language that is comprehensible to the average citizen.[196] As Sun Chaozhi remarks, "the law is not made for legal scholars and technicians, the law is made for the people".[197] Consequently, technical terms should be avoided unless absolutely necessary and words and phrases should be taken from those used in the everyday language of ordinary people.

Chinese commentators on legislation normally describe the principles of generality, flexibility and the use of ordinary language as requirements for primary legislation. However, many would acknowledge that secondary and tertiary regulations are often drafted in the same broad, indeterminate language.[198] Indeed the legislative drafting rules of the Beijing People's Government expressly require that all city regulations be, "simple, accurate, easy to understand and easy to remember" (*jianming, zhunque, yidong, yiji*).[199] Consequently, subordinate regulations often lack the very detail which in theory they are supposed to provide.

The generality of Chinese legislative language has important implications for the internal coherence of the law. In China's complex legislative hierarchy, which places few general limitations on the scope of secondary or tertiary regulations, the substantive content of primary legislation is in effect the principal ordering mechanism. However, if that content is expressed in apparently ambiguous language, the capacity of superior law to constrain subordinate law inevitably suffers. Subordinate law is in effect only minimally constrained by the content of superior law.

There is nonetheless much room for debate over the ambiguity of Chinese legislative language. As Michael Schoenhals points out, the official manipulation of language has been a key instrument of polit-

195. Supra at n. 85 and accompanying text.

196. Sun Chaozhi, "Weiguan Lifa Jishu," (A Microview of Legislative Technique), in Zhang Shangong, supra at n. 123, 230-65, 259.

197. Id.

198. Sun Changjun, "Difangxing Fagui de Yuyan Biaoshu," (The Linguistic Expression of Regional Regulations), in Tang Xiaokui, supra at n. 90, 126-38, 135. See also, Zhang Chunfa, supra at n. 183, 19.

199. Beijing Shi Renmin Zhengfu Guizhang Zhiding Chengxu Zanxing banfa, (Provisional Measures of the Beijing City People's Government concerning Procedures for Drafting Regulations), *Beijing Fazhi Bao* 2 (9 Dec. 1990).

ical control throughout the Communist era in China.[200] The Party has always made great efforts to control the language with which political, economic and social issues are discussed. For a Chinese official, failure to use approved terms and phrases can be a serious dereliction of duty and, in more turbulent times, even a fatal mistake.[201] One must therefore assume that Chinese law drafters are especially careful to ensure that legislation is expressed in approved language. This is moreover not inconsistent with the principle of generality and flexibility. Guo Daohui, for example, emphatically asserts that whilst flexible language should be "indistinct" (*mohu*), it should never be "imprecise" (*hanhu*), by which he means that legislative language should accurately convey a specific range of meaning.[202]

The close relationship between legislation and the vocabulary of Communist Party doctrines and policies illustrates the highly contextual nature of Chinese legislative language. In many instances, the law cannot be properly understood without a grasp of related Party policy documents. This of course presents a difficult barrier for individuals, whether Chinese or foreign, who do not have access to those materials. Yet an awareness of Party policy may still fail to resolve the textual ambiguities of the law. Carefully chosen language may merely reflect an underlying compromise and even the clearest decision can easily become outdated in the shifting sands of Chinese politics. Consequently critics of ambiguous legislative language, such as Shi Taifeng, argue that too many issues are left to be decided by the administrative officials who enforce the law.[203]

An argument could also be made that that Chinese law derives certainty and predictability from its broader social context. It is possible that the gaps and inconsistencies of legislative language are in part remedied in their application as they are filtered through the shared values and norms of Chinese society. This is certainly an aspect of Chinese law which deserves much greater attention.[204] However contemporary China is no longer a particularly homogenous society. Economic development coupled with increased exposure to the outside world is rapidly changing the nature of Chinese life. As divisions based on wealth, education, mobility and urbanization increase, the social context of Chinese law is less likely to stabilize legal practice in the ways its probably has in the past.

200. Michael Schoenhals, *Doing Things with Words in Chinese Politics* 5 (1992).

201. Id. at 24-25.

202. Guo Daohui, supra at n. 191, 19.

203. Shi Taifeng, supra at n. 131, 18.

204. Wen Dan's article, "Qiantan Ruhe Renshi ji Chuli "Hefa" yu "Heli" de Maodun," (A Short Discussion on How to Recognise and Resolve the Conflict between What is Lawful and What is Reasonable) 3 *Guangdong Faxue* 16-19 (1990), is one of the few scholarly pieces to appear in Chinese which discusses the importance of a commonly understood conception of reasonableness in the application of legal norms.

The subject of language and legal development in China is in itself a complex area for study. However some pertinent observations can be reached on the basis of this brief discussion. It is evident that Chinese law makers have not in general attempted to use legislative language, supported by rules of construction, to strengthen the internal structure and order of positive law. They prefer in fact, particularly in relation to primary legislation, that the specific meaning attached to legislative language should shift according to its context. The administrative advantages of indeterminate language are plain enough. Armed with formidable powers of interpretation, administrative bodies will inevitably prefer broadly drafted laws and regulations which leave them free to act as they see fit in specific circumstances. Yet it is important to be cautious in reaching conclusions about the apparent indeterminacy of Chinese legislative language. Indeterminacy is after all a matter of perspective. For officials, or even ordinary Chinese citizens, the law may well derive a degree of predictability from its political and social context which an outside observer may not perceive.

A Cooperative and Consultative Judiciary

In this article little has been said regarding the role of the judiciary in the current programme of legal modernization. This is perhaps surprising in view of the important position occupied by the courts elsewhere in providing the rules of interpretation which are thought to sustain the internal coherence of the legislative structure. However the Chinese courts play a much more circumspect role. Limited in their interpretational authority and fully integrated into the Party and state bureaucratic system, the courts have not had the opportunity or inclination to exert a disciplining force on the structure of legislation. This brief section cannot do justice to the complex role of the courts within China's legal order and serves only to outline the reasons why the judiciary have not policed the development of the legislative system.[205]

Despite the unitary structure of the court system, judicial practice within China is in fact quite diverse and reflects many of the country's geographic, economic and other disparities. It is nonetheless possible to identify two major factors which have limited the judiciary's influence over the legal system. Firstly, as described above, the formal powers of the courts to interpret law are tightly restricted. Only the Supreme People's Court (SPC) in Beijing is empowered to

205. The workings of China's judicial system are better described elsewhere. See S. Finder's extensive discussion of the organization and work of the Supreme People's Court, supra at n. 148; and D. Clarke's overview of various formal dispute resolution procedures and institutions in, "Dispute Resolution in China," 5 *Journal of Chinese Law* 245-96 (1991).

issue formal interpretations of law.[206] Whilst the application of law in the lower courts has an undeniable interpretational aspect, these courts are prohibited from expressing any formal opinion on the meaning of legislative language.[207] In principle all novel problems of interpretation must be referred to the SPC.

Furthermore, in accordance with the China's complex division of responsibility for legal interpretation, the SPC may only issue interpretations of primary legislation.[208] Consequently, when a problem arises concerning the interpretation of a secondary or tertiary regulation, the courts must defer to the issuing body in matters of interpretation.[209] And whilst in practice the courts may resist unreasonable interpretations, administrative law makers ultimately enjoy a near proprietary right to control the regulations they have issued. The judiciary's obligation to consult also extends to the SPC's interpretation of NPC legislation. In interpreting these laws, the SPC consults closely with the legislative staff of the NPC Standing Committee as well as the officials of any important administrative body affected by the law in question.[210]

The restricted interpretational powers of the Chinese courts may seem incomprehensible to a western lawyer, but they are entirely consistent with China's approach to law and legal administration. The courts are part of what is intended to be a fully integrated bureaucratic system. The judiciary's task is in principle to apply laws and regulations as they are given and, when in doubt as to the meaning of any provision, to inquire of the law maker. It is true that over the past decade the SPC has taken on greater responsibilities than were perhaps originally envisioned. It has, for example, issued several lengthy, official commentaries on NPC legislation which are recognized as important supplements to primary legislation.[211] Yet SPC interpretations are not binding outside the judicial system and may not be cited by lower level courts in their official decisions.[212] The SPC may yet play a stronger role in the development of Chinese law.

---

206. Guanyu Jiaqiang Falu Jieshi Gongzuo de Jueyi, supra at n. 144.

207. Guanyu Difang Geji Fayuan Buyi Zhiding Sifa Jieshi Xingzhi Wenjian de Pifu, (Reply concerning the Inadvisability of Regional People's Courts Formulating Documents which Resemble Judicial Interpretations) (1987) *Zhonghua Renmin Gongheguo Zuigao Fayuan Gongbao* 2, 19.

208. See supra at n. 145 and accompanying text.

209. Writer's interview, supra at n. 150.

210. Writer's interviews with officials of the Supreme People's Court, November 1988 and April 1992.

211. Zhou Daoluan, "Lun Sifa Jieshi ji qi Guifanhua," (A Discussion of Judicial Interpretation and its Standardization) 1 *Zhongguo Faxue* 87-96, 89 (1994). See also, Su Huiyu & You Wei, "Wanshan Xingfa Sifa Jieshi Ruogan Yuanze de Tantao," (An Enquiry into the Improvement of Certain Principles concerning the Judicial Interpretation of Criminal Law) *Zhongguo Faxue* 2, 61-68 (1992).

212. Guanyu Renmin Fayuan Zhizuo Falu Wenshu Ruhe Yinyong Falu Guifanxing Wenjian de Pifu (Reply Concerning the Treatment of Legal Normative Documents in the Formulation of Legal Documents by the People's Courts) (1986).

But this is unlikely to occur without the specific agreement of other powerful institutions.

Secondly, the courts have very little institutional autonomy. The participation of the courts in the consensual decision making processes of Chinese government is ensured through their integration into the Communist Party structure and their close links with other state institutions. The Party not only exerts it authority over the courts through its supervisory Political Legal Committees, but is also present within the courts through the Party affiliation of the senior judges.[213] In this way the Party maintains control over judicial policy; periodically altering sentencing guidelines and indicating new areas of emphasis for judicial work.[214]

The Chinese judicial system also spans the important division between central and regional administration. All courts are part of the national court system (*xitong*) and each one is therefore under the supervisory authority of the SPC as well as the higher courts of the same region and locality. But at the same time each court also forms part of the People's Government at the corresponding level of administration. The Higher People's Court of Shandong province is, for example, under the authority of both the Shandong provincial People's Government as well as the Supreme People's Court. As a result, this court is dependant on the Shandong People's Government for the allocation of buildings, personnel, transport and finances.[215] The courts are therefore particularly vulnerable to external pressure in sensitive cases. Thus where a court has cause to consider tertiary regulations issued by its own provincial People's Government, that court would be unwise to decide that those regulations were invalid or otherwise inapplicable without the acquiesence of the provincial officials concerned.

Conclusion

There are two distinct themes which have characterized the development of the formal sources of Chinese law during the 1980's and 1990's. The dominant theme is one which emphasizes the instrumental use of law and its essential openness to its context.[216] At a theo-

213. Wang Xinxin, "Sifa Duli Shi Zhengzhi Tizhi Gaige Zucheng Bufen," (The Independence of the Judiciary is an Aspect of Political Reform) (9 January, 1989) *Shijie Jingji Daobao* (World Economic Herald) 13.

214. Clarke, supra at n. 205, 261.

215. Writer's interview, supra at n. 152.

216. Other writers have characterized the dominant theme of contemporary Chinese law in similar terms. Edward Epstein has, for example, invoked a Weberian contrast between the prevailing use of law as an instrument of domination and the development of formal rational law which legitimates rather than dominates, supra at n. 34, 21-22. Yu Xingzhong uses the term "Chinese legal pragmatism" to describe the dominant, instrumental element within Chinese legal culture, supra at n. 42, 29-51.

retical level, this theme has found its expression in legal doctrines rooted in Vyshinsky's instrumentalism which deny a distinction between law and politics and perpetuate the principle of Communist Party supremacy. They have served to justify the use of Party directives to suspend or alter the operation of law and the use of Party policy documents to provide the necessary context for legal interpretation. These doctrines have also sustained the view that law derives its coherence of meaning more from its political and social context than from a reasoned interpretation of statutory language.

This dominant theme of instrumental, contextual law also involves a subtle interplay between China's contemporary legal practice and the background resonance of the Confucian based imperial legal tradition. The influence in this tradition in reinforcing the dominance of a contextual approach to law can be seen in two respects. It provides an important precedent for the idea that law is merely an aspect of a specific philosophy of social relations and that its rules can only be understood through the classical texts of that philosophy. It also affects the substance of contemporary Chinese legal practice. This can be readily seen in the continuing importance given to the repair of social relations between the parties to a dispute, even though this may involve the sacrifice of legal rights.

The minor theme of Chinese legal development emphasizes law's internal rationality and coherence and, hence, the separability of law and politics. The influence of liberal legal theory on this aspect of Chinese law is undeniable. Many Chinese academics and legislative officials have studied law in western liberal democracies since China's "open door" policy began in the late 1970's. In addition, closer contact with Taiwan has engendered an interest in the Republic of China's codified law and its origins in the law reforms of the Republican period. As a result, the idea that law can and should be rationally ordered, internally coherent and relatively autonomous is now a well known coin in the currency of Chinese intellectual exchange. Indeed, there are clearly some individuals within Chinese government and academia who are committed to the realization of some form of liberal democracy in China.

Nonetheless, the influence of liberal legal theory in China should not be overstated. Measures designed to increase the internal order and consistency of law are not incompatible with a desire to improve the efficacy of instrumental law. Coherence in law has a basic functional attractiveness because it obviates the need for continual reference to a decision maker.[217] It follows that improving legal coherence

217. H.L.A. Hart made this point much more elegantly in observing that, "If it were not possible to communicate general standards of conduct, which multitudes of individuals could understand, without further direction, nothing that we now recognize as law could exist." H.L.A. Hart, *The Concept of Law* (1961).

through the rationalization of its internal organization need not be linked to liberal theories of law which relate internal coherence and rationality to the separation of law and politics. It is moreover perfectly possible for internal rules which support the consistent interpretation and application of the law to be subject to a general principle that decision makers may override these rules at their own option.

Regardless of their sources of inspiration, Chinese legislative officials and academics have shown considerable interest in the rationalization and strengthening of the legislative structure. Writers have, for example, argued for the clarification of the issuing procedures for subordinate regulations[218] as well as the elimination of vague and inconsistent statutory language.[219] Other critics have even argued that the introduction of experimental reforms should be based on legislative measures rather than Communist Party directives.[220] But these rationalizing proposals and measures do not represent the dominant aspect of Chinese legislative development. They are small innovations in a system which is fundamentally orientated towards a contextual, instrumental approach to law.

This fundamental orientation has been particularly important to the development of China's legislative structure. Since the legal modernization programme began powerful state administrative bureaucracies have shaped the legislative structure to serve their interests. In doing so, they have pursued an instrumentalist understanding of law and have undermined the internal order of the law through their legislative practices. These institutions have in fact been so successful in forcing the structures of positive law to accommodate the exercise of administrative power, that the control of administrative law making has become one of the key issues of Chinese legal development.

Yet, because of the complicating effects of Chinese legislative theory, any attempt to address this issue through legislative reform will be particularly difficult. When the legal modernization programme began in 1979, legislative officials held a rigid, soviet inspired conception of positive law. In their view, legislatures, as the representative organs of the people, were exclusively competent to enact law. The norm creating activities of administrative bodies were brushed aside as "administrative" (*xingzheng*) rather than "legislative" (*lifa*) acts.[221] The resulting definition of positive law was a simple, two level hierarchy composed of direct or delegated NPC laws and regional People's Congress regulations. As legal reform got un-

218. Zhang Chunfa, supra at n. 183, 18.
219. Shi Taifeng, supra at n. 203.
220. He Jinhua, supra at n. 82.
221. Liu Han, supra at n. 41, 55.

derway, the complete exclusion of administrative law making from this definition proved to be too far removed from the reality of Chinese administration. China's legislatures, the NPC and the regional People's Congresses, barely existed as functioning institutions. Whereas the State Council and its ministries as well as the regional and local People's Governments were already entrenched as the country's effective law makers.[222]

The radical solution to this problem would have been to accept that all state and quasi-state institution create law through their rule making and rule enforcing activities. If this had been accepted, the difficult task of determining rules of precedence and competence to govern these activities would at least have embraced all possible forms of positive law. But China's leaders endorsed a much more conservative solution. They approved the creation of new categories of subordinate regulations, but only for the most important norms of the higher ranking administrative institutions of the state. The result was a trifurcated hierarchy of obscurely related legislative categories and powers and an equally complicated and unhappy distinction between law and normative documents.

This has created two distinct issues for Chinese legislative practice; how to define the outer boundary of positive law and how to distinguish its internal categories. These are in essence different aspects of the same problem. Distinctions between norms which have legal status and others which do not or between different types of law are pointless if practical consequences do not flow from these distinctions. Legislative officials in China are however divided in their approach to the resolution of this problem. One alternative has been to set out these practical consequences in the form of legislative organizational rules which would also serve to enhance the internal cohesion of the law. The other has been simply to allow the authority and meaning of different laws to be determined by external reference to the powers of the issuing body and the dictates of relevant Party and state policies.

The effort to create distinctions through internal rules has not been very successful. Most energy has gone into the creation of procedural distinctions. These have admittedly proven to be useful in providing a means of identifying the formal legal status of different documents, although it is still true at the tertiary level that procedures are so rudimentary that it is still hard to perceive the distinction between a regulation and a normative document issued by the same body.[223] Less time has been given over to the problem of identifying the substantive consequences which should result from these procedural distinctions. What has been suggested so far is poorly ar-

222. Supra at n. 64 and accompanying text.
223. Supra at n. 163 and accompanying text.

ticulated and appears to be unworkable in practice. For example, the purported principle that only primary legislation may be used to enact significant rights and obligations affecting Chinese citizens,[224] requires extensive doctrinal development before it could possibly serve as a guiding principle for the delimitation of legislative authority.

It could be argued that the reservation of substantive areas of law to different categories of Chinese legislation is unnecessary. The rule which prohibits subordinate law from infringing the provisions of relevant superior laws would appear to offer in itself a practical distinction between different categories of legislation. For example, it should be enough that Ministry of Public Security *ministerial regulations* are subordinate to State Council *administrative regulations* because the former must not contravene the latter. The problem with this argument is that it assumes the existence of highly developed principles and rules of statutory interpretation which can be used to stabilize the meaning of superior law and thereby determine the proper scope of subordinate legislative authority. This assumption is not borne out in the case of China. Firstly, statutory language is often vague and indeterminate, especially at the critical level of primary laws and secondary regulations.[225] Secondly and more importantly, authority over legal interpretation is decentralized and most often lies in the hands of the law makers themselves.[226] There is no single institution charged with final authority over the interpretation of all laws and regulations which could impose a unified vision of the legislative structure.

One must therefore conclude that direct reference to the context of Chinese law will continue to be the best means of understanding its complex division of legislative powers and categories. Although internal organizational rules have appeared, they are simply too crude to transform political and social conflicts into problems of legal doctrine and to produce their ultimate resolution. In this respect, the administrative structures and processes of the Communist Party and the state bureaucracies provide the most important context for the law. The authority of a regulation may be best described by reference to the rank and responsibilities of the issuing body and perhaps as well to the personal importance of its leaders. The substantive content of the law seems best approached in a similar contextualist manner, drawing much of its meaning in specific cases from national and local policies and culturally based normative expectations. But this conclusion also demonstrates that the accuracy of a directly contextual interpretation depends largely on each individual's knowledge and understanding of its proper context. An experienced Chinese of-

224. Zhou Xiaohong, supra at n. 108.
225. Guo Dahui, supra at n. 192 and accompanying text.
226. Writer's interview, supra at n. 150.

ficial well versed in Communist Party policy decisions is therefore more likely to find greater coherence in Chinese law than would, for example, a Chinese speaking, Hong Kong lawyer.

From a critical perspective, direct reference to law's context is of course often seen as a good thing, avoiding the charade of doctrinal indeterminacy. But even from this radical perspective China's legal system is not functioning well. However a legal system is conceived and organized, it must derive coherence and order from some source, be it internal doctrine or political and social context. Yet in China the disorder and instability of politics and society in the face of rapid economic change and dislocation has meant that context is not effectively providing the order which Chinese law so obviously needs.

[9]

COLUMBIA JOURNAL OF ASIAN LAW

VOL. 10 SPRING 1996 NO. 1

POWER AND POLITICS IN THE CHINESE COURT SYSTEM: THE ENFORCEMENT OF CIVIL JUDGMENTS

DONALD C. CLARKE*

According to reports from all regions of North China, there is a great accumulation of unexecuted cases at the level of the court of first instance. . . . In some of these cases, it has been two or three years since judgment; in some, the party frequently runs to the court to apply for execution but the problem is not resolved; in some, the party asks, "Is there any law in the court?" and "Does the judgment count for anything?" — this has been the cause of great dissatisfaction among the masses.

— North China Division of the Supreme People's Court, 1953[1]

---

* Professor of Law, University of Washington School of Law. This article is a revised and much expanded version of an article that appeared in the March, 1995 issue of the *China Quarterly*. I would like to thank the Committee on Scholarly Communication with China, the Committee on Legal Education Exchange with China, and the University of Washington School of Law for the funds and leave time that made possible the research on which this article is based. I would also like to thank William Alford, James Feinerman, Ellen Hertz, Nicholas Howson, Louis Wolcher, and Ping Yu for their comments and suggestions at various stages of this project.

Court officials, academics, lawyers, and others interviewed in China who were promised anonymity are identified in the notes only by profession. In addition to interviews and articles in legal journals, this article draws heavily on news reports published in the legal and popular press. These are not always reliable, and it would be a mistake to draw conclusions of any weight from a single report. I have tried to compensate for this unreliability by sheer volume, on the assumption that an inference is relatively reliable if it is supported by many news stories from different parts of the country.

1. Zuigao Renmin Fayuan Huabei Fenyuan [North China Division of the Supreme People's Court], *Guanyu Geji Renmin Fayuan Zhixing Panjue De Zhishi* [*Directive Concerning the Implementation of Judgments by People's Courts at All Levels*] (Aug. 1, 1953), *reprinted in* MINSHI SUSONGFA CANKAO ZILIAO [REFERENCE MATERIALS ON THE LAW OF CIVIL PROCEDURE], vol. II, part 2 [hereinafter 2 MSCZ], at 720, 720 (Zhongguo Shehui Kexueyuan Faxue Yanjiusuo Minfa Yanjiushi Min-Su Zu, Beijing Zheng-Fa Xueyuan Minshi Susong Jiaoyanshi [Civil Procedure Group of the Civil Law Research Section of the Institute of Law of the Chinese Academy of Social Sciences and the Civil Procedure Law Teaching and Research Section of the Beijing Institute of Politics and Law] eds., 1981) [hereinafter 1953 SPC-NC Directive].

At present, the most prominent problem in economic adjudication is the difficulty of executing judgments.

— Zheng Tianxiang, President of the Supreme People's Court, 1988[2]

When judgments are not executed, the law is worth nothing.

— "The masses"[3]

I. INTRODUCTION

It is a staple of Chinese legal literature that the judgments of Chinese courts in civil and economic cases are plagued by a low execution rate and that this is a serious problem. This perception should be taken seriously. When the President of the Supreme People's Court devotes significant space to it in his report to the National People's Congress, as did Zheng Tianxiang in 1988[4] and Ren Jianxin in subsequent reports, clearly something interesting is going on. Yet it would be a mistake to accept all reports uncritically. A critical examination of the claims and the evidence can yield a richer picture of reality than has been presented by the literature so far.

The issue of whether court judgments can be enforced is important for a number of reasons, among which is its bearing on the relationship between the legal system and the economic system. Laws, courts, and court judgments are part of the institutional framework within which economic reform is being carried out in China. Obviously, the rules of the game have to change. But the move from a hierarchically administered economy to a primarily market economy means more than just changing the content of the rules. It implies a whole new way of rule-making and rule-enforcing.

This article explores one particular way of making the rules mean something: the enforcement of a court decision that the implementation of a particular rule requires the performance of a particular act — typically, the delivery of money or goods. How does a court make A give something to B? If court decisions cannot be enforced, then the rules that they purport

2. Zheng Tianxiang, *Zuigao Renmin Fayuan Gongzuo Baogao* [*Supreme People's Court Work Report*] (Apr. 1, 1988), *reprinted in* ZUIGAO RENMIN FAYUAN GONGBAO [SUPREME PEOPLE'S COURT GAZETTE] [SPCG], No. 2, June 20, 1988, at 3, 8.

3. Quoted in Liu Yong, *Tantan Shen-Zhi Fenli De Biyao Xing* [*A Discussion of the Need to Separate Adjudication from Execution*], FAZHI JIANSHE [CONSTRUCTION OF THE LEGAL SYSTEM], No. 3, at 46, 46 (1984).

4. *See* Zheng, *supra* note 2, at 8.

to implement will have little significance,[5] and this has crucial implications for the direction of economic reforms.

It is important to stress what this article is *not* about. First, it is concerned only with civil judgments of the type outlined above. Because I am trying to look at cases in which there is no perceived direct threat to governmental authority, I do not discuss the enforcement of judgments in criminal matters or the enforcement of administrative decisions.

Second, I do not discuss the process by which the judgment to be enforced is produced. This is a key part of any full account of the enforcement of rights in China. A powerful opponent may be able to scare a weaker party out of bringing suit. Once suit is brought, many obstacles stand in the way of a correct judgment: judicial ignorance of the law and corruption, to name two, as well as the many factors detailed in this article that stand in the way of execution, such as favoritism of local enterprises.[6] This article deals only with what happens after the judgment is issued.

Third, this article is not about the enforcement of judgments, Chinese or foreign, involving foreigners. Since the beginning of large-scale foreign investment in China, the government has attempted to maintain a largely separate legal system for foreign businesses. In many cases there are special rules or practices applicable to foreigners and some of these are noted in passing. With the progress of economic reform, however, segregation is becoming less and less viable and the special status of foreigners is disappearing. What is true for domestic parties will increasingly be just as true for foreign parties, both for better and for worse.

Part II of this article explains the focus on court decisions. It argues that although not all the rules pertaining to economic activity, broadly defined, are enforced through courts, an important sub-class of those rules is given meaning through court decisions and their enforcement.

Part III introduces the legal institutional background to issues of execution, looking at legislation and the structure of the court system.

Part IV examines the evidence of the existence of a problem in enforcing civil judgments against recalcitrant defendants.

---

5. As will be shown later, however, there are some interesting ways in which even an unenforced and unenforceable court judgment can have significant real-world consequences.

6. For more on the factors that go into the production of a court decision, see Phyllis L. Chang, *Deciding Disputes: Factors That Guide Chinese Courts in the Adjudication of Rural Responsibility Contract Disputes*, 52 LAW & CONTEMP. PROBS. 101 (1989) and Donald C. Clarke, *What's Law Got To Do With It? Legal Institutions and Economic Reform in China*, 10 UCLA PAC. BASIN L.J. 1, 57-64 (1991).

Part V contains the detailed analysis of the problem, discussing precisely where problems seem to exist and why. In studying causes, it also suggests ways in which some problems could be overcome.

Part VI presents the conclusion and links difficulties in enforcement to the lack of fit between economic reform and legal institutional reform.

II. WHY LOOK AT COURT DECISIONS?

A focus on courts does not depend on the assumption that courts in China possess anything like the power and prestige they command in common-law countries and, to perhaps a lesser extent, in developed civil-law countries. It is instead the particular relationship among economic reforms, rules, and institutions that suggests a focus on court decisions and their enforcement.

The transition from a plan-centered to a market-centered economy requires an appropriate set of corresponding legal institutions, the most important feature of which is *general applicability*. The essence of the planned economy is production according to directives from above. A production directive to a firm is meaningless if it does not take into account the particular characteristics of the firm (for example, its production capacity). Firms producing in a competitive market, on the other hand, operate under a set of constraints common to all firms in their sector: prices, demand, environmental and labor regulations, etc.[7] If law in China is to be used in support of market institutions, it must apply indifferently to large numbers of economic actors. Otherwise the system will revert to the kind of specific directives and *ad hoc* bargaining whose inadequacies led to the drive for reform in the first place.[8]

A system of uniformly applicable rules needs an institution ready and able to undertake the task of enforcing them. For a number of reasons, the courts in China are the most likely candidate for this task.

First, individual courts, not just the system as a whole, have the putative authority to issue orders cutting across bureaucratic and territorial boundaries provided that jurisdictional requirements are satisfied. A judge sitting in a Hunan county and appointed by the county People's Congress could, under proper circumstances, legitimately order a state-owned, city-

7. This paragraph should not be read as a claim that firms in Western economies all actually function in this way. It is intended merely to highlight the differences between the ideal type of the planned economy and the ideal type of the market economy.

8. I make this argument more fully in Donald C. Clarke, *The Law, the State and Economic Reform*, *in* THE CHINESE STATE IN THE ERA OF ECONOMIC REFORM 190 (Gordon White ed., 1991).

run handicrafts factory in Harbin to pay a sum of money to a collectively-owned, township-run sandalwood supplier in Guangxi.

This type of formal authority is remarkable in China. No other institution, including the Communist Party, has it. The traditional way to solve disputes in post-1949 China has been to find the common superior with jurisdiction over both parties.[9] But this method invariably involves the problems of particularism and bargaining that economic reform was intended to move away from.

Second, norms enforced by courts can be less subject to dilution than norms enforced by other bureaucracies. Any authority system faces the problem of ensuring that policy formulated at the top is carried out properly below. The key advantage of court-enforced policy over bureaucratically implemented policy is that, if the system works properly, it minimizes the number of layers between policy making and policy implementation. A court can resolve a dispute between parties by direct reference to the original text of policy issued by the relevant policy maker, which could for example be the central government. In this case, there is only one intermediate layer between the central policy makers and the regulated parties. Thus, court enforcement of rules has the potential to provide a much greater degree of uniformity and consistency than enforcement by other bureaucracies — provided the courts can actually command obedience and have a system for ensuring consistent enforcement.[10]

A consistently enforced system of rights-granting rules of property and contract is often thought necessary for economic development.[11] Can

---

9. This principle applies not only to dispute resolution but sometimes also to the most basic kinds of communications or cooperative relationships. If two units in different systems (*xitong*) would gain from some mutually beneficial arrangement, they cannot just do it. They must go through proper channels. I discuss this principle at greater length in Donald C. Clarke, *The Creation of a Legal Structure for Market Institutions in China, in* REFORMING ASIAN SOCIALISM: THE GROWTH OF MARKET INSTITUTIONS 39, 45 (John McMillan & Barry Naughton eds., 1996).

10. It should be stressed that this is so far largely a question of potential, not reality. Law in China still works in much the same way as a bureaucratic command — in fact, it might be more accurately characterized as simply a species of bureaucratic command. A central law is passed down to the provincial level, where it is interpreted and sent down to the local level. The local gloss added at the intermediate levels is in fact expected, as the central regulation may be deliberately vague on certain points. Ultimately, local courts must follow the municipal authorities' interpretation of the provincial authorities' interpretation of the central document. In short, law in China tends to be like an army command: you follow only the orders of your immediate superior. Whether he gave the right orders or not is a matter between him and his superior, not for you to wonder about.

11. *See generally, e.g.*, DOUGLASS C. NORTH & ROBERT PAUL THOMAS, THE RISE OF THE WESTERN WORLD (1973); DOUGLASS C. NORTH, INSTITUTIONS, INSTITUTIONAL CHANGE, AND ECONOMIC PERFORMANCE (1990).

well defined property and contract rights — particularly property rights — reasonably be said to exist? Are rights of property and contract, however well defined, in fact reliably enforced? If not, does China's undeniably impressive growth provide a significant challenge to this theory? An examination of the enforceability of court decisions about rights can contribute to the discussion of the relationship between property and contract rights and economic development by providing a richer understanding of just what it means in practice to have a right in China.

III. INSTITUTIONAL BACKGROUND: COURT STRUCTURE AND LEGISLATION

A. *The Court System*

To understand the issue of execution in its full complexity, it is necessary to understand something about the structure of the courts.[12] China has a total of about 3,500 courts of general jurisdiction and various specialized courts[13] staffed by about 106,000 judges and 52,000 assistant judges.[14] There are four levels of courts of general jurisdiction, the lower two of which are the usual courts of original jurisdiction, although all can serve as such depending on the perceived importance of the case and the status of the parties.[15]

---

12. For more detail on the court system, see the accounts, on which the following paragraphs are based (although supplemented and updated) in Donald C. Clarke, *Dispute Resolution in China*, 5 J. CHINESE L. 245, 235-268 (1991) and Clarke, *supra* note 6, at 19-22, 57-69.

13. The structure of the court system is set out in Zhonghua Renmin Gongheguo Renmin Fayuan Zuzhi Fa [Law of the People's Republic of China on the Organization of People's Courts], *as amended*, 1983 ZHONGHUA RENMIN GONGHEGUO FAGUI HUIBIAN [COLLECTED LAWS AND REGULATIONS OF THE PEOPLE'S REPUBLIC OF CHINA] [FGHB] 4 [hereinafter Court Organization Law]. There are about 132 specialized courts, whose jurisdiction is by subject matter and is not limited by administrative boundaries. *See* Chang Hong, *Top Judge Feels Law Has Made Big Gains*, CHINA DAILY, Oct. 3, 1989, at 4.

14. *See Renmin Fayuan Zai Gaige Kaifang Zhong Quanmian Fazhan — Fang Zuigao Renmin Fayuan Yuanzhang Ren Jianxin* [*The People's Courts Are Developing in All Areas in the Course of Reform — An Interview With the President of the Supreme People's Court, Ren Jianxin*], ZHONGGUO FALÜ [CHINESE LAW], June 15, 1995, at 2, 7. Assistant judges are appointed by the courts themselves, not the local People's Congress or its Standing Commitee, *see infra* note 22 and accompanying text, and may be authorized to perform the same functions as judges. *See* Court Organization Law, *supra* note 13, art. 37.

15. For example, Intermediate Level People's Courts are the courts of original jurisdiction in all criminal cases where a foreigner is the accused or the victim. *See* Zhonghua Renmin Gongheguo Xingshi Susong Fa [Criminal Procedure Law of the People's Republic of China], 1979 FGHB 87, art. 15 [hereinafter Criminal Procedure Law]. In a system where court officials are simply bureaucrats, it is inappropriate for them to pass judgment on those of higher rank. Thus, regulations exist that assign original jurisdiction to courts of various levels depending on the administrative and social rank of the parties involved. *See, e.g.*, Zuigao Renmin Fayuan [Supreme People's Court],

At the top of the structure is the Supreme People's Court (*zuigao renmin fayuan*) (SPC).[16] Below it, at the provincial level, are the thirty Higher Level People's Courts (*gaoji renmin fayuan*) (HLPC): one for each province, autonomous region (*e.g.*, Tibet or Xinjiang), and centrally-administered city (*e.g.*, Beijing or Shanghai). Below the HLPCs are the 389 Intermediate Level People's Courts (*zhongji renmin fayuan*) (ILPC).[17] These are established just below the provincial level in prefectures (*diqu*), provincially-administered cities, and within centrally-administered cities.

At the bottom are the 3,000-odd[18] Basic Level People's Courts (*jiceng renmin fayuan*) (BLPC), which exist at the county level. Because it may be difficult for parties from outlying areas to attend court, a BLPC may establish branch courts known as People's Tribunals (*renmin fating*) (PT) outside the town in which it is headquartered.[19] The decision of a PT is the decision of the BLPC and is properly appealed to the court above the BLPC, not the BLPC.[20] There are over 18,000 PTs across the country.[21]

Guanyu Minshi Shenpan Gongzuo Ruogan Wenti De Yijian [Opinion on Several Issues in Civil Adjudication Work] (Aug. 28, 1963), *in* JIEFANG YILAI QUANGUO MINSHI, JINGJI SHENPAN GONGZUO HUIYI ZHENGCE WENJIAN XUANBIAN [SELECTED DOCUMENTS FROM NATIONAL MEETINGS ON CIVIL AND ECONOMIC ADJUDICATION SINCE LIBERATION] [hereinafter SELECTED DOCUMENTS] 1, 10-11 (Yunnan Zheng-Fa Zhuanke Xuexiao Minfa Jiaoyan Shi, Yunnan Sheng Gaoji Renmin Fayuan Yanjiushi [Civil Law Teaching and Research Section of the Yunnan Specialized Institute of Politics and Law and the Research Section of the Yunnan Province Higher Level People's Court] eds., June 1985) [hereinafter 1963 SPC Opinion]; Renmin Fayuan Shenpan Minshi Anjian Chengxu Zhidu De Guiding (Shi Xing) [Rules on the System of Procedure for the Adjudication of Civil Cases by People's Courts (for Trial Implementation)] (Feb. 2, 1979), *in* ZHIXING GONGZUO SHOUCE [HANDBOOK ON EXECUTION WORK] 73, 74-75 (Sun Changli ed., 1988) [hereinafter 1979 SPC Rules]. The Communist Party Central Committee may assign any case to the Supreme People's Court. *See id.*

16. For a detailed and well-informed account of the Supreme People's Court and its role in the legal system, see Susan Finder, *The Supreme People's Court of the People's Republic of China*, 7 J. CHINESE L. 145 (1994).

17. *See Renmin Fayuan Zai Gaige Kaifang Zhong Quanmian Fazhan*, *supra* note 14, at 2.

18. *See id.*

19. The establishment and functioning of PTs are governed by two regulations. The first, entitled "Experimental Procedures for the Work of People's Tribunals (Draft)" (*Renmin Fating Gongzuo Shixing Banfa* (*Cao'an*)), was circulated by the Supreme People's Court to lower courts in 1963. The second, entitled "Several Rules Concerning People's Tribunals" (*Guanyu Renmin Fating De Ruogan Guiding*), was formulated in July, 1988 by the Supreme People's Court and apparently circulated to lower courts. Neither document has to my knowledge been published. *See* Han Shuzhi, *Renmin Fating Shezhi Ji Gongzuo De Jige Wenti* [*Several Problems in the Establishment and Work of People's Tribunals*], FAXUE [JURISPRUDENCE] (Shanghai), No. 10, at 18, 18 (1990).

20. Court Organization Law, *supra* note 13, art. 20.

21. *See Renmin Fayuan Zai Gaige Kaifang Zhong Quanmian Fazhan*, *supra* note 14, at 2. The same source, the President of the Supreme People's Court, put the number at 18,500 in 1991. *See* Ren Jianxin, *Zuigao Renmin Fayuan Gongzuo Baogao* [*Supreme People's Court Work Report*],

The formal structure of the Chinese government and its relationship to the courts is shown in simplified form in Figure 1. Each court has a president, a vice president, and several judges. Generally, court presidents are chosen by the People's Congress at the same level, as shown, but vice presidents and other judges are chosen by the corresponding People's Congress Standing Committee.[22] This local control of personnel and funding[23] has crucial implications for the functioning of the court system that are discussed in more detail below.[24] Unlike federal judges in the United States, Chinese judges have no security of tenure and below the SPC are not appointed by the central government. Hence, BLPC judges are beholden to the county-level government, HLPC judges are beholden to the provincial-level government, and SPC judges are beholden to the central government.[25]

FAZHI RIBAO [LEGAL SYSTEM DAILY], Apr. 12, 1991, at 2, 2, *translated in* BRITISH BROADCASTING CORPORATION, SUMMARY OF WORLD BROADCASTS, PART 3: ASIA-PACIFIC [SWB/FE], Apr. 25, 1991, at C1/1. In 1994, however, another authoritative source put the number at 15,400. *See* ZHONGGUO FALÜ NIANJIAN 1994 [LAW YEARBOOK OF CHINA 1994], at 103 (1994).

22. This states only the formal rule. In fact, People's Congresses act as rubber stamps for the local Communist Party organizational department. *See, e.g.*, Zhonggong Zhongyang [Chinese Communist Party [hereinafter CCP] Central Committee], Guanyu Quan Dang Bixu Jianjue Weihu Shehui Zhuyi Fazhi De Tongzhi [Notice on the Need for the Whole Party to Firmly Uphold the Socialist Legal System] (July 10, 1986), *reprinted in* 3 SIFA SHOUCE [JUDICIAL HANDBOOK] 92, 94-95 ("Resolutions and decisions passed by People's Congresses and their Standing Committees at various levels must have prior approval in principle by the Party committee at the same level.").

23. Various internal Party documents state clearly that although court personnel are under a system of "dual leadership" (*shuangchong lingdao*), the leadership of the local Party organization is primary. *See* Zhonggong Zuigao Renmin Fayuan Dangzu [Communist Party Group of the Supreme People's Court], Guanyu Geji Renmin Fayuan Dangzu Xiezhu Dangwei Guanli Fayuan Ganbu De Banfa [Measures on Cooperation with Party Committees by Party Groups at Courts of All Levels in the Administration of Court Cadres] (transmitted Jan. 10, 1984 to Party branches in courts at the provincial level), *reprinted in* 3 SIFA SHOUCE [JUDICIAL HANDBOOK] 609 [hereinafter Corporation Measures] (citing Doc. 33 of CCP Organization Department (1983) and Doc. 15 of CCP Organization Department (1983)). For more on funding, see *infra* text accompanying notes 177-184.

24. *See infra* text accompanying notes 177-210.

25. Few ILPCs have a People's Congress at the same level. Prefectures, for example, are units of administration immediately below the provincial government established for the convenience of that government and have no People's Congress of their own. In that case, ILPC judges are officially appointed by the provincial People's Congress.

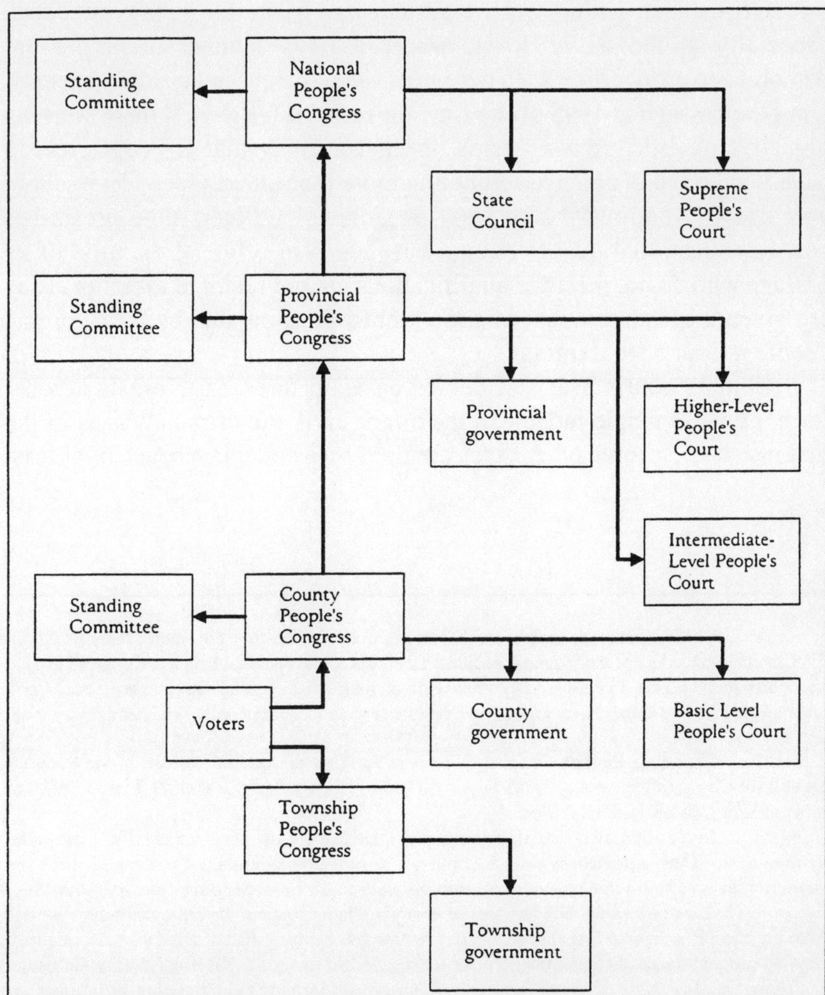

Figure 1: Formal relationship of government, courts, and People's Congresses. Arrows indicate power to appoint personnel.

Officials in China's court system are generally poorly educated, especially at the BLPC level, where a large number of judges are demobilized army officers.[26] There is as yet no career judicial bureaucracy. Until the passage in 1995 of the Law on Judicial Officers,[27] there were *no* objective qualifications in terms of legal training that all judges had to have,[28] although in practice something more than simply secondary school was usually required.[29] The Law on Judicial Officers now prescribes certain educational qualifications, but judges in office at the time of its passage who do not meet the qualifications are not required to resign. They are given a certain amount of time (yet to be stipulated by the Supreme People's Court) for training.[30]

China's courts hear and decide cases in three basic organizational forms. First, a single judge can try minor civil and criminal cases in the first instance. Second, other cases are tried by a collegiate bench of at least

---

26. These officers are simply assigned to a court whether they are wanted there or not. In 1988, the then-president of the Supreme People's Court asked the National People's Congress to give the courts more power to refuse assignments of unqualified personnel and begged local Party committees, People's Congresses, and governments not to send such people. *See* Zheng, *supra* note 2, at 4.

27. Zhonghua Renmin Gonghegua Faguan Fa [Law on Judicial Officers of the People's Republic of China] (effective July 1, 1995), FAZHI RIBAO [LEGAL SYSTEM DAILY], Mar. 3, 1995, at 2 [hereinafter Law on Judicial Officers].

28. Judges and clerks must, however, be qualified for the personal status of state cadre (*guojia ganbu*). Thus, a peasant or worker could not be suddenly elevated to a judgeship. He or she would first have to find some way to move into the state cadre class. *See* Academic Interview S.

The Law on Judicial Officers was several years in incubation. In 1988, Supreme People's Court president Ren Jianxin first announced that the law was being drafted and that it would establish a unified national standard of qualifications for judges. *See* Su Hongzi & Yu Xinnian, *Fayuan Gaige He Jinshe Shi Wancheng Shenpan Renwu De Zhongyao Baozheng* [*The Building and Reform of Courts Are Important Guarantees of the Fulfillment of Adjudication Tasks*], FAZHI RIBAO [LEGAL SYSTEM DAILY], July 19, 1988, at 1. Although this claim was consistently repeated in subsequent years, the law was not enacted until 1995.

29. *See* Academic Interview S.

30. *See* Law on Judicial Officers, *supra* note 27, art. 9. The educational qualifications are as follows:

> Graduation from an institute of higher education with a specialization in law, or graduation from an institute of higher education with a specialization not in law but with specialized legal knowledge, and two years' work experience; or a bachelor's degree in law and one year's work experience. Those who have achieved a master's or doctoral degree in law need not be subject to the above requirements of work experience. Adjudication personnel in office prior to the implementation of this law who do not meet the conditions stipulated [above] should undergo training in order to meet the conditions stipulated by this law within a prescribed period. Concrete measures shall be formulated by the Supreme People's Court.

three persons.[31] The bench is composed solely of judges or of judges and "people's assessors" (*renmin peishenyuan*) selected from the populace.[32] Third, each court has an Adjudication Committee, which is the highest decision-making body within the court. It is composed of the court president, the vice president, the head and deputy head of the various specialized chambers, and ordinary judges. The Adjudication Committee has the power to decide individual cases if it wishes and to direct the judge or bench that heard the case to enter a particular verdict.[33]

In addition to deciding cases by adjudication, courts can and indeed are encouraged to lead the parties to a mediated agreement. Until its 1991 revision, the Law on Civil Procedure instructed courts to "stress mediation"; when attempts at mediation failed, they were to proceed to adjudication.[34]

---

31. This requirement can create problems. According to one report, a number of People's Tribunals, when faced with cases that cannot be heard by a single judge, can attempt only mediation because they lack the third judge necessary to form a collegiate bench. *See Kunrao Renmin Fayuan De "Si Nan"* [*The "Four Difficulties" Vexing People's Courts*], FAZHI DAOBAO [LEGAL SYSTEM HERALD], Feb. 26, 1988, at 3.

32. It appears that the role of people's assessors is largely a formality and that they are not expected to disagree with the views of the presiding judge. See, for example, Liu Shouhai, *Peishenyuan Liangdi Shu* [*Letters from (People's) Assessors in Two Places*], FAZHI RIBAO [LEGAL SYSTEM DAILY], Aug. 25, 1988, at 1, where the writer recalls his service as a people's assessor. After the trial but before any discussion, he was informed that the court president had already decided how the case was to be disposed of and was presented with a copy of the judgment to sign. His career as a people's assessor ended when, in another case, he ventured to question the conclusions of the presiding judge.

33. The Adjudication Committee is discussed in greater detail in Clarke, *supra* note 6, at 60-61.

34. *See* Zhonghua Renmin Gongheguo Minshi Susong Fa (Shixing) [People's Republic of China Law on Civil Procedure (for Trial Implementation)], 1982 FGHB 133, art. 6 [hereinafter 1982 Law on Civil Procedure]. Article 6 is now article 9 in the revised Law on Civil Procedure. Where it formerly said that people's courts should "stress mediation," it now says they should "conduct mediation in accordance with the principles of voluntariness and lawfulness." Zhonghua Renmin Gongheguo Minshi Susong Fa [Civil Procedure Law of the People's Republic of China], ZHONGHUA RENMIN GONGHEGUO QUANGUO RENMIN DABIAO DAHUI CHANGWU WEIYUANHUI GONGBAO [PEOPLE'S REPUBLIC OF CHINA NATIONAL PEOPLE'S CONGRESS STANDING COMMITTEE GAZETTE] [NPCSCG], No. 3, July 10, 1991, at 3, art. 8 [hereinafter Law on Civil Procedure], *translated in* SWB/FE, May 8, 1991, at C1/1, *and in* CHINA L. & PRACTICE, No. 5, at 15 (1991). The translation here is my own.

In the view of the Economic Chamber of the Beijing Intermediate Level People's Court, to "stress" mediation meant that the court should attempt mediation in every case before it. *See* Liang Qinhan, *Chuli Jingji Jiufen Anjian Ying Zhuozhong Tiaojie* [*In Handling Cases of Economic Disputes One Should Stress Mediation*], FAXUE YANJIU [LEGAL STUDIES], No. 4, at 13, 13 (1981). Although this article predates even the old Law on Civil Procedure, to "stress mediation" appears to have been a well-settled policy directive for courts. Indeed, such was the need for courts to report large numbers of mediated settlements that even outcomes where one side got everything it asked for and the other side nothing were reported as successful mediations. *See, e.g., Changjia Laizhang, Fayuan Mingduan; Fang'ai Zhixing, Zhuren Shou Fa* [*Factory Welshes on Debts, Court Judges

An important feature of court mediation is that the mediation agreement has the same effect as a court judgment upon its delivery to the parties.[35] In fact, it arguably has a stronger effect, since, being in theory voluntary, it may not be appealed.[36] In addition, court mediation is the only kind of mediation attempt that can (in divorce cases) be required before a court will give judgment.[37]

Internally, courts are organized into several departments, all under the general authority of the Adjudication Committee and the court president. Several of these are adjudicatory chambers (*ting*) — the criminal chamber, the civil chamber, the administrative chamber, and so on. In addition to these chambers, there might also be a general office (*bangongshi*) and a personnel section (*renshi bumen*).[38]

The execution of judgments is generally consigned to a separate department within the court, the execution chamber (*zhixing ting*). Although the great majority of basic level and intermediate level courts[39] do now have such a chamber, it is not technically required. The relevant law requires only that particular personnel be placed in charge of execution work.[40] The execution chamber is administratively equal to the other adjudicatory chambers, and its officers are formally on the same bureaucratic ladder as adjudication officers.[41] Very few, however, have

---

Clearly; For Obstructing Execution, the Person in Charge Is Punished], ANHUI FAZHI BAO [ANHUI LEGAL SYSTEM NEWS], Apr. 6, 1988, at 1, 2.

35. *See* RENMIN TIAOJIE SHIYONG DAQUAN [PRACTICAL COMPENDIUM OF PEOPLE'S MEDIATION] 17 (Liu Zhitao ed., 1990).

36. *See id.*; Michael Palmer, *The Revival of Mediation in the People's Republic of China: (2) Judicial Mediation*, *in* YEARBOOK ON SOCIALIST LEGAL SYSTEMS 1988, at 161 (W.E. Butler ed., 1989).

37. *See* Zhonghua Renmin Gongheguo Hunyin Fa [Marriage Law of the People's Republic of China], 1980 FGHB 3, art. 25 [hereinafter Marriage Law].

38. *See* Academic Interview S; Court Interview K.

39. Execution chambers are most necessary at these levels, because they have original jurisdiction over almost all cases and are thus in charge of execution of the judgment whether or not it is appealed.

40. *See* Court Organization Law, *supra* note 13, art. 41; Law on Civil Procedure, *supra* note 34, art. 209.

41. *See* Academic Interview S. It is not clear what the effect of the new Law on Judicial Officers will be on execution officers. Because their work does not require the same level of legal training as that of a regular judge, the educational requirements of the Law clash with the principle that execution officers are essentially the same as judges in the other chambers. The Law on Judicial Officers essentially fudges the question by providing cryptically in article 48 that "execution officers of people's courts shall be administered with reference to (*canzhao*) the relevant provisions of this law." The legal significance of this formulation is that it makes it apparent that the drafters deliberately chose *not* to use one of several other formulations unambiguously meaning "in accordance with" (*yizhao*; *genju*; *anzhao*).

worked as such or have received specialized legal education,[42] and the prestige of the execution chamber is lower than that of the adjudicatory chambers.[43] According to a number of sources, young and capable cadres go to the adjudicatory chambers, while the execution chamber is the refuge of the tired, the mediocre, and the uneducated.[44] Nevertheless, one source reports that about one third of the funds spent on handling cases go toward execution.[45]

Reported statistics allow no more than a very rough picture of the operations of execution chambers in particular. While a 1987 article put the total number of execution personnel nationwide at 1301,[46] by 1990 there were 648 in Jiangsu province[47] and 635 in Heilongjiang province alone.[48]

---

42. *See* Beijing Shi Zhongji Renmin Fayuan Zhixing Ting [Beijing Intermediate Level People's Court Execution Chamber], *Wei Zhixing Gongzuo De Liangxing Xunhuan Gaijin Women De Gongzuo* [*Improve Our Work to Achieve a Virtuous Cycle in Execution Work*], at 5, *in* DI-ER-CI QUANGUO SHENGHUI CHENGSHI ZHONGJI RENMIN FAYUAN ZHIXING GONGZUO YANTAOHUI HUIYI CAILIAO [MATERIALS FROM THE SECOND NATIONAL CONFERENCE OF INTERMEDIATE LEVEL PEOPLE'S COURTS FROM PROVINCIAL CAPITALS ON EXECUTION WORK] [hereinafter CONFERENCE MATERIALS] (1992) [hereinafter Beijing ILPC].

43. *Id.*, at 2; Xi'an Shi Zhongji Renmin Fayuan Zhixing Ting [Xi'an Intermediate Level People's Court Execution Chamber], *Qiantan Zhixing Gongzuo De Diwei He Zuoyong* [*A Brief Discussion of the Position and and Role of Execution Work*], at 4-5, *in* CONFERENCE MATERIALS, *supra* note 42 [hereinafter Xi'an ILPC]. According to one court source, the chief of the execution chamber is, unlike the chiefs of the other chambers, often not on the court's Adjudication Committee (*shenpan weiyuanhui*), the organ of collective leadership in the court. To add insult to injury, execution chambers are apparently the last to get access to a car. Their officers have to ride about on bicycles. *Id.*, at 6.

44. *See, e.g.*, Xi'an ILPC, *supra* note 43, at 4-5; CHANG YI, QIANGZHI ZHIXING LILUN YU SHIWU [THE THEORY AND PRACTICE OF COMPULSORY EXECUTION] 5 (1990). In Fuzhou in Fujian province, about half of the execution chamber personnel in the city's one ILPC and 13 BLPCs had any post-secondary education. *See* Fuzhou Shi Zhongji Renmin Fayuan [Fuzhou Intermediate Level People's Court], *Qianghua Zhixing Gongzuo, Wanshan Shenpan Zhineng, Geng Haode Wei Gaige Kaifang He Jingji Jianshe Fuwu* [*Strengthen Execution Work, Perfect the Adjudication Function, Serve Even Better the Cause of Reform and Opening Up and Economic Construction*], at 1, *in* CONFERENCE MATERIALS, *supra* note 42 [hereinafter 1992 Fuzhou ILPC].

45. *See* Court Interview U. These expenses do not include funds for salaries.

46. *See* Gong Yiwei & Chen Yonghu, *Qiantan Jingji Hetong Zhongcai Jiguan De Zhixing Quan* [*A Brief Discussion of the Execution Powers of Economic Contract Arbitration Organs*], SHANGHAI FAZHI BAO [SHANGHAI LEGAL SYSTEM NEWS], Oct. 12, 1987, at 6, 6. To put this figure in context, recall that at this time there were well over three thousand BLPCs and ILPCs, the courts that mainly carry out execution.

47. *See* Jiangsu Sheng Gaoji Renmin Fayuan [Jiangsu Province Higher Level People's Court], *Renzhen Zuohao Zhixing Gongzuo, Wei Shehui Wending He Jingji Fazhan Fuwu* [*Conscientiously Do Execution Work Well to Serve the Cause of Social Stability and Economic Development*], RENMIN SIFA [PEOPLE'S JUDICATURE], No. 6, at 5, 6 (1990) [hereinafter Jiangsu HLPC]; Jiangsu Sheng Gaoji Renmin Fayuan [Jiangsu Province Higher Level People's Court], *Renzhen Zuohao Zhixing Gongzuo, Wei Shehui Wending He Jingji Fazhan Fuwu* [*Conscientiously Do Execution Work Well to Serve the Cause of Social Stability and Economic Development*], *in* JINGJI SHENPAN JINGYAN ZHUANTI HE ANLI XUANBIAN [SELECTED PROBLEMS AND CASES IN THE

These personnel handle well over a million cases a year,[49] of which approximately 85 percent are civil or economic cases.[50] Figures from Heilongjiang province give some indication of their workload. In 1988 and 1989, approximately two hundred courts with an execution staff of 635 executed almost 67,000 judgments.[51] On average, then, each court, with three specialized execution personnel, executed almost 170 judgments per year, or about one every two days.[52] In Guangzhou, the total execution caseload (not only successfully executed cases) was reported to be about 4,000 annually distributed among nine courts.[53]

EXPERIENCE OF ECONOMIC ADJUDICATION] [hereinafter SELECTED PROBLEMS] 234, 236 (Zuigao Renmin Fayuan Jingji Shenpan Ting [Supreme People's Court Economic Adjudication Chamber] ed., 1991) [hereinafter Jiangsu HLPC 2].

48. *See* Tang Langting (President, Heilongjiang Province Higher Level People's Court), *Jianchi Liang-Shou Zhua, Jiejue "Zhixing Nan" [Keep Grasping the Problem With Both Hands, Solve "Difficulty in Execution"]*, RENMIN SIFA, No. 6, at 3, 4 (1990).

49. In 1995, the figure was approximately 1.3 million. *See* Ren Jianxin, *Renmin Fayuan Gongzuo Baogao [Supreme People's Court Work Report]* (Mar. 12, 1989), *reprinted in* RENMIN FAYUAN BAO [PEOPLE'S COURT NEWS], Mar. 21, 1996, at 1. A figure of about one million was reported for 1992, *see* Ren Jianxin, *Jinyibu Quanmian Jiaqiang Shenpan Gongzuo, Genghaodi Wei Jiakuai Gaige Kaifang He Xiandaihua Jianshe Fuwu [Strengthen Adjudication Work in an Even More All-Around Way in Order to Serve Better the Causes of Accelerating Reform and Opening Up and Modernization]* (report to the 16th National Conference on Judicial Work, Dec. 21, 1992), SPCG, No. 1, Mar. 20, 1993, at 6, 12 [hereinafter Ren, *Strengthen Adjudication*], and 760,000 cases were reported for 1989, *see* Ke Changxin, *Guanyu Zhiding Qiangzhi Zhixing Fa De Huhuan [The Cry for Formulating a Law on Compulsory Execution]*, *in* "ZHIXING NAN" DUICE TAN [A DISCUSSION OF MEASURES TO DEAL WITH "DIFFICULTY IN EXECUTION"] 143, 145 (Zhengzhou Shi Zhongji Renmin Fayuan [Zhengzhou Intermediate Level People's Court] ed., 1992).

50. I have deduced this percentage from the figures provided in ZHONGGUO FALÜ NIANJIAN 1994 [LAW YEARBOOK OF CHINA 1994], at 1030 (Table 12) (1994).

51. *See* Tang, *supra* note 48, at 3-4.

52. According to one study of enforcement in several counties of New Jersey, each officer responsible for judgment collection handled (whether successfully or not) an average of 802 cases (writs and wage executions) per year. *See* Committee on Post-Judgment Collection Procedures in the Special Civil Part, *Report to the Supreme Court of New Jersey*, NEW JERSEY L.J., Nov. 1, 1993, at 2 [hereinafter *New Jersey Report*]. According to the Heilongjiang statistics, each officer there successfully executed an average of 53 judgments per year. Even if we pessimistically assume a successful execution rate of only 20 percent of all cases assigned, the total workload, 265 cases, still comes out to well under the New Jersey figure.

53. *See* Guangzhou Shi Zhongji Renmin Fayuan Zhixing Ting [Guangzhou Intermediate Level People's Court Execution Chamber], *Chongfen Fahui Zhixing Gongzuo De Zhineng Zuoyong, Genghaode Wei Shehui Anding He Jingji Fazhan Fuwu [Bring the Functional Role of Execution Work Into Full Play to Serve Better the Causes of Social Stability and Economic Development]*, at 1, *in* CONFERENCE MATERIALS, *supra* note 42 [hereinafter Guangzhou ILPC]. The figure for the number of courts is derived from ZHONGGUO YOUZHENG BIANMA: ZHENG-FA XITONG ZHUANJI [THE POSTAL CODES OF CHINA: THE POLITICAL-LEGAL SYSTEM SPECIAL EDITION] 180 (Zhongguo Youzheng Bianma Zheng-Fa Xitong Zhuanji Bianxie Zu [Editorial Group for the Political-Legal Special Edition of the Postal Codes of China] ed., 1992).

Assisting the execution chamber in addition to performing other functions are the court police (*fajing*).[54] These are recruited from the population at large and assigned through the personnel department of the local government.[55] Court police do not carry the same authority as regular police; they are part of a different bureaucratic system and do not instill the same fear.[56] According to one source, they do not carry the electric stun batons and guns that are the hallmarks of police authority,[57] but another source lists stun batons among the equipment possessed by the court.[58]

B. *Legislation and Procedure*

1. Legislation

Writers on execution complain constantly that there is insufficient legislation in this area, that what exists is too vague and general, and that courts therefore have no laws to follow.[59] The first major law on the subject is considered to be the 1982 Law on Civil Procedure;[60] this law was substantially revised and reissued in 1991,[61] apparently in part because of problems with execution.[62]

Despite general dissatisfaction with the state of legislation, however, execution has not been completely neglected. There is, in fact, a surprisingly rich tradition of legislation on execution. First, by the early

---

54. Court police are generally directly under the control of the court's general office (*bangongting*), which comes under the president. *See* Academic Interview S; Court Interview F.

55. *See* Court Interview F.

56. *See* Lawyer Interview R; Academic Interview B.

57. *See* Academic Interview L.

58. *See* 1992 Fuzhou ILPC, *supra* note 44, at 1.

59. *See, e.g.*, Pan Dingqu & Luo Shifa (officials of the Changsha Intermediate Level People's Court), *Qian Tan Zhixing Huanjing [A Brief Discussion of the Execution Environment]*, at 6, *in* CONFERENCE MATERIALS, *supra* note 42; Ding Haihu & Chen Xiuyan, *Shi Lun Qiangzhi Zhixing Lifa [An Exploratory Discussion of Legislation in the Field of Compulsory Execution]*, FAXUE ZAZHI [LEGAL STUDIES MAGAZINE], No. 5, at 38, 38-39 (1989). Ding Haihu, *Qiangzhi Zhixing Lifa Chuyi [A Proposal for Legislation in the Field of Compulsory Execution]*, FALÜ KEXUE [LEGAL SCIENCE], No. 6, at 71, 71-74 (1989); Xu Junying & He Congjian, *"Zhixing Nan" Fayuan Neibu Tanyin [A Look at the Causes Within the Court of "Difficulty in Execution"]*, FAXUE [LEGAL STUDIES], No. 10, at 16, 17 (1990); Kunming Shi Zhongji Renmin Fayuan [Kunming Intermediate Level People's Court], *"Zhixing Huizhan" Shi Huanjie "Zhixing Nan" Maodun De Youxiao Cuoshi [An "Execution Attack" Is an Effective Measure for Mitigating the Contradiction of "Difficulty in Execution"]*, at 4, *in* CONFERENCE MATERIALS, *supra* note 42 [hereinafter Kunming ILPC]; CHANG, *supra* note 44, at 4.

60. 1982 Law on Civil Procedure, *supra* note 34.

61. Law on Civil Procedure, *supra* note 34.

62. *See* Court Interview D.

1950s a number of municipal courts and regional judicial authorities formulated their own regulations governing execution procedures.[63] The peak of this trend is represented by a long and extremely detailed set of regulations formulated in 1955 by the court of Xuanwu District in Beijing.[64]

Second, a significant amount of legislation and regulations touching on execution was promulgated at the national level before the 1982 Law on Civil Procedure. The first of a series of proto-civil procedure laws was

---

63. *See, e.g.*, Harbin Shi Renmin Fayuan [Harbin City People's Court], Minshi Qiangzhi Zhixing (Tiaoli) [Civil Execution (Regulations)] (1949), *in* MINSHI SUSONGFA CANKAO ZILIAO [REFERENCE MATERIALS ON THE LAW OF CIVIL PROCEDURE], vol. I, part 1 [hereinafter 1 MSCZ], at 435 (Zhongguo Shehui Kexueyuan Faxue Yanjiusuo Minfa Yanjiushi Min-Su Zu, Beijing Zheng-Fa Xueyuan Minshi Susong Jiaoyanshi [Civil Procedure Group of the Civil Law Research Section of the Institute of Law of the Chinese Acadeny of Social Sciences and the Civil Procedure Law Teaching and Research Section of the Beijing Institute of Politics and Law] eds., 1981) [hereinafter 1949 Harbin Regulations]; Wulumuqi Shi Renmin Fayuan Minshi Anjian Zhixing Shi Xing Banfa [Urumchi City People's Court Trial Measures for the Execution of Civil Cases] (approved by Northwest Branch Court of the Supreme People's Court to take effect on Apr. 3, 1951), *in* 2 MSCZ, *supra* note 1, at 712 [hereinafter 1951 Urumchi Measures]; Shenyang Shi Renmin Fayuan Minshi Qiangzhi Zhixing Zanxing Banfa [Shenyang City People's Court Provisional Measures on Compulsory Execution in Civil Cases] (promulgated and effective for implementation on a trial basis on Mar. 26, 1951, revised version approved by Northeast People's Government), *in* 2 MSCZ, *supra* note 1, at 709 [hereinafter 1951 Shenyang Measures]; Dongbei Renmin Zhengfu Sifa Bu [Northeast People's Government Ministry of Justice], Guanyu Jiaqiang Minshi Qiangzhi Zhixing De Zhishi [Directive on Strengthening Compulsory Execution in Civil Matters] (June 5, 1951), *in* 2 MSCZ, *supra* note 1, at 714 [hereinafter 1951 Dongbei Directive]; Zuigao Renmin Fayuan Huabei Fenyuan [North China Division of the Supreme People's Court], Guanyu Geji Renmin Fayuan Zhixing Panjue De Zhishi [Directive Concerning the Execution of Judgments by People's Courts at All Levels] (Aug. 1, 1953), *in* 2 MSCZ, *supra* note 1, at 720.

64. *See* Beijing Shi Xuanwu Qu Renmin Fayuan [People's Court of Xuanwu District, Beijing], Minshi Zhixing Gongzuo Banfa [Civil Execution Measures] (June 20, 1955), *in* 2 MSCZ, *supra* note 1, at 723 [hereinafter 1955 Beijing Measures]. The Xuanwu court was at that time being held up as a model for other courts to follow.

issued as early as 1950.[65] This document established the general principle that coercive measures could be used to execute judgments:

> In civil cases, upon the application of the winning party, the court of first instance should effect compulsory execution of a confirmed judgment. When the court deems it necessary, it may also effect compulsory execution on its own [without such an application]. If the confirmed judgment orders the loser to pay money or to hand over articles of property for which substitution can be made, then when the court deems it necessary in the course of execution, it may, according to the concrete circumstances, seal up and auction the loser's property. When a ruling calls for provisional advance disposition of property or for provisional advance execution, the court making the ruling may, when it deems it necessary, carry out execution without waiting for an application.[66]

In subsequent years, the Supreme People's Court and the Ministry of Justice issued a number of notices and decrees dealing with specific problems of execution.[67] Indeed, a 1956 speech by the then-president of the

---

65. *See* Zhonghua Renmin Gongheguo Susong Chengxu Shi Xing Tongze [People's Republic of China General Principles for Trial Implementation on Litigation Procedures] (Dec. 31, 1950), quoted in CHANG, *supra* note 44, at 13 [hereinafter General Principles of Procedure]. I have not been able to find a copy of these regulations. Other substantial regulations dealing with matters of civil procedure were issued right up to the time of the first formal Law on Civil Procedure in 1982. In chronological order, they are as follows: Guanyu Beijing, Tianjin, Shanghai Deng Da Chengshi Gao-, Zhongji Renmin Fayuan Xing-, Minshi Anjian Shenli Chengxu De Chubu Zongjie [An Initial Summing-Up of Procedures for Adjudicating Criminal and Civil Cases in the Higher and Intermediate Level People's Courts of Large Cities Including Beijing, Tianjin and Shanghai], *in* ZUIGAO RENMIN FAYUAN [SUPREME PEOPLE'S COURT], GUANYU BEIJING, TIANJIN, SHANGHAI DENG SHISAN-GE DA CHENGSHI GAO-, ZHONGJI RENMIN FAYUAN XING-, MINSHI ANJIAN SHENLI CHENGXU DE CHUBU ZONGJIE [AN INITIAL SUMMING-UP OF PROCEDURES FOR ADJUDICATING CRIMINAL AND CIVIL CASES IN THE HIGHER AND INTERMEDIATE LEVEL PEOPLE'S COURTS OF THIRTEEN LARGE CITIES INCLUDING BEIJING, TIANJIN AND SHANGHAI], at 19 (July 1955) [hereinafter 1955 Procedure Summary]; 1963 SPC Opinion, *supra* note 15; Zuigao Renmin Fayuan [Supreme People's Court], Guanyu Guanche Zhixing Minshi Zhengce Ji-Ge Wenti De Yijian [Opinion on Several Problems in the Thorough Implementation of Civil Policies] (Aug. 29, 1963), *in* SELECTED DOCUMENTS, *supra* note 15, at 14; 1979 SPC Rules, *supra* note 15.

66. General Principles of Procedure, *supra* note 65, art. 72. A "confirmed" (*queren*) judgment is the same as a "legally effective" or final judgment from which there is no further appeal

67. Sifa Bu [Ministry of Justice], Wei Geji Renmin Sifa Jiguan Jin Hou Dui Weituo Diaocha Weituo Zhixing Huo Yiban Anjian Ying Jinsu Chuli De Tongbao [Circular Stating That Henceforth People's Judicial Organs Should Handle as Expeditiously as Possible Entrusted Investigation, Entrusted Exection and Transferred Cases] (Mar. 21, 1951), *in* 2 MSCZ, *supra* note 1, at 413 (1981) [hereinafter 1951 MOJ Notice]; Sifa Bu [Ministry of Justice], Gei Guangdong Sheng

Jiangsu Higher Level People's Court containing several detailed suggestions on execution shows that many of the techniques of the 1982 and 1991 Law on Civil Procedure were already in common use in the 1950s.[68] The 1980 Marriage Law made specific reference to compulsory execution "according to law" of unpaid judgments for maintenance and child support even though no formal law on civil procedure existed at the time.[69]

Execution is currently governed by the 1991 Law on Civil Procedure and its associated regulations, such as a lengthy Supreme People's Court opinion (*yijian*) of 1992 that supplements many of the law's provisions.[70] The status of the numerous administrative interpretations issued by the Supreme People's Court prior to the promulgation of the law is not entirely clear. Officially, they remain in effect provided they do not conflict with the provisions of the new law,[71] but it is not always easy to discern the

---

Chaoyang Xian Renmin Fayuan De Pifu Jieda [Reply and Answer to the People's Court of Chaoyang County, Guangdong Province] (1955), *in* 2 MSCZ, *supra* note 1, at 722; Caizheng Bu, Sifa Bu, Zhongguo Quanguo Gong-Xiao Hezuoshe Zongshe [Ministry of Finance, Ministry of Justice and National All-China General Office of Supply and Marketing Cooperatives], Guanyu Geji Renmin Fayuan Chuli Moshou, Zhuijiao, Paimai Wupin De Lianhe Tongzhi [Joint Notice on the Handling by People's Courts of Confiscation, Forced Payments and Auctions] (Sept. 10, 1956) (text not available); Sifa Bu [Ministry of Justice], Guanyu Weituo Zhixing Wenti De Tongzhi [Notice on Problems in Entrusted Execution] (June 18, 1957), *in* 2 MSCZ, *supra* note 1, at 418 [hereinafter 1957 MOJ Notice]; Zuigao Renmin Fayuan [Supreme People's Court], Guanyu Lihun Anjian Zhong Dui Caichan Chuli Ruhe Qiangzhi Zhixing Wenti De Pifu [Reply on the Question of How to Execute by Compulsion a Disposition of Property in a Divorce Case] (Dec. 9, 1963), *in* 2 MSCZ, *supra* note 1, at 743 [hereinafter 1963 SPC Reply]; Zuigao Renmin Fayuan [Supreme People's Court], Guanyu Qiangzhi Zhixing Minshi Caichan Anjian De Panjue Bu Xu Ling Xia Caiding De Pifu [Reply Stating That When Executing by Compulsion Judgments in Civil Cases Involving Property, It Is Not Necessary to Issue a Separate Ruling] (May 19, 1964), *in* 2 MSCZ, *supra* note 1, at 744 [hereinafter 1964 SPC Reply]; Zuigao Renmin Fayuan, Zhongguo Renmin Yinhang [Supreme People's Court, People's Bank of China], Zhuanfa Shanghai Shi Gaoji Renmin Fayuan Guanyu Renmin Fayuan Zhixing Minshi Panjue Xiang Yinhang Diaoqu Dangshiren Cunkuan Wenti De Tongzhi [Transmittal of the Shanghai People's Court Notice on the Problem of People's Courts' Levying on a Party's Bank Account When Implementing Civil Judgments] (June 16, 1980), *in* 2 MSCZ, *supra* note 1, at 745.

68. *See* Liu Shaotang, *Youguan Zhixing Gongzuo Ji-Ge Zhuyao Wenti De Yi-Xie Yijian* [*Some Ideas About Some Important Problems in Execution Work*], SIFA GONGZUO TONGXUN [BULLETIN OF JUDICIAL WORK], No. 12, at 13 (1956).

69. *See* Marriage Law, *supra* note 37, art. 35.

70. *See* Zuigao Renmin Fayuan [Supreme People's Court], Guanyu Shiyong Zhonghua Renmin Gongheguo Minshi Susong Fa Ruogan Wenti De Yijian [Opinion on Several Issues in the Application of the People's Republic of China Law on Civil Procedure], SPCG, No.3, Sept. 20, 1992, at 70 [hereinafter 1992 SPC Civil Procedure Opinion].

71. *See* Zuigao Renmin Fayuan [Supreme People's Court], Guanyu Xuexi, Xuanchuan, Guanche Minshi Susong Fa De Tongzhi [Notice on Studying, Publicizing, and Implementing the Law on Civil Procedure] (May 24, 1991), *in* ZHONGGUO FALÜ NIANJIAN 1992 [LAW YEARBOOK OF CHINA 1992], at 531 (1992) [hereinafter 1991 SPC Notice] ("With respect to judicial interpretations issued by the Supreme People's Court over the years in the field of civil procedure, all that conflict with the

existence of a conflict. If the new law declines to regulate a matter regulated under the old law, for example, is the rule of the old law in conflict?

Other gaps and ambiguities remain as well. For example, when a non-party objects to execution — generally on the grounds that property being seized is his and not the debtor's — execution officers are instructed by the Law on Civil Procedure to investigate the matter "according to the procedures prescribed by law."[72] This phrase was added in the 1991 revision — but there still exist no legally prescribed procedures for the investigation of such objections.[73]

2. Procedure

This section will introduce and classify the formal mechanisms of execution in order to set the stage for the analysis of the rest of the paper.

Execution in civil and economic cases is generally governed by the 1991 Law on Civil Procedure. Courts have the authority to execute a number of different documents. First are court judgments or rulings in civil cases in which appeals have been exhausted ("legally effective" judgments). These are to be executed by the court of first instance.[74] These judgments or rulings include court-sponsored mediation agreements[75] as

---

Law on Civil Procedure shall no longer be implemented."); *Zuigao Renmin Fayuan Dui Guanche Zhixing Minshi Susong Fa (Shixing) De Yi-Xie Yijian, Jieda, Pifu, Dafu Deng Shi Fou Hai You Xiao?* [*Are Various Opinions, Answers, Replies, Responses, Etc. Issued by the Supreme People's Court Respecting the Implementation of the Law on Civil Procedure (for Trial Implementation) Still in Effect?*], RENMIN SIFA, No. 1, at 46 (1992) (elaborating on 1991 SPC Notice).

72. Law on Civil Procedure, *supra* note 34, art. 208.

73. See Ke Changxin, *Guanyu Zhiding Qiangzhi Zhixing Fa De Jianyi* [*A Proposal on the Formulation of a Law on Compulsory Execution*], ZHENG-FA LUNTAN [POLITICAL-LEGAL FORUM], No. 2, at 95 (1992), who makes this complaint. It should be noted that the law of the Republic of China on Taiwan, which allows for objections from execution debtors as well as non-parties, does not provide much in the way of procedure either, although there are a few rules. *See* Qiangzhi Zhixing Fa [Law on Compulsory Execution], arts. 12-16, *in* ZUIXIN SHIYONG LIU FA QUAN SHU [NEWEST PRACTICAL COMPLETE BOOK OF THE SIX LAWS] 334 (Shi Maolin & Liu Qingjing eds., 1992).

74. *See* Law on Civil Procedure, *supra* note 34, art. 207. The same applies to any part of a criminal judgment or ruling calling for the transfer of property. *See id.*

75. *See* Law on Civil Procedure, *supra* note 34, art. 215; MINSHI SUSONG FA DE XIUGAI YU SHIYONG [THE REVISION AND APPLICATION OF THE LAW ON CIVIL PROCEDURE] 226 (Ma Yuan & Tang Dehua eds., 1991). It would seem that mediation agreements reached outside of court are not directly executable. Given the stipulation of article 215 ("The provisions of this book shall apply to the execution of bills of mediation issued by a People's Court"), this seems to be the only way of explaining the deletion of "mediation agreements" from the list of documents that can be executed by courts in the 1991 revision of the Law on Civil Procedure. *Compare* 1982 Law on Civil Procedure, *supra* note 34, art. 161 *with* Law on Civil Procedure, *supra* note 34, art. 207. For examples of execution of court-sponsored mediation agreements, see *Fushun Shi Zhongji Renmin Fayuan Dui Bu*

well as any ruling calling for the preservation of property during litigation or the preliminary transfer of property pending final resolution.[76] Courts may also in theory — although it is not known to have occurred — give direct effect to foreign judgments and arbitration awards by means of a ruling, and this ruling may be executed by compulsion.[77]

Second, "other legal documents" that are by law supposed to be executed by courts shall be executed by the court in the place of the execution debtor's residence or in the place of the property being executed against.[78] These "other legal documents" include orders of administrative

---

Zhixing Tiaojie Shu Zhe Caiqu Qiangzhi Cuoshi [*Fushun Intermediate Level People's Court Adopts Compulsory Measures Against Those Who Do Not Implement Bills of Mediation*], ZHONGGUO FAZHI BAO [CHINA LEGAL SYSTEM NEWS], Nov. 27, 1981, at 2; *Sihui Fayuan Fengtiao, Kangju Qiangzhi Zhixing, Xu Guilan Bei Yi Fa Juliu* [*Xu Guilan Rips Up Court Sealing Strips, Resists Compulsory Execution, Is Detained According to Law*], SHANGHAI FAZHI BAO [SHANGHAI LEGAL SYSTEM NEWS], Dec. 29, 1986, at 1; Qi Yaochao, Yu Maoqing, Chen Kezhi Fanghai Minshi Tiaojie Zhixing Bei Fakuan, Juliu An [The Case of Qi Yaochao, Yu Maoqing, and Chen Kezhi, Who Obstructed the Execution of Civil Mediation and Were Fined and Detained], *in* SPCG, No. 3, Sept. 20, 1991, at 44. On mediation in general and court-sponsored mediation in particular, see Donald C. Clarke, *Dispute Resolution in China*, 5 J. CHINESE L. 245, 256-257, 268-286, 294-296 (1996) (noting the sometimes coercive nature of mediation).

76. *See Nei-Xie Falü Wenshu Keyi Zuowei Fayuan Qiangzhi Zhixing De Genju?* [*Which Laws Can Form the Basis for Compulsory Execution by a Court?*], JIANGXI FAZHI BAO [JIANGXI LEGAL SYSTEM NEWS], July 22, 1988, at 3 [hereinafter *Which Laws?*].

77. *See* Law on Civil Procedure, *supra* note 34, arts. 268-269; *Which Laws?*, *supra* note 76. To execute a foreign judgment, a Chinese court must find that a relevant treaty or reciprocity exists between the foreign jurisdiction and China. A bilateral judicial assistance agreement is not, strictly speaking, necessary. In practice, enforcement by a Chinese court of a foreign judgment is virtually unknown. *See* Wang Changying, *Zhengque Yunyong Shenpan Jingji Anjian De Qiangzhi Cuoshi* [*Correctly Use Compulsory Measures in Adjudicating Economic Cases*], SHENZHEN FAZHI BAO [SHENZHEN LEGAL SYSTEM NEWS], July 23, 1990, at 7. In 1994, the Dalian Intermediate Level People's Court, essentially folding the reciprocity requirement into the treaty requirement, found a treaty lacking and thus rejected the application of a Japanese national to enforce the judgment of a Japanese court. *See* Riben Gongmin Wuwei Huang Shenqing Zhongguo Fayuan Chengren He Zhixing Riben Fayuan Panjue An [The Case of the Application of Japanese Citizen Gomi Akira to a Chinese Court for the Recognition and Execution of a Japanese Court Judgment], SPCG, No. 1, Mar. 20, 1996, at 29. This case is especially interesting because the judgment did not, strictly speaking, affect the wealth of Chinese nationals: a Japanese creditor was attempting to realize on the assets in China of a Japanese debtor.

78. *See* Wang, *supra* note 77. The language of the 1991 Law on Civil Procedure is an improvement on that of the 1982 Law on Civil Procedure, which spoke vaguely only of "the court having jurisdiction" without giving guidance on how to determine which court had jurisdiction. The 1991 law simply codifies the solution already reached in a 1984 Supreme People's Court document addressing precisely this issue. *See* Zuigao Renmin Fayuan [Supreme People's Court], Guanyu Renmin Fayuan Yi Shengxiao De Falü Wenshu Shi Fou Shiyong Minshi Susong Fa (Shixing) Di-Yibaishijiu Tiao Guiding De Shenqing Zhixing Qixian Deng Wenti De Pifu [Reply on the Question of Whether the Provisions of Article 169 of the Law on Civil Procedure (For Trial Implementation) on the Time Limit for Applications for Execution Apply to Legal Documents of a People's Court That Have Taken Effect, and Other Questions] (Aug. 15, 1988), *in* ZHIXING GONGZUO SHOUCE, *supra* note 15, at 180. On the other hand, it fails to address the problem that in any given place in China,

agencies that apply for compulsory execution,[79] final decisions of a state arbitration organ,[80] and an instrument evidencing debt that has been given compulsory effect by a state notarial organ.[81] The status of bills of

---

four courts — one at each level of the hierarchy — all have geographical jurisdiction. Probably the Basic Level or the Intermediate Level People's Court are intended, as they are the most likely to have execution chambers.

79. *See* MINSHI SUSONG FA DE XIUGAI YU SHIYONG, *supra* note 75, at 224. Such orders might come, for example, from the State Administration of Industry and Commerce, the Customs Administration, or a local land administration bureau. In one typical case, the defendant was ordered by the county land administration bureau to tear down an illegal structure; he refused but did not appeal to a court. The bureau then went to the court seeking compulsory execution of the order. The court then issued an order for compulsory execution, and tore the structure down itself when the defendant still refused. *See Shenpan Chengxu He Zhixing Chengxu; Shenqing Zhixing He Yisong Zhixing* [*The Adjudication Process and the Execution Process; Application for Execution and Transferred Execution*], JILIN FAZHI BAO [JILIN LEGAL SYSTEM NEWS], Sept. 20, 1988, at 1 [hereinafter *Adjudication Process*]. Similar cases are reported in *Minhe Xian Fayuan Zhixing Yi-Qi Zhaijidi Jiufen* [*Minhe County Court Executes a Judgment in a Dispute over Residential Land*], FAZHI DAOBAO [LEGAL SYSTEM HERALD], Aug. 26, 1988, at 3; *Weizhang Jianfang Bei Fayuan Qiangxing Chaichu* [*House Built in Violation of Regulations Is Forcibly Torn Down by Court*], ANHUI FAZHI BAO [ANHUI LEGAL SYSTEM NEWS], Sept. 7, 1988, at 1; *Yi Nong Hu Chaozhan Tudi Jian Fang Bei Qiangzhi Chaichu* [*House Built by Farmer Occupying Excessive Land Is Forcibly Torn Down*], YUNNAN FAZHI BAO [YUNNAN LEGAL SYSTEM NEWS], Nov. 11, 1988, at 2. According to one source, the State Council is in the process of formulating a set of regulations specifically addressing the issue of compulsory execution of administrative orders. *See* CHANG, *supra* note 44, at 14.

80. *See* 1992 SPC Civil Procedure Opinion, *supra* note 70, art. 256. Note, however, that the law allows defendants a number of grounds for in effect appealing the arbitration decision to the executing court — for example, errors of law or fact. *See* Law on Civil Procedure, *supra* note 34, art. 217.

81. *See* 1992 SPC Civil Procedure Opinion, *supra* note 70, art. 256. The general idea behind this provision is that if a notary office certifies the existence of a debt about which there is no question, a court may compel repayment of the debt without a trial. The proposition that courts may directly enforce documents evidencing indebtedness dates back as a legal matter at least to 1956. *See* Sifa Bu [Ministry of Justice], Guanyu Zhengming You Qiangzhi Zhixing De Xiaoli De Fanwei Deng Wenti De Pifu [Reply on the Scope of Certification of Compulsory Executability and Other Problems] (Sept. 20, 1956), *in* MINSHI SUSONGFA CANKAO ZILIAO [REFERENCE MATERIALS ON THE LAW OF CIVIL PROCEDURE], vol. II, part 3 [hereinafter 2A MSCZ], at 65 (Zhongguo Shehui Kexueyuan Faxue Yanjiusuo Minfa Yanjiushi Min-Su Zu, Beijing Zheng-Fa Xueyuan Minshi Susong Jiaoyanshi [Civil Procedure Group of the Civil Law Research Section of the Institute of Law of the Chinese Acadeny of Social Sciences and the Civil Procedure Law Teaching and Research Section of the Beijing Institute of Politics and Law] eds., 1982) [hereinafter 1956 MOJ Reply] ("With respect to documents evidencing debt about which there is genuinely no doubt, . . . if subsequently they should be carried out and are not carried out, the notarial organ may give a certification of compulsory executability."). It is not necessary that the original debt be evidenced by notarized documents. *See id.*

The provision may come from pre-1949 Republic of China (ROC) law. *See* Gongzheng Fa [Law on Notaries], art. 11, *in* XIANXING FALING DAQUAN (ZHONG) [COMPENDIUM OF CURRENT STATUTES (II)] 182 (Zhang Jingxiu ed., 1947), *as amended in* ZUIXIN SHIYONG LIU FA QUAN SHU, *supra* note 73, at 359. The PRC version is, however, a little different. The ROC law appears to give the defendant a chance to bring suit to overturn the notary's certification. The PRC version says that the notariat should provide certification only where there is "no doubt," but has no procedure for challenge. Article 218 of the 1991 Law on Civil Procedure states that courts should not execute such documents where it finds "genuine error," but provides no procedure for determining whether such error exists. Moreover, neither the Law on Civil Procedure nor the PRC Law on Notaries stipulates any procedure to be used by the notary office in determining whether any doubt exists about the indebtedness. *See* Guowu Yuan [State Council], Zhonghua Renmin Gongheguo Gongzheng Zanxing Tiaoli [People's Republic of China Provisional Regulations on Notarization] (Apr. 13, 1982), *in* ZHIXING GONGZUO SHOUCE, *supra* note 15, at 282.

There appears to be considerable confusion among the commentators on the point of procedure. One article asserts that notaries may provide certification only where no dispute exists, but goes on to specify a number of things that they should investigate — for example, whether the signer (in the case of a corporate debtor) had the authority to act, whether there was a genuine manifestation of intent, and other legally complex matters. *See* Huang Yongming & Tong Jianxin, *Dui Zhaiquan Wenshu Banli Qiangzhi Zhixing Gongzheng Zhi Chutan* [*An Initial Investigation Into the Giving by Notaries of Compulsory Executability to Debt Documents*], HEBEI FAXUE [HEBEI LEGAL STUDIES], No. 3, at 38 (1990). If there is no dispute over the debt, none of these matters should require investigation. If there is a dispute, then surely this is precisely where the rules of the Law on Civil Procedure should apply, and these quintessentially legal questions should be resolved in court.

According to the Supreme People's Court, notariats cannot certify the obligations contained in ordinary contracts as directly executable. *See* Zuigao Renmin Fayuan, Sifa Bu [Supreme People's Court and Ministry of Justice], Guanyu Yi Gongzheng De Zhaiquan Wenshu Yi Fa Qiangzhi Zhixing Wenti De Dafu [Response on the Question of Compulsory Execution According to Law of Debt Documents That Have Been Notarized] (April 9, 1985), *in* ZHONGHUA RENMIN GONGHEGUO FALÜ GUIFANXING JIESHI JICHENG [COLLECTED NORMATIVE INTERPRETATIONS OF THE LAWS OF THE PEOPLE'S REPUBLIC OF CHINA] [hereinafter NORMATIVE INTERPRETATIONS] 994 (1990). There must be something more — for example, a document showing that the person against whom execution is sought has agreed in advance to such execution if the debt is not paid. *See* ZHIXING DE LILUN YU SHIJIAN [THE THEORY AND PRACTICE OF EXECUTION] 7-9 (Liang Shuwen ed., 1993). In the words of one Western commentator,

> The probable intended meaning of [old] CPL Article 168 is that the creditor is required to produce a notarized document that establishes that the debtor is in default before a court will endorse execution proceedings. Such a document could not likely be produced if there were a dispute between debtor and creditor as to the existence of a default.

Christopher G. Oechsli, *The Developing Law of Mortgages and Secured Transactions in the People's Republic of China*, 5 CHINA L. REP. 1, 5 n.30.

In some cases, courts seem not to have paid sufficient attention to notarial certifications of executability. *See* Zuigao Renmin Fayuan, Sifa Bu [Supreme People's Court and Ministry of Justice], Guanyu Zhixing Minshi Susong Fa (Shixing) Zhong Sheji Gongzheng Tiaokuan De Ji-Ge Wenti De Tongzhi [Notice on Several Questions Related to the Provisions on Notarization in the Course of Implementing the Law on Civil Procedure (for Trial Implementation)] (Nov. 8, 1984) (on file with author) (instructing courts to give effect to such documents in accordance with the rules of the Law on Civil Procedure). In other cases, they seem to have gone too far, certifying as executable precisely those documents — ordinary contracts — they had been told to stay away from by the Supreme People's Court in 1985. *See Yinchuan Shi Gongzheng Chu, Yinchuan Shi Cheng Qu Renmin Fayuan Qiangzhi Zhixing Yi-Xiang Hetong* [*Yinchuan City Notary Office and Yinchuan City District Court Compulsorily Execute a Contract*], NINGXIA FAZHI BAO [NINGXIA LEGAL SYSTEM NEWS], Apr. 2, 1986, at 1; *Ju Bu Changfu Caizheng Zhouzhuanjin Yangniu Zhuanyehu Gao Mou Bei Qiangzhi Zhixing* [*Cattle-Raising Specialized Household Gao Refuses to Pay Back Circulating Capital Loan, Suffers Compulsory Execution*], TIANJIN FAZHI BAO [TIANJIN LEGAL SYSTEM NEWS], May 26, 1988, at 1; *Boyang Xian Gongzheng Chu Yunyong Qiangzhi Zhixing Shouduan Cujin Hetong Lüxing* [*Boyang County Notary Office Uses Compulsory Execution Methods to Promote the Carrying Out of Contracts*], JIANGXI FAZHI BAO [JIANGXI LEGAL SYSTEM NEWS], Dec. 14, 1990, at 1. In all these cases, plaintiffs took a contract they claimed had been breached to the notary office, obtained a

mediation issued by state arbitration organs was recently clarified after several years of confusion. In 1986, the Supreme People's Court issued a Notice saying that such bills could be executed by compulsion.[82] The statutory basis for this Notice, however, weak in the first place, later essentially disappeared as the provisions it cited in support were revised.[83] Nevertheless, it probably remained valid because subsequent legislation did not affirmatively rule out compulsory execution of such bills,[84] and a 1990 SPC document seemed to take for granted that they were executable by compulsion.[85] Although the 1991 Law on Civil Procedure makes no reference to the execution by courts of arbitration mediations, it does provide for the execution of arbitration decisions, and the recent Arbitration Law (effective on September 1, 1995) provides that arbitration mediations (*tiaojie shu*) have the same legal effect as arbitration decisions

---

certification of executability, and secured court execution of the certification.

82. *See* Zuigao Renmin Fayuan [Supreme People's Court], Guanyu Renmin Fayuan Dui Shenqing Qiangzhi Zhixing Zhongcai Jigou De Tiaojie Shu Ying Ruhe Chuli De Tongzhi [Notice on How People's Courts Should Dispose of Applications for the Compulsory Execution of Bills of Mediation Issued by Arbitration Organs] (Aug. 20, 1986), *in* NORMATIVE INTERPRETATIONS, *supra* note 81, at 995. *See also Xingzheng Tiaojie Shi Fou Keyi Qiangzhi Zhixing?* [*Is Administrative Mediation Subject to Compulsory Execution?*], TIANJIN FAZHI BAO [TIANJIN LEGAL SYSTEM NEWS], May 26, 1988, at 1 (citing other regulations in support of enforceability of arbitration mediations).

83. The Notice cited article 52, para. 3 of the 1981 Economic Contract Law (implying that any mediation agreement, let alone one sponsored by an arbitration organ, could be executed by compulsion) and article 166 and article 161, paragraph 2 of the 1982 Law on Civil Procedure. The last item was never convincing -- it just speaks to the executability of "other legal documents" without specifying further — and the references in the first two to the executability of mediation agreements of any kind were dropped in subsequent revisions. *Compare* Zhonghua Renmin Gongheguo Jingji Hetong Fa [People's Republic of China Law on Economic Contracts] (Dec. 13, 1981), 1981 FGHB 1, arts. 48, 49, translated in 2 CHINA'S FOREIGN ECONOMIC LEGISLATION 1 (1986), *with* Zhonghua Renmin Gongheguo Jingji Hetong Fa [People's Republic of China Law on Economic Contracts] (Sept. 2, 1993), art. 42, *in* SWB/FE, Oct. 6, 1993, at FE/W0302/WS1 (art. 52 of the old Economic Contract Law has been dropped entirely); *and compare* 1982 Law on Civil Procedure, *supra* note 34, art. 166 *with* Law on Civil Procedure, *supra* note 34, art. 216.

84. The relevant Supreme People's Court interpretation holds that prior interpretations, regulations, etc. remain in effect to the extent they do not conflict with subsequent legislation. As previously noted, *see supra* text accompanying note 71, whether a conflict exists is not as simple a question as the Supreme People's Court seems to think.

85. *See* Zuigao Renmin Fayuan [Supreme People's Court], Guanyu Shenqing Zhixing Gong-Shang Zhongcai Jigou Falü Wenshu Zhong De Bei Zhixing Ren Yi Bei Chexiao Ruhe Chuli Wenti De Pifu [Reply on the Question of What to Do when the Executee in an Application for the Execution of a Legal Document From an Industrial-Commercial Arbitration Organ Has Already Been Cancelled] (Nov. 14, 1990), *in* QUANGUO REN-DA FA-GONG-WEI, GUOWU YUAN FAZHI JU, ZUIGAO RENMIN FAYUAN, ZUIGAO RENMIN JIANCHAYUAN [NATIONAL PEOPLE'S CONGRESS LEGISLATIVE AFFAIRS COMMISSION, STATE COUNCIL LEGISLATIVE BUREAU, SUPREME PEOPLE'S COURT & SUPREME PEOPLE'S PROCURACY], GUOJIA FAGUI SHUJUKU [DATABASE OF STATE LAWS AND REGULATIONS] [hereinafter DATABASE] (CD-ROM database) [hereinafter 1990 SPC Reply].

(*caijue shu*).[86] That arbitration mediations may be subject to compulsory execution is also confirmed in passing by a recent Supreme People's Court Notice.[87]

Although nationwide statistics are hard to come by, what evidence there is suggests that the majority of cases sent to the execution chamber involve organizations such as enterprises, while only a minority of cases involve individuals.[88] The most common types of cases appear to be contract and debt cases between enterprises and individual debt cases.[89]

The execution process begins when a case is sent to the execution chamber, which can happen in a number of ways. When a court delivers an executable document or announces judgment, it is supposed to inform the parties of the rules regarding execution.[90] First, the judgment creditor can make an application (*shenqing*) for execution.[91] Second, the adjudicatory chamber that heard the case can transfer (*yisong*) it *sua sponte* to the

86. Zhonghua Renmin Gongheguo Zhongcai Fa [Arbitration Law of the People's Republic of China], NPCSCG, No. 6., Oct. 10, 1994, at 3, art. 51. An English translation can be found in SWB/FE, Oct. 6, 1994, at FE/2119/S1.

87. *See* Zuigao Renmin Fayuan [Supreme People's Court], Guanyu Renzhen Guanche Zhongcai Fa, Yi Fa Zhixing Zhongcai Caijue De Tongzhi [Notice on Conscientiously Implementing the Arbitration Law and Executing Arbitration Decision According to Law] (Oct. 4, 1995), *in* DATABASE, *supra* note 85.

88. *See* Court Interview F (70% of cases involve organizations, 30% involve individuals).

89. *See* Court Interview F; Guangzhou ILPC, *supra* note 53, at 1. Individual debt cases also appear to have the most potential for conflict. In one eleven-month period, a BLPC in Shanghai detained sixteen persons in fifteen cases, eleven of which involved debt. *See* Shanghai Shi Zhongji Renmin Fayuan [Shanghai Intermediate Level People's Court], *Dui Ju Bu Zhixing Fayuan Shengxiao Panjue Caiding De Xingwei Ren Shiyong Sifa Juliu Cuoshi De Tantao* [*An Exploration of the Use of Detention Against Persons Who Refuse to Carry Out Court Judgments and Rulings That Have Taken Legal Effect*], *in* CONFERENCE MATERIALS, *supra* note 42, at 2. Detention is a sanction used only in the most egregious circumstances.

90. *See* Zuigao Renmin Fayuan [Supreme People's Court], Guanyu Renmin Fayuan Yi Shengxiao De Falü Wenshu Shi Fou Shiyong Minshi Susong Fa (Shixing) Di-Yibaishijiu Tiao Guiding De Shenqing Zhixing Qixian Deng Wenti De Pifu [Reply on the Question of Whether the Provisions of Article 169 of the Law on Civil Litigation (For Trial Implementation) on the Time Limit for Applications for Execution Apply to Legal Documents of a People's Court That Have Taken Effect, and Other Questions] (Aug. 15, 1988), *in* ZHIXING GONGZUO SHOUCE, *supra* note 15, at 189 [hereinafter 1988 SPC Reply 2].

91. *See* Law on Civil Procedure, *supra* note 34, art. 216. For a detailed account of the process of applying for execution, see Song Jian, *Tantan Shenqing Zhixing Shu De Shizuo* [*A Discussion of the Formulation of an Application for Implementation*], HEBEI FAXUE [HEBEI LEGAL STUDIES], No.1, at 47-48 (1988). The applicant must provide, in addition to the judgment the execution of which is sought, details on what exactly she wants done and why she wants it done as well as information on the finances and property of the defendant. *See Adjudication Process*, *supra* note 79.

execution chamber.[92] Among cases deemed suitable for transferred execution are judgments awarding support or medical expenses;[93] presumably this is because the funds are typically urgently needed and the plaintiff may be weak and intimidated.[94] Third, one court can request the execution chamber of another court to execute a judgment through the process of entrusted execution (*weituo zhixing*) when the execution debtor or his property is within the second court's area of geographical jurisdiction.[95]

The time limit for the application is one year where at least one party is a "citizen" (*gongmin*) and six months where both parties are legal persons or other organizations.[96] This rule has been in effect since the 1982 Law on Civil Procedure. When the judgment was made before the 1982 law, the rule appears to be that it is treated as if made on the date that law came into effect.[97]

---

92. *See* Law on Civil Procedure, *supra* note 34, art. 216. While China's is by no means yet a litigant-driven legal system, a small sign of a move in that direction can be seen in the 1991 revision of the Law on Civil Procedure. Whereas article 166 in the old law listed transferred execution before execution upon application, the successor article 216 of the new law puts execution upon application first, implying that it is the normal, preferred method.

93. *See* 1988 SPC Reply 2, *supra* note 90, at 189.

94. In one reported case, officials of a BLPC in Guangzhou read a newspaper report about two sons who refused to obey a court judgment ordering them to pay support to their aged father. The execution chamber went out to investigate, filled out the necessary forms on behalf of the father, and obtained the money. *See* Guangzhou ILPC, *supra* note 53, at 2.

95. *See* Law on Civil Procedure, *supra* note 34, art. 210. On entrusted execution generally, see Hefei Shi Zhongji Renmin Fayuan Zhixing Ting [Execution Chamber of the Hefei Intermediate Level People's Court], *Qiantan Weituo Zhixing* [*A Short Discussion of Entrusted Execution*], *in* CONFERENCE MATERIALS, *supra* note 42; Zhang Yuqi, *Ruhe Zhixing Yidi Jingji Hetong Jiufen Anjian* [*How to Execute in a Different Region in Economic Contract Dispute Cases*], JIANGXI FAZHI BAO [JIANGXI LEGAL SYSTEM NEWS], May 5, 1987, at 3. The problems associated with entrusted execution are discussed *infra* at text accompanying notes 196-205.

96. *See* Law on Civil Procedure, *supra* note 34, art. 219. It seems likely that the one-year limitation would apply to natural persons of foreign citizenship as well. *See, e.g.*, ZHONGGUO RENMIN GONGHEGUO BAIKE QUANSHU: FAXUE [GREAT ENCYCLOPEDIA OF CHINA: JURISPRUDENCE] 829 (1984) ("In China and some other countries, the term *gongmin* refers to natural persons."). *But see id.* at 164 ("*Gongmin* refers to a person . . . with the citizenship of a particular country."); MIN FA TONG ZE SHIYI [EXPLICATION OF THE GENERAL PROVISIONS OF CIVIL LAW] 11 (1987); FAXUE CIDIAN (ZENGDING BAN) [DICTIONARY OF JURISPRUDENCE (ENLARGED EDITION)] 142, 344 (1984) (distinguishing between citizens (*gongmin*) and natural persons (*ziran ren*)). To add to the confusion, the 1986 General Provisions of Civil Law head Chapter Two with the ambiguous title "Citizens (Natural Persons)."

97. In 1987, the Supreme People's Court ruled that the judgment in one case would not be executed, given that it was made in the early 1950s, no application for compulsory execution had been made until 1984 (over two years after the coming into effect of the Law on Civil Procedure), and there was no excuse for the lateness of the application. *See* Zuigao Renmin Fayuan [Supreme People's Court], Guanyu Dui Shengxiao Duonian De Panjue Yuqi Shenqing Zhixing De Yi Fa Bu Yu Zhichi De Pifu [Reply Stating That According to Law Overdue Applications for the Execution of Judgments

Specific procedures for execution are often formulated by HLPCs, at the provincial level.[98] According to the account of one ILPC execution chamber, proceedings generally begin within five days of receiving the application. The chamber investigates the financial situation of the execution debtor and then, according to its reading of the situation, either directly takes measures to begin execution or summons the execution debtor to the court to attempt to persuade him to comply with the judgment.[99] According to another account, attempts to persuade the execution debtor to comply voluntarily would not go on for more than half a month.[100] The Beijing ILPC has formulated its own deadlines of three months to execute civil cases and six months to execute economic cases.[101]

Execution does not proceed forward inexorably once begun. In certain circumstances, such as when the execution debtor has no money, it can be suspended, to be revived when circumstances change.[102] In other

---

That Took Legal Effect Many Years Ago Will Not Be Supported] (Dec. 14, 1987), *in* ZHIXING GONGZUO SHOUCE, *supra* note 15, at 183. In 1989, the Court ruled in another case that execution should be granted where more than one year had passed between the judgment and the application, given that both events occurred before the passage of the 1982 Law on Civil Procedure and that the court in question was in part responsible for the fact that the judgment had not been executed for so many years following the application. *See* Zuigao Renmin Fayuan [Supreme People's Court], Guanyu Dui Minshi Susong Fa (Shixing) Shixing Qian Yijing Shenqing Zhixing Er Zhijin Wei Zhixing De Anjian Shi Fou Ying Yu Zhixing De Han [Letter on Whether Execution Should Be Had in Cases Where an Application for Execution Was Made Before Law on Civil Procedure (for Trial Implementation) Came Into Effect , But Execution Has Still Not Been Effected] (Aug. 15, 1989), *in* ZHONGHUA RENMIN GONGHEGUO FALÜ LIFA SIFA JIESHI ANLI DAQUAN [COMPLETE BOOK OF LEGISLATIVE AND JUDICIAL EXPLANATIONS AND CASES ON THE LAWS OF THE PEOPLE'S REPUBLIC OF CHINA] [hereinafter LEGISLATIVE EXPLANATIONS] 1238 (Xin Ru & Lu Chen eds., 1991). An example of a 1956 judgment executed in 1990 is reported in *Ershi-Nian Qian De Panjueshu Keyi Zhixing Ma?* [*May a Judgment From Twenty Years Ago Be Executed?*], YUNNAN FAZHI BAO [YUNNAN LEGAL SYSTEM NEWS], Feb. 23, 1990, at 3. For a full explanation of the statute of limitations issue, *see id.*

98. *See, e.g.*, Jiangsu HLPC 2, *supra* note 47, at 238.

99. *See* Guiyang Shi Zhongji Renmin Fayuan Zhixing Ting [Execution Chamber of the Guiyang Intermediate Level People's Court], *Zhengque Shiyong Falü Quebao Anjian de Zhixing* [*Use Law Correctly to Guarantee the Execution of Cases*], at 4, *in* CONFERENCE MATERIALS, *supra* note 42 [hereinafter 1992 Guiyang ILPC].

100. *See* Court Interview F.

101. *See* Beijing ILPC, *supra* note 42, at 5. Extensions are available when necessary. It is not clear what the consequences of failure both to meet a deadline and to get an extension are — perhaps a black mark in the record of the execution officer.

102. *See* ZHONGGOU MINSHI SUSONG FA JIAOCHENG [A COURSE IN THE LAW ON CIVIL PROCEDURE] 357 (Jiang Wei ed., 1990). Suspension occurs when the judgment creditor so requests, when a third party presents a well-founded objection, when a party dies or ceases to exist and it is necessary to wait for a successor to assume rights or bear obligations, and in "other circumstances" in the court's discretion. *See* Law on Civil Procedure, *supra* note 34, art. 234. Execution is also suspended after a court with proper jurisdiction decides to order a rehearing of the case. *See* Law on Civil Procedure, *supra* note 34, art. 183. Note that execution is not to be suspended in the time between the application for rehearing and the decision to order rehearing. On rehearing, see generally

circumstances, such as when the execution debtor has no prospects of ever having any money, execution can simply be terminated.[103]

IV. Scope of the Execution Problem

The issue of *zhixing nan* (difficulty in executing judgments) has received prominent coverage in the Chinese legal press for the last several years. From scattered complaints in the 1950s,[104] it has grown to become a regular feature of Supreme People's Court reports to the National People's Congress since 1988.[105] A recent report from a lower court pointed with alarm to the decline in the prestige of courts, attributing the unwillingness of enterprises and individuals with valid claims to litigate them to a simple reason: "The courts' judgments cannot be enforced. Not only can the debt not be recovered, but the expenses of litigation are lost as well."[106]

How bad are things really? It turns out that good statistics are simply not available on this matter. An extensive review of the literature failed to turn up a single serious study using well-defined categories. In particular,

---

infra text accompanying notes 160-171.

103. Article 235 of the Law on Civil Procedure lists the circumstances calling for an order terminating execution: where the judgment creditor revokes his request for execution, where the legal document forming the basis for execution is no longer valid, where the judgment debtor dies without property to satisfy the judgment, where the judgment creditor in a support case dies, where the judgment debtor is unable to pay because in "a difficult situation" without income and unable to work, and in other circumstances at the court's discretion. Interestingly, bankruptcy (either legal or actual) is not mentioned as grounds for termination.

104. *See, e.g.*, 1951 Dongbei Directive, *supra* note 63, at 714 (complaining that some court cadres don't even know what "compulsory execution" means); 1953 SPC-NC Directive, *supra* note 1, at 720 (noting failure to enforce judgments as a cause of "great dissatisfaction among the masses"); Tai Yingjie, *Tantan Women Fayuan De Zhixing Gongzuo* [*A Discussion of Our Court's Execution Work*], RENMIN SIFA GONGZUO [PEOPLE'S JUDICIAL WORK], No.3, at 20 (1957) (reporting complaints that courts could only talk, not act).

105. A mere thirteen characters ("Some judgments and rulings have not been executed") were allotted to the problem in Zheng Tianxiang's 1987 work report — a far cry from the three long paragraphs he devoted to it the following year, when he called it "the most outstanding problem in economic adjudication." Zheng Tianxiang, *Zuigao Renmin Fayuan Gongzuo Baogao* [*Supreme People's Court Work Report*] (April 6, 1987), SPCG, No. 2, June 20, 1987, at 12; Zheng, *supra* note 2, at 8.

106. Nanning Shi Zhongji Renmin Fayuan [Nanning Intermediate Level People's Court], *Guanyu Kaizhan Anjian Zhixing Huizhan De Yixie Zuofa He Tihui* [*Some Understandings Derived From Carrying Out an Execution Attack in Cases*], at 10-11, *in* CONFERENCE MATERIALS, *supra* note 42 [hereinafter 1992 Nanning ILPC]. Thus, although the supposed disinclination of the Chinese to litigate is frequently attributed to mysterious cultural forces, it may turn out that the Chinese, like practical people anywhere, do not engage in activities where the expected cost is greater than the expected return. For a now-classic exposition of this argument with relation to Japan, see John O. Haley, *The Myth of the Reluctant Litigant*, 4 J. JAPANESE STUD. 359 (1978).

the available literature often fails to distinguish between the referral rate — the number (or, depending on the context, the percentage) of judgments referred to the execution chambers for execution — and the overall success rate — the number (or, depending on the context, the percentage) of judgments actually enforced. Moreover, when discussing the success rate as a percentage, the literature often fails to make clear whether it is a percentage of judgments of a given type, or only of those referred to the execution chamber for execution.

In his often-cited 1988 report to the National People's Congress, Supreme People's Court president Zheng Tianxiang said that 20 percent of judgments in economic cases went unenforced in 1985 and 1986, while about 30 percent went unenforced in 1987.[107] Other authors say that of judgments having executable content in civil, economic, criminal, and administrative cases, about 30 percent are not enforced,[108] while still another author puts the number at over 50 percent.[109] (It is impossible to tell from the context whether the residual category is "fully enforced" or "fully or partially enforced.")

Unfortunately, it is not possible to confirm or dispute these claims using available statistics from other sources. The most commonly available statistics provide the number or percentage of judgments successfully enforced by the execution chamber. It is extremely difficult, however, to find a number indicating the total number of cases where execution could have been required — *i.e.*, where the defendant was required to hand over money or property or to perform some act. Thus, if defendants voluntarily performed their obligations in 95 percent of all cases where obligations were imposed, then a 10 percent execution rate on the remaining 5 percent, while certainly telling us something about the weakness of the execution chamber, would not indicate an alarming state of affairs in the legal system in general.

It is possible to construct a range of possible values using available statistics. First, we can find the maximum number of judgments and other

---

107. *See* Zheng, *supra* note 2, at 8. The sample of which this percentage represents a part would reasonably be the total number of cases resulting in a judgment having executable content in favor of the plaintiff. As Zheng did not say so, however, we do not know for sure. I believe that the sample is not limited to those cases that were referred for execution.

108. *See* Gu Lianhuang & Zhu Zhongming, *Qianghua Zhixing Gongzuo, Weihu Falü Zunyan* [*Strengthen Execution Work, Uphold the Dignity of the Law*], RENMIN SIFA [PEOPLE'S JUDICATURE], No. 4, at 3, 3 (1989). The authors provide no source for this number.

109. *See* Qian Yongchang, *Lun Shen-Zhi Fenli, Zhixing Fenliu* [*On The Separation of Adjudication from Execution and the Separate Process for Execution*], FAZHI JIANSHE [CONSTRUCTION OF THE LEGAL SYSTEM], No. 1, at 16, 16 (1990).

decisions that could possibly need execution in a given year, even though the real number is almost certainly lower. In 1989, a year for which there are fairly good numbers, courts completed first-instance proceedings in 1.8 million civil cases (mostly marriage and divorce, debts, and tort claims) and over 670,000 economic cases (among them bank loans, sales contracts, and rural contracting disputes).[110]

Next, we can obtain an approximation of the referral rate by finding the number of civil and economic cases referred to the execution chamber in that year.[111] In 1989, courts nationwide docketed 480,000 civil cases and 250,000 economic cases for execution.[112] If we assume that all first instance proceedings in 1989 resulted in judgments in favor of plaintiffs having executable content, then the referral rate is about 27 percent for civil cases and 37 percent for economic cases. Since that assumption is clearly unrealistic, the real referral rate must be higher. The minimum number of judgments in favor of plaintiffs having executable content is, of course, the number referred, which yields a referral rate of 100 percent.

We can also arrive at some estimates for 1992. In that year, courts accepted about 1.8 million civil cases[113] and about 600,000 economic cases.[114] The total number of cases sent to execution chambers was "almost

---

110. *See* Ren Jianxin, *Zuigao Renmin Fayuan Gongzuo Baogao* [*Supreme People's Court Work Report*] (Mar. 29, 1990), SPCG, No. 2, June 20, 1990, at 5, 8-9. Space constraints unfortunately forbid a full discussion of the methodological issues involved in using these numbers. They are obviously not perfect but I believe they will do. I should, however, highlight a few problems that can occur when using first-instance judgments as the denominator and judgments sent to the execution chamber as the numerator.

Not all judgments will be in favor of plaintiffs, and not all judgments in favor of plaintiffs (for example, adjustments of legal status) require execution. Because parties to litigation are allowed one appeal before they are obliged to perform under the terms of the judgment, a better upper-limit figure would be one for second-instance cases completed. I could not find this number. A first-instance case completed in 1989 might not be ready for execution until a subsequent year. On the other hand, first-instance cases completed in prior years would be coming on line for execution in 1989. Given a trend of increasing litigation, the number of cases lost to future years in this way probably slightly exceeds the number of cases picked up from prior years. This assumption is supported by a chart showing that in 1990, courts had an intake of 116,000 civil and 35,000 economic cases in second instance, while disposing of 114,000 civil and 33,000 economic cases: a real but minor difference. *See* ZHONGGUO FALÜ NIANJIAN 1991 [LAW YEARBOOK OF CHINA 1991], at 936 (1991).

111. It is only an approximation because there will be some cases in which the year of final judgment and the year of referral for execution are different. The extra referrals from the beginning of the year will not exactly match the lost referrals from cases judged but not referred at the end of the year if the rate of referral or the absolute number of cases heard changes from year to year.

112. *See* Yu Lingyu, *Guanyu Dangqian Zhixing Wenti De Ji-Dian Sikao* [*Some Thoughts About the Current Problems in Execution*], RENMIN SIFA [PEOPLE'S JUDICATURE], No.1, at 26, 26 (1991).

113. *See* Ren, *Strengthen Adjudication*, *supra* note 49, at 11.

114. *See id.*, at 6.

one million."[115] Since over 95 percent of execution cases are civil or economic,[116] this yields a minimum referral rate of about 40 percent and a maximum of, again, 100 percent. This is a higher number than that for 1989, but is of the same general order of magnitude, and squares with reports that the situation is getting worse.

Finally, we can derive an overall success rate by comparing the sum of the number of cases successfully enforced and the number of cases not referred against the total number of cases with executable content. Nationally, the reported success rate on referred cases was about 80 percent in 1993.[117] Assuming the 1992 and 1993 numbers are similar, it would mean that defendants paid in a maximum of 92 percent of all cases with an executable judgment in favor of plaintiffs (again, subject to some very unrealistic assumptions), and in a minimum of 32 percent of such cases.

There are also some interesting regional numbers. In 1989, execution chambers in Jiangsu claimed to have successfully executed about 70 percent of the cases sent their way.[118] In 1989 and 1990, slightly over half the cases brought to execution chambers in Wuhan could be executed according to the terms of the judgment.[119] A similar rate — about half — is reported for Shenzhen.[120] Other cities report remarkably high rates of execution. Xi'an reported an 82 percent success rate in execution from 1987 to 1991 inclusive.[121] From 1989 to early 1992, Fuzhou reported a success rate of 96 percent.[122] And the Intermediate Level People's Court (ILPC) of Urumqi reported a 100 percent success rate in economic cases in 1985, with a 99 percent success rate in economic and civil cases combined.[123]

---

115. *Id.*, at 12.

116. *See* Yu, *supra* note 112, at 26.

117. *See* ZHONGGUA FALÜ NIANJIAN 1994, *supra* note 21, at 102.

118. *See* Jiangsu Sheng Gaoji Renmin Fayuan, *supra* note 47, at 5. In that year, 19% of civil cases and 38% of civil cases required execution proceedings. *See id.* at 6.

119. *See* Ke, *supra* note 73, at 96. Another 43% had to be implemented through some kind of "alternate" execution process, meaning probably that the plaintiff did not get what it wanted. A loose interpretation of what counts as "successful execution" probably accounts for the 90% successful execution rate reported for the same period in the same city in *Wuhan Liangji Fayuan Like "Zhixing Nan"* [*Courts at Two Levels in Wuhan Firmly Overcome "Difficulty in Execution"*], FAZHI RIBAO [LEGAL SYSTEM DAILY], Feb. 22, 1993, at 1.

120. *See Weile Falü De Zunyan* [*For the Dignity of the Law*], SHENZHEN FAZHI BAO [SHENZHEN LEGAL SYSTEM NEWS], Sept. 26, 1990, at 1.

121. *See* Xi'an ILPC, *supra* note 43, at 3.

122. *See* 1992 Fuzhou ILPC, *supra* note 44, at 2.

123. *See Gongping Wu Si, Yan Yu Zhi Fa* [*Fair and Impartial, Strict in Upholding the Law*], XINJIANG FAZHI BAO [XINJIANG LEGAL SYSTEM NEWS], Dec. 26, 1987, at 2.

It would seem that the only lesson to be drawn from the available statistics is that they are not very useful. Even if we were able to arrive at some kind of number to represent a referral rate or an overall success rate, it would be risky to draw any conclusions from such a number.

First, the numbers given for "unexecuted judgments" typically include cases where the defendant is simply insolvent. Business is risky; bad debts happen. Failure to execute a judgment where the debtor is insolvent bears no relation to court power or state capacity. In many places, however, debtor insolvency accounts for a sizable proportion of unexecuted judgments: the Jiangxi Higher Level People's Court reported that out of 473 debt cases it surveyed, the decision in 277 had not been enforced; the failure to enforce in 166 of those cases was due simply to debtor insolvency, as opposed to the other 111 cases where it was due to debtor intransigence.[124] On the other hand, what is reported as insolvency *may* reflect court weakness if, for example, the debtor's administrative superior is by law responsible for the debt but succesfully resists paying it, or if the debtor, while short of cash in the bank, has a valuable factory building or other property that the court is for some reason unable or unwilling to exercise its legal right to seize.[125]

Second, the number given for "executed judgments" may include cases where the plaintiff was persuaded by the court to accept less than it was entitled to.[126] In one case, the court persuaded the plaintiff to forgive 50 percent of the interest due on a debt. The debtor then paid. This case was described as "smoothly executed" and no doubt went into the statistical records as such.[127]

---

124. *See* Jiangxi Sheng Gaoji Renmin Fayuan Jingji Shenpan Ting [Economic Adjudication Chamber of the Jiangxi Province Higher Level People's Court], *Ruhe Jiejue Zhaiwu Anjian Zhixing Nan De Wenti?* [*How to Solve the Problem of Difficulty in Executing Debt Cases*], JIANGXI FAZHI BAO [JIANGXI LEGAL SYSTEM NEWS], Oct. 2, 1987, at 3 [hereinafter Jiangxi HLPC]. Unfortunately, these categories are not as neat as they might seem at first. Failure to execute a judgment against an insolvent enterprise that "can't" pay may reflect the inability of the court to make its administrative superior bear responsibility even where it should do so. This problem is discussed in more detail below.

125. For more on the complex issue of real or apparent debtor insolvency, *see infra* text accompanying notes 227-240.

126. See the discussion in note 119 *supra*.

127. *See* SHENZHEN JINGJI TEQU SHENPAN SHIJIAN [ADJUDICATION PRACTICE IN THE SHENZHEN SPECIAL ECONOMIC ZONE] 140 (1990). See also Wuhan Shi Zhongji Renmin Fayuan [Wuhan Intermediate Level People's Court], *Yunyong Duozhong Biantong Zhixing Fangshi, Jiji Jiejue Jingji Jiufen Anjian Zhixing Nan Wenti* [*Actively Solve the Problem of Difficulty in Execution in Cases of Economic Disputes by Using Many Methods of Alternative Execution*], *in* "ZHIXING NAN" DUICE TAN, *supra* note 49, at 19, where cases executed via "alternative execution" (*biantong zhixing*) are counted as bringing up the execution rate. "Alternative execution" means execution

Third, for a number of reasons a judgment may simply not be issued against a defendant where it would be difficult to execute.[128] Courts have traditionally operated under a policy, formalized in Article 6 of the 1982 Law on Civil Procedure, of stressing mediation over adjudication. (The formal requirement of preferring mediation was abolished in the 1991 Law on Civil Procedure.) In practice, this meant that court officials were expected to dispose of about 80 percent of their caseload through mediation.[129] A policy that pressures courts to find a settlement gives an advantage to the stubborner party; it could artificially raise the execution rate because defendants would refuse to agree to a settlement that they were not prepared to carry out voluntarily.

Moreover, court officials have an incentive not to issue judgments that they foresee will be difficult to execute. They are assessed in part on the number of cases they handle. Because a case is not considered completed until successfully executed, their record looks bad if cases drag on and on. In addition, they may be subject to continued importuning and harassment by the dissatisfied judgment creditor until the judgment is executed.[130]

There is ample evidence that the perception of executability influences the substantive content of the judgment, and indeed whether the court accepts the case at all. As early as 1950, one court criticized its own erroneous past practice:

> [W]e held that the judgment should be based on the actual ability of the debtor to carry it out. For example, if *A* owed *B* 200 *yuan*, and in practice was able to repay only 100 *yuan*, then the judgment could only require him to repay 100 *yuan*.[131]

---

where the creditor takes something other than what the judgment says he is owed — for example, goods instead of cash. In practice it includes simply forgiving some of the indebtedness.

128. *See generally* Cheng Cheng, Liu Jiaxing & Cheng Yanling, *Guanyu Woguo Minshi Zhixing Zhong De Jige Wenti* [*On Some Problems in Civil Execution in China*], FAXUE YANJIU [STUDIES IN LAW], No. 1, at 44 (1982); ZHIXING DE LILUN YU SHIJIAN, *supra* note 81, at 35 (some courts "won't accept a case unless the judgment in it can be executed, and won't hand down a judgment that can't be executed.").

129. *See* Academic Interview L; Court Interview F.

130. *See* Lawyer Interview R.

131. Beijing Renmin Fayuan [Beijing People's Court], *Minshi Zhixing Gongzuo De Gaijin* [*Progress in Civil Execution Work*] (1950), *in* ZHONGHUA RENMIN GONGHEGUO XING MIN SHI SUSONG CANKAO ZILIAO [REFERENCE MATERIALS ON CRIMINAL AND CIVIL PROCEDURE IN THE PEOPLE'S REPUBLIC OF CHINA] 294, 295 (Wuhan Daxue Falü Xi Xing Min Fa Jiaoyanzu [Criminal and Civil Law Teaching and Research Group of the Wuhan University Department of Law] ed., 1954).

When I explored with one group of court officials in 1992 the question of how to enforce an eviction judgment against a tenant with no place to move to, they said the question would not arise because if the tenant had no place to go, the judgment would not have been issued in the first place.[132] Many courts are reluctant to accept divorce cases where the parties have not already solved the housing problem, since the result otherwise will be unmarried persons of different sexes sharing the same living quarters.[133] A Jiangsu court was praised by the provincial court for its rule whereby no chamber could send more than seven percent of its cases to the execution chamber. "This way, the adjudication officers are forced to give thorough consideration to execution when they are hearing the case."[134] An article praising a local court for having achieved a 95.5 percent execution rate explained how they did it: "The Lianhu court first of all . . . considers execution problems at the time of adjudicating the case, and exercises strict control over the acceptance of cases (*yange bahao li'an guan*)."[135] In other words, if the court foresees execution problems, it will not even give the plaintiff a chance to plead his case, let alone issue a favorable judgment.[136]

Finally, we simply do not know how much execution would constitute a good rate. If the marginal cost of execution rises as one approaches 100 percent, at some point it may not be socially worth it any more. Why should society bear the cost of recovering every ill-considered loan? As one academic remarked, "Courts are adjudication organs, not collection agencies."[137]

Moreover, it is extremely difficult to find systematic studies of the enforcement of judgments in courts in the United States, where the

132. *See* Court Interview K. This is not the philosophy of all courts. Other sources make it clear that although few if any courts will take coercive steps to evict a tenant who has no place to go, the hesitancy comes usually at the execution stage, *not* the judgment stage. Immunities and exclusions from execution are discussed further below.

133. In other words, courts can award the residence to one party, but they can't make the other party leave. *See* Lawyer Interview R; Academic Interview L; *see generally* Pan Xiaojun, *Guanyu Lihun Anjian Zhufang De Chuli* [*On the Handling of Living Quarters in Divorce Cases*], DANGDAI FAXUE [CONTEMPORARY LEGAL STUDIES], No. 2, at 60 (1990).

134. Jiangsu HLPC, *supra* note 47, at 237.

135. *Lianhu Fayuan Renzhen Jiejue "Zhixing Nan"* [*Lianhu Court Overcomes "Difficulty in Execution"*], FAZHI ZHOUBAO [LEGAL SYSTEM WEEKLY], Oct. 9, 1990, at 1.

136. Various sources suggest that courts will often strive to think up excuses to avoid accepting cases brought against army-run enterprises. *See, e.g.*, Academic Interview P; Cheng, Liu & Cheng, *supra* note 128, at 44.

137. Graduate Seminar on Enforcement of Civil Judgments with Professor Liu Jiaxing, Faculty of Law, Beijing University, Mar. 6, 1992.

enforcement rate, whatever it is, does not generate anything approaching the cries of alarm heard in China. There is reason to believe, however, that it is far from ideal, and indeed may not be very different from the rate of enforcement in China. A 1993 study commissioned by the New Jersey Supreme Court found, among other things, that almost all complaints about judgment collection procedures were from creditors, not debtors, and recommended that pro se litigants setting out to collect judgments be provided with a pamphlet outlining "the steps that can to be taken to collect a judgment so as to keep expectations realistic."[138]

The study found that in eleven New Jersey counties surveyed for the year 1987, only 25 percent of writs of execution in civil cases (this category excludes small claims and landlord-tenant cases) were returned fully satisfied. Seven percent were returned partially satisfied, and the remaining 68 percent were returned unsatisfied or simply dropped. The odds were somewhat better in small claims cases, where 37 percent of writs were returned satisfied and five percent were partially satisfied.[139] Difficult as it is to know the social reality actually reflected by these figures, and the degree to which they are comparable with Chinese numbers, it seems abundantly clear that the American public and legal community routinely put up with enforcement rates that the Chinese legal community would consider shockingly low.[140]

V. Analysis of the Problem

Despite the uncertainties of the statistics, it seems clear that there is a problem of some importance. It is therefore useful to understand why it might occur. The following discussion distinguishes problems common to all cases from problems specific to particular kinds of cases.

A. *General Problems in Execution*

General obstacles to execution can be divided roughly into those of external origin (those that operate to frustrate a court that wants to execute) and those of internal origin (those that make a court reluctant to take the

---

138. *See New Jersey Report*, *supra* note 52.

139. *Id.*

140. I would be very surprised to find that the Chinese legal community, any more than the American public (or indeed the author before beginning research for this article), had any idea how low these rates actually are.

steps needed to execute).[141] Obviously, if a court does not *wish* to enforce its own judgments, no amount of court power will change that fact.

1. Internal Obstacles

a. Reluctance to Use Coercive Measures

Primary and secondary sources on execution reveal a striking fact: courts and other wielders of state power are extraordinarily reluctant to use coercive measures in civil cases, especially when it appears that the defendant is not entirely morally wrong. A telling example is a case where a woman's jilted suitor, having unsuccessfully demanded the return of over 1,000 *yuan* worth of gifts, kidnapped the woman's baby as a debt hostage.[142] After five months of unsuccessful attempts by the go-between, the village committee, and "judicial departments" to persuade him to return the child, he was finally arrested.[143] If it took five months to get around to arresting a known kidnapper, one can imagine how long it would take to impose coercive measures against someone who simply owed some money.

Behind this reluctance is, of course, an idea that this is not *really* a criminal kidnapping. It is instead an admittedly deplorable development in what is essentially a messy domestic dispute. There is a very strong feeling among court personnel that coercive measures are simply not appropriate in civil cases — in Maoist terminology, contradictions among the people, not between the enemy and the people.

It would be a mistake to underestimate the continuing ideological force in China's legal system of the Maoist dichotomy between non-antagonistic and antagonistic contradictions. Coercion, like dictatorship, is something that one applies to the enemy; among the people, one uses persuasion and education.[144] Thus, Article 6 of the 1982 Law on Civil Procedure mandated a preference for mediation. In the words of one writer, "Economic cases fall within the category of disputes among the people and should usually be resolved by means of persuasion and

---

141. For a good general account of internal problems, *see* Xu & He, *supra* note 59.

142. This was not a custody battle; there is no indication in the report that the man was the child's father.

143. *See Ci An Gai Ding He Zui?* [*What Crime Should This Case Be Classified As?*], ZHENG FA LUNCONG [POLITICAL-LEGAL DISCUSSIONS], No. 1, at 17 (1992).

144. *See, e.g.*, Zeng Hanzhou (Vice President, Supreme People's Court), *Zai Di-Er-Ci Quanguo Minshi Shenpan Gongzuo Huiyi Shang De Baogao* [*Report at the Second National Conference on Civil Adjudication*] (Dec. 22, 1978), *in* SELECTED DOCUMENTS, *supra* note 15, at 28, 30 (1978). I discuss this issue at greater length in Clarke, *supra* note 75, at 286-288.

education."[145] The same philosophy was applied to the execution of court judgments — presumably after the failure of mediation:

> Because economic disputes belong to the category of contradictions among the people (*renmin neibu maodun*), and because the refusal of the execution debtor (*bei zhixing ren*) to implement a legally effective document is often due to all kinds of ideological and cognitive reasons, then as long as the court strengthens its educational work, patiently guiding the execution debtor, explaining the pros and cons and his legal responsibility, an execution debtor that is able to repay will generally change his attitude and voluntarily perform.[146]

This view is not simply that of academic commentators. The same caution toward coercive measures is reflected in a prototype civil procedure regulation issued by the Supreme People's Court in 1979, three years before the issuance of the first Law on Civil Procedure:

> Execution work must rely on the masses and the relevant departments. The court should work at educating and persuading the party involved and pay attention to work style. . . . Sealing up and selling off should be done with extreme caution and must be approved by the court's leadership. Important cases must be reported to the Party committee at the same level for approval.[147]

Given the apparent prevalence of this view among courts, it is not surprisingly shared by defendants, who are said to make comments such as, "I didn't steal or rob and haven't committed any crime; what can you do to me?" or "This is a civil case — they wouldn't dare grab anyone!"[148]

---

145. Fei Deping, *Jingji Shenpan Zhixing Gongzuo Qianlun* [*A Brief Discussion of Execution in Economic Adjudication*], FAXUE PINLUN [LEGAL STUDIES REVIEW], No. 1, 1986, at 63, 64. *See also* Xu Ping (Supreme People's Court Civil Chamber), *Duiyu Minshi Susong Fa* (*Shi Xing*) *Ji-Ge Wenti De Fayan* [*Speech on Several Problems on Implementing of the Civil Procedure Law* (*for Trial Implementation*) (no date; perhaps 1983)), *in* SELECTED DOCUMENTS, *supra* note 15, at 103, 112-113 ("[A] civil case is a manifestation of a contradiction among the people . . . . [It] arises on the basis of a unity of fundamental interests; it is not an irreconcilable contradiction.")

146. SHENZHEN JINGJI TEQU SHENPAN SHIJIAN, *supra* note 127, at 138.

147. 1979 SPC Rules, *supra* note 15, at 84.

148. *See* Li Wensen, Zhang Bingde & Wang Fengzhu, *Qiantan Zhixing Qian Dangshi Ren Duikang Xintai De Chengyin Ji Qi Fangzhi Cuoshi* [*A Brief Discussion of the Reasons for the Antagonistic Attitude of a Party Before Execution and Measures for Preventing It*], RENMIN SIFA [PEOPLE'S JUDICATURE], No. 5, 1990, at 41, 41. Similar language is cited in Yin Jiabao, *Renmin*

According to some lawyers interviewed, the reluctance of courts to use the power they have, not external interference, is the main reason for execution difficulties.[149] Nevertheless, there is some evidence that the patience of courts may be diminishing. A 1984 Supreme People's Court document to lower courts instructed them, in the spirit of the regulations noted above, first to carry out education and propaganda in the legal system, and to carry out compulsory execution only where education was ineffective.[150] A superseding document issued six years later omitted the admonition to educate; if a defendant refused to perform, he should be required to do so.[151] Similarly, a 1963 Supreme People's Court document, reprinted in 1981, contained an instruction to courts not to detain persons who refused to comply with the property portion of a divorce judgment.[152] Three different reprints from the 1990s, however, omit this instruction from the document.[153]

b. *Lack of Interest in Execution*

Execution of judgments has not traditionally been a matter of great concern for courts. Their main duty has been criminal adjudication and sentencing.[154] The execution of the sentence was in the hands of the other bodies such as the police and prison administration, so it was never an issue.[155] In addition to stressing criminal over civil cases, courts and scholars have traditionally stressed substantive law over procedural matters, which are considered less a matter of law than of work style

---

Fayuan De Panjue He Caiding Bixu Zhixing [*Judgments and Rulings of People's Courts Must Be Enforced*], RENMIN RIBAO [PEOPLE'S DAILY], Jan. 10, 1980, at 5. The view may also be shared by police, who are reported by some sources to be often uncooperative in locking people up as requested by a court. *See* Luo Shaocheng, *"Zhixing Nan" Qianxi* [*A Short Analysis of "Difficulty in Execution"*], *in* "ZHIXING NAN" DUICE TAN, *supra* note 49, at 78, 83.

149. *See* Lawyer Interview A. This view is not universally held. One prominent academic interviewed held that courts in general wanted to execute, but were stymied by the failure of other institutions — banks, government agencies, etc. — to cooperate. *See* Academic Interview L.

150. *See* Zuigao Renmin Fayuan [Supreme People's Court], Guanyu Guanche Zhixing "Minshi Susong Fa (Shi Xing)" Ruogan Wenti De Yijian [Opinion on Several Questions in the Implementation of the Law on Civil Procedure (for Trial Implementation)] (Aug. 30, 1984), *in* ZHIXING GONGZUO SHOUCE, *supra* note 15, at 87, 98 (art. 63).

151. *See* 1992 SPC Civil Procedure Opinion, *supra* note 70, at 89 (art. 254).

152. *See* 1963 SPC Reply, *supra* note 67.

153. *See* ZHIXING GONGXUO SHOUCE, *supra* note 15, at 198; NORMATIVE INTERPRETATIONS, *supra* note 81, at 975; LEGISLATIVE EXPLANATIONS, *supra* note 97, at 1227.

154. *See* Xi'an ILPC, *supra* note 43, at 4-5.

155. *See* CHANG, *supra* note 44, at 16.

(*zuofeng*).[156] As a subject of academic research, civil procedure did not even get off the ground until 1979.[157]

The very internal organization of courts reflects their priorities: the president takes charge of criminal adjudication, the vice president takes charge of civil adjudication, and the vice president's assistant takes charge of execution. When the adjudication committee discusses cases, criminal cases are at the top of the agenda. Problems in executing judgments come last — if there is any time left.[158]

A particularly extreme case of reluctance to execute was reported in 1994: after having mediated an agreement between the parties in 1988 (which had the legal effect of a court judgment), the court accepted 3,000 *yuan* in execution fees from the plaintiff but refused to do anything or even respond to inquiries for at least six years, despite an eventual direct order from the Supreme People's Court.[159]

c. *Lack of Finality*

Following European and Japanese practice, the Chinese system allows one appeal, with the second hearing a trial *de novo*. There is no third appeal, even on issues of law alone.[160]Although the judgment of the trial in second instance is supposed to be the final judgment and thus enforceable ("legally effective"), defendants in fact have numerous opportunities to relitigate the merits of the case, or at least to pose further procedural obstacles in the way of execution.

With its heavy emphasis on substance over procedure, Chinese law has been reluctant to enforce its own rules on finality. A 1964 Supreme People's Court document said that "[i]f the party refuses to perform [the judgment], the court should first investigate to see whether the original

---

156. *See* Academic Interview P.

157. *See* Academic Interview B.

158. *See* Xi'an ILPC, *supra* note 43, at 4-5.

159. *See* Zhang Wenrui, *Zhixing Nan Qi Neng Nan Zai Fayuan* [*How Can it Be That When Execution Is Difficult, the Difficulty Lies With the Court?*], FAZHI RIBAO [LEGAL SYSTEM DAILY], Apr. 5, 1994, at 2. Contrast this case with the system in New Jersey, where the remuneration of enforcement officers is dependent upon "how many items of process the officer serves and the officer's diligence in searching for assets." *New Jersey Report*, *supra* note 52, at 2.

160. Parties can still contest judgments that have become legally effective through a procedure known as *shensu* (petition). A petition is essentially a request to the court that made the judgment or its superior court to have another look at the case. The procuracy can also be petitioned to re-open the case. There are as yet no clear standards governing the grounds on which petitions may be brought or the number of times they may be brought. On petitions generally and their relationship to appeals, see Margaret Woo, *The Right to a Criminal Appeal in the People's Republic of China*, 14 YALE J. INT'L L. 118, 133-141 (1989).

judgment is correct"[161] — in effect giving the defendant the opportunity to force a rehearing of the issue even after formal appeals have been exhausted.

A more formal way for defendants to reopen a case after their single appeal (*shangsu*) is exhausted is through an application for readjudication (*shenqing zaishen*) on the grounds of mistake in the original judgment.[162] Although such an application is not supposed to stop the process of execution,[163] courts were authorized in 1989 should they deem it necessary to suspend execution while they are considering the application.[164] A later document appears to have rescinded this authorization to some degree: while higher courts are investigating the legally effective judgments of lower courts, they are not supposed to suspend execution until they have reached a decision that the judgment is definitely erroneous and have issued an order for rehearing.[165]

In one perhaps unusual case, the defendant, having lost both at the BLPC and at the ILPC, applied for readjudication at the HLPC and, when rejected, pursued his case to the Supreme People's Court. Although the judgment of the ILPC was the legally effective and immediately executable one, the defendant nevertheless succeeded through his subsequent applications in postponing execution by 22 months.[166]

If the decision being enforced by the court was issued by an administrative agency, the defendant gets another opportunity to contest it

161. 1964 SPC Reply, *supra* note 67.

162. The relevant procedure is set forth in articles 177-188 of the Law on Civil Procedure. Probably the only truly final judgment in Chinese civil law is a second-instance judgment of divorce, which under article 181 of the Law on Civil Procedure is not subject to an application for readjudication.

163. *See* Law on Civil Procedure, *supra* note 34, art. 178; 1990 SPC Reply, *supra* note 85, at 85.

164. *See* Zuigao Renmin Fayuan [Supreme People's Court], *Guanyu Jingji Jiufen Anjian Fucha Qijian Zhixing Wenti De Pifu* [*Reply on the Question of Execution During the Period of Reinvestigation of Cases of Economic Disputes*] (Aug. 8, 1989), *in* LEGISLATIVE EXPLANATIONS, *supra* note 97, at 1238.

165. *See* Zuigao Renmin Fayuan [Supreme People's Court], Guanyu Shenpan Jiandu Chengxu Zhong, Shangji Renmin Fayuan Dui Xiaji Renmin Fayuan Yijing Fasheng Falü Xiaoli De Panjue, Caiding, Heshi Caiding Zhongzhi Zhixing He Zhongzhi Zhixing De Caiding You Shei Shuming Wenti De Pifu [Reply on the Issues of Making a Ruling Suspending Execution During the Examination by a Superior Court in the Course of the Judicial Supervision Process of a Judgment or Ruling of an Inferior Court, and of Who Should Sign the Ruling Suspending Execution] (July 9, 1985), SPCG, No. 3, Sept. 20, 1985, *reprinted in* DATABASE, *supra* note 85. To the same effect is article 183 of the 1991 Law on Civil Procedure.

166. *See* Wang Aiying Yu Li Baosheng Zhaiji Jiufen Qiangzhi Zhixing An [The Case of Compulsory Execution in the Residential Land Dispute Between Wang Aiying and Li Baosheng], SPCG, No. 2, June 20, 1986, *reprinted in* DATABASE, *supra* note 85.

at the time of execution even if he did not appeal either administratively or to a court within the required time period.[167] This is because even where the defendant does not request a review, the court has the power, and perhaps the duty, to review the decision for "correctness" on its own.[168]

Defendants may also have a chance to reopen the case when execution of the judgment is entrusted to another court. In theory the entrusted court has no right to review the substance of the judgment,[169] and some courts assert that they follow this rule.[170] Other courts, however, assert that

> [b]efore executing an [entrusted] judgment, the execution chamber must strictly and conscientiously investigate the basis for execution. If it discovers that the judgment or mediation is in error, it should make a prompt report to the court president, who will turn it over to the Adjudication Committee.[171]

---

167. *See* Court Interview F. My conversation with the judges made it clear that it is simply not part of Chinese legal culture to say to the defendant, "Sorry — if you had an objection to make, you should have made it before when you had the chance."

168. *See* Zuigao Renmin Fayuan, Zhongguo Renmin Yinhang [Supreme People's Court, People's Bank of China], Guanyu Fayuan Dui Xingzheng Jiguan Yi Fa Shenqing Qiangzhi Zhixing Xuyao Yinhang Xiezhu Zhixing De Anjian Ying Ruhe Banli Wenti De Lianhe Tongzhi [Joint Notice on the Question of How Courts Should Handle Cases Where an Administrative Oragan Applies According to Law for Compulsory Execution and the Cooperation of a Bank in Execution Is Needed] (Jan. 11, 1989), *in* LEGISLATIVE EXPLANATIONS, *supra* note 97, at 1239; Zuigao Renmin Fayuan [Supreme People's Court], Guanyu Renmin Fayuan Yi Fa Zhixing Xingzheng Jiguan De Xingzheng Chufa Jueding Ying Yong He-Zhong Falü Wenshu De Wenti De Pifu [Reply on the Question of What Kind of Legal Document Courts Should Use When Executing According to Law the Administrative Punishment Decisions of Administrative Organs] (Sept. 14, 1985), *in* NORMATIVE INTERPRETATIONS, *supra* note 81, at 994.

169. *See* Zuigao Renmin Fayuan [Supreme People's Court], Guanyu Renmin Fayuan Xianghu Banli Weituo Shixiang De Guiding [Rules on the Mutual Handling of Entrusted Matters by People's Courts] (Sept. 25, 1993), SPCG, No. 4, Dec. 20, 1993, at 148 [hereinafter 1993 SPC Rules]; 1992 SPC Civil Procedure Opinion, *supra* note 70, at 89.

170. *See, e.g.*, Changchun Shi Zhongji Renmin Fayuan [Changchun Intermediate Level People's Court], *Bingqi Difang Baohu Zhuyi, Jiji Banli Shou Weituo Yu Xiezhu Anjian* [*Eliminate Local Protectionism, Actively Handle Cases of Entrustment and Cooperation*], *in* CONFERENCE MATERIALS, *supra* note 42 [hereinafter Changchun ILPC, *Eliminate Local Protectionism*]; Court Interview K; Court Interview U.

171. Jiangsu HLPC 2, *supra* note 47, at 237.

2. External Obstacles

a. *Local Protectionism*

Local protectionism is far and away the most frequently mentioned obstacle in the literature.[172] It manifests itself when officials in region *A* prevent the execution of a judgment in favor of a plaintiff from region *B* against a defendant from region *A*. Sometimes the court in region *A* will have rendered the unfavorable judgment only to find that it is not supported by other local government organs. More frequently — because a local court is less likely than an outside court to render a judgment unwelcome to the local leadership[173] — the judgment will have been rendered by a court in region *B*, and it will be attempting to execute it either directly or by entrusting execution to local court in region *A*.[174]

The general term "local protectionism" (*difang baohuzhuyi*) can describe a variety of practices. As a rule, they stem from the fact that local governments rely on local enterprises for revenues and employment, and so are reluctant to allow them to be financially damaged by having a

172. The citations are too numerous to list here. For a good general treatment of local judicial protectionism, see Chengdu Shi Zhongji Renmin Fayuan [Chengdu Intermediate Level People's Court], *Dizhi He Kefu Difang Baohu Zhuyi De Tantao* [*An Exploration Into Resisting and Overcoming Local Protectionism*], *in* CONFERENCE MATERIALS, *supra* note 42 [hereinafter 1992 Chengdu ILPC]; on local protectionism in economic adjudication in particular, see Zhang Yiping, *Jingji Shenpan Zhong Difang Baohu Zhuyi Wenti De Sikao* [*Thoughts About the Problem of Local Protectionism in Economic Adjudication*], SHENZHEN FAZHI BAO [SHENZHEN LEGAL SYSTEM NEWS], Nov. 14, 1990, at 3. *See also* Clarke, *supra* note 6, at 67-69. One group of court officials I spoke with agreed that while local protectionism was a problem, it was not the main problem. On the other hand, the same court later published an article, written at approximately the same time, saying essentially the opposite.

173. "Some leaders of Party and government organs even require that all economic contract cases involving the locality where the amount in dispute is relatively large be reported to them for instructions." Zhang, *supra* note 172. Despite the writer's indignation, however, such leaders are requiring from courts little more than what the Supreme People's Court itself has required of them. *See, e.g.*, 1979 SPC Rules, *supra* note 15, at 84 ("Important cases must be reported to the Party committee at the same level for approval."); Ren Jianxin, *Nuli Kaichuang Jingji Shenpan Gongzuo De Xin Jumian, Wei Shehuizhuyi Xiandaihua Jianshe Fuwu* [*Work Hard to Open Up a New Situation in Economic Adjudication, Serve the Construction of the Four Modernizations*] (report to the First National Conference on Economic Adjudication Work) (Mar. 28, 1984), *in* SELECTED DOCUMENTS, *supra* note 15, at 196, 216 ("Important issues and cases encountered in the course of work must all be reported to the Party committee with a request for instructions, in order to obtain the directions and support of the Party committee.").

174. Both procedures are explicitly permitted by 1993 SPC Rules, *supra* note 169.

judgment against them successfully executed.[175] In addition, a local enterprise may well be run by a local political leader, who will exert his influence to protect the enterprise.[176]

It is not simply some vague notion of respect for local leaders that makes courts reluctant to go against their wishes. This respect has a very specific institutional basis: the dependence of local court personnel upon local government at the same level for their jobs and their finances.[177] As one article noted, "Every aspect of local courts, including personnel, budgets, benefits, employment of children, housing, and facilities, is controlled by local Party and government organs, as are promotions and bonuses."[178] Courts generally may keep a portion of the fees they collect, and turn over the rest either to a higher court[179] or to the local government treasury.[180] These fees are not sufficient for salaries and other expenses, which must be met with funding from local government.[181] One urban BLPC reported that out of a total annual budget of about 800,000 *yuan*, half was received as a regular appropriation from the district (*qu*) government and half came from the portion of litigation fees they were allowed to retain.[182]

Stories abound of local governments using their power over courts to exercise influence. A judge in Fujian who executed a judgment against a local enterprise found his daughter transferred the next day by her employer, the county, to an isolated post on a small island.[183] In another

---

175. In 1985, the central government introduced a tax system that had the effect of giving local governments a much greater interest in local revenues. At the same time, court funding was made a local responsibility. Several sources attributed local protectionism mainly to the confluence of these two factors. *See, e.g.*, 1992 Chengdu ILPC, *supra* note 172, at 8; Court Interview D; Lawyer Interview R; Court Interview K; Zhang, *supra* note 172; Shi Youyong, *Shenpan Zhong Difang Baohu Zhuyi De Chengyin Ji Duice* [*Local Protectionism in Adjudication: Causes and Countermeasures*], FAXUE [LEGAL STUDIES], No. 6, at 15, 16 (1989).

176. A case in point is that of the Pingtan country salt plant discussed *infra* in note 220.

177. Sources making this diagnosis are too numerous to be cited here. The issue is discussed in more detail in Clarke, *supra* note 6, at 61-64. In one county, the local government's persistent favoring of the procuracy over the court led eventually to violence when the procuracy built its county-funded dormitory for dependents right up to the courthouse door, blocking vehicular access. *See* 1992 Chengdu ILPC, *supra* note 172.

178. Chen Youxi & Xue Chunbao, *Zaocheng Fayuan Zhixing Nan De San Da Jiben Yinsu* [*The Three Major Reasons Why Courts Have Difficulty in Execution*], ZHEJIANG FAZHI BAO [ZHEJIANG LEGAL SYSTEM NEWS], Aug. 16, 1990, at 3.

179. *See* Court Interview K.

180. *See* Academic Interview P.

181. *See* Court Interview K; Court Interview D; Court Interview F.

182. *See* Court Interview F.

183. *See* MINSHI SHENPAN RUOGAN LILUN YU SHIJIAN WENTI [SEVERAL THEORETICAL AND PRACTICAL PROBLEMS IN CIVIL ADJUDICATION] 391 (Tang Dehua ed., 1991).

case, local government officials, upon hearing that the local court was preparing to accept a case naming an important local enterprise as defendant, reportedly remonstrated:

> The Trust and Investment Company is an enterprise under district jurisdiction; a case as big as this will have an effect on the finances of the whole district. Don't you want your salaries paid? As for your application to the district to allocate funds for a dormitory, don't be ridiculous! You court people need to think of some excuse for blocking this case and not accepting it.[184]

Both direct execution and entrustment present their own problems. The chief problem with direct execution is that outside courts tend to lack the local clout needed to get their judgments enforced. Some banks in Shenzhen, for example, apparently had — and may still have — internal rules requiring that any freeze on customer accounts by an outside court be approved by a Shenzhen court,[185] although such a requirement is prohibited in notices issued in 1983 and 1993 by the Supreme People's Court and the People's Bank of China.[186] Numerous other banks have rules requiring that the freezing or seizure of funds be approved by higher bank authorities,[187] although such rules have also been declared unlawful by the Supreme People's Court.[188] On a more general level, some local governments have,

---

184. ZHANG, *supra* note 172, at 3.

185. *See Dangqian Jingji Anjian Weihe Zhixing Nan?* [*Why Is Execution Difficult in Economic Cases at Present?*], SHANGHAI FAZHI BAO [SHANGHAI LEGAL SYSTEM NEWS], Oct 2, 1989, at 1.

186. *See infra* text accompanying notes 250-254.

187. *See, e.g.*, Zhegjiang Sheng Gaoji Renmin Fayuan, Zhejiang Sheng Renmin Jianchayuan, Zhongguo Renmin Yinhang Zhejiang Sheng Feiyuan, Zhongguo Nongye YinHang Zhejiang Shen Fenyuan [Zhejiang Province Higher Level People's Court, Zhejiang Province People's Procuratorate, Zhejiang Provincial Branch of the People's Bank of China, Zhejiang Provincial Branch of the Agricultural Bank of China], Guanyu Chaxun, Zhifu He Chuli Susong Dangshiren Chuxu Cunkuan Wenti De Lianhe Tongzhi [Joint Notice on the Issues of Investigating, Stopping Payments from, and Handling Bank Deposits of Parties to Litigation] (Aug. 13, 1980), *in* 2 MSCZ, *supra* note 1, at 748 [hereinafter 1980 Zhejiang Notice] (requiring that freezes must have the approval of the bank director without indicating the grounds on which the director could legitimately disapprove); *Tian Da Gongsi Zongjingli Bei Zhikong Fanzui* [*General Manager of Tian Da Company Accused of Crime*], SHENZHEN FAZHI BAO [SHENZHEN LEGAL SYSTEM NEWS], May 31, 1989, at 1 (noting existence in several places, including Shanghai, of rule requiring approval at county level of bank for freezing of deposits).

188. *See* Zuigao Renmin Fayuan [Supreme People's Court], *Guanyu Renmin Fayuan Keyi Zhijie Yu Yinhang Xitong De Yingyesuo, Xinyongshe Lianxi, Chaxun, Dongjie Huozhe Kouhua Qi-Shiye Deng Danwei Cunkuan De Pifu* [*Reply* [*Saying*] *That People's Courts May Directly Contact Business Establishments and Credit Cooperatives Within the Banking System and Investigate, Freeze or Levy Upon Funds Held by Enterprises, Institutions and Other Units*] (Jan. 17, 1985), *in*

according to court officials both in interviews and in published writings, issued rules forbidding local banks from obeying court orders to remove funds from a local defendant's account if it is destined for an outside (*waidi*) plaintiff.[189] Such rules, if they exist, are unquestionably unlawful, but the rule in practice in China tends to be that a specific local regulation prevails over a general national one.[190]

Local courts may also attempt to interfere with direct execution within their jurisdiction by an outside court.

> When an outside court goes to another area to execute, the local court always refuses to cooperate, and may even obstruct execution. Even worse is when the local court has secret communications with the party, warning it to shift its funds and property, thus making it impossible for the outside court to execute.[191]

When officials of a Beijing court went to nearby Zhangjiakou to execute a judgment against a local defendant, they first cleared it with the local court. While they were in the process of removing property from the defendant's warehouse, however, the local court changed its mind and decided to "suspend execution," a measure beyond its authority because it was not the executing court. At this, the defendant's manager called on workers to block court personnel and a fight ensued.[192] When officials of the Chengdu ILPC went to Guangdong to execute a judgment, the president of the local court required the plaintiff to waive its claim to over half the amount of the judgment before he would allow the remainder to be transferred to the Chengdu court's account.[193]

One must have a certain sympathy, however, with a local court faced with an outside court coming in to enforce a judgment in favor of a plaintiff from its own jurisdiction. A suspicion that local protectionism might be at work is surely justified, since both courts face the same type of

---

ZHIXING GONGZUO SHOUCE, *supra* note 15, at 700 [hereinafter 1985 SPC Reply]. Whether this document can or should actually bind banks is open to question. Although the document states that it was issued after "liaison and study" with the People's Bank of China, the Bank chose not to be a co-issuer. Given that the Bank *is* a co-issuer of other similar documents, the absence of its name on this document could be significant.

189. *See* Court Interview E; 1992 Chengdu ILPC, *supra* note 172, at 1.

190. *See* Clarke, *supra* note 6, at 26-28.

191. 1992 Chengdu ILPC, *supra* note 172, at 4.

192. *See Kangju Zhixing Fayuan Panjue, Wang Zhihua Deng Reng Bei Juliu* [*For Resisting the Execution of a Court Judgment, Wang Zhihua and Others Are Still Detained*], BEIJING FAZHI BAO [BEIJING LEGAL SYSTEM NEWS], Feb. 24, 1990, at 1.

193. *See* 1992 Chengdu ILPC, *supra* note 172, at 5. Under prevailing law at the time, the Chengdu court had the authority to freeze a defendant's account, but needed approval of the local court before funds could be transferred out. *See infra* text accompanying notes 314-323.

pressures.[194] A court that ignored this reality would be doing an active disservice to defendants in its area of jurisdiction.[195]

When the person or property to be executed against is outside a court's geographical jurisdiction, it may also entrust (*weituo*) execution to the basic level[196] court of the relevant region instead of executing directly.[197] When a court is entrusted with execution, it must (*bixu*) begin

---

194. The Chengdu ILPC reported a case where a Henan court rendered a judgment *in absentia* in favor of a local plaintiff against a Chengdu defendant, and did not allow the defendant to appeal. When asked to cooperate in execution, the court discovered this "error" in procedure in time to prevent loss to the defendant. *See* 1992 Chengdu ILPC, *supra* note 172, at 3-4.

195. In one case, the plaintiff sued in its home court, a BLPC in Wuhan, because the defendant had made no payments on a automobiles it had leased with an option to buy. Plaintiff's lawyer then went to the defendant's home town in Sichuan with the Wuhan court's economic adjudication chamber *and* the execution chamber — suggesting that the result was something of a foregone conclusion. Upon investigation, they found that the defendant was delinquent in its payment of wages and did not intend to pay the debt owed to the plaintiff. The plaintiff's lawyer pointed out that the ownership of the cars did not change hands until all payments were made, and asked the court to impound the vehicles prior to the hearing. As this enraged the defendant's workers, the court quickly held a hearing and announced judgment against the defendant. After the announcement of the judgment, the plaintiff's lawyer hired drivers to take the vehicles back to Wuhan as quickly as possible, stopping for nothing. *See* YUNYONG FALÜ SHOUDUAN QING ZHAI BAI CE [ONE HUNDRED TACTICS FOR USING LEGAL METHODS TO CLEAR UP DEBTS] 229 (Li Bida ed., 1991). For other cases where the plaintiff's home court went to another jurisdiction to conduct the hearing, see *Dandong Fayuan Bodo Dangshiren Hefa Quanli Ying Chajiu [The Dandong Court's Stripping a Party of His Lawful Rights Should Be Investigated and Punished]*, FAZHI RIBAO [LEGAL SYSTEM DAILY], June 2, 1988, at 1; *Yi-Fen Bei Mieshile Liang-Nian Zhi Jiu De Tiaojie Shu [A Bill of Mediation That Was Looked on With Contempt for Two Long Years]*, SHANGHAI FAZHI BAO [SHANGHAI LEGAL SYSTEM NEWS], Aug. 15, 1988, at 1.

196. The level of court is stipulated in 1993 SPC Rules, *supra* note 169, art. 11. Before the issuance of this document, the proper level of court to entrust had been the subject of debate, with some arguing that execution should be entrusted to the court at the same level as the court that made the original judgment. *See, e.g.*, WEI JINFA, YIN SHIFENG & HE QIHUA, RENMIN FAYUAN ZHIXING DUICE [MEASURES FOR EXECUTION BY PEOPLE'S COURTS] 27-28 (1992).

197. See article 210 of the Law on Civil Procedure, *supra* note 34. The degree to which courts *should* entrust execution in such cases has remained an unsettled matter of policy. Article 165 of the 1982 Law on Civil Procedure said that courts "may" entrust execution. But a Supreme People's Court interpretation of 1984 said that courts "should" entrust execution. *See* Zuigao Renmin Fayuan [Supreme People's Court], Guanyu Zai Jingji Shenpan Gongzuo Zhong Guanzhe Zhixing "Minshi Susong Fa (Shi Xing)" Ruogan Wenti De Yijian [Opinion on Several Issues in the Implementation of the "Law on Civil Procedure Law (for Trial Implementation)" *in Economic Adjudication*] (Sept. 17, 1984), *in* ZHIXING GONGZUO SHOUCE, *supra* note 15, at 102, 107 (section VII, para. 4). In Chinese legal drafting, "should" is often close, and sometime equivalent, to "must." The 1991 Law on Civil Procedure and subsequent Supreme People's Court documents both restored the "may" formulation. *See* 1992 SPC Civil Procedure Opinion, *supra* note 70, at 89 (art. 259); 1993 SPC Rules, *supra* note 169 (art. 11). According to one court, however, the Supreme People's Court has a rule *requiring* entrustment. *See* Shanghai Shi Zhongji Renmin Fayuan [Shanghai Intermediate Level People's Court], *Zengqiang Fazhi Guannian, Banhao Weituo Anjian [Strengthen Legal-Mindedness, Handle Entrusted Cases Well]*, *in* CONFERENCE MATERIALS, *supra* note 42, at 5 [hereinafter 1992 Shanghai ILPC]. On entrusted execution in general, *see* ZHIXING DE LILUN YU SHIJIAN, *supra* note 81, at 83-96.

execution proceedings within fifteen days. The mandatory "must" is a deliberate change from the hortatory (and presumably ineffective) "should" (*yingdang*) of the 1982 Law on Civil Procedure.[198]

The main problem with entrusted execution is that the entrusted court is unlikely to devote a great deal of effort to it. From the earliest years of the People's Republic, a steady stream of documents attests to the difficulty of making courts take this procedure seriously.[199] As the Supreme People's Court complained in 1988,

> Recently, some courts have repeatedly reported some problems that deserve attention. These are principally as follows.
> (1) Some courts ignore entrustments from courts from other areas, or emphasize difficulties and procrastinate.
> (2) Some courts want to examine the records of the case from the entrusting court, or else they create obstacles, even to the extent of passing on information and giving suggestions to the party from their own locality, thus hindering implementation.
> (3) Some courts make reciprocity a condition, turning cooperation in entrustment between people's courts into an exchange relationship, and even demanding that the entrusting court pay expenses.
> (4) In handling entrusted matters, some courts, when they encounter any pressure or interference, do not dare to uphold

198. *See* 1992 Guiyang ILPC, *supra* note 99, at 1 (complaining that some courts wait months or years before executing entrusted cases).

199. *See* 1951 MOJ Notice, *supra* note 67; Zuigao Renmin Fayuan [Supreme People's Court], Guanyu Weituo Diaocha He Zhuanchu Huibao Gongzuo Shang Tuo La Zuofeng De Tongbao [Notice Regarding the Work Style of Procrastinating in Matters of Entrusted Investigation and Reporting Back on Disposition] (Apr. 19, 1956), *in* YOUGUAN SHENPAN YEWU WENJIAN HUIBIAN [COLLECTED DOCUMENTS RELATING TO ADJUDICATION WORK] 182 (1957); 1957 MOJ Notice, *supra* note 67; Sifa Bu [Ministry of Justice], Guanyu Renzhen Zuohao Daixun Daicha Liaojie Anqing Gongzuo De Tongzhi [Notice on Conscientiously Doing Well the Work of Substitute Questioning and Investigation in Order to Understand the Case] (Apr. 14, 1958), *in* 2 MSCZ, *supra* note 1, at 420; Zuigao Renmin Fayuan [Supreme People's Court], Guanyu Weituo Waidi Fayuan Diaocha Anqing He Chuanxun Dangshiren Ying Zhuyi De Wenti De Han [Letter on Problems to Which Attention Should Be Paid in Entrusting Courts From Other Regions to Investigate the Circumstances of a Case and to Summon a Party] (Feb. 20, 1962), *in* 2 MSCZ, *supra* note 1, at 421; Zuigao Renmin Fayuan [Supreme People's Court], Guanyu Zai Shenli Jingji Jiufen Anjian Zhong Renzhen Banhao Waidi Fayuan Weituo Shixiang De Tongzhi [Notice on Conscientiously Carrying Out Tasks Entrusted by Courts From Other Areas in the Course of Trying Cases of Economic Disputes] (Jan. 20, 1988), *in* ZHIXING GONGZUO SHOUCE, *supra* note 15, at 265 [hereinafter 1988 SPC Notice]; 1993 SPC Rules, *supra* note 169.

> principle or to do things according to law, and try to push the conflict onto the entrusting court.[200]

While courts generally report their own rate of successful execution of entrusted cases to be high,[201] they report a low rate of successful execution of cases entrusted to other courts. One court reported that in a ten-month period it made 115 entrustments to courts of twenty different provinces. By the time of the report, only fourteen (12 percent) had been executed. In thirty cases, the entrusted court reported back that it could not execute or requested termination of execution, and in fully seventy-one cases (62 percent) no response had been received at all.[202]

Local courts may be unwilling to help for the local protectionist reasons outlined above. In the face of determined stonewalling, the court wishing to execute may have little remedy.[203] Even a friendly court, as the quoted text suggests, may not dare to go against the wishes of local leaders. In one case, a sympathetic court president asked the outside court for understanding on the grounds that he was building a house and would never get it finished if he offended the county government — which, he said, "won't let us touch this case."[204] Finally, a court that is neither hostile nor afraid of local government may simply deem it too much of a bother to spend resources on executing the judgments of other courts when it may be hard pressed to execute its own. In such a case, the entrusted court might demand that the entrusting court pay the expenses of execution.[205]

As noted above, the principal cause of local judicial protectionism appears to be the combination of the local government's direct interest in the financial well-being of local enterprises with its power over court personnel and finances. Consequently, local protectionism could be

---

200. 1988 SPC Notice, *supra* note 199, at 265.

201. *See, e.g.*, 1992 Shanghai ILPC, *supra* note 197, at 1-2.

202. *See* Commentator, *"Liba Qiang" A, B, C — Shenpan Gongzuo Zhong De Difang Baohu Zhuyi Shu Ping* [*"Fence" A, B, C — An Account of Local Protectionism in Adjudication Work*], RENMIN SIFA [PEOPLE'S JUDICATURE], No. 10, 1990, at 2, 3.

203. In one case, a county court refused to help enforce an outside judgment despite two specific orders from the Supreme People's Court to do so. *See* Chen Shibin, *Dawu Sian Fayuan Jianchi Difang Baohu Zhuyi, Tuoyan San-Nian Ju Bu Xiezhu Zhixing Waidi Panjue* [*Dawu County Court Persists in Local Protectionism; After Delaying Three Years, Still Refuses to Assist in Execution of an Outside Judgment*], FAZHI RIBAO [LEGAL SYSTEM DAILY], June 4, 1988, at 1.

204. Liu Jian & Mu Xiaoqian, *Zhixing Zhong De Wu Da Nan Ti — Guangdong Sheng Jingji Jiufen Anjian Diaocha Zhi San* [*The Five Big Dilemmas in Execution — Part Three of an Investigation Into Economic Disputes in Guangdong*], FAZHI RIBAO [LEGAL SYSTEM DAILY], April 19, 1988, at 3, 3.

205. *See* 1988 SPC Notice, *supra* note 199, at 265.

expected to be less pronounced where either of these factors is weakened or absent. Indeed, lawyers and court officials interviewed suggested that local protectionism was much less of a problem with intermediate level and higher level courts, where the connection of the corresponding level of government with local finance was much more tenuous.[206]

Local judicial protectionism could also be expected to decline if the dependence of courts on local government could be reduced. On the financial side, this could be done by funding courts from the center instead of from various levels of local government.[207] At present, with the central government strapped for funds, there is no indication that such a reform is in the works.

On the personnel side, the picture is a little different. The general rule is that court presidents and vice presidents owe their jobs to local people's congresses at the same level — in practice the local Party organization.[208] Since late 1988, however, a small-scale experiment has been going on in Heilongjiang, Zhejiang, Fujian, and Inner Mongolia whereby superior courts have more say in appointments to inferior courts.[209] The spread of

206. *See* Lawyer Interview R; Court Interview K. One lawyer I interviewed was involved in a case against a Hangzhou defendant for 200,000 *yuan*. The Hangzhou court with jurisdiction, a Basic Level People's Court, refused to accept the case for hearing. The lawyer went to the Intermediate Level People's Court (directly above the first court) and obtained an order to the lower court to hear the case, but to no avail. Even after the lawyer procured a direct order from the Higher Level People's Court, at the provincial level, the Hangzhou court still refused to hear the case. *See* Lawyer Interview R. As one source points out, courts are more afraid to offend local government than they are to offend superior courts. *See* Wu Qingbao, *Di-Er-Ci Quanguo Jingji Shenpan Gongzuo Hiuyi Zongshu* [*A General Account of the Second National Conference on Economic Adjudication Work*], JINGJI FAZHI [ECONOMIC LEGAL SYSTEM], No. 6, at 25, 28 (1991). For a discussion of the prevalence of *kuai* (the principle of control at the same administrative level) over *tiao* (the principle of vertical control) in the court system, see Li Yaxiong, *Shi Lun Woguo Minshi Zhi Fa De Youhua* [*A Tentative Discussion of the Optimization of Implementation of Law in Civil Matters*], ZHONG-WAI FAXUE [CHINESE AND FOREIGN LEGAL STUDIES], No. 2, at 1, 1 (1992).

207. For proposals to this effect, see Zhang, *supra* note 172; 1992 Chengdu ILPC, *supra* note 172, at 13.

208. The dominant role of the Party in selecting judges is clearly spelled out in Cooperation Measures, *supra* note 23, which mentions only once the organs formally empowered to select judges: "After the above cadres have been approved within the Party, it is necessary to perform the procedures of appointment and removal in accordance with the provisions of the Organic Law of the People's Courts [*i.e.*, appointment must be by the appropriate People's Congress or its Standing Committee]. . . . Appointments to and removals from office may not be announced before the above legally-prescribed procedures have been followed." *Id.*, at 611.

209. For details, see Zuigao Renmin Fayuan Renshi Ting [Supreme People's Court Personnel Department], *Gaige Ganbu Tizhi, Jiaqiang Guanli Gongzuo, Baozheng Renmin Fayuan Yi Fa Duli Shenpan* [*Reform the Cadre System and Strengthen Supervisory Work; Guarantee the People's Courts' Independent Adjudication According to Law*], RENMIN SIFA [PEOPLE'S JUDICATURE], No. 9, at 16 (1990).

this reform would mean greater independence for courts from local government.[210]

For the time being, the best that courts seem able to do is to enter into what are essentially treaties of reciprocity with other courts. Under such agreements, each court party to the agreement promises to execute the judgments of the other signatories.[211] Courts are already, of course, statutorily required to execute the judgments of other Chinese courts, and the Supreme People's Court has specifically denounced the practice of requiring reciprocity.[212] Nevertheless, such agreements do exist and are even trumpeted as positive achievements in the press.[213] On the other hand, they have no real legal force, and will last only as long as the parties deem it in their interest to continue cooperating.

b. *Other Kinds of Interference by Administrative Bodies*

Local protectionism is merely one manifestation of a larger problem, that of interference by state administrative organs and local power-holders who do not want to see a judgment executed for whatever reason. Here the courts are on the horns of not one but two dilemmas.

---

210. A number of writers advocate centralizing the power of appointment of judges. *See, e.g.*, Yu Lianrui, *Shichang Jingji Huhuan Sifa Tizhi Gaigi* [*The Market Economy Cries Out for Reform of the Judicial System*], MINZHU YU FAZHI [DEMOCRACY AND THE LEGAL SYSTEM], No. 181, at 21 (1994).

211. *See* Academic Interview J (describing the practice in general); 1992 Chengdu ILPC, *supra* note 172, at 10.

212. *See* 1988 SPC Notice, *supra* note 199, at 265. *See also* Guangzhou Shi Zhongji Renmin Fayuan Zhixing Ting [Execution Chamber of the Guangzhou Intermediate Level People's Court], *Jianchi Yi Fa Ban Shi, Bingqi Difang Baohu Zhuyi* [*Uphold Doing Things According to Law; Do Away With Local Protectionism*], *in* ZHIXING GONGZUO SHOUCE, *supra* note 15, at 47, 48 (criticizing the principle of reciprocity).

213. *See* Yang Jisheng, *"East-West Dialogue" in China — The Strategy of Unbalanced Economic Development on the Mainland in Perspective* (in Chinese), LIAOWANG [OUTLOOK], No. 9, at 5 (1989), *translated in* FOREIGN BROADCAST INFORMATION SERVICE, DAILY REPORT: CHINA [FBIS], Apr. 10, 1989, at 37, 39 (describing agreements by Shanghai courts with those of nine other provinces); *Xiang-E Liushisi-Jia Fayuan Lianshou Gongpo Yidi Zhixing Nan Guan Jian Xiao* [*Sixty-Four Courts In Hunan and Hubei Join Hands, Achieve Results in Overcoming the Problem of Executing Judgments in Other Regions*], FAZHI RIBAO [LEGAL SYSTEM DAILY], July 24, 1991, at 1 [hereinafter *Sixty-Four Courts*] (reporting mutual execution agreement among courts of several cities along the Yangtse); Peng Changlin, *Jianli Jingji Shenpan Sifa Xiezhu Zhidu, Xieshou Gongke Anjian Yidi Zhixing Nanti* [*Establish a System of Judicial Cooperation in Economic Adjudication, Join Hands to Attack and Overcome the Problem of Executing in a Different Region*], JINGJI FAZHI [ECONOMIC LEGAL SYSTEM], No. 7, at 30 (1992) (article enthusiastically praising the same agreement). According to the agreement described in the sources cited here, participating courts agreed *inter alia* to give priority to executing each other's judgments (as opposed to the judgments of non-participating courts).

The first dilemma is that of conflicting policy signals. On the one hand, courts are told to administer justice independently according solely to the requirements of the law. The days of seeking advice from the local Party committee on specific cases are supposed to be over, as stated by no less than Jiang Hua, then President of the Supreme People's Court, in the *People's Daily* as early as 1980.[214] In addition, a series of academic articles and news reports over the last several years has noted the persistence of Party decisionmaking in legal cases only to deplore it.[215]

On the other hand, however, courts are at the same time receiving policy documents from both the Party and the Supreme People's Court that specifically provide for Party committee decisionmaking in specific cases. In 1980, for example — the same year as President Jiang's remarks — a Central Committee document noted that one of the duties of the Party's Political-Legal Committees at various levels was to "dispose of important and difficult cases."[216] A string of Supreme People's Court policy directives to lower courts through the late 1970s and the 1980s reflects the Party's position: "Important cases must be reported to the Party committee at the same level for approval" (1979);[217] in important or difficult cases, courts "must always . . . report . . . to the Party committee with a request for instructions" (1984);[218] it is more necessary than ever "to strengthen the system of reporting to the Party committee for instructions" (1984).[219]

The second dilemma is an outgrowth of the first: if the courts try to go their own way and not to involve the local Party organization in their decisions, they may find that their judgments, however independently

---

214. *See Baozheng Fayuan Duli Shenpan, Feichu Dangwei Shenpi Anjian Zuofa* [*Guarantee the Independent Adjudication of Cases by the Courts in Accordance With the Law; Abolish the Practice of the Party Committee Examining and Approving [Decisions in] Cases*], RENMIN RIBAO [PEOPLE'S DAILY], Aug. 25, 1980, at 1.

215. The sources are too numerous to list here. I discuss the issue, with citations, in Clarke, *supra* note 6, at 61-64.

216. Zhonggong Zhongyang Guanyu Chengli Zheng-Fa Weiyuanhui De Tongzhi [Notice of the Central Committee of the Chinese Communist Party on the Establishment of Political-Legal Committees] (Central Committee Doc. No. 5 (1980)), *cited in* Zhonggong Zhongyang Guanyu Jiaqiang Zheng-Fa Gongzuo De Tongzhi [Chinese Communist Party Central Committe Notice on Strengthening Political-Legal Work] (Jan. 13, 1982), *reprinted in* ZHONGGONG NIANBAO 1983-84 [YEARBOOK OF CHINESE COMMUNISM 1983-84], at 8-6 (1984).

217. 1979 SPC Rules, *supra* note 15, at 84.

218. Wang Zhanping, *Zhenfen Jingshen, Nuli Kaichuang Minshi Shenpan Gongzuo De Xin Jumian* [*Get Spirits Up, Work Hard to Open Up a New Situation in Civil Adjudication*] *in* SELECTED DOCUMENTS, *supra* note 15, at 121, 142 (report to 4th National Conference On Civil Adjudication Work, June 28, 1984).

219. Ren, *supra* note 173, at 216. Ren was vice president of the Supreme People's Court at the time.

arrived at, are unenforceable. Party involvement may not be bad; in paying due respect to the Party organization, courts may simply be doing what is necessary to ensure political backing for their judgments.[220] As one source noted, "The practice of execution shows that if court work is supported and assisted by local Party and government departments, execution work goes smoothly."[221] If local authorities oppose the court, however, it may find (in the words of one threatening official) that it has "bitten off more than [it] can chew" (*chibuliao douzhe zou*).[222] In one reported case, a single telephone call from the local Party secretary brought execution to a halt.[223] In another case, a defendant used what were evidently police connections to disrupt court activities, including blocking the entrance to the court for

---

220. As one court put it,

> When a court experiences difficulty in executing judgments in cases that are doubtful, complex, widely influential, or subject to a great amount of interference, it should promptly report to the Party committee and the People's Congress, asking them to make an appearance in order to request the relevant departments to assist the court in getting its judgment executed.

Jiangsu HLPC 2, *supra* note 47, at 239. For similar sentiments, see Guangzhou ILPC, *supra* note 53, at 3; 1922 Beijing ILPC, *supra* note 42, at 8; Su He (vice president of the Huhehot Intermediate Level People's Court), *Tantan Jiejue 'Zhixing Nan' De Juti Cuoshi* [*A Discussion of Concrete Measures for Solving "Difficulty in Execution"*], at 5, *in* CONFERENCE MATERIALS, *supra* note 42. Of course, going to the People's Congress won't always work. The court of Tongan county in Fujian wrote six times to the court of Pingtan county in the same province requesting that it carry out entrusted execution against the Pingtan county salt plant. Nothing happened because the head of the salt plant was a member of the local People's Congress standing committee. *See* Fuzhou Shi Zhongji Renmin Fayuan Zhixing Ting [Fuzhou Intermediate Level People's Court], *Renzhen Zuohao Waidi Fayuan Weituo Huo Xiezhu Zhixing De Gongzuo* [*Conscientiously Do Well the Work of Execution Entrusted by or in Cooperation With Courts From Other Regions*], at 8, *in* CONFERENCE MATERIALS, *supra* note 42 [hereinafter 1992 Fuzhou ILPC 2].

Kevin O'Brien has observed the same imperatives at work in the attitudes of people's congress deputies toward "independence" from the Party — they don't necessarily *want* it. *See* Kevin J. O'Brien, *Chinese People's Congresses and Legislative Embeddedness: Understanding Early Organizational Development*, 27 COMP. POL. STUD. 80 (1984).

221. Chen & Xue, *supra* note 178. In one reported case, it was only after the head of the local government expressed his firm support for "the independent handling of cases by the court" that the court was able to get its judgment enforced. *See Linfen Xing Shu Zhuanyuan Wang Min Zhichi Fayuan Yi Fa Ban'an* [*Linfen Administrative District Chief Wang Min Supports the Court in Handling Cases According to Law*], SHANXI FAZHI BAO [SHANXI LEGAL SYSTEM NEWS], Dec. 14, 1986, at 1.

222. The case is reported in Liu Jian & Mu Xiaoqian, *Shei Zai Wei Beigao Dang Houtai? — Guangdong Sheng Jingji Jiufen Anjian Zhixing Nan Diaocha Zhi Er* [*Who Is Backing Up the Defendant? — Part Two of an Investigation Into Difficulty in Executing in Cases of Economic Disputes in Guangdong*], FAZHI RIBAO [LEGAL SYSTEM DAILY], April 5, 1988, at 3.

223. *See Shi-Wei Shuji Neng Ganshe Fayuan De Zhixing Ma?* [*Can the Municipal Party Committee Secretary Interfere With the Court's Execution?*], MINZHU YU FAZHI [DEMOCRACY AND THE LEGAL SYSTEM], No. 5, at 5 (1983) (letter to the editor).

three days with a vehicle loaded with toughs, who refused to let anyone enter or leave.[224]

Sometimes the power balance may be so one-sided that courts are simply not in the picture at all. In a Shaanxi village, a Party secretary forged a contract and unlawfully appropriated 20,000 *yuan* rightfully belonging to a peasant. The county Party and People's Congress investigated, found the peasant's complaint well founded, and ordered the money returned. The culprit, however, refused to do so, and evidently there was no way to require him. The most interesting thing about the report of this affair, however, is that while it uses terms such as "bringing a suit" (*gaozhuang*) and "a case of contract dispute" (*hetong jiufen an*), it never mentions the involvement of courts.[225]

The problem of local government interference appears to remain substantial. Chinese courts are not, along the Anglo-American model, powerful arbiters of last resort who can decide important questions involving powerful state leaders. Instead, they are in practice just one bureaucracy among many with a limited jurisdiction. When a court is on the same administrative level as a defendant, it simply lacks the rank to enforce.[226]

c. *Insolvency of Defendant*

Sometimes execution of a judgment will be impossible because the defendant either no longer exists or is insolvent.[227] Failure to execute a judgment here might have nothing to do with the adequacy of legal remedies or the strength of courts.[228] The strongest legal system in the world cannot prevent bad debts. On the other hand, the picture becomes more complicated when we realize that failure to execute against an insolvent corporate defendant also means failure to hold anyone else —

---

224. *See Xiayi Fasheng Ruma Fayuan Ganbu An* [*A Case of Humiliating and Cursing Court Cadres Occurs in Xiayi*], SHANGHAI FAZHI BAO [SHANGHAI LEGAL SYSTEM NEWS], Oct. 12, 1987, at 7.

225. *See id.*, at 1. It should be noted that *gaozhuang*, before the modern era, meant simply bringing a grievance to a government official.

226. *See Zhei-Ge Zao Yi Shenjie De Anzi Yao Tuo Dao He Ri Zhixing?* [*How Long Will This Long-Adjudicated Case Drag on Until Execution?*], FAZHI ZHOUBAO [LEGAL SYSTEM WEEKLY], May 17, 1988, at 3 ("We can't execute against the town government [in a suit that the latter lost]; we're on the same administrative level.") (letter to the editor).

227. On this problem, see generally Pan & Luo, *supra* note 59; Su, *supra* note 220; Kunming ILPC, *supra* note 59, at 3; Fei, *supra* note 145, at 63.

228. This argument is made in Court Interview F and Changchun ILPC, *Eliminate Local Protectionism*, *supra* note 170.

investors, for example, or an administrative superior — accountable for the debt. If someone else *should*, by some standard, be held accountable, then the failure to execute is significant.

It is important to examine this question because insolvency or dissolution of the debtor enterprise appears to account for a very large proportion of unexecuted judgments — according to one estimate, 30 to 40 percent.[229] In many cases, however, it may be that somebody else should be made responsible and is somehow getting off the hook. Suppose, for example, that the Bureau of Light Industry of City *X* runs an enterprise that is deeply in debt. It can try to pre-empt creditors by simply closing it down. During the "company fever" of the 1980s, this was a popular way of reducing risk. Government organs would establish undercapitalized "briefcase" companies; if they made money, well and good. If not, creditors would be left holding the bag.[230]

Several regulations have attempted to deal with this problem. A 1985 State Council notice provided that where companies were negligently approved, the approval organ bore responsibility for debts.[231] A joint Central Committee-State Council notice of the following year made approval organs responsible where unlawful operations resulted in unpayable debts.[232] A 1987 Supreme People's Court document provided — somewhat tautologically — that where a branch enterprise established by an enterprise closed down, it bore its debts itself if it was a legal person

229. *See* Xue Chunbao, *Dui Dangqian Fayuan Panjue Huo Caiding De Jingji Anjian Zhixing Wenti De Pouxi* [*An Analysis of Current Difficulties in Execution of Court Judgments or Rulings in Economic Cases*], ZHENJIANG FAXUE [ZHENJIANG LEGAL STUDIES], No. 2, at 25, 25 (1989). Other sources very roughly corroborate this figure. Out of 473 debt cases surveyed by the Jiangxi Higher Level People's Court, for example, 166 were unexecuted because the defendant had no money. *See* Jiangxi HLPC, *supra* note 124, at 3. In one group of unexecuted judgments before the Shenzhen Intermediate Level People's Court, 30 percent were for amounts exceeding one million *yuan* (there are about 8.3 *yuan* to the U.S. dollar). *See Jingji Anjian Zhixing Nan De Yuanyin He Duice* [*Difficulty in Execution in Economic Cases: Causes and Countermeasures*], SHENZHEN FAZHI BAO [SHENZHEN LEGAL SYSTEM NEWS], Sept. 20, 1989, at 3. *See also* Kunming ILPC, *supra* note 59, at 3-4.

230. For an account of one of these "briefcase" companies, see *Panjue Ruhe Zhixing?* [*How Can the Judgment Be Executed?*], SHENZHEN FAZHI BAO [SHENZHEN LEGAL SYSTEM NEWS], Aug. 8, 1990, at 1.

231. *See* State Council, Guanyu (Yao) Jinyibu Qingli He Zhengdun (Gelei) Gongsi De Tongzhi [Notice on Further Cleaning Up and Rectifying (All Kinds of) Companies] (words in parentheses omitted in some versions) (Aug. 20, 1985), *in* 4 JINGJI SHENPAN SHOUCE [HANDBOOK OF ECONOMIC ADJUDICATION] 70 (1988).

232. *See* Zhong-Gong Zhongyang, Guowu Yuan [Chinese Communist Party Central Committee, State Council], Guanyu Jinyibu Zhizhi Dang-Zheng Jiguan He Dang-Zheng Ganbu Jing Shang, Ban Qiye De Guiding [Rules on Further Putting a Stop to Party and Government Organs and Party and Government Officials Engaging in Business and Running Enterprises] (Feb. 4, 1986), *in* 1 JINGJI SHENPAN SHOUCE [HANDBOOK OF ECONOMIC ADJUDICATION] 209 (1987).

(because legal persons have limited liability). If it was not, then debts were to be borne by the superior enterprise. If the debtor in question was a "company" (*gongsi*), however, then the 1985 and 1986 regulations noted above would apply.[233] A 1990 State Council notice may or may not have modified the 1985 notice: it states, *inter alia*, that debts incurred by a company after it has become administratively separated from its founding government agency are not the responsibility of the founder.[234] It does not address the question of negligent approval. Finally, a 1994 Supreme People's Court notice abolished that part of its 1987 notice that said that debts of "companies" should be dealt with according to the 1985 State Council notice.[235] This would appear to mean that negligent approval is no longer grounds for imposing liability on a superior agency.

In the face of these regulations, government departments have come up with a new way of avoiding responsibility for indebted companies: instead of closing the company down, which would expose them to liability, they leave the company formally in existence as an empty shell with no substantial assets. As long as the company exists, the entity that approved it is not responsible for its debts. The company itself is, but its liability is limited to the property it has been given to manage — which has been largely stripped away.[236]

---

233. *See* Zuigao Renmin Fayuan [Supreme People's Court], Guanyu Xingzheng Danwei Huo Qiye Danwei Kaiban De Qiye Daobi Hou Zhaiwu You Shei Chengdan De Pifu [Reply on the Question of Who Should Bear the Debts of Enterprises Run by Administrative Units or Enterprise Units After They Have Become Insolvent] (Aug. 29, 1987), *in* ZHONGHUA RENMIN GONGHEGUO FALÜ QUANSHU [COMPENDIUM OF THE LAWS OF THE PEOPLE'S REPUBLIC OF CHINA] [hereinafter LAW COMPENDIUM] 1188 (1989).

234. *See* Guowu Yuan [State Council], Guanyu Zai Qingli Zhengdun Gongsi Zhong Bei Chebing Gongsi Zhaiquan Zhaiwu Qingli Wenti De Tongzhi [Notice Concerning the Issue of Debts and of Amounts Owing to Companies Merged or Closed in the Course of Cleaning Up and Rectifying Companies] (Dec. 12, 1990), ZHONGHUA RENMIN GONGHEGUO GUOWU YUAN GONGBAO [PEOPLE'S REPUBLIC OF CHINA STATE COUNCIL GAZETTE] [SCG], No. 28 [1990 volume], Feb. 5, 1991, at 1043, 1044 [hereinafter Notice on Company Debt].

235. *See* Zuigao Renmin Fayuan [Supreme People's Court], Guanyu Qiye Kaiban De Qita Qiye Bei Chexiao Huozhe Xieye Hou Minshi Zeren Chengdan Wenti De Pifu [Reply on the Question of the Bearing of Civil Liability After the Cancellation or Closing of Other Enterprises Run by Enterprises], SPCG, No. 2, June 20, 1994, at 71 [hereinafter Reply on Civil Liability]. The cumulative effect of all these notices and instructions from different bodies is far from clear. To attempt a strictly logical analysis may be missing the point, since Chinese judges — often recently demobilized army officers with little or no legal education — are not necessarily going to conduct the same analysis.

236. *See* Wuhan Shi Zhongji Renmin Fayuan Zhixing Ting [Execution Chamber of the Wuhan Intermediate Level People's Court], *Guanyu Zhixing Chengxu Zhong Zhuijiu Zhuguan Danwei Qingchang Zeren De Jige Wenti* [*Some Problems in Enforcing the Responsibility of the Unit in Charge to Clear Up Debts in the Course of Execution Proceedings*], at 3, *in* CONFERENCE MATERIALS, *supra* note 42 [hereinafter Wuhan ILPC]; Liu & Mu, *supra* note 204, at 3.

Courts and legal scholars are not unaware of this subterfuge. Thus, one court has suggested that at least where it is clear that the shell is maintained for the purpose of avoiding liability on the part of the company's administrative superior (*zhuguan bumen*), liability should be imposed.[237] Unfortunately, this sensible idea is seriously compromised by the limitation of the superior's liability to its extrabudgetary funds (*yusuanwai zijin*).[238] These are unlikely to be ample. Moreover, at least one scholar has proposed that creditors' recovery be further limited to the insolvent company's registered capital — that is, the original investment made in it.[239] This makes no sense for a number of reasons, the most obvious of which is that undercapitalization is the whole justification for going after the administrative superior in the first place. The most recent pronouncement on the subject, a 1994 Supreme People's Court document, rules that where a wound-up debtor as a practical matter met the requirements for legal personality, the liability of a superior agency cannot exceed the difference, if any, between registered capital and actual initial investment. Where the debtor did not as a practical matter meet the requirements for legal personality, the superior agency is responsible for the whole amount of the debt.[240]

d. Lack of Cooperation by Other Units

In a number of circumstances, the court cannot execute a judgment on its own, but needs the cooperation of other units that control various resources. The degree to which other units must cooperate with courts remains remarkably unclear even after more than a decade of legal reform. What is clear is that as a practical matter units such as banks can

---

237. *See* Wuhan ILPC, *supra* note 236, at 4. In a general discussion of the liability of superior administrative departments for the debts of subordinate enterprises, the court went on to propose handling this kind of case according to the general principle that the party receiving the benefits should bear the responsibility. Given that superior departments take profits and management fees, they should be expected to bear liability when things go wrong as well in accordance with the principle of the unity of rights and responsibilities. *See id.*, at 8. This apparently sensible rationale would, however, mean nothing less than the abolition of limited liability.

238. *See* Notice on Company Debt, *supra* note 234; Wuhan ILPC, *supra* note 236, at 9; Zhang Baoqin, *Qiantan Bei Zhixing Ren De Biangeng* [*A Brief Discussion of a Change in the Identity of the Executee*], FAXUE PINGLUN [LEGAL STUDIES REVIEW], No. 2, at 78, 79 (1992).

239. *See* Zhang, *supra* note 238, at 9.

240. *See* Reply on Civil Liability, *supra* note 235. This document is especially interesting because it defines legal personality in terms of substance, not in terms of the fulfillment of formal requirements such as registration.

sometimes ignore court requests or orders with impunity.[241] Thus, when a court wishes to freeze or seize funds in a defendant's bank account, the banks can often as a practical matter — lawfully or unlawfully — pose many obstacles if they wish to. Similarly, a defendant's work unit may simply refuse to garnish wages by the amount the court requests, and the court appears to have little recourse.

The ability of banks and others to resist court orders to assist in execution stems from the fact that the court is essentially just another bureaucracy, with no more power to tell banks what to do than the Post Office. Traditionally, it appears that organizations outside the court bureaucracy had no more than a kind of moral obligation to cooperate with a court. In one case from the 1950s, the court ordered that eight *yuan* per month be withheld from the defendant's wages to pay a debt. The defendant's work unit thought this was unreasonable and withheld five *yuan* instead. The court, it was reported, realized its error and agreed to five *yuan*.[242] The case is presented positively as one of consultation between equals, not as a struggle for power between a giver and a receiver of orders. In a similar case in the 1980s, the court told the defendant's work unit to garnish ten *yuan* per month from his wages for child support after divorce. This time, however, the work unit simply refused to cooperate outright.[243] In Harbin, a district real estate administration bureau, having received a direct order from the provincial level court to transfer housing

241. *See* Pan & Luo, *supra* note 227, at 6; *Dangqian Jingji Anjian Weihe Zhixing Nan?*, *supra* note 185, at 1; Huang Shuangquan, *Guanyu Minshi Zhixing De Qingkuang Diaocha* [*An Investigation Into Execution in Civil Cases*], ZHENGZHI YU FALÜ [POLITICS AND LAW], No. 2 at 64, 66 (1984); CHANG, *supra* note 44, at 5.

242. *See* Beijing Shi Xuanwu Qu Renmin Fayuan [People's Court of Xuanwu District in Beijing], *Guanyu Minshi Zhixing Anjian Zhong Kouchu Gongzi De Chubu Jingyan* [*Initial Experience in Garnishing Wages in Executing Civil Cases*], RENMIN SIFA GONGZUO [PEOPLE'S JUDICIAL WORK], No. 4, at 23, 24 (1957) [hereinafter Xuanwu Court].

243. *See Renmin Fayuan Yijing Shengxiao De Panjue Bixu Zhixing* [*Judgments of the People's Court That Have Taken Legal Effect Must Be Executed*], RENMIN RIBAO [PEOPLE'S DAILY], Oct. 25, 1982, at 4 (1982) (letter to the editor). In another case from the mid-eighties, a defendant refused to pay ten *yuan* in court costs (almost certainly a matter of face, not finances). The court then issued a notice to the defendant's work unit asking it to pay over the sum from his wages. According to art. 171 of the 1982 Law on Civil Procedure in effect at the time, such a notice had to be obeyed. Nevertheless, the order came back with a pencilled message on the envelope saying,

> The court comrades handling this case are requested to do more mediation work in order to avoid the exacerbation of contradictions among the people. The circumstances are unclear and it is impossible to execute by compulsion.

According to the report, the relevant official at the defendant's work unit was later shocked when informed that it was a serious offense not to carry out a court order. *See Gongran Tuihui Fayuan Xiezhu Zhixing Tongzhi Shu* [*Brazenly Returning the Court's Notice to Cooperate in Execution*], SHANGHAI FAZHI BAO [SHANGHAI LEGAL SYSTEM NEWS], May 20, 1985, at 1.

to a party, refused to issue the necessary documents. In fact, it requested guidance from the bureau at the municipal level regarding what it was supposed to do about the judgment with which it did not agree.[244]

Although generally applicable law and Party policy[245] now make clear that all units have a duty to obey court orders, the regulations that really count when it comes to cooperation between bureaucratic "systems" (*xitong*) are those to which all the relevant parties have signed on. A prime example is a 1980 regulation on procuratorial investigation of bank accounts issued jointly by the People's Bank of China, the Supreme People's Court, the Supreme People's Procuracy, the Ministry of Public Security, and the Ministry of Justice.[246] This is far more binding on banks than, say, a 1985 Supreme People's Court regulation[247] that was issued apparently after "liaison and study" with the People's Bank of China, but nevertheless without its co-signature.

---

244. *See Zhongshen Panjue Yi Liang-Nian; Zhi Jin Tuotan Bu Zhixing* [*Final Judgment Already Two Years Old; Still Delaying Execution to This Day*], HAERBIN FAZHI BAO [HARBIN LEGAL SYSTEM NEWS], Sept. 3, 1989, at 1.

245. *See* Chinese Communist Party Central Committee, Guanyu Jianjue Baozheng Xingfa Xingshi Susong Fa Qieshi Shixing De Zhishi [Directive on Firmly Guaranteeing the Thorough Implementation of the Criminal and Civil Procedure Laws] (Sept. 9, 1979) ("Relevant units and individuals must resolutely execute judgments and rulings issued according to law by judicial organs."), *in* 1 SIFA SHOUCE [JUDICIAL HANDBOOK] 67; *Renmin Fayuan De Panjue He Caiding, Youguan Danwei He Geren Bixu Jianjue Zhixing* [*Relevant Units and Individuals Must Firmly Implement Judgments and Rulings of People's Courts*], SHANGHAI FAZHI BAO [SHANGHAI LEGAL SYSTEM NEWS], Apr. 16, 1984, at 3. Despite the existence of this specific mandate to Party members, as well as the general duty (in fact a heightened duty) of Party members to obey state law, my interviews made it clear that courts and plaintiffs do not and cannot use the threat of Party disciplinary sanctions against Party member defendants who do not obey court orders.

This issue, in fact, exposed an interesting clash of legal cultures. To most of my interlocutors, the idea of using Party discipline seemed absurd. To me, the idea that this was out of the question seemed strange, since with any other administrative or criminal violation by a Party member, Party disciplinary sanctions can be used in addition to, and indeed often in place of, the regular administrative or criminal punishment called for.

In the view of one group of judges, Party sanctions were not appropriate because we were talking of civil matters — "contradictions among the people" — not criminal matters. In other words, they did not distinguish between liability on the original claim, which is civil, and liability for refusing to perform a judgment imposing civil liability, which they had just informed me could be criminal. *See* Court Interview F.

246. Zhongguo Renmin Yinhang, Zuigao Renmin Fayuan, Zuigao Renmin Jianchayuan, Gongan Bu, Sifa Bu [People's Bank of China, Supreme People's Court, Supreme People's Procuracy, Ministry of Public Security, Ministry of Justice], Guanyu Chaxun, Tingzhi Zhifu De Moshou Geren Zai Yinhang De Cunkuan Yiji Cunkuan Ren Siwang De Cunkuan Guohu Huo Zhifu Shouxu De Lianhe Tongzhi [Joint Notice Concerning Investigating, Stopping Payments From, and Confiscating Funds of Individuals Held in Banks as Well as the Procedures for Making Payments From or Transferring Ownership Over Funds Belonging to Deceased Depositors] (Nov. 22, 1980), *in* ZHIXING GONGZUO SHOUCE, *supra* note 15, at 686 [hereinafter 1980 SPC Joint Notice].

247. *See* 1985 SPC Reply, *supra* note 188.

In general, courts (as well as the procuracy and the police) appear to encounter extraordinary problems in getting access to a defendant's bank records or account.[248] Banks are jealous guardians of their prerogatives — a jealousy that has been enhanced by the effect of economic reform on their need to compete for customers — and the duty of banks to assist law enforcement agencies has been the subject of repeated rulemaking in the 1980s and 1990s.

The 1980 joint regulation noted above provided that neither the court nor the procuracy could directly review bank records; they had to specify to bank officials what they wanted and get the approval of the bank director at a certain administrative level, who was then supposed to order the subordinate bank to provide the information requested.[249]

Subsequent notices and regulations have, with some exceptions, marked an effort to increase the power of courts and other law enforcement institutions vis-à-vis the banks. In 1983 the Supreme People's Court and the People's Bank of China jointly issued a key notice (the "1983 Joint Notice") that governed court-bank relations for about a decade.[250] On the one hand, this notice noted "some problems" in the implementation of rules governing the access of courts to bank records, and admonished banks not to interfere with the seizure of funds belonging to judgment debtors. Instead of specifying a minimum level in the bank hierarchy at which approval of the court order had to be obtained, it merely instructed courts to deliver the appropriate documents to "the bank" or to the "responsible person."[251]

On the other hand, whereas the 1982 Law on Civil Procedure said that courts "may" (*ke*) entrust the execution of a judgment against a non-local defendant to a court in the locality of the defendant, the 1983 Joint Notice

248. Indeed, when one bank cooperated with a court it made headlines. *See Ning'an Xian Er-Shang Yinghang Jiji Xiezhu Fayuan Zuohao Zhixing Gongzuo* [*Number Two Commercial Bank in Ning'an County Actively Cooperates With the Court in Doing Execution Work Well*], HEILONGJIANG FAZHI BAO [HEILONGJIANG LEGAL SYSTEM NEWS], Feb. 24, 1987, at 1.

249. *See* 1980 SPC Joint Notice, *supra* note 246. At least one provincial regulation made equally stringent demands. *See* 1980 Zhejiang Notice, *supra* note 187. It would in practice have taken precedence over the central regulations.

250. Zuigao Renmin Fayuan, Zhongguo Renmin Yinhang [Supreme People's Court, People's Bank of China], Guangyu Chaxun, Dongjie He Kouhua Qiye Shiye Danwei, Jiguan, Tuanti De Yinhang Cunkuan De Lianhe Tonzhi [Joint Notice on Investigating, Freezing, and Levying on Bank Accounts of Enterprises, Institutions, Organs, and Organizations] (Dec. 28, 1983), *in* ZHIXING GONGZUO SHOUCE, *supra* note 15, at 695 [hereinafter 1983 Joint Notice].

251. A subsequent interpretive document issued only by the Supreme People's Court specified that "responsible person" meant the person in charge of the local branch, not an official at any particular level, thus watering down the 1980 requirement completely. *See* 1985 SPC Reply, *supra* note 188.

went beyond this to say that when levying from a non-local bank account, courts "should" (*yingdang*) entrust the local court to issue a required notice to the local bank. This is not quite as strong as "must" (*bixu*), but considerably stronger than the merely permissive "may". Indeed, the 1983 Joint Notice's use of "should" was criticized by Chinese legal scholars as contrary to law and supportive of local protectionism.[252]

Although the 1991 revised Law on Civil Procedure maintained the formulation of "may" with respect to entrusted enforcement and made no special exception for the seizure of bank deposits, courts and banks remained confused.[253] After all, the 1982 Law on Civil Procedure had said the same thing, with no apparent effect on the validity of the 1983 Joint Notice. The issue may finally have been settled, at least in terms of concrete regulations if not in terms of practice, by a notice issued in 1993 by several interested agencies: the People's Bank of China, the Supreme People's Court, the Supreme People's Procuracy, and the Ministry of Public Security (the "1993 Joint Notice").[254]

This notice apparently supersedes the 1983 Joint Notice, although it does not say so specifically. It repeats the requirement of earlier notices that requests for bank cooperation in investigating, freezing, or seizing deposits must come from a court, procuracy, or police bureau at the county level or above. It specifies (this time over the seal of the People's Bank of China, and thus in a manner that is binding on banks) that the "responsible person" at the bank whose signature is needed can be the head of the local branch and need not be someone higher up. Finally, it states clearly that any court, procuracy, or police bureau may request the cooperation of a bank without regard to jurisdictional boundaries, thus resolving the issue of whether a local court had to be entrusted with execution if a bank account was involved.

---

252. *See* Xu & He, *supra* note 59, at 17.

253. *See generally* 1992 Guiyang ILPC, *supra* note 99, at 8; 1992 Fuzhou ILPC, *supra* note 44, at 9 (noting need for guidance in the matter).

254. Zhongguo Renmin Yinhang, Zuigao Renmin Fayuan, Zuigao Remnin Jianchayuan, Gongan Bu [People's Bank of China, Supreme People's Court, Supreme People's Procuracy, Ministry of Public Security], Guanyu Chaxun, Dongjie, Kouhua Qiye Shiye Danwei, Jiguan, Tuanti Yinhang Cunkuan De Tongzhi [Notice on Investigation, Freezing, and Levying on Bank Accounts of Enterprises, Institutions, Organs, and Organizations] (Dec. 11, 1993), *in* DATABASE, *supra* note 85. The final section of the notice reveals the ways in which the conflict between courts and banks is manifested: banks are forbidden to transfer or unfreeze frozen funds or to warn the depositor in advance of freezing, while courts for their part are told that when there is a difference of opinion with a bank, the matter should be resolved through consultation between the superiors of both court and bank instead of by detaining bank personnel.

e. *Inadequacy of Legal Means of Coercion*

An important general obstacle to enforcement is the lack of tools of coercion available to courts. As noted in the preceding section, courts have few means of forcing units whose cooperation is needed in execution to go along. In the 1991 revision of the Law on Civil Procedure — inspired in part by execution problems — courts actually *lost* the power to detain bank personnel for failure to cooperate in freezing or seizing bank deposits.[255] Unlike Anglo-American courts, Chinese courts have no general contempt power. Any exercise of coercion over the person or property of a party must have a specific statutory basis. This is not, of course, to say that courts never act without a statutory basis, but the lack of one does make things more difficult. Generally, a defendant's resistance to execution must be quite egregious before courts will resort to coercive measures, and the press is full of stories of court officials being beaten and humiliated by arrogant execution debtors.[256] It is still a matter of debate in the Chinese legal community whether the mere failure by a defendant to carry out a judgment, without more, is sufficient to justify administrative detention or criminal punishment.[257]

A number of sources complain about the lack of useful national legislation on the subject of execution. The 1992 revision of the Law on Civil Procedure was intended in part to redress this problem. In addition,

---

255. Compare article 77 of the 1982 Law on Civil Procedure (allowing detention or criminal prosecution of those with an obligation to assist the court in a civil case who fail to do so) with article 103 of the 1991 Law on Civil Procedure (allowing only the fining of bank personnel who refuse to assist courts). According to one Supreme People's Court official I interviewed, this weakening of court powers was the result of strong lobbying during the revision process by the People's Bank, which did not want courts to be able to lock up bank officials. *See* Court Interview D. The brief detention of a bank manager for refusing to transfer funds from the defendant's account — he wanted to use the money to ensure that the bank's own outstanding loan to the defendant was repaid — is reported in Heilongjiang Sheng Gaoji Renmin Fayuan Yanjiu Shi [Research Office of the Heilongjiang Higher Level People's Court], *Hangzhang Wei Fa Bei Yi Fa Juiliu* [*Bank Manager Violates Law, Is Detained According to Law*], RENMIN SIFA [PEOPLE'S JUDICATURE], No. 4, at 7 (1989) [hereinafter 1989 Heilongjiang HLPC].

256. *See, e.g.*, Lü Huichang & Xiong Fasheng, *Ju Bu Zhixing Fayuan Panjue Bing Ouda Zhifa Renyuan* [*Refuses to Implement Court Judgment, Even Beats Law Implementation Personnel*], HUBEI FAZHI BAO [HUBEI LEGAL SYSTEM NEWS], July 14, 1988, at 1; Li Dezhang, *Minshi Shenpan Faguanmen De Kuzhong* [*The Bitterness of Judges in Civil Adjudication*], SICHUAN FAZHI BAO [SICHUAN LEGAL SYSTEM NEWS], June 20, 1988, at 1 (listing complaints of judges); Gao Fa, *Weigong Wuru Ouda Ban'an Renyuan De Wenti Yingdang Yinqi Zhongshi* [*The Problem of Personnel Handling Cases Being Surrounded and Attacked, Humiliated, and Beaten Should Attract Attention*], FAZHI DAOBAO [LEGAL SYSTEM HERALD], Jan. 20, 1990, at 3 (catalog of abuses suffered by court officials from beating to imprisonment).

257. I discuss the coercive tools available to courts in detail in the next section below.

there is a long tradition of courts formulating their own execution procedures that continues to this day.[258]

B. Specific Problems in Execution

This section looks at how judgments can vary in their executability depending on a number of different characteristics they might have. Specifically, it looks at how the executability of a judgment can be affected by the nature of the defendant and the plaintiff as well as by the method of execution.

1. Who Is the Defendant?

While it is reasonable to think that defendants of different status will have differing abilities to resist execution, the sources do not always tell an unequivocal story. According to some sources, execution against large state-owned enterprises is generally not a problem.[259] They are less likely than small enterprises to be strapped for immediate cash.

On the other hand, when they do not have the money or for some other reason do not wish to pay, execution can be very difficult.[260] It seems clear from interviews and published sources that in 1992 (and probably still) courts were to show special solicitude for large and medium-sized state-owned enterprises when asked to execute a judgment against them.[261] In particular, seizing their fixed assets in satisfaction of a debt was, and

---

258. *See* Xu & He, *supra* note 59, at 17. Court rules from the 1950s include 1951 Shenyang Measures, *supra* note 63; 1951 Urumchi Measures, *supra* note 63; and 1955 Beijing Measures, *supra* note 64. Recently, court rules have been issued by the Jiangsu Higher Level People's Court, *see Jiangsu Sheng Fayuan Shouci Zhixing Gongzuo Huiyi* [*Jiangsu Provincial Court Holds First Meeting on Execution Work*], *in* RENMIN FAYUAN NIANJIAN 1989 [YEARBOOK OF PEOPLE'S COURTS 1989], at 759 (1989), and the Heilongjiang Higher Level People's Court, *see Heilongjiang Sheng Fayuan Zhixing Gongzuo Huiyi* [*Execution Work Meeeting of the Heilongjiang Provincial Court*], *in* RENMIN FAYUAN NIANJIAN 1989 [YEARBOOK OF PEOPLE'S COURTS 1989], at 751 (1989).

259. *See* Lawyer Interview H; Academic Interview G.

260. *See* Court Interview U; Lawyer Interview O; Court Interview F.

261. *See* Lawyer Interview O; Lawyer Interview H; Guangzhou ILPC, *supra* note 53, at 4; Su, *supra* note 220, at 4; Academic Interview J.

probably remains, virtually forbidden.[262] As a general rule, courts are not supposed to stress execution "one-sidedly" to the neglect of other factors:

> When adopting coercive legal measures to resolve economic cases, we must never pay attention only to finishing up the case; we must at the same time pay attention to unity and stability in society, to stabilizing relations of socialist ownership, and to developing the socialist economy.[263]

In practice, this means "Don't execute where it will mean closing the defendant enterprise and throwing workers onto the street."[264] In the words of one high-ranking judge, "[t]o promote a unified and stable social situation is the overriding task above all else."[265] This principle is entirely

---

262. *See* Lawyer Interview A ("Normally, one doesn't execute against means of production; one executes against circulating funds."). The same self-imposed prohibition against touching capital assets can be found in the report of a meeting to discuss execution problems held by the HLPC of the province of Jiangsu. *See* RENMIN FAYUAN NIANJIAN 1990 [YEARBOOK OF PEOPLE'S COURTS 1990], at 620 (1989). There is no basis in the Law on Civil Procedure or the Enterprise Bankruptcy Law for distinguishing between the two. Some writers hold that one can seize means of production, even if needed by the debtor enterprise for production, if they are needed even more by the creditor enterprise. *See* Liao Degong & Yu Mingyong, *Lun Wanshan Minshi Caichan Baoquan Zhidu He Minshi Zhixing Zhidu* [*On Perfecting the System of Property Preservation in Civil Matters and the System of Execution in Civil Matters*], FAXUE YANJIU [STUDIES IN LAW], No. 4, at 47, 50 (1992). For a detailed discussion of what types of property can be executed against and in what circumstances, see CHAI FABANG, JIANG WEI, LIU JIAXING & FAN MINGXIN, MINSHI SUSONG FA TONGLUN [GENERAL TREATISE ON THE LAW OF CIVIL PROCEDURE] 454 (1982) [hereinafter CIVIL PROCEDURE TREATISE]; ZHIXING DE LILUN YU SHIJIAN, *supra* note 81, at 48.

263. Wang, *supra* note 77, at 7 (the author at the time of writing was the President of the Shenzhen Intermediate-Level People's Court). For almost identical language, see Guangzhou ILPC, *supra* note 53, at 2. Other court officials spoke to me of the need to take into account not only the legal effects, but also social and economic effects of the judgment. *See* Court Interview F; *see also* Beijing ILPC, *supra* note 42, at 8 ("We oppose the tendency of not considering social or political effects, of considering individual cases in isolation [when undertaking execution]."). This is not to suggest that courts in common law systems never take practical consequences into account when rendering judgment or undertaking execution. The difference — and it is a significant one — is that they must never admit to doing so, while Chinese courts are urged to. *Fiat justitia, ruat cœlum* is not a maxim of the Chinese legal system. For an interesting history of how the United States Supreme Court tried to take social reality into account while appearing not to do so in the school desegregation case, *Brown v. Board of Education* (believing that an order requiring immediate desegregation, while just, would have been unenforceable), see Philip Elman, *The Solicitor-General's Office, Justice Frankfurter, and Civil Rights Litigation, 1946-1960: An Oral History*, 100 HARV. L. REV. 817 (1987) (describing the use of the formula "with all deliberate speed").

264. For a case where a court refused to enforce its own judgment against an enterprise on precisely these grounds ("The township government leaders don't approve of its being put to death; we must consider the matter from the standpoint of what's advantageous to economic development"), see Zhang, *supra* note 172.

265. Wang, *supra* note 77, at 7.

the result of Party policy and is not sanctioned by any published document with the status of law.[266]

Among state-owned enterprises, those run by the military are particularly proof against execution. As the Chengdu ILPC complained,

> Military funds can't be investigated; anything to do with assets or funds they say is all military funds and can't be executed against. There is no rule [addressing this issue] in law or policy. . . . . We have not been able to have compulsory execution in a single case against a military enterprise.[267]

In the words of the Nanning ILPC, judgments against government departments or the military were generally "impossible to execute."[268] The best hope, albeit a thin one, for courts in these cases is to go through the enterprise's administrative superior.[269]

Contrary to the view of the Chengdu ILPC, there are — and were at the time its article was written — rules addressing the issue of execution against military funds. In 1985, banking authorities and the General Logistics Department of the PLA jointly issued a document providing that military units should use a special bank account for certain commercial activities.[270] In 1990, in response to two requests for instructions from

---

266. *See, e.g.*, Li Peng, *The Current Economic Situation and the Issue of Further Improving State-Owned Large and Medium-Sized Enterprises*, *in* SWB/FE, Oct. 23, 1991, at FE/1210/C1/1 (speech by Li Peng at a CCP Central Committee work conference on September 23, 1991).

267. Chengdu Shi Zhongji Renmin Fayuan [Chengdu Intermediate Level People's Court], *Qiantan Jingji Anjian Zhixing Zhong De Youguan Wenti* [*A Brief Discussion of Problems Related to Execution in Economic Cases*], *in* "ZHIXING NAN" DUICE TAN, *supra* note 49, at 60, 67.

268. 1992 Nanning ILPC, *supra* note 106, at 13.

269. *See* Academic Interview G. It should be noted that the difficulty of executing against military enterprises is not limited to enterprises engaged in military production. It includes any business in any sector run by the military, such as the Palace Hotel in Beijing. The difficulty is caused not by a legal bar on execution against military assets, but by the practical difficulty of moving against such a powerful defendant.

270. *See* Zhongguo Renmin Yinhang, Zhongguo Gong-Shang Yinhang, Zhongguo Nongye Yinhang, Zhongguo Renmin Jiefang Jun Zong Houqin Bu [People's Bank of China, Industrial-Commercial Bank of China, General Logistics Department of the Chinese People's Liberation Army], Jundui Danwei Zai Yinhang Kaishe Zhanghu He Cunkuan De Guanli Banfa [Measures for the Administration of Accounts and Deposits Established in Banks by Military Units], *Cai Zi* No. 110 (1985). This document appears to be an internal regulation not publicly available, but it is referred to in Zuigao Renmin Fayuan [Supreme People's Court], Guanyu Jundui Danwei Zuowei Jingji Jiufen Anjian De Dangshiren Ke Fou Dui Qi Yinhang Zhanghu Shang De Cunkuan Caiqu Susong Boaquan He Jundui Feiyong Neng Fou Qiangxing Huabo Changhuan Zhaiwu Wenti de Pifu [Reply to the Questions of Whether It Is Permitted to Apply Litigation Protection Measures to the Bank Deposits of Military Units That Are Parties in Economic Disputes, and Whether Military Funds May be Coercively Seized for the Repayment of Debt] (Oct. 9, 1990), *in* ZHONGHUA RENMIN GONGHEGUO

lower courts made three years earlier, the Supreme People's Court issued a reply ruling that funds from the special bank account, as well as from other accounts that were unlawfully used for business, were available for execution.[271] Given that no PLA department was a co-issuer of this document, however, its binding power is questionable.

Small enterprises and *getihu* (individual businesses) present their own problems. Because they may have relatively more at stake, they may be more stubborn about resisting execution, even if they have less actual power to do so.[272]

Finally, enterprises that provide employment for the disabled seem to enjoy a certain immunity from execution.[273]

Geographical location of the defendant also appears to play a role. Several sources mentioned that execution was more difficult against defendants in poorer and inland provinces. Henan in particular was mentioned by three different sources.[274] It is not clear why execution should be more difficult in poorer provinces. It may be that defendants are more likely to be insolvent; it may be that local enterprises are especially valued and thus protected. As more than one source points out, however, such a strategy can backfire in the long run. People will be reluctant to do business with enterprises from places where courts and government always protect their own. Backward regions may simply remain backward for lack of trade and investment.[275]

Finally, it is worth saying a word about individuals subject to execution. Individuals have long had a limited immunity from execution when money or property is sought. A number of local court rules from the 1950s all provide that courts must leave with the judgment debtor sufficient funds and property for the livelihood of debtor and his or her dependents.[276] The same rule appears in Article 171 of the 1982 Law on

---

FALÜ (ZENGBU BEN) 1990-1992 [COMPENDIUM OF THE LAWS OF THE PEOPLE'S REPUBLIC OF CHINA (SUPPLEMENTARY EDITION) 1990-1992], at 364-365 (1993) [hereinafter 1990 SPC Reply 2].

271. *See* 1990 SPC Reply 2, *supra* note 270.

272. *See* Lawyer Interview H; Academic Interview G.

273. *See* Nanjing Shi Zhongji Renmin Fayuan Zhixing Ting Nanjing Intermediate Level People's Court Execution Chamber], *Zhixing Zi Bu Di Zhai Anjian De Jidian Tihui Ji Sikao* [*Some Understandings and Thoughts About Executing in Cases of Liabilities Exceedings Assets*], *in* "ZHIXING NAN" DUICE TAN, *supra* note 49, at 38, 39.

274. Lawyer Interview O; Academic Interview J; Lawyer Interview R.

275. *See* 1992 Chengdu ILPC, *supra* note 172, at 6; Academic Interview J.

276. *See, e.g.*, 1949 Harbin Regulations, *supra* note 63, at 437 (arts. 21, 25); 1951 Dongbei Directive, *supra* note 63, at 714 (art. 6); 1951 Shenyang Measures, *supra* note 63, art. 7; 1951 Urumchi Measures, *supra* note 63, art. 10; 1955 Beijing Measures, *supra* note 64, part IV, art. 5; 1955 Procedure Summary, *supra* note 65, at 34.

Civil Procedure and in Article 222 of its 1991 revision. It would be a mistake to suppose that this exemption is always interpreted generously. In 1989, a Shenzhen defendant was allowed to keep only 150 *yuan* per month from his income in order to support himself, his mother, and his daughter — less than two *yuan* per day per person at a time of significant inflation.[277]

It is a different story entirely with individuals subject to judgments for eviction. Such judgments can be among the most difficult to execute of all.[278] Primary and secondary sources agree that "coercive measures are undertaken only when the execution debtor genuinely has a place to move to and still refuses to move."[279] In virtually all cases, a person with no place to go is immune from execution.[280]

---

277. *Fayuan Yao Baoliu Bei Zhixing Ren De Shenghuo Feiyong Ma?* [*Should the Court Leave Enough for the Living Expenses of the Executee?*], SHANGHAI FAZHI BAO [SHANGHAI LEGAL SYSTEM NEWS], Dec. 18, 1989, at 7. Compare this stingy immunity with that of the bankruptcy laws of, say, Florida, which exempt from seizure among other things *all* wages and the debtor's personal residence, regardless of its value. As one bankruptcy judge complained, "[Y]ou could shelter the Taj Mahal in this state and no one could do anything about it." Larry Rohter, *Rich Debtors Finding Shelter Under a Populist Florida Law*, N.Y. TIMES, July 25, 1993, at 1.

278. *See* Court Interview U; Court Interview E; 1992 Fuzhou ILPC, *supra* note 44, at 10; Luo, *supra* note 148, at 78. The difficulty has existed for decades. *See* Tai, *supra* note 104, at 21. On housing cases generally, see Fuzhou Shi Gulou Qu Fayuan [Fuzhou City Gulou District Court], *Dui Zhixing Shoufang Anjian Ruogan Wenti De Tantao* [*An Investigation Into Several Problems of Execution in Cases Involving the Recovery of Housing*], *in* CONFERENCE MATERIALS, *supra* note 42 [hereinafter Gulou BLPC], whose "solution" merits quotation on the grounds of sheer fatuousness:

> Practice proves that with respect to the problem of cases involving the recovery of housing being difficult to execute, provided we have confidence, address this problem correctly, approach it with the actual circumstances in mind, adopt effective measures, and in the course of execution work earnestly to ensure that the execution activities are well founded, the processes are lawful, work is done carefully, methods are appropriate, measures are effective, and procedures are complete, then the problem of cases involving the recovery of housing being difficult to execute can be resolved in a relatively satisfactory way.

Id. at 4.

279. Cheng, Liu & Cheng, *supra* note 128, at 43. *See also* Academic Interview C; Court Interview U.

280. This policy appears to apply only to cases deemed to be "internal contradictions" and thus can be waived in the case of political dissidents and their families. The wife and daughter of Ren Wanding, jailed both in the late 1970s and the late 1980s for human rights advocacy, found the door to their flat nailed shut with all their belongings still inside upon arriving home one afternoon. *See* Sheryl WuDunn, *Wife of Jailed China Dissident Is Left Homeless by Eviction*, N.Y. TIMES, Apr. 19, 1992, at A7.

I did find one case of eviction where the tenant appears to have had no place to go. An individual business operator (*getihu*) was forcibly removed from a space rented to her as a workshop about a year after she began living in it (precisely because she had no other residence). This case may, however, be the exception that proves the rule: first, unlike the typical tenant, she was living in a space that was not intended for residential use; second (and probably most important), the space belonged not to a private landlord but to a local supply and marketing cooperative, and was thus

This policy has a long history in the People's Republic and can perhaps be considered a kind of customary law — I have been unable to find any authoritative documentary basis for it outside of a 1955 set of internal rules of the court of Xuanwu District in Beijing.[281] A 1992 article refers to "provisions of law" supporting this immunity but provides no concrete reference.[282] It appears to be one of those things that everyone "just knows." It has been justified on the grounds that just as a court suspends execution against a debtor who has no money, it should suspend execution against a tenant who has no place to go.[283]

In an eviction case, the defendant might be given an initial deadline of half a year or a year within which to move out, with extensions available.[284] The plaintiff-landlord might be encouraged to find another place for the defendant and to help him out with the first few rent payments.[285] When both tenant and landlord refuse to look for another place for the tenant, the result is not eviction but paralysis: the maintenance of the status quo.[286]

Even when there is another important policy at stake — for example, that of returning possession of property wrongfully taken from overseas

---

considered government property. *See Zhou Haiqing Zhanyong Gonggang Bei Qiangzhi Tengtui [Zhou Haiqing Occupies Public Quarters, Is Forced to Move Out]*, SICHUAN FAZHI BAO [SICHUAN LEGAL SYSTEM NEWS], July 25, 1988, at 1.

281. "Coerced moving from a residence should be effected under the premise that the applicant still has a place to live." 1955 Beijing Measures, *supra* note 64, part. VII, art. 1. This principle is repeated in identical language (not surprisingly, given that the author is an official in the same court) in Tai, *supra* note 104, at 21. The earliest mention I have found of this policy is in Shenyang Renmin Fayuan [Shenyang People's Court], *Minshi Zhixing Gongzuo Zhong De Ji-Dian Jingyan Jiaoxun [Some Experience and Lessons From Work in Civil Execution]* (1951), *in* ZHONGHUA RENMIN GONGHEGUO XING MIN SHI SUSONG CANKAO ZILIAO [REFERENCE MATERIALS ON THE LAW OF CRIMINAL AND CIVIL PROCEDURE OF THE PEOPLE'S REPUBLIC OF CHINA] 295, 295-296 (Wuhan Daxue Falü Xi Xing Min Fa Jiaoyanzu [Criminal and Civil Law Teaching and Research Section of the Wuhan University Department of Law] ed., 1954). In this source, however, the court considers the practice to be a shortcoming in its own work.

282. *See* Gulou BLPC, *supra* note 278, at 6.

283. *See* ZHIXING DE LILUN YU SHIJIAN, *supra* note 81, at 44. On the other hand, debtors generally have an incentive to find money, whereas tenants under this rule have no incentive to find another place to live.

284. *See* Academic Interview J. The deadline is a hollow threat, since if the tenant has not found a place by the time it expires, he still cannot be forced to move. *See id.*

285. This was suggested by one court in interviews. *See* Court Interview E. It is confirmed in articles by courts from other parts of the country entirely. *See, e.g.*, 1992 Fuzhou ILPC, *supra* note 44, at 10 ("When the execution debtor has no place to move to, we ask the landlord to help him find a place and to provide funds for moving."). Another court reports two cases: in one, the landlord found the tenant a new place for 60 *yuan* a month and made a one-time payment to the tenant of 900 *yuan*; in the other, the court persuaded the tenant to reduce his demand for "moving expenses" from 20,000 *yuan* to 1,400 *yuan*. *See* Gulou BLPC, *supra* note 278, at 7-8.

286. *See* Gulou BLPC, *supra* note 278, at 1.

Chinese — the burden of that policy falls on the work units of those wrongfully occupying the property, not on the occupants themselves. Until their units find alternative housing, the occupants will not be forced to leave.[287] One court went so far as to blame "execution difficulties" on landlords who obstinately insisted on getting their property back in accordance with the judgment. In such cases, wrote the court, "we should resolutely suspend execution in accordance with the provisions of Article 234, Paragraph 5 of the Law on Civil Procedure."[288]

In evictions as in other areas, execution policy essentially mirrors legal policy. As seen already in the discussion of the lack of finality of judgments,[289] courts do not seem to draw a strict distinction between pre-judgment and post-judgment procedure. Even after a landlord overcomes the obstacles in the way of obtaining a favorable judgement, however, the same policies continue to operate at the stage of execution. A local rule on execution in Fujian province states that where a tenant has no place to go, he should be given a period of time (normally not to exceed one year) within which to find a new place. If by the end of the period the tenant has still not found a place to go, the execution officer should conduct diligent ideological work on the *landlord* and give another extension.[290]

2. Who Is the Plaintiff?

Who the plaintiff is can significantly affect the likelihood of a judgment's being executed. First, courts tend to work harder on behalf of a plaintiff who will need support from the state if the judgment is not executed.

Claims for payment of support for children, spouses, or aged parents are given high priority in adjudication and in execution.[291] At the time the claim is made but before it has been judged, the court can order an advance payment (*xianxing geifu*), a measure similar to a preliminary injunction

---

287. *See* Guowu Yuan Qiaowu Bangongshi, Cheng-Xiang Jianshe Huanjing Baohu Bu [State Council Office of Overseas Chinese Affairs, Ministry of Urban and Village Construction and Environmental Protection], Guanyu Luoshi "Wen Ge" Qijian Bei Jizhan De Huaqiao Sifang Zhengce De Ruogan Guiding [Several Rules on Carrying Out Policies Regarding Private Residences Belonging to Overseas Chinese That Were Occupied During the "Cultural Revolution"] (June 8, 1982), *in* ZHIXING GONGZUO SHOUCE, *supra* note 15, at 203, 204.

288. Gulou BLPC, *supra* note 278, at 11. The relevant paragraph allows a court to suspend execution when it deems it "necessary" to do so for any reason.

289. *See supra* text accompanying notes 160-171.

290. *See* Gulou BLPC, *supra* note 278, at 3.

291. *See, e.g.*, Court Interview K; Guangzhou ILPC, *supra* note 53, at 2.

imposing an affirmative duty on the defendant.[292] After the plaintiff has won, courts are supposed to put extra effort into execution.

In addition, the policy of supporting large and medium-sized state-owned enterprises has a plaintiff-side effect as well: where the plaintiff is a favored enterprise that desperately needs the money, courts are supposed to put extra effort into execution of judgments in their favor.[293]

Second, there are some cases in which the plaintiff will be *less* interested in execution than the average plaintiff and thus may not push the court as hard as other plaintiffs might. As long as an enterprise manager has a realistic hope that losses can be made up out of state funds, the bottom line is less important than an allocation of responsibility for the loss. Even if an enterprise manager cannot hope to collect on a debt, a judgment in the enterprise's favor serves a purpose: it declares unambiguously that there is an amount of money owing to the enterprise. The manager can then explain to his superiors any shortfall in revenues, for example, by means of the judgment in the enterprise's favor. As one lawyer explained, "In the end it's all about justifying yourself" (*zuihou shi 'ge jiaodai wenti*).[294]

3. Methods of Executing Judgments

a. Sanctions for Refusal to Carry Out Court Orders

When persons or organizations do not carry out a court's orders, the court can try to perform the act itself. If a defendant refuses to pay a sum of money to the plaintiff, the court can attempt to take money from the defendant's bank account. It can also send a bailiff to the defendant's home to remove valuable property that can later be auctioned off for the plaintiff's benefit. In many cases, however, it is much simpler if the party simply does as it is told in the first place. What threats can the court bring to bear?

---

292. *See* Article 97, Law on Civil Procedure, *supra* note 34.

293. *See* Court Interview K.

294. Lawyer Interview R; a similar point is made in Lawyer Interview X; Academic Interview M; Academic Interview C.

When the person subject to the order is the defendant (as opposed, for example, to the defendant's bank or employer),[295] the court can attempt to impose both administrative and criminal sanctions.

Article 102 of the Law on Civil Procedure allows a court to fine or detain (*juliu*) any person (including the responsible person of an organization) who refuses to carry out a legally effective judgment or ruling of the court. This detention is considered administrative in nature and is imposed by the court president without the necessity of any sort of hearing. Although the period is limited to fifteen days, there is no limit on the number of times a person may be detained.[296] Because of the sensitivity of such a coercive measure, a 1987 Supreme People's Court document, probably unaffected by the 1991 amendments to the Law on Civil Procedure, stipulates that detention under Article 102 in areas outside of the detaining court's geographical jurisdiction should be effected by a personal entrustment request to the local court. Not even sending the request through the mail is sufficient.[297]

Execution measures directed against the person, as opposed to the property, of the defendant are politically very sensitive in China. It is an article of faith among Chinese legal scholars and officials that, unlike in the pre-Communist era, courts may not execute against the person of the defendant. In the 1982 Law on Civil Procedure, mere refusal by a defendant to carry out a judgment, without more (such as threatening or beating court personnel), was not grounds for detention — although, curiously, mere refusal by a *non*-party such as a bank manager to cooperate in execution was.[298] An authoritative 1985 textbook explains:

> To detain the debtor, making him suffer in order to force him to perform his duty to pay off the debt, is a method used by the exploiting classes to oppress the working people . . . . If a party does not use violence or similar methods to resist execution, and

---

295. The power of courts to require cooperation in execution from non-parties is discussed briefly above at text accompanying note 256.

296. *See* Court Interview F.

297. *See* Zuigao Renmin Fayuan [Supreme People's Court], Guanyu Jueding Caiqu Minshi Juliu Cuoshi De Fayuan Neng Fou Weituo Bei Juliu Ren Suozaidi Fayuan Dai Wei Zhixing De Pifu [Reply On the Question of Whether a Court That Has Decided to Impose Civil Detention Measures May Entrust the Court of the Detainee's Locality to Execute on Its Behalf] (Oct. 15, 1987), *in* NORMATIVE INTERPRETATIONS, *supra* note 81, at 48.

298. *See* 1982 Law on Civil Procedure, *supra* note 34, arts. 77, 164. This interpretation is supported by *Dui Bei Zhixing Ren De Zhei-Zhong Xingwei Gai Zenme Ban?* [*What Should Be Done in the Face of This Kind of Behavior by the Executee?*], RENMIN SIFA [PEOPLE'S JUDICATURE], No. 4, at 48 (1990) (letter to the editor).

> merely refuses to perform [his duty], the implementing officer (*zhixing yuan*) . . . cannot use force with respect to his person.[299]

Despite this accepted taboo, debate and controversy are still possible because there is no agreement on what it actually means to execute against the person. For example, some scholars hold that one cannot enforce child custody awards through criminal or administrative sanctions against the non-custodial parent who takes or hides the child because that would constitute execution against the person.[300] Others hold that it is permissible on the grounds that the "object" of execution is behavior — the act of handing over the child to the custodial parent — and not the person of the defendant or the child.[301]

Academic sources consistently distinguished detention under the 1982 Law on Civil Procedure from detention under Republican law by holding that detention under the former was imposed not for the failure to carry out the judgment, but for some other act. Although Article 102 of the 1991 Law on Civil Procedure seems to have destroyed the viability of this distinction, it appears that in general the mere passive refusal to carry out a judgment will in practice result in nothing more than a fine, even though detention is technically possible.[302] On the other hand, it is possible to go very quickly beyond the threshold of mere passive resistance. A company manager in Shenzhen, for example, was detained for three days when he cursed court cadres who had come to investigate company records and threatened to call the police.[303] This may be the kind of abuse of detention powers that the Supreme People's Court had in mind when it issued a

299. MINSHI SUSONG FA SHIXING WENTI TANTAO [AN INVESTIGATION INTO PROBLEMS IN THE IMPLEMENTATION OF THE LAW ON CIVIL PROCEDURE] 231 (Chen Yanling, Yang Rongxin, Liu Jiaxing, Zhao Huifen, Tang Dehua & Cheng Cheng eds., 1985).

300. *See* WEI, YIN & HE, *supra* note 196, at 116-117; Jin Xinnian, *Zi-Nü Renshen Anjian Juyou Zhixingxing Ma?* [*Are Cases Involving the Persons of Children Executable?*], FAXUE [LEGAL STUDIES], No. 4, at 33 (1987). The views of these writers are prefigured in 1951 Urumchi Measures, *supra* note 63, which instructs the courts to use persuasion and education.

301. *See* Wu Peizhong, *Lihun Anjian Keyi Qiangzhi Zhixing?* [*Can Divorce Cases Be Coercively Executed?*], FAXUE [LEGAL STUDIES], No. 4, at 22, 22-23 (1987); Liu, *supra* note 3, at 46-47.

302. *See* Lawyer Interview T.

303. *Yuan Sanda Zu'ai Sifa Renyuan Zhifa Bei Luliu* [*Yuan Sanda Obstructs Judicial Personnel in Carrying Out the Law, Is Detained*], SHENZHEN FAZHI BAO [SHENZHEN LEGAL SYSTEM NEWS], Aug. 22, 1991, at 1.

notice in 1992 reminding courts that detention in civil cases was a coercive measure to be used only with the greatest of caution.[304]

Although passive resistance is at least in theory now grounds for administrative detention, there is disagreement about whether mere refusal to perform is by itself enough to justify criminal sanctions. Article 157 of the Criminal Law allows for the imposition of punishment including imprisonment upon anyone who "by means of threats or violence obstructs state personnel from carrying out their functions according to law or refuses to carry out judgments or orders of people's court that already have become legally effective." Unfortunately, the original Chinese is arguably ambiguous on the issue of whether "by means of threats or violence" applies to refusal to carry out judgments as well as obstructing state personnel. According to some sources, it does — passive refusal to perform cannot be criminally punished.[305] Other sources, including court officials, disagree: no threats or violence are required.[306]

In practice, of course, the views of courts count for more than the views of academics because it is the former that have the power to sentence. Thus, although proposals during the latest revision (in 1991) of the Law on Civil Procedure to spell out that mere refusal to perform could be a crime were defeated,[307] some courts seem to have gone their own way and made it one regardless.[308] In one case dating from 1980, just after the promulgation of the Criminal Law, a Tianjin defendant was prosecuted

---

304. *See* Zuigao Renmin Fayuan [Supreme People's Court], Guanyu Zai Zhixing Jingji Jiufen Anjian Zhong Yanjin Weifa Juliu Ren De Tongzhi [Notice on Strictly Prohibiting the Unlawful Detention of Persons in the Course of Executing Cases of Economic Disputes] (Aug. 29, 1992), *in* DATABASE, *supra* note 85.

305. *See* Huang Xianping, *Tan Ju Bu Zhixing Renmin Fayuan Panjue (Caiding) Zui [A Discussion of the Crime of Refusing to Execute Judgments (Rulings) of People's Courts]*, JIANGXI FAZHI BAO [JIANGXI LEGAL SYSTEM NEWS], June 7, 1983, at 64; Li Junjie, *Lun Ju Bu Zhixing Panjue Zui De Fanzui Goucheng [A Discussion of What Constitutes the Crime of Refusing to Execute Judgments]*, HEBEI FAXUE [HEBEI LEGAL STUDIES], No. 1, at 1 (1992); Lawyer Interview T; CHANG, *supra* note 44, at 27 (who views this limitation as a weakness).

306. *See* Court Interview F; Court Interview E; Wang Wei, *Ju Bu Zhixing Renmin Fayuan Panjue Caiding Zui Ji Qi Shenli Chengxu De Tantao [An Investigation Into the Crime of Refusing to Execute Court Judgments and Orders and the Process for Its Adjudication]*, RENMIN SIFA [PEOPLE'S ADJUCATION], No. 10, at 15, 16 (1990) (viewing violence and threats as aggravating circumstances instead of necessary elements); Zhu Xianghong, *Ju Bu Zhixing Fayuan Panjue, Caiding Zui Liang Yi [Two Proposals on the Crime of Refusal to Implement Court Judgments and Rulings]*, XIANDAI FAXUE [MODERN LEGAL STUDIES], No. 2, at 23, 23 (1992); Xiao Li, *Qianghua Dui Zhixing Dangshiren De Falü Yueshu [Strengthen the Legal Constraints on Parties Being Executed Against]*, FAXUE [LEGAL STUDIES], No. 9, at 14, 15 (1992).

307. *See* Academic Interview P.

308. Space limitations preclude discussion here of the fascinating issue of who is supposed to prosecute in such cases.

under Article 157 for the non-violent refusal to perform a judgment requiring him to move from a house.[309] In another more recent case, a woman was sentenced to fifteen days' detention — apparently under Article 157 — because she "wept and wailed and made a big fuss" when court personnel came to seize her property in satisfaction of a tort judgment against her.[310]

The last word on the subject — for the time being — may have come from the Supreme People's Court, which issued an official Opinion in 1992 specifying that the mere failure, without more, to carry out a judgment, ruling, mediation, or payment order of a court when one had the ability to do so constituted an offense under Article 102(6) of the Law on Civil Procedure.[311] A 1993 case published as a model in the Supreme People's Court Gazette then demonstrated that such an act, when the "circumstances are serious" (*qingjie yanzhong*), could constitute a crime punishable under Article 157 of the Criminal Law.[312]

b. *Freezing and Seizure of Bank Deposits*

If the execution debtor refuses to pay an amount owing under a judgment, the court can try to take funds owned by it but held by others. To this end, Article 221 of the Law on Civil Procedure allows a court to freeze funds held in a defendant's bank account and to have them transferred to a judgment creditor. This measure is most useful against enterprises and other organizational defendants subject to rules requiring them to keep

---

309. *See Tianjin Shi Heping Qu Renmin Fayuan Chengli Zhixing Zu, Jiji Kaizhan Minshi Zhixing Gongzuo* [Tianjin City Heping District People's Court Establishes Execution Group, Actively Launches Execution Work], *in* 2 MSCZ, *supra* note 1, at 755.

310. *See Wang Zhanshu Bei Juliu Fakuan* [*Wang Zhanshu Detained and Fined*], BEIJING FAZHI BAO [BEIJING LEGAL SYSTEM NEWS], May 23, 1990, at 1.

311. *See* 1992 SPC Civil Procedure Opinion, *supra* note 70, art. 123(3). Article 102 of the Law on Civil Procedure reads in relevant part as follows:

> If a participant in litigation or other person commits any of the following acts, the people's court may, according to the seriousness of the circumstances, fine or detain the person; where the act constitutes a crime, the person shall be subjected to criminal liability according to law
>
> [...]
>
> (6) Refusing to perform decisions and rulings of a people's court that have already become legally effective.

312. *See* Chen Jianming Ju Bu Zhixing Renmin Fayuan Panjue An [The Case of Chen Jianming's Refusal to Implement the Judgment of a People's Court] (Hangzhou City Gongshu District Basic Level People's Court, Sept. 17, 1993), *in* DATABASE, *supra* note 85. In this case, the seriousness of the circumstances seems to have had to do with the amount owed and the defendant's reneging on a mediation agreement.

their funds in banks, often in a single account.[313] Nevertheless, these rules are often violated, making it hard for creditors to find all the defendant's funds.[314] Given the importance of the rules for execution of judgments, it is curious that the rules have been in existence for over a decade, and yet have not been codified into an authoritative law. They are nothing more than notices (*tongzhi*) from the People's Bank of China, which arguably has no authority to tell organizations not administratively under it what to do.

The 1991 revision of the Law on Civil Procedure saw a significant strengthening of these measures. Whereas under the 1982 law courts could only freeze, but not transfer, funds in banks outside of their geographical jurisdiction,[315] the 1991 revision and subsequent interpretation make it clear that this disability has been abolished in law.[316] Nevertheless, it appears to persist in practice at least in some places, where banks insist on an order from the local court before consenting to transfer funds.[317]

Despite its potential for circumventing a defendant's resistance to execution, the freezing or seizure of bank deposits faces a number of obstacles. First, as noted, it is difficult to prevent parties anticipating litigation from keeping their funds in several bank accounts, some of them secret.

Second, banks themselves now operate under a much more competitive regime and are anxious to avoid offending customers. To this end, they will often drag their heels and in other ways attempt to block the

---

313. *See, e.g.*, Zhongguo Renmin Yinhang [People's Bank of China], Yinhang Zhanghu Guanli Banfa [Measures on the Administration of Bank Accounts] (Oct. 28, 1977), *in* 3 JINGJI SHENPAN SHOUCE [HANDBOOK OF ECONOMIC ADJUDICATION] 56, 57 (1988).

314. *See* Luan Yixin, Peng Yingjie & Shi Heping, *Dui Dangqian Shenli Jingji Jiufen Anjian Youguan Chafeng, Dongjie, Kouhua Kuanxiang De Diaocha Yu Tantao* [*An Investigation and Inquiry Into Sealing, Freezing, and Levying Upon Funds in the Adjudication of Economic Dispute Cases*] HEBEI FAXUE [HEBEI LEGAL STUDIES], No. 1, at 25, 26 (1992); Jiangsu Sheng Xuzhou Shi Zhongji Renmin Fayuan [Intermediate Level People's Court of Jiangsu Province, Suzhou City], *Zenyang Chaxun Bei Zhixing Ren De Zhanghu* [*How to Investigate the Executee's Bank Accounts*], RENMIN SIFA [PEOPLE'S JUDICATURE], No. 8, at 18, 18 (1990).

315. *See* 1983 Joint Notice, *supra* note 250, at 697; 1992 Fuzhou ILPC 2, *supra* note 220, at 9. Despite the existence of a Supreme People's Court notice recommending entrustment to the local court of matters pertaining to seizure of funds, a 1989 article in the *Legal System Daily* found "no legal basis" for the practice. *See Yinhang Xiezhu Fayuan Dongjie Cunkuan De Liang-Ge Wenti* [*Two Issues in Banks' Cooperation With Courts in Freezing Deposits*], FAZHI RIBAO [LEGAL SYSTEM DAILY], Nov. 15, 1989, at 3.

316. *See* Court Interview F; 1992 SPC Civil Procedure Opinion, *supra* note 70, at 91 (art. 180).

317. *See* Court Interview U.

efforts of courts to take their customers' money.[318] Moreover, in many cases banks will have outstanding loans to the debtor. Thus they may attempt to ensure that their own loan is repaid before they freeze any funds,[319] although this practice has been forbidden.[320]

Third, banks remain sensitive to their status and will not easily take orders from courts, whom they perceive to be another parallel bureaucracy.[321]

Fourth, local governments in some areas have formal or informal rules forbidding the forcible transfer of funds from local parties to outside parties.[322] Although such rules are technically unlawful, local banks must in practice obey them.

c. *Sealing and Seizure of Property*

Sealing (*chafeng*) and seizure (*kouya*) of property are both measures authorized by Article 223 of the Law on Civil Procedure to ensure that a judgment is paid. The defendant is deprived of possession until the judgment is paid; if it is not paid within a specified period, the court can sell off the property. In one typical case of sealing, court officials broke the locks on the defendant's building, inventoried and removed the property inside, put a new lock on, and pasted up strips of paper over the door announcing the sealing.[323] Seizure is much simpler: the court simply removes the property.

The problem with sealing is that it is largely a symbolic measure; there is little to stop defendants from removing the seals and continuing to use the property except their fear of court sanctions. If they greatly feared

---

318. *See* Liu & Mu, *supra* note 204, at 3; *Yinhang "Xiezhu Zhixing Ban'an" Duo Fang Tuiwei; Lüshi Chuanzhe Jingfu Chumian Hengjia Ganshe* [*Bank in "Cooperating in the Execution of a Case" Avoids It in Various Ways; Lawyer Wearing Police Uniform Recklessly Interferes*], SHANGHAI FAZHI BAO [SHANGHAI LEGAL SYSTEM NEWS], Nov. 26, 1990, at 7.

319. *See* 1992 Chengdu ILPC, *supra* note 172, at 2; Liu & Mu, *supra* note 204, at 3.

320. *See* 1983 Joint Notice, *supra* note 250; Zuigao Renmin Fayuan [Supreme People's Court], Guanyu Yinhang Shanzi Huabo Fayuan Yi Dongjie De Kuanxiang Ruhe Chuli Wenti De Han [Letter on How to Deal With the Problem of the Bank's Levying on Its Own Authority on Funds That Have Already Been Frozen by the Court] (Mar. 26, 1989), *in* LEGISLATIVE EXPLANATIONS, *supra* note 97, at 1239. A Heilongjiang bank manager was briefly detained by court order for attempting this tactic. *See* 1989 Heilongjiang HLPC, *supra* note 255.

321. *See* Lawyer Interview R.

322. *See* Court Interview E.

323. *See Li Jianyi Baisu Zhan Fang Bu Ban, Nantou Qu Fayuan Qiangzhi Zhixing* [*Li Jianyi Loses Lawsuit but Continues to Occupy House Without Moving; Nantou District Court Coercively Executes*], SHENZHEN FAZHI BAO [SHENZHEN LEGAL SYSTEM NEWS], Jan. 18, 1989, at 1. The article is accompanied by a photograph.

court sanctions, however, sealing would not be necessary in the first place. In one case, when a defendant refused to pay a judgment, the court went to his house to "seal" his television set. Instead of seizing the appliance to satisfy the judgment, court officials "sealed" it by instructing him not to sell or otherwise transfer it — which of course he immediately did.[324]

Courts are also reluctant to take the drastic step of sealing in the case of assets needed for production by an enterprise because it could lead to needless waste. Thus, it is recommended that courts instead seize the ownership certificates of the assets in question in order to prevent their unlawful transfer, and allow them to continue to be used.[325]

Auction has increasingly come to be the method of choice in realizing the value of sealed and seized property. The traditional method of realizing value was *bianmai*: "selling off" at a price deemed appropriate by the court and the buyer. Behind this method is the idea that every asset has an objective value independent of the vagaries of supply and demand. Moreover, some assets such as land might have been deemed unsuited to market transactions.

The 1991 Law on Civil Procedure explicitly provides for the auctioning (*paimai*) of sealed and seized property. It is viewed as superior because the competition of an auction will produce a better price, something that benefits both the debtor and the creditor. As more types of property become subject to market pricing, auctioning will become more common. In 1991, the *Supreme People's Court Gazette* published the proceedings of an otherwise unremarkable case in which a house was auctioned to pay a judgment, apparently just to show that even something as sensitive as housing could be subject to auction.[326] On the other hand, the law still contains large gaps: courts are to turn the seized property over to "the relevant unit" for auctioning, but there is no law or regulation indicating who that "relevant unit" might be.[327]

---

324. *See* Li Wentong Ju Bu Zhixing Fayuan Panjue Bing Yinni Caichan Bei Soucha An [The Case of Li Wentong, Who Refused to Implement a Court Judgment, Hid Assets, and Was Searched], SPCG, No. 4, Dec. 20, 1991, at 21.

325. Huang Changqing & Zheng Haishi, *Shiyong "Susong Baoquan" He "Zhixing Cuoshi" De Ji-Dian Changshi [A Few Points of Common Sense About Using "Litigation Preservation" and "Execution Measures"]*, RENMIN SIFA [PEOPLE'S JUDICATURE], No. 5, at 39 (1990).

326. *See* Lin Jinzhang Ju Bu Lüxing Fayuan Panjue, Bei Qiangzhi Bianmai Fangchan Zhixing An [The Execution Case of Lin Jinzhang, Who Refused to Carry Out the Court's Judgment and Whose House Was Coercively Auctioned], SPCG, No. 4, Dec. 20, 1991, at 22.

327. *See* Zhang Jingxue, *Zhixing Chengxu Zhong De "Yi Wu Di Zhai" ["Paying Debts in Kind" in the Execution Process]*, FAXUE [LEGAL STUDIES], No. 5, at 17 (1994).

d. Labor Service

An intriguing and controversial method of execution that may become more common is labor service (*laowu dizhai*; *laowu daichang*; *zhedi laoyi*) whereby the judgment debtor works off the debt. There is little now to stop a creditor from agreeing to hire a debtor and to pay him at a certain rate for his labor.[328] The issue is whether the court should be involved in coercing the labor of a debtor.

One proposal suggests that morally blameworthy debtors could be required to work in labor re-education camps for a period of time in order to pay off their debts.[329] Another proposal suggests that debtors with no money but the ability to labor could be sent to work off their debts in some kind of factory.[330]

The legal community in China is extremely cautious about the idea of labor service. A prominent concern is whether the public will accept what is essentially the imposition of servitude for civil obligations.[331] Another concern is whether it might, given the "current judicial circumstances" (*muqian zheizhong sifa zhuangkuang*), lead to abuses of power.[332]

Although a proposal to include it in the latest revision of the Law on Civil Procedure was rejected,[333] labor service is still apparently imposed by some courts on their own.[334]

---

328. A 1991 Supreme People's Court document allows labor service where both parties agree and the arrangement harms the interests neither of society nor of third parties. *See* Zuigao Renmin Fayuan [Supreme People's Court], Guanyu Renmin Fayuan Shenli Jiedai Anjian De Ruogan Yijian [Several Opinions on the Adjudication by People's Courts of Borrowing-Lending Cases] (Aug. 13, 1991), art. 20, *in* ZHONGGUO FALÜ NIANJIAN 1992 [LAW YEARBOOK OF CHINA 1992], at 532 [hereinafter 1991 SPC Opinions].

329. *See* Yang Duoming, *Shi Xi Jingji Jiufen Anjian Zhixing Nan De Yuanyin He Duice* [*A Tentative Analyis of Causes and Countermeasures for the Difficulty of Executing in Cases of Economic Disputes*], SHEHUI KEXUE JIA [SOCIAL SCIENTIST], No. 4, at 87, 88 (1989).

330. *See* Lawyer Interview W.

331. *See* Zuigao Renmin Fayuan [Supreme People's Court], Guanyu Fushun Shi Fayuan Suo Qingshi De Li Fusheng, Pi Yanxiang Er An Ying Ruhe Chuli De Fuhan [Reply to the Request for Instructions from the Fushun City Court on How to Handle the Two Cases of Li Fusheng and Pi Yanxiang] (Jan. 6, 1955), *in* ZHONGHUA RENMIN GONGHEGUO ZUIGAO RENMIN FAYUAN [PEOPLE'S REPUBLIC OF CHINA SUPREME PEOPLE'S COURT], YOUGUAN SHENPAN YEWU HUIBIAN [COLLECTED DOCUMENTS RELATED TO ADJUDICATION] 30 (1958) (barring labor service in one case because of fear of losing "social sympathy"); MINSHI SUSONG FA DE XIUGAI YU SHIYONG, *supra* note 75, at 266 (expressing concerns about negative public reactions).

332. *See id.*

333. *See* Academic Interview P.

334. *See* Academic Interview L.

e. *Payment in Kind*

It frequently happens that a debtor has goods but no cash. In such a case, the court may encourage the creditor to take the goods in lieu of cash (*yi wu di zhai*).[335] The obvious problem with this method is that the reason the debtor has no cash is precisely that nobody wants to buy its products. The Supreme People's Court has endorsed this method where the plaintiff agrees to it.[336] This hardly seems necessary, since debtors usually do not need anyone's permission to make a sale to creditors. The problem is that courts sometimes force this method of execution upon plaintiffs against their will.[337]

Payment in kind, when forced on the judgment creditor, runs against the grain of economic reform because it relies on the notion of innate, objectively determinable value instead of value determined by supply and demand. If the creditor does not wish to accept the goods at the value placed on them by the court, according to one treatise, the goods will be returned to the execution debtor and execution suspended.[338] According to another treatise, if property cannot be sold at the price originally asked by the court, the court cannot simply "sell it off cheaply" for whatever it will bring.[339]

f. *Other Non-Statutory Methods*

Courts have at times shown remarkable ingenuity in fashioning remedies that will go some way toward solving problems created by post-Mao reforms while respecting the ideological strictures of an earlier day. A serious problem can arise, for example, when a state body has large debts but where it is unlawful to sell or otherwise transfer for value the assets under its control (which formally belong to the state and of which it

335. *See* Xining Shi Zhongji Renmin Fayuan [Xining Intermediate Level People's Court], *Wo Shi Fayuan Zai Zhixing Zhong Caiyong "Yi Wu Di Zhai" Fangshi De Jidian Zuofa* [*Some Ways in Which Our Court Adopted the Method of "Payment of Debt in Kind" in the Course of Execution*], *in* CONFERENCE MATERIALS, *supra* note 42; Chen Xiangli, *Jiejue "Zhixing Nan" Wenti De Yi-Zhong Duice — Dui "Biantong Zhixing" De Ji-Dian Renshi* [*A Method for Solving the Problem of "Difficulty in Execution" — Some Ideas About "Alternative Execution"*], FAXUE PINGLUN [LEGAL STUDIES REVIEW], No. 6, at 71, 72 (1990).

336. 1991 SPC Opinions, *supra* note 328, art. 21.

337. *See* Liao Mujie, *Minshi Zhixing Zhong De Yi Wu Di Zhai Chutan* [*An Initial Investigation Into the Payment of Debt in Kind in Civil Execution*], RENMIN SIFA [PEOPLE'S JUDICATURE], No. 3, at 25, 25-26 (1992); for general criticisms, see Zhang, *supra* note 327.

338. *See* CIVIL PROCEDURE TREATISE, *supra* note 262, at 448.

339. *See* ZHONGGUO MINSHI SUSONG FA JIAOCHENG, *supra* note 102, at 352.

is the steward). An enterprise, for example, might have non-transferable mining rights; a scientific research institute might have land and buildings that cannot be auctioned without compromising its state-assigned mission. Compulsory administration (*qiangzhi guanli*) meets this problem of market failure (more accurately, market non-existence) by having the court "administer" the rights of the execution debtor and turn the revenues over to the judgment creditor. While not authorized by statute, this procedure has apparently been used by at least one court, which appointed an administrator to be paid from the revenues derived from the managed property.[340]

Another creative method designed to deal with the same type of problem is a transfer of ownership plus leaseback where selling the execution debtor's property — for example, a factory building — is deemed undesirable because it would create unemployment. Here, the court transfers ownership of the fixed assets to the judgment creditor, which then leases them back to the execution debtor. The rent is set at the bank interest rate on the value of the assets as assessed by "relevant units." If the execution debtor misses rent payments or stops using the property in question, it can be sold by the creditor in satisfaction of the debt.[341] Unfortunately, a number of questions about this method of execution remain unanswered. For example, is the assessed value of the transferred assets supposed to equal the amount of the debt? What standards will the "relevant units" use to assess value?

A similar solution was reached by a court when faced with an execution debtor that had no property except a number of taxis whose use it subcontracted out to drivers. The drivers had a right to purchase the cars after a certain period of time and upon the payment of a sum of money. Instead of seizing the cars, the court seized the ownership certificates and instructed the drivers to make future payments to the judgment creditor.[342]

---

340. *See* Nanchang Shi Zhongji Renmin Fayuan Zhixing Ting [Nanchang Intermediate Level People's Court Execution Chamber], *Qiangzhi Guanli Chutan* [*An Initial Investigation Into Compulsory Administration*], *in* CONFERENCE MATERIALS, *supra* note 42.

341. *See* Sichuan Sheng Zigong Shi Zhongji Renmin Fayuan [Sichuan Province Zigong City Intermediate Level People's Court], *Gan Yu Zhi Fa, Shan Yu Zhi Fa, Tupo Zhixing Nan* [*Dare to Implement the Law, Be Good at Implementing the Law, Make a Breakthrough in Execution Difficulty*], *in* SELECTED PROBLEMS, *supra* note 47, at 249, 258.

342. *See* Huang & Zheng, *supra* note 325, at 39.

g. *Self-Help*

When plaintiffs feel that courts are unable to give them what they desire — a favorable ruling that is promptly executed — they may resort to self-help. Self-help should be discussed in a survey of execution techniques because not only is the line between pre-judgment and post-judgment remedies sometimes obscure, but so is the line between officially-sanctioned and private remedies. Moreover, there is no sharp distinction between courts and police.

The result is that whether before or after judgment, a well-connected plaintiff may be able to enlist the aid of public security forces in achieving its objective. It may also choose to go it alone with the acquiescence of the police and courts.

In one frequently reported type of self-help case, a plaintiff from city (or county or town) *A* will have the police from the same city detain a defendant from outside city *A* until the claimed debt is paid.[343] The police cooperate because the plaintiff is an important local enterprise. In reports of such cases, the detention is typically justified as part of an investigation into charges of fraud against the defendant, but the extortionate motive is only thinly disguised. In one case, for example, police from Renxian county in Hebei traveled to Zhengzhou in Henan, where they arrested and brought back to Renxian the manager of a department store involved in a dispute over nails supplied by a Renxian enterprise. Police said they were acting under instructions from county leaders and would not release the manager until the nails were paid for.[344] In another case report in the book *One Hundred Strategies for Using Law to Clear Up Debts*, the writer mentions as an aside that a plaintiff trying to collect a debt asked the police and the procuracy to assist. They helpfully detained three people from the defendant organization for up to eight months, but were unsuccessful in collecting.[345]

This strategy appears to have become quite widespread and is international in scope. While judicial kidnapping of foreign citizens originally appears, interestingly enough, to have been limited to ethnic

---

343. *See generally* Zhou Shihua, *Dui Zhaiquan Zhaiwu Jiufen Yinqi De Feifa Jujin An De Pouxi* [*An Analysis of Cases of Unlawful Detention Arising Out of Debt Disputes*], ZHONG-WAI FAXUE [CHINESE AND FOREIGN JURISPRUDENCE], No. 6, at 56 (1993); Zhang Ya & Wei Zhi, *Zhongguo "Renzhi Xianxiang"* [*China's "Hostage Phenomenon"*], FAZHI RIBAO [LEGAL SYSTEM DAILY], Jan. 2, 1994, at 5; 1992 Chengdu ILPC, *supra* note 172. These are only a few of the numerous articles on the subject that could be cited.

344. *See Illegal Detention in Hebei Condemned,* CHINA DAILY, Aug. 11, 1993, at 3.

345. *See* YUNYONG FALÜ SHOUDUAN QING ZHAI BAI CE, *supra* note 195, at 234.

Chinese, it has lately been extended to those from other ethnic groups as well. In all cases, it was made clear that the victim would be released when the sum demanded was forthcoming.[346]

Although the central government has been unwilling or unable to respond in concrete cases, there is a series of regulations since 1990[347] — all apparently ineffective, given their similar content — that spell out the details of the problem. The most recent such regulation, from 1993, repeats the admonition to local procuracies not to arrest people in ordinary economic disputes.[348] In particular, they are instructed not to get involved in contract, debt, and other economic disputes; not to get involved in the recovery of debts or the taking of debt hostages; not to make arrests outside their geographical jurisdiction without notifying local authorities; and not to charge fees for their services or take a portion of the amount recovered.[349]

In a case reported in 1993, a local court invalidated the detention of a man who had been captured from another county by local police solely on the basis of allegations by a rival. His whereabouts were discovered shortly after his disappearance when the police cabled his family informing them that he had been detained for investigation and instructing them to come and "resolve" the matter.[350] The court's decision was based not on

346. *See generally* Jonathan Manthorpe, *Sour Business Deals a Risk for Canadians; Hostage-Taking, Arrests Become a Major Problem*, OTTAWA CITIZEN, Nov. 25, 1994, at E8.

347. Zuigao Renmin Jianchayuan [Supreme People's Procuracy], Guanyu Bu De Yi Jiancha Jiguan De Mingyi Wei Dangdi Zhuikuan Taozhai De Tongzhi [Notice That It Is Not Permitted to Seek Repayment of Debts in the Name of the Procuracy on Behalf of the Locality] (Apr. 16, 1990), *in* LAW COMPENDIUM, *supra* note 233, at 173; Zuigao Renmin Jianchayuan [Supreme People's Procuracy], Guanyu Yi-Xie Jiancha Jiguan Yuequan Ban'an Canyu Zhuikuan Taozhai De Qingkuang Tongbao [Bulletin on the Situation in Which Some Procuratorial Organs Handle Cases Outside the Scope of Their Authority and Get Involved in Seeking Repayment of Debts] (Jan. 10, 1991), *in* LAW COMPENDIUM, *supra* note 233, at 173; Zuigao Renmin Jianchayuan [Supreme People's Procuracy], Guanyu Yanjin Jiancha Jiguan Yuequan Ban'an Chashou Jingji Jiufen Weifa Buren De Tongzhi [Notice Strictly Forbidding Procuratorial Organs From Handling Cases Outside the Scope of Their Authority, Interfering in Economic Disputes, and Unlawfully Arresting People] (July 20, 1993), *in* ZUIGAO RENMIN JIANCHAYUAN GONGBAO [SUPREME PEOPLE'S PROCURACY GAZETTE], No. 1, Apr. 15, 1993, at 28 [hereinafter 1993 Procuratorial Notice].

348. A 1995 Supreme People's Court Reply spells out that there is no legal basis for procuracies to lodge protests (*kangsu*) against decisions to execute the same way they can against other court decisions. *See* Zuigao Renmin Fayuan [Supreme People's Court], Guanyu Dui Zhixing Chengxu Zhong De Caiding De Kangsu Bu Yu Shouli De Pifu [Reply That Protests Against Rulings in the Course of Execution Proceedings Shall Not Be Accepted] (Aug. 10, 1995), *in* DATABASE, *supra* note 85.

349. *See* 1993 Procuratorial Notice, *supra* note 347.

350. *See* Wu Peisheng & Zhou Qiang, *Danyang Fayuan Chexiao Yi Shou-Shen Jueding* [*Danyang Court Cancels a Decision on Custody and Investigation*], FAZHI RIBAO [LEGAL SYSTEM DAILY], July 12, 1993, at 1.

the unlawful grounds for detention, however, but on the technical ground that the detention had exceeded the three months allowed by the Ministry of Public Security's regulations on administrative detention.[351]

VI. CONCLUSION

This article began with the proposition that some but not all court judgments and decisions are difficult to execute, and that this affects the practical significance of economic and other rights apparently granted by law.

The available evidence, while often contradictory, suggests certain patterns. It will be difficult, for example, to execute against a large and locally-important but cash-poor state-owned enterprise in a poor province. All eviction cases against individuals will be difficult, but there is no special difficulty in evicting organizational tenants.

It is surprisingly difficult, however, given the attention that has been devoted to the problem of execution difficulties, to come to a firm conclusion about its seriousness, particularly in comparison with other societies. The reality of what Chinese courts do and don't do is simply too messy to provide neat answers to the questions posed at the beginning of this article. Nevertheless, the evidence canvassed here does throw a surprising amount of light on a number of other issues of importance.

A. *Legal Culture*

It is impossible to read a large number of news reports and articles dealing with execution without realizing that a certain legal culture beyond the written rules is at work. In the realm of execution policy and practice, legal culture means a sense of the arguments and considerations that should count in deciding whether or not a person shall be required to perform (or to refrain from performing) a certain act. Some of these ideas may well be

---

351. The point of invalidating the detention, from which the plaintiff had already been released, was simply to clear his name. The particular regulations breached by the local police, those pertaining to a form of detention called "custody and investigation" (*shourong shencha*; also sometimes translated as "shelter and investigation"), have never been publicly issued and remain in effect a state secret. *See generally* Donald C. Clarke & James V. Feinerman, *Antagonistic Contradictions: Criminal Law and Human Rights in China*, CHINA Q., No. 141, at 135, 143-144 (Mar. 1995); LAWYERS COMMITTEE FOR HUMAN RIGHTS, CRIMINAL JUSTICE WITH CHINESE CHARACTERISTICS 67-71 (1993). A number of regulations building on the original authorizing regulations, such as the 1985 Notice of the Ministry of Public Security Concerning Strict Control of the Use of the Method of Custody and Investigation, are translated in the September-October 1994 issue of *Chinese Law and Government*.

written into the law, but others may not. Indeed, some of the arguments and considerations that are deemed to count may contradict what the written law says.

There are numerous examples of the unwritten rules that courts go by even though there is no statutory support.[352] Some of those unwritten rules have a basis in policy; others have a basis in no more than popular perceptions of what is right and reasonable.

A recurring example of a legal idea that has actual force (in that courts and other legal officials feel constrained by it) is the principle of widened responsibility. I say "widened" not only because Chinese notions of responsibility are often much wider than those of Anglo-American law, but also because they are often wider than what Chinese law itself calls for. Although this principle is apparent in many areas of the legal system,[353] it will be discussed here only insofar as it is relevant to execution: in cases where although the mandate of the law is clear, Chinese legal officials will hesitate to act because the defendant can plausibly (but without, strictly speaking, any legal basis) argue that others are equally if not more responsible for his situation.

Take, for example, the recurring problem of evictions. It is commonplace that the landlord is expected to help the tenant find another place to live and perhaps help out with the rent, at least at first. Since the tenant has a place to go, she can no longer argue that eviction will mean putting her out on the street, an argument that is sure to paralyze the court. After being forcibly evicted and moved to new quarters, however, apparently some tenants will refuse to pay the rent, telling the new landlord to look to the court for it, since it is the court's "fault" that they are where they are. According to one court writing about this phenomenon, this puts the court in a difficult position because "it has no way to solve the problem."[354] Of course, it does have a way: the new landlord can bring an action to evict for non-payment of rent, and the court can evict. But the court doesn't want to evict. Where the defendant has a unit, it can garnish

352. See, for example, the rules on eviction and on seizure of capital stock in satisfaction of debt discussed respectively *supra* at text accompanying notes 278-290 and at text accompanying note 262.

353. For example, both traditional and modern Chinese criminal law accept the notion that one can be criminally responsible for driving another to suicide through acts which, by themselves, are lawful.

354. Guiyang Shi Zhongji Renmin Fayuan Zhixing Ting [Guiyang Intermediate Level People's Court], *Jiji Kaizhan Zhixing Huodong, Weihu Falü De Zunyan* [*Actively Launch Execution Activities, Uphold the Dignity of the Law*], *in* "ZHIXING NAN" DUICE TAN, *supra* note 49, at 118, 124.

his wages to pay the rent, but where the defendant has no salary income, garnishment is impossible.[355]

The same phenomenon is visible when enterprises refuse to pay a debt on the grounds that it was incurred by a former manager, not the current one.[356] Obviously, the validity of the debt cannot be made to depend on whether the debtor agrees that it is owed. Yet courts cite managerial changeovers as an obstacle to execution different in kind from a general reluctance on the part of the debtor to pay. By distinguishing the two circumstances, courts grant a certain validity to the argument and disarm themselves.

Interestingly, we can see the same phenomenon in reverse when a creditor attempts to collect from an enterprise whose sole relation to the debt is that it was formerly under the management of the current debtor's manager.[357] I would predict that one can find cases of attempts to collect from a particular enterprise on the grounds that it is now managed by the person who managed the debtor enterprise when the debt was incurred.

This study also illuminates other aspects of Chinese legal culture. It confirms, for example, the generally observed reluctance of the system to give teeth to rules respecting finality if it were ever to be at the cost of getting the right substantive result. In short, the system simply does not assign a high relative cost to delay and uncertainty. Both at the adjudicatory and the execution stage, defendants are given many more chances to make their case than a reading of the letter of the law would indicate. This reluctance to accept finality is part of a broader reluctance to allow any aspect of procedure to dictate a substantive result, a reluctance that finds expression throughout the legal system. It is inconceivable, for example, that a wrongdoer in China could escape punishment on a technicality. A sharply contrasting view of the importance of procedure relative to substance can be found in a recent dissent by Justice Antonin Scalia: "What the Fourteenth Amendment's procedural guarantee assures

---

355. *See id.*, at 124.

356. *See, e.g., id.*, at 123; Li Honghe & Yang Dianwen, *Yao Yan Yu Zhi Fa Bixu Zuohao Zhixing Gongzuo* [*To Be Strict in Implementing the Law Means We Must Do Execution Work Well*], HEILONGJIANG FAZHI BAO [HEILONGJIANG LEGAL SYSTEM NEWS], July 19, 1986, at 3, 3; Fei, *supra* note 145, at 63.

357. In one case, enterprise *A*'s truck was essentially hijacked and its driver beaten by unidentified persons. The enterprise later discovered the they had been sent by a court trying to collect on behalf of a local plaintiff from enterprise *B*. The connection was that the manager of enterprise *B* was the former manager of enterprise *A*. *See* Legal Advisor, *Qingyuan Xian Fayuan Zheiyang Zhixing Panjue Dui Ma?* [*Is It Correct for the Qingyuan County Court to Execute Its Judgment in This Way?*], FAZHI RIBAO [LEGAL SYSTEM DAILY], Feb. 22, 1993, at 1.

is an opportunity to contest the reasonableness of a damages judgment in state court; but there is no federal guarantee a damages award actually *be* reasonable."[358] This way of thinking is profoundly alien to the legal culture apparent in this study. It would be the duty of any court at any stage of the process to remedy unreasonableness or injustice whenever it found it.

The concern for a substantively correct outcome is not, however, overriding. While substance may trump procedure, it does not trump everything else. The imperative to keep up appearances can be so strong that it crowds out all other values. Consider the courts cited earlier that maintained a high rate of execution by ensuring that problematic judgments were not issued or problematic cases not even heard. So normal and acceptable was this practice, even with its clear cost to plaintiffs with a sound case, that some courts were praised for their success with these gatekeeping techniques.[359]

B. *Anomalous Position of Courts in the Chinese Polity*

As argued in Part II of this article, the establishment and maintenance of market institutions in the reforming Chinese economy requires — or at least is substantially aided by — a particular kind of rule making and rule application. This rule making and application is characterized by generality and should be understood in opposition to the traditional system of ad hoc bargaining between individual enterprises and their superiors.

The problem with a system of general rules is that there is currently no system of institutions in China willing and able to enforce them. First, there is a chicken-and-egg problem. In the absence of complete economic reform, economic activity does not take place on a level playing field. Thus, applying general rules without taking individual differences into account is not only seen as unfair, but actually is so. Moreover, it may be counterproductive as well, if efficient enterprises that nevertheless lose money find themselves in trouble, for example, under the Enterprise Bankruptcy Law. However, the development of a market economy is obstructed to the extent that the principle of particularism reigns.

Second, making general rules stick implicates important questions of political power. It means drastically weakening the power of some institutions to grant exemptions and building institutions that can enforce the rules. Courts have seemed the natural candidate for the task because of

358. BMW of North America v. Gore, 64 U.S.L.W. 4335, 4347 (1996) (Scalia, J., dissenting).

359. *See supra* text accompanying notes 134-136.

their sweeping formal authority and their ability to keep to a minimum the amount of noise in policy transmission. They are not, however, capable of carrying it out as currently structured.

Two principles, *tiao* and *kuai*, govern the flow of power in the Chinese political system. *Tiao* is the principle of vertical control: superiors in a given bureaucratic hierarchy dictate to inferiors. *Kuai* is the principle of horizontal control: a particular body at a given level of adminstration — say, the Party committee — has control over certain other bodies at the same level of administration in a given jurisdiction.[360] Individual courts are subject to both in varying degrees. As noted previously, they are subject to the principle of *kuai* in the key field of personnel decisions, but subject to the principle of *tiao* when the correctness of their decisions is in question. But the exercise of power by courts fits comfortably into neither principle, and this is the key to their continued weakness. Courts are, and are seen by other bureaucracies as, a separate but equal bureaucratic hierarchy. They are conceded their own sphere of authority, to be sure, but they do not have the overarching authority of courts in common law and, to a lesser extent, continental European legal sytems. The only power that a court can exercise by virtue of *tiao* is over a lower court. Courts have real power over other bodies only by virtue of *kuai*: provided they are supported by local government, they can exercise real power over local actors. But this is not supposed to be the source of court power. Court power is supposed to stem from their authority to pass judgment on disputes involving anyone in accordance with rules validly promulgated by a large number of local and national bodies.

Courts are thus in the position of occupying a doubly anomalous position in the Chinese polity: exercising a power that is supposed to stem neither from *tiao* nor from *kuai*, and enforcing a set of rules that are essentially alien to the system: rules that purport to operate horizontally, across bureaucracies, and to bind all citizens and institutions equally.

C. *Lag of Legal Reform Behind Economic Reform and Other Social Changes*

While China's courts are hampered in one sense by being too far in front of the rest of reform, in other important ways they suffer from being too far behind. While there have been significant legal reforms in the Deng

360. For a much fuller but still concise summary of the workings of *tiao* and *kuai*, *see* KENNETH LIEBERTHAL, GOVERNING CHINA 169-70 (1995).

era, in many crucial areas the legal system remains as before and is thus unable to perform the task of enforcing the rules of economic reform. First, there is no evidence to suggest that courts have more real power now than they did a decade ago. The observance of court judgments for many institutions remains essentially voluntary. Despite the increasing reliance of the government upon statutory law as a means of policy implementation (as opposed, for example, to political campaigns), surprisingly little has been done to enable courts to enforce these laws effectively.

Moreover, the social and economic milieu in which courts operate has changed as well. What used to work is no longer so effective as before. For example, when virtually all urban residents worked within an organization responsible to the state, a good deal of enforcement could be carried out within the organization. When the income of most defendants is in the form of a wage, then support payments can be deducted from the wage. On the other hand, garnishing wages is completely ineffective as an execution measure against individual businesspeople (*getihu*) who have no wages to garnish.[361]

Yet another reason for the apparent increase in execution difficulties is the change in the nature of cases heard by courts. Divorce cases were traditionally the mainstay of civil litigation.[362] The divorce declaration itself needs no execution, and the amount of property to be redistributed was small. What urban residents had that was most valuable was their right to live and work in the city, something not subject to division as property. The majority of cases that did feature defendants reluctant to pay were family cases involving duties of support.[363] With the progress of economic reform, courts have found themselves called on to do what they had almost never been called on to do before: enforce judgments against state

---

361. A 1957 article noted the same phenomenon when economic reform was moving, as it were, in the opposite direction: after the "socialist transformation" of industry in the 1950s, debt cases between individual businesspeople (artisans, merchants, etc.) essentially disappeared. The debtors seen by courts after that were typically salaried employees. This made the garnishing of wages a much more effective tool of execution that it had been before. *See* Xuanwu Court, *supra* note 242, at 23.

A study of judgment collection procedures in New Jersey found that wage execution orders were notably more effectively than other collection procedures. *See* New Jersey Report, *supra* note 52.

362. Indeed, even in 1992 divorce cases constituted some 70% of the civil case load at one court I visited. *See* Court Interview V.

363. *See* Jiamusi Shi Zhongji Renmin Fayuan Yanjiushi [Jiamusi Intermediate Level People's Court], *Jingji, Minshi Caipan Zhixing Nan De Yuanyin Ji Duice* [*Causes and Countermeasures for Difficulty in Execution in Economic and Civil Adjudication*], FAXUE YU SHIJIAN [JURISPRUDENCE AND PRACTICE], No. 4, at 41, 41 (1988).

enterprises. At the same time, however, they remain under the *de facto* control of the same power that controls local enterprises.

The persistence of local control over courts demonstrates that establishing a system where courts would have real power involves grasping some very thorny political nettles. If anything stands out from a study of execution difficulties, it is the confirmation at a fine level of institutional detail of the impression of many observers that the central government faces serious problems in making its writ run in the provinces. Interviews and published sources all make clear that a good part of the execution problem stems from the willingness and ability of local governments simply to ignore central regulations and directives when it suits them. Even when the central authorities are directly aware of the problem, they seem in some cases unable or unwilling to do anything about it. The plight of courts is in this case a symptom, not a cause, of this larger problem. Reforms in the staffing of courts, long promised and long delayed, as well as reforms in the way courts are financed — reforms that have *not* been promised — are necessary before courts can be used to overcome the obstacles to reform caused by local protectionism and particularism, because they are now part of the very structure causing the problem.[364]

D. Proper Role of State in Establishment of Efficient Social Institutions

From a broader perspective, the prominence of local and regional centers of political power on the list of obstacles to execution of judgments in China may shed light on the question of the proper role of the state in the establishment of economically efficient social institutions. Recent writing in law and economics has attacked the "legal-centralist" view, attributed to scholars from Hobbes to Calabresi, that the state is the exclusive creator of property rights.[365] Instead, these writers say, property rights may arise "anarchically out of social custom" and "from the workings of non-hierarchical social forces."[366]

---

364. This point is made by a number of sources. *See* Academic Interview P; Luo, *supra* note 148, at 84.

365. *See* Robert C. Ellickson, *A Hypothesis of Wealth-Maximizing Norms: Evidence from the Whaling Industry*, 5 J. L. ECON. & ORG'N 83 (1989); R. Zerbe, The Development of Institutions and the Joint Production of Fairness and Efficiency in the California Gold Fields (Right Makes Might) (May 8, 1990) (unpublished manuscript).

366. *See* Ellickson, *supra* note 365, at 83.

It may be, of course, that the debate will turn out to be about what the participants mean by "rights." Just how compulsory must the corresponding duty be before we will find that a "right" exists? Ellickson's study of norms established spontaneously in the whaling industry hardly disproves the legal-centralist thesis when the writer concedes that the system broke down as economic pressures led some whalers simply to defect.[367] The assurance of enforcement, the confidence that others *cannot* defect at will, is the whole point of having a right, and the key to the arguments of Douglass C. North and others that well-defined rights are necessary for sustained economic development to occur.[368]

If we adopt a strong definition of "rights," however, the Chinese case suggests that the spontaneous-rights thesis, while not necessarily wrong, has limits in a complex economy. Efficient economic organization doesn't just happen: there are powerful political forces opposed to it that can be overcome only by more powerful political forces. State intervention is just as necessary to a complex market economy as it is to a planned economy. Local governmental power made the Commerce Clause necessary in the United States Constitution; federal governmental power is needed to enforce it.

E. Relevance for North Hypothesis

An important issue raised by the weakness of rights-enforcing institutions in China is the extent to which that observed weakness challenges the connection made by North and others between economic development and well-defined and enforceable rights of property and contract. The intuitive appeal of the hypothesis is undeniable: it seems beyond dispute that the unavailability or unenforceability of property rights is going to deter useful investment that would otherwise occur. Consider the predicament of the Chinese peasant interviewed below:

> When asked, Mr. Yang says that agricultural production and income could increase even further if the family made some irrigation improvements, terraced more of their land, and planted fruit trees. Mr. Yang, though, is unwilling to make such capital improvements to the land. The profits from such investments would only be realized after several years, and Mr.

367. *See id.*, at 95 n.39.
368. *See* NORTH & THOMAS, *supra* note 11.

> Yang considers his family's use rights to the land too uncertain. Although the local leaders told him they could use the land for at least fifteen years, the [Yang family's] land use contract has no such term. And Mr. Yang notes that his neighbors were required to give up a portion of their land, on which they had recently planted fruit trees, for a road. The neighbors received no compensation.[369]

One might interpret the much-vaunted consumption boom in the Chinese countryside as evidence of agricultural investments forgone for the reasons cited by Mr. Yang.

Although it seems clear that investment by Mr. Yang and others similarly situated is the type of transaction that is going to suffer if courts, who have been given the task of guaranteeing Mr. Yang's rights, are unable to do so, it remains to be seen whether the discouragement of such transactions is a major problem.

The evidence so far suggests that economic development in China has not been significantly hampered by the lack in some circumstances of effective enforcement of rights. Nobody who was in China in, say, 1978 can doubt the reality of the tremendous economic growth and rise in prosperity that has occurred since that time. How can that undeniable fact be reconciled with the evidence adduced here that legal institutions remain essentially unreformed and ill-suited to the institutions of a market economy, that property and contract rights are not reliably enforced? Apparently, either the popular connection drawn between economic development and the effective protection of rights is mistaken, or the Chinese system does indeed provide such protection where it counts.

It is possible, of course, that the observations are simply wrong: perhaps, despite surface appearances, legal institutions in China provide far more predictability and stability than they appear to. The news on

---

369. Tim Hanstad, *The Effects of Rural Reforms on a Chinese Family*, RURAL DEV. INST. REV., at 1, 2 (Spring 1993). In another work based on the same set of interviews, the researchers write:

> If land is taken, little legal assurance is afforded the farmer in obtaining compensation — either for the disturbance of his usership or for improvements he may have made in the land. It appears that only nominal compensation, if any, is given. . . . [T]he farmer will not keep the continuing benefit of long-term improvements . . . .

ROY L. PROSTERMAN & TIM HANSTAD, LAND REFORM IN CHINA: A FIELDWORK-BASED APPRAISAL 37 (1993). For a recent summary of the authors' research and arguments about the relationship between secure rights and productive investment, see Roy L. Prosterman, Tim Hanstad & Li Ping, *Can China Feed Itself?*, SCI. AM., Nov. 1996, at 90.

execution of judgments is not all bad. While courts still do not have a great deal of general power to impose their will, in a number of well-defined circumstances, they are not the paper tigers that some of the Chinese (and Western) literature makes them out to be. As one court official pointed out, "'Difficult to execute' does not mean 'impossible to execute' (*zhixing nan bu dengyu zhixing bu liao*)."[370]

Another possibility is that both the North hypothesis and the findings of this paper are right. China's current growth would then be explained as taking place in spite of the absence of appropriate legal institutions. The tremendous advance over the pre-reform period would be explained not as a function of how hospitable the current institutional structure is to economic development, but instead as a function of how unimaginably inhospitable and restrictive the pre-reform system was. The thunderclap of growth we have witnessed over the past several years is, in this view, nothing more than the air of entrepreneurship rushing in to fill a vacuum. It is, essentially, a one-time-only advance that will stall out when further gains from exchange can be obtained only from a division of labor and institutional complexity not supported by China's legal institutional structure.

A final possibility is that the North hypothesis is simply wrong: perhaps stable and predictable rights of property and contract, effectively enforced, are only a small part of the explanation of why economic growth occurs. It may be that while they matter at the margin, reasonably effective institutional substitutes are available and other factors are much more important contributors to economic development. Macauley, for example, demonstrated the discontinuity between contract law and the contracting practices of businesses in the United States; what mattered more to the parties than the law was that they were in a relationship that was beneficial to both.[371] According to this theory, I keep my promise to you not because of the threat of legal sanctions, but because I want to do business again either with you or with those who would hear about any promises I broke. A great deal of business can be done on the basis of trusted go-betweens and the desire for a long-term relationship. In such circumstances, legally enforceable rights are simply not very important. Court-enforced rights are most needed in the case of transactions between strangers who do not

370. Court Interview K.

371. *See* Stewart Macauley, *Non-Contractual Relations in Business: A Preliminary Study*, 28 AM. SOC. REV. 55 (1963). On the theory of relational contracting, see Ian Macneil, *Contracts: Adjustment of Long-Term Economic Relations Under Classical, Neo-Classical, and Relational Contract Law*, 72 NW. U.L. REV. 854 (1978).

expect to have further dealings with each other and are indifferent to reputational damage. But how important are such transactions to an economy? Even what might seem the paradigmatic example of such a transaction, anonymous buying and selling on the stock market, takes place within an institutional framework where market authorities can, in order to attract customers and encourage repeat transactions, impose their own sanctions such as expulsion on wrongdoers and set up a private insurance scheme for cheated investors.

This theory, of course, has its limits. If the promise of further business is the only glue that holds contractual relations together, then an entire class of necessary and useful contracts — those between parties who have no need or desire for anything more than a one-shot deal — will be unenforceable and thus discouraged. There are, however, reasons for thinking that in China this class of contract is relatively rare, and that therefore this problem is relatively unimportant, at least for the moment.

First of all, China's population is not very mobile. Although mobility has increased tremendously in the economic reform era, changing one's residence is still difficult. Therefore, a party who prepays on a contract has less reason (although not of course no reason) to fear that the other party will simply disappear with the money.

Second, only a small percentage of economic activity measured by value is conducted by individual entrepreneurs, with most of the rest conducted by units of government at various levels.[372] These are much more likely to be known quantities to a prospective business partner. Altogether, then, it may be that relational contracting can carry economic development in China a long way even in the absence of a well functioning formal system.

A further question raised by the North hypothesis is whether we might expect to see not economic development as a response to institutional innovation, but rather institutional innovation as a response to economic development. Can demand create supply? Under this conjecture, the growth and increasing complexity of economic activity in China will eventually tend to generate the institutions needed to keep it going. The difficulty here is supplying a mechanism whereby demand elicits supply. Many societies in history would have been much better off with a well developed legal system, but they didn't all get one.

---

372. *See* Table 1 in Barry Naughton, *Distinctive Features of Economic Reform in China and Vietnam, in* REFORMING ASIAN SOCIALISM: THE GROWTH OF MARKET INSTITUTIONS, *supra* note 9, at 282. A small percentage of output is attributable to joint ventures and wholly foreign-owned enterprises.

The most plausible scenario may be one founded on the increasing power of regional governments coupled with an increased mobility of capital. While the central government has not so far shown much capacity for creating a set of institutions that can effectively enforce property rights, it may be more possible for the provinces (and perhaps governments at even lower levels) to do so. Why should they want to? The answer here lies in competition for resources. The region that provides the most hospitable environment for economic activity will reap the rewards of increased employment and tax revenues.[373] This may be one of the reasons behind the judicial cooperation agreements signed by Shanghai with several other cities in the late 1980s[374] and more recently by courts of several cities along the Yangtse.[375] The key to this scenario is that provinces must be independent enough to be able to offer meaningful differences in economic environment, but not independent enough to obstruct the free movement of capital.

373. One should also note that in the absence of strong, *enforceable* central policies on environmental protection, such competition is likely to lead to severe pollution that "will make Eastern Europe look like a nature park." Ann McIlroy, *An Economic Boom Is Fuelled by Environment-Destroying Material*, VANCOUVER SUN, May 1, 1993, at B2 (quoting Western diplomat in Beijing).

374. *See supra* note 213 and sources cited therein.

375. *See Sixty-Four Courts*, *supra* note 213; Peng, *supra* note 213.

[10]

POLICE POWERS AND CONTROL IN THE PEOPLE'S REPUBLIC OF CHINA: THE HISTORY OF *SHOUSHEN*

KAM C. WONG*

I. INTRODUCTION

In 1961, the public security bureau of the People's Republic of China ("PRC" or "China") adopted a measure called *shourong shencha* (*"shoushen"*), meaning "sheltering for examination," to deal with the increasing flow of migrants throughout China.[1] *Shoushen* was designed as a measure whereby the police could detain and investigate suspected criminals who had no known status or confirmed residence or suspected "itinerant criminals" (*liucuan fan*).[2]

In the 1960s, *shoushen* was used primarily as a means of population control. By the 1980s, it was being used to promote criminal justice and social control. More recently, *shoushen* has been used as a measure for collecting debts. *Shoushen* was never a legislatively sanctioned police power, being at all times since its inception purely an administrative measure. *Shoushen* was never officially adopted by the National People's Congress ("NPC") or by the NPC Standing Committee, but *shoushen* received favorable legal interpretations from the NPC.[3] As originally

---

* B.A. (Hons.) 1975, Indiana University; J.D. 1977; Dip., National Institute of Trial Advocacy, 1980; M.A. 1988, Ph.D. candidate, State University of New York (Albany) - School of Criminal Justice; Member, State of Michigan Bar. I thank the Universities Service Center (USC) at the Chinese University of Hong Kong for offering me a challenging place to collect my data and nurture my thoughts as a visiting scholar (1993-1994). Particularly, I thank Dr. Hsin Chi Huan, the Director, and Ms. Jean Hung the Assistant Director of the USC, for their indefatigable help and assistance. An abbreviated version of this paper has been presented at the USC as a luncheon seminar, entitled: "PRC police powers and control" and as a staff seminar at the Senior Command Course, Staff Training Institute, Correctional Services Department, Hong Kong. I am indebted to the participants of the seminars who gave me valuable feedback.

1. For a brief history of *shourong shencha* [hereinafter *"shoushen"*], *see Wang Cuihua Bufu Suxian Diqu Xingzhengshu Gongan Chu Shourong Shencha An* [*The case of Wang Cuihua's Refusal to Accept Sheltering for Examination by the Su County District Government Administration Police Office*] [hereinafter *"Case of Wang Cuihua"*], *in* ZHONGGUO SHENPAN ANLI YAOLAN [IMPORTANT OVERVIEW OF CHINESE ADJUDICATED CASES] 1183 (1992) [hereinafter "IMPORTANT OVERVIEW OF CHINESE CASES"].

2. *Guanyu Jian Qiangzhi Laodong He Shouron Shencha Liang Xiang Cuoshi Tongyi Yu Laodong Jiaoyang De Tongzhi, Guofa (1980) 56 Hao* [*Circular Regarding the Merger of Labor Reform and Investigative Detention, State Council (1980) No. 56*] (promulgated February 29, 1980) [hereinafter *"State Council Circular"*], *in* ZHONGGUO JINGCHA FALU FAGUI GUIZHANG SHIYI DAQUAN [COMPILATION OF INTERPRETATIONS OF CHINESE POLICE LAWS, REGULATIONS AND RULES] 618-19 (1993).

3. *Chuanguo Renda Changweihui Fazhi Gongzuo Weiyuanhui, Guanyu Ruhe Lijie He Zhixing Falu Ruogan Wenti De Jieda (Er)* [*Regarding Answers to Certain Questions Concerning the Understanding and Execution of the Law* (2)] (promulgated March 2, 1988) [hereinafter *"Jiangxi Province Answers"*], *in* ZHONGHUA RENMIN GONGHEGUO FALU GUIFANXING JIESHI JICHENG (ZENGBU BEN) [ANNOTATED COMPILATION OF THE LAWS AND RESTRICTIVE INTERPRETATIONS OF THE

conceived, *shoushen* had few procedural safeguards. Eventually, the State Council and the Ministry of Public Security issued a number of directives concerning the proper use of *shoushen*, including directives covering the jurisdictional scope, approval authority, time limits, and administration of the practice of *shoushen*. However, these directives were largely inconsistent, unclear, over-broad, and open-ended.[4] The NPC Standing Committee, the State Council, the Supreme People's Court, the Supreme People's Procuracy, and the Ministry of Public Security all attempted to control the exercise of *shoushen*, but met with little success.

On March 17, 1996, the NPC adopted the amended Criminal Procedure Law of the People's Republic of China[5] ("Criminal Procedure Law"). The Criminal Procedure Law, while not mentioning *shoushen* by name, acknowledges the functional necessity of the *shoushen* type of investigative powers and accordingly provides for its regulation and control.[6] With this in mind, the Criminal Procedure Law places all public security coercive measures,[7] including *shoushen*,[8] under one unified procedural control scheme. Henceforth the public security authority "must

---

PEOPLE'S REPUBLIC OF CHINA (SUPPLEMENT)] [hereinafter "COMPILATION OF LAWS AND RESTRICTIVE INTERPRETATIONS OF THE PRC (SUPPLEMENT)"] at 8-9 (1991) (explaining that the NPC Standing Committee has approved the use of *shoushen*, citing approvingly a circular promulgated in response to a legal issue brought forth by the Jiangxi Province People's Congress Standing Committee). *See Guanyu Yange Kongji Shiyong Shourong Shencha Shouduan De Tongzhi, Gongfa (1985) 50 Hao [Circular Regarding the Serious Control Over the Use of the Sheltering for Examination Measure, Public Security (1985) No. 50]* (promulgated July 31, 1985) [hereinafter *"1985 Public Security Circular"*].

4. Chen Weidong & Zhang Tao, *Shourong Shencha De Ruogan Wenti Yanjiu [Research Into Certain Questions Regarding Sheltering for Examination]*, ZHONGGUO FAXUE [CHINESE LEGAL SCIENCE], Feb. 1992, at 82-87 [hereinafter "Chen & Zhang I"].

5. The Criminal Procedure Law of the People's Republic of China adopted by the Second Session of the Fifth National People's Congress [hereinafter "NPC"] on July 1, 1979 [hereinafter "Criminal Procedure Law"] was amended in accordance with the "Decision on Amending The Criminal Procedure Law of the People's Republic of China" made by the Fourth Session of the Eighth NPC on March 17, 1996. For an unofficial English translation, see FBIS-CHI-96-069, April 9, 1996. For a detailed discussion of the amended Criminal Procedural Law, see LAWYERS COMMITTEE FOR HUMAN RIGHTS, OPENING TO REFORM? AN ANALYSIS OF CHINA'S REVISED CRIMINAL PROCEDURE LAW (1996).

6. For a detailed discussion, see "Legislative response to *shoushen* in 1996" *infra*.

7. *See generally* Chapter VI Coercive Measures, the Criminal Procedure Law, *supra* note 5. The term coercive measure is not defined. Article 50 provides a contextual understanding of coercive measures: "People's courts, people's procuratorates, and public security organs, according to circumstances of the case, may summon a criminal suspect or defendant for detention, allow him to obtain a guarantor and await trial out of custody, or allow him to live at home under surveillance." Coercive measures thus conceived included police summon, investigative detention, home surveillance, and prosecution arrest.

8. *See supra* note 3.

strictly observe this law and relevant provisions" in investigating, arresting, and detaining suspects.[9]

This paper explores the historical development of *shoushen* as an exercise of police powers in China up to the present time. Part II details the historical development, abuses and control of *shoushen*. Part III describes the latest NPC effort in regulating and controlling the *shoushen* in promulgating the amended Criminal Procedure Law. Part IV concludes by observing that the Criminal Procedure Law is just the latest chapter in the PRC's continuous effort to control abuse of police powers.

II. THE HISTORY OF *SHOUSHEN*

A. *Developments Through 1980*

Shoushen was originally conceived in 1961. On November 31, 1961, the Ministry of Public Security filed a report with the Chinese Communist Party Central Committee entitled "A Report Regarding Resolutely Stopping the Free Movement of the Population," calling attention to the growing "*mangliu*" (floating population) problem facing China, and calling for effective and immediate management and control of the population.[10] The report noted that as a result of three years of natural catastrophes, from 1959-1961, the rural population had increasingly migrated into the cities for food, shelter, and jobs; in short, for survival and a better life.[11] The

---

9. *See* Criminal Procedure Law, Chapter 1, Article 3, paragraph 3, which provides, in pertinent part: "In conducting criminal proceedings, the people's courts, the people's procuratorates, and the public security organs must strictly observe this law and relevant provisions of other laws." *See also* Article 14: "The people's courts, the people's procuratorates, and the public security organs shall safeguard the procedural rights that participants in proceedings enjoy according to the law."

10. *Guanyu Jianjue Zhizhi Renkou Ziyou Liudong De Baogao* [*Report Regarding Resolutely Stopping the Free Movement of the Population*] (promulgated November 31, 1961), in ZHA ZHENJIAN, ZHONGGUO FAZHI SIXI NIAN (1949-1989)) [FORTY YEARS OF THE CHINESE LEGAL SYSTEM (1949-1989)] 286 (1989).

11. For a short account of the population 'tug-of-war' between urban and rural China, see Ge Xiangxian & Qiu Weiying, ZHONGGUO MINGONG CHAO [CHINA'S LABOR WORKER EXODUS] 167 (1990) [hereinafter "CHINA'S LABOR WORKER EXODUS"]; *Report to The Second Plenary Session of the Seventh Central Committee of the Communist Party of China* (promulgated March 5, 1949), *in* IV SELECTED WORKS OF MAO TSE TUNG 368-69 (1961); *see also Guanyu Quanzhi Nongmin Mangmu Liuru Chengshi De Zhishi* [*Instruction Regarding Dissuading Peasants From Blindly Moving Into Cities*] (promulgated April 17, 1953), *in* CHINA'S LABOR WORKER EXODUS, *supra*, at 178; *Jixu Quanche 'Guanyu Quanzhi Nongmin Mangmu Liuru Chengshi De Zhishi' De Tongzhi* [*Circular on the Continued Implementation of 'Instruction Regarding Dissuading the Peasants From Blindly Moving Into the City'*] (promulgated March 12, 1954), *id.*; *Guanyu Zhizhi Nongcun Renkou Mangmu Weiliu De Zhishi* [*Directive Regarding Stopping the Peasant Population From Blindly Flowing Outward*] (promulgated December 18, 1957), *in* RENMIN RIBAO [PEOPLE'S DAILY],

report suggested a three prong attack on the problem, including the use of *shoushen*.[12]

Since its inception in 1961, *shoushen* has never been formally incorporated into China's regulatory scheme concerning police powers. The 1954 Regulations of the PRC on Arrest and Detention provided the first set of regulations on police arrest powers but did not incorporate *shoushen*.[13] These regulations were replaced by the 1979 Regulations of the PRC on Arrest and Detention ("1979 Arrest Regulation").[14] On January 1, 1980, the PRC Criminal Procedure Law provided the first comprehensive legal framework for the exercise of police investigative and arrest powers.[15] The PRC Criminal Procedure Law was clarified by circulars and resolutions from the Supreme People's Court and Supreme People's Procuratorates.[16] It was also supplemented by various directives,

December 19, 1957, at 1; *Shelun: Zhizhi Nongcun Renkou Mangmu Weiliu* [*Editotial: Stopping the Peasant Population from Blindly Flowing Outward*], in RENMIN RIBAO [PEOPLE'S DAILY], Dec. 19, 1957, at 1.

12. The other two measures were: (1) stopping people from emigrating; and (2) perfecting the control of transportation. *See* Zha, *supra* note 10, at 286.

13. *Regulations of the PRC on Arrest and Detention* (adopted at the third meeting of the Standing Committee of the National People's Congress on December 20, 1954), *translated in* ARREST AND DETENTION REGULATIONS OF THE PEOPLE'S REPUBLIC OF CHINA in FHKP, 1:239-242 [hereinafter *"1954 Arrest Regulations"*]. *See* Zhao Cangbi, *Guanyu Xiugai 'Zhonghua Renmin Gongheguo Dibu Juliu Tiaoli' De Shuo Ming* [*Explanation on the Revision of 'Arrest and Detention Regulations'*] (promulgated February 21, 1979), *in* ZHONGHUA RENMIN GONGHEGUO LIFA SIFA JIESHI ANLI DAIQUAN [COMPENDIUM OF LEGISLATION, JUDICIAL INTERPRETATIONS AND CASE LAWS OF THE PEOPLE'S REPUBLIC OF CHINA] 989-90 (1990) [hereinafter "COMPENDIUM OF LEGISLATION, JUDICIAL INTERPRETATIONS AND CASE LAWS OF THE PRC"] (explaining that the 1954 Arrest Regulations were practically abandoned during the Lin period from 1966-76).

14. *Zhonghua Renmin Gongheguo Daibu Juliu Tiaoli* [*Regulations of the People's Republic of China on Arrest and Detention*] (adopted at the Sixth Meeting of the Standing Committee of the Fifth National People's Congress and promulgated for implementation by Order No. 1 of the Standing Committee of the National People's Congress on February 23, 1979), *in* ZHONGHUA RENMIN GONGHEGUO FALU QUANSHU [COLLECTION OF LAWS OF THE PEOPLE'S REPUBLIC OF CHINA] [hereinafter "COLLECTION OF LAWS OF THE PRC"] 87-93 (1989) [hereinafter *"1979 Arrest Regulations"*]. For an English translation, see THE LAWS OF THE PEOPLE'S REPUBLIC OF CHINA (1979-1982) (Beijing: Foreign Language Press) 47-49. *1979 Arrest Regulations*, art. 15 ("[t]he Regulations on Arrest and Detention of the People's Republic of China promulgated on December 20, 1954 shall be invalidated simultaneously").

15. Criminal Procedure Law of the People's Republic of China (adopted July 1, 1979), *translated in* CRIMINAL PROCEDURE LAW OF THE PEOPLE'S REPUBLIC OF CHINA, THE LAWS OF THE PRC (1979-1982) 120-50 (1987) [hereinafter "Criminal Procedure Law"]; *see* RESOLUTION OF THE STANDING COMMITTEE OF THE NPC ON THE PLAN FOR IMPLEMENTING THE CRIMINAL PROCEDURE LAW (adopted April 16, 1980), *id.* at 198-99.

16. *See Guanyu Renmin Jianchayuan Dibu Juliu Renfan You Gongan Jiguan Zhixing De Tongzhi* [*Circular Regarding the Arrest and Detention of Prisoners by the People's Procuracy Should Be Conducted by the Public Security Organs*] (promulgated March 27, 1979), *in* ZHONGGUO GONGAN BAIKE QUANSHU [CHINESE PUBLIC SECURITY ENCYCLOPEDIA] [hereinafter "PUBLIC

instructions, and orders from the Ministry of Public Security.[17] However, except for certain circulars and directives, none of these laws explicitly sanction *shoushen*, and *shoushen* does not appear in the PRC Constitution (1982), the PRC Criminal Procedure Law, the PRC Criminal law, or the 1979 Arrest Regulations.

At the Third Plenum of the Eleventh Central Committee in 1978, the Chinese Communist Party ("Party") called generally for a more reliable and accountable legal system.[18] The Ministry of Public Security responded with its first attempt to restrict what had been an unstructured *shoushen* power. The Ministry of Public Security "Circular Regarding the Reorganization and Strengthening of *Shoushen* for Itinerant Criminals" provides a rudimentary procedural framework for the employment of *shoushen* by the police.[19] The Circular provides that *shoushen* detention should be centralized[20] and limited.[21] *Shoushen* should follow strict approval procedures[22] with a time limit.[23] The Circular was clearly designed as an interim measure to address a growing concern over the use of *shoushen*, allowing more time for experimentation and reflection.

SECURITY ENCYCLOPEDIA"] 831 (1989); *Guanyu Renmin Fayuan Jueding Juliu Renfan You Gongan Jiguan Zhixing De Juti Banfa De Tongzhi* [*Circular on Concrete Measures Requiring the Police to Execute People's Court Decisions to Arrest an Offender*] (promulgated March 27, 1979), *id.*

17. *See Gonganju Yushen Gongzuo Guize* [*Ministry of Public Security Regulations on Examination*] (adopted August 20, 1979), *in* COLLECTION OF LAWS OF THE PRC, *supra* note 14, at 266-74; *Gongan Jiguan Banli Xingshi Anjian Chengxu Guiding* [*Stipulations on Criminal Case Handling Procedures by the Public Security Organs*] (promulgated March 10, 1989), *in* ZHONGHUA RENMIN GONGHEGUO JIANCHA YEWU QUANSHU [THE COMPREHENSIVE BUSINESS MANUAL OF PRC PROCURATORATE] 499-512 (1990) [hereinafter "BUSINESS MANUAL OF THE PRC"].

18. See "*Zhongguo gongchangdang di shiyijie zhongyang weiyuanhui disanci quanti huiyi gongbao*" [*Public declaration of the Chinese Communist Party, Eleventh Central Committee, Third Plenary Session*] (passed on December 22, 1978), *in* DI SHISAN JIE SANZHONG QUANHUI YILAI ZHONGYAO WENXIAN XUANBIAN [COLLECTION OF IMPORTANT DOCUMENTS SINCE THE ELEVENTH CENTRAL COMMITTEE, THIRD PLENARY SESSION] (Zhonggong zhongyang dangxiao chubanshe, 1981 (RJ 05321)), 1-11 ("In order to protect people's democracy, it is necessary to strengthen the socialist legal system." at 11).

19. *Guanyu Zhengdun He Jiaqiang Dui Liucuan Fanzui Fenzi Shourong Shencha Gongzuo De Tongzhi, Gongfa (1978) 87 Hao* [*Circular Regarding the Reorganization and Strengthening of Shourong Shencha for Itinerant Criminals, Public Security (1978) No. 87*] (promulgated November 1, 1978), *in* PUBLIC SECURITY ENCYCLOPEDIA, *supra* note 16, at 224.

20. *Id.* (*Shourong* centers should be located only at local (*difang*) and city first class public security organs. Those established at the county level are to be abolished).

21. *Id.* (*Shoushen* should be used only against current *liucuan fan* or important *liucuan fan*).

22. *Id.* (*Shoushen* should first be fully documented by the local police, then endorsed by the fenju or county public security, and finally approved by the local or city public security bureaus. Further, complicated cases should be discussed by the *Shoushen* leadership and approved by the local or city public security bureaus.

23. *Id.* (*Shourong* should not last for more than one month).

Beginning in 1978 and through 1980, the Supreme People's Court used its constitutional interpretation power to issue eight key opinions dealing with *shoushen*.[24] Substantively, the Court's pronouncements served as official endorsements of *shoushen*, previously a dubious legal practice. In making explicit legal provision for offsetting time spent during *shoushen* against subsequent criminal sentences, the Court implicitly acknowledged the validity and legitimacy of *shoushen*. The Court also clarified that any illegal investigative detention measure, no matter under what name or for what purpose, constitutes a deprivation of freedom and may not be used. The Court demonstrated its concern for the abusive uses and deleterious effects of onerous powers of investigative detention, particularly during the Gang of Four era. Thus, these opinions served important education and propaganda functions.

The opinions of the Supreme People's Court affirm that by 1978, *shoushen* had captured the attention of the PRC political leadership. The political leadership was very concerned with the abuse of police authority.[25] It was committed to putting any unfettered exercise of police power, especially *shoushen*, under close scrutiny. The respective actions taken on *shoushen* , first by the Ministry of Public Security and later by the Supreme People's Court, should be read in the context of an overall attempt, and a coordinated effort, by the political authority to limit the use of the police power through law and education.[26] And, in a still larger context, they reflected the nation's attempt to introduce the "rule-of-law."[27]

---

24. *See, e.g., Guanyu Zuifan Beibu Qian Zai Kanshou Suo Geli Shencha Riqi Kefou Zhedi Xingqi De Pifu, Xian Gaofa (1978) 18 Hao Qingshi* [*Official Reply Regarding Whether the Time Spent by Offenders During Investigative Separation in Detention Centers Can Be Used to Offset Against a Criminal Sentence, Xian Higher People's Court (1978) Request for Instruction No. 18*], *mentioned in* COMPILATION OF LAWS AND RESTRICTIVE INTERPRETATIONS OF THE PRC, at 121.

25. The concern with police abuse of power is best expressed in Peng Zhen's address to the NPC in introducing the 'seven draft laws.' *See Guanyu Qige Falu Caoan De Shuoming* [*Explanation Regarding the Seven Draft Laws*] (adopted July 26, 1979), *in* COMPENDIUM OF LEGISLATION, JUDICIAL INTERPRETATIONS AND CASE LAWS OF THE PRC, *supra* note 13, at 55-57.

26. *See* RENMIN RUHE YU GONGAN DA JIADAO [HOW THE PEOPLE CAN DEAL WITH PUBLIC SECURITY] 4-6 (1990) (describing the magnitude of police powers).

27. *See* Li Xue, *Lun Woguo Xingshi Zhengce Yu Xingfa De Guanxi* [*A Discussion of the Relationship Between Our Country's Criminal Policy and Criminal Law*], FAXUE [LEGAL STUDIES], Aug. 1992, at 91-97; ZHANG YOUYU, GUANYU SHEHUI ZHUYI FAZHI DE RUOGAN WENTI [REGARDING CERTAIN QUESTIONS ON SOCIALIST LEGAL SYSTEM] (1980) (there continues to be debate about the nature and functions of law in China). For a discussion of Peng Zhen's rule-by-law philosophy, see Pitman B. Potter & Peng Zhen, *Evolving Views on Party Organization and law*, in CAROLE L. HAMRIN & TIMOTHY CHEEK, CHINA'S ESTABLISHMENT INTELLECTUALS 21-51 (1986). For a more recent study on Peng Zhen's rule-by-law philosophy, see PITMAN B. POTTER, FROM LENINIST DISCIPLINE TO SOCIALIST LEGALISM, IN USC SEMINAR SERIES NO. 10 (Hong Kong Institute of Asia-Pacific Studies, Chinese University of Hong Kong, 1995). During the anti-crime campaigns (1983-

B. *Shoushen in the 1980s*

Since the economic opening of China in the 1980s, the police have faced a sharply increasing crime rate,[28] as police resources have shrunk and police responsibilities have grown.[29] Along with market reforms, the number of economic crimes, such as theft and fraud, have increased.[30] One of the most pressing problems is the *mangliu*[31] and *liucuan* problem.[32]

1987) criminal procedure rules were dispensed with to expedite the handling of criminals. *See Guanyu Xunsu Shenpan Yanzhong Weihai Shehui Zhian De Fanzui Fenzi De Chengxu* [*Regarding the Procedure for Prompt Adjudication of Cases Involving Criminals Who Seriously Endanger Public Security*] (adopted Sept. 2, 1983), *in* ZHONGHUA RENMIN GONGHEGUO FALU GUIFANXING JIESHI JICHENG [COMPILATION OF LAWS AND RESTRICTIVE INTERPRETATIONS OF THE PRC] *supra*, note 24 (1990).

28. *Xin Zhongguo Fazhi Jianshe Sishi Nian Yao Lan: 1949-1988 (1990)* [*New China Legal System Construction: Overview of Significant Events Over 40 Years: 1949-1988*] 409 (1990) (the concern with crime led to successive nationwide anti-crime champaign (1983-1987)). *See Quanguo Gaoji Renmin Fayuan Chang Zuotan Hui Jiyao* [*Summary of Nationwide Higher People's Court President's Meeting*] (published May 1, 1989), *in* COMPILATION OF LAWS AND RESTRICTIVE INTERPRETATIONS OF THE PRC (SUPPLEMENT), *supra* note 3, at 193-94. (demonstrating that overall criminal cases handled by the people's courts during the first quarter of 1989 increased by 14.75%, including an increase in major burglaries and thefts of 78.7%, robberies of 59.98%, and murders of 13.05%).

29. *See Guanyu Jiaqiang Gongjian Fa Bumen Fame Shouru Guanli He Baozheng Banan Jingfei De Tongzhi, Caiyizi (1990) 79 Hao* [*Circular Regarding Strengthening the Management of Penalties and Confiscation and Guaranteeing of Case Handing Expenditure of the Police, Procuratorate, Court Departments, Ministry of Finance (1990) No. 79*] (promulgated October 9, 1990), *in* COMPILATION OF LAWS AND RESTRICTIONS OF THE PRC (SUPPLEMENT), *supra* note 3, at 12 (cited to by the Supreme People's Court, and alluding to problems of insufficient case handling expenses leading to various illegal efforts to obtain operational funding, including the imposition of fines instead of legal punishments). *Id.* For a discussion on the changing role and responsibility of the PRC police in the economic reform, see Kam C. Wong, *Public Security Reform in China in the 1990s*, CHINA REVIEW (1994), ch. 5, 5.5 to 5.44, esp. 1-5 (explaining that the PRC Police faces changes in its mission, values, powers, structure and process).

30. Theft cases grew from 744,374 cases in 1981 to 1,122,105 cases in 1991. Serious thefts grew from 16,873 cases in 1981 to 355,201 cases in 1994. Fraud cases grew from 18,665 in 1981 to 57,706 in 1994. For 1981 figures, see LAW YEAR BOOK OF CHINA (1987), 887, Table 18. For 1994 figures, see LAW YEAR BOOK OF CHINA (1996), 1069, Table 1.

31. "*Mangliu*," meaning "blind flow," has come to signify a significant group of people, mainly younger men, who move in and out of Chinese cities looking for work. *See generally* Li Mengbai, LIUDONGRENKOU DUI DACHENGSHI FAZHAN DE YINGXIANG HE DUICE [EFFECT OF FLOATING POPULATION ON THE DEVELOPMENT OF BIG CITIES AND POSSIBLE SOLUTIONS] 32-74 (1991) (Statistical Analysis of the Problem); CHINA'S LABOR WORKER EXODUS, *supra* note 11, at 167-82 (humanistic account); Willy Wo, *Comment*, SOUTH CHINA MORNING POST, Aug. 10, 1993, at 3 (describing *mangliu* as civilian workers, mostly rural peasants, who go to cities en masse to look for job opportunities).

32. *Guanyu Zai Daji Liucuan Fanzui Huodong Zhong Xuyao Zhuyi Jige Wenti De Tongzhi* [*Circular Regarding Paying Attention to Certain Questions When Cracking Down on Cases Involving Itinerant Criminals*] (promulgated December 13, 1989), *in* COMPENDIUM OF LEGISLATION, JUDICIAL INTERPRETATIONS AND CASE LAWS OF THE PRC, *supra* note 13, at 601-02 (explaining that

The *mangliu* are part of an even larger group known as the "floating population" (*renkou liudong*) who move in and out of the cities for a variety of reasons, including visiting, shopping, conducting business or working.[33] This floating population problem is particularly serious for certain regions of China, including coastal areas such as Guangzhou, industrial cities such as Shanghai, economic zones such as Shenzhen, and transportation hubs such as Beijing.[34]

economic opening and social reforms led to a huge increase in population mobility, resulting in itinerant criminals intermingling with the population and taking advantage of slack public security controls).

33. The 'floating population' can be defined as those people who have no proper permanent residence and stay in the city to conduct any number of activities, from social visits to business. *See* Li Mengbai, *supra* note 31, at 6. A survey of 74 cities and township (43 cities and 31 towns) in 1986 showed mass movement of rural people into the cities and towns since the economic reform in 1979:

Table 1: People moving in cities and towns as a percentage of local residence

Year	Big cities*	Small Cities*	Towns
1977-1978	12.5%	12.6%	6.0%
1979-1980	19.5%	20.2%	12.5%
1981-1982	9.7%	19.8%	11.3%
1983-1984	15.6%	21.1%	12.0%
1985-1986	17.0%	23.6%	16.3%

Source: *Zhongguo Renkou Qianyi Yu Chengshihua Yanjiu* [*Chinese Population Movement and Urbanization Research*] 8 (1988).
*Big cities include especially big cities, and small cities include medium size cities.

34. According to one survey, the average daily population movement into Shanghai in 1988 was 2.09 million people, into Beijing in 1988 was 1.31 million, into Guangzhou in 1989 was 1.30 million and into Wuhan in 1990 was 1.20 million. Li Mengbai, *supra* note 31, at 8.

Statistically, *mangliu* are predominately male,[35] below 35 years of age,[36] and have less than average education.[37] They are predominantly manual laborers, and hold temporary or unstable jobs.[38] They predominantly congregate in city centers or on the outskirts of town.[39]

35. Table 2: Sex make up of mobile populations in 5 cities in 1988 (extracted from 11 cities)

Cities	Male	Female	Ratio: female = 1
Total	3804595	1487251	2.56
Shanghai	5568667	260133	2.14
Beijing	627033	192618	3.25
Guanzhou	616687	297533	2.07
Wuhan	458967	295608	1.55
Hangzhou	342264	161606	2.12

Li Mengbai, *supra* note 31, at 13.

36. Table 3: Age distribution of mobile population:

Sex	Total	< 18	18 - 35	35 - 50	> 50
Male	100%	6.32%	55.6%	30.38%	7.7%
Female	100%	15.27%	54.01%	18.25%	12.48%

Id.

37. Table 4: Education achievement of Shanghai residents vs. mobile population (1988)

Educational achievement	Residents	Mobile population
illiterate	7.0%	9.4%
primary school	18.8%	24.0%
junior middle school	41.3%	47.6%
senior middle school	25.3%	14.6%
university	5.6%	3.3%
university graduates	2.0%	0.6%

See Li Mengbai, *supra* note 31, at 14.

38. A Beijing survey showed that 94% of the mobile population who moved there engaged in building construction, restaurant services, agriculture trading, coal manufacturing and transportation, refuse hauling, road maintenance, and toilet cleaning. They were not entitled to social benefits and were subjected to the vicissitudes of the markets. *See id.* at 16.

39. Table 5: Beijing mobile population geographic distribution

Year	Town Center	Suburban District	Remote Suburb
1979	63.56%	30.57%	5.87%
1987	17.5%	57.00%	25.50%

See Id. at 18.

The *mangliu* population creates social problems as the massive influx of non-local residents burdens the cities' limited physical infrastructure — such as roads, communications, electrical utilities, and the water supply. In addition, the limits of the cities' fragile social support services such as birth control, education, medicine, food subsidies, public security, and environmental protection are challenged and often surpassed.[40] *Mangliu* exist outside the residential registration system.[41] It has been suggested that the *mangliu* problem destabilizes Chinese society and threatens the normative order, resulting in recurring social harms.[42] *Mangliu* criminals are also disproportionately involved in more serious crimes.[43] *Mangliu* are also said to be populated with petty thieves, hooligans, gamblers, drug addicts, and prostitutes, and living on the fringes of society and at the expense of local communities.[44] More significantly, crimes committed by *mangliu* appear to be increasing.[45]

Shoushen came to the rescue as an all-purpose crime fighting and social control device. *Shoushen* was used in the 1980s as a stop gap measure between the failing traditional social control networks and the nascent criminal justice system. A Ministry of Public Security circular recognized that *shoushen* was designed to deal with "those who reside in

---

40. *Id.* at 58-73.

41. For an excellent discussion of the Chinese social control system, see MICHAEL DUTTON, POLICING AND PUNISHMENT IN CHINA (1992).

42. As demonstrates by the table below, they commit a disproportionate amount of crimes. Table 6: Mobile criminals as a percentage of all criminals in seven major cities.

Cities	Date	Mobile criminals as a % of total criminals
Hangzhou	Jan. - Nov., 1989	90.0%
Shenyang	1988	69.8%
Guangzhou	1989	57.9%
Chongqing	1988	42.9%
Shanghai	1989	31.4%
Wuhan	1988	33.0%
Tianjin	Jan. - July, 1989	23.0%

See Li Mengbai, *supra* note 31, at 49.

43. In 1989, *mangliu* criminals were responsible for 1/3 of all robberies, 1/8 of all murders, and 2/3 of all serious fraud and misrepresentation cases in Shanghai. *Id.*

44. *Id.*

45. In Guangzhou, crimes by *mangliu* grew from 109 criminal arrests in 1983 to 5703 in 1988, an increase of 520%. *Id.* at 48. Similarly, in Shanghai, *mangliu* criminal arrests as a percentage of the total arrests grew from 6.8% in 1983 (778 arrests) to 31.4% in 1989 (5285 arrests), an increase of roughly 520 times. *Id.* at 160. The figures over seven years figures were: 6.8% in 1983; 10.8% in 1984; 11.3% in 1985; 17.8% in 1986; 19.9% in 1987; 29.9% in 1988; 31.4% 1989. *Id.*

the village and have come to commit crimes in the cities, along the railway, and at large factories and mines."[46] Eventually, *shoushen* extended the reach of the traditional rural social control network into the urban centers and brought administrative control to what was considered an otherwise unruly and mobile crowd.

C. 1980 State Council Circular

The growing use of *shoushen* as an administrative social control and crime fighting measure prompted the State Council to issue a circular ("State Council Circular") on February 19, 1980, providing for the placement and treatment of *shoushen* persons in re-education camps.[47]

The State Council Circular defines the permissible scope and jurisdictional reach of *shoushen* and sets forth some minimal guidelines for its use. Essentially, it addresses the question, which had previously escaped serious attention, of who the intended targets of *shoushen* are. The State Council Circular has been interpreted to require that two separate conditions be met before *shoushen* be allowed: the person must have committed a minor legal violation or criminal conduct,[48] and the person must belong to at least one of the following five categories: (a) one who does not give a true name or address; (b) one who is without a known origin (*laili buming*); (c) one who is suspected of committing crimes from place to place (*licuan zuoan*); (d) one who is suspected of committing

---

46. *Guanyu Zuohao Laojiao Gongzuo De Baogao (Jielu)* [*Report Regarding Perfecting Labor Education Work (Summary)*], *in* GONGAN JIGUAN BANLI LAODONG JIAOYAN ANJIAN FAGUI HUIBIAN [COLLECTION OF PUBLIC SECURITY REGULATIONS ON HANDLING LABOR EDUCATION CASES], at 11-16 (1992) (calling for the expeditious handling of itinerant criminals, instructing against prolonged investigations and advising against requiring unnecessary evidentiary proof, calling for the preventing of suspected itinerant criminals from escaping and committing more crimes, allowing for the uninterrupted investigation of suspects, and providing for the work, education and reform of a group of economically displaced *mangliu*).

47. State Council Circular, *supra* note 2. *See Guanyu Xian, Zhen Shoushen Laodong Jiaoyan He Diqu Juban Laodong Jiaoyang Changsuo Wenti De Pifu, 80 Gongfa (Jiao) 137 Hao* [*Official Reply to Question Regarding County, Township Labor Education Farm, and Local Area Establishing Labor Education Farm, 80 Public Security (Education) No. 137*] (by which all those subject to *shoushen* were supposed to be processed at *shoushen* farms especially established for *shoushen*, set up by the respective provinces, autonomous regions, independent cities and larger cities, such that there is no separate facility for *shoushen* at the local level; the labor-education farm is to be supervised and administered by a labor-reform committee which is staffed with people from civil administration, public security and labor departments).

48. This excludes the use of *shoushen* to deal with serious criminals, who should be processed by compulsory measures under the PRC Criminal Procedure and corresponding Arrest and Detention Regulations (1979).

crimes repeatedly (*duoci zuoan*); or (e) one who is suspected of committing crimes in a group (*jiehuo zuoan*).[49]

Having been promulgated by the State Council, the State Council Circular is significant because it serves and has been cited as an empowering administrative regulation for *shoushen*.[50] While the State Council Circular does not confront directly the issue of the legality of *shoushen*, in providing for the placement of those subject to *shoushen*, it arguably legitimizes the use of *shoushen* to deal with itinerant criminals. The State Council Circular is also significant in that it provides, for the first time, a clearly articulated operational definition of *shoushen* power, defining when *shoushen* is to be used and to whom *shoushen* applies. It further functions as a jurisdictional benchmark for the regulation and control of its exercise.

However, the State Council Circular leaves many questions unanswered, such as where the legal foundation of the power comes from, whether the measure is to be regarded as criminal or administrative, how the measure is to be reconciled with existing police powers to investigate, detain, and arrest individuals under the PRC Criminal Procedure Law, and which investigative measure is preferred when alternative measures are available, as in the case with minor criminals, such that if both measures may alternatively be used, such discretionary use of powers could properly be controlled.[51]

D. 1985 Ministry of Public Security Circular

Having become disturbed by the indiscriminate and abusive use of *shoushen* in carrying out the then on-going anti-crime campaign, the Ministry of Public Security released a report in 1985.[52] The Ministry

---

49. *See Case 104: "Weifa shoushen zhiren sunhai, yingdang peichang" [Harm resulting from illegal sheltering for examining, should be compensated] (Liu Jiaqiang vs. Public Security of A Certain City), in* XINGZHENG PEICHANG ANLIE XUANPING (SELECTION OF ADMINISTRATIVE COMPENSATION CASES) 179-84 (1992) [hereinafter "ADMINISTRATIVE COMPENSATION CASES"].

50. *Guanyu Gongan Jiguan Guanche Shishi 'Xingcheng Susongfa' De Ruogan Wenti De Tongzhi [Circular Regarding Certain Questions on the Thorough Implementation of the 'Administrative Procedure Law'], in* COMPILATION OF LAWS AND RESTRICTIVE INTERPRETATIONS OF THE PRC (SUPPLEMENT), *supra* note 3, at 45-49 [hereinafter *"Administrative Procedure Law Circular"*] (pronouncing that before any new *shoushen* law is promulgated, the public security is supposed to follow the State Council Circular). *See Guanyu Shoushen De Pifu Yiju De Fuyi Wenti [On the Question Regarding the Reconsideration of the Determination Basis for Sheltering for Examination]*, *id.* at 46.

51. *See* Chen & Zhang I, *supra* note 4.

52. *1985 Public Security Circular*, *supra* note 3.

observed that *shoushen* had been inappropriately used over the past 20 years as a substitution for investigation (*daijin*), adjudication (*daishen*), and punishment (*daixing*).[53] In response, the Ministry of Public Security promulgated a circular ("1985 Public Security Circular"), defining *shoushen* and detailing procedural guidelines for its use.[54]

First, the 1985 Public Security Circular provides that the people's procuratorate is responsible for *shoushen* supervision. In addition, according to the 1985 Public Security Circular, *shoushen* should only be used against itinerant criminals and criminal suspects who refuse to disclose their true names, addresses, places of origin and backgrounds. *Shoushen* should not be used against local offenders when their status is unmistaken or the evidence against them is clearly established. Also, *shoushen* must be approved by the county level public security party section or party committee.

Regarding the timing and duration of *shoushen* investigations, the 1985 Public Security Circular provides that *shoushen* subjects must be questioned within twenty-four hours, and the family and work unit (*danwei*) of the individual subject to *shoushen* must be informed within twenty-four hours of the reasons for the *shoushen* and the location of the investigation. Further, the *shoushen* examination must be completed within one month. If the case is too complicated or involves an inter-province or inter-regional crime, the *shoushen* period can be extended to two months upon the approval of a higher level public security bureau. For a further extension, the public security bureau or department of the province, autonomous region or independent municipality must give its approval, with the maximum period of *shoushen* not to exceed three months. The time for calculating the *shoushen* period for suspects who refuse to give their names or addresses commences when the name and address have been established.

Regarding the examination itself, the 1985 Public Security Circular provides that the examination should be based on evidence, and that hitting, yelling, insults, and torture are not allowed. Those subject to *shoushen* enjoy civil rights as guaranteed by the PRC Constitution and laws. They are to be separated from regular criminals, given a right to complain against any violation of their rights, and must be given adequate food and lodging just like any other local suspect.

---

53. *Id.*
54. *Id.*

Regarding the outcome of a *shoushen* investigation, the 1985 Public Security Circular provides that those who are found guilty of crimes are to be prosecuted according to the PRC Criminal Procedure Law, and should be subject to labor education or administrative sanctions if they are deemed necessary. In cases of wrongful detention, the mistake should be openly acknowledged and steps taken to ameliorate any adverse consequences (*shanhou gongzuo*).

The 1985 Public Security Circular replaced all previous circulars, instructions, decisions, and notices on the subject matter of *shoushen* issued by the national or local public security organs.[55] The 1985 Public Security Circular has since been accepted as the de facto "administrative procedure" for *shoushen*. It was applied by the Public Security of Railroads, the Civil Aviation Administration, and both the Ministries of Forestry and Transportation.[56] It has been referred to by the NPC Standing Committee,[57] adopted by the people's procuratorate,[58] cited by the people's courts, and accepted by legal scholars.[59]

However, the 1985 Public Security Circular continued to fuel debate over the nature, scope, interpretation and constitutionality of *shoushen*, the main contention focusing on whether *shoushen* should be considered a criminal or administrative measure, and whether there was a need to provide for a separate administrative detention power beyond the powers provided by the PRC Criminal Procedure Law.[60]

---

55. *Id.* art. 9 (providing that "[a]ll previous circulars and instructions by the Ministry of Public Security or local public security bureaus are void to the extent to which they conflict with this circular").

56. *See Guanyu Tielu Ruhe Zhixing Dui Shoushen Duixiang Yanchang Shoushen Qixian Shenpi Wenti De Qingshi Baogao De Pifu* [*Official Reply to Report Requesting for Instruction Regarding How Railways Can Extend Sheltering for Examination Period for Examination Subjects*] October 16, 1985, *in* PUBLIC SECURITY ENCYCLOPEDIA, *supra* note 16, at 879.

57. *Jiangxi Province Answers, supra* note 3.

58. *Guanyu Renmin Jianchayuan Zhijie Shouli Zhencha De Tanwu, Huilu, Qinquan, Duzhi Deng Fanzui Anjian Bushiyong Shoushen De Tongzhi* [*Circular Regarding not Using Sheltering for Examination for the Crimes of Corruption, Bribery, Infringement of Rights, and Dereliction of Duty Cases Directly Investigated by the Supreme People's Procuracy*] (promulgated 21 March, 1990) [hereinafter "*Supreme People's Procuratorate Circular*"], *in* ZHONGGUO FALU NIANJIAN (1991) [LAW YEARBOOK OF CHINA (1991)], at 623 (1991) (incorporating, by reference, the 1985 Public Security Circular, *supra* note 2).

59. Chen Weidong & Zhang Tao, *Zai Tan Shourong Shencha Buyi Feichu* [*The Taking-In Examination System Must not be Abolished*] *in* ZHONGGUO FAXUE, March, 1993, at 113 [hereinafter "Chen & Zhang II"].

60. Wang Xinxin, *Shoushen Zhidu Yingyu Feichu* [*The Taking-in and Examination System Must be Abolished*] *in* ZHONGGUO FAXUE, March, 1993, at 110. Chen & Zhang II, *supra* note 59, at 113.

E. *Limitation of Shoushen into the 1990s*

Into the 1990s, the Chinese government has remained interested in curbing abusive uses of the *shoushen* power.[61] The overall trend has been toward more restrictive uses of *shoushen*, and in particular, the trend has moved away from using *shoushen* in commercial disputes.[62] On September 8, 1990, the Ministry of Public Security, Supreme People's Procuracy, and the Supreme People's Court issued a notice ("Notice"), summing up the general sentiment against the use of *shoushen* in commercial cases.[63] The Notice cited twelve reported cases of illegal detention from Shenzhen, Guangdong province in 1989, and noted that illegal detention cases had arisen elsewhere.[64]

61. *See* Yang Yichen, *Zui Gao Renmin Jianchayuan Gongzuo Baogao* [*The Supreme People's Procuratorate Work Report*] (promulgated April 1, 1988), *in* ZHONGGUO JIANCHA NIANJIAN (1989) [PROCURATORIAL YEARBOOK OF CHINA (1989)], at 21-28; LAW YEARBOOK OF CHINA 802 (1991) (reporting on the First national Procuracy meeting on "rights violation" and dereliction of duty, held in Beijing from April 3-9, 1990); LAW YEARBOOK OF CHINA 720 (1992) (reporting on the Second national procuracy meeting on "rights violation" and dereliction of duty held in Beijing from May 18-23, 1990).

62. *Guanyu Gongan Jiguan Bude Feifa Yuequan Ganyu Jingji Anjian De Chuli Tongzhi, (89) Gong (Zhi) Di 30 Hao* [*Circular Regarding the Fact that Public Security Organs Should not Interfere Illegally with Commercial Dispute Cases*], *in* COMPILATION OF LAWS AND RESTRICTIVE INTERPRETATIONS OF THE PRC, *supra* note 3, at 22 (a circular issued by the Ministry of Public Security in April, 1989, strictly forbidding public security from using *shoushen* and other forms of detention to interfere with commercial disputes). *See Guanyu Chachu Zai Shangmao Huodong Zhong Yi Bangjia, Kouliu Renzhi Deng Fangfa Bihuan Zhaiwu Feifa Jujin Taren De Anjian Tongbao, Gaojainfa Fazi (1990) Di Er Hao* [*Circulation of Notice Regarding Investigating and Handling Cases of Illegal Detention and Using of Kidnaping and Holding of Hostages to Coerce Repayment of Debts in Commercial Activities*], *id.* (in which the Supreme People's Procuracy reinforced the general theme of the 1985 Public Security circular). *See also Gonganbu guanyu yanjin gongan jiguan chashou jingji doufen weifa zhuaren de tongzi* [*Ministry of Public Security Notice Regarding Strictly Forbidding Public Security Organs in Interfering with Economic Disputes and Illegally detaining People*] (promulgated on April 25, 1992) (Gong Tong Zhi (1992) 50 hao) *in* ZHONGGUO JINGCHA FALU FAGUI GUIZHANG SHIYI DAQUAN, 1327-1328. The Notice observed that the Circular Regarding the Fact that Public Security Organs Should Not Interfere with Commercial Dispute Cases has not been strictly followed. Public security organs was admonished to (1) stay away from contractual cases and commercial disputes; (2) not use *shourong shencha* in commercial cases and against foreigners; (3) not place commercial agents under custody as hostage for debt collection; (4) follow proper procedures when conducting police business outside ones jurisdiction.) *Id.*, at 1328.

63. *"Circular of Notice Regarding the Situation of Illegal Detention Cases in Commercial and Trade Disputes"* [*Guanyu Zai Shangye Maoyizhong Feifa Jujin Anjian Qingkuan de tongzhi*] *in* COMPILATION OF LAWS AND RESTRICTIVE INTERPRETATIONS OF THE PRC (SUPPLEMENT), *supra*, note 3, at 20-22.

64. Four of the cases involved local people, four others involved people from other areas of Guangdong, and the rest were from outside the province. Five of the 12 cases involved public security and procuratorial officials.

After the discussion of the cases, the Notice went on to explain:

> There were also some local public security officers and procurators who exceeded their legal authority by unilaterally protecting local economic interests in the handling of economic disputes. They treated what should have been mere commercial disputes as economic crimes and used illegal detention to help certain work units or individuals collect their debts. These practices violate state laws and party discipline. They severely interfere with citizens' personal freedom and destroy the normal functioning of the economic order. The public security organs, procurator offices, and courts should pay special attention and adopt effective measures to prevent and rectify the problem.[65]

On November 6, 1990, the Ministry of Public Security issued another circular ("1990 Public Security Circular"), expounding the abuses of *shoushen* in aiding local economic interests.[66] The 1990 Public Security Circular noted that public security officers violated their jurisdictional authority by treating contract and debt disputes as economic crimes involving fraud and using *shoushen* and detention to coerce the repayment of debts. In so doing, the 1990 Public Security Circular noted that public security officers applied *shoushen* to the wrong people, and often detained those people for three to four months, and sometimes even up to one or two years, which is much longer than the one month period allowed by law.

The 1990s witnessed a tightening of control over who can carry out *shoushen*, who can be made a target of *shoushen*, when one subject to *shoushen* may be interrogated, how a target of *shoushen* can complain of abuses, and what remedies were available to an aggrieved party.

On December 13, 1989, the Ministry of Public Security, Supreme People's Procuracy, and Supreme People's Court issued a Circular dealing with the handling of cases involving itinerant criminals ("Itinerant

---

65. *Id. See Guo Debing Bufu Xinjiang Jinghexian Gonganju Shoushen Juedingan* [*Case of Guodebing Refusal to Except the Sheltering for Examination Determination of Xinjiang Province Jinghe County Public Security Bureau*] (1990) [hereinafter "*Case of Guo Debing*"], in IMPORTANT OVERVIEW OF CHINESE CASES, *supra* note 1, at 1177.

66. *Guanyu Qieshi Jiuzheng Gongan Jiguan Banli Zhapian Caiwu Anjian Zhong De Buzheng Zhifeng De Zhongzhi* [*Circular Regarding Realistically Correcting Inappropriate Style of Public Security Organs in Handling Swindling of Goods and Money Cases*] (promulgated November 6, 1990), *in* COMPILATION OF LAWS AND RESTRICTIONS OF THE PRC (SUPPLEMENT), *supra* note 3, at 103-6.

Criminals Circular").[67] The Itinerant Criminals Circular acknowledged the difficulties in the investigation, arrest, prosecution, and adjudication of such criminals. It called for the arrest and prosecution of itinerant criminals when the facts are clear and basic evidence exists.[68] On March 21, 1990, the Supreme People's Procuracy issued a circular further clarifying in what cases *shoushen* can be used ("Procuracy Circular").[69] This circular prohibits the use of *shoushen* for cases involving corruption, bribery, infringement of rights or dereliction of duty.[70] In May 1990, the Minster of Public Security issued a document admonishing public security at all levels not to extend the scope of *shoushen* at will or illegally overstep the administrative time limits on *shoushen*. The document also provides that any person subject to *shoushen* may appeal the decision to impose *shoushen* to the next level of public security authority. If a person subject to *shoushen* decides to challenge the decision to impose *shoushen*, the *shoushen* process continues except as provided by the PRC Administrative Procedure Law.[71]

In 1991, the Ministry of Public Security issued a circular to take further steps to exercise control over the use of *shoushen* ("1991 Public

---

67. *See Guanyu Zai Daji Liucuan Fanzui Huodong Zhong Xuyao Zhuyi Jige Wenti De Tongzhi* [*Circular Regarding Certain Questions on the Handling of Cases Involving Itinerant Criminals"*], *in* COMPENDIUM OF LEGISLATION, JUDICIAL INTERPRETATIONS AND CASE LAWS OF THE PRC, *supra* note 13, at 601-2 (setting forth one of the most comprehensive definitions of itinerant criminals: criminals who commit crimes across city and county jurisdictions, and particularly, either those who commit a series of crimes across city and county jurisdictions, or those who commit crimes in their places of residence but escape to other cities and towns and continue to commit other crimes; itinerant criminals do not include those who are out of town tourists, businessmen, workers who commit occasional crimes and those who, while living in a local area, commit crimes in cities and towns across the border).

68. *See* Xu Youjun, *Zhongguo Xingshi Susong Yu Renquan* [*Chinese Criminal Process and Human Rights*], ZHONGWAI FAXUE (CHINESE AND FOREIGN LEGAL STUDIES), Feb. 1992, at 38-43 (demonstrating the tension existing between protecting individual rights and advancing social welfare).

69. *Supreme People's Procuratorate Circular, supra* note 58.

70. It is argued that *1985 Public Security Circular* only authorizes the *shoushen* of criminals without known name, address, or place of origin. Legally, the power does not apply to cases of bribery, corruption, infringement of rights, and dereliction of duty because these offenses are usually committed by state officials with clear identity and known address. Practically, there is little need to resort to such power because state officials are not likely to escape investigation.

71. *Guanyu Yinfa "Quanguo Gongan Fazhi Gongzuo Huiyi Jiyao" Tongzhi, Gong Fa (1990) 10 Hao* [*Notice Regarding the Publication and Circulation of "Summary to National Public Security Legal System Work Meeting", Public Security Release (1990) No. 10*], (promulgated May, 1990), *referenced in* item 3 "*Guanyu Shourong Shencha De Pifu Yiju He Fuyi Wenti*" [*Issue concerning the basis for approving and reviewing of sheltering for examination*] *in Gonganbu Guangyu Gongan Jiguan Guanche Shishi "Xingzheng Susong Fa" Rugan Wenti De Tongzhi* [*Ministry of Public Security: Notice regarding certain questions on the thorough implementation of the "Administrative Procedure Law"*] *in* ZHONGGUO JINGCHA FALU FAGUI GUIZHANG SHIYI DAQUAN, 963-967, 964.

Security Circular").[72] The 1991 Public Security Circular largely reiterates rules proscribed in the 1985 Public Security Circular regarding the time limits within which *shoushen* must be completed.[73]

On July 29, 1992, the Ministry of Public Security issued a definitive statement to clarify the jurisdictional ambiguity between the State Council Circular and 1985 Public Security Circular. In response to a query by the Jiangsu public security bureau,[74] the Ministry of Public Security clearly and unequivocally endorsed the jurisdictional requirement of the State Council Circular in making the *shoushen* applicable to "four targets" (*si zhong duixiang*).[75]

A more recent attempt to control the wrongful use of *shoushen* has been made through administrative law.[76] The PRC Constitution (1982) provides a cause of action for compensation against the government for administrative wrongdoing.[77] The PRC Administrative Procedure Law

---

72. *See Case of Guo Debing*, *supra* note 65 (citing *Guanyu Jinyibu Kongzhi Shiyong Shoushen Shouduan De Tongzhi* [*Circular Regarding Further Steps to Exercise Serious Control of the Use of Shoushen Measure*]), ((91) Gongfa 37 Hao Wenjian).

73. First, those subject to *shoushen* must be examined within the first 24 hours after detention. Second, those found to be inappropriate subjects for *shoushen* should be released promptly. Third, suitable *shoushen* subjects should not be examined for more than the legal time limit, *i.e.* one month unless under exceptional circumstances; fourth, no *shoushen* should be extended over three months.

74. "*Guangyu Shourong Shencha Fanwei Wenti De Qingshi Baogao*" (*Su Gong Ting (95) 211 Hao*) ["*Request (for Instruction) and Report Regarding the Jurisdictional Scope of Shelter for Examination*"] *in* "*Gonganbu Guanyu Dui Shourong Shencha Fanwei Wenti de Pifu*" [*Ministry of Public Security: Reply Concerning the Question of Scope in Sheltering for Examination*] (Gongfu Zhi (1992) 6 Hao) *in* ZHONGGUO JINGCHA FALU FAGUI GUIZHANG SHIYI- DAQUAN [CHINA ENCYCLOPEDIA OF LAWS, REGULATIONS AND RULES REGARDING POLICE], at 950.

75. *Id.* The Ministry of Public Security issued another clarifying statement on the jurisdictional scope of *shoushen*. In reliance to an inquiry by Sichuan province public security bureau - "Guanyu Dui Fazheng Daolu Jiaotung Shigu Taoyi De Jidongche Jiashiyuan Kefu Shiyong Shencha Shouduan Qingshi" [Request (for Instruction) Regarding Whether Sheltering for Examination Measure can Be Used Against Drivers of Motor Vehicle Accidents Who Fled] - the Ministry of Public Security cited *1985 Public Security Circular* and "*Guangyu Jinyibu Yange Kongzhi Shiyong Shourong Shencha Shouduan De Tongzhi*" [*Notice on Further Serious Control of the Use of Sheltering for Examination Measures*] (Gong Tong Zhi (1991) 37 Hao) in issuing the opinion that only drivers who refused to give true name and address or otherwise with unknown background should be sheltered for examination, while others should be released. *See Gonganbu Guanyu Dui Jiaotung Shigu Hou Taoyi De Jidongche Jiashiyuan Shiyong Shencha Shouduan Qingshi Pifu*" [*Reply to Request Regarding Using Sheltering For Examination against Motor Vehicle Drivers Who Fleed from the Scene of Traffic Accident*] *Id.*, at 951.

76. Wang Liming, *Lun Wanshan Qinquanfa Chuangjian Fazhi Shehui De Guanxi* [*A Discussion on the Relationship Between Perfection of the Law of Tort and Building a Legal Society*], FAXUE [LEGAL STUDIES], July, 1992, at 14-19.

77. CONSTITUTION OF THE PEOPLE'S REPUBLIC OF CHINA, art. 41(3) (adopted Dec. 4, 1982) ("Citizens who have suffered losses through infringement of their civil rights by any state organ or functionary have the right to compensation in accordance with the law."), *translated in*

allows an aggrieved person to sue the government for administrative wrongdoing.[78] The Supreme People's Court has since issued comments providing that any person can challenge the public security's decision to practice *shoushen* administratively in court.[79]

Subsequently, the legal status of *shoushen* was put into doubt by the People's Supreme Procuratorate in an official reply to an inquiry from the Guangdong province regarding whether an escaped *shoushen* person should be prosecuted as an escapee under the Criminal Law.[80] The Supreme People's Procuratorate answered that one subject to *shoushen* who escapes should be prosecuted and punished as an escapee, but opined that further prosecution and additional penalties are only warranted for a guilty escapee and not for an innocent one.

In March 1996 the PRC political leadership and policy makers took a dramatic step forward to control the abuse of police powers, including that of *shoushen*, when the NPC adopted the amended Criminal Procedure Law. We now turn to a discussion of how the Criminal Procedure Law regulates and controls *shoushen* as an investigative power.

CONSTITUTION OF THE PEOPLE'S REPUBLIC OF CHINA AND AMENDMENTS TO THE CONSTITUTION OF THE PEOPLE'S REPUBLIC OF CHINA 11 (Legislative Affairs Commission of the Standing Committee of the National People's Congress ed., 2d ed. 1990) [hereinafter "CONSTITUTION"]; *see* Hu Xiaohua, *Guanyu Goujia Xingzheng Qinquan Sunhai Peichang Zeren De Goucheng Yu Xianzhi Wenti* [*On the Question of Constitution and Limitation of Compensation of State Administrative Infringement of Rights*], FAXUE [LEGAL STUDIES], July, 1992, at 86-89.

78. ADMINISTRATIVE PROCEDURE LAW OF THE PEOPLE'S REPUBLIC OF CHINA (adopted April 4, 1989), art. 2, *translated in* ADMINISTRATIVE PROCEDURE LAW OF THE PEOPLE'S REPUBLIC OF CHINA (Legislative Affairs Commission of the Standing Committee of the National People's Congress ed., 2d ed., 1990) (gives citizens the right to sue in the court when their legal rights have been violated by administrative actions); *id.*, art. 11(1) and 11(2) (providing that a person can file a complaint challenging any coercive measures which deprive one's liberty or restrict one's freedom); *see* ZHONGHUA REMIN GONHEGUO BAIFA SHIJIE ANLIE QUANSHU [EXPLANATION OF 100 PRC LAWS AND CASES] (1993), at 1077-1129 [hereinafter "PRC LAWS AND CASES"]; Hu Xiaohua, *supra* note 77 (identifying the five necessary elements for the successful prosecution of an action brought under the Administrative Procedure Law).

79. GUANYU GUANCHE ZHIXING 'ZHONGHUA RENMIN GONGHEGUO XINZHEN SUXONG FA' RUGAN WENTI DE YIJIAN (SHIXING) [COMMENTS ON CERTAIN QUESTIONS REGARDING RESOLUTE EXECUTION OF PRC ADMINISTRATIVE LAW].

80. *Guanyu Shoushen Jiancha Renyuan De Taopao Xingwei Shifou Zhuisu Wenti De Pifu* [*Official Reply Regarding the Question of Whether the Escape Conduct of Sheltering for Examination Persons Should be Prosecuted*], *in* BUSINESS MANUAL OF THE PRC, *supra* note 17, at 1171. Article 161 of the Criminal Law provides that "a criminal who escapes after being arrested or held in custody according to law" will receive an additional sentence on top of that for the original offense.

III. LEGISLATIVE RESPONSE TO *SHOUSHEN* IN 1996

The final chapter to the *shoushen* saga was written in 1996. On March 17, 1996 the NPC adopted tho Criminal Procedure Law of the People's Republic of China. The law was passed to promote socialist legality as well as to protect people's rights.[81] The Criminal Procedure Law, while not mentioning *shoushen* by name, effectively places all public security coercive measures, including *shoushen*,[82] under one unified procedural control scheme. Henceforth the public security authority "must strictly observe this law and relevant provisions" in investigating, arresting, and detaining suspects.[83]

Jurisdictionally, the Criminal Procedure Law specifically authorizes the public security organs to detain active criminals or major suspects under the following circumstances:

> "(6) If he/she does not reveal his/her true name and address or his/her identity is unclear.
> (7) If there is strong suspicion that he/she is a person who goes from place to place committing crimes...."[84]

---

81. Article 2 provides, in pertinent part: "The tasks of the Criminal Procedure Law of the People's Republic of China are to guarantee accurate and timely clarification of the facts of crimes, to apply the law correctly, to punish criminal elements, to safeguard innocent people from criminal prosecution ... to protect the citizens' ...rights..." *See also* Article 14: "The people's courts, the people's procuratorates, and the public security organs shall safeguard the procedural rights that participants in proceedings enjoy according to the law."

82. *See* note 88, *infra*.

83. *See* Criminal Procedure Law, Chapter 1, Article 3, paragraph 3 which provides in pertinent part: "In conducting criminal proceedings, the people's courts, the people's procuratorates, and the public security organs must strictly observe this law and relevant provisions of other laws." *See also* Article 14: "The people's courts, the people's procuratorates, and the public security organs shall safeguard the procedural rights that participants in proceedings enjoy according to the law."

84. Article 61 provides: "Public security organs may first detain an active criminal or a major suspect under any of the following circumstances:
(1) If he is preparing to commit a crime, is committing a crime, or is discovered immediately after committing a crime.
(2) If he is identified as having committed a crime by the victim or by an eyewitness on the scene.
(3) If he is discovered to have criminal evidence near his person or at his residence.
(4) If after committing the crime, he attempts to commit suicide or to escape, or if he is a fugitive.
(5) If he may possibly destroy or fabricate evidence, or conspire to make false confessions.
(6) If he does not reveal his true name and address, or his identity is unclear.
(7) If there is strong suspicion that he is a person who goes from place to place committing crimes, who repeatedly committed crimes, or who teamed up with others to commit crimes.

The above jurisdictional provisions echo the *shoushen* language in the State Council Circular[85] and the 1985 Public Security Circular.[86] These provisions are a major departure from past legal policy and administrative practice dealing with *shoushen*.[87] The NPC clearly and unequivocally acknowledged *shoushen* as a proper exercise of police investigative powers, and to be regulated by the Criminal Procedure Law.

Procedurally, the Criminal Procedure Law provides clear and explicit guidelines for investigative detention including *shoushen*. It prescribes the jurisdictional limits for investigative detention (Article 61), procedure for detention (Article 64), procedure during detention (Article 65), procedure for release (Article 65), procedure for arrest (Article 69), procedure for extension of detention (Article 69), procedure for challenging illegal detention (Article 75) and procedure for oversights (Article 76).

Generally, under the Criminal Procedure Law all investigative detentions must be accompanied by a detention warrant.[88] The police, with a few exceptions, must inform the detainee's family or work unit of his arrest within 24 hours.[89] The procedure during an investigative detention is strictly prescribed by Article 65:

> The public security organ should conduct an interrogation of the detained person within 24 hours after detention. When it is discovered that he should not have been detained, the detained person must be released immediately and be issued a release certificate.[90]

---

85. *See* note 2, *supra*.
86. *See* note 3, *supra*.
87. *See* Part II, The History of *Shoushen*, *supra*.
88. Article 64 provides:

> When a public security organ is detaining a person, it must produce a detention warrant.
>
> The family of the detained persons or his unit shall be notified 24 hours after detention of the reasons for detention and the place of custody, except in circumstances where notification would hinder investigation or there is no way to notify them.

It is clear that this provision will be of little use in protecting the rights of one group of *shoushen* targeted criminals, *i.e.* "a person who goes from place to place committing crimes; who repeatedly committed crimes ..." (Article 61(6)).

89. *Id.*
90. *See also* Article 9, para. 2 to the Police Law which provides that investigative detention by the police should not exceed 24 hours, and with the approval of the next level of public security organs, no more than 48 hours. The Police Law provides for a shorter initial detention period (12 hours) before approval is necessary.

Specifically, the Criminal Procedure Law provides strict time limits to guide the proper exercise of and effective supervisory control over investigative detention powers. Investigative detentions, under normal circumstances, should last no more than 72 hours, at which time a formal request for arrest approval should be made to the procuratorates. An extension of one to four days is possible, but only under special circumstances.[91] This can be further extended for 30 days in cases involving "a major suspect who is on the run and who allegedly commits crimes repeatedly." [92]

The Criminal Procedure Law sets forth outer limits for investigative detention. The period for holding the crime suspect in custody during investigation may not exceed two months, with a possible extension for another one month period with the approval of the prosecurtorate at the next level if the case is complicated.[93] Beyond this outer limit, an extension can only be granted by provincial autonomous regional, and municipal people's procuratorate for special types of cases, which include "major and complicated cases in which the suspect's crimes have been committed at various locations."[94] It is significant to observe that the Criminal Procedure Law makes clear that the procedural time clock on criminals or suspects

---

91. Article 69 provides: "In cases where a public security organ considers it necessary to arrest a detained person, it shall, within three days after detention, submit a request to the people's procuratorate for review and approval. Under special circumstances, the time for requesting review and approval may be extended by one to four days." What constitutes special circumstances is not defined under the Criminal Procedure Law. In light of the comprehensive nature of the law, it does not appear to be the intent of the NPC to allow for a liberal interpretation of "special circumstances."

92. Article 69, para. 2 provides: "For a major suspect who is on the run, who repeatedly commits crimes, or who partners with others to commit crimes, the time for requesting review and approval may be extended by up to 30 days." A liberal construction of this provision will include all "*licuan fan*" who by definition are wandering criminals from place to place (itinerant criminals.)

93. Article 124 provides in pertinent part: "The period for holding a crime suspect in custody during investigation may not exceed two months. If a case is complicated and cannot be concluded before the period expires, the period may be extended by one month with the approval of the procuratorate at the next level up."

94. Article 126: "If investigation of any of the following cases cannot be concluded within the period specified by Article 124 of this law, the period may be extended by two months with the approval of or decision by a provincial, autonomous regional, or municipal people's procuratorate: (1) A major and complicated case in a remote region with very poor transport facilities; (2) A major criminal gang case; (3) A major and complicated case in which the suspect's crime has been committed at various locations; (4) A major and complicated case involving a broad spectrum of crimes for which evidence is difficult to obtain."

detained for investigation does not start to run if the criminal suspect refuses to disclose his true name, address, and identity."[95]

The Criminal Procedure Law also provides for citizen challenge and official supervision of any illegal exercise of investigative detention powers. First, the aggrieved citizen has a right to file a complaint against the police.[96] Article 75 of the Criminal Procedure Law provides the aggrieved citizen with a statutory avenue to challenge any illegal detention:

> A suspect or a defendant and his or her legal representative and close relatives, or counsels appointed by a suspect and the defendant, have the right to demand rescission of the coercive measures taken by ... the public security organ that have exceed the legal limit. The ...public security organ shall release the suspect or defendant against whom the coercive measures exceeding the legal limit have been taken..."

The people's procuratorate is also charged with the responsibility of rectifying any illegal investigation activities in the process of reviewing and approving arrests by the public security.[97]

IV. CONCLUSION

In this paper, I have attempted to trace the historical development of *shoushen* from a well intended social control device to a much abused police power. The paper ends appropriately with the passage of the amended Criminal Procedure Law on March 17, 1996. The NPC, in promulgating the Criminal Procedure Law, effectively brought all police investigative powers under one roof. In so doing, the NPC clearly demonstrated its resolution in bringing law and order to the widespread

---

95. Article 128 provides, in pertinent part: "If the criminal suspect refuses to disclose his true name, address, and identity, the period under which he can be held in custody starts from the date identity is clarified ...." If this provision is literally applied, the Criminal Procedure Law will be of little use in protecting a large group of criminal suspects against prolonged investigative detention., *e.g.* those from the *mangliu* ranks; this is the same problem which existed under the *shoushen* investigative system.

96. Article 14, para. 3: "Participants in proceedings have the right to bring complaints against ... investigators for acts that violate their procedural rights as citizens..."

97. Article 76: "In the course of its work of reviewing and approving arrests, if a people's procuratorate discovers that there are illegalities in the investigation activities of a public security organ, it shall notify the public security organ to rectify them, and the public security organ shall notify the people's procuratorate of the circumstances of the correction."

abuse of police powers in the PRC, particularly the misuse of *shoushen*. This is a propitious beginning. What remains to be seen is how the Criminal Procedure Law will be received and applied in the field. If our own experience with legal control over police misconduct is any guide,[98] the Criminal Procedure Law is just another chapter in the long fight against *shoushen* abuses.

98. WILLIAM A. GELLER (ed.), LOCAL GOVERNMENT POLICE MANAGEMENT (1991), 11-13. ("The police response to the High Court's rulings of the 1960s was largely one of bitterness and outrage: criminals would have all the advantage; police would be shackled and impotent to deal with serious crime...")

[11]

Citizens v. Mandarins: Administrative Litigation in China*

Minxin Pei

The Chinese government has, in the last 20 years, devoted enormous political resources and effort to revamping its legal system. The resultant legal reforms, part of the government's programme of political institutionalization, have been the subject of intense scholarly interest in the West.[1] One of these legal reforms was the Administration Litigation Law (ALL), passed in April 1989 and implemented in October 1990. The theoretical significance of this law can hardly be exaggerated because, if fully enforced, it would afford Chinese citizens an important legal instrument with which to defend themselves against the abuse of state power by government agencies and officials. Like other legal reforms, the ALL has attracted the attention of both Chinese and Western legal scholars. However, most early studies do not offer in-depth empirical analysis of the implementation of the law, its effects on China's administrative practices and its political implications. A possible exception was a 1992 study by a group of Chinese scholars who used polling data to assess the public perception of the ALL and relied on two case studies to investigate how the law was implemented at the grassroots level.[2] Nevertheless, the 1992 study has its limitations. Apart from the issue of the reliability of polling in China, it contains no national data on the implementation of the law; nor does it provide an in-depth analysis of sample court cases that went to trial according to the provisions of the ALL. Furthermore, it covers only a very brief period following the implementation of the law and relies on insufficient data, especially at the national level. Other works on the ALL suffer from similar problems, as lack of empirical data apparently restricted their authors mostly to a historical review of the evolution of administrative litigation in China, an analysis of the legal provisions of the ALL and speculation about its effectiveness.[3]

* The financial support for the research was provided by the United States Institute of Peace (SG-71–94). The opinions, findings, and conclusions or recommendations expressed in this article are those of the author and do not necessarily reflect the views of the United States Institute of Peace. The author wishes to thank the helpful comments from Larry Diamond, Elizabeth Perry, Stanley Lubman and Jonathan Hecht.

1. See Anthony Dicks, "The Chinese legal system: reforms in the balance," *The China Quarterly*, No. 119 (September 1989), pp. 540–576; Pitman Potter (ed.), *Domestic Law Reforms in Post-Mao China* (Armonk, NY: M. E. Sharpe, 1994); and Stanley Lubman, *China's Legal Reforms* (New York: Oxford University Press, 1996).

2. See Gong Ruixiang (ed.), *Fazhi de lixiang yu xianshi* (*The Ideal and Reality of the Rule of Law*) (Beijing: Zhongguo zhengfa daxue chubanshe, 1993).

3. Susan Finder, "Like throwing an egg against a stone? Administrative litigation in the People's Republic of China," *Journal of Chinese Law*, Vol. 3, No. 1 (Summer 1989), pp. 1–28; Pitman Potter, "The Administrative Litigation Law of the PRC: judicial review and

This study attempts to address several important empirical and theoretical questions left hitherto unanswered. For example, are any patterns demonstrated by the disposition of the lawsuits filed under the ALL since its implementation; and what do such patterns reveal about the political and institutional constraints on the Chinese legal system? Which groups have been the primary beneficiaries of the ALL? Which types of government administrative abuses are more likely to trigger lawsuits under the ALL? What do the results of the implementation of the ALL so far suggest about whether this new institution is undergoing consolidation? How did the institutional innovations in the Deng Xiaoping era reshape state–society relations?

This article uses newly available court cases and official national data on administrative litigation in 1986–96 to explore these issues.[4] The first section analyses the main provisions of the ALL; the second section evaluates its implementation based on the national data for the period between 1987 and 1996; and the third section examines 236 cases that went to trial in China in the early 1990s.[5]

The Administrative Litigation Law

Prior to the passage of the ALL in April 1989, the principal legal basis of administrative litigation was Article 3 of China's Civil Procedure Law (Interim), which was promulgated in 1982. Specifically, Article 3 stated that "this law applies to administrative litigation cases which are legally stipulated to be tried in the People's Court." The legal implications of this were profound. Before the establishment of a legal basis for adjudicating disputes between citizens and the government over various administrative decisions, the only recourse for private citizens who believed they had been unjustly treated or penalized by the government and its officials was to send their written appeals to higher government agencies, the media and China's top leaders; many travelled to provincial capitals and Beijing trying to make direct appeals to high-ranking officials. Such individual efforts rarely succeeded in redressing the grievance, however. One

---

footnote continued

bureaucratic reform," in Potter, *Domestic Law Reforms in Post-Mao China*, pp. 270–304; Song Bing, "Assessing China's system of judicial review of administrative actions," *China Law Reporter*, Vol. 8, Nos.1–2 (1994), pp. 1–20.

4. Lawsuits against government officials and agencies had been filed and tried even before the passage of the ALL, but the number of such cases grew dramatically after the passage of the law.

5. These 236 cases include 189 from a series of textbooks for Chinese judges. They are collected in *Zhongguo shenpan anli yaolan* (*Selected Major Trial Cases in China*); this series is edited by Zhongguo gaoji faguan peixun zhongxin (The National Training Centre for Senior Judges) and the Law School of the People's University; it is published by Zhongguo renmin gongan daxue (The Chinese People's Public Security University) Publishing Company. The 189 cases were from *Zhongguo shenpan anli yaolan* (hereafter *ZSAY*) (1992, 1993, 1994, 1995). Forty cases were published in *Renmin fayuan anli xuan* (*Selected Cases from the People's Court*), Nos. 11–15 (Beijing: Renmin fayuan chubanshe, 1995). Seven cases were published in *Zhongguo falu nianjian* (*Law Yearbook of China*), various years.

official report revealed that 95 per cent of all the administrative disputes that were appealed to higher government agencies were eventually returned to lower-level (and often the same) government agencies with which the dispute originated in the first place. This practice rarely satisfied the aggrieved individuals. The same report said that more than half the citizens who initiated the complaints were forced to repeat their appeal process.[6]

Although Article 3 of the Civil Procedure Law established a minimum legal basis of administrative litigation after 1982, this provision alone did not constitute a working law, nor did it specify procedural rules. Thus, private citizens seeking judicial relief from injurious and unjust government acts face serious hurdles. The absence of an administrative litigation law and the practical problems it had created attracted the attention of China's law-makers. Under the auspices of the Judiciary Committee of the National People's Congress (NPC), a group of legal scholars began drafting the ALL in 1986 and completed the first draft in 1987.[7] Initial response from government officials was predictably sceptical: a 1987 poll showed that of the 80 municipal, county, and district agencies surveyed, 95 per cent of the officials polled considered the ALL "premature" and urged the passage of the law be delayed.[8]

Despite such reservations on the part of government officials who would probably face legal challenges and restrictions if the law were passed, the leadership of the Chinese Communist Party (CCP) seemed committed to the codification of procedures of administrative litigation.[9] In October 1987 the Political Report of the 13th Congress of the CCP (delivered by Zhao Ziyang, then the CCP General Secretary) cited, as the Party's legislative priorities, the promulgation of administrative laws and the establishment of an appeals system for Chinese citizens. Another legal development made the passage of the ALL both more necessary and desirable. After the PRC Code on Penalties Imposed in the Course of Maintaining Public Order went into effect in January 1987,[10] the judicial branch of the Chinese government was reportedly forced to establish special tribunals to handle legal cases involving the administrative penalties imposed under the Code. These administrative tribunals (*xingzheng shenpan ting*),[11] established an institu-

6. Liu Jinghuai, "Min gao guan you fa keyi" ("The legal basis for private citizens to sue government officials"), *Liaowang* 29 October 1990, p. 14.

7. Also see Potter, "The Administrative Litigation Law of the PRC," pp. 274–76; Finder, "Like throwing an egg against a stone?" pp. 8–10.

8. Liu Jinghuai, "Min gao guan you fa keyi," p. 14.

9. The CCP Politburo reportedly held two special meetings on the ALL. Peng Zheng, the chairman of the National People's Congress, strongly supported the ALL. Interview with the head of the Institute of Law at the Shanghai Academy of Social Sciences, May 1997.

10. The Chinese title of this law is "Zhonghua renmin gongheguo zhi an guanli chufa tiaoli." It gave the Chinese law-enforcement authorities broad powers to impose penalties (including administrative detention) on Chinese citizens.

11. For a brief discussion on this development, see Tong Shuisheng, "Min gao guan beiwanglu" ("A memo on citizens suing officials"), *Falü yu shenghuo* (*Law and Life*), No. 82 (October 1990), p. 20.

tional arena in which citizens could seek judicial relief from official abuse of power.[12]

In October 1988 the draft version of the ALL was presented to the Standing Committee of the NPC for debate; the same draft was also circulated to the public for comment.[13] Several revisions later, in March 1989, the ALL was tabled at the second session of the Seventh NPC for passage; and on 4 April 1989, the NPC passed it. Although the ALL did not take effect nationally until October 1990, the government implemented it before then on an experimental basis in several provinces.[14]

The passage of the ALL was hailed in the Chinese legal community. Optimists felt it had the potential to be the key legal instrument for protecting human rights and laying the foundations of the rule of law in China. Preliminary assessment by Western legal scholars was also positive.[15] Judging by the provisions of the law, such optimism was not entirely misplaced.[16] Among other things, the ALL provides ordinary Chinese citizens, "legal persons," and even foreigners the right legally to challenge administrative decisions (various penalties or other measures) that adversely affect their freedom or economic interests.[17] It also sets stringent procedural standards and places the burden of proof on government agencies whose decisions are being challenged. The ALL gives the court the power to uphold, revoke, revise or compel administrative actions. However, it contains several important flaws.[18] Its definition of "concrete administrative actions" subject to judicial review is vague, thus immunizing many government actions from legal challenges. It may not be used to challenge certain government policies that violate citizens' constitutional rights but are "generally binding" (the family planning policy being a clear example). Finally, it makes no provisions regarding administrative actions taken by the CCP, giving the ruling party immunity from judicial review.

12. At the end of 1988 there were 1,400 administrative tribunals; in 1990 the number rose to 2,638. *Xinhua yuebao*, No. 534 (April 1989), p. 36; Liu Jinghuai, "Min gao guan you fa keyi," p. 15.

13. According to Wang Hanbin, the chairman of the Judiciary Committee, the NPC received commentaries on the law from 130 government agencies and courts and only 300 commentaries directly from private citizens. *Xinhua yuebao*, No. 534 (April 1989), p. 36.

14. Henan, Guangdong, Sichuan and Tianjin were mentioned in Liu Jinghuai's report. Liu Jinghuai, "Min gao guan you fa keyi," p. 15.

15. Yang Haikun, "Baituo xingzheng susong zhidu kunjing de chulu" ("A solution to the besieged administrative litigation system"), *Zhongguo faxue* (*Chinese Legal Science*), No. 3 (1994), p. 51; Potter, "The Administrative Litigation Law of the PRC," pp. 287–290; Finder, "Like throwing an egg against a stone?" pp. 27–28.

16. The official text of the ALL can be found in *Xinhua yuebao*, No. 534 (April 1989), pp. 32–36; an English translation is available in *China Current Laws*, Vol. 1, No. 9 (October 1989), pp. 6–16. The references to the text of the ALL in this article are mostly based on this translation.

17. For detailed analysis of the provisions of the ALL, see Potter, "The Administrative Litigation Law of the PRC," pp. 276–281; Finder, "Like throwing an egg against a stone?" pp. 11–27.

18. See Potter's excellent analysis of the limits of the ALL, in "The Administrative Litigation Law of the PRC," pp. 282–87.

Table 1: **Number of Cases Accepted (*shouli*) and Tried (*shenli*) by the Court, 1986–96**

	Accepted	*Change (%)*	*Tried*	*Change (%)*
1986	632	—	—	—
1987	5,240	729	4,677	—
1988	9,273	77	8,751	88
1989	9,934	7	9,742	11
1990	13,006	31	12,040	24
1991	25,667	97	25,202	109
1992	27,125	6	27,116	8
1993	27,911	3	27,958	3
1994	35,083	26	34,567	24
1995	52,596	50	51,370	49
1996	—	—	79,527	55

Sources:
Zhongguo fazhi nianjian (*Law Yearbook of China*), various years; *Falü yu shenghuo* (*Law and Life*), No. 82 (October 1990), p. 19; *Renmin ribao*, 21 March 1997, p. 2.

The Implementation of the ALL

Increase of administrative litigation lawsuits. The data on administrative litigation in China are reported in *Zhongguo falü nianjian* (*Law Yearbook of China*). In addition, the annual reports by the Chief Justice of the Supreme Court of the People contain some data on administrative litigation. Provincial supreme courts also report the number of administrative litigation cases (ALCs) tried and their disposition (these reports are published in the provincial yearbooks). Although one must treat official data with caution, it appears that the data reported in these yearbooks are relatively reliable because they reflect the patterns of change consistent with the findings by more independent analysts.[19]

The statistical data on ALCs gathered for this study indicate that the ALL has had a considerable impact since its implementation in 1990. It is true that similar lawsuits against government agencies and officials had been filed and tried prior to the passage of the ALL, but the number of such cases was relatively small in the late 1980s (fewer than 10,000). In the 1990s the number of such cases processed by the legal system each year continued to rise, reaching 79,527 in 1996 (Table 1).

The pattern of the increase in the number of ALCs seemed to have been influenced in part by the stop-and-go nature of political liberalization in the Deng era and by the changes in the Chinese legal system. The rapid increase in 1988 was apparently the result of the relatively relaxed political environment created by the policies of then CCP General Secretary Zhao Ziyang. Conversely, in the aftermath of the crackdown on

19. See, for example, Gong Ruixiang, *Fazhi de lixiang yu xianshi*.

the pro-democracy movement in 1989, the increase of ALCs slowed down.

On the whole, however, other changes in China's legal system had a greater impact on the number of ALCs accepted and tried in the court. The spectacular rise in 1987 was a result of the implementation that year of the PRC Code on Penalties Imposed in the Course of Maintaining Public Order. The enforcement of this code occasioned more opportunities for disputes between citizens and state agents over the latter's discretionary power in imposing penalties; it also entailed, as mentioned earlier, the establishment of the administrative tribunals to process cases involving administrative penalties. The doubling of ALCs in 1991 was clearly the consequence of the implementation of the ALL after October 1990. The rapid rise registered in 1994 (up 24 per cent), 1995 and 1996 (up almost 50 per cent) was not the direct result of any specific legal changes affecting the ALL. As will be demonstrated, this upward trend reflected a higher level of public awareness of the ALL and its legal implications. Although the results of the implementation of the ALL since 1990 showed that the law remained an imperfect legal instrument for Chinese citizens, the very fact that filing a lawsuit based on the ALL can lead to some form of judicial relief has probably encouraged an increasing number of citizens to take this option.

Regional variation. The regional distribution of ALCs filed in 25 of China's 27 provinces and three municipalities is presented in Table 2.[20] Using the differential between a province's share of the national population and its share of ALCs filed in 1994 as a measure of the level of administrative litigation (a proxy for citizens' assertiveness of their legal rights), it is shown that more economically developed areas do not necessarily lead the nation in litigation against the government. The provinces with the highest positive differentials were either among the poorest (Hunan and Henan) or the mid-income (Shandong and Heilongjiang). Indeed, some of the most prosperous regions (such as Guangdong, Beijing and Fujian) lagged behind the poorest regions (such as Henan, Hunan and Guizhou) in this respect. This evidence casts doubts on a positive relationship between the level of economic development and frequency of administrative litigation. However, there does seem to be a negative relationship between economic development and administrative litigation because the less developed provinces in China made up the majority of the laggards shown in Table 2. Of the 14 provinces with negative differentials, seven were among the poorest provinces (Sichuan, Anhui, Jiangxi, Yunnan, Gansu, Ningxia and Shaanxi); two were relatively poor provinces (Qinghai and Inner Mongolia).

20. The 1994 data for several provinces are unavailable. We use the data for 1993 and 1992 for these provinces to estimate their share of ALCs. Our estimates show that Tianjin's share (based on 161 ALCs in 1993) was 0.78% with a differential of − 0.72; Shanxi's share (631 in 1993) was 2.2% with a differential of − .03; Jiangsu's share (906 in 1992) was 3.3% with a differential of − 2.55. The number of cases accepted for trial by individual provinces seemed slightly to exceed the number given by the Supreme People's Court.

Table 2: **Regional Distribution of ALCs Accepted by the Court in 1994**

Provinces	*Number*	*Percentage*	*Share of population*	*Differential*[a]	*Wealth rank*[b]
Hunan	4,857	13.84	5.3	8.54	20
Henan	5,187	14.78	7.53	7.25	26
Shandong	3,961	10.5	7.23	3.27	10
Guizhou	1,609	4.58	2.88	1.70	30
Heilongjiang	1,602	4.56	3.0	1.56	11
Jilin	917	2.6	2.1	0.5	13
Shanghai	478	1.36	1.1	0.25	1
Hubei	1,761	5.0	4.77	0.23	15
Xinjiang	552	1.57	1.36	0.21	12
Liaoning	1,247	3.5	3.3	0.2	4
Zhejiang	1,282	3.65	3.58	0.07	6
Shaanxi	1,047	2.98	2.9	− 0.08	27
Ningxia	115	0.3	0.4	− 0.1	21
Beijing	246	0.7	0.9	− 0.2	2
Qinghai	70	0.19	0.39	− 0.2	17
Hainan	22	0.06	0.59	− 0.53	9
Inner Mongolia	462	1.31	1.88	− 0.57	16
Fujian	725	2.06	2.65	− 0.59	8
Gansu	465	1.32	1.98	− 0.66	29
Guangdong	1,675	4.77	5.58	− 0.81	5
Yunnan	829	2.36	3.28	− 0.92	25
Jiangxi	766	2.18	3.35	− 1.17	22
Hebei	1,327	3.78	5.3	− 1.52	14
Anhui	702	2.0	4.96	− 2.96	23
Sichuan	2,118	6.0	9.3	− 3.3	24
Subtotal	34,022	96.97	—	—	—
Other	1,061	3.03	—	—	—
Total	35,083	100	—	—	—

Notes:
a. The difference between the province's share of ALCs and national population. A positive number indicates above-average use of the law in the province.
b. Per capita income in 1994.
Sources:
Provincial Yearbooks and *Zhongguo falü nianjian* (1995), pp. 823–885; per capita income data were from Zhou Zhenghua (ed.), *Zhongguo jingji fengxi 1995* (*Analysis of the Chinese Economy in 1995*) (Shanghai: Shanghai renmin chubanshe, 1996), p. 94.

One possible explanation of the regional variation in administrative litigation is that it may be related to differing degrees of judicial fairness in different regions. In regions where the system of judicial review has been better established and fairer, citizens are less fearful of filing ALCs. Evidence from Henan, which led the country in the number of ALCs filed in both absolute and relative terms in 1994, provides some support for this view. The disposition of ALCs in Henan in 1993 and 1994 shows that the proportion of rulings favourable to plaintiffs is much higher than the national average. Of the 4,910 ALCs tried in the courts in 1994, administrative actions were upheld in 13.9 per cent of the cases and revoked in 27.2 per cent; of the 3,764 ALCs tried in the courts in 1993, administrative actions were upheld in 16 per cent of the cases and revoked in 16 per cent, but in addition, the courts changed administrative actions in 2.4 per cent of the cases and compelled government agencies to perform their legal responsibility in 15 per cent. Altogether, plaintiffs obtained favourable or partially favourable rulings in nearly 33 per cent of the cases (compared with 16 per cent for the government). The data for 1993 and 1994 show that plaintiffs enjoyed a two-to-one advantage over the government in all the cases that went to trial in Henan. Moreover, the rate of withdrawal in Henan was also lower than the national average. In 1993, 39.3 per cent of ALCs were withdrawn (the national average was 41 per cent); in 1994, 34.8 per cent (14.8 per cent of ALCs were withdrawn after the defendants changed the disputed administrative actions). Henan's withdrawal rate in 1994 was 9 per cent lower than the national average.[21] The data for Hunan and, to a lesser degree, Shandong were similar. The data for 1994 showed that the courts in Hunan revoked administrative actions in 15.2 per cent of the cases and upheld them in 13.8 per cent (with a withdrawal rate of 50 per cent). Shandong's courts revoked administrative actions in 9.6 per cent of the cases and upheld them in 9.5 per cent (with a high withdrawal rate of 65 per cent).[22] The above data indicate that the greater likelihood of obtaining favourable rulings from the court may be an important reason for the large number of ALCs filed against the government in Henan and Hunan. The data from Shandong suggest that out-of-court settlement may have become a principal form of dispute resolution between the state and private citizens.

Scope of administrative litigation. As the number of ALCs rose, the scope of the ALL also expanded. Given the intrusiveness of the Chinese state, the broad discretion enjoyed by government agents and the lack of clearly defined property rights, the ALL provided one of the few state-sanctioned means for private citizens to challenge the actions of government officials on many regulatory and administrative issues. According to an official report, more than 40 types of administrative branches of the state (such as law enforcement, urban development, commercial administration, tax collection, environmental protection and so on) were targets of lawsuits in 1995.[23] The breakdown of the type of ALCs in the court from 1988 to 1994 reveals two trends. First, the composition of such cases is basically consistent over time, with most ALCs involving disputes over law-enforcement agencies (the public security bureau and committee of reform through labour), land use, forestry, urban zoning, and real estate (see Table 3). Disputes in these four areas constituted

21. *Zhongguo falü nianjian* (1994), p. 236; *Zhongguo falü nianjian* (1995), p. 847.

22. *Hunan nianjian* (*Hunan Yearbook*) (1995), p. 88; *Shandong nianjian* (*Shandong Yearbook*) (1995), p. 844.

23. *Renmin ribao*, 22 March 1996, p. 3.

Table 3: **Composition of Cases, 1988–95**

Type	*1988*[a] *number* *(%)*	*1990*[b]	*1992*[b]	*1993*[b]	*1995*[b]
Public security	3,385 (38.6)	4,519 (34.7)	7,863 (29.0)	7,018 (25.1)	11,427 (22.2)
Land use	2,719 (31.1)	4,038 (31.0)	8,330 (30.7)	8,063 (28.9)	10,009 (19.5)
Urban zoning and real estate	433 (4.9)	—	—	2,038 (7.3)	2,949 (5.7)
Forestry	422 (4.8)	—	—	1,971 (7.1)	2,568 (5.0)
Industrial and commercial adm.	204 (2.3)	—	710 (2.6)	571 (2.0)	1,388 (2.7)
Public health	250 (2.9)	—	548 (2.0)	456 (1.6)	892 (1.7)
Traffic	—	—	—	—	1,275 (2.5)
Other	1,253 (14.3)	4,449 (34.3)	9,674 (35.7)	7,794 (28.0)	20,862 (40.7)
Total	8,753	13,006	27,125	27,911	51,370

Notes:
a. The number of cases tried by the court.
b. The number of cases accepted by the court.
Sources:
Zhongguo falü nianjian, various years; *Renmin fayuan nianjian* (1992) (Beijing: Renmin fayuan chubanshe, 1995), p. 839; figures for 1988 were obtained from Susan Finder, "Like throwing an egg against a stone? Administrative litigation in the People's Republic of China," *Journal of Chinese Law*, Vol. 3, No. 1 (Summer 1989), p. 11.

about 80 per cent of all ALCs in 1988 and 52 per cent in 1995. Secondly, the scope of the ALL has been expanded over the years, as the law has been increasingly invoked to challenge government actions in many other areas; this has led to a relative decline of the proportion of ALCs involving law-enforcement agencies and land use, and a gradual rise in the proportion of cases labelled as "other" (about 41 per cent in 1995).[24]

The data in Table 3 also reflect a stark political reality in China. Citizens sue the government to protect their liberty and property only as a last resort. Thus, they often refrain from suing not because their rights have not been violated, but because the stakes are not high enough. A survey of plaintiffs showed that 57 per cent stated that they filed suits under the ALL because they felt they had no other choice.[25] According to

24. Court cases provide some clues as to what are labelled under the "other" category. They include the following: cases against the bureau of standards, against the patent bureau, against local governments on matters other than land use or zoning, against tax collection agencies, against the supervisory agencies of state-owned enterprises, and against the bureau of civil affairs.

25. Tang Yongjin, "Yichang jingqiaoqiao de geming" ("A quiet revolution"), in Gong Ruixiang, *Fazhi de lixiang yu xianshi*, p. 60.

one study, disputes over land use made up most of the ALCs in an agrarian region in Henan because the very livelihoods of the aggrieved peasants were at stake. Similarly, a large number of lawsuits were filed against law-enforcement agencies because the aggrieved citizens felt their liberty was threatened. From this perspective, one should not view the relatively small share of suits filed against the state's regulatory and extractive agencies (industrial and commercial administration and tax collection agencies) as evidence that they are less likely to be embroiled in disputes with citizens. According to the same study, fewer suits were filed against those two agencies because they were in a better position to retaliate against plaintiffs even if they lost. A private citizen could thus "win once but lose the rest of his life."[26]

Analysis of outcome: who wins. A key test of the effectiveness of the ALL is whether the Chinese legal system has displayed judicial impartiality in adjudicating ALCs. This test is conducted in the following section, based on the data from 1987 to 1995 (Table 4). Despite the incompleteness of the official data on the implementation of the law, this analysis indicates that its success at providing impartial judicial review has been mixed, for a number of reasons.

A relatively high percentage of suits were dismissed. An examination of official data on the disposition of ALCs shows that the proportion of dismissed suits was unusually high and has been climbing steadily since 1991. Although this category (ALCs dismissed by the court of first instance) was not explicitly identified in most official annual reports on administrative litigation, the data for 1992 revealed that 8 per cent of ALCs were dismissed by the court of first instance. The Supreme People's Court's annual report for 1995 showed that about 16 per cent of all the ALCs (8,349) were dismissed by the courts after the first ruling (*caiding*).[27] This shows that dismissed cases constituted most of the court decisions under the "other" category (comprising 10–15 per cent of the ALCs processed in 1987–95). The rest of the "other" category includes the transfer of the cases to a different judicial branch (such as the civil litigation court) and "termination" of the proceedings (presumably without rendering any judgment).

Low probability of winning ALCs against government agencies. Data for this period show that plaintiffs had only a 15–21 per cent chance of obtaining a favourable ruling from the courts of first instance that tried the cases (a favourable ruling results in revoking or, on rare occasions, changing the disputed administrative actions).[28] In comparison, the government had a higher chance (17–50 per cent) of having its actions

26. Zhang Shuyi and Zhan Zhongle, "Qiantu guangming, daolu quzhe" ("Bright future and tortuous road"), in Gong Ruixiang, *Fazhi de lixiang yu xianshi*, pp. 113, 121.

27. Compared with the data for previous years, the number of dismissed cases in 1995 might be too high.

28. Few court decisions change original administrative actions because the ALL restricts the court's authority to modify administrative actions. Such actions may be revised only when administrative penalties are deemed "clearly unjust."

Table 4: **Disposition of Tried Cases (%)**

	RAA	*UAA*	*SWP*	*CAA*	*Other*[a]
1988	11	49	27	5	8
1989	14	42	31	6	7
1990	17	36	36	3	8
1991	19	32	37	2	10
1992	21	28	38	2	11
1993	19	23	41	2	15
1994	19	21	44[b]	1	15
1995	15	17	51[b]	1	16

Notes:
RAA: Revoking administrative actions.
UAA: Upholding administrative actions.
SWP: Suits withdrawn by plaintiffs.
CAA: Administrative actions revised by the court.
a. The "other" category remains a mystery. In the data for 1988 "other" explicitly consisted of two types of disposition: cases that were "terminated" (*zhongjie*) and presumably dismissed, and cases that were transferred (*yisong*) to other authorities. The data for 1992 explicitly identified the number of cases dismissed (*bohui qisu*) (2,116) for that year. This accounted for about 8% of all the cases processed by the courts. The data for 1995 explicitly identified the number of dismissed and terminated cases (8,349) for that year.
b. In 1994, 38% of all the cases in this category were withdrawn after the defendants changed "concrete administrative acts"; in 1995, about 45% of all the cases in this category were withdrawals after original administrative actions were revised or changed.
Source:
Zhongguo falü nianjian, various years.

upheld by the court. One should observe, however, that there has been a remarkable convergence between the ratio of rulings favourable to the plaintiff and those favourable to the defendant since the early 1990s. Such a convergence resulted not from a rising ratio of rulings favouring plaintiffs (which remained constant), but from a falling ratio of rulings favouring defendants (from 50 per cent in 1987–88 to 17 per cent in 1995). The data for the disposition of the ALCs in 1995 show that, for all the ALCs that went to trial that year, the odds of winning their cases were about the same for plaintiffs and defendants. If we include the percentage of the ALCs dismissed by the courts without trial (8 per cent in 1992 and possibly 16 per cent in 1995), the government maintained a nearly two-to-one advantage in having its actions effectively upheld by the court.

The puzzle of withdrawn cases. The most intriguing puzzle in analysing the effect of the ALL is presented by the large proportion of ALCs filed but later withdrawn by plaintiffs. Data in Table 4 indicate that the rate of withdrawal was increasing rapidly in the early 1990s – from 37 per cent in 1991 to 51 per cent in 1995. The share of withdrawn ALCs in 1995 nearly doubled that in 1988.

A closer examination of the data on the withdrawn ALCs shows, however, that a large number of such withdrawals represent out-of-court settlements (with the government agencies being sued unilaterally rescinding or changing their administrative actions). Official data reported (Table 4) that of the suits withdrawn by plaintiffs in 1994, 38 per cent of them (or 16.7 per cent of the total cases processed by the courts that year) were withdrawn after the defendants (government agencies) rectified the disputed administrative actions. Of the suits withdrawn in 1995, 45 per cent (or 22.5 per cent of the total cases processed that year) were withdrawn after the defendants rectified the disputed actions. In the sample cases, there were altogether 14 cases of withdrawal of suits by plaintiffs. In 12 of the 14 cases, plaintiffs withdrew their suits after the defendants rescinded the disputed administrative actions to the satisfaction of the plaintiffs. There were only two cases in which plaintiffs withdrew their suits after realizing that their suits lacked merit or were not covered under the ALL.[29]

These results show that the very act of filing a lawsuit can generate substantial benefits for the plaintiffs even without going to trial. Compared with either not filing the suit (and enduring the adverse consequences of unjust government actions) or going to trial (facing poorer odds of winning), filing a suit and then hoping that the government agency being sued will rectify its original actions before trial amounts to taking a calculated risk that redress can be achieved indirectly. In fact, according to the preceding analysis, filing a suit to induce the government agency to change its actions before trial has about the same probability of obtaining effective relief as filing the suit and receiving a favourable ruling after trial (about 16 and 20 per cent in 1995 and 1994, as shown in Table 4). The costs are, of course, much lower.

Thus, if the ratio of court-revoked administrative actions and administrative actions rectified by the government agencies without going to trial are combined, it seems that the very act of filing an ALC gives the plaintiff a considerable chance (36.7 per cent in 1994 and 38.3 per cent in 1995) of obtaining the desired judicial relief one way or another. The risk of filing an ALC is therefore justified. This may be the reason why the rate of filing ALCs rose rapidly in the mid-1990s (especially 1994 and 1995), even without major legal or political reforms that would increase the effectiveness, impartiality and enforceability of the ALL.

This analysis is counter to the assertion made by some Chinese legal scholars that the large number of withdrawn ALCs was indicative of the failure of the ALL as a legal instrument to provide judicial relief to ordinary citizens.[30] Such criticism is based on the fact that of all the withdrawn ALCs in 1994 and 1995, 62 per cent and 55 per cent, respectively, were withdrawn by plaintiffs "abnormally"; that is, they withdrew their complaints without having the disputed actions rescinded

29. See cases nos. 11, 12, 13, 22, 35 in *Yaolan 1992*; nos. 15, 23, 38, 43, 44 in *Yaolan 1993*; nos. 47, 59 in *Yaolan 1994*; nos. 10 and 30 in *Yaolan 1996*.

30. Yang Haikun, "Baituo xingzheng susong zhidu kunjing de chulu," p. 51; Zheng Hangsheng (ed.), *Report on Social Development by Renmin University of China, 1994–1995* (Beijing: Renmin daxue chubanshe, 1995), p. 68.

by the government authorities being sued. However, our analysis of the data suggests a different explanation. The decision to withdraw ALCs seemed to be based on rational reasoning, not merely fear of reprisal or distrust of the legal system. Plaintiffs decided not to pursue their cases against government agencies and officials in the court because of the high odds against winning. As analysed above, when the ratio of dismissal by the court of first instance (roughly 10 per cent) and winning ratio for the government (averaging about 28 per cent over the same period) are combined, the government had a probability of effectively winning 38 per cent of all ALCs tried in the court, double the probability of winning for plaintiffs (19 per cent).

Such odds may force a rational plaintiff to adopt a different strategy, one aimed at obtaining judicial relief without the negative ramifications of winning a suit against the government. This strategy consists of filing an ALC in the hope of obtaining a pre-trial settlement (not very different from the practice in civil litigation in the United States). Clearly, administrative litigation is a costly process both to the aggrieved citizens and to the government agencies being sued. For the plaintiffs, there is a higher probability of losing the case than winning it in the courts; the benefits of actually winning were dubious because of the difficulty in enforcing rulings against the government; and the government agency and officials that lose in court may then retaliate against the plaintiffs in the future.

Government agencies and officials face real risks in fighting ALCs in the courts. Although their overall probability of effectively winning is about 40 per cent, the 20 per cent probability that they will lose poses a non-trivial threat. Losing an ALC may undermine the authority of the government agency and blemish the record of the responsible officials. In the court proceedings government agencies and officials risk unfavourable public scrutiny. If their abuse of official power is rampant, such misdeeds may be publicized or reported to higher authorities. Although the Chinese political system is undemocratic and unresponsive, certain egregious cases of abuse of citizens' rights, if subjected to sufficient exposure, can force national authorities to take drastic action against the culpable officials in order to appease public opinion and popular demands for justice.

This means that both sides have a considerable incentive for an out-of-court settlement. Moreover, the administrative tribunals, caught in the middle of the legal proceedings, apparently see out-of-court settlement as the most convenient way out of a no-win situation. On the one hand, given the lack of judicial independence, the court can ill afford to rule consistently against the government's administrative authorities even if their actions must be revoked under the ALL. On the other hand, the court's persistent bias in favour of the government may not only jeopardize its credibility, public image, institutional identity and sense of professionalism, but also force determined plaintiffs to pursue their grievances with higher-level government authorities or make appeals to higher courts. Thus, the administrative tribunals, too, have a strong incentive to encourage a settlement. According to one source, many ostensibly out-of-court settlements were actually mediated by the administrative court. Especially in cases in which the administrative court found it hard to uphold the government's action, the court would informally ask the defendants to rescind the disputed actions while trying to persuade the plaintiffs to withdraw the suits.[31]

Variation in disposition of ALCs against different agencies. Not all government agencies are equal in terms of their influence on judicial proceedings. Everything else being equal, the more powerful government agencies should enjoy greater advantages in the judicial proceedings in administrative litigation. Such advantages should be reflected in the disposition of ALCs filed against these agencies. Based on available data on the disposition of ALCs filed against different government agencies (Table 5), there is evidence that more powerful agencies (local governments and important functional departments) are likely to receive more favourable treatment in the court. The data for 1992–94 show that local government (which is often sued in cases of disputes over land ownership, land use, forestry, urban real estate and zoning) consistently enjoyed a significant advantage in the court. This advantage can be measured in terms of two comparisons. First, the percentage of court rulings favourable to the local government in these cases is compared with the overall percentage of rulings favourable to the government in all cases. This reveals that, with the exception of urban zoning, the percentage of rulings favourable to local governments was consistently above the national average. Law-enforcement agencies enjoyed a similar advantage in administrative litigation proceedings although their advantage has been shrinking over the years and, in 1995, disappeared altogether. Secondly, the percentage of rulings favourable to defendants is compared with that favourable to plaintiffs. Here local government also enjoyed a visible, though gradually shrinking, edge over plaintiffs (2–8 per cent).

Conversely, second-tier, less powerful administrative agencies may have no inherent advantage in administrative litigation proceedings. It is clear from Table 5 that, with the exception of 1995, industrial and commercial administrations enjoyed no advantage when compared with other government agencies, as reflected in a lower-than-average percentage of favourable rulings for these administrations (3–5 per cent). Moreover, the advantage for industrial and commercial administrations as defendants disappeared completely in 1993 and 1994 (but not in 1995). The story was the same for other local government agencies. The data for 1992–94 show that cultural and public hygiene agencies were less likely to have their administrative actions upheld and more likely to have them revoked.[32]

31. This claim was based on a report on the implementation of the ALL conducted by the Sichuan Supreme People's Court. It was cited in Tang Yongjin, "Yichang jingqiaoqiao de geming," pp. 43–44.

32. For cultural agencies, the court upheld their administrative actions in 20% of the lawsuits in 1992, 12.5% in 1993, 9.2% in 1994 and 11.4% in 1995 while revoking their

Table 5: **Disposition of Major Categories of ALCs (%)**

	UAA	*RAA*	*CAA*	*SWP*	*Other*
1992					
Law-enforcement	31	19	3	37	10
Land use	32	26	1	35	6
Industrial and commercial adm.	25	16	1	44	14
All cases	28	21	2	38	11
1993					
Law-enforcement	26	17	2	43	12
Land use	31	23	1	37	8
Urban zoning	20	12	1	33	34
Industrial and commercial adm.	19	18	1	45	17
All cases	23	19	2	41	15
1994					
Law-enforcement	20	16	2	47	15
Land use	30	25	1	34	10
Urban zoning	19	13	0.5	54	13.5
Industrial and commercial adm.	16	17	0	46	21
All cases	21	19	1	44	15
1995					
Law-enforcement	17	16	2	50	15
Land use	29	22	1	34	14
Urban zoning	22	15	0	50	13
Industrial and commercial adm.	30	17	0	40	13
All cases	17	15	1	51	16

Notes:
UAA: Upholding administrative action;
RAA: Revoking administrative action;
CAA: Changing administrative action;
SWP: Suits withdrawn by plaintiffs;
SD: Suits dismissed.
Source:
Zhongguo falü nianjian, various years.

The appeals. The ALL gives the losing party the right to appeal. Based on the data for 1988, 1990, 1992 and 1995 (Table 6), the rate of appeal of the rulings of the first trials was within the range of 19 to 31 per cent. The appellate court makes four types of rulings: upholding first-trial decisions; changing first-trial decisions; returning the case to the lower court for retrial; or an unspecified other decision. Appellants can also

footnote continued
administrative actions in 22% of the cases in 1992, 26.7% in 1993, 17% in 1994 and 16.2% in 1995. The court upheld the actions of public hygiene agencies in 16.3% of the cases in 1993 and 17.2% in 1994, while revoking their actions in 18% of the cases in 1993 and 13% in 1994. *Zhongguo falü nianjian* (1994), p. 1029; (1995), p. 1065; (1996), p. 959; *Renmin fayuan nianjian* (*Yearbook of the People's Court*) (1992), p. 839.

Table 6: **Disposition of Appealed Cases, 1988–95**

	1988	*1990*	*1992*	*1995*
First trial cases completed	8,029	12,040	27,116	51,370
Appeals accepted	2,359	3,431	8,334	9,694
Appeals completed	2,218	3,325	8,273	9,536
FTDU	1,573	2,192	5,333	6,086
FTDR	246	662	1,332	1,408
RFRT	—	258	687	676
AW	—	102	397	658
Other	399	111	524	708

Notes:
FTDU: First-trial decisions upheld;
FTDR: First-trial decisions revised;
RFRT: Returned for re-trial;
AW: Appeals withdrawn.
Source:
Zhongguo falü nianjian, various years.

withdraw their appeals. Available data on the disposition of the appealed cases for 1992 and 1994 indicate a stable pattern. First, the appellate courts tended to uphold the first-trial decisions in most cases (64 per cent in 1992 and 1995). Secondly, a modest percentage of the rulings by the appellate court (16 per cent in 1992 and 15 per cent in 1995) favoured the appellants. Thirdly, an even smaller percentage of the appealed cases were sent back to the lower courts for retrial (8 per cent in 1992 and 7 per cent in 1995). Finally, unlike the high rate of withdrawals in the first trial, few appellants withdrew their appeals (5 per cent in 1992 and 7 per cent in 1995).

Given the fact that for 1992, the government had a higher chance of obtaining a favourable first-trial ruling than the plaintiff (28 per cent versus 21 per cent), it seems that the appellate court decisions also favoured the government (since 64 per cent of all first-trial decisions were upheld, assuming that losing plaintiffs and defendants were equally likely to appeal). This bias, if the assumption about the defendants' and plaintiffs' equal propensity to make appeals holds, seemed almost to have disappeared by 1995. Since the probability of obtaining a favourable first trial ruling was nearly identical for plaintiffs and defendants that year (15 versus 17 per cent), the appellate courts appear to have reduced their pro-government bias. Given the higher professional qualifications of judges and legal staff in the appellate courts and their relative insulation from local government agencies involved in the lawsuits, it is reasonable to assume that Chinese appellate courts exercise a higher level of impartiality and autonomy in judicial review.

How the ALL Works: Evidence from Case Studies

This section analyses the information provided by 236 cases that were tried in China's administrative tribunals in the early 1990s. Because these cases were not randomly selected by the Chinese sources that published them, they should not be considered fully representative. Indeed, they may contain one major bias. Intended mainly as legal precedents and textbook cases for future Chinese judges and lawyers, they may include cases considered exemplary in terms of compliance with the procedures of the ALL. In other words, the application of the ALL documented in these cases may reflect the ideal image of the ALL held by those who selected the cases, rather than the reality. Another problem caused by the non-random selection is that these cases cannot be used to generate information on how different factors (such as socio-economic backgrounds of litigants, the branches of government agencies being sued and access to legal representation) may affect trial outcomes.

However, the pitfalls caused by these two short-comings can be avoided if they are not relied upon to analyse either procedural fairness or factors that affect trial outcomes. On the other hand, several factors enhance the value of the these cases. First, most of them were contained in specialized volumes edited by leading legal Chinese scholars. The small number of copies printed (8,000 for each volume) and high prices (110–198 *yuan*) were evidence that these case books were not intended by the authorities as mass propaganda tools. The government was thus less likely to put pressures on the editors concerning the selection and presentation of the cases. Secondly, the non-random selection of the original data may have less effect in terms of understanding several important issues about the ALL, such as who sues, who sues whom, who has legal representation and what types of violation are most frequently committed by government agencies. Thirdly, if the composition of the 236 sample cases included in this study resembles that of the general population of ALCs (Table 3), it means that, at least in one important aspect, the sample cases represent the general population.

A breakdown of the 236 cases is presented in Table 7. On the whole, the composition of the sample cases collected here is similar to that of the general population (Table 3) although the cases here over-represent the ALCs involving taxation and industrial and commercial administration. A close analysis yields answers to a number of questions.

Who sues? Although no study has been conducted to examine the composition of plaintiffs in ALCs, the 236 cases studied here shed some light on this problem (Table 8). A surprising finding is that state-owned enterprises (SOEs) and private firms/entrepreneurs made up the largest proportion of plaintiffs (20 per cent each). However, the over-representation of cases against industrial and commercial administrations may be responsible for the large number of SOEs in the sample (see Table 9). In any case, the ALL has provided SOEs a useful legal instrument for resolving their disputes with state agencies that regulate them. Compared with aggrieved private individuals, SOEs are less afraid of

Table 7: **Types of Cases in the Sample**

Type	*Number*	*Percentage*
Law-enforcement	59	25
Land use, urban zoning and real estate	50	21
Industrial and commercial adm.	36	16
Taxation	13	6
Public health	8	3
Environment	5	2
Traffic	5	2
Other	60	25
Total	236	100

taking government agencies to court. Another explanation for their legal activism is related to disputes over property rights. Since the property rights of SOEs are poorly defined in China, they are subject to local interference in their managerial affairs and often become attractive targets for other government agencies hungry for various fees. The ALL enables them to use the legal system to challenge such illegal levies and interference.

China's emerging private entrepreneurs and firms also have taken advantage of the legal protection provided by the ALL. They account for

Table 8: **Who Sues: Types of Plaintiffs from the Sample**

Plaintiffs	*Number of cases*	*Percentage*
State-owned enterprises	48	20
Private entrepreneurs/firms	47	20
Peasants	39	17
Workers	27	11
Collective firms/organizations[a]	22	9
Unemployed	9	4
Foreign joint ventures	9	4
Professionals	9	4
Cadres	9	4
Collective suits[b]	7	3
Other	10	4
Total	236	100

Notes:

a. Collective firms and organizations include urban collective firms, township and village enterprises, villagers' committees and villagers' teams.

b. Collective suits are filed by a group of individuals, ranging from 25 households to 505 individuals in the sample.

20 per cent of the plaintiffs in the sample cases.[33] Given the unpredictable regulatory environment in which China's new private entrepreneurs and firms operate, they are more likely to encounter bureaucratic intrusion and harassment than are other individuals. Moreover, their relative economic autonomy from the state and their enormous personal stake in the success (and often the very existence) of their businesses give them both more economic resources and greater incentives to seek judicial relief by filing ALCs against government agencies that interfere with their private enterprise. Therefore, despite the small share of private entrepreneurs in the Chinese population, they seem to be the most active litigants against the state.

Data in Table 8 show that peasants and workers accounted for, respectively, 17 and 11 per cent of the plaintiffs in the sample. It may be that more peasants than workers file ALCs against the government because they account for the majority of the population and their relatively low social status makes them more likely to be victims of the abuse of power by low-level state agents. In comparison, ALCs filed by individuals of higher socio-economic status (such as professionals and cadres) accounted for a small percentage of the sample cases (4 per cent for both groups), reflecting their relatively privileged positions, as well as their small presence in the Chinese population.

The analysis of the data in Table 8 suggests that the ALL has benefited the three social groups with relatively low political or social status: private entrepreneurs, peasants and workers.[34] Therefore, if the implementation of the ALL becomes more effective and impartial, it can become a valuable institutional device to reduce the tensions between the state and the three largest social groups in China.

Table 8 shows that there are two types of collective suits, one filed by urban and rural collectives such as township and village enterprises and villagers' committees, and the other filed by *ad hoc* groups of private citizens whose rights were violated by government actions. Most of the actual cases filed by urban and rural collectives resemble those filed by SOEs and involve disputes over government regulations and rights to land and mineral resources. The second type of collective suits is politically more interesting. Although such spontaneously organized collective lawsuits were only 3 per cent of the sample, they serve as a telling indicator of *organized* political and civic activism in present-day China.

33. Because the sample includes many lawsuits against industrial and commercial administrations, the share of the suits filed by private entrepreneurs and firms might be larger than in a random sample. However, the information in Table 9 shows that only 11 private entrepreneurs and firms were plaintiffs in cases against industrial and commercial administration, indicating that the selection bias is not too severe in this sample. In terms of the outcome of the suits, private firms and entrepreneurs won 25 cases (53%), obtained partial favourable rulings in six cases (13%), lost 12 cases (26%), and withdrew in four cases (three cases were withdrawn after the defendants revoked the disputed actions).

34. The previously cited 1992 study based on primary research reported similar findings. Of the 96 plaintiffs surveyed, about 19% reported that their economic status was "relatively poor or poor"; 68% reported that their economic status as "average." Tang Yongjin, "Yichang jingqiaoqiao de geming," p. 7.

Table 9: **Who Sues Whom: Plaintiffs and Defendants in Most Frequently Filed Cases**

Defendants	*Law enforcement*	*Land use, zoning and real estate*	*Industrial and commercial adm.*	*Taxation*	*Other*
Plaintiffs					
State-owned enterprises	3	6	15	2	22
Private firms/ entrepreneurs	13	3	11	4	16
Peasants	12	11	0	3	13
Workers	18	5	0	0	4
Collective firms/ organizations	1	8	4	2	7
Unemployed	4	1	0	0	4
Professionals	4	4	0	0	1
Collective suits	0	3	1	2	1
Foreign joint ventures	1	1	2	0	5
Cadres	3	5	0	0	1
Other	0	3	3	0	4
Total	59	50	36	13	78

Of the seven cases included in the sample, five were filed by urban residents and two by rural residents. Plaintiffs in three of the five cases filed by urban residents tried to stop construction of commercial projects that would threaten their property and impair their quality of life, suggesting that the ALL might become a potentially useful legal weapon for community activists in the future.

The two sample cases from rural China, both in 1992, show that the ALL could provide limited legal protection against unlawful taxes imposed by local government. In the first case, 32 peasants in a village in Sichuan sued the local township government for imposing taxes that exceeded the legal limit set by the provincial government. They won the case. In the second case, 25 peasants in Sichuan sued the local township government for imposing various illegal levies in violation of the provincial government's limits on taxes and fees. They also won the suit.

Who sues whom? The preceding section analyses the socio-economic and organizational backgrounds of plaintiffs; this section examines whether certain types of plaintiffs are more likely to sue certain types of government agencies. Such analysis may yield important clues as to the relative role of different government agencies in regulating the lives and activities of different social groups and economic organizations in China. The data from the sample (Table 9) reveal several patterns.

First, state-owned enterprises are more likely to sue government regulatory agencies, such as industrial and commercial administrative agen-

Table 10: **Access to Legal Counsel, 1991–95**

Year	*Percentage of plaintiffs with professional counsel*	*Percentage of defendants with professional counsel*
1991	21	36
1992	38	28
1993	35	19
1994	30	17
1995	21	14

Source:
Zhongguo falü nianjian, various years.

cies. One-third of the ALCs in the sample filed by SOEs was against such agencies. Of the remaining 22 cases under the category of "other" in Table 9, all were against various government regulatory agencies (the environmental protection department, public health bureau, the department of standards and others).

Secondly, most lawsuits against Chinese law-enforcement agencies were filed by individuals of low socio-economic status. Workers, private entrepreneurs, peasants and the unemployed accounted for 47 of the 59 ALCs against law-enforcement agencies. The implications are twofold. First, those agencies may be more abusive of their power in their dealings with lower-status individuals than in their dealings with higher-status citizens. In addition, China's lower-status groups seem to have a rising level of awareness of their legal rights and to be growing more assertive in seeking judicial relief from abuse of power by law-enforcement authorities.

Thirdly, judging by the relatively large number of ALCs involving disputes over land ownership and use filed by peasants and rural collectives (19 of 50), the determination of property rights appears to have become a major source of conflict in rural China.

Finally, as shown by the fact that a large portion (23 per cent) of the ALCs filed by private entrepreneurs was against industrial and commercial regulatory agencies, it may be inferred that despite two decades of economic reform, Chinese private entrepreneurs still operate in a difficult regulatory environment.

Access to legal counsel. The ALL allows plaintiffs to represent themselves in the proceedings, or they may appoint others to do so: professional lawyers, social groups, their close relatives, individuals recommended by their work units or other citizens permitted by the court to represent their cases. For plaintiffs, access to professional legal counsel is a reasonable indicator of the extent of their economic resources and, perhaps more importantly, of their determination to pursue judicial remedy of unjust government actions (assuming that the more determined plaintiffs tend to devote more resources to such lawsuits). For defendants, the decision to seek representation by professional counsel may be an indication of how seriously they treat ALCs filed by ordinary citizens.

The national data (Table 10) on legal representation in administrative litigation show that, with the exception of 1991, more plaintiffs retained legal counsel than defendants. This suggests that plaintiffs tended to invest more resources in ALCs than defendants. However, the rate of legal representation for plaintiffs, after first rising dramatically from 21 per cent in 1991 to 38 per cent in 1992, fell gradually in the following years. There are three likely explanations.

First, the rate of professional legal representation for plaintiffs nearly doubled from 1991 to 1992, perhaps as a response to the government's high rate of legal representation at that time. The decline of legal representation thereafter might be related to the perceived impact of such representation on trial outcomes. More specifically, the lawyers' role turned out to be less critical in litigation proceedings than expected because, according to the findings of a 1992 study, plaintiffs thought that their own legal knowledge was the most important factor in winning a case (a good lawyer ranked as the fourth most important factor, behind a "sense of justice" and "good social *guanxi* (connections))."[35] China's legal system also prescribes a limited role for lawyers, a factor that hampers their ability to defend the rights of their clients. The same study found that 90 per cent of the lawyers surveyed agreed that the "limited role of lawyers" was one of the factors that made administrative litigation difficult in China.[36]

Secondly, plaintiffs who filed suits in 1992–93 might have been more determined to pursue their cases to the end and thus hired professional lawyers to increase their chances of winning. But as out-of-court settlement between plaintiffs and defendants began to predominate, plaintiffs might not need to retain professional legal service in order to reduce the financial costs of litigation.[37]

Finally, decreasing rate of professional legal representation might be the result of the rapid increase of administrative litigation cases. The rate of legal representation fell in relative terms when the rate of growth of ALCs was faster than the rate of growth of professional lawyers. This may be the case in 1994 and 1995, when the number of ALCs rose 26 per cent and 50 per cent, respectively. In the same period, the growth of the legal profession was slower. In 1994, the total number of lawyers rose by 22 per cent; in 1995, the growth of the number of lawyers was only 8 per cent.[38]

The data on the legal representation for defendants show a steady decline, from 36 per cent in 1991 to only 14 per cent in 1995. This trend

35. Tang Yongjin, "Yichang jingqiaoqiao de geming," p. 35.

36. *Ibid.* p. 29.

37. According to two Chinese researchers, most peasants were unwilling to spend money on legal representation. Zhang Shuyi and Zhan Zhongle, "Qiantu guangming, daolu quzhe," p. 117.

38. The data on the number of lawyers in China were obtained in *Zhongguo falü nianjian* (1994), p. 1045; (1995), p. 1079; (1996), p. 975.

has several implications. The high rate of legal representation for the government in 1991 is an indication that the formal implementation of the ALL that year might have caused much anxiety among government officials about their chances of winning ALCs under more formalized and stringent rules stipulated by the law. The high rate of legal representation in 1991 was a defensive measure. But as the court continued to maintain its pro-government bias (albeit the bias declined in the early 1990s), the government might have decided to forego the precautionary measure of retaining professional counsel. Another significant factor for the low rate of legal representation for the government was that most law-enforcement agencies – in this sample 90 per cent – did not retain professional counsel (probably because these powerful agencies did not view legal representation very seriously). The most important reason for this general trend is, however, the emergence of out-of-court settlement as the dominant form of resolution, which greatly reduced the need of professional counsel.

Comparatively speaking, the rate of legal representation in administrative cases was lower than that in criminal cases (ranging between 47 to 41 per cent from 1993 to 1995) but higher than those in civil and economic cases. However, because official Chinese data on civil and economic cases are not detailed enough to show the rate of legal representation for plaintiffs and defendants, it is only possible to draw estimates from such data. To be precise, official data on legal representation in civil and economic cases should be termed "rate of lawyer participation." This rate specifically means the number of lawyers who participated in a given year's civil and economic cases, without revealing which side they represented. If it is assumed that plaintiffs and defendants in civil and economic cases are equally likely to hire professional legal counsel, the rate of legal representation for each side may be derived by halving the rate of lawyer participation. The rate of lawyer participation in civil cases was stable in the early 1990s: 10.2 per cent in 1993, 11.1 per cent in 1994 and 11.6 per cent in 1995. The rate in economic cases fluctuated in the same period: 20.6 per cent in 1993, 26.5 per cent in 1994 and 25.6 per cent in 1995.[39] Thus the rate of legal representation for each side may be in the range of 5–6 per cent for civil cases and 10–14 per cent in economic cases – considerably lower than that in administrative cases.

Table 11 shows the access to professional legal counsel by plaintiffs in the 203 of the sample cases for which such information was given. Although the rate of legal representation in the sample (71 per cent) is much higher than the overall national rate described above, it is the case that access to professional legal counsel depended on the plaintiffs' economic resources. Plaintiffs who were commercial or collective organizations (SOEs or township and village enterprises) had above-average rates of professional legal representation (about 83 per cent for SOEs and rural collectives). Private entrepreneurs also had high rates of professional

39. *Zhongguo falü nianjian*, 1993, 1994, 1995.

Table 11: **Plaintiffs' Access to Legal Counsel in 203 Sample Cases**

Plaintiffs	*Represented by professional counsel*	*No legal counsel*	*Represented by non-professional counsel*
State-owned enterprises	37	7	1
Private entrepreneurs/firms	33	6	3
Peasants	17	11	4
Workers	16	8	1
Collective firms/organizations	15	1	2
Unemployed	6	1	–
Collective suits	4	3	–
Other	17	8	2
Total (%)	145 (71%)	45 (22%)	13 (7%)

legal representation (79 per cent). Plaintiffs with fewer economic resources had below-average rates of professional legal representation. For workers, the rate in the sample was 64 per cent; for peasants, the rate was 53 per cent.[40] Unemployed plaintiffs had a high rate of professional legal presentation in the sample (six out of seven) because the unemployed plaintiffs who had income-earning family members all had hired professional legal counsel. The only unemployed plaintiff who did not have professional legal counsel was a homeless migrant labourer.

Bones of contention: administrative violations. The ALL permits private citizens, commercial entities and other organizations to challenge specific administrative actions in court. The analysis in the preceding sections gives some clues as to the types of plaintiffs and the suits they are likely to file. This section studies the types of violations committed by government agencies or agents that may prompt aggrieved citizens or commercial entities to file ALCs.

According to Article 54 of the ALL, seven types of violations by government agencies may cause the court to rule in favour of the plaintiffs by revoking or partially revoking the disputed administrative acts, ordering the defendant to perform a new specific administrative act, modifying administrative penalties, and ordering the defendant to perform its legal duties. The seven are as follows:[41]

1. The disputed specific administrative actions are based on insufficient principal evidence.
2. The disputed specific administrative actions are reached through an incorrect application of law or rules and regulations.

40. In addition to lack of economic resources, Chinese peasants have less access to legal counsel because there are very few lawyers in the countryside.

41. The following text is based on "Administrative Procedure Law," *China Current Laws*, Vol. 1, No. 9 (October 1987), p. 10.

Table 12: **Types and Frequency of Violations by Government Agencies in Sample Cases**

Type of violations	*Law enforcement*	*Land use zoning and real estate*	*Industrial, commercial administration*	*Taxation*	*Other*	*Total*
ELA	14	12	11	4	19	60
IPE	9	11	3	3	22	48
IAL	12	10	7	3	8	40
VLP	12	8	3	1	8	32
AOA	6	1	3	2	4	16
FPL	6	7	0	0	1	14
UAP	7	1	1	0	0	9
Total	66	50	28	13	62	219

Notes:
ELA: exceeding legal authority, including acts with no legal basis;
IPE: insufficient principal evidence;
IAL: incorrect application of law and rules;
VLP: violation of legal procedures;
FPL: failure to perform legal responsibility;
AOA: abuse of authority;
UAP: unjust administrative penalties.

3. The defendant violated legally prescribed procedures.
4. The defendant exceeded its legal authority.
5. The defendant abused its power.
6. The disputed administrative penalties are clearly unjust.
7. The defendant failed to perform or delayed the performance of its legal responsibility.

The final rulings favourable to plaintiffs issued by the courts of first instance and by the appellate courts are examined in the sample to ascertain the frequency with which such violations occur. The court may rule in favour of the plaintiffs on the basis of one or more violations in the same case. These legal rulings provide a rare look at how power is exercised by the Chinese government. The findings are reported in Table 12.

The court-established violations by government agencies tabulated in Table 12 suggest the following features of China's administrative system and offer some clues as to why actions taken by state agencies are often subject to legal challenges under the ALL.

Agency-specific characteristics.

Law-enforcement. It is evident that China's law-enforcement agencies, as shown by Table 12, seem most prone of all state agencies to all types of violations. The three most frequent violations committed by law-enforcement agencies are exceeding their legal authority; violating legal procedures; and incorrectly applying laws and rules or taking actions with no legal basis. That law-enforcement agencies have engaged in widespread violation of Chinese laws – such as abuse of authority, gathering insufficient evidence, imposing unjust penalties and failing to perform their legal duties – is a troubling indicator of their organizational problems and corroborates the widespread popular impression that China's law-enforcement agencies are plagued by serious abuse of power.

Land use and zoning agencies. The most frequent violations committed by such agencies are exceeding legal authority; taking actions on the basis of insufficient principal evidence; incorrectly applying laws and rules; and violating legal procedures. These agencies (mostly local governments) exceed their legal authority chiefly because China's national and local laws on property rights are relatively new, unclear and often non-existent.

Industrial and commercial administration. Like law-enforcement agencies, China's regulatory agencies in the industrial and commercial sectors are particularly prone to exceed their legal authority because they are not accountable to other supervisory bodies. More importantly, they also frequently misapply laws and rules because China does not have a uniform commercial code. Furthermore, its laws and regulations governing commerce are simultaneously excessive and insufficient: excessive because there are too many restrictive regulations (especially on the private sector), insufficient because existing laws and regulations lack precision and transparency.

The institutional origins of violations. Table 12 shows that government agencies tend to commit some types of violation more frequently than others. The four most often-committed violations are:

1. Exceeding legal authority, including making administrative decisions without any legal basis (60 out of 219 violations).
2. Actions based on insufficient principal evidence (48).
3. Incorrect application of laws and rules, or no legal basis for administrative actions (40).
4. Violation of legal procedures (32).

It is suspected that the high frequency of such administrative violations is symptomatic of three major problems in China's legal, economic and political systems. First, the Chinese state still maintains excessive control over socio-economic activities through its system of laws and regulations. Secondly, the laws, rules and regulations that govern socio-economic activities are in great need of clarification. Close analysis of the sample cases shows that national, provincial and local laws often conflict with and even contradict each other. Many also lack transparency, thus allowing administrative authorities unwarranted additional power to interpret them to their advantage. Such systemic legal confusion and opaqueness is also exacerbated by unclear specification of the limits of jurisdictional authority and power of the various government agencies. The combined effects of imprecise, opaque and conflicting laws, rules and regulations inevitably lead to a high rate of the misapplication of laws and the exceeding of legal authority by government agencies.

Thirdly, decision-making in Chinese administrative agencies remains highly arbitrary, such that there is no accountability. Rather, there is a tendency to reach important administrative decisions that affect the lives and livelihoods of ordinary citizens on the basis of insufficient evidence. Legal procedures are frequently violated, and the limits of agencies' legal authority are often exceeded. The analysis in this study shows a consistent pattern of "administrative opportunism" whereby government agencies tend to base their decisions on laws and regulations that would favour them, even though such laws and regulations did not apply. In other words, misapplication of laws was often not accidental but intentional. In many sample cases reviewed in this study, government agencies misapplied laws and exceeded their authority primarily to impose heavy fines or seize the property of ordinary citizens and commercial entities.

Fruits of victory: what did plaintiffs get? In the 236 sample cases, plaintiffs obtained 148 favourable or partially favourable rulings from the court, excluding cases where plaintiffs withdrew their lawsuits after the defendants voluntarily revoked or changed the disputed administrative actions. Most favourable rulings led to a complete revocation of an administrative action, a partial revocation of an administrative action, an order to compel the performance of a delayed legal responsibility by the defendant, or an order to take a new administrative action. When plaintiffs won ALCs, defendants usually paid more than half, and sometimes nearly all, of the litigation costs. A litigant who lost an appeal was responsible for the costs of the appeal.

Of the favourable rulings obtained for plaintiffs in the sample, most did not award compensation to plaintiffs because such compensation was not demanded. Out of the 148 rulings for plaintiffs, this was the case for 96 (65 per cent). Of the remaining rulings favourable to plaintiffs, 17 plaintiffs demanded compensation but the court denied it; 18 demanded compensation but were awarded lower amounts (some then appealed to the higher court for more compensation); and 17 demanded compensation and received amounts apparently satisfactory to them. All compensation awards were for direct economic losses resulting from disputed administrative actions; there were no consequential compensation or damage awards. This suggests that the primary motive for plaintiffs was to revoke an injurious and unjust administrative action. Although many plaintiffs demanded compensation, the sample cases show that it was difficult to get the court to award such compensation or award it in a satisfactory amount.[42]

42. Before the implementation of the Law on State Compensation on 1 January 1995, citizens could not sue the state for damages.

Conclusions

The evidence presented and analysed in this study shows that, although the constraints of China's closed political system seriously limit the effectiveness of the ALL, the institution of judicial review of administrative actions is gradually being consolidated. The findings tend to support some of the earlier predications made of the ALL by one scholar who noted that it could be used by more powerful organizations (such as SOEs) in challenging government administrative agencies; he also saw the ALL as a useful legal instrument for China's emerging private sector.[43] Indeed, SOEs and private entrepreneurs and firms were among the most active litigants in the sample. Analysis of the national data on the increasing scope of administrative actions subject to challenge under the ALL similarly bears out the predication by another scholar who foresaw the expansion of the application of the ALL to "include within the ambit of judicial scrutiny an increasingly broad range of administrative activity."[44] Moreover, the embedded flaws of the ALL identified earlier by other scholars were also reflected in the results of the implementation. For example, the law's "focus on judicial review of the legality rather than the propriety of administrative decisions" has prevented Chinese citizens from invoking the ALL to challenge substantive government policies, as shown by the fact that none of the sample cases contained such suits.[45] The lack of judicial autonomy was also an important factor in the court's persistent bias in favour of the government (as indicated by their greater odds of winning these suits).

Therefore, in several important aspects, one may argue that the ALL has failed to live up to the expectations of its liberal proponents: it has not become a fully reliable or effective legal instrument that enables ordinary citizens to defend themselves against government infringements of their rights. But it has not been a total failure. The evidence indicates that it has gained a limited role in curbing and rectifying unjust treatment of citizens by government officials. One of the important findings of this study, which was not foreseen by other scholars in their earlier studies of the ALL, is the rising rate of settlements that provide effective judicial relief to the plaintiffs. The evidence gathered in this study offers some preliminary signs of the gradual consolidation of the ALL as a legal institution, including the consistent and dramatic rise of administrative litigation suits since its implementation; the decline in the percentage of rulings in favour of government agencies; the rise in the percentage of effective victories for plaintiffs; and the public perception of the ALL as a useful, albeit limited, legal instrument for protecting their rights.

A 1992 poll showed that 92 per cent of the respondents agreed that "it is better to have the ALL than not have it because, although the ALL is

43. Potter, "The Administrative Litigation Law of the PRC," p. 288.

44. Finder, "Like throwing an egg against a stone?" p. 28.

45. Potter's insight on the "legality" focus of the ALL is invaluable in understanding why it was enacted and how it was implemented. Potter, "The Administrative Litigation Law of the PRC," p. 288.

not perfect, citizens' rights have gained some protection."[46] In the same poll, 68 per cent of the ordinary citizens surveyed agreed that the ALL made a difference in limiting unlawful practices in society.[47] Under it, administrative litigation has also become an important option for ordinary citizens. When asked what recourse they would have when their rights are violated by the government, 35 per cent of the respondents said that they would bring their complaints directly to "relevant government agencies," while 30 per cent said that they would sue the government in the court (under the ALL).[48] The ALL also had an impact on government officials. The 1992 poll found that 74 per cent of the government officials surveyed said that they had begun to exercise greater caution in their work because of the ALL.[49]

This initial evidence of the institutional consolidation of China's administrative litigation system also sheds some light on the process of institutional evolution. The case of the ALL offers some evidence that institutions evolve through a process of *mutual adaptation* – new institutions adapt to the existing political system and its constraints and the existing political system adapts to the new norms and rules stipulated and embodied in the new institutions. As a result, the proposed institutional experiment tends to realize less than its full potential in terms of structuring political behaviour and enforcing new norms. At the same time, even such partially effective institutional experiments have a real impact on the existing political system, with its components (that is, various bureaucracies and organizations) struggling to adjust their behaviour to meet at least some of the requirements set by the new institutional experiments. There is evidence of such adjustments made by various agencies of the Chinese state. For example, a one-in-five chance that they may lose a case forces them to be increasingly open to settling with plaintiffs. Government officials also admitted that the ALL made them more careful in exercising administrative power. The immediate result of this mutual adaptation is a novel and complex arrangement of conflict resolution between the Chinese state and its citizens unanticipated by the designers of the ALL.

On the one hand, the ALL has set a series of legal precedents and procedures for citizens to seek judicial relief through a complete litigation process. On the other hand, the high costs of this process and the severe constraints placed by the Chinese political system on the judiciary induced plaintiffs and defendants to seek compromises through court-mediated settlements in many cases. This has certainly fallen short of the ideal of the rule of law, but even this imperfect outcome has generated real benefits both for the Chinese state (in terms of opening an institu-

46. Zhan Zhongle, "Xingzheng susongfa shishi xianzuang yu fazhan fangxiang diaocha wenjuan baogao" ("Report on the survey on the implementation and trends of the ALL"), in Gong Ruixiang, *Fazhi de lixiang yu xianshi*, p. 280.

47. Tang Yongjin, "Yichang jingqiaoqiao de geming," p. .11.

48. *Ibid.* p. 59.

49. *Ibid.* p. 14.

tional channel for addressing public discontent) and for individual citizens (in terms of redressing government-inflicted wrongs).

An intriguing question is why the old political system should accommodate the requirements of new institutions and refrain from reversing such accommodations. Scholars who have followed recent Chinese legal reforms argue that such accommodation was necessitated by the post-Mao regime's search for a new basis of legitimacy.[50] Other than legitimation concerns, it is contended that such accommodations, once made, may be difficult to withdraw unilaterally because of the high political costs that would entail. First, in many cases, the accommodations were initiated by reformers within the old regime who saw political benefits of a more institutionalized legal system. An attempted reversal of reform would lead to a bitter intra-elite struggle with high risks for both sides. Secondly, institutional development tends to be path-dependent. Legal reforms are no exception. The path-dependency of legal reform in China has been recognized also by other scholars, as one wrote, "... the operation of law is subject to evaluation and challenge by reference to external standards: once a principle of law is enunciated it becomes part of the public domain and open to uses that the regime may not be able to control."[51] In addition to setting new norms that eventually become benchmarks for evaluating individual or organizational behaviour, a new institution also acquires its defenders who are beneficiaries of the new system. Therefore, although institutional innovations may start as experiments, the longer such experiments continue, the higher the costs entailed in their reversal. Initially, the costs of reversing an institutional experiment are mainly reputational; the ruling elite risks losing political legitimacy or credibility if part of its new policy package is abandoned without justifiable reasons. In the Chinese context, since the ALL was promoted and implemented as an important element of China's overall legal reforms, any official action that overtly suspended or weakened its enforcement would have discredited the entire programme of legal reform.

Gradually, as an institutional experiment continues, political and economic entrepreneurs begin to perceive its potential benefits and capture them. Consequently, despite the limited nature of most institutional experiments, they attract entrepreneurs who then become the beneficiaries of these experiments (it is no mere accident that, in this sample, Chinese private entrepreneurs were the most active private litigants). The benefits won by these entrepreneurs are widely publicized by the reformers, who try to disseminate the information to more groups and attract a larger political following to defend the new institutional arrangement. Hence in the early days, lawsuits filed under the ALL received enormous publicity in the media. Once the benefits of the experiments have been conferred

50. See Pitman Potter, "Riding the tiger: legitimacy and legal culture in post-Mao China," *The China Quarterly*, No. 138 (June 1994), pp. 325–358; Edward J. Epstein, "Law and legitimation in post-Mao China," in Potter, *Domestic Law Reforms in Post-Mao China*, pp. 19–55.

51. Potter, "Riding the tiger," pp. 325–26.

on many important groups (as the ALL has done for SOEs, township and village enterprises, the legal community, village groups, peasants, workers and entrepreneurs), it becomes more politically costly to reverse the reform.

This study also suggests that China's legal reforms, though far from establishing the rule of law in the short term, have made measurable progress in promoting legal norms and awareness of such norms at the grassroots level. For example, a majority of Chinese citizens know of the existence of the ALL.[52] The 185 cases examined here reveal that private citizens are more assertive of their rights. In the sample cases there are citizens who sued authorities for illegal search, seizure, fines and detention, who challenged regulatory agencies for failure to issue permits or licences, and who demanded rectification of unjust administrative penalties levied against them. The fact that a considerable proportion of suits filed under the ALL (about 39 per cent in 1995, according to this analysis) led to full or partial correction of wrong or unjust administrative actions shows that such legal risk-taking by ordinary Chinese is not completely futile. If this trend continues, a virtuous cycle may emerge: rising public awareness of legal norms and resources leading to increasing assertiveness by citizens and more frequent use of laws like the ALL, which creates more a credible threat to arbitrary government agents and places greater pressure on them to be accountable for their exercise of power.

Finally, this study indicates that state–society relations are changing in post-Mao China and that the boundaries between the state and society are being redrawn. A principal force of such changes is undoubtedly China's economic reforms that have restructured authority relations in virtually all sectors of the economy and society as a result of redistribution of economic resources from the state to society. However, the study shows that institutional changes such as legal reforms are a critical factor in the redefinition of state–society relations in China. These changes have more explicitly set limits on state power and established procedures for citizens to defend themselves against intrusion or infringement by the state and its agents. If such institutional changes continue, the new state–society relations in China will be not only based on structural factors (the distribution of economic resources and organizational capital between the state and society) but also underpinned by an increasingly sophisticated set of institutions that embodies norms and enforcement mechanisms which make such relations more sustainable and less prone to open conflict.

52. According to a 1992 poll, 88% of the ordinary people surveyed said that they had heard about the ALL. Tang Yongjin, "Yichang jingqiaoqiao de geming," p. 10.

[12]

TINGMEI FU

Legal Person in China: Essence and Limits

As little as a decade ago, "legal person" or *faren* was a strange concept to the great majority of lawyers, not to mention the general public, in the People's Republic of China ("PRC" or "China'). Today not only lawyers but even economists and enterprise managers have widely accepted this notion.[1] Indeed, the concept of legal person has become an inseparable part of the contemporary Chinese legal system. It would be difficult to understand Chinese law without an adequate knowledge of the concept and its implications.

Since the promulgation of the General Principles of Civil Law ("GPCL") in 1986,[2] the concept of legal person has been discussed, broadly and specifically, inside and outside of China.[3] Many of the early discussions, however, tend to give descriptive accounts of the concept. It has become clear that recent developments have provided an improved opportunity and also a renewed need to review the essence and limits of this important concept in Chinese law.

This paper starts with a discussion of the establishment of the

---

TINGMEI FU, LL.B. (Suzhou, China), LL.M. (London), Ph.D. (London), is an investment adviser with Peregrine Capital (China) Limited, Hong Kong. The research for this paper was mainly carried out when the author was a Ph.D. candidate and part-time lecturer in Chinese law at the School of Oriental and African Studies, University of London. The main theme of this paper formed a part of the author's Ph.D. dissertation entitled, "Law and Policy of State Enterprises in Post-Mao China". While accepting full responsibility for the views expressed in this paper, the author wishes to thank Michael Palmer for Ph.D. dissertation supervision, and Yuan Cheng, Joseph Gote and Andrew Bell for their valuable help in preparing this paper.

1. For a discussion by economists, see Ji Peng & Yang Mu, "Jiejian Xifang Faren Zhidu, Chonggou Woguo Qiye Xingtai" (Learning the Legal Person System from the West, and Restructuring Our Enterprise Pattern), *Zhongguo: Fazhan Yu Gaige* (China: Development and Reform), 23-8 (No. 6, 1988). Reprinted in *Jingjifa* (Economic Law), 53-8 (No. 4, 1988). Enterprise directors and managers come to acknowledge the concept of legal person mainly by accepting that they are "the legal representatives of legal persons" (for a definition of this concept, see art. 38 of the GPCL, also see infra n.55).

2. Adopted at the Fourth Session of the Sixth National People's Congress (NPC) on Apr. 12, 1986, and effective as of Jan. 1, 1987. For an English translation of the GPCL by W. Gray & H.R. Zheng, see 34 *Am. J. Comp. L.*, at 715-43 (1986).

3. For a general discussion, see H.R. Zheng, "China's New Civil Law," id. 669, esp. 677-80. For a specific analysis of enterprise legal persons, see Zhao Zhongfu (translated by Winston Zhao), "Enterprise Legal Persons: Their Important Status in Chinese Civil Law," 52 *L. and Contemp. Prob.* 1 (Summer 1989). In addition, Stanley Lubman, in his excellent review of the study of Chinese law, also noted this concept. See "Studying Contemporary Chinese Law: Limits Possibilities and Strategy," in 39 *Am. J. Comp. L.* 293-341 (1991), at 329.

legal person concept in Chinese civil law, and to a lesser extent its application to administrative law and civil procedure law, is also noted. The second part of the paper assesses the nature of legal personality in Chinese law. The discussion attempts to analyze the Chinese perception of legal personality from the perspectives of both civil and criminal law. The third part of the paper examines the character of independence of Chinese legal persons more specifically from the aspects of property rights and civil liability. In particular, the discussion assesses the so-called "management right" authorized by law to state enterprises, and the possibility of lifting the corporate veil.

I. Establishment of the Legal Person Concept in Chinese Law

A. *Adoption of the Legal Person Concept in Chinese Civil Law*

1. Legal Person: A Background

In China, although it was not impossible for various organizations to hold property and to take part in social and economic activities in their own names, the idea of legal personality was not legally accepted until the adoption of the Civil Code (1929) of the Republic of China—the first comprehensive civil legislation in China.[4] After the foundation of the PRC in 1949, all the laws previously adopted by the Republican authorities were abolished in mainland China, though some legal concepts were able to survive. "Legal person", as one of these surviving concepts, first formally appeared in the Temporary Measures Concerning the Conclusion of Contracts Between State Organs, State Enterprises, and Cooperatives (hereinafter "Measures").[5] Article 5 of the Measures provided that "a contract or deed must be concluded between legal persons represented by their responsible persons". Despite this provision, the meaning and implication of legal person was far from clear, as no other legislation was available which dealt with this concept. Furthermore, the Provisional Regulations Concerning Private Enterprises,[6] promulgated later in the same year, though referring to the five types of company existed under the Company Law (1929) of the Republic of China, did not even mention the concept of corporate personality. In fact, apart from some academic discussions,[7] no evidence is available to demon-

4. For an early and general discussion, see Hu Changqing, *Zhongguo Minfa Zonglun* (General Discussion on Chinese Civil Law), at 102 (1933).

5. Adopted by the Financial and Economic Committee under the State Administration Council (predecessor of the State Council) on Sept. 27, 1950. For the text of these Measures, see *Zhonghua Renmin Gongheguo Zhongyang Renmin Zhengfu Faling Huibian* (Collection of Laws and Regulations of the PRC Central Government) (1949-1950), at 696 (1982).

6. Promulgated on Dec. 29, 1950. See the text in id., 705-11.

7. For example, one book on civil law defined a legal person as a "social organi-

strate the continuous use of this term by Chinese authorities until the early 1980s. Indeed, for most years of this period, law was put aside in the PRC, and the notion of legal person was attacked as a bourgeois legal concept.

When China started its legal construction drive in the late 1970s, the concept of legal person was revived in the mind of some Chinese lawyers who became aware of its importance and began to advocate the establishment of the legal person concept.[8] In the early 1980s, the fact that the notion of legal person was the invention of the capitalist law did seem to restrain some people from unconditionally welcoming its adoption.[9] But this did not turn out to be a critical obstacle as many advocates sought to reinforce their argument by expressly citing the precedent established in the Soviet civil law regarding the institution of the legal person.[10] Indeed, earlier discussions among Chinese lawyers showed that they approached the concept of legal person and its features in a way similar to their Soviet counterparts.[11]

Despite the enthusiasm of academics, the concept of legal person remained uncertain for several years. The Economic Contract Law (1981)[12] was the first Law in which "legal person" was formally employed. But this law used this term to a great extent as a conven-

---

sation which is established in accordance with legal procedure, which is able to independently participate in civil activities in its own name, and which can be plaintiff and defendant in court proceedings." The term "legal person" was described as being applicable to state enterprises, official organs, cooperatives, state-capitalist enterprises and social organizations. See "Teaching and Research Section of the Central School of Political and Legal Cadres," *Zhonghua Renmin Gongheguo Minfa Jiben Wenti* (Fundamental Issues in the Civil Law of the PRC), at 68 (1958). However, it appears that even at this stage, the discussions had to distinguish carefully between the socialist or capitalist nature of legal persons.

8. See Liu Qishan & Bai Youzhong, "Yingdang Queli Faren Zhidu, (The Legal Person System Should be Established)," *Renmin Ribao* (People's Daily), Apr. 23, 1981, at 5; Gao Shuyi, "Faren Zhidu Dui Woguo Shixian Sihua de Xianshi Yiyi, (Practical Importance of the Legal Person System on Realising Our Four Modernisations)," *Faxue Yanjiu* (Studies in Law, Beijing), 15-17 (No. 4, 1980); Yu Nengbin & Yang Zhenshan, "Minshi Zhuti—Faren (Civil Subjects—Legal Persons)," *Zhongguo Fazhi Bao* (China Legal News), Sept. 4, 1981, at 3; also see Chen Kecong, "Zuowei Minshi Zhuti Zhi Yi de Faren (Legal Persons As a Kind of Civil Subjects)," *Guangming Ribao* (Enlightment Daily), Nov. 17, 1981, at 3.

9. For a summary of different opinions concerning the adoption of the legal person concept, see Wang Baoshu & Cui Qingzhi, *Jingji Faxue Yanjiu Zongshu* (Summary of Research on Economic Law), at 72-4 (1989).

10. See, e.g., Liu & Bai, supra n.8.

11. For example, one commentator attempted to define a legal person as "a social organisation which possesses organisational structure and independent property, and which is able, in its own name, to participate in civil activities, to enjoy civil rights and bears civil liabilities, and to initiate and to defend legal proceedings in accordance with the law". See Yu & Yang, supra n.8. Also compare with supra n.7.

12. Adopted at the Fourth Session of the Sixth National People's Congress on Dec. 13, 1981. The Economic Contract Law has been amended by the Standing Committee of the Eighth National People's Congress on Sept. 2, 1993. For the text in Chinese, see *Renmin Ribao* (overseas ed.), Sept. 6, 1993 at 2.

ience for defining the capacity of business organizations to enter into contracts. This is because the Economic Contract Law, like the Measures of 1950, required that an economic contract should only be concluded between legal persons.[13] Apart from that enterprises were formally granted the capacity to make contracts, there was little evidence to suggest that the concept of legal person was used positively to grant enterprises significant independence and autonomy. Furthermore, due to the absence of comprehensive civil legislation, the definition and relevant requirements for a Chinese legal person were far from clear. In fact, the Economic Contract Law, in many articles,[14] still tended to use the term "*danwei*" (unit), rather than *faren*, to refer to various economic organizations. This reflected the fact that, at that time, the term "legal person" was not yet familiar to many Chinese legislators and lawyers. Indeed, the unpopularity of the concept of legal person was confirmed by the fact that neither the Civil Procedure Law (For Trial Implementation)[15] nor the 1982 Constitution employed this term. Instead, the Constitution, for example, employed "social groups", "enterprises and non-business organisations" to embrace various entities,[16] many of which would have qualified as "legal persons".

2. State Enterprise Reform and Adoption of the Concept of Legal Person

It is indisputable that to a great extent the construction of the entire post-Mao legal system has been prompted by a fundamental need to serve the Chinese economic reforms. In this respect, the history of the legal person in the 1980s was no exception.

In the beginning of the economic reforms, the Chinese leadership was very concerned with "invigorating" state enterprises—the main economic force in Chinese socialist economy. Prior to the economic reforms, Chinese state enterprises were under extensive government control. Every state enterprise, from the supply of its materials to the production and distribution of products, from the appointment of its directors and managers to the administration of labour, strictly had to follow rigid state plans and compulsory government orders. Having been deprived of autonomy in important decision-making, state enterprises were little concerned with making profits or suffering losses. The government, as owner, would

13. Art. 1. However, the newly amended Economic Contract Law (1993) has formally abolished such restriction by providing that economic contracts are contracts concluded between legal persons and between "legal person and other entrities such as individual households (see art. 2).

14. E.g., arts. 4 and 5.

15. Adopted on Mar. 8, 1982 and effective from Oct. 1, 1982. This law has been replaced by the Civil Procedure Law of 1991 (see infra n.34.).

16. E.g., art. 5.

take away all the profits they made and at the same time bear all the liabilities for their losses. Accordingly, state enterprises had no "independence" from government manipulation, a situation widely seen as an obstacle to economic efficiency and modernisation.

Inspired by the need to grant autonomy to state enterprises, Chinese lawyers were quick to pick up the notion of corporate personality. Thus, in one authoritative civil law textbook published in 1983, a legal person was defined as "a social organization that has self-operated property, and that can independently enjoy civil rights and assume civil duties".[17] After explaining the roles played by the legal person institution in capitalist societies, this book continued to enumerate many potential functions of the concept of legal person in Chinese socialist legal system. One of these functions was described as "a legal device to increase the vitality of enterprises".[18] This conclusion was based on the assumption that, unlike previous state enterprises that were heavily dependent on government authorities, state enterprises as legal persons would have independent interests and independent property.[19]

At almost the same time, Chinese concept of legislation began to take constructive steps towards defining the concept of legal person. On April 1, 1983, the State Council issued Provisional Regulations Concerning State Industrial Enterprises (hereinafter "Enterprise Regulations")[20] which provided:

> [State industrial] enterprises are legal persons. Their directors are the representatives of the legal persons. Enterprises shall exercise, in accordance with the law, the right to possess, use and dispose of the state assets which the state authorises them to manage and administer, shall independently engage in production and operation, shall bear the responsibility to which the state prescribes, and shall independently initiate and defend legal proceedings in the court.[21]

As such, the Enterprise Regulations not only assumed the legal person status of state enterprises, but also actually set out the principal characteristics of enterprise legal persons.

As a further attempt, in 1984 the Central Committee of the Chinese Communist Party adopted the Decision on Economic System Reforms (hereinafter "the Party Decision"), which has been re-

17. Tong Rou (ed.), *Minfa Yuanli* (Civil Law Jurisprudence), at 51 (1983). For an English translation of the most parts of the Second Impression (1987) of this book, see W.C. Jones (ed.), *Basic Principles of Civil Law in China* (1989).

18. *Basic Principles of Civil Law in China*, id. at 65.

19. Id.

20. For the text, see *Zhonghua Renmin Gongheguo Fagui Huibian* (Laws and Regulations of the PRC), at 383 (1983).

21. Id. art. 8.

garded as milestone in China's urban economic reforms. The Party Decision, which for the first time officially declared that the Chinese economy was a "socialist commodity economy", expressly listed one of the most important objectives of the urban economic reforms as:

> to make every (state) enterprise become truly relatively independent economic entity, and become a socialist commodity producer and manager which runs itself and assumes sole responsibility for its profits and losses, and has the capacity of reforming and developing itself, and becoming a legal person that enjoys its rights and bears its duties.[22]

Here the concept of legal person was employed and stressed deliberately and officially. In less than two years, the GPCL was adopted to provide detailed treatment for the legal person concept. According to the GPCL, a legal person shall be an organization that has capacity for civil rights and capacity for civil conduct and independently enjoys civil rights and assumes civil obligations in accordance with the law.[23] This definition, though echoing many academic discussions in the early 1980s, was clearly the expression of the perception by the Chinese authorities of the legal person concept as reflected in the Party Decision.

The process of gradual reception of the legal person concept in Chinese civil law shows that without economic reforms the concept of legal person would not have been accepted so widely and so positively in China. Although it was apparently necessary for China to accept the notion of legal person before it could adopt a comprehensive civil law, the acceptance of the concept would have seemed impossible had it not been made applicable to state enterprises—the dominating operators in Chinese socialist economy. In this context, the state policy of granting a degree of operational autonomy, with concomitant corporate personality, to state enterprises played a decisive role in the reception of the concept of legal person in Chinese civil law.

2. Legal Persons as Outlined by the GPCL

In the GPCL, "legal person" is used as a concept in opposition to "citizens (natural persons)". Indeed, the legal framework established by the GPCL concerning legal person is relatively detailed. Of the 156 articles of the GPCL, eighteen are devoted to it.[24] The term is also used in many other articles of the GPCL.[25]

The GPCL expressly sets out the legal requirements for a legal

22. *Renmin Ribao*, Oct. 21, 1984, at 4.
23. Art. 36, GPCL.
24. Art. 36-53.
25. See, e.g., art. 54 (civil legal act), art. 63 (agency), and arts. 94-96 (intellectual property).

person.[26] Article 37 of the GPCL provides:

(i) establishment in accordance with the law;
(ii) possession of the necessary property or funds;
(iii) possession of its own name, organization and premises, and
(iv) ability to independently bear civil liability.

Theoretically, every entity which accords with these basic requirements is able to obtain legal personality and become a Chinese legal person. As far as enterprises are concerned, apart from state enterprises that are automatically granted legal personality, all collective enterprises with the proper qualifications are able to become legal persons.[27] Furthermore, all Sino-foreign equity joint ventures,[28] some Sino-foreign cooperative joint ventures,[29] and some wholly foreign owned enterprises[30] qualify as Chinese legal persons. In addition, according to the GPCL, official organs, institutions and social organizations which have met the basic requirements are also capable of obtaining legal personality.[31]

---

26. These requirements, however, were stated differently in the drafts prior to the GPCL. See Henry R. Zheng, supra n.3, at 678. Also see the discussion below concerning the civil law perspective of legal personality.

27. See art. 41, GPCL.

28. The Law on Sino-Foreign Equity Joint Ventures, being adopted in July 1979, did not refer to the legal personality of joint ventures. However, subsequently, the legal person status of equity joint ventures was officially acknowledged in art. 2 of the Implementing Rules of the Law on Sino-Foreign Equity Joint Ventures (promulgated by the State Council on Sept. 20, 1983). Also see art. 41, GPCL.

29. See art. 2 of the Law on Sino-Foreign Cooperative Joint Ventures (promulgated on Apr. 16, 1988). Also see art. 41, GPCL.

30. See art. 8 of the Law on Wholly Foreign-Owned Enterprises (promulgated on Apr. 12, 1986). Also see art. 41, GPCL.

31. Art. 50, GPCL. Since this legal provision, regulations governing these legal persons are emerging. For example, as far as social organizations are concerned, on Sept. 27, 1988, the State Council adopted Measures on the Administration of Foundations. See the text in *Zhonghua Renmin Gongheguo Guowuyuan Gongbao* (Bulletin of the PRC State Council), at 779-81 (1988). On Nov. 1, 1989, the State Council promulgated the Regulations Concerning the Administration of Registration of Social Organizations. See the text, id., 779-83 (1989).

A new PRC Trade Union Law was adopted on Apr. 3, 1992. See the text in *Gongren Ribao* (Workers' Daily), Apr. 8, 1992, at 1. Art. 14 of this Law provides: "the national Trade union Association, local Trade Union Associations and industrial Trade Union Associations shall have the status of social organization legal persons. Grassroot trade union organizations, if meeting the qualifications of a legal person provided by the GPCL, shall become social organization legal persons in accordance with the law."

It should also be noted that political parties are not included in the concept of legal person in Chinese law. This is mainly because they are not regarded as ordinary "social organizations". For an explanation concerning the exclusion of political parties from "social organizations", see "Responsible Persons from the Ministry of Civil Affairs Answer Questions Concerning the Application of the Regulations Concerning the Administration of Registration of Social Organizations," *Fazhi Ribao* (Legal Daily), May 21, 1990, at 4.

B. *Application of the Concept of Legal Person in Chinese Law Other Than Civil Law*

Since the acceptance of the legal person concept in the GPCL, the notion of legal person has been incorporated into a number of newly adopted or amended laws and regulations. Its use in two of the basic laws in Chinese context—Civil Procedure Law and Administrative Litigation Law is illustrated below.

1. Civil Procedure Law

As mentioned earlier, the Civil Procedure Law (For Trial Implementation) of 1982 did not employ the term of legal person. However, the new Civil Procedure Law, adopted on April 9, 1991,[32] uses the concept. Article 3 of this law provides:

> This Law shall apply to civil actions heard by the People's Court involving relationships concerning property and personal relationships between citizens, between legal persons or between other organizations, and among citizens, legal persons and other organizations.

As such, the Civil Procedure Law has formally and explicitly recognised that legal persons may stand as plaintiffs and defendants in civil proceedings. Furthermore, the Civil Procedure Law provides that legal persons shall be represented in litigations by their legal representatives.[33]

2. Administrative Litigation Law

The Administrative Litigation Law of the PRC was adopted on April 4, 1989 and came into effect on October 1, 1990.[34] Before the Administrative Litigation Law took effect, administrative litigation was governed by the Civil Procedure Law (For Trial Implementation) of 1982.[35]

The Administrative Litigation Law which began to be drafted in 1986 at first did not expressly acknowledge the *locus standi* of legal persons. Although many Chinese scholars advocated the adoption of the concept of legal person in administrative litigation law,[36] the term "legal person" was absent until the draft dispatched for consul-

32. Effective Apr. 9, 1991. For the English text of this law, see *China L. and Prac.* 15-16 (No. 5, 1991).

33. Art. 49. For a definition and brief discussion on "legal representative" in Chinese law, see infra n.51 and accompanying text.

34. For an English text, see *China L. and Prac.* 37 (No. 5, 1989).

35. Art. 3 of this law provided that "the provisions of this law are applicable to administrative cases that by law are to be tried by the people's court."

36. See, e.g., two articles in *Faxue* (Law Monthly, No. 4, 1988): Xiong Wenzhao, "Xingzheng Faren Lun (On Administrative Legal Persons)," at 11-14; Chen Zizhong, "Xingzheng Jiguan de Falü Diwei Yu Xingzheng Faren Zhidu (Legal Status of Administrative Organs and Administrative Legal Person System)," at 8-10.

tation in July 1988.[37] Nevertheless, just a few months later, the approved Administrative Litigation Law was able to single out legal persons as a type of plaintiff in administrative litigations, as opposed to other non-legal person organisations as well as citizens. Article 2 of this Law provides:

> citizens, legal persons and other organizations shall have the right to sue in accordance with this Law if they think their legal rights have been infringed by the administrative acts of some administrative organs and their staff.

The Administrative Litigation Law, however, does not identify the legal person status of defendants in administrative cases. Instead, the Law refers to "administrative organs" as the defendants in most cases[38] though in some cases "organisations" other than administrative organs may also become defendants.[39] Nevertheless, since the GPCL has assumed the legal person status of administrative organs,[40] it seems logic for the court to apply general laws concerning official organ legal persons as provided by the GPCL. For example, only the legal representative of an administrative organ may represent that organ in administrative litigations.[41]

The fact that the concept of legal person has been incorporated into a number of newly adopted laws such as the Administrative Litigation Law and newly amended laws such as the Civil Procedure Law illustrates that the legal person has become an important concept in shaping and sustaining the emerging Chinese legal system.

II. Legal Personality: Fictional or Realistic?

A. *Nature of Legal Personality: the Civil Law Perspective*

During the last century, Western jurisprudence has presented

37. In that draft, the term "*zuzhi*" (organisations) was employed to embrace all plaintiffs excluding natural persons.

38. See arts. 2 & 25.

39. See art. 25. As far as "organizations" are concerned, the Administrative Litigation Law adopts different approaches towards their status. Par. 4 of art. 25 provides: where specific administrative acts are performed by organisations empowered pursuant to laws or regulations, such organizations shall be the respondents; where specific administrative acts are performed by organizations entrusted by administrative authorities, the administrative authorities which entrust such organizations shall be the respondents. One example of "organization" as defendant may be the health and antiepidemic stations or food hygiene and inspection offices at the county level or above, which are not government administrative organs but are administered by the health authorities. See arts. 31 & 33, Food Hygiene Law of the PRC adopted on Nov. 19, 1982 and effective from Jul. 1, 1983.

40. Art. 50, GPCL.

41. It is, however, not clear whether an "organization" which does not qualify as a legal person may be sued in its own name in administrative litigations. The provisions of the Administrative Litigation Law may be interpreted as to give such "organization" the status as defendant in such litigation.

several theories to reveal the nature of legal personality.[42] Traditionally, "fiction theory" regards a legal person as an entity created by proper authority, but "association theory" characterizes corporate personality as an association of shareholders. Moreover, while "realistic theory" sees the legal personality as the legal recognition of group interests which as a practical matter already exist, a new theory has recently taken the lead in reinterpreting corporate personality in the light of the corporate group (or enterprise).[43]

In China, the GPCL basically defines a legal person as an "organisation" (*zuzhi*).[44] Attempts have been made by Chinese lawyers to explain the organizational features of legal person. For example, it is suggested that a legal person as an organization shall have its unity and entirety.[45] Moreover, it is generally agreed that a legal person must have a relatively fixed organizational structure; it must have formal patterns through which various internal units or persons are integrated; and it must have express rules concerning the ways, objectives and coverage of its activities.[46] In addition, a legal person may act in its own name in external activities, including initiating and defending legal proceedings.[47]

The GPCL itself, however, does not contain any express rules regarding the ways through which a legal person operates. In academic discussions, it is widely believed that a legal person has its own "mind". The prevailing theory in China concerning the mind of a legal person is the "organ theory".[48] According to this theory,

42. For a brief summary of the vast West literature, see, e.g., Harry H. Henn & John R. Alexander, *Laws of Corporations*, 144-7 (3rd ed. 1983). Also see Phillip I. Blumberg, "The Corporate Personality in American Law: A Summary Review," 38 *Am. J. Comp. L.* 49-69 (Supplement 1990).

43. See Blumberg, id.

44. Art. 36. In China, the identity of legal persons can be so confusing that individuals (managers, directors, etc.) are frequently regarded by laymen as legal persons. Therefore, e.g., Zhuhai Special Economic Zone Daily has to explain "whether or not village heads and accountants are legal persons". For an extract of this explanation (presumably selected as an instructive explanation), see *Baokan Wenzhai* (Digest of Newspapers and Periodicals), Feb. 11, 1992, at 2-3.

45. See Wang Jiafu (ed.), *Jingjifa* (Economic Law), at 33 (1988).

46. Id. Also see Tong Rou (ed.), *Minfa Zongze* (General Rules of Civil Law), at 51 (1990).

47. The GPCL, in art. 37, does not expressly make it a condition that a legal person must be able to be plaintiff and defendant in the court. Nor does art. 36 of the GPCL defines a legal person in this way. This absence also contrasts with the academic discussion of legal person in the 1950s (supra n.7) and the Enterprise Regulation of 1983 (supra n.21). In fact, recent Chinese legal practice has shown that a non-legal person entity may also be a plaintiff or defendant in court proceedings. One such example is that a workshop within a state enterprise may sue the enterprise over a contract (*chengbao* contract) by which the liabilities and interests of both parties are ascertained in advance. For a discussion of such developments, see Gu Peidong, "Zhongguo Xianshi Jingji Chongtu Jiqi Susong Jizhi de Wanshan (Current Economic Conflicts and the Perfection of Litigation Mechanisms in China)," in *Zhongguo Shehui Kexue* (Social Sciences in China), at 211-23 (No. 1, 1990).

48. A theory contrasting to the organ theory is the "agency theory". According

apart from acting through its agents, a legal person can enjoy legal rights and execute legal acts through its organ. Here the "organ" (*jiguan*) means "either an individual or a collective body that, in accordance with the law or the articles of association, is able to represent the legal person in its external relations when engaging in business operations."[49] The acts of managing organ are invariably seen as the acts of the legal person, as the organ represents the mind of the legal person.[50] At the heart of the organ theory is the concept of the "legal representative," defined as the person with responsibility who in accordance with law or the provision of the articles of association exercises authority on behalf of a legal person.[51] A legal person is unconditionally bound by the acts performed by its legal representative within its business capacity.[52]

At first sight, the organ theory seems to suggest that legal personality is "real," as a legal person has a "mind." That assumption, however, is far from true. In fact, most leading civil lawyers in China take the view that corporate personality is "created" by law, and is therefore merely a "legal fiction" (*falü nizhi*).[53] The mind of the legal person is just a metaphor, not a reality.

The most effective weapon widely used by Chinese lawyers for defending the artificial nature of legal personality is their firm belief that every legal person must have limited capacity.[54] Indeed, Chinese law has developed a very strict limited capacity rule regarding enterprise legal persons. For example, enterprise legal persons must have clearly stated objectives, approved by the government departments responsible for enterprise legal person registration.[55] While it

---

to the latter, the legal person being a legal creature does not have its own mind or capacity to act, therefore its activities have to be carried through its agents such as its directors. However, the agency theory has no support in Chinese law.

49. See Tong Rou (ed.), supra n.46, at 163.

50. Id. at 161.

51. Art. 38, GPCL. The concept of "legal representative" (*fading daibiaoren*) was developed from the term "responsible person" (*fuzeren*) as used in the Measures of 1950 (see supra n.5). In practice, the legal representative may be the director, the manager, the chairman of the board of the directors, or the general manager. In some cases, legal representatives may be other persons in charge of legal persons. See the explanation made by the Supreme People's Court, in Henry Zheng, *China's Civil and Commercial Law*, (1988), at 312. According to art. 38 of the GPCL, the status of legal representative enables an appropriate person to represent a legal person in its external relations, in such matters as signing contracts and initiating and defending court proceedings on behalf of an enterprise.

52. Art. 43, GPCL. A legal representative is therefore not an agent for the enterprise.

53. See Wang Jiafu, supra n.45, at 32; Tong Rou (ed.), supra n.46, at 146. Also see Liang Huixing, *Minfa* (Civil Law), at 105 (1988).

54. See Tong Rou (ed.), supra n.46, at 157-62; Liang, supra n.53, at 105.

55. See the Regulations Concerning the Administration of Registration of Legal Persons (hereafter "Registration Regulations"), promulgated by the State Council on Jun. 3, 1988. For the text in English, see *China L. and Prac.* 33-41 (No. 7, 1988). Also see the Implementing Rules for the Regulations Concerning the administration of Registration of Legal Persons (hereafter "Registration Implementing Rules"),

is viable for a company established in some Western jurisdictions to have the same capacity as that of a natural person,[56] in China, the proposition that a legal person may be founded for unlimited purposes or unlimited capacity remains an impossibility.[57] In fact, an enterprise applying for more than one major business objective is certain to end with the disapproval of its application for enterprise legal person registration.[58]

The fictional nature of legal personality is also widely believed to have been reinforced by the compulsory requirement that a legal person must be established in accordance with the law.[59] An organization which meets all the requirements of a legal person as provided by the GPCL is not necessarily a legal person. Unlike a natural person, who is born with legal personality, enterprises are not legal persons until the completion of registration with the relevant government authority.[60] The legal personality of enterprises only comes into existence when a business license is issued.[61] Before it obtains a business license, an organization is not allowed to engage in business operations.[62] Otherwise it is vulnerable to sanctions.[63]

The fiction theory of legal personality, however, is likely to create problems concerning liabilities arising from the activities per-

---

promulgated by the State Administrative Bureau for Industry and Commerce on Nov. 3, 1988. For the text in English, see id. 29-53 (No. 3, 1989).

There are four levels of such bureaux: national, provincial, city (prefectural), and county.

56. This is especially true in many common law countries where the ultra vires doctrine has been effectively abolished.

The abolition of the ultra vires doctrine not only brings greater freedom for companies themselves, but also puts third parties dealing with the companies in a better position for seeking legal protection in, e.g., enforcing ultra vires contracts. This contrasts to most civil law countries where, although not having the tradition of the ultra vires doctrine, less favourable protection is now provided to third parties who knew or should have shown the limits on the capacity of companies they are dealing with. For a comparative study, see my paper, "Gongsifa Zhong de Yuequan Yuanze Jiqi Gaige (The Ultra Vires Doctrine and Its Reform in Company Law)," in *Faxue Yanjiu*, 61-7 (No. 4, 1991).

57. In Chinese law, an enterprise must have strictly stated "business coverage" (*jingying fanwei*) and specific "business pattern" (*jingying fangshi*) which means the way through which the approved businesses are to be carried out. For example, an enterprise engaged in retailing business is not allowed to do wholesale business. The acts which are not consistent with either the business coverage or the business pattern are void.

58. In July 1989, the State Administrative Bureau for Industry and Commerce issued the Circular Concerning Several Issues Regarding Approving Business Capacity (see the text in Chinese, in *Zhonghua Renmin Gongheguo Gongsi Fagui Huibian* (Collection of PRC Company Laws and Regulations, at 199-201 (1991).) Par. 3 provides that an enterprise may have one main business and several other collateral businesses, but not vice versa.

59. Arts. 36 & 37, GPCL.

60. See art. 3, Registration Regulations, supra n.59.

61. Id.

62. Id.

63. See art. 66, Registration Implementing Rules supra n.59. An organization engaging in business before registration may be fined up to 20,000 Renminbi Yuan.

formed by its managing organ. It is stipulated by law that a legal person must act within the limits of its business capacity.[64] But in practice, the organ as an independent body may perform illegal acts that may be either within or outside the business capacity of the legal person. It appears that a strict application of the fiction theory of legal personality would suggest that only lawful acts performed by the organ of a legal person might be attributable to the legal person having limited capacity. Indeed, in the early 1980s, it was held by some leading Chinese lawyers that illegal contracts signed by the organ in the name of the legal person (including those ultra vires contracts signed with third parties who knew or ought to have known the ultra vires nature of the contracts concerned) "do not have any legal effect against the legal person that is entitled to refuse to accept any liability".[65] But other scholars seemed to adopt cautious approach. They attempted to make distinctions between illegal acts conducted within the business capacity and those outside. Therefore, while a legal person should be responsible for illegal contracts concluded within its business capacity, it should not be responsible for illegal contracts signed outside its business capacity.[66] However, the GPCL of 1986 rejected both theories. This is because, the GPCL assumes that a legal person should be unconditionally responsible for the business activities of its legal representative and other personnel.[67] Moreover, the GPCL holds a legal person, as well as its legal representative responsible for illegal activities conducted outside its approved business capacity.[68] Consequently, a legal person is responsible for various illegal civil acts, regardless of whether they are intra vires or ultra vires.

The imposition on legal persons of liability for illegal acts appears to suggest that a legal person represented by its organ is able to conduct illegal acts. However, this is only true when and if such acts are within the capacity of the legal person. This is only those acts that are performed by the legal representatives or the "organ" and fall within the business capacity of a legal person are attributable to the legal person. Furthermore, the liability for illegal operations outside the business capacity of the legal person is imposed not on the presumption of the validity of the said acts, but on the belief

64. Art. 42, GPCL.

65. See Tong Rou (ed.), *Minfa Yuanli*, supra n.17, at 63. Also see Jones, *Basic Principles of Civil Law in China*, supra n.17, at 73.

66. See Li Zuotang & others, *Minfa Jiaocheng* (Textbook on Civil law), at 66 (1982).

67. Art. 43. This article has also been interpreted as actually holding legal persons liable for torts performed by its legal representatives and other personnel in the course of business activities. See Tong Rou, supra n.46, at 162. Indeed, many other articles of the GPCL also provide for the tort liability of legal persons. See, e.g., arts. 106, 121-6.

68. See art. 49, par. 1, GPCL.

that these acts are absolutely void simply for the lack of capacity.[69] In other words, the "mind" of the legal person is always restricted by its business capacity.

Therefore, there appears to be a contradiction between the limited capacity rule and liability for acts outside this capacity. A legal person is *not able to* perform illegal acts but is nevertheless made liable for many illegal acts performed in its name. As a matter of fact, this contradiction has to be resolved by reference to policy considerations. On the one hand, the limited capacity of the legal person is underlined by the state policy of controlling various enterprises. First, this is evidenced by the strict rule in approving the business capacity by relevant government authorities, as discussed above. Secondly, it is provided by law that failing to act within the limits of its capacity may cause not only civil liabilities,[70] but also administrative and criminal liabilities for the legal representatives of the legal persons.[71] In particular, the administrative accountability is the most significant sanction. Government authorities responsible for the registration of enterprise legal persons are more than registration agencies. They are also empowered to supervise the operation of all enterprises.[72] In addition, these government authorities may impose sanctions on enterprise legal persons. For example, if a contract signed by an enterprise legal person falls outside its approved business capacity, then the registration authority may have a number of options available for penalizing the enterprise. These options include: warning, fines, confiscation of unlawful earnings, stopping or rectifying business activities, and withholding or withdrawing the business license.[73] Therefore, in addition to its legal bearing, the limited capacity rule also has administrative implications. Accordingly, it appears that it is highly unlikely for this rule to be relaxed, unless a free market is to prevail in China. In other words, the limited capacity rule, which operates to defend the fictional nature of legal personality, will continue to

69. See Tong Rou (ed.), supra n.46, at 160. It should be noted that in Chinese law there is no explicit provision to this effect. In fact, the voidness of such activities may only be deduced from relevant legal provisions. Art. 42 of the GPCL provides that "an enterprise legal person must conduct business within its registered scope of business". And art. 58 of the GPCL, which is concerned with civil acts provides that acts that violate the law are void. Therefore, it may be inferred that the acts of an enterprise legal person conducting activities outside its business capacity are void because these activities violate art. 42 of the GPCL.

For a report on a case involving a problem of ultra vires and void contracts, see *China L. and Prac.* 17-8 (No. 1, 1992).

70. See art. 49, GPCL; art. 30, Registration Regulations, supra n.55. Also see the discussion below.

71. Id.

72. See art. 62, Registration Regulations, supra n.55.

73. See art. 30, id.

function as long as the state policy of controlling enterprises is sustained.

On the other hand, if a legal person were to be allowed to rely on the fiction theory and freely reject liabilities arising from illegal activities performed by their legal representatives and other personnel, it is innocent third parties who would suffer most. Accordingly, in order to protect third parties and constrain the operation of legal persons, the law has chosen to hold a legal person responsible for all illegal operations performed in its name. This policy is especially exemplified by the bold legal declaration that a legal person should be responsible for the business operations of not only its legal representatives but also "other personnel". In particular, the liability for "other personnel"[74] is believed to be based on two factors: first, a legal person bears a duty of care and supervision towards its personnel; and secondly, a legal person is under a duty not to harm third parties.[75] Indeed, it is these policy factors that have advanced Chinese jurisprudence concerning the liability of legal persons, especially for activities outside their business capacity, despite the fact that they do not have the capacity to perform such activities. In essence, the imposition of civil liability does not break the limited capacity rule, and this development may still be reconciled with the fiction theory of legal personality. In some cases, legal persons bear vicarious liability. But in other cases, legal persons' liabilities are not vicarious. This is mainly because the acts that are performed by the legal representatives as the organ and within their business capacity are deemed to be the managing acts of the legal persons concerned.

As such, Chinese civil law in principle insists upon the traditional fictional view of corporate personality. Furthermore, as Chinese state enterprises—the principal subjects possessing legal personality—are in fact "one man enterprises", that is, wholly owned by the state, the associational feature of legal persons is not very apparent.[76] As will be discussed later, to some extent, it may

74. The GPCL does not clarify the precise meaning of "other personnel". In Chinese legal circles, two different theories are presented. One theory argues that "other personnel" refer to members other than the legal representative within the legal person, but others seem to adopt restrictive interpretation by limiting "other personnel" to those members of the legal person's organ, who are not the legal representative but who are nevertheless able to represent the legal person in its external business activities. See Tong Rou, supra n.46, at 164. However, it seems that while the latter theory is appropriate in, e.g., assuming contractual liabilities for the legal persons (as the conclusion of contracts always requires definite authority, preferably member of the organs), this theory may still appear too strict in the case of torts liability, as ordinary members of the legal person, in performing their duties (not necessarily their authority), may also damage the interests of third parties.

75. See Tong Rou, supra n.46, at 165.

76. This must be subject to qualification that limited companies may have to be associated, as Chinese law does not accommodate the one-man company. See Tong

be possible to argue for the enterprise (corporate group) theory in the light of "independent liability" of legal persons. But it seems certain that the realist theory of corporate personality receives little support in Chinese civil law.

The fiction theory may have profound effects on the legal treatment of legal persons. One such example concerns personality rights. Traditionally, socialist civil law tended to deny compensation for non-property damages. This was mainly due to the fear that such compensation might encourage the commercialization of personality and to the practical difficulty of assessing such damages. The GPCL, however, does offer legal protection of personality rights to both natural and legal persons. While compensation may be claimed by individuals in respect of a limited number of personality rights,[77] legal persons are also entitled to certain personality rights.[78] However, although most Chinese lawyers seem to agree that the GPCL provision may be used by individuals to claim non-property damages, it is debatable as to whether a legal person as legal fiction can claim non-property relief. Some lawyers maintain that non-property damages may only be awarded to persons who are capable of physical and mental activities, thus denying the possibility of compensation of non-property damages for legal persons.[79] But others contend that legal persons are also entitled to non-property damages, as they have their special mind and mental activities.[80] In Chinese legal practice, compensation for non-property damages seems to have received mixed reactions. While one local court is quoted as having awarded relief to non-property claims to a legal person whose name was abused,[81] the PRC Supreme People's Court seems to hold firmly that non-property claims concerning, for example, the damages of legal persons' reputations, shall not be supported.[82] This division of views reflects the different understandings of the nature of legal personality. In the future, it seems that it is highly unlikely, if at all possible, that Chinese law will allow legal

Rou, supra n.46, at 150. For the different treatment of "companies" and general "enterprises", see infra n.162 and discussion below concerning the independent liability of legal persons. In fact, the Provisional Regulations Concerning Private Enterprises (1988, infra n.111) require that a limited liability company must have at least two members.

77. Art. 120, par. 1. Personality rights refer to rights of name, picture, reputation and honor. Many other personality rights, such as privacy, are not protected in Chinese law.

78. Art. 120, par. 2. The coverage is name, reputation and honor.

79. See, e.g., Peng Wangming, "Jingshen Sunhai Ji Shu'e Chutan (Preliminary Discussion on Non-Property Damages and the Assessment of Damages)," in *Faxue Pinglun* (Law Review), 67-9 (No. 2, 1988).

80. See, e.g., Guan Jinhua, "Faren Rengequan Jiqi Sunhai Peichang (Corporate Personality and Its Compensation for Damages)," in *Faxue Yanjiu*, 45-49 (No. 6, 1991).

81. Id. That local court is seated in Fujian Province of Southern China.

82. See id.

persons to claim non-property damages if legal personality continues to be characterized as fictional nature.

B. *Nature of Legal Personality: The Criminal Law Perspective*

Legal person crimes have been recognized in a number of jurisdictions, including both civil and common law countries.[83] In China, since the mid-1980s, the criminal liability of legal persons has experienced a revolution that has again brought a need as well as an opportunity to examine the nature of legal personality.

The PRC Criminal Law, being adopted in 1979, did not use the concept of legal person. But this Law can be interpreted as indicating that crimes may be committed by enterprises and other organizations. For example, article 127 of the Criminal Law provides:

> where an industrial enterprise violates the law and regulation on trademark administration and counterfeits the registered trademark of another enterprise, the person directly responsible shall be sentenced to fixed-term imprisonment of not more than three years, criminal detention or a fine.

But since the criminal liability under this provision is to be attached to natural persons, it is arguable whether such a crime is in nature committed by natural persons or enterprises themselves. In fact, no Chinese enterprise is known to have been prosecuted under this provision.

Indeed, the criminal liability of enterprises as legal persons has for nearly ten years been a very controversial subject in China. In the mid-1980s, fierce debates went on between proponents and opponents of the idea of legal person crimes.[84] During the debates, many basic issues concerning criminology were raised. They included the application and aims of punishments. For example, physical punishments are obviously not applicable to legal persons as organizations. Moreover, there was disagreement among Chinese lawyers as to whether the imposition of criminal liability on legal persons might accomplish the aim of criminal penalty, that is, to educate "responsible persons" and prevent them from committing further crimes. However, throughout the debates, a fundamental question asked by most participants was whether legal persons were capable of having

---

83. For example, English law has since 1944 been willing to attach criminal liability to companies as legal persons. For a specific discussion, see L.H. Leigh, *The Criminal Liability of Corporations in English Law* (1969). For an examination of American corporate crimes in the legal and social policy context, see F.T. Cullen, W.J. Maakestad & G. Cavender, *Corporate Crime Under Attack—The Ford Pinto Case and Beyond* (1987), especially, Chapter 3, "Corporate Criminal Liability: An Historical Review".

84. For a summary of different views, see Gao Minxuan (ed.), *Xin Zhongguo Xingfaxue Yanjiu Zongshu* (Summary of Research on Criminal Law in the PRC), at 192-215 (1986).

criminal intent and committing crimes. Obviously, different perceptions concerning legal personality would lead to different answers on this central issue.

Proponents of legal person crimes held that a legal person was a "realistic" entity and it therefore, like natural persons, was capable of committing crimes. They contended that, since a legal person had its independent legal personality and "organs" as its mind, actions taken by the organ and other responsible persons in the name and for the benefits of the legal person should be treated as crimes committed by the legal person itself.[85]

Opponents, however, sought to draw a distinction between actions taken by legal persons and actions conducted by natural persons. They argued that legal personality was not realistic but fictional in nature, and that the capacity of legal person was always restricted.[86] A legal person did not have the ability to perform crimes, which were illegal in nature and outside the scope of its capacity. Accordingly, although crimes might be committed in the name of a legal person, they should only be attributable to its legal representatives and other responsible persons.[87] In a word, a legal person should never be responsible for crimes, whatsoever, committed in its name.[88]

As such, the debates regarding the criminal liability of legal persons seem to raise the possibility of choice: if legal personality was realistic, then a legal person itself, with its organ acting as its "head" and "mind", should be able to commit crimes. On the other hand, if a legal person was purely artificial, then it lacked the capacity in the first place to commit any crime.

The confusion continued to grow in the mid-1980s. As a result, the GPCL of 1986 attempted a compromise. Although the GPCL seemed to admit that a legal person might commit crimes,[89] it merely intended to impose punishment on their legal representatives,[90] leaving unanswered the issue of criminal liability of the legal person *per se*.

Despite the confusion, however, the Customs Law, adopted on June 22, 1987, made a significant move in the direct of recognising

85. See Chen Guanjun, "Lun Faren Fanzui de Jige Wenti (Several Issues Concerning Legal Person Crimes," in *Zhongguo Faxue* (Laws in China), at 7 (No. 6, 1986).

86. See Gao Minxuan & Jiang Wei, "Guanyu 'Faren Fanzui' de Ruogan Wenti (Several Issues Concerning 'Legal Person Crimes')." Id., at 17.

87. Id.

88. Id. Also see Ji Susheng, "Qianxi Woguo 'Faren Fanzui Xingwei' (Preliminary Discussion on 'Legal Person Criminal Acts in China')," in *Zhongguo Faxue*, at 33 (No. 4, 1990). Ji argued that socialist legal persons should not conduct illegal acts.

89. GPCL, arts. 49 & 110.

90. For a definition, see supra n.51.

legal person crimes in China. Article 47 of the Customs Law provides,

> if enterprises, non-business institutions, official organs and social organizations commit smuggling, judiciary organs shall investigate the criminal liability of their chargers and direct wrongdoers in accordance with the law; the committed unit shall be fined, the smuggled goods and products, tools for smuggling and illegal gains shall be expropriated.

Although the Customs Law did not expressly employ the concept of legal person, it may be presumed that this concept is implied, as most enterprises, non-business institutions, official organs and social organisations are in fact legal persons.

Following the adoption of the Customs Law, there have been an increasing number of laws, regulations, and judicial explanations that specify legal person crimes.[91] For example, the Standing Committee of the National People's Congress on January 21, 1988 adopted "Supplementary Provisions Concerning Punishing Smuggling Crimes" and "Supplementary Provisions Concerning Punishing Corruption and Bribery", both of which contain express provisions as to the punishment of legal persons committing crimes.[92] As a result, it appears settled that in Chinese law a legal person *per se* may be made a defendant in criminal prosecutions. And in such cases, not only the legal representatives and connected persons of the legal person but also the legal person itself shall be investigated as to possible criminal liability.

This new development, however, does not automatically resolve the controversy concerning the nature of legal personality. This is because relevant legal stipulations have not explicitly answered whether or not a legal person *can* commit crimes. Nor has consensus been achieved among Chinese lawyers that legal person is capable of committing crimes. Although it is widely accepted that the civil liability of legal persons may be assumed to be vicarious, the vicarious nature of criminal liability may be strongly criticized as contradicting the basic principle of criminal law that one should only be responsible for what one has actually done. In fact, this issue was repeatedly raised by the opponents of the notion of legal person crimes.[93] Therefore, the logical precondition to the positive ac-

91. According to one estimate, this number as over 40. See He Bingsong, "Faren Xingshi Zeren de Shijiexing Fazhan Qushi (The World Tendency of the Development of Criminal Liability of Legal Persons)," in *Zhengfa Luntan* (Tribune of Political Science and Law), at 7 (No. 5, 1991).

92. Art. 5 of the Smuggling Provisions, in *Quanguo Renmin Daibiao Dahui Changwu Weiyuanhui Gongbao* (Bulletin of the Standing Committee of the National People's Congress), at 21-4, (No. 1, 1988). Also see arts. 6 and 9 of the Corruption and Bribery Provisions, id. at 25-7. The punishments of legal persons are represented by *fajin* (fines) and confiscation of illegally obtained property.

93. See, e.g., Jie, supra n.88.

knowledgment of legal person crime would seem to be that the crime for which a legal person is responsible was actually committed by the legal person itself. Fundamentally, this presumption would seem totally to reverse the fiction theory of legal personality. This may, however, be unacceptable, not only to some Chinese criminal lawyers but also certainly to most civil lawyers.

In fact, one has to look at the underlying decisive factor that had prompted the legal recognition of legal person crimes. This factor is the policy consideration relating to the crackdown on serious economic crimes committed in the name of legal person. Since the Chinese economic reforms have provided opportunities for legal persons to participate in social and economic activities, they may improperly exploit such opportunities and commit crimes, especially economic crimes. And it is mainly owing to the serious nature of widespread economic crimes committed in the name of enterprise legal persons that the Chinese authorities have decided to take a pragmatic approach by introducing criminal liability for legal persons.

One obvious example is the example of the crime of smuggling, which was the first example of liability for legal persons in Chinese law. In 1985, the number of smuggling cases alleged by the PRC Customs to have been committed in the name of legal persons and organizations amounted to more than 2,000—double the number in 1984.[94] Although this amounted to only ten percent of the total number of cases investigated by the Customs in 1985, the value of the goods smuggled accounted for more than ninety percent of the total value of all smuggled goods in such cases for the year.[95] It was clear that legal persons, being enterprises and organizations, possessing more economic capacity than individuals, were more likely to commit economic crimes of serious nature. And it was for such serious matters that legal persons, together with other organizations, were made accountable for smuggling in 1987 by the Customs Law. Moreover, criminal liability was imposed on legal persons despite the widely accepted notion that smuggling as a crime necessarily requires the proof of criminal's "direct intent" (*zhijie guyi*) to smuggle.[96] In fact, similar policy considerations can also be found for the legal recognition of other crimes such as bribery which is frequently resorted in the new era of economic reforms and which is often carried out in the "name" of a legal person.

94. See Liu Baibi & Lin Yongsheng, *Jingji Xingfaxue* (Economic Criminal Law), at 211 (1989).

95. Id.

96. In other words, a person who "smuggles" as a result of "negligence" (*guoshi*) cannot be presecuted as a smuggler. See Gao Mingxuan (ed.), *Xingfaxue* (Criminal Law), at 389 (1982). Also see Zhang Qiang (ed.), *Zhongguo Jingji Fanzui Zuixing Lun* (Crimes and Punishment for Economic Crimes in the PRC), at 29 (1989).

As a result of underlying policy considerations, legal person crimes in China have come into being almost exclusively through special provisions in special legal documents. The Criminal Law of 1979 has not been amended to acknowledge the notion of legal person crimes.[97] As a result, orthodox criminology, which only assumes the criminal accountability of natural persons, still occupies a leading position. It follows that legal persons may not be prosecuted for crimes that are not yet explicitly recognised by special laws and regulations as applicable to legal persons. For example, the issue of whether or not a legal person can be prosecuted for murder and manslaughter is very likely to be answered in the negative in Chinese law.[98] As such, although some lawyers insist that legal persons as realistic entity are able to commit crimes,[99] many eminant criminal lawyers are far from convinced that legal persons themselves can be said to have the "mind" of criminal intent.[100]

It seems, therefore, that although problem of the pragmatic attitude has been adopted in admitting legal person crimes, Chinese law has failed to provide a clear and definite answer to the criminal capability of legal persons. Underlying policy considerations have in fact succeeded in forcing legal recognition of legal person crimes. But this has been done without a serious commitment to clarify the nature of corporate personality. As a result, considerable confusion still continues to exist in the interpretation and further development of criminal liability of legal persons.

III. Legal Personality: Absolute or Relative?

In discussing the essence and functions of the legal person concept, many Chinese lawyers and policy-makers prefer not to get entangled in the complicated theories concerning legal personality. Instead, they tend to put emphasis on the independence of legal persons. Such emphasis has been particularly underlined by the fact

97. Some Chinese scholars have advocated general rules to deal with legal person crimes. One way to do it is to amend the Criminal Law to acknowledge legal person crimes. And the other way is to consolidate into special law existing provisions concerning legal person crimes. For a discussion of different methods and their merits, see, e.g., Li Mingliang, "Faren Fanzui Lifa Fangshi Zhi Wojian (My Opinion on the Legislation Concerning Legal Person Crimes)," in *Xiandai Faxue* (Modern Legal Science), 61-2 (No. 2, 1991).

98. Such crimes can be prosecuted in many common law countries. See Leigh, supra n.83, at 51-2.

99. See Liu & Lin, supra n.94.

100. See Gao, supra n.84. Also see Zhao Bingzhi, "Guanyu Faren Buying Chengwei Fanzui Zhuti de Sikao (Some Considerations about that Legal Persons Should Not Be the Criminals)," in *Faxue Yanjiu*, at 56-62 (No. 5, 1989). Zhao particularly argues that since the Criminal Law as a basic law was adopted by the National People's Congress (NPC)—the highest legislative body in China, it should have the authority to override those laws and regulations recognising legal person crimes that have been merely adopted by the Standing Committee of the NPC and other bodies (e.g., the Supreme People's Court).

that, as revealed earlier, the notion of "legal person" was primarily introduced to facilitate the self-management and self-responsibility of state enterprises. Obviously, in order to carry out self-management, state enterprises, and indeed all enterprises, must be guaranteed sufficient independence. By "independence", Chinese lawyers usually refer to two main aspects: independent liability and independent property.[101] Indeed, in the Chinese case, such independence must be regarded as a principal test for assessing the achievements reached in adopting the legal person concept. Is this independence, derived from legal personality, absolute or just relative?

A. *Legal Personality and Property Rights*

1. Defining Property Rights for Different Enterprises: Towards Legal Person Ownership?

As required by the GPCL, "necessary property or funds" is an essential condition for the acquisition of the legal person status.[102] As far as enterprises are concerned, the minimum amounts of the property or funds as required by relevant laws and regulations for registration purpose are the same for all enterprises of the same trade.[103] A fundamental distinction, however, exists in respect to the nature of property rights. In the West, a judge could conclude without hesitation that "the capital is the property of the corporation".[104] Moreover, it is widely believed among Western lawyers that the property of a company differs from the property of its members and investors, and that the company is the legal owner of its property.[105] But in China, the issue of property ownership is particularly sensitive.[106] In fact, Chinese law has shown a strong reluc-

101. See generally Editorial Department of "Studies in Law," *Xinzhongguo Minfaxue Yanjiu Zongshu* (Summary of Researches in Civil Law in the PRC), at 121 (1990).

102. Art. 37.

103. See art. 15 of the Rules for Implementing the Regulations Concerning the Administration of Registration of Enterprise Legal Persons adopted by the State Administrative Bureau for Industry and Commerce on Nov. 3, 1988. According to this provision, for example, the registered capital of production companies may not be less than Renminbi 30,000; the registered capital for commercial companies which are mainly engaged in wholesaling may not be less than Renminbi 500,000.

104. Per Lord Wrenbury, in Brandery v. English Sewing Cotton Co. Ltd. (1923) A.C. 744, at 767.

105. See Henn & Alexander, supra n.42, at 146.

106. For a general discussion, see Howard Chao & Yang Xiaoping, "The Reform of the Chinese System of Enterprise Ownership," 23 *Stan. J. Int'l L.* 365-97 (1987); Wang Liming & Liu Zhaonian, "On the Property Rights System of the State Enterprises in China," 52 *L. and Contemp. Prob.*, 19-42 (1989); Edward Epstein, "The Theoretical System of Property Rights in China's General Principles of Civil Law: Theoretical Controversy in the Drafting Process and Beyond," 52 *L. and Contemp. Prob.* 177-216 (1989); Paul Cantor & James Kraus, "Changing Patterns of Ownership Rights in the People's Republic of China: A Legal and Economic Analysis in the

tance to make unified and clear declaration as to the property ownership of various enterprise legal persons.[107] Instead, existing laws and regulations, by maintaining that different types of legal persons shall have different property rights, have created chaos and confusion.

Property rights concerning various enterprises as legal persons may be tentatively summarized as follows:

First, a *de facto* two-tier property ownership structure exists in respect of collective enterprise legal persons. A collective enterprise as a legal person enjoys the property ownership right,[108] but the collective which invested in the first place to establish the enterprise is also entitled to ownership rights over the property of the enterprise.[109]

Secondly, the law provides that foreign investment enterprises as legal persons own their property.[110]

Thirdly, as far as private enterprises are concerned, only those which take the form of a limited liability company may obtain legal personality.[111] But the only provision concerning the property rights of private enterprises in Chinese law is that "investors of private enterprises shall enjoy ownership rights in respect of the property of the enterprises".[112]

Fourthly, and as will be examined later, state enterprises are

Context of Economic Reforms and Social Conditions," 23 *Vand. J. of Trans. L.* 479-538 (1990).

107. Such a unified approach seems to have been adopted by the Hong Kong Basic Law, which promises to protect "enterprise ownership right" (*qiye suoyouquan*). See art. 105, par. 3 of the Hong Kong Basic Law, adopted by the National People's Congress on Apr. 4, 1990.

108. Art. 48 of the GPCL provides, inter alia, "collective enterprises as legal persons shall bear civil liability with respect to the property which the enterprises own."

109. See, e.g., the definition of the different meaning of the "collective ownership" in Regulations Concerning the Collective Enterprises in Cities and Towns (adopted by the State Council on Jun. 21, 1991 and effective from Jan. 1, 1992; for the text in Chinese, see *Renmin Ribao*, Sept. 18, 1991, at 2.). Art. 4 states, the collective ownership by the working people may mean one of the following three circumstances: (1) collective ownership by the working people of the enterprise concerned; (2) collective ownership by the working people of the joint economic organisation to which the collective enterprises belong; or (3) collectively owned assets of the working people in above stipulations (1) and (2) should occupy a dominant role (i.e., not lower than 51%).

110. Art. 48, GPCL.

111. See art. 10, Provisional Regulations Concerning Private Enterprises, adopted by the State Council on Jun. 3, 1988 and effective from Jul. 1, 1988. Apart from limited liability companies, a private enterprise may be also run as a sole trader enterprise, or partnership enterprise. However, both these forms are denied legal personality in Chinese law.

112. Id. art. 20. It must be noted that when the GPCL was adopted in 1986, the legality of private enterprises in China was uncertain. Therefore, the GPCL did not provide for the property right of private enterprises. For a discussion on private enterprises, see Alison W. Conner, "To Get Rich Is Precarious: Regulation of Private Enterprise in the People's Republic of China," *J. of Chin. L.* at 1-46 (No. 1, 1991).

exclusively owned by the state, though they may enjoy the right to manage the property which the state has authorized them to manage and administer.[113]

Finally, in regard to companies limited by shares, due to the lack of a Company Law and the absence of express legal provisions, it is not clear whether or not a company limited by shares can enjoy ownership rights over its property. Some scholars maintain that a limited company should have the right of ownership to its property.[114] But others argue that, while a limited company has the ownership right over its property, its shareholders should also be able to enjoy the ownership right.[115] In other words, the property ownership rights in a limited company constitute a two-tier structure. In addition, there are still some who insist that the property of a limited company is owned by its shareholders, and is merely managed by its managers.[116]

The above brief summary suggests that enterprises possessing the same legal personality may not have the same property rights. The notion of corporate personality has therefore failed to provide a unified basis for the property rights of different enterprise legal persons.

In fact, as early as 1981 Chinese lawyers began to advocate "legal person ownership" (*faren suoyouquan*).[117] The essence of this notion was to provide all enterprises possessing corporate personality with property ownership rights. In addition to the argument that legal person ownership would help achieve the aim of enterprise independence, advocates of this notion sought to reinforce their argument by claiming that equity joint ventures, as Chinese legal persons, had already been granted the right of property ownership.[118] The case of Sino-foreign equity joint ventures had at least two implications. First, in spite of the lack of a company law, a legal person taking the form of a limited liability company—the only offi-

113. See Arts. 48 & 82, GPCL.

114. See Guo Feng, "Gufenzhi Qiye Suoyouquan Wenti de Tantao (Discussion of the Issue of Ownership Right of Joint Stock Companies)," in *Zhongguo Faxue*, at 3-13 (No. 3, 1988).

115. See Wang Liming, "Lun Gufenzhi Qiye Suoyouquan de Erchong Jiegou (On the Two-tier Structure of Ownership Rights of Limited Companies)," id. at 47-56 (No. 1, 1989).

116. See Tong Rou & Shi Jichun, "Woguo Quanmin Suoyouzhi 'Liangquan Fenli' de Caichanquan Jiegou (The Property Rights Represented by the Separation of Ownership and Management in Our State Ownership System)," in *Zhongguo Shehui Kexue*, at 159-74 (No. 3, 1990). Although this article focuses on the property right of state enterprises, in order to reinforce their argument the authors also discuss in detail the issue of property rights for limited companies.

117. See, e.g., Liang Huixing, "Lun Qiye Faren Yu Qiye Faren Suoyouquan (On Enterprise Legal Persons and Legal Person Ownership Right)," in *Faxue Yanjiu*, at 26-31 (No. 1, 1981).

118. Id. at 30.

cial form for equity joint ventures[119]—is widely believed by Chinese lawyers to be the sole owner of its property. Secondly, the involvement of state property in Sino-foreign joint ventures does not prevent the joint ventures, as legal persons, from acquiring property ownership. Consequently, some scholars came to the conclusion that it was possible to establish a unified legal person ownership, though the state should be kept as the ultimate owner in the case of the state enterprises.[120]

The idea of legal person ownership achieved partial success. This was illustrated by the legal stipulation that foreign investment enterprises, as legal persons, have full ownership over their property.[121] Moreover, the notion of legal person ownership was also partially reflected in the legal treatment of collective enterprises, which as legal persons are allowed to "share" property ownership with their investors, that is, the collectives. However, the idea of legal person ownership was separately blocked and eventually defeated by the case of state enterprises which, though endowed with legal personality, have been denied property ownership.

2. Management Rights, Legal Personality and Enterprise Autonomy

In the early 1980s, Chinese lawyers as well as economists presented many theories to define the property rights of state enterprises.[122] Generally speaking, those theories can be divided into two categories. One was concerned with the conferment on state enterprises of property ownership. Within this category, there existed two different approaches. One was the radical approach advocating that enterprises should possess full ownership rights over their property.[123] Another approach, which was less radical, was concerned with "relative ownership". This school, which included the idea of "legal person ownership" as discussed above,[124] though encouraging state enterprises to obtain certain property ownership did stress the importance of keeping the state as the ultimate legal owner. As such, a structure of two-tier property ownership rights was meant to be applied.

119. See art. 4 of the Law on Sino-Foreign Equity Joint Ventures. In some areas such as Guangdong, however, other forms of companies such as companies limited by shares may also be used as a result of local legislation. For an examination of such legislation in Guangdong, see Clement Shum, "Companies with Foreign Equity Participation in China," *J. Bus. L.* 185-95 (Mar. 1991).

120. Id. at 30-31. Also see the discussion below.

121. Art. 48, GPCL.

122. For a summary review and comments, see Wang Liming & Liu Zhaonian, "On the Property Rights System of the State Enterprises in China," 52 *L. and Contemp. Prob.* 19-42 (Summer 1989).

123. See id. at 31-2.

124. See Liang Huixing, supra n.117.

The attempt to confer state enterprises with ownership rights, however, proved unacceptable. This was mainly because both approaches were seen as inevitably undermining state ownership. Facing with the unchangeableness of complete state ownership, many scholars looked for compromise in defining the property rights of state enterprises. On the one hand, state enterprises as legal persons would be able to possess certain property right to pursue self-management. On the other hand, the sole state ownership should be carefully preserved.

Different theories were aired to express such a compromise. They included, to mention a few, possession theory, trust theory, and the right of beneficial use theory.[125] However, none of these theories was able to convince the Chinese authorities. Instead, only the theory concerning "the right to manage and administer" (*jingying guanli quan*) finally succeeded. The term, "the right to manage and administer", actually originated in Soviet legislation,[126] and first appeared in Chinese legislation in 1979.[127] Although the use of this term in the early 1980s met some criticism,[128] it nevertheless came to be widely accepted. The reasons for the popularity of this term were several. First, this term was seen by many as being able to give enterprises sufficient legal rights to defend their independence and autonomy. Secondly, this term was acceptable to economists as well as to the public. At least, this term appeared to be more comprehensible to the lay person than "the right to possess", "trust", and "the right of beneficiary use", which were seen by many as pure legal terms. Thirdly, and most importantly, this term, by preserving the state as the legal owner of state enterprises, avoided any direct damage to the state ownership. Therefore, it proved acceptable to the Chinese authorities.

In the mid 1980s, "the right to manage and administer", or alter-

125. See Wang & Liu, supra n.122, 27-31.

126. This term was first suggested by a Soviet jurist, Wynijilatov, in the 1940s, and was then incorporated into Soviet civil legislations in the 1960s. This term was later accepted by many eastern European countries, including Hungary and Czechoslovakia. See Wang & Liu, supra n.122, at 28.

127. On July 13, 1979, the State Council promulgated "Some Provisions Concerning Expanding State Industrial Enterprises' Autonomous Right to Manage and Administer". See the text in Chinese, in *Laws and Regulations of the PRC*, supra n.20, 249-52 (1979).

128. See Jiang Ping and others, "Guojia Yu Guoying Qiye Zhijian de Caichan Guanxi Yingshi Suoyouquan He Jingyingquan de Guanxi (The Property Relationship Between the State and State Enterprises Should Be the Relationship Between the Owner and the Possessors)," *Faxue Yanjiu*, at 6-11 (No. 4, 1980). The main criticisms were: first, the term "administer" (*guanli*) was likely to be misunderstood as an administrative function; secondly, the right to manage and administer was not an independent right. Nor did it reflect the independent interests of enterprises; thirdly, "manage and administer" was an economic term, and not a legal term; finally, "manage and administer" was not only the right but also the duty of enterprises.

natively "the right to manage" (*jingying quan*),[129] was gradually recognised by Chinese legislation. In 1986, the GPCL provided that state enterprises shall lawfully enjoy the right of management over the property that the state has authorized them to manage and administer.[130] Furthermore, the GPCL employs "necessary" (*biyao de*), rather than "own" (*suoyou de*), to describe the independent property of a legal person.[131] It follows that, though many other enterprises as legal persons do have property ownership right, state enterprises do not have to "own" property to become legal persons. Instead, it is sufficient for them to have the right to "manage" the property.

Following the formal recognition in the GPCL of the management right, the most comprehensive approach towards defining this right is contained in the State Enterprise Law of 1988.[132] As a principle, this Law provides that state enterprises have the rights of possession, use, and disposal, in accordance with the law of the property they are authorized by the state to manage and administer.[133] The rights to possess and to use the property coincide with those embodied in property ownership;[134] but the management right does not include the right to "benefit" (*shouyi*), though enterprises are encouraged to make profits. Furthermore, the right to dispose of property is especially qualified by the wording "in accordance with the law".[135] As such, theoretically, the absence of the right to benefit and the strict qualification concerning the right to dispose of state property symbolize the crucial aspects as to which the right of man-

---

129. It seems that a certain confusion exists as to whether these two terms possess the same meaning. In legal contexts, they are sometimes mixed. The law tends to provide that an enterprise has the right to "manage" the property which the state authorizes it to "manage and administer". But some Chinese scholars hold that there are substantial differences between "the right to manage and administer", and "the right to manage". They see that "the right to manage" was used deliberately to counteract the negative effects arising from "the right to manage and administer" which inherited the administrative function of state enterprises and the unequal relationship between enterprises and government departments. See Shi Jichun, "Tong Rou Xianshen de Jingyingquan Sixiang (The Right to Manage In the Mind of By Professor Tong Rou)," *Fazhi Ribao* (Legal Daily), Mar. 4, 1991, at 3. It seems that even the right to manage was not new, as Hungarian law had once adopted this term. See Wang & Liu, supra n.122, at 28.

130. Art. 82.

131. Art. 37.

132. Adopted on Apr. 13, 1988, effective from Aug. 1, 1988. For the text in English, see *China L. and Prac.* 35-50 (No. 5, 1988).

133. Art. 2.

134. The GPCL, in art. 71, lists the main rights embodied in the property ownership rights. They include: the right to possess, use, benefit from and dispose of the property concerned.

135. Thus, art. 29 of the State Enterprise Law provides that enterprises shall be entitled to lease or assign for value in accordance with stipulations of the State Council, fixed assets given to them by the state to operate and manage. Benefits derived from such assets must be used for renewing equipments or improving technology.

agement differs from that of property ownership. In addition, the State Enterprise Law sets out detailed illustrations and limitations of the management right granted to state enterprises. Such rights consist of thirteen different aspects, including production, sale of products, selection of materials, pricing, foreign trade, use of retained funds and disposal of assets.[136]

To some extent, by acquiring legal personality and management, Chinese state enterprises have gained a better position than they used to have. Theoretically speaking, they are no longer unconditionally dependent on the government departments, which should respect the independence and autonomy of state enterprises. In dealing with third parties other than government departments, state enterprises may, like other enterprise legal persons, act independently and autonomously.

Since 1987, the most popular form adopted for implementing the management right is the "contracting" (*chengbao*) system currently carried out by the overwhelming majority of large and medium-sized state enterprises.[137] By signing with the government a contract that usually includes financial and other targets to be fulfilled,[138] state enterprises were expected to obtain management independence. However, practice has shown that considerable difficulties are present in enforcing management rights. On the one hand, many state enterprises led by their directors[139] tend to make the best of the resources available in the enterprises without pooling substantial investments. Consequently, they not only remain indifferent to the accumulation and protection of state property, but also lack the potential for further development. On the other hand, and more disappointingly, various government departments still frequently interfere with enterprise management and brutally infringe the legal interests of enterprises by, for example, illegally appropriating enterprises.[140]

---

136. State Enterprise Law, arts. 22-34. But it should also be noted that many of these rights are qualified by restrictions such as "in accordance with the provisions of the State Council", leaving the State Council and subordinate Ministries with great discretionary powers to withdraw or limit these rights.

137. For a brief introduction of this system, see Wang & Liu, supra n.122, at 39-41. On Feb. 27, 1988, the State Council promulgated the Provisional Regulations Concerning the Contracting System of State Enterprises. Smaller state enterprises may, however, be leased out for management.

138. Id. art. 16.

139. Directors or managers play a very important role in the contracting system. Although it is the enterprises that are contractors, directors nevertheless have independent interests in the sense that the remuneration and rewards for their performance are expressly provided in the contract signed between the enterprises and government authorities. In the event of disputes concerning the contract, directors also have a limited right to bring suits against government authorities.

140. In order to protect enterprises' independent interests, on Apr. 28, 1988, the State Council promulgated the Provisional Regulations Concerning Prohibiting Misappropriation to Enterprises. See the text in *Laws and Regulations of the PRC*,

It has become clear that the ineffective implementation of management rights is inherently due to the fact that state enterprises do not have property ownership rights. Despite the attribution of legal personality to state enterprises, various government departments as the representatives of the state as the legal owner still tend to intervene extensively into the management of state enterprises which simply cannot refuse.[141] Consequently, as far as state enterprises are concerned, legal personality has failed to guarantee their autonomy.[142]

In fact, as far as state enterprises are concerned, legal personality is only able to confer relative independence upon them. The relative autonomy of state enterprises was actually characterized by the Party Decision of 1984[143] as one of the fundamental aims of the economic reforms. Legal personality of state enterprises cannot be absolute, but has to be relative. At least, the legal personality of state enterprises should never be regarded as so unconditional as completely to exclude government supervision and administration of state enterprises. In this sense, the state policy that emphasizes the preservation of state ownership has played a vital role in merely granting relative legal personality to state enterprises.

B. *Independent Liability and "Piercing the Corporate Veil"*

1. Independent Liability

The GPCL employs the notion of "independent liability" to describe the liability feature of all Chinese legal persons. However, within Chinese legal circles, considerable confusion exists as to the exact meaning of this term. In particular, this term has been misunderstood by some as being equivalent to "limited liability".[144] In

supra n.22, 745-9 (1988). Despite this legal document, Chinese enterprises, especially state enterprises, have been reportedly suffering heavily from misappropriations by various government authorities. For a detailed analysis of the difficulty in preventing such appropriation and an legal examination of the difficulty in implementing the state enterprise reform, see Donald Clarke, "What's Law Got to Do with It? Legal Institutions and Economic Reform in China," 10 *UCLA Pacific Basin L.J.* 1-76 (No. 1, Fall 1991).

141. It is theoretically possible for state enterprises to bring suits against government authorities that have infringed the management autonomy of state enterprises. In addition to relying on the contract signed between state enterprises and government authorities, state enterprises may also rely on the provisions of the Administrative Litigation Law (see art. 11). However, as government authorities possess great discretionary powers, a state enterprise which wins a case is very likely to lose far greater interests in the future. This explains why no suit has ever been brought by state enterprises under the provisions of the Administrative Litigation Law.

142. It is also the case that state enterprises have not been effectively made responsible for their operations.

143. See text accompanying supra n.22.

144. An example can be found in the Regulations Concerning Foreign-Related Companies in the Special Economic Zones of the Guangdong Province (adopted on Sept. 28, 1986, effective from Jan. 1, 1987). While art. 3, para. 2 of the Regulations

fact, "independent liability" and "limited liability' differ in their meaning and substance.[145] Fundamentally, "independent liability" is reserved for legal persons, whereas "limited liability" is meant for shareholders of companies. For example, an unlimited company as legal person is able to bear "independent liability", but its shareholders may nevertheless be obliged to bar unlimited liability. Moreover, to hold that a company (legal person) bears limited liability is not only against the law,[146] but also detrimental to the interests of the shareholders.[147]

In an attempt to clarify the meaning of "independent liability", the GPCL defines the scope of civil liability for several types of enterprise legal persons.[148] Therefore, collective enterprises and foreign investment enterprises, if qualified as legal persons, shall be responsible with all the property which they own. But in the case of state enterprises, the extent of their civil liability is the property which the state has authorized them to manage and administer. As such, despite the fact that the state is the sole owner of state enterprises, it is no longer responsible for the debts of the latter. Such limitation of the state's liability contrasts greatly with the situation before the economic reforms, when the state actually bore unlimited liability for state enterprises.

The concept of independent liability is also significant in that organizations which do not have legal personality are not able to bear independent liability. For example, as indicated earlier, not all cooperative joint ventures may qualify as Chinese legal persons. For those that are not legal persons, the liability has to be determined in accordance with relevant contracts or the general law governing partnership.[149]

The notion of independent liability has paved the way for the

---

assumes that "all foreign-related companies in the Special Economic Zones are limited liability companies," art. 149 seems to impose unlimited liability on partners of cooperative joint ventures. For a brief discussion, see Edward J. Epstein, "China and Hong Kong: Law, Ideology and the Future Interaction of the Legal Systems," in Raymons Wacks (ed.), *The Future of the Law in Hong Kong*, 37-75, at 73. Here if art. 2 had been expressed as "all foreign-related companies . . . are companies assuming *independent* liability", then there would not have been such conceptual confusion.

145. See *Farrar's Company Law*, at 67-8 (1988).

146. See art. 48, GPCL. Also see art. 106 of the Implementing Regulations of the Law on Equity Joint Venture, which states that an equity joint venture shall be liable with "all its assets".

147. See *Boyle and Bird's Company Law*, at 49 (1987) ("It is wrong to insert, as has been done, 'The Liability of the Company is Limited'. Such a variation, if passed by the Registrar, might produce results disastrous to the members."). Compare with the misleading expression that "a legal person has limited liability", in Zheng, supra n.51, at 310.

148. See art. 48, GPCL.

149. The GPCL only makes stipulations concerning partnership between natural persons (see arts. 30-35). Therefore the partnership between enterprises may have to be decided by reference to the rules concerning "economic associations" (see arts. 52-3, GPCL).

development of enterprise bankruptcy in Chinese law. For many years following the foundation of the PRC, the concept of bankruptcy was not applicable in China. But in just a few months after the adoption of the GPCL, the Enterprise Bankrupty Law was promulgated.[150] Due to the enormous controversies involved, this law was meant for trial implementation and only applicable to state enterprises.[151] Nevertheless, the newly-adopted Civil Procedure Law[152] contains a chapter (Chapter Nineteen) regarding the "Procedures for the Repayment of Debts Owed by Bankrupt Enterprise Legal Persons". This chapter consists of eight articles containing provisions similar to those stipulated by the Enterprise Bankruptcy Law,[153] and is applicable to all enterprises possessing legal personality other than state enterprises, which are still under the exclusive jurisdiction of the Enterprise Bankruptcy Law.[154]

2. Piercing the Corporate Veil?

In the West, in the early days after the recognition of corporate personality, it was taken for granted that the legal personality of corporations should be preserved in determining their civil liability. Shareholders should not be made accountable, in excess to their promised contribution, for the debt liability of corporations which possessed legal personality. From the early Twentieth Century, however, courts in many jurisdictions have followed the American

150. Adopted on Dec. 2, 1986, effective from Nov. 1, 1988. For an introduction to this Law, see Henry Zheng, "Bankruptcy Law in the People's Republic of China—Principles, Procedure and Practice," 19 *Vand. J. Trans. L.* 683 (1986).

151. For a detailed review of the drafting process of the Chinese Enterprise Bankruptcy Law, see Ta-Kuang Chang, "The Making of the Chinese Bankruptcy Law: A Study of the Chinese Legislative Process," 28 *Harv. Int'l L.J.*, 333-72 (1987).

Many restrictions have been imposed on by this bankruptcy law. For example, state enterprises as debtors have to get the approval form relevant government departments in charge before they are able to file for bankruptcy (see art. 8). In addition, government departments are also entitled to play an important role in the process of reorganisation and liquidation. In addition, due to the grave concern over various issues such as unemployment and social instability, the Enterprise Bankruptcy Law remains far from effectively enforced in China. According to the information provided by the Economic Chamber of the Supreme People's Court, by the end of 1991, the number of bankruptcy cases accepted by courts at local levels was just 252. In 1991, the courts declared bankruptcy on 57 enterprises. For the source of this information, see *Baokan Wenzhai* (Digest of Newspapers and Periodicals), Mar. 24, 1992, at 1. (The report did not indicate whether all these cases were concerned with state enterprises. It is possible that other types of enterprises may have also been involved.)

152. Supra n.32.

153. For example, apart from the absence of the requirement "due to poor management", the test for enterprise bankruptcy as adopted in the Civil Procedure Law (art. 199) is similar to that provided in the Enterprise Bankruptcy Law (art. 3). In addition, the order for the repayment of debts as provided in the Civil Procedure Law (art. 204) is the same as that provided in the Enterprise Bankruptcy Law (art. 37).

154. See art. 206, Civil Procedure Law (1991), supra n.32.

experiences in lifting corporate veil which has been abused. "Piercing the veil" is both possible and desirable when, for example, corporate personality is used for the purpose of fraud or as a means to avoiding legal obligations, or when a legal person is controlled by another legal person in the same group, with the latter being potentially made liable for the former's debts.[155] For some observers, "piercing the veil jurisprudence" has initiated a new enterprise theory concerning corporate personality.[156]

In China, piercing the veil jurisprudence is still largely unknown. In fact, both the Enterprise Bankruptcy Law and the State Enterprise Law[157] have in principle denied any civil liability owed by the state (or government) to a state enterprise or its creditors in case the former's actionable interference led to the latter's bankruptcy. In theory, therefore, enterprise legal persons should only be responsible for their debts to the extent of all the property which they own or "manage".

In practice, however, corporate personality has been lifted at least once. In August 1987, the Supreme People's Court issued an "Opinion" (*pifu*) on the debt liability of enterprises and companies promoted by administrative organs or enterprises.[158] According to this Opinion, while the debts of "enterprises" or "companies" established by administrative units should be first paid out of the property of the enterprises or companies, the part they could not afford to pay had to be made up for by those administrative units that approved and established the enterprises or companies, or that reported the establishment of the enterprises or companies. On the other hand, when a "branch enterprise" (*fenzhi qiye*) was established by an enterprise, if the branch enterprise was actually qualified as a legal person, its debt should be paid with its own independent assets; if the "branch enterprise" was not qualified as a legal person, the enterprise which established the branch enterprise should have joint and several liability with the branch. But if the branch was a "company" (*gongsi*), "*regardless of its being qualified as a legal person or not*," the enterprise that promoted the branch company had to be responsible for making up the debts which the branch company could not afford to pay in full.[159] As such, the Opinion of the Supreme People's Court actually lifted corporate per-

155. For a summary of European Continental law on this issue, see E.J. Cohn & C. Simitis, " 'Lifting the Veil' in the Company Laws of the European Continent," 12 *Int'l and Comp. L.Q.*, 189-225 (1963). For an account of English law, see *Farrar's Company Law*, supra n.145, at 73-81.

156. See Blumberg, supra n.42.

157. Adopted on Apr. 13, 1988 and effective as of Aug. 1, 1988. For an English translation, see *China L. & Prac.*, 35-50 (No. 5, 1988).

158. See *Zhonghua Renmin Gongheguo Zuigao Renmin Fayuan Gongbao* (Bulletin of the Supreme People's Court of the PRC), at 21 (No. 4, 1987).

159. Id.

sonality by asking certain connected entities (including administrative units and "enterprises") that established the bankrupt enterprises and companies in question to be responsible for their debts.

The move towards lifting the corporate veil immediately caused great concern and shock among Chinese lawyers.[160] They argued strongly that as legal persons should bear "independent liability", their corporate veil should not be lifted.[161] As such, they resorted to the notion of independent liability to defend the corporate veil of legal persons.

In fact, one has to look at the general background underlying the move towards lifting the corporate veil. At the time when the Supreme People's Court issued its Opinion, China had just begun to "consolidate" (*zhengdun*) enterprises, especially "companies" formed by administrative organs. This consolidation was a mass movement launched under the guidance of the Party and state policies. Indeed, the Supreme People's Court, in its Opinion, directly cited and referred to those policy documents jointly issued by the State Council and the Central Committee of the Chinese Community Party. Accordingly, these policy documents to a great extent formed the very basis of the Opinion issued by the Supreme People's Court. The Opinion also expressed the intentional differentiated treatment between ordinary "enterprises" (*qiye*) and "companies" (*gongsi*)[162] in the case of enterprises that functioned as their "promoters and sponsors" (*kaiban ren*). The fact that "enterprises" were discriminately held liable to pay up the debts of the "companies" which the enterprises had promoted, regardless of the companies being legal persons or not, can only be explained as a kind of penalty imposed on those enterprises which were keen to establish "companies" in order to make profits.

It is therefore clear that the decision to lift the corporate veil as instructed by the Opinion was taken less on the basis of logical and

160. See, e.g., Lin Yi, "Guanu Qiye Kaiban De Gongsi Daobi Hou Zhaiwu Qingchang Wenti de Jidian Sikao (Some thoughts about the Payment of Debts Sustained by Bankrupt Companies Promoted by Enterprises)," in *Faxue Pinglun*, at 84-88 & 69 (No. 1, 1991).

161. Id.

162. The relationship between "enterprise" and "company" is very controversial in the Chinese context. Generally speaking, except for some "administrative companies" which have both business and administrative functions, "enterprises" are usually understood to include "companies". However, for certain purposes such as registration, "companies" may be put under different legal regime from that governing ordinary "enterprises". In fact, the controversial relationship between "enterprise" and "company" has been one of the major obstacles frustrating the promulgation of company law in China. For the purpose of "consolidating companies", "companies" refered to enterprises whose titles included the term of "company" (*gongsi*), though in fact those companies might belong to neither limited liability companies nor companies limited by shares as prevailing in the West.

legal reasoning than under the guidance of the particular state policy. As a result, the challenge made by Chinese lawyers against this move sounds understandable.

Indeed, as a response to the concerns expressed over the lifting of the corporate veil, on December 21, 1990, the State Council issued a Circular concerning the settlement of debts of abolished or merged companies in the campaign to consolidate companies.[163] This Circular to a considerable extent modified the position set by the Opinion of the Supreme people's Court. It required that companies which met the requirements of a legal person as provided by the GPCL, and "which had dissociated themselves from the Party or government organisations as their promoters and sponsors", should as a rule pay their debts with the property they were authorised by the state to manage or which they owned.[164] As such, the shock caused by the Supreme Court's Opinion was partially redressed. Although it seems that the Circular continued to lift the veil of companies that failed to disconnect themselves from government or Party authorities, it is clear that many other companies whose veil would have been lifted in accordance with the Opinion were eventually relieved by the new state policy as recognised in this Circular.

The campaign to consolidate companies was officially ended in late 1991. But the experience during this campaign clearly demonstrates that corporate personality in China is not so absolute as to be preserved in all circumstances. The corporate veil can be lifted as a result of special state policy. Furthermore, it has also been suggested by some Chinese lawyers that the idea of holding both natural and legal persons behind the veil liable for the debts of subordinate legal persons may be relevant both in domestic civil law[165] and even in foreign investment enterprise law.[166] However, the opposition to the practice of lifting the corporate veil cannot be underestimated. This is not only because some factors such as conceptual confusion are present, but because many Chinese lawyers still tend to overemphasize the function of legal personality in separating enterprises and their investors (shareholders or owners).[167]

---

163. For the text, see *Collection of PRC Company Laws and Regulations*, supra n.58, at 316.

164. Id.

165. It may be necessary to ask holding companies to be responsible for the debts of their subsidiaries. For an discussion, see Wang Baoshu, "Woguo Qiye Lianhe Zhong de Kangcaien Xianxiang Jiqi Falü Duice (On Newly Emerged Concern and Legal Disposition in China)," in *Faxue Yanjiu*, 47 (No. 6, 1990).

166. The corporate veil may be lifted as a matter of reference to "international practice". Consequently, foreign investors may be held liable for the debts of foreign investment enterprises established in China. For a brief mention, see Yao Meizhen (ed.), *Waishang Touzi Qiyefa Jiaocheng* (Textbook on Foreign Investment Enterprise Law), at 67 (1990).

167. One Chinese scholar has this comment on the Western concept of piercing the corporate veil: "considering the (low) standard of our legal system and the (in-

Consequently, it remains to be seen whether piercing the corporate veil jurisprudence will be introduced in Chinese law on legal grounds similar to those already widely accepted in the West.

IV. Conclusion

In Chinese law, legal person, or *faren*, is one of the most notable legal concepts that have been established during the process of economic and legal reforms initiated since the late 1970s.[168] In their treatment of this concept, many Chinese lawyers have tended to idealize its image and functions. In particular, it has been advocated that legal persons shall be definitely independent, that corporate personality shall not be pierced in any circumstances, and that legal persons are not able to commit crimes—and for some observers, not even civil wrongs. Furthermore, some Chinese scholars would simply dismiss those entities that do not possess many of these characteristics of autonomy as not being proper legal persons.[169] However, the idealization of the concept of legal person has met a number of setbacks, which have in turn created contradictions and considerable uncertainty as to the explanation and comprehension of the concept itself.

Fundamentally, Chinese civil law has insisted that a legal person is a legal fiction. But the legal recognition of legal person crimes has posed a serious challenge to the fiction theory of legal personality. Indeed, no consensus has been achieved among Chinese lawyers in explaining legal person crimes within the theories of legal personality.

Independence and autonomy are widely assumed to be inherently attached to all legal persons, but such independence has proved far from absolute in Chinese law. The corporate veil may be lifted. Moreover, legal personality has proved to have apparent limits in providing state enterprises with the very degree of independence and autonomy required for their successful self-management.

In fact, of the various factors that have informed the develop-

---

adequate) professional knowledge of judges, the adoption of this theory or practice (i.e., piercing the corporate veil) is likely to produce considerable discretion and to reduce the positive function of the legal person system". See Shi Jichun, "Woguo Jiben Jiti Jingji Lifa Chuyi (My Humble Opinion on Basic Legislation Concerning Collective Economy in China)," *Zhongguo Faxue*, 33-41, at 39 (No. 2, 1992).

168. Other concepts introduced and established in the past decade in China include bankruptcy and many new terms regarding intellectual property.

169. For example, commenting on state enterprise reform, a prominent law professor takes the view that the failure of state enterprises in effectively and flexibly engaging in their own production as real commodity producers and managers clearly has much to do with the fact that they are not "real legal persons". See Jiang Ping, "Qiye Ying Chengwei Zhenzheng de Faren (Enterprises Shall Become Real Legal Persons)," *Zhongguo Jingji Tizhi Gaige* (China's Economic System Reforms), at 27 (No. 4, 1992).

ments concerning the notion of legal personality in Chinese law, policy considerations are predominant. The establishment of the concept of legal person was driven by state policy of transforming state enterprises into independent and self-governing entities. However, in spite of their possession of the same legal personality, different types of enterprise legal persons may eventually have markedly different features. In particular, while many enterprises do have property ownership rights, state enterprises are prohibited by law from becoming property owners. Instead, they are only granted the right of management. This restriction has significant political and ideological implications, underscored by the preservation of the state ownership of state enterprises. As a result, the notion of legal personality has failed to surmount the fence of property ownership and to form a solid basis for unified legal person ownership. Indeed, as demonstrated in the discussions, the property rights of different enterprise legal persons are still far from clarified and settled in Chinese law.

Many other policy factors are also prominent in advancing the developments relating to legal persons in Chinese law. For example, the practice of "piercing the veil" of certain enterprises and companies as legal persons was solely based on the special state policy of penalizing official organizations that "abusively" established and operated businesses. Similarly, criminal liability of legal persons has been predominantly pushed by the state policy to crack down on economic crimes. In these cases, although underlying policy considerations can effect rapid developments concerning the notion of legal personality, as illustrated in the discussion, such developments may also bring chaos and confusion.

In essence, therefore, the legal person in China is not merely a legal fiction but more of a policy creature. While the written laws do not provide clear and ready answers to many problems concerning the notion and theory of legal personality, the essence of Chinese legal persons has to be, and can be, better understood by taking into consideration various policy factors that have in one way or another underlined and shaped legal persons and corporate personality in China. Failure to consider these factors may lead to an unrealistic hope that the mere adoption of legal concepts such as legal person would bring about fundamental changes to the existing social, economic, and political systems. In fact, as demonstrated in the discussions, the features and functions of newly established concepts such as legal personality are bound to be characterized and conditioned by the existing systems.

The notion of legal personality in Chinese law is not fully developed. Much important legislation—in particular a comprehensive company law[170]—needs to be promulgated in order to place the concept of legal person in a broader spectrum for a more detailed examination. Nevertheless, many basic ideas concerning legal personality have taken shape. Indeed, it is little more than a decade since the concept of legal person was first formally employed in post-Mao legislation. Although this concept has apparent limits and, contrary to the original design, has not greatly benefited state enterprises, it has been accepted and used widely in the context of civil law. In fact, the legal person concept may play an important role in facilitating the establishment and operation and in ascertaining the legal liabilities of various enterprises as well as official organs, institutions and social organizations. Furthermore, the concept of legal person has also had far-reaching implications in many branches of Chinese law other than civil law. Indeed, the concept of legal person is still evolving, as evidenced by its application in criminal and administrative laws. Therefore, in spite of many problems, legal person or *faren* must be treated as a fundamental and promising concept to be developed and elaborated in the emerging Chinese legal system.

170. China's venture in drafting company legislation in the new era of economic reforms started as early as 1985. But the drafting of a general law governing limited liability companies and joint stock limited companies has met considerable difficulty. In addition to some outstanding technical issues, a major obstacle of the drafting had for some time been the uncertainty and confusion regarding the role to be played by Western style limited companies in China. Despite the official endorsement of certain experimentation since the mid-1980s, joint stock limited companies were suspected by some to be alien to the socialist system. It is since 1992 that the significance of joint stock limited companies has been widely affirmed. This is evidenced by the fact that a considerable number of Chinese state enterprises have been selected to be reorganised into joint stock limited companies and some of them have even issued shares to the public including foreign investors. The experimentation of joint stock limited companies in China is currently guided by administrative rules on limited companies issued by relevant central authorities and by relevant local company legislation. A comprehensive national company law which purports to govern both limited liability companies and joint stock limited companies is being reviewed and subject to approval by Chinese legislature.

[13]

Legal and Institutional Uncertainties in the Domestic Contract Law of the People's Republic of China

Daniel Rubenstein*

This article attempts to link characteristics of Chinese contracts to the specific ideological, legal and institutional arrangements that govern them. In the context of Hong Kong's reversion to Chinese sovereignty, this analysis of the domestic law of the People's Republic of China may now have important implications for Hong Kong.

Since Chinese scholars often trace peculiarities in China's contract law to the pre-1980 planned economy, the article begins by rehearsing key characteristics of contracts under planning. After a brief analysis of the function of post-Mao legal reform, of the civil law, and of the relations between the legislature, judiciary, and Communist Party, the article examines, in turn, three stages of the contractual process: (1) On capacity, the author maintains that economic contracts are still restricted to "juristic persons" (*faren*), and that this empowers the state to "screen" economic actors. (2) On formation and performance, the author argues that "liberalizing" changes implemented by the 1993 Economic Contract Law still leave the state considerable "principled ambiguity" to interfere. Moreover, Chinese versions of liquidated damages, anticipatory repudiation, *force majeure*, and the absence of *rebus sic stantibus* all reflect vestiges of the planned economy's emphasis on specific performance. (3) On dispute resolution, the author discusses mediation, resolution by a common superior, arbitration, and the courts. He stresses control of mediation by the state, and the tendency for mediation to blur into arbitration; the influence on courts from local cadres and the Ministry of Justice; and the inability of the judiciary to form an internally consistent, self-referential corpus of case law.

This analysis concludes that despite the importance of legal reform (*viz.*, a prospective "unified" contract law), real private-law protection for contracts will require a fundamental rethinking of the institutional arrangements which make up party-state rule.

Le présent article vise à expliquer certains principes du droit chinois des contrats à la lumière de leur contexte idéologique, légal et institutionnel. Au moment du retour de Hong-Kong à la Chine, cette analyse pourrait avoir des conséquences importantes pour tous ceux qui font affaires à Hong-Kong.

La plupart des juristes chinois expliquent les particularités du droit chinois des contrats à partir de l'économie planifiée d'avant 1980. L'auteur débute donc par une analyse des contrats dans une économie planifiée. Après une brève analyse de la réforme du droit civil dans l'ère post-Mao et des relations entre la législature, le système judiciaire et le parti communiste, l'article explore une à une trois étapes du processus contractuel. (1) À propos de la capacité, l'auteur note que les contrats à caractère économique demeurent l'apanage des «personnes juridiques» (*faren*) et que cela permet à l'État de sélectionner les acteurs économiques. (2) À propos de la formation et de l'exécution, l'auteur affirme que les réformes «libérales» mises en place par la *Loi sur les contrats de 1993* laissent à l'État une marge d'intervention importante. (3) À propos de la résolution de différends, l'auteur discute de la médiation, de la résolution «interne» des conflits, de l'arbitrage et du recours judiciaire. Il souligne l'importance du contrôle exercé sur la médiation par l'État et la tendance de la médiation à se muer en arbitrage, ainsi que l'influence des cadres locaux et du ministère de la justice sur les tribunaux et l'impossibilité pour les tribunaux de former un corps de décisions qui soit cohérent et qui démontre une certaine logique interne.

Cette analyse conclut que malgré l'importance de la réforme légale (soit la possibilité d'un droit «unifié» des contrats), une protection réelle des contrats en droit privé chinois exige une réforme en profondeur des arrangements institutionnels qui sont à la base de l'État à parti unique.

---

* A.B. (University of Illinois, Urbana), M.A., Ph.D. (University of Minnesota, Twin Cities); adjunct professor of political science, Wayne State University (Detroit, Michigan), and special lecturer in political science, Oakland University (Rochester Hills, Michigan). The author would like to thank Daniel Kelliher and Raymond Duvall of the Department of Political Science at the University of Minnesota and Tahirih Lee of the University of Minnesota Law School for their comments and suggestions on earlier versions of the research presented in this article. He would also like to acknowledge his obvious debt to Donald Clarke's pioneering research on dispute resolution and the enforcement of civil judgments in China. The author, of course, bears sole responsibility for any errors of fact, interpretation or inference.

To be cited as: (1997) 42 McGill L.J. 495
Mode de référence : (1997) 42 R.D. McGill 495

Introduction

In the wake of Hong Kong's handover to the People's Republic of China ("P.R.C.") on 1 July 1997, foreign business and political leaders will be monitoring Hong Kong's legal protection of commercial contracts for signs of mainland influence. Western business executives say that a contract in the P.R.C. is "more a sense of moral obligation than absolute rights", "vaguely worded mush", "arbitrary justice", and "a piece of wastepaper".[1] Lack of enforcement is written off as "part of the cost of doing business" while editorialists admonish China to start following the "rules of the road".[2] This study aims to shed light on how the legal and institutional milieu in which contracts function in the P.R.C. generates the sorts of behaviors and transaction costs feared by foreigners.

China's *domestic* contract law[3] may have reverberations outside the domestic sphere for several reasons. Contracts involving foreigners, though currently regulated by a distinct piece of legislation, may in future be brought under the aegis of a unified, monolithic contract law,[4] and there is no guarantee that this unified legislation

---

[1] See respectively H. Sender, "Party of the First Part: China Tries to Improve Contract Law" *Far Eastern Econ. Rev.* (11 February 1993) 42 at 42; "China Business" (Editorial) *The Wall Street Journal* (18 November 1994) A18; N. Holloway, "Arbitrary Justice: Breach of Contract in China Becomes Test Case" *Far Eastern Econ. Rev.* (20 July 1995) 78 at 78; K. Chen, "The Extent of the Law" (A Report on China) *The Wall Street Journal* (10 December 1993) R5. See also generally R.L. Homan, "World Wire: Beijing Orders U.S. Cafe Closed" *The Wall Street Journal* (22 November 1994) A18; E. Guyot, "Contract Disputes Imperil China's Bid to Raise Foreign Capital, S & P Warns" *The Wall Street Journal* (15 December 1994) A10. Throughout the mid-1990s a continuous stream of such articles has bemoaned contract practices in China.

[2] See respectively Holloway, *ibid.*; "China Business" (Editorial), *ibid.*

[3] China has separate domestic, foreign, and technology contract laws. These are, respectively, (1) Economic Contract Law of the People's Republic of China, 4th Sess., 5th National People's Congress ("N.P.C."), 13 December 1981 (effective 1 July 1982) (translated into English in (1982) 2 China L. Rptr. 61, and reprinted in Chinese in C.P. Li, ed., *Shiyong Falü Shouce (Zhushiben)* [*Practical Handbook of Law (Annotated)*] (Beijing: China Economic Press, 1986) 185) [hereinafter 1982 Contract Law] as am. by 3d Sess., Standing Committee of the 8th N.P.C., 2 September 1993 (bilingual text in S. FitzGerald, ed., *China Laws for Foreign Business*, vol. 1 (*Business Regulation*) (Australia: CCH International, 1993) para. 5-500) [hereinafter 1993 Contract Law]; (2) Foreign Economic Contract Law of the People's Republic of China, 10th Sess., Standing Committee of the 6th N.P.C., 21 March 1985 (bilingual text in FitzGerald, ed., *ibid.*, para. 5-550; other unofficial English translation in 24 I.L.M. 799, Documents, Beijing Rev. (8 July 1985) I) [hereinafter Foreign Contract Law]; (3) Law of the People's Republic of China on Technology Contracts, 21st Sess., Standing Committee of the 6th N.P.C., 23 June 1987 (bilingual text in FitzGerald, ed., *ibid.*, para. 5-577) [hereinafter Technology Contract Law].

[4] Although I was unable to obtain a recent draft of the "proposed unified contract law" (*hetong fa jianyi cao'an*), it has been reported that a copy of it appears in [1995] no. 4 *Minshang Fa Luncong* [*Review of Civil and Commercial Law*]. This draft was submitted to the Judicial System Work Committee of the N.P.C. Standing Committee in January 1995. See H. Liang, "Cong 'Sanzuding Li' zouxiang Tongyi de Hetong Fa" ["Moving from 'Three-legged Legislation' towards a Unified Contract Law"] [1995] no. 3 *Zhongguo Faxue* [*Chinese Legal Science*], reprinted in [1995] no. 9 *Faxue* [*Legal Studies*] (Chinese People's University reprint series topic D41) 109 at 112. In addition to

will privilege doctrines from today's foreign contract law. Moreover, until such a unified law is implemented,[5] it appears that Hong Kong companies may be regulated in their dealings with mainland enterprises by the P.R.C.'s domestic contract law, not its foreign contract law. Neither the *Joint Declaration*[6] nor the Basic Law[7] indicate that mainland—Hong-Kong contracts will be treated as Chinese-foreign contracts. In fact, article 13 of the Basic Law states that the P.R.C. shall retain control over Hong Kong foreign policy, suggesting that Hong Kong will not be a "foreign" entity. More importantly, the National People's Congress Standing Committee may invalidate contracts and other laws which "contravene" its own interpretation of the Basic Law.[8] As well, the legislature of the Hong Kong Special Administrative Region — currently hand-picked by Beijing — may amend provisions of Hong Kong's pre-1997 common law, including rules of equity.[9] Until the question is settled which contract law controls under different sorts of circumstances in Hong Kong, understanding the potential commercial-law implications of Hong Kong's handover requires an appreciation of the P.R.C.'s current domestic contract law.

This article begins with a brief rehearsal of the contract system under communist planning. Although far fewer items are covered by the plan than in the past, the *principles* by which planning officials are authorized to interfere in various aspects of contract form, content, formation and dissolution are legacies of the planned economy. Part II discusses three variables that are key to understanding the larger socio-political context in which Chinese contract law operates: a lack of separation of powers (and an attendant lack of *stare decisis* and judicial review), the persistent importance of Party committees and "Party groups" (*dang zu*) at many key levels of the

---

Liang's article, numerous commentaries by scholars who were active in overseeing and writing the revised law have appeared in Chinese journals (see *e.g.* L.M. Wang, "Tongyi Hetong Fa Zhiding zhong de Ruogan Yinan Wenti Tantao" ["Probing Studies on Several Complicated Problems in the Enactment of a Unified Contract Law"] in [1996] no. 4 *Zhengfa Luntan* [*Tribune of Political Science and Law*] 49 (part 1), [1996] no. 5 *Zhengfa Luntan* 52 (part 2)). One such participant has also published a commentary in English, a translation of a speech given in March 1996 at the Center for Chinese Legal Studies of Columbia University Law School: P. Jiang, "Drafting the Uniform Contract Law in China" (1996) 10 Colum. J. Asian L. 245. To the extent the present article touches on the prospective unified contract law, which it does only sparingly, it draws primarily from these sources.

[5] The date for passage keeps being pushed back, apparently due to the immense political difficulties associated with finding principles acceptable to free marketers and planners, proponents of voluntary exchange and defenders of administrative prerogative, central and local leaders, etc. In the latest development, the unified law was to be enacted at the Fifth Meeting of the N.P.C. in March 1997, but it was not (on planned enactment at the Fifth Meeting, see Jiang, *ibid.* at 245).

[6] *Sino-British Joint Declaration on the Question of Hong Kong*, 19 December 1984, U.K.T.S. 1984 No. 26, reprinted in 23 I.L.M. 1366 [hereinafter *Joint Declaration*].

[7] Basic Law of the Hong Kong Special Administrative Region of the People's Republic of China, 3d Sess., 7th N.P.C., 4 April 1990, reprinted in 29 I.L.M. 1519 [hereinafter Basic Law]. Also available at http://www.cityu.edu.hk/Basic Law/b1.htm (17 June 1997).

[8] Basic Law, *ibid.*, arts. 158-60, 17.

[9] *Ibid.*, art. 8.

Chinese economy and bureaucracy, and the fact that the contract law is not unequivocally subordinate to China's *General Principles of Civil Law.*[10]

The substantive analysis which then follows is divided along three elements or stages of the contractual process. These stages are drawn from the textbook definition of "freedom of contract":

> The ability at will, to make or abstain from making, a binding obligation enforced by the sanctions at the law. The right to contract about one's affairs, including the right to make contracts of employment, and to obtain the best terms one can as the result of private bargaining.[11]

First, Part III addresses the question of who may enter a contract. The P.R.C. not only imposes strict legal requirements on who may assume the "juristic person" status necessary to enter into legally protected contracts, but, I argue, direct or indirect state control over vital economic resources continues to render the ability to become a contractor highly dependent on personal and professional connections.

Second, Part IV asks how much negotiation and bargaining is customary or permitted in setting and adjusting contract terms? In essence, voluntary negotiation, a key ingredient in legitimating contracts under Western ideals of freedom of contract, is attenuated by often hidden differences in the legal status of contractors, the still common practice of state interference in pricing decisions, and emphasis on legal doctrines like specific performance.[12] Other factors, such as the lack of a system of offer and acceptance separate from administrative approval, and official emphasis on form contracts, have been much-discussed in the drafting of the unified contract law. They are touched upon accordingly.

Third, Part V surveys the basic characteristics of dispute-resolution forums and contract enforcement. Whether Hong Kong will indeed maintain an independent judiciary is uppermost in the minds of many Hong Kong residents. This section connects legal and institutional arrangements in China's judiciary with many of the maladies that affect the resolution of contract disputes and the enforcement of court decisions in China. Based on this analysis, I conclude that even should China's unified contract law bring China into line with Hong Kong and other foreign legal systems, it is the preservation of Hong Kong's institutional arrangements for mediation, arbitration and adjudication (*e.g.*, which branch of government staffs and finances tri-

---

[10] *General Principles of Civil Law of the People's Republic of China*, 4th Sess., 6th N.P.C., 12 April 1986 (effective 1 January 1987) [hereinafter *General Principles of Civil Law*] (bilingual text in FitzGerald, ed., *supra* note 3, para. 19-150; Chinese text also in Li, ed., *supra* note 3, 126. See text below, accompanying notes 67-70.

[11] H.C. Black, *Black's Law Dictionary: Definitions of the Terms and Phrases of American and English Jurisprudence, Ancient and Modern*, 6th ed. (St. Paul, Minn.: West, 1990) at 918 ("liberty of contract").

[12] In Anglo-American law, "specific performance" is the principle that "where money damages would be an inadequate compensation for the breach of an agreement, the contractor or vendor will be compelled to perform specifically what he has agreed to do" (*ibid.* at 1138). This definition does not entirely capture the principle of specific performance as it is practiced in the P.R.C.

bunals, how are personnel appointed and fired) which will most effectively safeguard contracts in Hong Kong.

I. Background: P.R.C. Contract Practice and Law in the Era of Socialist Planning

The post-1949 political earthquake that transformed China's economy culminated by 1956 in a more-or-less fully planned economy. Under planning, ministries set provisional targets based on input and output information from immediately subordinate organs and extrapolation from previous years. These "control" figures would then be sent back to the subordinate organs which rectified them based on figures culled from enterprises and industrial bureaus (in urban areas) or brigades, communes, prefectures, and provinces (in agriculture). This process, sometimes called "planning and counterplanning", is meant to produce a plan which is feasible for individual enterprises yet ensures that the resources of each enterprise are used in accordance with national goals.[13] It has been well-documented how this process can be rife with bargaining, tactical prevarication, implicit threats and peer pressure, and, of course, fiat from above.[14]

Within this system, "contracts" were essentially administrative devices characterized by involuntariness in term-setting and performance. For example, most industrial and wholesale contracts were signed at "goods-ordering conferences" (*dinghuo huiyi*) attended by those who would produce and deliver products under the plan. At these conferences ministries would assign "dancing partners", *i.e.*, a supplier and outlet, for every product. Information shared between the dancing partners and the ministry might influence the terms of the resulting agreement, but the "contract" was not signed on the basis of voluntarism or free negotiation.[15] The function of state-sector contracts was to clarify responsibilities between units, concretize plan targets to workers and managers, and enable responsibility for performance failures to be traced.[16]

---

[13] See M. Ellman, "Economic Calculation in Socialist Economies" in J. Eatwell, M. Milgate & P. Newman, eds., *The New Palgrave: Problems of the Planned Economy* (New York: W.W. Norton, 1990) 91 at 91.

[14] On the planned economy in this period, see A. Donnithorne, *China's Economic System* (New York: Praeger, 1967) and D.H. Perkins, *Market Control and Planning in Communist China* (Cambridge, Mass.: Harvard University Press, 1966). On central, ministerial and provincial interaction in formulating plans, see K. Lieberthal & M. Oksenberg, *Policy Making in China: Leaders, Structures, and Processes* (Princeton: Princeton University Press, 1988) at 128-34. On rural teams and brigades setting agricultural production targets, see J.C. Oi, *State and Peasant in Contemporary China: The Political Economy of Village Government* (Berkeley: University of California Press, 1989), especially at 57-62.

[15] See R.M. Pfeffer, *Understanding Business Contracts in China, 1949-1963* (Cambridge, Mass.: Harvard University Press, 1973) at 10-28; L. Cheng & A. Rosett, "Contract with a Chinese Face: Socially Embedded Factors in the Transformation from Hierarchy to Market, 1978-1989" (1991) 5 J. Chinese Law 143 at 169.

[16] See R.M. Pfeffer, "The Institution of Contracts in the Chinese People's Republic (Part I)" (1963) 14 China Q. 153 at 162.

Enforcement was also an administrative matter. Although a much smaller number of commodities than in the Soviet Union was subject to planned allocation,[17] substituted performance — the ability to get one's contract fulfilled elsewhere — was generally unavailable. Since plan inputs and outputs were mutually dependent, failure to perform by one enterprise could produce a chain reaction that might snowball into huge problems for downstream industries. And payment of monetary damages was tainted by the notions that the purpose of exchange was not profit but fulfillment of social need, and that monetary losses would simply accrue to "the whole people". Even had ideology encouraged enterprises to assume financial responsibility for their own performance failures, however, the fact that prices under planning were essentially artificial made it impossible to rationally calculate damages.

In 1950, the new regime had promulgated two laws which decisively shaped dispute resolution and enforcement practices: the "Provisional Methods"[18] and what may be called the "Decision".[19] Their provisions dealt mainly with the newly established cooperatives. They required that the financial committee of higher-level supervisory organs be notified of contract signings and gave responsibility for ensuring proper signing and implementation to the appropriate central ministry. Thus, grain contracts would be supervised by the ministry of agriculture, cooperative consumer goods contracts by the ministry of trade, and so on.[20] In addition to being brought under ministerial control and made to serve the state's financial planning, large categories of contracts were forced to include "guarantor" (*baozhengren*) clauses. The guarantor (a higher-level ministerial office) bore responsibility in case of breach.[21] This codified a core principle of contracts, and economic life generally, under socialist planning — losses do not accrue to the enterprise.

These regulations also established a three-tiered hierarchy for resolving disputes,[22] which reflected the state's preference for "internal" dispute resolution, that is, resolution by a body that is organizationally related to the parties and financially impacted

---

[17] Although comparisons are difficult because they used different classification schemes, China's unified allocation system included at its peak in the mid-1960s some 500 goods; the Soviet's included over 5,000 (see C. Wong, "Material Allocation and Decentralization: Impact of the Local Sector on Industrial Reform" in E.J. Perry & C. Wong, eds., *The Political Economy of Reform in Post-Mao China* (Cambridge, Mass.: Council on East Asian Studies, Harvard University, 1985) 253 at 261).

[18] "Jiguan, Guoying Qiye, Hezuoshe Qianding Hetong Qiyue Zanxing Banfa" ["Provisional Methods for Signing Contracts by Organs, State Enterprises, and Collectives"] in Guowuyuan Jingji Fagui Yanjiu Zhongxin Bangongshi [Office of the Economic Laws and Regulations Research Center of the State Council], ed., *Jingji Hetong Fagui Xuanbian* [*Compilation of Laws and Regulations on Economic Contracts*] (Beijing: Worker's Press, 1982) [hereinafter *Compilation of Economic Contract Laws*] 24 [hereinafter Provisional Methods].

[19] "Zhongyang Renmin Zhengfu Maoyibu Guanyu Renzhen Dingli yu Yange Zhixing Hetong de Jueding" ["Decision of the Central People's Government Trade Section Concerning the Conscientious Signing and Strict Implementation of Contracts"] in *Compilation of Economic Contract Laws*, *ibid.*, 27 [hereinafter Decision].

[20] See Provisional Methods, *supra* note 18, art. 9; Decision, *ibid.*, art. 14 and preface. For a discussion of how the state exerted control through such contracts, see Perkins, *supra* note 14.

[21] Provisional Methods, *ibid.*, art. 6; Decision, *ibid.*, art. 3, s. 12.

[22] See Part V below.

by the outcome of the dispute. Post-Mao reforms have challenged this institutional principle but it has not been entirely displaced. Mandating that disputes be resolved by organs with internal relations to the parties creates incentives for mediators to minimize financial damages (since their parent organ would absorb the loss) and to press for specific performance.

Despite experimentation with more economically liberal policies in 1956-57 and 1961-63, vacillations in economic policy before 1978 mask a fundamental continuity in contract use. Three factors account for this: specific regulations, bureaucratic organization, and law. First, regulations have indirectly restricted prices in contracts even during periods of marketization. For example, in the spring of 1955, when cooperatives increased the differential between wholesale and retail prices so that private merchants could earn more profit, they were told what that differential should be. Wholesale prices were determined administratively, not by the market or negotiation. Similarly, although retail outlets could purchase some goods directly from factories under the "selective purchase" system, prices were set by commercial organs, not the factories themselves.[23] Detailed regulations ensured that wholesale prices, and hence contract prices, continued to be determined by the state's perception of social need.

Second, on the bureaucratic level, the historic decentralization of 1957-59 for the most part simply made the province a planning unit like the state writ small. It was felt that decentralization of economic decision-making was required to combat increasingly obvious inefficiencies of the centrally planned economy.[24] Prime among these inefficiencies was "blindly signing contracts" (*mangmu ding hetong*), that is, failure of ministries to investigate market needs and the capabilities of parties before setting the terms of enterprise contracts.[25] But the reform ultimately adopted, as Franz Schurmann has noted, gave more power to provinces (especially local party committees), not production units (central ministries with jurisdiction over specific industries).[26] Specifically, provinces were given control over most light industrial enterprises (except textiles) and non-strategic heavy industry. Even centrally-owned enterprises came under "dual control", meaning management decisions were subject to approval by provincial party committees as well as ministerial organs at the same level. Provinces assumed more control over distribution of materials, pricing and taxes, and they were permitted to include the activities of centrally owned enterprises in their

---

[23] See D.J. Solinger, *Chinese Business Under Socialism: The Politics of Domestic Commerce, 1949-1980* (Berkeley: University of California Press, 1984) at 220-21.

[24] Despite elite consensus on the problem, the solution adopted was, of course, a product of political struggle and compromise. For discussion of decentralization, see H. Harding, *Organizing China: The Problem of Bureaucracy 1949-1976* (Stanford: Stanford University Press, 1981) at 107-15 and 175-77; Solinger, *ibid.* at 93-98; C. Riskin, *China's Political Economy: The Quest for Development Since 1949* (Oxford: Oxford University Press, 1987) at 104-107; and R. MacFarquhar, *The Origins of the Cultural Revolution*, vol. 1 (*Contradictions Among the People 1956-1957*) (New York: Columbia University Press, 1974).

[25] See P.B. Potter, *The Economic Contract Law of China: Legitimation and Contract Autonomy in the PRC* (Seattle: University of Washington Press, 1992) at 21-25, esp. nn. 15 and 31.

[26] See F. Schurmann, *Ideology and Organization in Communist China*, 2d ed. (Berkeley: University of California Press, 1968) at 175-76.

own provincial plans. What this reform did *not* do, however, is more important for contracts. Beijing continued to write the price-fixing principles by which localities could alter prices. The center had to approve changes in targets, and the Ministry of Commerce retained the significant powers of "guidance" (*lingdao*), "management" (*guanli*) and "approval" (*pizhun*).[27] Most importantly, the still quite large provincial territorial unit basically performed the same planning functions previously performed by the centre. The logic of planning was unchanged: resource allocation did not occur through freely negotiated exchange. The plan that controlled it was now mostly provincial or regional, not national.

Third, legal developments codified the nature of contracts and the position of contractors. By 1958, a famous civil-law textbook[28] appeared which asserted that civil relations must serve the end of socialism. Some civil relations were to be fostered, others were to be abolished. The property interests of "antagonistic" classes were not granted protection, while state property was inviolable. Law was to be interpreted in terms of state policy; realization of the state economic plan was paramount. Permanent laws were still eschewed lest they become a barrier to socialist transformation.[29] In keeping with the practices of the planned economy, it advised judicial and mediatory bodies to pursue performance rather than compensatory or punitive damages.[30] Clearly, this "civil" law was primarily a bulwark for statist aims. Yet even this dubious foundation for contract freedom was never adopted. In the aftermath of the anti-rightist campaign of 1957 and at the start of the Great Leap Forward in 1958, law was explicitly subordinated to policy.

Similar points could be made about the 1960-62 round of liberalization. At any rate, by March 1962, control over pricing (which had been decentralized to provinces and localities in 1957-58) was recentralized. Later that year the National Price Commission was established. It set prices on all goods except for a handful of agricultural commodities.[31] Although price negotiation in contract formation was thus strictly curtailed, the regime did seek to increase enterprise efficiency through a new approach to contract enforcement. In 1962-63, two regulations evinced unprecedented concern with assigning responsibility for nonfulfillment.[32] No longer were losses

---

[27] Solinger, *supra* note 23 at 95-98, emphasizes the powers of the Ministry of Commerce.

[28] Zhongyang Zhengfa Ganbu Xuexiao Minfa Jiaoyanshi [Teaching and Research Section of the Central Political and Legal Cadres' School], ed., *Zhongguo Renmin Gongheguo Minfa Jiben Wenti* [*Basic Issues of Chinese Civil Law*] (Beijing: Legal Press, 1958).

[29] On the points cited, see *ibid.* at 7-12, 21, 25-30.

[30] See Pfeffer, *supra* note 15 at 29-47.

[31] See J.J. Guo, *Price Reform in China, 1979-86* (New York: St. Martin's Press, 1992) at 19.

[32] "Zhonggong Zhongyang Guowuyuan Guanyu Yange Zhixing Jiben Jianshe Chengxu, Yange Zhixing Jingji Hetong de Tongzhi" ["Circular of the Chinese Communist Party Central Committee and State Council Concerning the Strict Enforcement of Basic Construction Procedures and the Strict Fulfillment of Economic Contracts"] in *Compilation of Economic Contract Laws, supra* note 18, 35 [hereinafter Circular]; and "Guojia Jingji Weiyuanhui Guanyu Gong Kuang Chanpin Dinghuo Hetong Jiben Tiaokuan de Zanxing Guiding" ["Provisional Regulations of the State Economic Committee on the Basic Clauses in Contracts for the Ordering of Factory and Mining Products"] in *Compilation of Economic Contract Laws, ibid.*, 53 [hereinafter Ordering Regulations].

simply to be absorbed by ministries. Liabilities were specified according to the nature of the breach. The supplier bore liability for untimely delivery or deficient quality, while the buyer bore liability for failure to accept delivery or last-minute changes in specifications. In contrast to the emphasis of the 1958 civil law textbook on specific performance or compensation, these regulations permitted penalty clauses, *i.e.*, punitive damages.[33]

Such moves toward contract freedom and responsibility were weakened, however, by provisions regarding dispute resolution. Higher-level management bodies were to mediate, or relevant economic committees were to arbitrate.[34] Pitman Potter has discovered through interviews with Hong Kong émigrés that compensation in the 1960s was almost never total but took the form of a negotiated reduction in payment, echoing traditional norms like "splitting the difference".[35] Still being ultimately responsible, ministerial bodies (who were the mediators) would simply alter production quotas to account for nondelivery. This was more practical than waiting to receive payment or performance. Chronic shortages and quality problems in manufactures often meant buyers faced a "Hobson's choice of accepting the defective goods or waiting for the party in breach to attempt to produce conforming goods."[36] While waiting for performance, no compensation or punitive damages would be levied. In inter-ministerial disputes brought to arbitration before an Economic Committee, perception of social need could determine which ministry would absorb more of the loss.

A draft civil law submitted to the National People's Congress ("N.P.C.") in mid-1964[37] attempted to place the contract principles laid down by the Circular[38] and Ordering Regulations[39] into a larger legal framework. It omitted such principles as equality between parties and voluntary participation in civil-law relations, and defined contract as "an important tool for implementing economic plans, for strengthening economic co-operation, and for facilitating people's lives."[40] Hope of passing even this plan-oriented legislation faded, however, with the onset of the Cultural Revolution in 1966. In 1969, most of the staff of the National Price Commission was sent to the countryside for "re-education through labor", leaving the State Planning Commission of the State Council responsible for price policy. Implementation problems notwithstanding, only fixed prices were permitted for the rest of the Cultural Revolution. No further legal or contract reforms were attempted until after Deng recharted China's economic course in 1978.

---

[33] Ordering Regulations, *ibid.*, s. 9, arts. 32-35. See also Potter, *supra* note 25 at 25-26, nn. 45 and 46.

[34] Ordering Regulations, *ibid.*, art. 36.

[35] See Potter, *supra* note 25 at 28.

[36] *Ibid.*

[37] Draft Civil Code of the People's Republic of China (1 July 1964), issued by the General Office of the Standing Committee of the N.P.C. [hereinafter Draft Civil Code].

[38] *Supra* note 32.

[39] *Supra* note 32.

[40] Draft Civil Code, *supra* note 37, art. 68, quoted in J. Chen, *From Administrative Authorisation to Private Law: A Comparative Perspective of the Developing Civil Law in the People's Republic of China* (Dordrecht: Martinus Nijhoff, 1995) at 44.

II. The Nature of the Post-Mao Legal Reforms

The Third Plenary Session of the Eleventh Central Committee of the Chinese Communist Party (December 1978) is generally viewed as the first time China's leadership linked the success of economic reform to the development of a legal system.[41] China's leaders have viewed political reform ("democracy"), economic reform and legal reform as inseparable, but in a very specific manner. Order, control and stability were prime goals in the aftermath of the Cultural Revolution. It was felt that lower-level Party members had been given too much authority to interpret and implement central directives, resulting in near chaos. "Anarchism" and "ultra-individualism", epitomized by Lin Biao and the Gang of Four, were vilified.[42] The leadership sought law that could, on the one hand, protect citizens against official arbitrariness (the main element in the government's definition of "democracy") and, on the other, control the terms of citizens' participation in politics and economics. Only law could guarantee that increased individual participation in the economy and professionalization of enterprise management would occur in an orderly fashion according to principles laid down by Beijing. Law would undergird a renewed "democratic centralism". Lower-level Party cadres would for the first time not just apply law to citizens, but also be subject to it. The inaugural statement of the five-year legal education movement begun in 1985 captures the interrelatedness of democracy, strengthening of central Party control, and economic reform:

> It is necessary to popularize knowledge of the law among the masses of people to enable them to have a good grasp of the law and to cultivate the habit of doing things in accordance with the law. ... When the people are familiar with their rights and obligations, they will enhance their sense of responsibility of being their own masters. ... Only then will they supervise the implementation of the law and the work of state functionaries.[43]

In essence, law was to be a new mechanism for channeling central Party guidance of the economy, bypassing local cadres. One of the central questions for contracts in

---

[41] "Communiqué of the Third Plenary Session of the 11th Central Committee of the Communist Party of China" (22 December 1978), trans. in *Beijing Rev.* (29 December 1978) 6.

[42] From 1966 to 1970, Lin Biao, leader of the People's Liberation Army (P.L.A.), implemented Mao's tactic that the army lead the Party in conducting the "movement" politics of the Cultural Revolution. The Gang of Four, led by Mao's wife, Jiang Qing, also led the Cultural Revolution and tried to carry it on after Mao's death, steadfastly opposing any restoration of pre-Cultural Revolution policies aimed at political stability or marketization of the economy. Although frequently at odds, these two "cliques" were tried simultaneously in 1980 and found, ultimately, to be "ultraleftists". When all is said and done, their shared crime seems to have been to disregard norms of intra-elite co-operation, to make grabs for personal power, and to completely nullify party structures, administrative procedures and economic stability — hence, the labels "anarchist" and "ultra-individualist" (see T.W. Wu, *Lin Biao and the Gang of Four: Contra-Confucianism in Historical and Intellectual Perspective* (Carbondale, Ill.: Southern Illinois University Press, 1983), esp. c. 2, 9 and 10; F.C. Teiwes, *Leadership, Legitimacy, and Conflict in China: From a Charismatic Mao to the Politics of Succession* (Armonk, N.Y.: M.E. Sharpe, 1984), s. III).

[43] "Turn Law Over to the People" *Renmin Ribao* [*People's Daily*] (16 June 1985) at 2, quoted in E. Donahoe, "The Promise of Law for the Post-Mao Leadership in China" (1988) 41 Stanf. L. Rev. 171 at 179.

contemporary China, then, is whether the reliability and predictability that in the West derive from embedding contracts in a civil- or private-law framework can be achieved under a regime that views law as a statist tool of policy implementation.

A. The View from the Top: Government Inter-Branch Relations

Deng repeatedly stressed that legal reform was not meant to create an American-style tripartite separation of powers and system of checks and balances.[44] China's legislature, the N.P.C., not only approves legislation, but is empowered by the Constitution to "interpret" laws, a function assumed by the judiciary in many other political systems.[45] Legislative authority over judicial interpretation was clarified in a 1981 N.P.C. resolution which states that the N.P.C. shall "clarify the limits of laws or make supplementary regulations" (*jinyibu mingque jiexian huo zuo buchong guiding*) while the Supreme Court shall interpret "questions of the concrete use of such laws in judicial work" (*shenpan gongzuo zhong juti yingyong ... de wenti*).[46] This seems to mean that the Supreme Court, for example, may say when the circumstances of a case warrant application of a specific law, but, unlike the U.S. Supreme Court, may not elaborate on the case's implications or relationship to other laws, including the Constitution. This resolution terminated any hope of developing a system of judicial review in China. The "court of final appeal" on questions of a law's scope or meaning is clearly the legislative, not judicial, branch. And despite the growing autonomy of the N.P.C. in the reform era, its interpretations of "important economic or administrative laws" are still subject to review and approval by the Party's Politburo or full Central Committee.[47]

The judiciary is also subject to the Party's specific notion of "judicial independence". As Jerome Cohen observed years ago, judicial independence in China means that individual courts are independent from other administrative hierarchies, not from higher courts.[48] A higher court need not wait to hear an appeal to intervene in a case being heard by a lower court. Moreover, the Party is not considered an

---

[44] See *e.g.* his speech to military commanders delivered on 9 June 1989 (full text reproduced in "Deng's Talks on Quelling Rebellion in Beijing" *Beijing Rev.* (10-16 July 1989) 18).

[45] The Constitution of the People's Republic of China, 5th Sess., 5th N.P.C., 4 December 1982, as am. by 1st Sess., 8th N.P.C., 29 March 1993 (bilingual text in FitzGerald, ed., *supra* note 3, para. 4-500 at 4-500(67)), art. 67(1) and 67(4) [hereinafter Constitution].

[46] "Quanguo Renmin Daibiao Dahui Changwu Weiyuanhui Guanyu Jiaqiang Falü Jieshi Gongzuo de Jueding" ["Resolution of the N.P.C. Standing Committee Providing an Improved Interpretation of the Law"], adopted 10 June 1981, in *Zhonghua Renmin Gongheguo Fagui Huibian* [*Compendia of Laws and Regulations of the PRC*] [hereinafter *PRC Compendia of Laws*] (1981) 27.

[47] See M.S. Tanner's discussion (in "The Erosion of Communist Party Control over Lawmaking in China" (1994) 138 China Q. 381 at 384 and 399) of "Zhonggong Zhongyang guanyu jiaqiang dui lifa gongzuo lingdao de ruogan yijian" ["Several Opinions of the CCP Central Committee on Strengthening Leadership over Legislative Work"], CCP Central Committee Document No. 8 (1991), a "secret" document obtained by Tanner. The Politburo is a core leadership of fifteen to twenty individuals elected by the Central Committee, which has roughly 175 members.

[48] See J.A. Cohen, "The Chinese Communist Party and 'Judicial Independence': 1949-1959" (1969) 82 Harv. L. Rev. 967.

"administrative hierarchy". A practice known as *shuji pi an* ("approval of cases by the [local] Party Secretary") was commonplace in the Mao era and may still be operative in important cases. Even if it isn't, court presidents, who usually belong to local Party committees, have authority to override decisions of particular judges in particular cases. The Supreme Court, for its part, is called not the highest "court" but the highest "judicial organ", exercising "the adjudicatory aspect of the state's unified power."[49] Finally, the judiciary is permitted only a very weak form of *stare decisis*, further undermining independence. Each of these issues will be elaborated momentarily under the topic of dispute resolution in court adjudication.

B. Two Basic Institutional Channels of Party Control

The Party's ubiquitous presence throughout Chinese society is often taken for granted, but two modes by which its power is institutionalized are worth noting. First is the institution of "dual rule" or "parallel rule". Every governmental level is paralleled by a Party committee to which it is directly subordinate. Conflicts between ministries and across localities can be resolved in Party committees both because of their superior authority and because key government officials also belong to them, thus allowing jurisdictional and bureaucratic differences to be hashed out.[50]

Second, government agencies themselves contain "Party groups" (*dang zu*) which, for central ministries, are appointed directly by the Party's personnel office, called the Organization Department.[51] Some observers believe Party groups are even more powerful than Party committees because they play a direct decision-making role (not just supervision) in the policies within each ministry. Whatever the case, Party leaders evidently view them as important sites for establishing control; after briefly being made optional in 1988, they were quickly reinstituted during the post-Tiananmen retrenchment.[52] These basic institutional relations between the judiciary, legislature, Party and all ministerial organs should be kept in mind when reference is made to powers that allow planners and Party officials to intervene in contract formation, dispute resolution, and enforcement.

---

[49] S. Finder, "The Supreme People's Court of the People's Republic of China" (1993) 7 J. Chinese L. 145 at 148. See also Constitution, *supra* note 45, art. 123.

[50] The classic treatment of dual rule is Schurmann, *supra* note 26, especially at 188ff. On the importance of Party committees, see Schurmann, *ibid.* at 190-94.

[51] For more on the Organization Department's current role in staffing and monitoring government agencies, see Y. Huang, "Research Note: Administrative Monitoring in China" (1995) 143 China Q. 828.

[52] For a concise discussion of Party committees, Party groups, and the latter's fall and rise, see S. Shirk, *The Political Logic of Economic Reform in China* (Berkeley: University of California Press, 1993), c. 3.

C. The Ambiguous Relationship of Civil Law to Contract Law

The 1993 Contract Law (like the 1982 law it amended) applies to contracts for purchase and sale, construction, processing,[53] transport of goods, supply of electricity, storage, property leasing, loans, insurance, and "other economic contracts".[54] Any contract involving a foreign entity is governed by the Foreign Contract Law,[55] and any contract for commissioning, cooperatively conducting, or transferring technological research and development is governed by the Technology Contract Law.[56] That said, it should be stressed that the nature of the Contract Law — even whether it falls under the scope of 1987's *General Principles of Civil Law*[57] — is quite cloudy, even to Chinese legal scholars. To appreciate the ambiguities involved, we must begin with the reform context in which the 1982 Contract Law[58] and 1987 *General Principles of Civil Law* came into existence.

1. Economic Reform and the Need for Civil Law

One of the central acts in reforming the planned economy, begun in 1979 on a trial basis and affirmed by the N.P.C. in 1982, was to bifurcate the state economic plan into a traditional "mandatory" (*zhilingxing*) plan and a new "guidance" (*zhidaoxing*) plan. The mandatory plan continued to fix quotas and arrange inputs for vital sectors of the economy while the guidance plan set general allocation goals for the localities that could be implemented and adjusted, with central permission, according to local conditions and the availability of inputs on the market.[59] This created a two-track price system. Goods subject to mandatory purchase and allocation traded at state-set prices; goods sold above quota, or those exempt from mandatory planning, floated at market prices or within bands set by local or central officials.[60] During the decade-and-a-half of reform, certain goods have remained in the mandatory plan, some have remained in the guidance plan, and some have shifted back and forth. Periods when government fought inflation (*e.g.*, 1995) usually saw an increase in the scope of the mandatory plan and controlled prices. The government does not publish a comprehensive list of products subject to price controls, so it is impossible to say

---

[53] "Processing contract" (*jiagong chenglan*) is a peculiarly Chinese term that refers to one party contracting to labour on and thereby transform certain materials. It includes "fixed work" (*dingzuo*, in which one party stipulates the labor to be performed on some object, often in reference to transforming fabric into clothing); "renovation" (*xiushan*, often used in reference to housing repair); "repair" (*xiuli*, typically used in reference to repairs on small objects like bicycles and appliances); "printing" (*yinsha*); "advertising" (*guanggao*); and "surveying" (*cehui*) (see R. Liu, ed., *Hetong Falü Cidian* [*Dictionary of Contract Law*] (Beijing: China Auditor's Press, 1993) at 259).

[54] 1993 Contract Law, *supra* note 3, art. 8.

[55] *Supra* note 3.

[56] *Supra* note 3.

[57] *Supra* note 10.

[58] *Supra* note 3.

[59] See Z. Zhao, "Report on the Sixth Five-Year Plan" in *Fifth Session of the Fifth National People's Congress* (Beijing: Foreign Languages Press, 1983) 169.

[60] See B. Naughton, "China's Experience with Guidance Planning" (1990) 14 J. Comp. Econ. 743; Guo, *supra* note 31, c. 6.

with precision which transactions use "free market" pricing. Chinese officials claim that prices are currently set by the market for ninety-five percent of consumer goods and eighty to eighty-five percent of industrial inputs, but it is unclear whether goods subject to price "bands" are included, and officials have recently advocated stricter price "management" and detailed laws clarifying local, central and business responsibilities in pricing decisions. The government has clearly used price ceilings and fiscal subsidies as anti-inflationary devices in the recent past.[61] Despite a definite long-term trend towards price freedom, then, prices floating at market rates at one time may easily be re-controlled, fixed within bands, or otherwise interfered with.

The 1982 Contract Law was enacted precisely to regulate the inevitably expanding number of transactions falling outside the mandatory plan and state-determined prices. The rights and obligations of parties involved in a mandatory planning contract are not governed by the Contract Law but by "relevant laws and administrative regulations."[62] The Contract Law only covers the "market" transactions of China's "market reforms", that is, guidance-plan and no-plan contracts. However, while transactions under the guidance plan (and therefore the Contract Law) are supposed to be characterized by voluntarism, negotiation and equal status between parties, the Contract Law reflects some of the same tentativeness and ambiguity of guidance planning and the dual-track price system. Exactly which transactions are "free" and which subject to some regulation is unclear. Nowhere has the tension between plan and price controls, on the one hand, and contract freedom, on the other, been more apparent than in debates surrounding passage of the *General Principles of Civil Law* in 1987.

First, a terminological clarification. China's government distinguishes civil law from "economic" law. Law governing mandatory-plan contracts is "economic" law. It is administrative in nature. Broadly speaking, the law governing voluntary economic transactions is civil law. The "Economic Contract Law" (the full name of the Contract Law) is, somewhat confusingly, *not* economic law, as it does not regulate contracts that fall under mandatory planning. It is usually considered civil law.[63]

In the lead-up to passage of the *General Principles of Civil Law*, adherents of stronger economic law argued that economic law should govern both hierarchical administrative relations between enterprises and ministries as well as enterprise-to-enterprise relations wherever state or collective resources (*e.g.*, land, materials and finances) are involved. They believed that civil law should be limited to relations involving "consumption" and in which the means of livelihood is under personal ownership. Inter-firm relations under economic law, the argument went, should not be based on equal status, and state intervention should always be possible.[64] On the other side, adherents of the "commodity relations theory" argued that "socialist commodity

---

[61] See National Trade Data Bank, U.S. Dept. of Commerce, Market Research Reports No. IMI964011, "China: Price Reform on Hold" (1996).

[62] 1993 Contract Law, *supra* note 3, art. 11.

[63] For more on the civil law/economic law distinction, see M. Kato, "Civil and Economic Law in the People's Republic of China" (1982) 30 Am. J. Comp. L. 429.

[64] For these sorts of views, see "Guanyu Min Fa, Jingji Fa de Xueshu Zuotan" ["Academic Forum on Civil and Economic Law"] [1979] no. 4 *Faxue Yanjiu* [*Studies in Law*] 14.

relations", defined as exchange carried out in the production, allocation, transfer and consumption of material goods, regardless of ownership, should be governed by civil law.[65] Thus, this argument went, enterprise-to-enterprise relations — even between state or collective units — should adhere to principles of voluntariness and equal status; civil-law principles should govern within the sphere of the commodity economy, but state authorities (*i.e.*, the Party) should determine the size of that sphere through policy decisions. These two schools of thought are sometimes called the "small civil law" and "big civil law" schools. The "small civil law" approach would obviously have permitted administrative interference in virtually all significant contract transactions.

In the end, the *General Principles of Civil Law* did not penetrate vertical relations between state administrative organs and enterprises, but did claim exclusive jurisdiction over horizontal (*i.e.*, inter-ministerial), enterprise-to-enterprise commodity relations regardless of the form of enterprise ownership. In theory, all such transactions are between "equal subjects" (*pingdeng zhuti*) whose actions enjoy "equal status" (*diwei pingdeng*).[66] This was considered a victory for the "big civil law" school. Regarding contracts, however, closer examination of both the *General Principles of Civil Law* and the Contract Law reveals it was a partial victory at best.

2. The Relation of the *General Principles of Civil Law* to Contract Law

Chinese law is divided into fundamental (*genben*), basic (*jiben*) and specifically enacted (*danxing*) law. The fundamental law is the Constitution; basic law regulates specific spheres of activity; and "special enactments" (*danxing fagui*) govern in a more specific manner activities discussed in fundamental and basic law. That is, basic law is subordinate to fundamental law and assumes a "leading role" over specific enactments.[67] In actuality, relations of subordination between laws can be unclear and sometimes chaotic. Clearly, the *General Principles of Civil Law* is a basic law on a par with the Administrative Law or the Criminal Law.[68] The Contract Law, however, is sometimes referred to as a "basic law for regulating economic contractual relations", yet is otherwise identified as specially enacted legislation.[69] The Contract Law is generally presumed to be regulated by the *General Principles of Civil Law*, but

---

[65] The commodity relations theory was advocated by perhaps China's foremost expert on civil law, Tong Rou, who died in 1991. For a discussion in English of his thought, see W.C. Jones, ed., *Basic Principles of Civil Law in China* (Armonk, N.Y.: M.E. Sharpe, 1989), a translation of Tong's *Minfa Yuanli* [*General Principles of Civil Law*].

[66] *General Principles of Civil Law*, *supra* note 10, arts. 2 and 3.

[67] R. Tong, trans. J.K. Ocko, "The *General Principles of Civil Law of the PRC*: Its Birth, Characteristics, and Role" (1989) 52:2 Law & Contemp. Probs. 151.

[68] See Q. Liu, ed., *Min Fa Jiaocheng* [*A Course in Civil Law*] (Beijing: China People's Public Security University Press, 1993) at 6.

[69] On the Contract Law as "basic" contract law, see Z. Liu, ed., *Xin Jingji Hetong Fa* [*The New Economic Contract Law*] (Beijing: China Auditor's Press, 1994) at 1. On the Contract Law as specially enacted legislation, see Liu, *A Course in Civil Law*, *ibid.* at 7.

there has been some debate on that subject.[70] Even the Contract Law's dominant status in the contract realm is uncertain. A high-level Commerce Bureau official recently argued that its paramount status over contracts is being undermined by a proliferation of contract laws that govern specific kinds of transactions; that is, it is sometimes treated as just one of many contract-related specific enactments.[71]

Such confusion is exacerbated by the fact that the *General Principles of Civil Law* was enacted five years *after* the 1982 Contract Law. This meant it could not serve as a foundation for the Contract Law (as civil codes usually ground specific legislation), but is an attempt to harmonize and codify previously unarticulated general principles that underlie a broad spectrum of statutes and regulations (of which the Contract Law is one) which predate it. The *General Principles of Civil Law* also lacks the "Special Parts" which in most civil-law systems illustrate how principles apply to specific situations. Specific topics are instead addressed in specially enacted laws like the Contract Law. The Chinese government views this arrangement as "an innovation in the history of civil legislation" designed to facilitate state control and flexibility during the "unique historical circumstances" generated by reform.[72] Unfortunately, it also creates confusion as to what law governs in particular situations and what general principles apply.

A cursory comparison of the conceptual underpinnings of the *General Principles of Civil Law* and the Contract Law reveals obvious tensions. The *General Principles of Civil Law* regulates property and personal relations between equal subjects based on German civil-law concepts such as "civil legal act", "juristic person", and "agency". It appears to conceive of a highly individualistic world quite compatible with freedom of contract. For example, it defines a contract as "an agreement between parties to establish, alter, or terminate a civil law relationship" and allows the contract or agreement between the parties to establish such crucial terms as quality, duration, place and price.[73] Nonetheless, the Chinese state does not go so far as to equate civil law with "private" law, as is usually done in the West.

> Our country's civil law is public law, not private law. ... "Private law" assumes that in handling matters between private individuals the state cannot interfere unless one party brings a lawsuit. ... Economic activity in our country is basically made up of economic transactions between social organizations made up of juristic persons and such organizations and citizens. ... State procuratorial

[70] See *e.g.* J. Liu, "Dui Xiuding 'Jingji Hetong Fa' Ruogan Jiben Wenti de Tantao" ["An Inquiry into Several Basic Issues Concerning Revising the Economic Contract Law"] [1992] no. 6 *Faxue Yanjiu* [*Studies in Law*] 48 [hereinafter "Inquiry"].

[71] In addition to the current Foreign Contract Law and Technology Contract Law, recently proposed legislation includes a Commercial Contract Law (*Shangye Hetong Fa*), Insurance Contract Law (*Baoxian Hetong Fa*) and Credit Contract Law (*Xindai Hetong Fa*) (see "Inquiry", *ibid.*).

[72] Tong, *supra* note 67 at 158.

[73] *General Principles of Civil Law*, *supra* note 10, arts. 85 and 88.

organs (*guojia jiancha jiguan*) not only supervise criminal matters, but also supervise (*jiandu*) certain economic activities.[74]

Perhaps more in the public-law spirit, the Contract Law by contrast explicitly limits who can enter into contracts and under what circumstances. Price terms may only be negotiated if state policy and the plan allow. All contracts must be in writing. The Contract Law, with a few exceptions, only governs contracts between juristic persons. And Commerce Bureau and government offices at the county level or above possess vague, potentially intrusive authority to "supervise" (*jiandu*) contracts according to administrative regulations.[75] Although the Contract Law is generally called a civil-law enactment, its spirit is so administrative that scholars actually talk about the need to co-opt contract law *into* civil law. One scholar suggested first drafting a unified economic-contract code (containing general provisions pertaining to all economic contracts, including foreign and technology contracts), to be followed by a civil-contract code, which would pave the way towards eventual absorption of the economic- and civil-contract codes into whatever complete Civil Code is ultimately adopted.[76]

Contract legislation whose scope is unclear, and that may or may not be subordinate to what is at any rate a public-law-spirited civil law, is bound to be a less than hearty guarantor of contract freedom. With this background in mind, let us now examine the issues of who may enter a contract, the role of bargaining and equal status, and dispute resolution and enforcement processes.

III. Who May Enter a Contract? Legal Personality and Juristic Personhood

In civil-law countries, "legal person" is usually defined as a "right and duty-bearing unit" and includes juristic persons (legally constituted entities like corporations) and natural persons (individuals). In most civil-law countries, juristic and natural persons — in their capacity as legal persons — enjoy roughly the same right to enter into legally protected contracts. In China, that right is reserved for juristic persons.

This point is often obscured in writings on Chinese law because the Chinese use a single term, *faren* (literally "law-person"), that may be translated as either juristic or legal person. But *faren* does not include natural persons and is therefore comparable to "juristic person". The tradition of limiting participation in contracts to juristic persons dates back to the 1950 Provisional Methods, which stipulated that a contract cannot be made with an individual, but must be "executed by a juristic person."[77] The 1982 Contract Law reiterated this restriction (art. 2) but added that individual household enterprises and members of agricultural communes, though not juristic persons, could form contracts between themselves and juristic persons "with reference to"

---

[74] Liu, *A Course in Civil Law*, *supra* note 68 at 6. The word *jiandu* implies a before-the-fact control even more comprehensive than the after-the-fact investigation and rectification implied by *jiancha*.

[75] Provisions cited are from the 1993 Contract Law, *supra* note 3, arts. 17(3), 3, 2 and 44, respectively.

[76] See "Inquiry", *supra* note 70.

[77] Provisional Methods, *supra* note 18, art. 5.

(*canzhao*) the Contract Law (art. 54). Some scholars argued that article 54 in fact permitted natural persons to sign economic contracts, and thus contradicted article 2.[78] This interpretation may exaggerate the 1982 law's liberality. The regime probably never saw itself granting natural persons such rights. Why? First, contracts formed "with reference to" the Contract Law may not enjoy protection *under* it. Second, household enterprises and commune officials are not natural persons: "they are not the same as ordinary individual citizens."[79] Later developments confirm that the state never intended to relax the juristic-person requirement. Although household enterprises and "agricultural contract management households" were eventually incorporated into the 1993 Contract Law (art. 2), an authoritative 1994 Commerce Bureau contract reference book still states that "any unit that does not possess juristic person 'qualifications' (*zige*) cannot sign an economic contract."[80] "Citizens" (*gongmin*), it notes, enjoy some civil-law rights (such as the right to work and to inherit personal property), but do not, in their capacity as citizens, enjoy rights reserved to juristic persons, including the right to engage in foreign trade, banking and insurance business.[81] In short, if an entity is not a properly approved and registered juristic person, it runs the risk that its contracts might not be protected by the provisions of the Contract Law.

How is juristic personhood administered by law? Requirements from the 1987 *General Principles of Civil Law* are clear only as far as they go: A juristic person must be established in accordance with law, possess property or funds, and possess a name and premises. But a juristic person must also be "able to assume civil obligations independently."[82] Who decides when an applicant is qualified to do so? The *General Principles of Civil Law* goes on to state that civil obligations may be assumed by state-owned, collective and various foreign enterprises that meet state capital requirements and are properly registered.[83] Again, qualifications for approval to register are nowhere spelled out. In effect, there is a tautology: the right to *be* a juristic person — a *prerequisite* for assuming civil obligations — is restricted to those who *may* assume civil obligations. This tautology is resolved by neither the 1982 and 1993 Contract Laws, which do not address business registration, nor later regulations governing the establishment and registration of various sorts of enterprises. State Council regulations (1988) govern the process by which private enterprises register with the Industrial-Commercial Administrative Management Bureau ("Commerce Bureau"). They require that applicants either be created or approved by a government

[78] For example, Cheng & Rosett argue that article 54 mandates the actors it mentions to "follow" the Contract Law (Cheng & Rosett, *supra* note 15 at 206). Potter suggests that the 1982 law meant to extend contracting rights to "units (or individuals) who had the requisite financial capacity to perform their obligations ..." (*supra* note 25 at 32).

[79] "... *tamen ye butong yu yiban de gongmin geren*" (Li, ed., *supra* note 3 at 222 (annotation to art. 54, 1982 Contract Law)).

[80] Z. Wang *et al.*, *Zhongguo Hetong Daquan (Xiudingban)* [*Handbook of Chinese Contracts (Revised Edition)*] (Beijing: Economic Management Press, 1994) at 1313.

[81] *Ibid.* at 24-26.

[82] *General Principles of Civil Law*, *supra* note 10, arts. 36-40.

[83] *Ibid.*, art. 41.

or ministerial body, or be pre-approved by the Commerce Bureau itself.[84] The (pre-)approval procedures which governments or Commerce Bureau offices must follow are nowhere defined. Even the eagerly anticipated Company Law of 1994 (governing privately-held and share corporations) did not clear things up: accompanying registration regulations also stipulate that companies must be pre-approved by a governmental body or the Commerce Bureau itself.[85] In other words, a would-be contractor does not possess a "right" to become a juristic person provided he or she meets some objective standard; he or she is granted permission to become a contractor based upon the good will or internal policy directives of local governments and Commerce Bureau offices.

The history of the concept of juristic person in China suggests that the state probably keeps approval criteria intentionally vague. Briefly introduced under the Kuomintang ("KMT") civil code of 1930, the concept of juristic person was initially rejected in the P.R.C. because it was seen as a pillar of the legal superstructures attending "commodity (*i.e.*, capitalist exchange) economies".[86] The landmark 1958 legal textbook simply classified juristic persons administratively according to forms of ownership (*e.g.*, state, collective, etc.).[87] The 1964 draft civil law did not mention them at all. Academic discussion of legal personality then reappeared in 1980 in the context of policy debate over granting state enterprises greater operational autonomy.[88] Some argued that greater enterprise autonomy required separating enterprise liabilities from state liabilities and that the institution of legal personality would perform just that function. When "juristic person" was finally reintroduced, beginning with the 1982 Contract Law, it was intended to implement this change in economic administration, not to recognize associations or groups as analogs to rights-bearing individuals, as in the Western tradition.[89] This is, in the main, why individuals and enterprises without authority over state property were excluded from the definition of juristic person. The purposes of "enterprise juristic persons" are to recognize enterprises as relatively independent, to protect their business activities, to allow them to use the property they own or manage, to separate the enterprises' property from the state's for the purpose

[84] "Zhonghua Renmin Gongheguo Qiye Fa Ren Dengji Guanli Tiaoli" ["Regulations of the P.R.C. for Managing the Registration of Enterprise Juristic Persons"], effective 3 June 1988, in *PRC Compendia of Laws*, *supra* note 46 (1988) 900, arts. 4, 5, 7, 14 and 15.

[85] "Zhonghua Renmin Gongheguo Gongsi Dengji Guanli Tiaoli" ["Administrative Rules of the P.R.C. Governing the Registration of Companies"], State Council of the P.R.C., 24 June 1994, arts. 4 and 7 (in FitzGerald, ed., *supra* note 3, para. 13-568). The Company Law is "Zhonghua Renmin Gongheguo Gongsi Fa" ["Company Law of the P.R.C."], 5th Meeting (Standing Committee), 8th N.P.C., December 1993 (effective 1 July 1994) in (1994) 9:2 China L. & Prac. 7.

[86] H.F. Cui, "Lun Faren Zhidu" ["On the System of Legal Personality"] [1984] no. 6 *Zhengzhi yu Falü* [*Politics and Law*] 51 at 52.

[87] See *Basic Issues of Chinese Civil Law*, *supra* note 28.

[88] See *e.g.* S.Y. Gao, "Faren Zhidu Dui Woguo Shixing Sihua de Xianshi Yiyi" ["The Practical Significance of the Institution of Legal Personality to the Realization of China's Four Modernizations"] [1980] no. 4 *Faxue Yanjiu* [*Studies in Law*] 15.

[89] On how contending theories of legal personality in the West have revolved around the question of what it means to say a group is a "person", see R. Pound, *Jurisprudence*, vol. 4 (St. Paul, Minn.: West, 1959) at 220-61.

of liability, and to assure foreigners that they are dealing with independent companies.[90] As the civil-law scholar Tong Rou put it, legal personality "is an important legal tool of a ruling class for maintaining and developing the economy."[91] But,

> treating legal personality as a legal tool and as being a product of the will of the ruling class, Chinese "theory" effectively rejects the real essence of this private law institution, that is, treating individuals and organizations as well as the state as equal and abstract subjects of rights.[92]

What are the basic goals the state has pursued through control over who enters contracts? Essentially, non-state-owned businesses — household, private and collective — have been promoted to reduce unemployment and augment production and services in the tertiary sector, a sector ignored or suppressed under the planned economy. Opportunities are rationed accordingly. Household enterprises, for instance, may only be established by unemployed youth, laid off or "idle" (*xiansan*) personnel, or skilled retirees, and they are restricted to trades like retail, transportation, personal services (*e.g.*, haircutting), and small-scale repair.[93] A number of policies that usually function in the "background" also support the rationing of these opportunities. The Constitution still upholds socialism as the "fundamental system" (*jiben zhidu*) and the state-managed economy as its "leading force" (*zhudao liliang*). And the reforms are guided by Deng's famous Four Cardinal Principles: to uphold the socialist road, the people's democratic dictatorship, leadership by the Party, and Marxism-Leninism/Mao Zedong Thought.[94] In general, the business approval process is meant to ensure that enterprises "satisfy the necessities of the state and the society" to promote production, convenience, and efficiency.[95]

The state has taken great care to ensure that it does not lose control over the decision to permit or deny someone the right to engage in legally protected economic exchange. Behind a veneer of civil-law language lie carefully constructed "veto points". These make it impossible for would-be businesspersons who are denied juristic personhood to assert against the state a "right" to contract; *i.e.*, they cannot accuse the state of violating the law or their rights. The formal institutional barriers to engaging

---

[90] Z. Zhao, trans. W. Zhao, "Enterprise Legal Persons: Their Important Status in Chinese Civil Law" (1989) 52:3 Law & Contemp. Probs. 1 at 3-6.

[91] R. Tong *et al.*, *Zhongguo Minfa* [*Chinese Civil Law*] (Beijing: Legal Press, 1990) at 94-95.

[92] Chen, *supra* note 40 at 107.

[93] "Guowuyuan Guanyu Chengzhen Feinongye Geti Jingji Ruogan Zhengcexing Guiding" ["Several State Council Policy Regulations Concerning City and Township Non-Agricultural Household Economies"], issued July 1981, in *PRC Compendia of Laws*, *supra* note 46 (1981) at 283; and "Guowuyuan 'Guanyu Chengzhen Feinongye Geti Jingji Ruogan Zhengcexing Guiding' de Buchong Guiding" ["State Council Supplementary Regulations to 'Several Policy Regulations Concerning City and Township Non-agricultural Household Economies'"], issued April 1983, in *PRC Compendia of Laws*, *supra* note 46 (1983) 511.

[94] See X.P. Deng, "Uphold the Four Cardinal Principles" (30 March 1979) in *Selected Works of Deng Xiaoping, 1975-1982* (Beijing: Foreign Languages Press, 1984) 166 at 172.

[95] Zhao, *supra* note 90 at 4.

in productive economic activity are very real and potentially high; how high depends largely on how local officials use their considerable discretionary power.[96]

IV. Equal Status and Negotiation: Contract Formation and Performance

Having been passed before the 1987 *General Principles of Civil Law*, the 1982 Contract Law is, in theory, more influenced by "economic" law than the 1993 Contract Law. Indeed, the 1982 Contract Law was instituted when the state plan still regulated most economic activity. Its *raison d'être* includes "safeguarding the socialist economic order, improving economic 'effectiveness' (*xiaoli*), and ensuring implementation of the state plan."[97] It states that contracts must accord with the demands of the state plan and declares void any contracts that violate the state plan or "state interests or society's public interests" (*guojia liyi huo shehui gonggong liyi*).[98] Any disputes over contracts involving the mandatory plan are to be handled administratively by the "higher-level planning bodies responsible" (*shangji jihua zhuguan jiguan*). And contracts under guidance planning should be signed "with reference to" (*canzhao*) plan targets while conforming with the "real situation" (*shiji qingkuang*) of the enterprises involved.[99]

On the surface, the changes which resulted in the 1993 Contract Law free contracts from the strictures of the plan. The 1993 law's *raison d'être* replaces "implement the state plan" with "safeguard healthy development of the socialist market economy."[100] Contracts no longer must accord with the requirements of state policy and planning, but only with laws and administrative regulations.[101] These changes imply less direct state intrusion into the economy. Deeper analysis seems to indicate, however, that the state has not really relinquished much discretion to interfere in contracts. Broadening the types of entities that fall under the Contract Law's scope certainly did not dilute the principle of state control over who enters contracts. In addition, "administrative regulations" may be issued by planning authorities and may be just as intrusive and oriented to the plan as policy or the plan itself. Moreover, the prohibition against contracts that violate state or public interests remains. This in itself grants Chinese courts much broader grounds for nullifying contracts than are avail-

---

[96] For more on the practical realities of obtaining juristic-person status (*i.e.*, getting one's business approved and registered), see S. Young, *Private Business and Economic Reform in China* (Armonk, N.Y.: M.E. Sharpe, 1995); W. Kraus, trans. E. Holz, *Private Business in China: Revival between Ideology and Pragmatism* (Honolulu: University of Hawaii Press, 1991); D. Rubenstein, *Transaction Costs and Market Culture under China's Contract Law Reform* (Ph. D. dissertation, University of Minnesota, 1996).

[97] 1982 Contract Law, *supra* note 3, art. 1.

[98] *Ibid.*, arts. 4 and 7. A contract may also be found only partly invalid, in which case the unaffected parts remain valid.

[99] *Ibid.*, art. 11.

[100] 1993 Contract Law, *supra* note 3, art. 1.

[101] Compare 1982 Contract Law, *supra* note 3, art. 4 with 1993 Contract Law, *ibid.*, art. 4.

able to U.S. courts, for example.[102] In fact, many provisions of the 1993 Contract Law continue to leave the state "principled ambiguity" to do as it pleases.

"Freedom of contract" implies, among other things, that neither party has "more rights" than the other and that the contract terms the parties freely negotiate and agree to should govern their relationship. In China, the state, through its economic plans and state-owned enterprises, endows certain "civil law" actors with special powers that may conflict with the principle of equal status. Contract principles that potentially impinge on equal status and negotiation basically fall into two categories: contract formation and contract performance. In the analysis that follows, special attention is paid to whether principles in each category tend to guarantee, or leave room for interference with, equal status and free negotiation.

A. Contract Formation

Article 5 is the main provision of the 1993 Contract Law that appears aimed at increasing parties' freedom to form a contract according to their will. The 1982 law stated, in the same article, that contracts "must adhere to the principles of equality and mutual benefit, agreement through consultation, and compensation for equal value." The 1993 law replaces "must adhere to" (*bixu guanche*) with the less strict "should abide by" (*yingdang zunxu*) and omits "compensation for equal value". Courts had used the latter phrase to overturn freely negotiated price terms that they deemed unfair.[103] Some scholars thus touted the change in article 5 as heralding greater freedom of contract.[104]

But, in the context of Chinese jurisprudence, the meaning of this change is not so clear. The "principle of compensation for equal value" (*dengjia youchang de yuanze*) did not originally mean equal, fair or just division of the benefits of an exchange, but rather that parties possessed a *right* to compensation, a right not recognized by the state under economic law, administrative law, or plan-oriented policy.[105] In this light,

---

[102] In the landmark case of *Home Building & Loan Association* v. *Blaisdell*, 290 U.S. 398, 54 S. Ct. 231 (1934) [hereinafter cited to U.S.], the U.S. Supreme Court reinterpreted the "contract clause" of the U.S. Constitution (art. I, § 10), which states that "No State shall ... pass any ... Law impairing the Obligation of Contracts." However, the judgment, upholding moratoriums on farm foreclosures during the Depression, sanctioned state laws that achieve a "rational compromise between individual rights and public welfare" (*ibid.* at 442) in responding to economic "crises" that threaten the very "economic structure upon which the good of all depends" (*ibid.*). This ruling may in practice allow governments broad discretion to interfere with contracts, but the *principle* on which it rests — ameliorating economic *crises* — is much more restrictive than preventing "harm" to "state or public interests".

[103] For examples, see P.B. Potter, "Riding the Tiger: Legitimacy and Legal Culture in Post-Mao China" (1994) 138 China Q. 325 at 343-44, nn. 91-93.

[104] Pitman Potter, referring to article 5 in notes to his translation of the 1993 Contract Law revision, wrote, "parties have been granted more autonomy in concluding their bargains" ("Economic Contract Law Revision" (1993) 9 China L. & Prac. 40 at 48).

[105] This is made quite clear in S. Qi, "Jingji Fa shi yi ge Zhongyao de Duli de Falü Bumen" ["Economic Law is an Important, Independent Branch of Law"] in "Academic Forum on Civil and Economic Law", *supra* note 64 at 15.

that it has been omitted from the 1993 Contract Law may mean that the right to compensation has been attenuated. If so, one of the characteristics that distinguished the Contract Law from economic law would be diluted, resulting in a weakening of principles of contract freedom. It is too early to tell what was intended by this change and what its result will be.

Whatever standards of equal value are brought to bear on contractors, however, it is the very fact that China has until now used administrative approval instead of a system of "offer and acceptance" which has continued to lend Chinese contracts a highly administrative flavour. That is, generally speaking, a contract becomes binding only when it is duly authorized, typically by the local office of the Commerce Bureau or ministry of justice.[106] Although a systematic concept of offer and acceptance is on the agenda of the unified contract law,[107] it is currently nonexistent in China.

B. Contract Performance and Nonperformance

The changes in the 1993 Contract Law which most influence equal status and negotiation involve contract performance. Under mandatory planning, parties were subject to "specific performance"; that is, contracts were administrative orders, so administrators could order a party to perform specifically what he had "agreed" to do, no matter how impractical or costly.[108] Anglo-American law also recognizes the doctrine of specific performance, but conceives of it in terms of remedying loss, not in terms of fulfilling administrative orders.[109] That is, the need for performance is evaluated in terms of the cost or benefit to the parties themselves. Parties are usually free to break an agreement so long as they are willing to pay the price. Chinese law still tends to view specific performance in terms of administration, not freedom, of contract.

One of the most common methods for determining the cost of terminating an agreement is "liquidated damages", defined as "the sum which party to contract agrees to pay if he breaks some promise ..."[110] It is a pre-estimate of probable loss and is often paid up front (like a deposit). It thus differs from compensatory damages, which are determined after the breach by a court or other third party. China's reform-era legislation has emphasized something that appears very similar to liquidated damages, called "breach fees" (*weiyue jin*), but with a distinctly administrative flavor.

---

[106] Whether or not Commerce Bureau or ministry of justice approval is required has in fact been an area of some disagreement among legal scholars. Though I would argue such approval is almost always optional, courts certainly may be more likely to void a contract that is without it, and approval may be required from other administrative organs via rules that remain unpublished. For a more extended discussion, see the author's *Transaction Costs and Market Culture under China's Contract Law Reform*, *supra* note 96 at 184-88.

[107] See Jiang, *supra* note 4 at 249; Liang, *supra* note 4 at 111.

[108] On the importance of "specific performance" under planning, see J.V. Feinerman, "Legal Institution, Administrative Device, or Foreign Import: The Roles of Contract in the People's Republic of China" in P.B. Potter, ed., *Domestic Law Reforms in Post-Mao China* (Armonk, N.Y.: M.E. Sharpe, 1994) 225.

[109] See *supra* note 12.

[110] *Black's Law Dictionary*, *supra* note 11 at 391.

An American court, when addressing a breach of a contract that contains a liquidated-damages clause, will ask: Was the intention of the parties that the contract actually be performed (in which case specific performance may be invoked simultaneously with liquidated damages), or was it that the liquidated-damages clause constitute "a price fixed for the exercise of an option to terminate" (in which case payment of liquidated damages would suffice)?[111]

Chinese law does not make this distinction. The 1982 and 1993 Contract Laws state that even if "breach fees" are paid, the breachor "should" still carry out the contract "if the other party so requests."[112] The ambiguous term "should" (*yingdang*) has allowed proponents of civil law (who interpret it as an admonition) and economic law (who interpret it as an imperative) to press their own interpretations. For instance, one advocate of economic law argues that, under this clause, courts should have the option of ordering specific performance to ensure that fulfilling the state economic plan remains the economy's top priority; under socialism, the *raison d'être* of economic exchange should be to satisfy social demand, not simply create profit.[113] Courts that favor this interpretation might invalidate a freely agreed-upon price for termination if they determine performance is in the public good. And, as has been oft criticized by legal scholars (but will probably change under the unified contract law), the 1982 and 1993 Contract Laws depart from prevalent international practice in *requiring* parties to include "breach fee" clauses and, in many cases, stipulating the amount.[114] Breach fees have been viewed as administrative punishment, not just compensation.[115] Bolstering court discretion to order strict performance is a provision which prohibits either party from changing a contract "without authorization" (*shanzi*).[116]

It might be that judges not only *may* enforce specific performance but are often compelled to do so by governmental or ministerial officials. There have been some calls to introduce a Western doctrine — *rebus sic stantibus* or fundamental change of circumstances — that would expand the grounds available to contractors (and judges) for altering contracts.[117] *Rebus sic stantibus* is "a tacit condition, said to attach to all treaties, that they shall cease to be obligatory so soon as the state of facts and condi-

[111] For precedents as early as the 1920s that establish this distinction, see J.D. Calamari & J.M. Perillo, *The Law of Contracts* (St. Paul, Minn.: West, 1970) §§ 14-34.

[112] 1993 Contract Law, *supra* note 3, art. 31. The actual wording is "[If] the other party requests continued performance of the contract, [the breachor] should continue to carry it out" (*duifang yaoqiu jixu lüxing hetong de, ying jixu lüxing*).

[113] W. Wang, "Lun Hetong de Qiangzhi Shiji Lüxing" ["On the Coercive Enforcement of Contract"] [1984] no. 3 *Faxue Yanjiu* [*Studies in Law*] 46.

[114] For criticisms of this system, see Jiang, *supra* note 4 at 250.

[115] L. Wang *et al.*, "Wanshan Woguo Weiyue Zeren Zhidu Shi Lun" ["Ten Views on Perfecting China's System of Responsibility for Breach of Contract"] [1995] no. 4 *Zhongguo Shehui Kexue* [*Chinese Social Science*] 4, reprinted in [1995] no. 12 *Faxue* [*Legal Studies*] (Chinese People's University reprint series topic D41) 85 at 93-94.

[116] 1993 Contract Law, *supra* note 3, art. 6.

[117] Z. Yang, "Shilun Woguo Minfa Queli 'Qingshi Biangeng Yuanze' de Biyaoxing" ["On the Necessity of Establishing 'The Principle of Changed Circumstances' in China's Civil Law"] [1990] no. 5 *Zhongguo Faxue* [*Chinese Legal Science*] 53.

tions upon which they were founded has substantially changed."[118] It would allow courts to rescind or modify contracts in light of changes in background conditions that are external to the parties, fall under *force majeure* (discussed next), and result in manifest inequity. The perceived need for such a doctrine may suggest that contractors and judges are groping for a doctrinal counterweight to the administratively-oriented Chinese version of specific performance. To my knowledge there have been no plans to introduce *rebus sic stantibus* into China's contract law.

Vestiges of the planned economy's performance imperative touch even rather arcane doctrines like "anticipatory repudiation", when one party suspends performance of or rescinds a contract because he has unequivocal evidence that the other party "will not render its performance under the contract when that time [time fixed for performance in the contract] arrives ..."[119] Under articles 2-609 and 2-610 of the U.S. Uniform Commercial Code ("U.C.C."), suspension or rescission is justified if one merely has "reasonable grounds" for believing one's partner will not (*e.g.*, through verbal statements) or cannot (*e.g.*, because of financial or production difficulties) perform.[120] Under a similar doctrine from the German BGB, *exceptio adimpleti non contratus*, one may suspend performance if there is a "significant deterioration in the financial position of the other party" which endangers one's claim for counterperformance.[121]

In China, one may suspend performance due to another's anticipatory repudiation only under the Foreign Contract Law, not the 1993 Contract Law, and that provision[122] seems to have been added, reluctantly, only because of international standards.[123] Even under the Foreign Contract Law, stricter conditions are put on its exercise than in either the U.C.C. or BGB. First, the party exercising its right to suspend performance must have "conclusive evidence" (*queqie zhengju*) that the other party cannot perform; "reasonable grounds" will not do. Second, one may only suspend, not rescind, performance.[124] Third, one is liable for breach if he later cannot prove that the other party could not perform. In addition, the Chinese law does not encompass what one analyst has called "clear repudiation" (*mingshi huiyue*), or explicit statements by

---

[118] *Black's Law Dictionary*, *supra* note 11 at 1267.

[119] *Ibid.* at 93 ("anticipatory breach of contract"). The phrase "anticipatory repudiation" refers to the act of the party who is unable or unwilling to perform (his "repudiation", or breach, is "anticipatory", or prospective, not actual). Somewhat confusingly, using another's anticipatory repudiation as a justification for your own breach is also often called "anticipatory repudiation".

[120] See also Y. Zhao, "A Comparative Study of the Uniform Commercial Code and the Foreign Economic Contract Law of the People's Republic of China" (1988) 6 Int'l Tax & Bus. Law. 26 at 46 n. 133.

[121] *The German Civil Code: Revised Edition (as amended to January 1, 1992)*, trans. S.L. Goren (Littleton, Colo.: Rothman, 1994), art. 321 [hereinafter BGB].

[122] Foreign Contract Law, *supra* note 3, art. 17.

[123] For details, see B. Gong, "The Future Direction of the PRC Economic Contract Law" (Shanghai: Law School of Fudan University, 1995) at 19-20 [unpublished].

[124] In this, art. 17 of the Foreign Contract Law, *supra* note 3 approaches art. 321 of the BGB, *supra* note 120.

one's partner that he is unwilling to or will not perform. It only covers "tacit repudiation" (*moshi huiyue*), that is, an inability to perform.[125]

Obviously, the Foreign Contract Law's stance on suspending performance in response to anticipatory repudiation makes it difficult for creditors to suspend or rescind deals even when they may have good reason to believe their partner may default. Under domestic-contract law, no form of the principle exists. As part of China's transition from a planned economy to a socialist market economy, however, the performance imperative implicit in China's approach to this doctrine is giving way to a recognition that a strong form of the anticipatory-repudiation doctrine would be good for creditors; it is one of the doctrines, in its Anglo-American form, that is being pushed most heavily by scholars involved in drafting the unified contract law.[126] Nonetheless, there are apparently no plans to relax the requirement of "conclusive evidence" and the attendant liability for breach if one fails to produce it, or to explicitly recognize "clear repudiation".[127] In other words, until the unified contract law is passed, and depending upon how it addresses the issue of anticipatory repudiation, the state continues to emphasize performance. In general, contractors lack the right to decide for themselves, based on the relative costs (and risks) of performing, whether to perform.

The power to order specific performance (at the request of one party) is clearly an access point for state interference in negotiation — a negotiated price for termination may be overridden. Court authority to mandate performance is mirrored by considerable discretion in deciding what counts as a valid excuse for *non*performance. Such discretion results from ambiguity in a change to the 1982 Contract Law that, at first glance, seems to reduce the possibility of outside interference in freely negotiated contract terms. Under the 1982 Contract Law, one permissible excuse for nonperformance was a change in the state plan that made it impossible or excessively costly to carry out a contract (*e.g.*, either expected materials were not allocated or prices changed).[128] This clearly subordinated contracts to planning and was rescinded in the 1993 Contract Law. Now, the only permissible grounds for modifying or rescinding a contract are failure of the other party to perform and *force majeure* (*buke kangli*).[129] But due to ambiguities in the doctrine of *force majeure* under Chinese law, courts retain discretion to decide when a party can back out of contract responsibilities.

Force majeure, "superior (or irresistible) force", is when part or the entirety of a contract "cannot be performed due to causes which are outside the control of the parties and could not be avoided by exercise of due care." It is similar to, but subsumes, "act of God", or *vis major*, which refers to natural disasters.[130] In the context of China,

---

[125] See Wang, *supra* note 115 at 85-87.

[126] See Wang, *ibid.*; L. Wang, "Yuqi Weiyue Zhidu Ruogan Wenti Yanjiu" ["Research on Some Problems of the System of Anticipatory Breach of Contract"] [1995] no. 2 *Zhengfa Luntan* [*Tribune of Political Science and Law*] 18; Liang, *supra* note 4 at 115.

[127] See *e.g.* the comments made by Jiang, *supra* note 4 at 251.

[128] Art. 27.

[129] 1993 Contract Law, *supra* note 3, art. 26.

[130] *Black's Law Dictionary*, *supra* note 11 at 33 ("act of God"), 645 ("*force majeure*") and 1572 ("*vis major*").

the first question that must be asked is, can the actions of state officials and planners count as *force majeure*? Many contracts depend on inputs, financing and licenses from state organs. Does refusal of a state official to provide these things constitute *force majeure*? Courts in fact frequently applied the 1982 provision permitting changes in contracts due to the state plan (especially price changes).[131] Would such changes now be considered *force majeure*? If so, how close can a relationship between an enterprise and the state officials responsible for such policy changes be before *force majeure* no longer applies? Clearly, the opportunity exists for enterprises and ministries to collude in using *force majeure* to relieve enterprises of their obligations, especially with so many pricing and planning decisions devolved to provincial or local officials. The doctrine of *force majeure* as it appears in Chinese law does not resolve these issues.

Chinese law merely defines *force majeure* as "objective conditions" (*keguan qingkuang*) that are "unforeseeable" (*buneng yujian*), "unavoidable" (*buneng bimian*), and "insurmountable" (*buneng kefu*).[132] But no legislation, regulations or legal interpretations say whether the actions of planning officials fall inside or outside of these categories. Moreover, the phrase *buneng* ("not able") in each of the three major conditions elides a distinction that has assumed great importance in Anglo-American law: impossible versus impracticable. "[A] thing is impossible in legal contemplation when it is not practicable; and a thing is impracticable when it can only be done at an excessive and unreasonable cost."[133] *Buneng* can mean either. Courts are thus able to invoke the standard of impossibility when they want to make it difficult for a party to avoid specific performance, and a more relaxed standard like impracticability when they want to relieve a party of certain obligations. Indeed, courts have been known to permit stronger, state-connected parties wider latitude for nonperformance despite propaganda supporting consistent, objective enforcement.[134]

In sum, a negotiated price for contract termination is vulnerable to myriad legal grounds for ordering specific performance — social good, the request of one party, indirect orders from planners, etc. In this vein, judicial discretion generated by ambiguity in the doctrine of *force majeure* may allow the state to pick and choose when performance is required. Just as importantly, it provides opportunities for enterprises to parlay even indirect connections with planning authorities into real status inequalities. By colluding with planners, or even local courts, such enterprises may not be held to contract terms as strictly as their co-contractants. All in all, the 1993 Contract

---

[131] *E.g.*, [1988] no. 2 *Zhonghua Renmin Gongheguo Zuigao Renmin Fayuan Gongbao* [*Gazette of the Supreme People's Court of the PRC* 16 [hereinafter *Supreme Court Gazette*]. See also L. Ross, "Force Majeure and Related Doctrines of Excuse in Contract Law of the People's Republic of China" (1991) 5 J. Chinese L. 58 at 96; P.B. Potter, *supra* note 103 at 344.

[132] *General Principles of Civil Law*, *supra* note 10, art. 153. Article 24 of the 1985 Foreign Contract Law, *supra* note 3, essentially restates this definition.

[133] *Black's Law Dictionary*, *supra* note 11 at 755 ("impossibility").

[134] On propaganda, see D. Zweig *et al.*, "Law, Contracts, and Economic Modernization: Lessons from the Recent Chinese Rural Reforms" (1987) 23 Stanf. J. Int'l L. 319; on reality, see Ross, *supra* note 131.

Law does not clearly do a better job of upholding principles of free negotiation and equal status than its 1982 counterpart. Obvious references to planning have been omitted, but the loopholes have not been plugged. "Principled ambiguity" permitting official interference in contracts continues to pervade the state's legal framework. Its vision of even "civil law" freedom of contract is, ultimately, still tentative and based less on individual rights than on state guidance of the economy.

V. Dispute Resolution: Vertical and Horizontal Pressures

Freedom of contract requires that contracts be enforceable at law. Also, institutional economists view enforcement as perhaps the most salient aspect of contracts. Without reliable, impartial and predictable dispute resolution and enforcement, they postulate, the ability of contracts to foster long-distance and impersonal trade will be impaired.[135]

Excluding extremely informal mediators (like clan leaders, neighbours, relatives and friends), dispute-resolution bodies, or forums, in China include: (1) People's Mediation Committees (*Renmin Tiaojie Weiyuanhui*) ("Mediation Committees"); (2) common administrative superiors ("superiors") (typically a ministerial official); (3) the Commerce Bureau; and (4) People's Courts ("courts"). In the countryside, Party secretaries, public-security officials, and brigade leaders sometimes still conduct mediation, but this study focuses on urban China.[136]

Among these four forums, China (like Western nations) recognizes three modes, or types, of dispute resolution: mediation (*tiaojie*), arbitration (*zhongcai*) and adjudication (*shenpan*). Each is recognizable to its Western counterpart but may function very differently. Mediation involves a third party who helps bring the parties to voluntary agreement but (in theory) lacks authority to impose a solution. Arbitration involves a non-judicial body who by the parties' agreement — usually by a pre-arranged "arbitration clause" in the contract — may impose a solution. And adjudication involves a court that enjoys jurisdiction despite the wishes of the parties and possesses authority to impose a solution.

In China, Mediation Committees may only mediate. Superiors may conduct mediation or, in some cases, something akin to arbitration. The Commerce Bureau is the primary arbitral body, operating through its Economic Contract Arbitration Committees (*Jingji Hetong Zhongcai Weiyuanhui*) ("Arbitration Committees").[137] Theoreti-

[135] See D.C. North, *Institutions, Institutional Change and Economic Performance* (Cambridge: Cambridge University Press, 1990), especially at 121. See also O.E. Williamson, *The Economic Institutions of Capitalism: Firms, Markets, Relational Contracting* (New York: Free Press, 1985).

[136] On the *de facto* mediation authority of these officials, see D. Barnett, *Cadres, Bureaucracy, and Political Power in Communist China* (New York: Columbia University Press, 1967); S.M. Huang, *The Spiral Road: Change in a Chinese Village Through the Eyes of a Communist Party Leader* (Boulder, Colo.: Westview Press, 1989).

[137] The 1993 Contract Law, *supra* note 3, art. 42, declares that parties may use "arbitral organs", which are defined as Commerce Bureau Arbitration Committees in "Zhonghua Renmin Gongheguo Jingji Hetong Zhongcai Tiaoli" ["Regulations of the PRC for Arbitration over Economic Contracts"],

cally, Arbitration Committees may also be used for mediation. Courts, though required in civil cases to first attempt mediation, alone possess authority to adjudicate.[138]

Aside from a requirement in the 1982 Contract Law that parties attempt consultation before availing themselves of any other method of dispute resolution, the 1982 and 1993 Contract Laws both grant parties great discretion in choosing a dispute-resolution forum. They may attempt mediation first. If it fails or if they are not willing to submit to mediation, they may go directly to the Commerce Bureau for arbitration, or even directly to court for adjudication.[139] Determining how and when these options can actually be exercised requires a closer look at each forum.

A. People's Mediation Committees

After the communists took power, all independent associations eventually either became state associations or were eliminated, and mediation bodies were no exception. Of the three modes of dispute resolution, mediation in China perhaps differs most from its Western incarnation. Anglo-American law recognizes mediation as a "[p]rivate, informal dispute resolution process in which a neutral third person, the mediator, helps disputing parties to reach an agreement [and] [t]he mediator has no power to impose a decision on the parties."[140] Although mediation in China is informal, Mediation Committees are not private and mediators seem to possess authority to impose decisions or make their decisions virtually binding. It is estimated that up to ninety percent of civil disputes are resolved through Mediation Committees and other informal (ministerial, enterprise, etc.) mediating bodies.[141]

From the founding of the P.R.C., Mediation Committees have been an important organization for sociopolitical control at the local level, part of the system of "comprehensive control" (*zonghe zhili*). Although the government refers to the activity of Mediation Committees as informal or "mass" (*qunzhong*) mediation — as opposed to the formal or "judicial" (*fayuan*) mediation that occurs in court — Mediation Committees in fact operate under the direct bureaucratic control of local sections of the Ministry of Justice. They merely receive guidance from local governments and basic-level courts.[142] Their day-to-day work is guided by a locally appointed "judicial

---

promulgated August 1983 by the State Council, in FitzGerald, ed., *supra* note 3, vol. 2 (*Business Regulation*) para. 10-620.

[138] The "principle of 'emphasizing mediation'" ("*zhuozhong tiaojie*" *de yuanze*) is described in Liu, ed., *supra* note 53 at 909. It is set out in *Zhonghua Renmin Gongheguo Minshi Susong Fa* [*Code of Civil Procedure of the PRC*] [hereinafter *PRC Code of Civil Procedure*], adopted April 1991, in Fitzgerald, ed., *ibid.*, vol. 3 (*Business Regulation*) para. 19-201.

[139] See 1982 Contract Law, *supra* note 3, art. 48, and 1993 Contract Law, *supra* note 3, art. 42.

[140] *Black's Law Dictionary*, *supra* note 11 at 981 ("mediation").

[141] M. Palmer, "The Revival of Mediation in the People's Republic of China: (1) Extra-Judicial Mediation" in W.E. Butler, ed., *Yearbook on Socialist Legal Systems, 1987* (Dobbs Ferry, N.Y.: Transnational, 1987) 219 at 223 n. 14.

[142] See "Renmin Tiaojie Weiyuanhui Zanxing Zuzhi Tongze" ["Provisional Organizational Principles for People's Mediation Committees" [hereinafter Mediation Principles] in *Zhongyang Renmin Zhengfu Faling Huibian* [*Compilation of Laws and Decrees of the Central People's Government*]

assistant" (*sifa zhuli yuan*) who operates under the leadership of the local Ministry of Justice.[143] Most are established by Residence Committees (*Jumin Weiyuanhui*) in cities and by Villagers' Committees (*Cunmin Weiyuanhui*) in the countryside, but they also exist as "mediation small groups" (*tiaojie xiaozu*) in factories and among every ten households in a village.[144] They are charged with upholding Party policy, they channel information to the Party, they have close relations with local police, and most mediators are Party members.[145]

In light of how Mediation Committees are organized, it is perhaps not surprising that they often violate their own avowed "principle of voluntariness" (*ziyuan yuanze*) and act more as arbitrators than as mediators.[146] That settlements are imposed is suggested by peculiar reports that parties "repudiate" (*fanhui*) or "refuse to accept as final" (*bufu*) mediation agreements. In fact, judicial assistants have in practice often gone beyond "guiding" the work of Mediation Committees and imposed settlements. Far from being seen as an aberration, some scholars have actually defended this practice.[147] And judicial assistants have *de facto* authority to impose decisions in minor cases because courts will simply not accept them for adjudication. In a way, then, "Mediation Committee" is a misnomer; these bodies are more like small-claims courts.[148]

Because Mediation Committees are extensions of the Party-state, they can neither develop nor adhere to their own professional standards. That is, how they resolve disputes is always a function of the current policy line. During the Cultural Revolution conflicts were politicized, used for mobilizing the masses. Mediation, in the sense of meeting your opponent halfway, was condemned as pernicious promotion of "class harmony" (*jieji tiaohe*).[149] Persons combating "rightist tendencies", or those with good class backgrounds, were encouraged never to compromise. Mediators sided with the party who was convincingly more "left".

In the Deng era the pendulum has swung the other way. "Compromise" (*rang*) is now encouraged. Class conflict is downplayed. The state views mediation as a tool

---

(January-September 1954) (Beijing: Legal Press, 1954) 47, arts. 2 and 10; "Renmin Tiaojie Weiyuanhui Zuzhi Tiaoli" ["Regulations on the Organization of People's Mediation Committees" [hereinafter Mediation Regulations], issued June 1989 by the State Council, in *PRC Compendia of Laws*, *supra* note 46 (1989) 131, art. 12.

[143] Mediation Regulations, *ibid.*, art. 2.

[144] See Palmer, *supra* note 141 at 269.

[145] On personnel and organization, see Stanley Lubman's pathbreaking "Mao and Mediation: Politics and Dispute Resolution in China" (1967) 55 Calif. L. Rev. 1284.

[146] The argument that follows is made by D.C. Clarke in "Dispute Resolution in China" (1991) 5 J. Chinese L. 245. That Mediation Committees should follow the principle of voluntariness is stipulated in the *PRC Code of Civil Procedure*, *supra* note 138, art. 16.

[147] See Z. Yao, "Sifa Xingzheng Tiaojie Caijuequan Chuyi" ["A Preliminary Discussion of Adjudication Powers in Judicial Administrative Mediation"] [1986] no. 2 *Faxue* [*Jurisprudence Monthly*] 38.

[148] See Clarke, *supra* note 146 at 293.

[149] J. Wang, "Renmin Tiaojie zai Zhongguo de Yanxu he Fazhan" ["The Continuity and Development of People's Mediation in China"] [1985] no. 6 *Faxue Yanjiu* [*Studies in Law*] 28 at 30, *passim*.

for soothing the jealousies, called "red-eye disease" (*hongyan bing*), that have accompanied Deng's policy of "let some get rich first".[150] Rather than *replace* courts' legal formality with class struggle, Mediation Committees now work *with* courts to reduce their caseloads and foster a sense of legality. In line with a re-emphasis on Mao's more conciliatory writings, civil matters like contract disputes are called "nonantagonistic" contradictions "among the people" (not "antagonistic" contradictions "among the people and the enemy") which should be resolved using persuasion (not coercion).[151] But mediators have understandably been confused by the tension between upholding contractors' lawful rights and "soothing" conflicts. In the mid-1980s, mediators were finally told to stop using the term *tiaohe* ("conciliation"), which implies exalting social harmony and forcing compromise at the expense of individuals' rights, and start using *tiaojie* ("mediation"), which implies discerning right from wrong and adhering to the principle of voluntariness.[152] The habit of imposing solutions based on Party policy can be expected to die hard, however, especially among older mediators.

Although mediation agreements are not supposed to be legally binding, a party who hopes to challenge a mediation agreement that was coerced or is otherwise unsatisfactory faces serious obstacles.[153] Appeals are first referred back to the Mediation Committee's judicial assistant, who is charged to uphold any agreement that does not violate "law or policy".[154] Appeal after this point is impossible for smaller cases because, again, courts will not accept them. If one's case is large enough, one may appeal to court, but only if the other party reneges on the mediation agreement (or never agreed to submit to mediation in the first place).[155] And, once in court, judges seem much more likely to enforce the original agreement than allow it to be amended. Both the Mediation Regulations and the *Code of Civil Procedure* indicate parties "should" (*yingdang*) carry out mediation agreements.[156] Recall from earlier discussion of breach fees and specific performance that *yingdang* may be interpreted as an admonition ("ought to") or an imperative ("must").[157] Although no law formally defines *yingdang* in this context, authoritative legal textbooks have interpreted it as "must".[158] At any

---

[150] See examples in Palmer, *supra* note 141 at 246-47, nn. 93-97.

[151] This of course refers to Mao's speech, "On the Correct Handling of Contradictions Among the People" (27 February 1957) in *Selected Readings from the Works of Mao Tse-tung* (Peking: Foreign Languages Press, 1967) 350.

[152] See W.D. Ji, "Fazhi yu Tiaojie de Beilun" ["A Contrary View of Legality and Mediation"] [1989] no. 5 *Faxue Yanjiu* [*Studies in Law*] 21.

[153] On supposed lack of bindingness, see Liu, ed., *supra* note 53 at 909: "they do not possess legal effect" (*bu juyou falüshang de xiaoli*).

[154] See "Minjian Jiufen Chuli Banfa" ["Procedures for Handling Disputes Among Citizens"], issued April 1990 by the ministry of justice, in *Zhonghua Renmin Gongheguo Guowuyuan Gongbao* [*Gazette of the State Council of the PRC*] [hereinafter *State Council Gazette*], no. 16 (28 August 1990) 597, arts. 4 and 18(1).

[155] See *PRC Code of Civil Procedure*, *supra* note 138, art. 16.

[156] Mediation Regulations, *supra* note 142, art. 9; *PRC Code of Civil Procedure*, *ibid.*

[157] See text above, accompanying note 112.

[158] In a legally nonbinding but authoritative annotation to art. 48 of the 1982 Contract Law, a 1986 legal handbook averred, "if the parties reach a new agreement through mediation, this agreement

rate, article 16 of the *Code of Civil Procedure* states merely that if a Mediation Committee "violates law" (*weibei falü*) in mediating a dispute, the court should "put it right" (*jiuzheng*).

In short, Mediation Committees are an extension of the party-state. Mediators are guided by the policy of the moment, not professional standards intrinsic to the practice of mediation. And imposed or unsatisfactory mediation agreements are difficult to challenge in court. Rhetoric aside, Chinese mediation is thus fundamentally different from the Western ideal of private, voluntary, nonbinding mediation. Its differences do not derive merely from informal bargaining and power dynamics, however, but are a direct result of how the state organizes Mediation Committees and the formal rules it uses to govern them and their relation to courts.

B. Common Administrative Superiors ("Internal" Dispute Resolution)

Especially under the planned economy, "internal" dispute resolution — resolution by a body that is organizationally related to the parties and affected financially by the dispute's outcome — was the norm. In 1950, a three-tiered system of dispute resolution was established:[159] (1) "consultation" (*xieshang*) between the management (i.e., ministerial) offices of the enterprises involved. If they could not agree, either party could (2) appeal to a district or, if they were from different districts, a prefectural finance committee. Finally, in rare cases, they could (3) appeal to court. 1963 regulations reiterated that dispute resolution involving factory and mining-goods contracts should take the form of mediation by higher-level management or arbitration by the economic committee concerned.[160]

Ministerial superiors and finance or economic committees exemplify the same sort of "internal" dispute resolution that a corporate president engages in when she resolves a dispute between two wholly-owned subsidiaries. The interests of the organization are generally placed above the rights of the parties or the terms of the agreement. In "internal" dispute resolution, considerations "external" to the contract govern. "Both parties can be viewed as pockets of their common superior, and the decision how much to take from one pocket and put in the other is decided by considerations such as convenience and efficiency, not justice and fault."[161] The entire economy under planning thus approximates what institutional economists call "unified governance": transactions do not truly take place across a market interface, for they are governed by a single authority who can resolve disputes by fiat.[162]

Resolution by an administrative superior continues today for certain classes of contracts. A common governmental administrative superior is automatically granted jurisdiction to mediate trade disputes between state and collective enterprises, and

should be viewed as a new contract which possesses legal binding force on both parties" (Li, ed., *supra* note 3 at 217).

[159] See Provisional Methods, *supra* note 18, art. 10; Decision, *supra* note 19, art. 4.

[160] Ordering Regulations, *supra* note 32 at 53, art. 36.

[161] Clarke, *supra* note 146 at 248-49.

[162] See Williamson, *supra* note 135 at 75-79.

mediation agreements between enterprises within a ministerial "system" (*xitong*) must be carried out on pain of disciplinary sanction.[163] Such "mediators" are instructed to "enable" (*shi*, also meaning "cause" or "make") parties to resolve their dispute based on Party and state programs and policies in ways "beneficial" (*youliyu*) to construction of the "four modernizations".[164] Yet private enterprises trading across systems may forgo mediation by an administrative superior, and even an intraministerial dispute may be brought to the Commerce Bureau or court if the internal mediator cannot resolve it. If societal economic actors are increasingly choosing to use "external" forums, that may mean they are viewing contracts in terms of rights that merit strict enforcement. That is, they are rejecting "internal" forums' use of "external" considerations. Although some research has addressed contractors' changing preferences regarding different dispute-resolution forums, results have been inconclusive, inconsistent or difficult to interpret.[165]

C. The Commerce Bureau: Economic-Contract Arbitration Committees

Shortly after Deng's ascension to power, Commerce Bureau offices were granted supervisory authority over certain industrial contracts and commercial contracts (*e.g.*, contracts among factories, their wholesalers, supply and marketing cooperatives, and retail outlets).[166] While intraministerial industrial contracts remained under the supervision of economic committees, the Commerce Bureau was established as an interagency organ that handled transactions that cut across vertical ministerial systems.[167] The gradual move from ministerial to Commerce Bureau supervision is reflected in differences between the 1982 and 1993 Contract Laws. Under the 1982 law, both Commerce Bureau offices and ministries were charged with contract "supervision and inspection" (*jiandu jiancha*). In addition, ministries were to establish targets for and check up on enterprises' contract performance.[168] Under the 1993 Contract Law, Commerce Bureau offices are the only institution named as responsible for contract "supervision" (*jiandu*). "Inspection" and target-setting are not mentioned at all.[169]

The bindingness of Commerce Bureau arbitration was also strengthened under the 1993 Contract Law, bringing it more in line with Western arbitration practices.

---

[163] "Shangye Jingji Jiufen Tiaojie Shixing Banfa" ["Trial Procedures for the Resolution of Commercial Economic Disputes"], promulgated November 1989 by the Commerce Bureau, in *PRC Compendia of Laws*, *supra* note 46 (1989) 267, arts. 10 and 19.

[164] Wang, *supra* note 80 at 1359.

[165] See Potter, *supra* note 25; my Ph. D. dissertation, *supra* note 96.

[166] "Gongshang Xingzheng Guanli Zongju Guanyu Gong Shang, Nong Shang Qiye Jingji Hetong Jiben Tiaokuan de Shixing Guiding" ["Provisional Regulations of the Central Commerce Bureau Concerning the Basic Provisions in Contracts Between Industrial and Commercial Enterprises and Between Agricultural and Commercial Enterprises"] in *Compilation of Economic Contract Laws*, *supra* note 18, 107.

[167] See Potter, *supra* note 25 at 52.

[168] 1982 Contract Law, *supra* note 3, art. 51.

[169] 1993 Contract Law, *supra* note 3, art. 44. However, supervision responsibilities are shared with "other relevant competent departments of the People's Government at the county level or above" (1993 Contract Law, *ibid.*).

The 1982 Contract Law permitted arbitration judgments to be appealed to court within fifteen days of being issued; arbitration judgments may not be appealed under the 1993 law.[170] The state has been urging contractors to include in their contracts "arbitration clauses" that stipulate whether disputes are subject to Commerce Bureau arbitration or court adjudication. Official policy encourages arbitration (most contracts, however, still do not even contain arbitration clauses; of those, it is unknown what percentage opt for arbitration).[171] As administrative bodies, Arbitration Committees are probably not subject to rules of evidence or a principle of adherence to law as stringent as those which apply to courts. In addition, since Commerce Bureau offices also register business enterprises and regulate trade, they have an (albeit tenuous) "internal" relation to contractors.[172] State strengthening of arbitration judgments and promotion of arbitration clauses may thus be interpreted one of two ways: either as willingness to let parties freely decide who will resolve their disputes, or as an effort to reassert administrative control over contracts.

All dispute-resolution bodies — Arbitration Committees and courts included — are instructed to begin the process of dispute resolution with mediation. Mediation carried out under Arbitration Committees is perhaps even less like Western notions of mediation, however, than mediation carried out under Mediation Committees. A recent Commerce Bureau contract reference book describes Arbitration Committee mediation as "arbitration-mediation" (*zhongcai tiaojie*) and states,

> Only if mediation is unsuccessful can arbitration be carried out. ... This is an important "symbol" (*biaozhi*) of the difference between our country's arbitration system and the arbitration systems of capitalist countries.
>
> Mediation during arbitration activities and arbitration are two different stages in a "unitary process" (*tongyi jincheng*). ... Mediation should "permeate" (*guanchuan*) the arbitration process from start to finish.[173]

That is, Commerce Bureau mediation is subsumed into an essentially arbitral process. It might be somewhat unclear whether mediation agreements reached through Mediation Committees or internal supervisors are enforceable in court, but Arbitration Committee "mediation agreements" definitely are. In this they differ in name only from Arbitration Committee "arbitration agreements". The distinction between mediation and arbitration under the Commerce Bureau is thus very slippery; it may well be that even cases brought for mediation are ultimately subject to arbitration. Indeed, mediation is described merely as a "litigation process" (*shenli guocheng*) by which Arbitration Committees handle cases.[174] These facts suggest Arbitration Committees have more power to impose solutions than some propaganda implies. They also suggest that Chinese statistics on the proportion of cases resolved through mediation (measured by "mediation agreements") must be interpreted cautiously.

---

[170] Compare 1982 Contract Law, *supra* note 3, art. 49, and 1993 Contract Law, *ibid.*, art. 42.

[171] 1993 Contract Law, *ibid.*, arts. 42 and 43.

[172] This point is emphasized repeatedly in Potter, *supra* note 25.

[173] Wang, *supra* note 80 at 1361.

[174] *Ibid.* at 1360-62.

It is difficult to know much more about the workings of arbitration, however, because the Commerce Bureau does not publish cases and businesspersons are often secretive about such dealings (one reason they may have chosen arbitration in the first place).

D. People's Courts: Neither Administration nor Law

China has 3,000-odd Basic-level People's Courts at the county level. The next highest courts are the Intermediate-level People's Courts at the prefectural level, followed by the Higher-level People's Courts at the provincial, autonomous region, or centrally-administered city level. The Supreme People's Court rarely hears cases; it generally comments on cases already ruled on by provincial courts.[175] Regarding contracts, courts have two important functions: resolving disputes and enforcing the decisions of other types of dispute-resolution forums. Only courts possess the power of enforcement (*e.g.*, one must bring suit in court to force a party to live up to an arbitration agreement). Dispute resolution and enforcement are discussed in turn. Special attention is paid to constraints on court impartiality.

Parties may bring a contract case to court if they cannot reach agreement through mediation or if either party is unwilling to submit to mediation or arbitration.[176] A court will first mediate the dispute.[177] Somewhat ironically, agreements reached through court "mediation" are considered voluntary and therefore, unlike adjudicated settlements, cannot be appealed.[178] An adjudicated settlement, by the doctrine "the second trial is the final trial" (*liang shen zhong shen*), may be appealed one time.[179] Judges can thus make their decisions more binding by pressuring parties to accept a mediated settlement. For this, they can use techniques similar to those of magistrates in imperial China such as "telegraphing" their likely decisions, forcing parties to settle "in the shadow of the law".[180]

---

[175] See "Zhonghua Renmin Gongheguo Renmin Fayuan Zuzhi Fa" ["Law of the PRC on the Organization of People's Courts"], amended, *PRC Compendia of Laws*, *supra* note 46 (1983) 4.

[176] 1993 Contract Law, *supra* note 3, art. 42.

[177] *PRC Code of Civil Procedure*, *supra* note 138, art. 9. In trying contract cases they "must" (*bixu*) follow "the principle of "emphasizing mediation"" ("*zhuozhong tiaojie*" *de yuanze*) (Liu, ed., *supra* note 53 at 909).

[178] See M. Palmer, "The Revival of Mediation in the People's Republic of China: (2) Judicial Mediation" in W.E. Butler, ed., *Yearbook on Socialist Legal Systems, 1989* (Dobbs Ferry, N.Y.: Transnational, 1989) 145 at 161.

[179] See M.Y.K. Woo, "The Right to a Criminal Appeal in the People's Republic of China" (1989) 14 Yale J. Int'l L. 118. Woo describes a procedure called *shensu* ("petition" or "appeal") whereby a party can ask the court or its superior court to re-examine a case after the second trial. It appears to apply only to criminal cases and, even then, is rarely used. Standards governing *shensu* do not appear to be published.

[180] Qing era magistrates' use of "telegraphing" during the stage after a plaint was filed but before judgment was rendered is discussed in P.C.C. Huang, "Between Informal Mediation and Formal Adjudication: The Third Realm of Qing Civil Justice" (1993) 19 Modern China 251, especially at 266, 275-78. A worthwhile theoretical discussion of settling disputes "in the shadow of the law" may be found in M. Galanter, "Justice in Many Rooms: Courts, Private Ordering, and Indigenous Law"

Like so many organizations in China, courts are situated within a web of vertical and horizontal interests. Vertical pressures arise from the bureaucratic position of the entire court system in Communist ideology and organization. Again, the N.P.C. Standing Committee, not courts, is responsible for judicial interpretation. "Judicial independence" in China means that individual courts are independent from other administrative hierarchies, not from higher courts.[181] The Constitution designates the Supreme Court the highest "judicial organ" (not the highest "court") and allows it to "supervise" lower-level courts, suggesting it exercises "the adjudicatory aspect of the state's unified power".[182]

From the top of this judicial hierarchy, the Supreme Court, in its regularly published *Gazette*, issues comments on and amendments to provincial-level decisions that indicate to what extent they are models to be followed.[183] These "precedent-like" statements differ significantly, however, from the principle of *stare decisis*. *Stare decisis* holds that once a court decision settles a point of law, the same interpretation shall be applied to all cases with similar facts coming before that and lower courts.[184] In China, no court but the Supreme Court may publish its decisions; higher-level and intermediate-level courts therefore cannot issue "precedent".[185] Might such decisions circulate through internal channels and form a sort of "secret" precedent? Possibly, but we simply do not know. Lower courts are prohibited from citing even Supreme Court comments and opinions (*i.e.*, those they are instructed to follow!).[186] It seems unlikely they would be instructed to follow lower-court rulings, but they might do so anyway.

In the end, since courts do not publish their decisions, and since, even if they did, they could not cite Supreme Court opinions, it is impossible to know how Supreme Court "precedent-like" statements influence lower courts. We do know that the Anglo-American "principle of 'following precedent'" ("*zunxun xianli*" *de yuanze*) has been criticized as ill-suited to China on the grounds that it allows obscure precedents to be misused to subvert the intent of the law.[187] In addition, in 1986 the president of the Supreme Court stated that the purpose of printing decisions in the *Gazette* is to

---

(1981) 19 J. Legal Pluralism 1, which traces the phrase to R.H. Mnookin & L. Kornhauser, "Bargaining in the Shadow of the Law: The Case of Divorce" (1979) 88 Yale L.J. 950.

[181] See Cohen, *supra* note 48.

[182] Finder, *supra* note 49 at 148. See also Constitution, *supra* note 45, arts. 123 and 127.

[183] See N.P. Liu, "'Legal Precedents' with Chinese Characteristics: Published Cases in the Gazette of the Supreme People's Court" (1991) 5 J. Chinese L. 107 at 121.

[184] *Black's Law Dictionary*, *supra* note 11 at 1406.

[185] "Guanyu Difang Geji Renmin Fayuan Buying Zhiding Sifa Jieshixing Wenjian de Pifu" ["Instruction that Lower Courts at Each Level Should Not Issue Any Documents Concerning Judicial Interpretations"] [1987] no. 2 *Supreme Court Gazette*, *supra* note 131, 19.

[186] Liu, *supra* note 183 at 122 n. 61, citing an unpublished 1986 Supreme Court "reply" (*pifu*).

[187] G.Z. Chen & Z.Q. Xie, "Guanyu Wo Guo Jianli Panli Zhidu Wenti de Sikao" ["Observations on the Question of Establishing a Legal Precedent System in China"] [1989] no. 2 *Zhongguo Faxue* [*Chinese Legal Science*] 86 at 91-92.

enhance "specific guidance" (*juti zhidao*), not to set "precedent".[188] The Party-state appears to be making a distinction between decisions that have authority over lower courts, and decisions that have authority over lower courts, legislative branch interpretations, and new legislation. The former are permissible; the latter are not. That is, Supreme Court decisions are not permitted to form a body of authoritative, self-referential, and internally consistent doctrine independent from and binding on the Party. There is a distinct resemblance between the Party's use of Supreme Court opinions and imperial-era case compilations that only assumed precedent-like status after receiving the Emperor's imprimatur. "Precedent" as Party guidance is quite different from *stare decisis*.

Vertical pressures to adjudicate according to Party policy or the wishes of higher-level courts are therefore securely institutionalized. Yet vertical pressures on courts to rule in a biased manner in contract disputes are usually exerted from mid-level (especially provincial) Party Committees, not the centre. This is reflected in endemic complaints of "local protectionism" (*difang baohuzhuyi*) among courts. That is, in a dispute between a local and non-local enterprise, a court will often give more weight to the effect on local finance and employment of a local firm bearing liability than to the letter of the contract or equity. Local protectionism is not necessarily a symptom of a weakened centre or state disintegration, as many assume. As Li Jianqiang has argued, the root cause of local protectionism is post-Mao cadre-promotion policy. Essentially, cadres now win promotion by attaining higher economic growth in their province and contributing more revenue to the central coffers.

> When this standard for judging local leaders cannot be challenged, what provincial leaders ... can do is to use all means within their jurisdiction to strive for economic growth. ... It is economic growth rather than their cooperation with other regions that is judged by the Center.[189]

Regional competition, in short, affirms the centre's policies and authority; it doesn't challenge them. What are the organizational links between courts and local authorities that engender this dynamic of inter-court local protectionism?

The fundamental source of court protectionism seems to be that, although they belong to a hierarchy of higher courts, local courts are financed and staffed at the local level. Courts at each level are under the control of the corresponding People's Government (court presidents, for example, are appointed by local People's Congresses). Judicial appointments lack any sort of tenure so judges may be removed at any time. Judges are thus beholden to the local People's Government which is in turn subordinate to the local Party Committee. Judges are dependent on local Party and government organs for their jobs, benefits, housing, promotions, bonuses, and even employment of their children. As one legal official wrote, "This personnel power ex-

---

[188] T.X. Zheng, "Zuigao Renmin Fayuan Gongzuo Baogao" ["Work Report of the Supreme Court of the PRC"], presented to the N.P.C., 8 April 1986, in [1986] no. 2 *Supreme Court Gazette*, *supra* note 131, 3 at 11.

[189] J.Q. Li, "Regionalism without Regional Identity: Provincial Leaders and Inter-regional Competition in the PRC" (Paper presented at the annual meeting of the Western Conference of the Association for Asian Studies, Ogden, Utah, 24-26 October 1996) at 21.

ercised by a small group of leaders hangs like the sword of Damocles over those who would do things according to law."[190] It is also unknown how widely the Mao-era doctrine of "approval of cases by the local Party Secretary" (*shuji pi an*) is still practiced. Though now considered irregular, the Supreme Court mandated it for cases involving foreigners as late as 1979.[191] Moreover, the decisions of individual judges who actually hear a case may be overridden by the court president (often a member of the local Party Committee).[192] With more and more contract disputes arising between "township and village enterprises" (*xiangzhen qiye*) with direct ownership, fee and tax ties to local governments, it is hardly surprising that these organizational arrangements (combined with current cadre-promotion policy) have generated severe local protectionism among courts.

China tries to minimize these conflicts of interest in contract cases through a doctrine called "avoidance" (*huibi*). It is unclear how it could actually be very useful, though. It holds that if judicial officials or their relatives are parties to a dispute, stand to profit from the result of a case, or have a relationship to the disputants that may influence their impartiality, they may dismiss themselves from hearing the case. But counties have a financial interest in any dispute involving a township-owned enterprise or even a private enterprise that pays taxes and fees. Since county officials can harass or fire judges, judges conceivably stand to profit (or lose) from any commercial case they hear. They certainly have a relationship *to individuals who have a relationship* with the disputants that may influence their impartiality. Avoidance might be more effective in Intermediate-level People's Courts, which are the courts of first instance in cases that have a "major influence" (*zhongda yingxiang*) in a locality (*i.e.*, which involve large sums of money, or influence fulfillment of plan targets).[193] Local protectionism may be weaker because the relationship between local finance and the corresponding level of government under which intermediate courts function may be much more tenuous.[194] But most disputes will go to basic-level courts.[195]

The ultimate Achilles heel of impartial court adjudication seems to be the Party-state's desire to preserve "principled ambiguity" in the law. Principled ambiguity maintains flexibility for Party intervention. Party policy can decisively influence the implementation of the law without explicitly contravening it. Maintaining principled ambiguity requires maintaining a monopoly over legal interpretation. An integral

---

[190] Quoted in Clarke, *supra* note 146 at 263.

[191] See "Renmin Fayuan Shenpan Minshi Anjian Chengxu Zhidu de Guiding (Shixing)" ["Rules on the System of Procedure in the Adjudication of Civil Cases by People's Courts"], issued 2 February 1979, art. 2, cited in Clarke, *supra* note 146 at 261-62, n. 58.

[192] See "Law of the PRC on the Organization of People's Courts", *supra* note 175, art. 11.

[193] On the doctrine of avoidance and rules governing courts of first instance, see Wang, *supra* note 80 at 1420-21.

[194] See D.C. Clarke, "The Execution of Civil Judgments in China" (1995) 141 China Q. 65 at 72.

[195] This suggests that contracts are much more problematic than even the most vocal foreign critics of Beijing believe. Most cases that make headlines in the West involve non-Chinese and large sums of money. They are thus handled by higher-level courts, are subject to the more Western-oriented Foreign Contract Law, and are treated gingerly to preserve China's world image. How many smaller, domestic cases of local protectionism are never heard of?

element of principled ambiguity is thus prohibition of an independent system of precedent, or *stare decisis*. As mentioned before, courts cannot even publish their decisions or cite Supreme Court opinions. Civilian legal systems that ban precedent usually compensate with detailed codification. That is certainly not the case in China. The net effect is that judges are more likely to be left to their own devices, especially since laws and regulations are published by a bewildering array of bureaucracies, and there is no overall index. In short, the power of horizontal pressures might be considerably weaker if courts were permitted to develop a countervailing corpus of legal interpretation through *stare decisis*, but this would conflict with the fundamental constitutional principles of the Party-state. Local protectionism — and its attendant undermining of respect for contracts — is thus an unintended but direct consequence of fundamental organizational principles of Party-state rule.

The general dynamics of local protectionism combine with several other institutional arrangements to make court enforcement a serious problem in China. Although courts are the only dispute-resolution forum granted the authority to enforce or "implement" (*zhixing*) agreements or decisions, they have no general contempt power. That is, the mere refusal to carry out a court order is not in itself a criminal offense. This problem is magnified when a court tries to execute a judgment against a non-local enterprise. Some provinces have passed laws, against central policy, that require an order from a local court before local banks can freeze the assets of a local enterprise.[196] Thus, a court must often seek the cooperation of another court in the locality of the enterprise it is trying to enforce against — a court utterly dependent on its own Party and government superiors. That second court, even if it is willing, may be unable to get a local bank to cooperate. Incredibly, when the new *Code of Civil Procedure* was passed in 1991, the Ministry of Finance apparently lobbied (successfully) to abolish courts' powers to detain and imprison bank officials who refuse to cooperate with court orders to freeze or transfer funds. Courts may only issue fines, but even these must be enforced in the noncooperative party's locale.[197]

But local protectionism is not the sole impediment to enforcement that undermines the capacity of contracts to lower transaction costs. Legally-sanctioned status inequalities have not entirely disappeared. As late as 1992 courts were ordered to show "special solicitude" (in the name of social stability) when asked to execute against large and medium-sized state-owned enterprises.[198] And execution against enterprises run by the military has been called "impossible".[199]

---

[196] Shenzhen apparently has such regulations (see "Dangqian Jingji Anjian Weihe Zhixing Nan?" ["Why is There Currently an Execution Problem in Economic Cases?"] *Shanghai Fazhi Bao* [*Shanghai Legal System Daily*] (2 October 1989) 1).

[197] See Clarke, *supra* note 194 at 79. See also *PRC Code of Civil Procedure*, *supra* note 138, arts. 221 and 222. For a more recent and expanded presentation of Clarke's unparalleled research, see his "Power and Politics in the Chinese Court System: The Enforcement of Civil Judgments" (1996) 10 Colum. J. Asian L. 1.

[198] See Clarke, *ibid.* at 74, citing Guangzhou Shi Zhongji Renmin Fayuan Zhixing Ting [Guangzhou Intermediate-Level People's Court Execution Chamber], "Chongfen Fahui Zhixing Gongzuo de Zhineng Zuoyong, Genghaode Wei Shehui Anding he Jingji Fazhan Fuwu" ["Give Full Play to the

Conclusion

This overview of domestic contract law in the P.R.C. has highlighted how black-letter law or institutional arrangements structure the practical reality of entering, forming and enforcing a contract on the mainland. It is clear that the contract discourse the Chinese state has promoted under its socialist market economy diverges in fundamental ways from Western notions of freedom of contract.

The ability at will to enter a contract? The state maintains control over who may enter economic contracts through the institution of juristic personhood and restrictions on to whom and for what purpose it may be awarded. Juristic persons are not viewed as individuals writ large with bundles of inalienable rights, but as public-law creations meant essentially to serve the ends of state policy. Moreover, due to ambiguities in the registration process, the ability to obtain juristic personhood is often a function of one's personal and professional connections. Once this hurdle is cleared, one may still have to have a contract approved before courts will recognize it as binding, due in part to the absence of a well-established doctrine of offer and acceptance.

The right to order one's affairs through contracts and bargaining, and to be free of external pressures? Contrary to the spirit of its own civil law, which stresses "equal status" between contractors, the state has not given contracts clear legal protection from interference by the actions of planning officials, ministries and state enterprises. Without sophisticated legal doctrines like impracticability, courts are left with significant discretion to decide when an event falls under *force majeure*. At the same time, courts can use the doctrine of specific performance to force a party to carry out a contract even after he has paid compensation. Domestically, contractors are not permitted to freely negotiate a price for termination.

The right to enforcement? All of the forums the state provides — including those for "mediation" — possess legal and statutory powers to render their decisions binding or practically binding. Mediation Committees are suffused with pressures from the Ministry of Justice and the Party. Internal dispute resolution by a common administrative superior explicitly elevates the collective good above the rights of the parties or terms of the contract. And People's Courts are beset by a host of crisscrossing vertical and horizontal pressures that can influence their decisions; they are simultaneously prohibited from developing a corpus of legal precedents that might aid them in making more consistent, law-based judgments.

Although institutional arrangements play a crucial role in diluting legal protection for contracts, the P.R.C. continues to refine the law itself in ways that promise to bring it more in line with international practice. Yet the very rapidity with which the law changes in the P.R.C. today means that its impact on the actual practice of legal offi-

---

Function of Execution Work, Serve Social Stability and Economic Development Even Better"] in *Di'er ci Quanguo Shenghui Chengshi Zhongji Renmin Fayuan Zhixing Gongzuo Yantaohui Huiyi Cailiao* [*Materials from the Second National Conference of Intermediate-Level People's Courts from Provincial Capitals on Execution Work*] (June 1992).

[199] Clarke, *ibid.*

cials is highly unpredictable. In the end, it is probably the institutional arrangements which will dictate continuity or change in the mainland's contract regime. If so, maintaining the uniqueness and integrity of Hong Kong's legal institutions, rather than the independence of its contract law *per se*, is probably the best guarantee that contracts in Hong Kong will continue to enjoy the legal protections they did before 1 July 1997.

---

[14]

Regulating Labour Relations in China : The Challenge of Adapting to the Socialist Market Economy

Pitman B. POTTER*
LI Jianyong**

Cet article analyse la nouvelle Loi de la RPC *sur le travail, entrée en vigueur le 1er janvier 1995, dans le contexte historique et actuel des relations de travail en Chine. Les auteurs accordent une attention particulière aux dispositions relatives au contrat de travail et au règlement des différends. Ils examinent également les difficultés soulevées par l'introduction des conventions collectives dans les entreprises chinoises, et par les relations entre les syndicats et le Parti communiste. Tout en reconnaissant, dans leur appréciation globale de la loi, qu'elle pourrait marquer une étape importante vers la protection juridique des droits des travailleurs, ils signalent que sa portée réelle pourrait être amoindrie par la prépondérance de la politique de croissance économique, par le souci de préserver le contrôle politique et par des difficultés pratiques de mise en œuvre.*

This paper examines the new Labour Law of the PRC, *effective January 1, 1995, in the light of current and historical conditions of labour relations in China. Provisions regarding the labour contract system and dispute resolution are discussed in greater detail. Issues related to the introduction of collective bargaining and to the relationship between trade unions and the Communist Party are also examined. In their overall assessment, the authors recognize the potential significance of the* Labour Law

* Associate professor of Law and Director of Chinese Legal Studies at the University of British Columbia Law Faculy.

** Researcher at East China Institute of Politics and Law and is currently in the LLM program at UBC Law Faculty.

Les Cahiers de Droit, vol. 37, n° 3, septembre 1996, pp. 753–775
(1996) 37 *Les Cahiers de Droit* 753

as a major step towards the legal protection of workers' rights, but point out that its effectiveness could be undermined by the preeminent policy of economic growth, by concerns about political control, and by obstacles to full implementation.

Introduction

China's transition to a socialist market economy has brought on new challenges for labour relations. No longer is economic production the province of a comprehensive state bureaucratic administration. Rather the economy is increasingly dominated by an ever-expanding number of private and quasi-private actors, which pose new challenges for doctrines of labour control articulated by the Communist Party of China (CPC) and enforced through the state labour bureaucracy. On one hand the ideological justifications no longer exist for strict labour discipline, politically subservient labour unions, the absence of collective bargaining and denial of the right to strike. On the other hand, China's economic development (and continued political stability) require a tightly controlled labour force, even as the demands of efficiency restrict investment in working conditions and benefits. China's first comprehensive labour law went into effect on January 1, 1995, and represents the regime's most recent efforts to grapple with problems brought on by the transition to a socialist market economy[1]. This paper will examine the new *Labour Law of the PRC* in light of current and historical conditions of labour relations in China.

1. Foundations for PRC Labour Policy

The *Labour Law of the PRC* reflects current policy priorities of the Chinese government, but these operate in the context of the Party's historical relations with urban workers. During the pre-Liberation period, the CPC's problematic attempts to mobilize urban workers into a revolutionary force contributed to labour policies that placed a premium on political control. During the Maoist period, the ideological conceit that China was a workers' state led to policies of material coaptation of workers, but accompanied by the price of continued discipline and control.

1.1 Revolutionary Relations Between Cadres and Urban Workers

During the revolutionary period prior to 1949, the CPC had a conflictive relationship with urban workers. Initial successes at labour organizing in the southern cities of Guangzhou and Shanghai in the 1920s were met with vigorous counter-measures by the Nationalist Party (KMT) leadership and local capitalists[2]. In Guangzhou, despite sporadic strikes and labour unrest the Communist Party had difficulty consolidating its gains and mobilizing workers to accomplish its revolutionary goals. In Shanghai, the first United Front brought tentative successes, as the Party used strikes and labour organization efforts to strengthen its position, only to see these efforts wiped out by the Nationalist coup in 1927[3]. In the North, the CPC faced similar problems. Despite active labour organizing work in the northern

1. For an authoritative review of the Labour Law of the PRC that reviews the law's efforts to re-order labour relations in light of changing conditions of China's socialist market economy, see Guo Xiang, «Laodong fa : Weihu zhigong hefa quanyi de jiben fa» (The Labour Law : A basic law for protecting the lawful rights of staff and workers), in *Gongren ribao* (Worker's Daily) Jan. 5, 1995, p. 5. Also see Commentator's article «Conscientiously safeguard labourer's legitimate rights and interests», *Renmin ribao* (People's Daily) Jul. 6, 1994, p. 1, in *FBIS Daily Report-China* Jul. 12, 1994, pp. 17-18 and Wang Yantian and Fu Gang, « A channel begins to open up as the tide of reform surges forward — A commentary on the passage of the Labour Law of the PRC », Beijing *Xinhua* Domestic Service Jul. 28, 1994, in *FBIS Daily Report-China* Aug. 3, 1994, pp. 17-19.
2. See generally, C.M. Wilbur, « The Nationalist Revolution : from Canton to Nanking, 1923-1928 », in D. Twitchett and J. K. Fairbank eds., *The Cambridge History of China*, (Cambridge : Cambridge University Press, vol. 12, Part One, 1983) 527-720, at 541-549.
3. See generally E.J. Perry, *Shanghai on Strike : The Politics of Chinese Labor* (Stanford, Ca. : Stanford University Press, 1993).

cities and along the major railroad lines, the Party was generally unable to translate these efforts into successful political revolution[4]. These failures contributed to policies toward urban workers which, on the one hand saw labour organizing as a basis for revolution, and yet on the other remained circumspect about the practical potential of such efforts.

The regulatory frameworks erected by the CPC in its revolutionary base areas reflected this ambivalence. In the Jiangxi Soviet for example, the enactment of a labour law based on the Soviet Model gave vent to two policy aims : improving conditions and establishing trade unions as the focus of the CPC's Party-building efforts, to ensure that the workers' movement remained subservient to the Party's revolutionary programme[5]. In the northern base areas, labour regulations were used in a similar way to articulate policies of improving labour conditions while ensuring disciplined compliance by workers to CPC policy directives through the labour union system[6]. Party doubts about the reliability of workers as political allies were brought home during the campaign to retake Manchuria after 1945, where concerns about worker support contributed to the Party Centre's decision to build rural base areas and in effect abandon the cities[7].

Thus, during the pre-Liberation period, the CPC's experience with difficulties in developing the revolutionary consciousness of Chinese workers and bending them to the political needs of the Party had a significant influence of the Party's labour policies. As well, the gradual displacement of the urban leadership of the CPC and the emergence of Mao Zedong led to further disregard of urban issues generally and an ambivalence toward urban workers. By the time the CPC gained control of the entirety of China, a pattern of labour policy was well established that emphasized political control over worker organizations — control that was mandated in no small part by doubts about the political reliability of the urban proletariat.

---

4. See generally, J. ISRAEL and D.W. KLEIN, *Rebels and Bureaucrats : China's December 9ers* (Berkeley, Los Angeles and London : University California Press, 1976).
5. See W. E. BUTLER, *The Legal System of the Chinese Soviet Republic 1931-1934* (Dobbs Ferry, N.Y. : Transnational Publishers, 1983) at 107-117.
6. See LAN Quanpu, *Jiefangqu fagui gaiyao* (Outline of laws and regulations in the liberated areas) (Beijing : Masses Publishers, 1982), pp. 118-121.
7. See SHAN Siyi, *Zai jiefang zhanzheng zhong fengfu fazhan* (Rich development during the war of liberation) (Beijing : PLA Press, 1991), pp. 22-23 ; LI Ying, ed., *Wenhua da geming zhong de ming ren zhiyu* (Cases of famous personalities in the Cultural Revolution) (Beijing : Nationalities Institute Press, 1993), pp. 77ff ; ZHENG Xiaofeng and SHU Ling, *Tao Zhu zhuan* (Biography of Tao Zhu) (Beijing : Youth Publishing, 1992), p. 188.

1.2 Labour Policy in Mao's China

Labour policies during the Maoist period entailed a combination of coaptation with material benefits and the imposition of political discipline and control. Following the general pattern of oscillation between formal and informal patterns of rule[8], methods of labour regulation tended to shift between alternatives of enactment and enforcement of formal rules and reliance on informal Party policy directives.

During periods of more formal regulation (1954-1958, for example), reliance was placed on the « labour contract system ». At that time, China's economy was characterized as undergoing the transition from the private to the public ownership, and the labour contract system was considered a useful mechanism for bringing labour relations in private ownership enterprises within the ambit of Party control. The Party-organized trade unions played a central role in setting the terms of collective labour contracts in particular, by which terms and conditions of employment were set for an entire enterprise. Thus, Section 32 of the Common Program of the Chinese People's Political Consultative Congress authorized the trade unions to represent staff and workers in signing collective contracts with private enterprises[9]. The *Provisional Methods for Mutual Signing of Collective Contracts Between Capitalists and Workers in Privately Operated Industrial and Commercial Enterprises* (1949) promulgated by All China Federation of Trade Union (ACFTU) prescribed detailed regulations concerning collective labour contracts on such issues as hours of work, sick leave, benefits and working conditions[10]. Sections 5 and 6 of the *Trade Union Law* (1950) authorized the trade unions to represent workers and staff in signing collective contracts[11]. The labour contract system was also recognized in the *Directive Concerning Signing Collective Contracts in State-Owned Enterprises* (1953) and the *Directive Concerning Signing Collective*

---

8. See V.H. LI, « The Evolution and Development of the Chinese Legal System », in J. M. H. LINDBECK, *China: Management of a Revolutionary Society* (Seattle and London: University of Washington Press, 1971).
9. See: CHEN Hefu, *Zhongguo xianfa leibian* (Compilation of Chinese Constitutions) (Beijing: Chinese Academy of Social Sciences Press, 1980), p. 189. Also see LIN Jia, *Zhonghua renmin gongheguo laodongfa jianghua*, (Speaking of China's Labour Law) (Beijing: Chinese Procuracy Press, 1994), p. 66.
10. « Guanyu siying gongshang qiye lao zi shuang fang dingli jiti hetong de zanxing banfa » (Provisional methods for mutual signing of collective contracts between capitalists and workers in privately operated industrial and commercial enterprises), in *Renmin shouce* (People's handbook) 1950, p. A115.
11. See SONG Xiangguan, ed., *Shiyong laodong fa daquan* (Encyclopedia on the use of labour law) (Changchun: Jilin Documentary History Press, 1989), p. 364.

Contracts in Productive Mines (1955)[12]. This regulatory structure was aimed at ensuring improved conditions for labour, and also Party control of workers through the medium of trade unions.

With the completion of Socialist Transformation, and particularly during the period 1958-1962, labour policy was the province of flexible Party directives. Workers were viewed as members of a collectivist organism in which there was little need for formal regulations. Informal policy edicts and administrative directives were sufficient. During these periods, labour policy presumed that workers were the masters of the enterprises under the ideology of socialist public ownership and there were no longer any basic conflicts of interests between workers, enterprises and the state. The labour contract system was considered a vestige of capitalist private ownership, and so was abolished[13]. The importance of political control over workers remained, however, and during the Cultural Revolution competing factions issued conflicting rules on worker participation in the movement[14].

Chinese labour policies were articulated in several constitutions enacted between 1954 and 1982. The 1954 Constitution articulated worker rights to employment, improved working conditions and wages, rest (*xiuxi*), sick and retirement pay and other benefits[15]. The so-called « Cultural Revolution » Constitution of 1975 enshrined a right to strike without making reference to labour discipline, while the 1978 Constitution reflected the post-Mao reversals of radical policies and added provisions on labour discipline[16]. The 1982 Constitution deleted the right to strike altogether[17].

These varying approaches to labour relations reflected conclusions about class struggle held by contending elements of the CPC elite[18]. At one end of the spectrum were views associated with Liu Shaoqi and Peng Zhen, who had concluded as early as 1956 that class struggle was no longer a problem and the emphasis should shift to developing China's productive

12. See *Zhonghua renmin gongheguo fagui xuanbian* (Compilation of laws and regulations of the PRC), 1954, 1956.
13. See LEE Lai To, *Trade Unions In China* (Singapore : Singapore University Press, 1986), p. 111.
14. See generally, H.Y. LEE, *The Politics of the Chinese Cultural Revolution* (Berkeley : University of California Press, 1978) at 129-139.
15. See 1954 Constitution Articles 91-93, in CHEN Hefu, *op. cit.*, fn. 9, p. 233.
16. See J.A. COHEN, « China's Changing Constitution », in *76 China Quarterly*, 794-841 (1978).
17. See 1982 PRC Constitution (Beijing : Foreign Languages Press, 1983), art. 42-44.
18. See P. VAN NESS and S. RAICHUR, « Dilemmas of Socialist Development : An Analysis of Strategic Lines in China, 1949-1981 », in BULLETIN OF CONCERNED ASIAN SCHOLARS, ed., *China From Mao to Deng : The Politics and Economic of Socialist Development* (Armonk, N.Y. : M.E. Sharpe, 1983) at 77-89.

forces — entailing greater emphasis on labour discipline. Radical views associated with Mao Zedong on the other hand held that class struggle would continue for a long time and insisted that worker rights be given priority over obligations concerning labour discipline and productivity. Despite these differences however, the theme of political domination continued, and resulted in what has been termed a neo-Confucian relationship of patronage and control between workers and unit leaders[19].

2. Transition to a Market Economy

China's transition to a socialist market economy is ongoing and likely will continue to evolve significantly in the future. During the first fifteen or so years of reform, three distinct phases can be identified : (i) an initial phase of market liberalization, (ii) an acceleration phase during which price reforms were central, and (iii) a privatization phase during which the role of state enterprises has been transformed dramatically.

2.1 Initial Efforts at Reform

The economic reform programs initiated following the 3rd Plenum of the 11th Central Committee in 1978 were tentative at first, but soon moved beyond the confines of either the Maoist or Soviet models that had influenced China previously[20]. Key to this was the political re-emergence of those who emphasized the decline of class struggle and the need to focus on productive forces[21]. For with the end of class struggle, the Party/state need no longer concern itself with resolving the problem of exploitation, and could recognize greater degrees of autonomy by individuals and groups in the economy. Thus contracts, business firms, and labour relations all could be directed not by the Party/state charged with eliminating and avoiding class exploitation, but rather by autonomous actors increasingly freed of state intrusion.

These ideological changes and their policy implications emerged slowly at first. In labour relations, for example, little attention was paid to reforming the state enterprise labour system initially. Instead, the emphasis was placed on reforming enterprise management. Reforms in state planning permitted enterprises managers to contract with a wider variety of business partners, while the two-track pricing system permitted managers greater

---

19. See A.G. Walder, *Communist Neo-Traditionalism : Work and Authority in Chinese Industry* (Berkeley, Los Angeles and London : University of California Press, 1986).
20. See generally, H. Harding, *China's Second Revolution : Reform After Mao* (Washington, D.C. : Brookings Institution, 1987).
21. See « Communique of the Third Plenum of the 11th Central Committee », in *Hongqi* (Red Flag) no. 1, 1979, p. 14.

flexibility in obtaining production inputs[22]. Regulations were enacted to strengthen the autonomy of factory managers from interference by Party secretaries[23]. Thus the initial policy focus was on increasing the efficiency and productivity of state enterprises, with little attention paid to reforming relations between state enterprises and their workers. In labour relations, the neo-Confucian patrimonial relationship continued.

However, in an effort to address the employment problem for an increasing number of migrant workers — primarily young people seeking work outside their assigned residence (*hukou*) location (often these were Cultural Revolution youth who were returning to the cities after having been sent down to rural areas, or peasants seeking escape from the drudgery of village life), the government enacted rules on contract labour. The 1986 *Regulations on Administration of Labour Contracts by State Enterprises* permitted state enterprises to hire occasional workers without actually incorporating them into the enterprise work unit and providing the standard array of accompanying benefits[24]. The labour contracts executed under these rules were generally not available to workers already formally assigned to the enterprise, and in view of the lower level of benefits available under them were not considered desirable.

Even though labour contracts formed pursuant to the 1986 Regulations were essentially « gap-fillers » for workers who were not already part of state enterprise system, the new measures did encourage the gradual emergence of a somewhat free labour market[25]. Even as unskilled workers began to do contract labour in areas of construction and goods transport — to the extent of reducing the staff needs and costs of state enterprises, skilled workers began to find ways to secure their release from former employers to gain more remunerative employment. This was, despite the resistance of state enterprise employers who were often unwilling to freely release their skilled workers to seek higher paid employment. Employment agencies

22. For a review of Chinese economic policies and conditions in the 1980s, see JOINT ECONOMIC COMMITTEE OF U.S. CONGRESS, *China's Economy Looks Toward the Year 2000* (Washington, D.C. : U.S. Government Printing Office, 1986).

23. See « Zhongguo renmin gongheguo quanmin suo you zhi gongye qiye fa » (Law of the PRC on Enterprises Owned by the Whole People), in STATE COUNCIL LEGAL AFFAIRS BUREAU, ed., *Zhonghua renmin gongheguo xin fagui huibian* (Compilation of new PRC laws and regulations) 1988, n° 1 (Beijing : Xinhua, 1988), p. 27.

24. See « Guoying qiye shixing laodong hetong zanxing guiding » (Provisional regulations for implementation of labour contracts by state enterprises), in SONG Xiangguan, *op. cit.*, fn. 11, p. 58. Also see generally, H. K. JOSEPHS, *Labour Law in China : choice and responsabiliy* (Salem, N.H. : Butterworths, 1990).

25. See J. HOWELL, *China Opens its Doors : The Politics of Economic Transition* (Boulder, Colo. : Lynne Rienner, 1993) at 209-243.

began to spring up which would serve as « headhunters » for firms seeking to hire skilled workers and professionals and arrange payment of the release fee demanded by state enterprises as the price of releasing their staff members to other units. As well, the sidewalk labour markets became an increasingly important source of unskilled workers being hired for short-term projects. In sum, the initial reforms culminated in the emergence of a proto-market for labour.

2.2 Accelerated Reform

By the late 1980s, many of the initial reforms had run their course. Enterprise managers were increasingly independent, production inputs and outputs were gradually being freed of state regulatory constraints, and labour was becoming more widely available under the labour contract system. Taking the decision to push reforms one step further, the government embarked on a risky and controversial course of price reform — permitting commodity prices to respond to market forces instead of state planning mandates[26]. This meant that while there was little adjustment in the output quotas demanded of state enterprises, production inputs were subject to ever-increasing prices. The dilemmas for enterprise brought on by the problem of price spiralling often resulted in reduced benefits to industrial workers. For those workers formally attached to state enterprises, this meant that bonuses were cut back or eliminated, forced purchasing of state bonds was enforced, upgrading of worker facilities was postponed or cancelled, and general working conditions declined[27]. While much attention was focused on the role of unemployed itinerant workers in the demonstrations, factory workers formally attached to state enterprises were also extremely active.

For contract workers, the results of price reform were two-fold. In many cases labour contracts were cancelled or not renewed — thus rendering large numbers of workers unemployed. Yet these workers were often unable to return to the rural villages from whence they had come : these areas had adjusted to the migrant labourers' absence, there was no work for them to do and moreover their families remained dependent on their remissions of money from the cities. The result was increasing numbers of

---

26. For a general review of the late stages of reform and many of the attendant consequences, see JOINT ECONOMIC COMMITTEE OF U.S. CONGRESS, *China's Economic Dilemmas in the 1990s : The Problems of Reforms, Modernization, and Interdependence* (Washington, D.C. : U.S. Government Printing Office, 1991).
27. See K. HARTFORD, « The Political Economy Behind Beijing Spring », in T. SAICH, ed., *The Chinese People's Movement : Perspectives on Spring 1989* (Armonk, N.Y. : M.E. Sharpe, 1990) at 50-82.

unemployed labourers wandering the streets of major cities in search of work. A second consequence was that when short term labour contracts were available, the terms were even more unfavourable that had been the case previously. In the employers' market that dominated at the time, itinerant labourers had little bargaining power and the inflation resulting from price reform was reducing the ability of employers to offer generous compensation and benefits under these labour contracts. The participation of urban workers in the democracy demonstrations of Spring 1989 provided ample testimony to the extent of dissatisfaction.

The Chinese government's response was indicative of its concern over worker unrest. A vigorous campaign was launched of discipline and control over urban workers that saw public executions of workers accused of participating in the democracy demonstrations dominate the Chinese public media throughout much of 1989. Indeed, the harshest punishments were reserved for worker demonstrators, particularly in comparison to the relatively lenient treatment of intellectuals and students. Repression was also directed at attempts to form independent labour unions, as labour organizers such as Han Dongfang were arrested and harassed[28].

2.3 Privatization and the Socialist Market Economy

A third stage of reform has emerged following Deng Xiaoping's Southern Tour (*Nanxun*) in 1992. Responding to Deng's call for accelerated and expanded economic reform, increased attention has been paid to privatization of Chinese enterprises. While debate continues over the extent of true privatization in the Chinese economy — particularly in light of the evidence that many so-called private enterprises are in fact owned and operated by local government agencies —, it is clear that the structure of enterprise control has changed[29]. Transformation of state enterprises through securitization has been accompanied by policies approving expansion of the village and township enterprise sector and the development of private enterprises limited by shares in urban areas[30]. Enterprises now respond to the local interests of corporatist elites who embody both the economic determinism of business managers with the political power of Party cadres. Along with local corporatism has come greater attention to efficiency and reduced production costs, which in turn has contributed to continued declines in

28. See « China : New Arrests Linked to Worker Rights », in *Human Rights Watch/Asia*, Mar. 11, 1994.
29. See A.G. WALDER, « China's Transitional Economy : Interpreting Its Significance », 144 *China Quarterly*, 963-979 (1995).
30. For a collection of insightful articles on the latest stages of the reform process, see the special issue of the *China Quarterly* on China's transitional economy, December 1995.

labour conditions for industrial workers[31]. In response to these concerns, the Chinese government has re-emphasized long-standing regulations on worker health and safety, and in some instances issued new regulations[32]. In addition, new rules have been enacted governing reporting on worker accidents and injuries, in the hope that increased reporting requirements would induce greater compliance with health and safety regulations[33].

Unfortunately, enforcement of these regulations has been problematic and as a result increased worker unrest has become a major challenge for Chinese labour policy. Between 1986 and 1994, 60,000 labour disputes were recorded (probably matched by a sizeable number of unreported disputes), and 3,000 labour disputes were noted during first three months of 1994 alone[34]. The upsurge of labour disputes has been accompanied by renewed attempts to establish autonomous workers federations: e.g. the Beijing Workers Autonomous Federation and the China Workers Autonomous Federation[35]. While these events have been dismissed by the PRC Labour Ministry as an «inevitable» component of economic modernization, the matter is clearly a source of concern — particularly in light of the Tiananmen experience[36].

The Chinese government's labour policies are caught in a dilemma of conflicting imperatives. Economic reform and the privatization (or at least corporatization) of production enterprises would appear to justify granting greater rights to workers in the areas of collective bargaining, work stoppages, and so on. Yet the regime also faces the need for continued economic growth, which mandates greater control over worker discipline even as it permits declining conditions of employment. The PRC *Labour Law* represents the regime's effort to address these issues.

31. See Generally, M. C.F. GAO, «On the sharp end of China's economic boom — migrant workers», in *China Rights Forum*, Spring 1994, pp. 12-13, 27; LIU Ping, «Dying for Development», in *China Rights Forum*, Fall, 1994, pp. 14-15, 27.
32. For a review, see SONG Xiangguan, *op. cit.*, fn. 11, pp. 128-205.
33. See e.g. «Qiye zhi gong shangwang shigu baogao he chuli guiding» (Regulations on the reporting and resolution of injuries and accidents involving enterprise workers and staff), in XIN Shanyin and YE Xiaoli, ed., *Xinbian changzhang jingli shiyong jinji falu quanshu* (Newly compiled compendium of practical economic laws for factory directors and managers) (Beijing: Procuracy Press, 1993), p. 1787.
34. See «Labour Minister: Strikes «inevitable» with reform» (Hong Kong, AFP, Jul 15, 1994), in *FBIS Daily Report-China* July 15, 1994, pp. 12-13.
35. See B. GILLEY, «Shen Yuan Escapes 27 Jul», in *Eastern Express* (HK) Aug. 9, 1994, in *FBIS Daily Report-China* Aug. 9, 1994, pp. 18-19; B. GILLEY, «Further on Labor Activist», in *Eastern Express* (HK) Aug. 9, 1994, in *FBI Daily Report-China* Aug. 9, 1994, p. 19.
36. *Supra*, fn. 34.

3. An Overview of China's New *Labour Law*

The *Labour Law of the PRC* was enacted at the 8th session of the Standing Committee of the 8th National People's Congress July 5, 1994, and went into effect January 1, 1995[37]. The law went through a tortuous drafting process, involving thirty drafts since Deng Xiaoping first proposed drafting such a law during a 1978 central work conference[38]. While the delay revealed the extent to which managing labour relations is an essential basis for the distribution of patronage within China's hierarchical and vertically integrated administrative systems, the enactment of the legislation revealed the extent of consensus that workers presented a fundamental source of tension in the course of the transition from the planned to the market economy. The final draft was pushed through in response to obvious challenges resulting form changing ownership conditions of enterprises[39]. While private enterprises and foreign invested enterprises were the primary source of concern initially[40], state-owned and cooperative enterprises are also targeted[41].

3.1 Basic Principles

The PRC *Labour Law* extends a number of specific benefits to workers. These include « guarantees » respecting equal opportunity in employment, job selection, compensation, rest, leave, safety and health care, vocational training, social security and welfare, and the right to submit disputes to arbitration. Hiring units are required to fulfill various labour requirements in the areas of hours of employment, rest, leave, worker safety, health care and protection for female and juvenile workers. Juxtaposed to these benefits are a number of obligations that workers must honour, including the duties to fulfill work requirements, improve vocational skills, carry out work safety and health regulations, observe labour discipline and vocational ethics. The law also contains various enforcement provisions, by which

37. All references to the Labour Law of the PRC are to the text in *China Law and Practice*, August 29, 1994, pp. 21-36.
38. See WANG Yantian and FU Gang, *loc. cit.*, fn. 1, 17-18.
39. See « Labour Law should be adopted soon », *Xinhua* Domestic Service Jun 30, 1994, in *FBIS Daily Report-China*, July 1, 1994, p. 21.
40. See ZHANG Xia, « Foreign-funded ventures in China told to unionize », in *China Daily* Jul. 15, 1994, p. 4, in *FBIC Daily Report-China* Jul 15, 1994, pp. 20-21, wherein labour abuses by foreign investment enterprises (usually Hong Kong owned or managed) are cited as the reason for increased attention to labour conditions. See also *supra*, fn. 39, and GUO Xiang, *loc. cit.*, fn. 1.
41. See « Offenders of labour regulations exposed », *Xinhua* English service July 28, 1994, in *FBIS Daily Report-China*, July 28, 1994, p. 34.

local Labour Administration Departments are charged with supervision and inspection of labour relations.

Subject to these broad principles, the new *Labour Law* contains a multitude of specific provisions as summarized below. A range of implementing regulations are currently being drafted to address these matters in greater detail.

1. *Labour Contract System* : Following the 1978 economic reforms, the labour contract system has undergone a rebirth. The *Labour Law* provides rules for contract provisions on term and description of employment, labour protection, remuneration, discipline, termination, liability for breach and limits to the use of probationary work periods during which benefits may be limited.

2. *Limits to Working Hours and Overtime* : Overtime pay is required for work in excess of eight hours per day and 44 hours per week. One day per week is guaranteed for rest. Approval may be obtained for alternative arrangements.

3. *Wages* : The *Labour Law* establishes a principle of equal pay for equal work. This is intended to bring about greater gender equality in employment[42]. The state-mandated minimum wage must be taken as base pay. Factors to be considered in setting the state-mandated minimum wage include cost of living, the average wages being paid in the locality, productivity levels, and regional variations.

4. *Social Insurance System* : Employers must provide for benefit payments in cases of retirement, illness or injury, incapacity, unemployment, child birth, and so on.

5. *Labour Disputes* : The *Labour Law* provides institutional rules for resolving conflicts arising during the course of (a) contract drafting (administrative resolution of the dispute by the local Labour Administration Department) ; (b) contract enforcement (resolution by an arbitration commission comprised of representatives from the local Labour Administration Department, the trade union, and the employer) ; and (c) disputes between employers and employees generally (resolution through a mediation by a commission comprised of representatives of staff and workers, the employer, and the local trade union, or arbitration by a commission comprised of representatives of the local Labour Administration Department, the trade union and the employer). Arbitral decisions may be appealed to the courts.

---

42. There are doubts about the likelihood of reaching this goal, however. See M. Woo, « Biology and Equality : Challenge for Feminism in the Socialist and Liberal State », (1993) 42 *Emory Law Journal* 143 at 143-146.

6. *Supervision and Enforcement*: The relevant institutions for dispute resolution include the local Labour Administration Departments, Local People's Governments, and Trade Unions.

7. *Legal Liability*: Employers who violate provisions of the *Labour Law* are potentially liable for compensation for harm, administrative penalties and criminal sanctions.

8. *Foreign Enterprise Labour Rules*: The *Labour Law* contains provisions for foreign investment enterprises that augment regulations already in place.

Of the basic issues discussed above, the labour contract system and the dispute resolution provisions are of particular importance and will be discussed in greater detail below.

3.2 The Return to the Labour Contract System

With the post-Mao economic reform policies beginning in 1978, the labour contract system that had been used during the 1950s was revitalized. After the All China Federation of Trade Unions (ACFTU) approved the use of the labour contract system in State-owned enterprises in April 1979, the labour contract system was increasingly seen as a positive mechanism for improving labour conditions and enterprise efficiency[43]. Initially, the emphasis of regulations was on the foreign business sector. Thus, in July, 1980, the *Regulations on Labour Management in Joint Venture Enterprises* were promulgated by the State Council, and provided for individual and collective labour contracts in joint ventures[44]. These measures were augmented by the *Procedures for Implementation of the Regulations on Labour Management in Joint Venture Enterprises* (1984)[45].

The labour contract system was also gradually being extended to the domestic economy as well. At the First Session of the 6th NPC in June 1983, Premier Zhao Ziyang alluded to the need for greater flexibility in arrangements for workers in the economy[46], and the following year's CPC Central Committee « Decision on Reform of the Economic System » asserted the

43. See e.g., « Jiji anpai chengshi daiye qingnian » (Positively arrange urban employment for youth), in *Renmin ribao* (People's Daily), June 7, 1979, p. 3, « Ben shi quanmin qiye shou ci zhijie zhao shou hetong gong » (This city's public enterprises accept recruitment through the contract labour for the first time), in *Jiefang ribao* (Liberation Daily) (Shanghai), Aug. 16, 1980, p. 1.

44. See MINISTRY OF LABOUR *et al.*, *Laodong fa shouce* (Labour law handbook) (Beijing: Economic Management Press, 1988), p. 288.

45. *Id.*, p. 290.

46. See ZHAO Lukuan, « Lun laodong hetong zhi » (On the labour contract system), in *Renmin ribao* (People's Daily), Sept. 7, 1983, p. 5.

need to expand the labour contract system[47]. The labour contract system was formally extended to state enterprises in July, 1986, with the *Interim Provisions on the Implementation of the Labour Contract System for State Owned Enterprises*[48]. Private enterprises were included as well under the *Provisional Regulations on Private Enterprises* (1988)[49] and the *Provisional Regulations on Labour Management in Private Enterprises* (1989)[50], which required private enterprises to sign labour contract with workers based on the principles of equality, voluntariness and agreement through consultation, and which authorized the trade unions to represent staff and workers in concluding collective contracts. Since Deng's « Southern Tour » in early 1992, the labour contracts system received even greater attention. The 1992 *Regulations for Transferring the Management Mechanism in the State-Owned Industrial Sectors* granted enterprises broader rights to determine the terms of employment through the use of labour contracts with individual workers[51].

China's new *Labour Law* requires in Article 106 that every province, autonomous region and centrally governed municipality should stipulate the steps for implementation of the labour contract system in accordance with the *Labour Law* and with the existing conditions. By the end of 1994, a total of thirteen provinces and municipalities had implemented the labour contract system for staff and workers covering in all some 40 million contract workers — about 25 % of the total work force[52]. Provincial and municipal regulations are gradually coming into force, such as the Shanghai Municipal Government's *Regulations on Labour Contracts of Shanghai Municipality* (1995), which call for popularization of the labour contract

47. See CHEN Wenyuan, « Guanyu laodong hetong de jige jiben wenti » (Some basic issues concerning labour contracts), in *Zhongguo fazhi bao* (Chinese legal system gazette), Aug. 25, 1986, p. 3.
48. « Guoying qiye shixing laodong hetong zhi zanxing guiding », in *Zhongguo fazhi bao* (China legal system gazette) Sept. 10, 1986, p. 2.
49. « Zhonghua renmin gongheguo siying qiye zanxing tiaoli », in *Siying qiye changyong falu shouce* (Handbook of commonly used laws for private enterprises) (Beijing : Law Publishers, 1988), p. 1.
50. « Siying qiye laodong guanli zanxing guiding », in *Laodong fa yu laodong zhengyi shiyong shouce* (Practical handbook on labour law and labour disputes) (Beijing : Chian Economy Press, 1994), p. 672.
51. « Quanmin suoyouzhi gongye qiye zhuanhuan jingying ji zhi tiaoli », in XIN Shanyin and YE Xiaoli, *op. cit.*, fn. 33, p. 122.
52. See LI Boyong, « Speech at the National Meeting on Labour Work : Implementation of the Labour Code » in *People's Daily* (overseas edition) Dec. 14, 1994. LI Boyong is PRC Minister of Labour.

system in Shanghai Municipality beginning in 1996[53]. While the contract system is intended to bring greater discipline and control to enterprises in managing labour relations, to a certain extent, the new Labour Law maintains the systems of patronage and coaptation that characterized the Maoist system. Thus, where a Shanghai worker voluntarily sought cancellation of a labour contract in order to take a job at another factory, the original employer was expected still to provide severance pay[54].

3.3 Continued Importance of Party-Dominated Trade Unions

A critical element of the new labour contract system is the continued role of the CPC-led labour unions under the ACFTU. Article 26 of the 1983 *Charter of China's Trade Unions* passed by the Tenth National Congress of China's Trade Unions authorized basic level trade union committees to represent staff and workers to sign collective labour contracts[55]. This authorization was repeated in the various regulations on foreign investment enterprises and on Chinese state and privately owned enterprises. Under the 1992 *Trade Union Law* trade unions receive once again the authority to represent staff and workers in concluding collective contracts with enterprises and institutions[56].

While labour unions can of course play a positive role in achieving better working conditions and other benefits, the record of the ACFTU system is somewhat problematic. The ACFTU's primary role as a guarantor of Party power and a « transmission belt » for Party policies undermines its capacity for independent action. And since all local trade unions are subject under law to the overall authority of the ACFTU, there is no legal sanction for the creation of independent labour unions that might challenge the Communist Party's official policies[57]. In addition, recent case reports suggest that the temptation to draw on worker dues for improper purposes may be overwhelming—raising again concerns that workers' interests are not particularly high matters of concern for union officials[58].

53. See Shanghai Municipality : « Stipulations on Labour Contracts for Shanghai Municipality », in *Shanghai Legal System*, Dec. 18, 1995.
54. See « Jiechu laodong hetong, gai bu gai fa jingji buchangjin ? » (In case of cancellation of a labour contract, must the compensation fee still be paid ?), in *Gongren ribao* (Workers Daily), Jan. 5, 1995.
55. « Zhongguo gonghui zhangcheng », in *Gonghui fa shouce* (Handbook of trade union law) (Beijing : Democracy and Legal System Press, 1994), p. 380.
56. « Zhonghua renmin gongheguo gonghui fa », *op. cit.*, fn. 55, p. 63.
57. See generally, S. BIDDULPH and S. COONEY, « Regulation of Trade Unions in the People's Republic of China », (1993) 19 *Melbourne University Law Review*, 255-292.
58. See e.g., « Fayuan cuo jiang huifei di zizuo susong fei » (The court improperly takes union dues to pay litigation fee), in *Laodong ribao* (Workers's Daily) Oct. 10, 1995, p. 5.

3.4 Dispute Resolution

The *Labour Law*'s provisions on dispute resolution may offer workers a basis for appealing or perhaps avoiding altogether arbitrary decisions by management. In one case, for example, workers were accused of stealing electrical equipment and arbitrarily docked in pay — the public security officials being only too willing to enforce management orders with little if any investigation[59]. In another case, a worker was summarily suspended for three days without pay after getting into an argument with a supervisor[60]. The supervisor's superiors backed the suspension and the (reportedly innocent) worker was left without a remedy. Similar incidents have been reported at other enterprises[61]. The hope is that implementation of the *Labour Law* will impose more formalized processes for investigation and dispute resolution.

The dispute resolution provisions of the *Labour Law* build on experiments developed earlier[62]. Of particular importance were the 1987 State Council *Regulations on Resolution of Labour Disputes in State Enterprises*[63], which provided for mediation and arbitration of labour disputes. Summarizing previous experiences, the State Council's 1993 *Regulations for Handling Labour Disputes* provided a framework for the labour disputes that would later be incorporated into the PRC *Labour Law*[64]. The Ministry of Labour articulated the reasons for the labour dispute system by reference mainly to the increased numbers of labour disputes that accompanied enterprise reforms[65].

The primary methods for resolving disputes included mediation, which is to be used through the whole process of handling labour disputes. According to the *Labour Law*, mediation should be based on the voluntariness of both parties. Both the process and content of dispute resolution should be in accordance with the law and follow the principle of fairness. The *Labour*

59. See « Qiye yao zijue weihu laodong zhe hefa quanyi » (The enterprise should take the initiative to safeguard the legitimate rights and interests of workers », in *Gongren ribao* (Workers Daily) Feb. 28, 1995.
60. See « Zheiyang jiechu hetong dui ma ? » (Is this kind of cancellation of contract proper ?), in *Gongren ribao* (Workers Daily) Jan. 9, 1995, p. 6.
61. See e.g. « Laodong fa shi jingying zhe you fa ke yi » (The « Labour Law » will cause managers to have a law to follow), in *Gongren ribao* (Workers Daily) Jan. 5, 1995.
62. See D. Hunter, « Chinese Labour Dispute Arbitration Procedures : An Early Review in Zhejiang Province », (1990) 11 *Comparative Labor Law Journal* 340.
63. « Guoying qiye laodong zhengyi chuli zanxing guiding », *op. cit.*, fn. 49, p. 10.
64. See *FBIS Daily Report-China* Aug. 2, 1993, p. 27.
65. See « Answers to Questions About the Policy of Handling Labour Disputes », Ministry of Labour, *Zhongguo laodong fa zhengce fagui quanshu* (Encyclopedia of China's labour laws and policies) (Jilin : Science and Technology Press, 1994), p. 648.

Law requires that equality be accorded to the parties in matters of legal status, rights to apply for a mediation, arbitration or court judgment, and the various rights to present and explain pertinent facts in labour disputes. The new law requires that mediators, arbitrators and judges should be impartial to the parties involved and, in order to protect both parties' rights and interests and especially those of workers, the labour mediation committee, the labour arbitration committee and the people's court should handle labour disputes in a prompt and timely fashion. These broad principles are taken as the foundation upon which the various procedures for dispute resolution are based.

The first step in dispute resolution is mediation through the mediation committee. If this fails, the dispute will go to arbitration through an arbitration committee, and possibly to the third step of litigation before the People's Court. Under Article 80 of the *Labour Law*, the labour dispute mediation committee is established inside the employing unit and is composed of representatives of the staff and workers, representatives of the employer, and representatives of the trade union. The committee Chair is to be held by a representative of the trade union. Under Article 81, the labour dispute arbitration committee is composed of representatives of the local Labour Administrative Department (who also chairs the committee), representatives from the trade union at the corresponding level, and representatives of the employer. Arbitration is the first level of binding dispute resolution, and the prominent role of the trade union in reviewing its own mediation decision, as well as the absence of direct representation of staff and workers are particularly noteworthy. While litigation before the People's Courts is possible, both as a matter of first instance and to appeal an arbitral decision, the practical significance is minimal in light of the institutional and political weaknesses of the court system in China[66]. The continued inability of the courts to enforce judgments against powerful economic enterprises may render irrelevant the *Labour Law*'s provisions for judicial enforcement[67]. Moreover, courts have been seen to lack sufficient expertise to permit them to coordinate dispute resolution proceedings without compromising other aspects of enforcement of the *Labour Law*[68].

---

66. See generally, D. C. CLARKE, « Dispute Resolution in China », (1992) 5 *Journal of Chinese Law*, 246.
67. GUO Xiang, *loc. cit.*, fn. 1.
68. See « Fayuan cuo jiang huifei di zuo susong fei » (The court erroneously reduces union fees to pay litigation fees), in *Gongren ribao* (Workers Daily) Oct. 10, 1995, p. 5, in which the court handling a dispute over investment funds improperty deducted litigation fees from the union membership fund.

4. Continuing Challenges

While the PRC *Labour Law* represents an important step toward building an effective legal framework for protecting workers' rights in China, there are a number of issues remaining to be resolved. Coinciding with the law's promulgation were official accounts bemoaning the general lack of awareness and basic knowledge of the law[69], and cautioning against lax implementation by administrative departments concerned[70]. In addition, as with other aspects of China's legal regime, the law represents a formalistic expression of specific rights and obligations, but does little to serve as a foundation for meaningful enforcement of fundamental rights for workers. Official reviews of the PRC *Labour Law* describe it as the complete articulation of the rights of workers[71]. In other words workers' rights are only those articulated in the law, and do not extend beyond the text of the legislation. Of particular interest are statements that the rights of workers in China must be based on China's unique situation, and cannot be addressed by reference to foreign labour law criteria[72]. Such an approach to workers' rights leaves little room for articulating and enforcing generalized norms for employer behaviour, or for making workers rights unconditional and independent of various contractual duties.

Although China's labour conditions are of course unique, two matters discussed by labour specialists in the PRC are of particular importance concerning the *Labour Law*, namely collective bargaining and dispute resolution. The *Labour Law* makes reference to collective labour contracts, but it fails to provide meaningful protection for collective bargaining. The obvious unequal bargaining power between individual workers and employers has caused many to view collective bargaining as an essential element of modern labour law. Unfortunately, the *Labour Law* leaves direct

---

69. Guo Xiang, *loc. cit.*, fn. 1.
70. « Laodong fa zhi jianshe de lichengbei » (The milestone established by the Labour Law system), in *Gongren ribao* (Workers Daily) Jan. 9, 1995, p. 1 ; « Qixin xieli tuijin laodong fa zhi jianshe » (Make consolidated efforts to promote the establishment of the labour law system), in *Gongren ribao* (Workers Daily), Jan. 27, 1995, p. 1 ; Cao Min, « State vows to protect interests of labourers », *China Daily* Jul 8, 1994, p. 1, in *FBIS Daily Report-China*, July 8, 1994, pp. 17-18.
71. See e.g., Ji Yanxiang, « Weihu laodongzhe hefa quanyi de jiben falu » (A basic law for safeguarding the legitimate rights and interests of workers), in *Jingji jingwei* (Economic transit) (Zhengzhou) June 1994, pp. 30-32, 69 ; Guo Xiang, *loc. cit.*, fn. 1.
72. *Id.* While China claims adherence to international treaties on the rights of workers, it claims as a developing country that some international labour standards are inapplicable to China. See Zhang Zuoyi, « Zhongguo laodong lifa » (China's labour legislation), in *Zhengfa luntan* (Theory and discussion on politics and law) 1994 no. 6, pp. 1-4 at pp. 1 and 4.

representatives of staff and workers out of the contract bargaining process, and omits specific reference to the importance of collective bargaining.

The power disparity between employers and employees is entrenched further through provisions concerning termination of labour contracts. According to section 25 of the Law, the employing unit may revoke a labour contract if the worker is « proved not up to the requirements for recruitment during the probation period ». Unfortunately, the case record suggests that some staff and workers have been terminated improperly during the probation period[73]. Furthermore, Article 26 (3) permits the employer to demand and ultimately to impose revocation of a labour contract with written notification in cases of changed circumstances. This section has been seen as a a source of potential abuse, because it lacks provisions concerning the employer's burden of proof, and thus leaves room for employers to use changed circumstances improperly as an excuse to summarily dismiss employees. In contrast, while employees have the right to revoke labour contracts « where the employer resorts to violence, intimidation or illegal restriction of the personal freedom » or « fails to provide working conditions as agreed upon in the labour contract », it is difficult for the worker to meet the burden of proof in these cases.

The general inattention to collective bargaining to redress power imbalances in the new *Labour Law* is puzzling in light of the fact that the concept has been well accepted in the PRC for some time[74]. Shortly after Liberation, collective bargaining rights were reserved for the employees of private enterprises[75]. During the economic reform period of the 1990s, several administrative units noted the importance of collective bargaining in labour relations in foreign investment enterprises. For example, the « Announcement » co-issued by the Labour Department, the Public Security Bureau and the ACFTU March 4, 1994 requires that foreigners' invested and private enterprises should establish systems for negotiation and collective bargaining[76]. Apparently, despite a willingness to impose collective bargaining on foreign capitalist enterprises, the Chinese government is not yet ready to accept that the socialist market economy entails potential exploitation of workers by domestic enterprises to the same degree.

73. See ZHANG Shuqing, «The employees in the joint-venture, cooperative, and foreigners' invested enterprises ask for the protection for their rights and interests», in *Minzhu yu fazhi fazhi* (Democracy and Legal System), no. 20, 1995, p. 24-25.
74. See CHEN Wenyuan, «Guanyu laodong fa de jige jiben wenti chusuo» (Preliminary inquiry on several basic issues of the Labour Law), in *Zhengfa luntan* (Theory and discussion on politics and law) June 1994, pp. 55-59, 62.
75. See Article 6 of the Trade Union Law promulgated by ACFTU, June,1950.
76. See PRC Supreme People's Court, *Laodong zhengyi shenpan shouce* (Judicial handbook on labour disputes) (Beijing: Law Publishers, 1994), p. 216.

A second major issue concerns the independence of trade unions. The new *Labour Law* entrenches the Party-dominated labour union system as the basic mechanism for enforcing workers' rights[77]. The *Labour Law* places significant reliance on the trade union in representing and safeguarding the legitimate rights and interests of labourers (Article 7) in requesting reconsideration of termination of a contract by the employer unit and in supporting workers' application for arbitration or litigation (Article 30) ; in representing workers in concluding collective labour contracts (Article 33) ; in representing workers on the labour dispute mediation committee (Article 80) and arbitration committee (Article 81) ; and in representing workers in supervising implementation of laws and regulations by the employer (Article 88). However, the law contains no provisions concerning the formation and the structure of a trade union. The PRC *Trade Union Law* (1992) does include such provisions, but contains nothing to suggest that trade unions under the ACFTU will be independent. According to Article 3, all salaried workers are eligible for the membership of a trade union. This would extend to enterprise directors and managers, thus permitting those in charge of the employing unit to join or even to dominate the trade union in their unit. Moreover, the *Trade Union Law* also grants CPC cadres close access to trade union leadership. And in fact, CPC cadres have dominated the ACFTU since 1948, as appears from the data presented in Table 1.

Table 1 : CPC cadres in the leadership of the ACFTU 1948-1965[78] :

	Number of Presidium Chairs and Vice Chairs	*Number of CPC cadres serving as Chair and Vice Chair*
1948	4	3
1953	4	2
1956	5	3
1957	5	3
1958	6	4
1962	7	4
1965	6	4

The pattern continued following the Cultural Revolution with the renewal of the ACFTU. The leader of ACFTU when it resumed its activities after the Cultural Revolution was Mr. Ni Zhifu, a Politburo member of the

77. See « Laodong fa jiaqiangle gonghui de weihu zhineng » (The Labour Law has strengthened the safeguarding capacity of the unions), in *Gongren ribao* (Workers Daily) Jan. 5, 1995, p. 4 ; « Jiaqiang gonghui gaige he jianshe de qiaoji » (A useful scheme for strengthening reform and construction of the unions), in *Gongren ribao* (Workers Daily), Jan. 23, 1995, p. 1 ; GUO Xiang, *loc. cit.*, fn. 1.

78. See LEE Lai To, *op. cit.*, fn. 13, p. 71.

CPC[79], and the current Chair of the ACFTU, Mr. Wei Jianxing, is a member of the CPC Politburo[80]. In state enterprises, almost 80 % of leadership positions in trade unions are occupied by the Party Secretaries of the respective units[81]. Similarily, in foreign enterprises, almost all leaders of trade unions are concurrently Party directors of the Personnel Department of those units[82]. The close linkage between the unions and the local Party leadership means that aggressive union action to protect workers rights over the interests of the Party is unlikely[83].

Aside from issues inherent in the text of the *Labour Law*, a variety of other questions arise concerning effective implementation. Technical issues arise for example concerning the standards for workplace safety, environmental conditions, workers' health, and similar matters. These matters likely will be left to individual ministries and commissions, such as the Ministry of Health, National Environmental Protection Agency, and of course the Labour Ministry. However, detailed regulations will be needed and trained implementation staff will be essential.

Socio-economic problems will also complicate the problem of enforcement. Of particular importance is the crisis of so-called « migrant workers ». Current figures of migrant workers approach fifty million, with official estimates of 120 million « surplus labourers » and the expectation that by the year 2000 China will have 200 million surplus agricultural workers on the non-agricultural employment marke[84]. These conditions have already outstripped the capacity of the government to respond. Many of these migrants are only too happy to take factory jobs -whether in the relatively more secure state sector or the higher paying village and township enterprise sector — without regard to working conditions and legal rights.

In the context of problems of technical complexity and the swelling numbers of surplus and migrant workers, enforcement of the *Labour Law*'s provisions on workers' rights is hampered further by local corporatist

79. *Id.*, p. 146.
80. See WEI Jianxing : « The Implementation of the Labour Law Should Highlight the Function of Protection », in *Legal System Daily*, July 23, 1995.
81. See SHI Tanjing, *Laodong fa* (Labour Law) (Beijing : Economic Science Press, 1990) p. 257.
82. See CHANG Kai, « Legal issues concerning the collective bargaining and collective contract system in foreigners' invested enterprises », in *Zhongguo Faxue* (Chinese Jurisprudence) Beijing, Jan. 1995, p. 56.
83. For an indication of the closeness of the links between Party organs and labour unions, see « Sheng shi dang lingdao tan gonghui » (Provincial and municipal Party leaders discuss labour unions), in *Gongren ribao* (Workers Daily), Jan. 27, 1995, p. 3.
84. See LI Tian, « Population flow into big cities », *Beijing Review*, July 18-24, 1994, pp. 15-19, in *FBIS Daily Report-China* July 20, 1994, pp. 20-21.

alliances between administrative officials and business enterprises[85]. The economic incentives underlying local corporatist relations have even subverted the financial integrity of the labour unions themselves, as cases have arisen where labour union funds were improperly invested thus putting worker pensions at risk[86]. Furthermore, the local CPC cadre evaluation system places premium on stability, production, and full employment, while giving little attention to strict enforcement of workers rights[87].

Conclusion

The People's Republic of China has seen many changes in the structure of its economy and in the treatment of workers employed by economic enterprises. While the *Labour Law* of the PRC represents a major step toward articulating legal norms on the protection of workers rights, it still reflects the imperatives of Chinese government policies of economic growth and the Chinese Communist Party's concerns with political control. Thus provisions on contract labour and the role of trade unions appear to serve the interests of the Party/state to a greater extent than they do the interests of Chinese workers. The new law also faces significant impediments to full implementation. Nonetheless, in the context of the transition to a socialist market economy the new labour code does represent significant progress in the ongoing challenge of managing labour relations in China.

---

85. For a discussion of corporatism in Chinese reforms, see K. PARRIS, « Local Initiative and National Reform : The Wenzhou Model of Development », 134 *China Quarterly* 242 (1993).
86. See e.g., « Wei han bu zhixing Gonghui fa, (Nonsensically failing to enforce the Trade Union Law), in *Gongren ribao* (Workers Daily), Oct. 10, 1995, p. 5.
87. See generally, J.P. BURNS and J.P. CABESTAN, « Provisional Chinese Civil Service Regulations », in *Chinese Law and Government*, Winter 1990-1991.

Name Index